WIDER BOUNDARIES
OF DARING

WIDER BOUNDARIES OF DARING

The Modernist Impulse in Canadian Women's Poetry

DI BRANDT &
BARBARA GODARD, *editors*

Wilfrid Laurier University Press

This book has been published with the help of a grant from the Canadian Federation for the Humanities and Social Sciences, through the Aid to Scholarly Publications Programme, using funds provided by the Social Sciences and Humanities Research Council of Canada. We acknowledge the support of the Canada Council for the Arts for our publishing program. We acknowledge the financial support of the Government of Canada through the Book Publishing Industry Development Program for our publishing activities.

Library and Archives Canada Cataloguing in Publication

Wider boundaries of daring : the modernist impulse in Canadian women's poetry / Di Brandt and Barbara Godard, editors.

Includes bibliographical references and index.
ISBN 978-1-55458-032-3

1. Canadian poetry (English)—Women authors—History and criticism. 2. Canadian poetry (English)—20th century—History and criticism. 3. Canadian poetry (English)—21st century—History and criticism. 4. Modernism (Literature)—Canada. I. Brandt, Di II. Godard, Barbara

PS8103.W6W44 2009   C811'.5409112   C2008-904549-1

Cover image: *The Dance* by P.K. Irwin (1962; egg tempera, 36.5 cm × 32 cm), from the collection of P.K. Page. Cover design by Angela Moody, Moving Images. Text design by C. Bonas-Taylor.

© 2009 Wilfrid Laurier University Press
Waterloo, Ontario, Canada
www.wlupress.wlu.ca

Every reasonable effort has been made to acquire permission for copyright material used in this text, and to acknowledge all such indebtedness accurately. Any errors and omissions called to the publisher's attention will be corrected in future printings.

No part of this publication may be reproduced, stored in a retrieval system or transmitted, in any form or by any means, without the prior written consent of the publisher or a licence from The Canadian Copyright Licensing Agency (Access Copyright). For an Access Copyright licence, visit www.accesscopyright.ca or call toll free to 1-800-893-5777.

CONTENTS

A New Genealogy of Canadian Literary Modernism
Di Brandt 1

THE MAKING OF CANADIAN LITERARY MODERNISM

The Writing Livesays: Connecting Generations of Canadian Modernism *Ann Martin* 29

Feminist and Regionalist Modernisms in *Contemporary Verse, CV/II*, and *CV2* *Christine Kim* 49

P.K. Page: Discovering a Modern Sensibility *Sandra Djwa* 75

Tradition, Individual Talent, and "a young woman / From backwoods New Brunswick": Modernism and Elizabeth Brewster's (Auto)Poetics of the Subject *Bina Toledo Freiwald* 97

"And we are homesick still": Home, the Unhomely, and the Everyday in Anne Wilkinson *Kathy Mezei* 125

Anne Marriott: Modernist on the Periphery *Marilyn J. Rose* 147

Discontinuity, Intertextuality, and Literary History: Gail Scott's Reading of Gertrude Stein *Lianne Moyes* 163

Literary Modernism as Cultural Act

"They cut him down": Race, Class, and Cultural Memory in Dorothy Livesay's "Day and Night"
Pamela McCallum 191

Dorothy Livesay and CBC Radio: The Politics of Modernist Aesthetics, Gender, and Regionalism *Peggy Lynn Kelly* 213

Phyllis Webb as Public Intellectual *Pauline Butling* 237

"A Collection of Solitary Fragments": Miriam Waddington as Critic *Candida Rifkind* 253

"Our hearts both leapt / in love with metaphor": P.K. Page's Professional Elegies *Sara Jamieson* 275

The Passionate and Sublime Modernism of Elizabeth Smart
Anne Quéma 297

Jay Macpherson's Modernism *Miriam Nichols* 325

Word, I, and Other in Margaret Avison's Poetry
Katherine Quinsey 347

Reading P.K. Page in English/Italian; or, On the Politics of Translating Modernist Gender *Elena Basile* 373

Contributors 397

Index 403

A New Genealogy of Canadian Literary Modernism

DI BRANDT

We Are Alone

We are alone, who strove to be
Together in the high sun's weather.

We are bereft, as broods a tree
Whose leaves the river sucks forever.

We are as clouds, which merge and vanish
Leaving breathless the dead horizon—

We are as comrades, whose handshake only
Comes rare as leap-year and mistletoe morning.

Each one ploughing a one-man clearing
Neither one alive to see

In wider boundaries of daring
What the recompense might be.

—Dorothy Livesay

Dorothy Livesay's poem "We Are Alone," written in the 1930s, expresses simultaneously dismay and hope: dismay that the grandly conceived collective cultural project she and her colleagues are engaged in has become a fragmented, isolating one; and hope that its benefits will nevertheless be recognized and valued beyond their place and time, and beyond the realm of current influence and experience of its members. Livesay was engaged in many collective cultural projects in her long career; by the time she wrote this poem (probably still in her twenties), she had already published two well-received volumes of poetry, studied French Symbolist poetry at the Sorbonne in Paris, joined the Communist Party, trained as a social worker at the University of Toronto, and become a caseworker and political activist in Montreal and New Jersey. She would go on to write many more books of poetry, essays, and reviews, frequently announcing subjects and strategies that would become mainstream attentions in Canadian poetry a decade or two later, winning the Lorne Pierce Gold Medal of the Royal Society in 1947, and the Governor General's Awards for Poetry in 1944 and 1984. She established two literary magazines, *Contemporary Verse* in Vancouver in 1941 (together with Anne Marriott, Doris Ferne, and Floris Clark McClaren, appointing Alan Crawley as editor); and *Contemporary Verse II* in Winnipeg in 1975 (later renamed *Contemporary Verse 2*). Livesay was the self-appointed mentor of several generations of poets across the country for many decades, actively overseeing the development of an internationally inflected Canadian poetry scene and going out of her way to encourage younger women and men in every region to explore their poetic talents as deeply as possible. Her prolific, outspoken, and influential career spanned nearly the whole century, inhabited numerous locations and intellectual engagements across Canada and internationally, and addressed an impressive array of subjects—from romance to nationalism, racism, war, ecology, eroticism, reproduction, feminism, intergenerational relations, and aging—in a range of genres and poetic forms, from precise imagist portraits to energetic agitprop chants to politically astute radio dramas, to influential critical essays, to rhythmically charged, visionary, documentary long poems, prose autobiography, and fiction.

"With so dazzling a track record," Lee Thompson asks in her 1987 critical study of Livesay's work, "why has Livesay been comparatively neglected by literary critics in her homeland?" Thompson cites the omission of Livesay from F.R. Scott's 1936 anthology *New Provinces*, which "claimed to illustrate the new directions Canadian modernists were taking"; from Gary Geddes's 1970 first edition of *15 Canadian Poets*; and from the very male-dominated 1983 York University conference on the Canadian long poem, where "Livesay, one of its senior and most accomplished practitioners, was noticeably unfêted and even slighted while a tight circle of male poets and critics gave congratulatory papers upon one another's work" (147). Gender discrimination, asserts Thompson, along with a good dose of Ontario and Quebec centric regionalism, must be considered the basis for these omissions: how could a woman, a social worker and mother from

Winnipeg and Vancouver, be the leader of one of Canada's most important and innovative literary movements? The same pattern of neglect continues into the present. Brian Trehearne, in his otherwise fascinating history of the rise of literary modernism in Canada, *Aestheticism and the Canadian Modernists* (1989), makes the astonishing claim that Canadian modernism began in part in "the early volumes of Livesay" (252), and then mentions her only two more times in his 370-page book! Louis Dudek and Michael Gnarowski never mention her in their pioneering history of the rise of modernism in Canada, *The Making of Modern Poetry in Canada* (1947).

Dean Irvine, whose archival and editorial work has brought Livesay's and Anne Wilkinson's unpublished and uncollected works to recent critical and public attention, nevertheless reverts to the same masculinist genealogy in his 2005 anthology of essays, *The Canadian Modernists Meet*. The title is an overt nod to F.R. Scott's satirical poem, "The Canadian Authors Meet" (1927), which posited a muscular and implicitly masculine rebellion against the (feminine) "tea party" aesthetics of the Canadian literary establishment of the period. The poem is often cited as the birth announcement of Canadian modernism; one can read in it a subtext of a masculinist self-birthing, "bootstrapping," as is the fashionable term among scientists, through the rejection of maternity and women's collegial presence and influence: T.S. Eliot's daunting women "talking of Michelangelo" are reduced here to "twittering" Miss Crotchets. It is a narrative of origins that has been obediently adhered to by most Canadian literary historians into the present, even though it is, as Carole Gerson characterized it in an essay on literary canon formation in *Canadian Literature* in 1992, "a nasty [if witty] poem by an otherwise progressive poet" (62), that effectively dismissed the growing influence of women writers in the Canadian literary scene at the time. (From 1924 to 1933, the period Scott is writing about, for example, the membership of the 800-member Canadian Authors' Association grew from 45% to 58%). Gerson's essay is a perceptive call for the re-examination of Canada's modernist origins with an eye to gender consciousness, citing the well-known work of Shari Benstock in *Women of the Left Bank* (1986), Sandra Gilbert and Susan Gubar in *Madwoman in the Attic* (1988), and Bonnie Kime Scott in *The Gender of Modernism* (1990) as models of revisionary feminist literary scholarship. These groundbreaking texts brought the contribution of women writers to English, French, and American modernist aesthetics and culture to the foreground of literary consciousness, and thereby altered our understanding of the period and its workings and preoccupations immensely, both in highlighting the prodigious importance of women's writing and cultural activism to the period, and in revealing experimentalism in sexual expression and gender performance as one of its central concerns. In the case of Kime Scott, the inclusion of writers of the Harlem Renaissance in her profile of American modernism opened the door, additionally, to a much more racially and ethnically inflected understanding of the cultural project of the period. Kime Scott's current work is on the "greening of modernism," particularly in the work of Virginia Woolf, a new and timely direction of enquiry about the period that we address tangentially in this volume with an eye to further enquiry.

Irvine's collection aims to decentre the received canonicity of Canadian modernism by "shifting our gaze" from canonized figures and texts to more "peripheral" figures, institutions and texts, including a "revaluation of women modernists' marginality" (Introduction 8–9), celebrating the "tea party" of his contemporaries that Scott's poem satirized. A good half of the essays published in his anthology are written by women scholars, including several of the contributors to *Wider Boundaries*. In spite of these egalitarian intentions, however, Irvine's introduction resolutely repeats the standard masculinist genealogy, positing F.R. Scott and A.J.M. Smith as the originary fathers of the movement, and E.J. Pratt and Leo Kennedy as their sons and inheritors (omitting Klein, whom Dudek included in his trinity of fathers in Peter Stevens's 1969 collection of essays, *The McGill Movement*). Strong, central, pioneering women like Livesay, who began publishing several years before they did, who prominently appeared "in the vanguard of poetic modernism in Canada" from its beginning (Thompson 143), and whose literary career dramatically outshone theirs in numerous remarkable ways, are relegated to the margins of the movement. Celebrating the importance of "margins" and "peripheries" doesn't alter this fact. There have been several appreciative book-length feminist appraisals of Livesay's work in recent decades, notably by Lee Thompson (1987), Peter Stevens (1992), and Nadine McInnis (1994), but they have been primarily biographical and individual in emphasis. Trehearne, for his part, uses Livesay's stature to exclude her from *Aestheticism and the Canadian Modernists*, astonishingly asserting that because her work outlived the "aestheticist" moment of modernism, becoming "overwhelmed" by "more powerful influences," she had to be omitted from his study (313). One wonders which influences, darkly referred to but unspecified, Trehearne might be thinking of: Livesay's Communist affiliations? Her women's rights activism? Her agitprop work on the breadlines?

Why would these affiliations exclude her from his study, since she herself was actively and influentially engaged in the public discussion of aestheticism as a cultural project on numerous occasions during the formative years of Canadian modernism? We think, for example, of her well-known polemic, "Decadence in Modern Bourgeois Poetry," on the need for social conscience as a corrective to the solipsistic risk of aestheticism, given as a radio talk on CBC in 1936 (published in *Right Hand Left Hand*, 1977).

P.K. Page, despite her extensive poetic and artistic accomplishments over nearly a century, suffered a critical fate similar to Livesay's: "To read the table of contents in Louis Dudek and Michael Gnarowski's book *The Making of Modern Poetry in Canada*," observes Wanda Campbell (in Irvine's anthology), "one would assume that there were no female contributors at all to the modernist movement in Canada (only P.K. Page has a minor three-sentence entry)" (79). Campbell neglects to mention that the "minor entry" is followed by a copy of her letter to the editors of the fledgling literary magazine *Northern Review*, protesting the publication of a vicious review of a new poetry collection by Robert Finch; here she was distancing herself from the editorial policy of the magazine and declaring intellectual independence from the group. It is interesting that Gnarowski and Dudek saw fit to include her presence only with reference to this declarative moment, neither before nor after; interesting, too, that Campbell and Irvine missed the opportunity to comment on this point. Trehearne's *Aestheticism and the Canadian Modernists* has not even one reference to Page, Waddington, or Phyllis Webb, or any other woman poet of note, other than his three brief references to Livesay. His 1998 study of the McGill movement, *The Montreal Forties*, offers certain amends to these glaring omissions; its first chapter is devoted to Page's early poetry, and he goes so far as to call Page "the exemplary poet of the Montreal forties" (105). Interestingly, though, that the chapter begins with an extended discussion of the lengthy silence of her "middle period," followed by a lengthy excursion into local and international influences, most of them male, including Pound and Joyce and her often reluctant colleagues at *First Statement*. Trehearne's discussion of Page's poetics is insightful, positing a "tension between the compulsion to aesthetic brilliance and the force of experiential sympathy" in her poetry—precisely the topic of Livesay's polemic in her "Decadence" article. It is a problem that bedeviled most modernist poets, Trehearne observes, after the initial heady wave of radical dislocation and fragmentation of traditional lyric and narrative form (*Montreal Forties* 89, 66).

Page, like Livesay, was a prime mover in the development of Canadian modernism, and her poetry has continued to impress and influence her contemporaries into the present, undergoing several significant metamorphoses over her long career. Like Livesay, Page travelled widely, acquiring rich internationalist inflections in her work in the process. Both poets were interested in multimedia experimentation as well as poetry, Livesay exploring radio, agitprop theatre, and literary magazine publishing, and Page acquiring a second professional career as a recognized painter, under the name P.K. Irwin. Both garnered national and international success and celebrity, Livesay being named an Officer of the Order of Canada in 1986, Page in 1999. Page's early experiments with imagism and surrealism, and what we would now call ecopoetics, were succeeded by formal experiments in prose poetry and explorations of relational subjectivities, most recently through her popular resurrection of the Spanish glosa with its intricate intertextual possibilities.

Page's writing has inspired a conference and several essay collections, but as in the case of Livesay, these events and publications have been focussed on the individual poet.[1] A recent exception is the *Journal of Canadian Studies / Revue d'études canadiennes*'s special issue on Page's work, titled *Extraordinary Presence: The Worlds of P.K. Page / Une présence extraordinaire: Les univers de P.K. Page* (ed. Zailig Pollock), which features several critical reassessments of her work vis-à-vis the modernist canon. Irvine, for example, examines "the sociality of gender in modernist little magazine culture," citing *Contemporary Verse* as the first and most important publishing venue for Page's developing poetics as a young poet, predating her contact with the *Preview* group in Montreal (24). Trehearne reassesses his previous comments on Page's poetics as Montreal-derived, by highlighting its internationalist surrealist gestures. He posits, however, somewhat oddly, that the influence of international surrealism on her work may be no more than a "fascinating coincidence" (59).[2]

A similar case of critical neglect over a long and influential career can be made for Phyllis Webb. Her life was a public one indeed, including stints in radio broadcasting, as the founding organizer and later producer of the prestigious *Ideas* program on CBC from 1965 to 1969, and in politics, running for public office as a CCF (Co-operative Commonwealth Federation) candidate for Victoria in 1949—at the ripe age of 22! Webb published critically acclaimed collections of poetry, received numerous accolades and prizes, including, most famously, a private award in 1980, from Michael

Ondaatje, bp Nichol, Margaret Atwood, and Page, who felt the Governor General's Award for Poetry should have gone to her that year. She was given the Governor General's Award for Poetry two years later, in 1982, and was made an Officer of the Order of Canada in 1992. In his Notes on Contributors in *West Coast Line*'s special issue on Phyllis Webb, guest-edited by Pauline Butling, Roy Miki calls Webb a "prominent" West Coast Canadian poet "who, over four decades, has advanced a line of contemporary poetic thought on the cutting edge of what matters in this country" (6). Her experiments in imagism, mythopoetic archetypalism, and new subjectivities, including feminist but also more contemplative, transcultural, Haida- and Buddhist-derived transpersonal and impersonal being-states, produced what many consider to be an exemplary and certainly widely influential poetics; yet the first booklength study of her life and writing did not appear until 1997, when Butling's reading of Webb's oeuvre came out, titled *Seeing in the Dark: The Poetry of Phyllis Webb* (1997). Countering the long years of critical neglect and even denigration Webb had suffered at the hands of certain male critics, Butling asserts that Webb's writing ranks among the best in the country, both in its formal and visionary innovative practices, and is "pivotal to a politics of social change in which 'new' subjectivities are garnering increased visibility and value" (viii).

Miriam Waddington, Anne Marriott, Margaret Avison, Elizabeth Brewster, Anne Wilkinson, Jay Macpherson, and Elizabeth Smart, the other modernist women writers featured in this anthology, all became similarly prolific and important writers, deeply engaging a broad array of modernist concerns: the interrogation of subjectivity in the domestic and public arenas; new definitions of sociality and the implications of new media on the local, national, and transnational level; and experimental mythopoetic, surreal, "decadent," imagist, and what we would now call feminist and ecopoetic approaches to language and creative expression. Many of these women poets occupied prominent public positions in universities across the country, collected the country's top literary prizes, and inspired numerous imitators and admirers, and yet have suffered similar omission from major anthologies and critical genealogies. We note much appreciated important exceptions in this regard: *The New Oxford Book of Canadian Verse in English* (1982), edited by Margaret Atwood, and Garry Geddes's revised editions of *20th Century Poetry and Poetics* (2006) and *15 Poets x 3* (2001). All of the poets named here, with the exception of Wilkinson, who died in 1961, continued to metamorphose poetically into the height of the postmodern period, occupying positions of national and international influence until their deaths, Livesay in 1996, and Waddington in 2004. Page is still writing and publishing prominently and influentially in the present, in her nineties. The span of these poets' careers and the range of their artistic activities thus vastly exceeded the poetics of a single moment in the 1920s and 1940s, a point Patricia Smart has similarly made about the women of the Automatiste movement in Quebec in her feminist revisionary history of the period, *Les femmes du Refus Global* (1998). Thompson observes that Livesay's poetic subjects were often several decades ahead of the general literary fashion (144), a statement that applies to these women poets generally, who pioneered political modern content and form in ways that spoke powerfully to their own time and who brought new imaginative energies and new social spaces into Canadian literary life. Echoing Patricia Smart in the Quebec context, we assert that the depth, breadth, and longevity of these writers' literary productivity and influence should not be used to disqualify them from histories of the period, but rather to enrich their parameters and definition.

Wider Boundaries of Daring: The Modernist Impulse in Canadian Women's Poetry thus hopes to offer a corrective to the current telling of Canada's literary history by highlighting the achievement and legacy of our best modernist women poets, not "alone" but "together," not as solitary and marginal receivers of modernist influence but as important makers of it, consciously engaging in a collective, revisionary, "new" cultural project. Such a revaluation has been long called for. In 1983, David Arnason gave a paper at the Dorothy Livesay conference at the University of Waterloo titled "Dorothy Livesay and the Rise of Modernism in Canada," declaring Livesay the progenitor of Canadian modernism and proposing that the project of modernism needs to be rethought in light of her central place in the making of it. Arnason's paper emphatically sets aside Scott's and Smith's literary experiments in the *McGill Fortnightly Review* as "the juvenilia of two writers who later became well known in Canada [but who] represented neither a breakthrough nor even a beginning of modernist writing in Canada," championing in their stead the young Livesay's "stunning" and thoroughly modern first two poetry collections, *Green Pitcher* in 1928 and *Signpost* in 1932. These accomplished books, argues Arnason, exhibit a consciousness "steeped in modern poetics," which he defines broadly as "a rejection of conventional nineteenth-century poetic structure" in favour of highly charged language," often "suffused with irony and objectivity" (6). Arnason also identifies a feminine, indeed feminist, genealogy in Canadian letters in observing that

Livesay's accomplished poetics at such a young age derived, in part, from her innovative poet mother, Florence Randal Livesay, who taught her to experiment with modern form. Arnason proposes a radical revision of our history and understanding of the period, given that important writers like Livesay rejected the alienated, aristocratic, and masculinist "high modernism" typified by Eliot, in favour of a more socially committed, and accessible, "humane and democratic vision" (17).

Barbara Godard's influential feminist essay, "Ex-centriques, Eccentric, Avant-Garde: Women and Modernism in the Literatures of Canada," appeared in the premiere issue of *Tessera*, a new feminist journal co-founded by Godard (with Gail Scott, Daphne Marlatt, and Kathy Mezei) in 1984. Godard announces the project of decentring the masculinist and ahistorical Canadian literary canon prevalent at the time, by championing experimental, liminal, and avant-garde prose writing by women in the forties and fifties. She points out that Robert Kroetsch's provocative remark in the American journal *boundary 2* in the early seventies—that Canada had skipped the modernist phase and gone straight from the Victorian to the postmodern—had effectively stopped critical investigation into Canadian literary modernism, and particularly the central role played by women writers and artists in its creation. Countering the widely held view that Canadian fiction of the period was dominated by "social realism" and mostly written by men, Godard champions the stylistically innovative novels of Elizabeth Smart, Sheila Watson, Gabrielle Roy, and Thérèse Tardif, which introduced a visionary, surreal, and highly self-reflexive sensibility into Canadian fiction that was identifiably modernist, as well as feminist, in the tradition of the lyrical novel introduced by Virginia Woolf and Djuna Barnes, and the language writing of Gertrude Stein. Novels such as Smart's *By Grand Central Station I Sat Down and Wept* and Sheila Watson's *The Double Hook*, argues Godard, are characterized by repetition, syntactic disruption, lack of plot, and moments of epiphany, and exemplify modernist preoccupations with experimental subjectivities and new definitions of sociality that should put them in the vanguard of Canadian literary history rather than its margins. Her valorization of innovative women's writing in the essay and elsewhere in the same period (notably in oft-cited essays on Sheila Watson in *Studies in Canadian Literature* and Quebec women's writing in *Fireweed*), was highly significant in changing the direction of critical attention in Canadian literary studies toward greater interest in experimental prose writing and toward the consideration of a much broader range of women writers in defining a literary tradition in Canada. Glen Willmott, for example, acknowledges Godard's influence in his detailed study of the Canadian novel as an experimental form, with Sheila Watson's work as a major example (*Unreal Country*, 2002); Dean Irvine's critical and editorial work on modernist women poets such as Livesay (*Archive for Our Times*, 1998) and Wilkinson (*Heresies: The Complete Poems of Anne Wilkinson*, 2003), and in his edited collection *The Canadian Modernists Meet* (2005), as well as Diana Relke's project to delineate a women's literary genealogy in Canada along ecopoetic lines in *Greenwor(l)ds* (1999), are similarly indebted to Godard's reframing of the Canadian modernist literary project in more experimental and egalitarian ways. The essays in this volume take up Godard's challenge in several important further directions.

Wider Boundaries of Daring highlights the central contribution of women writers to the movement we now refer to as modernism and assesses the cultural achievements of our best modernist women writers in multi-faceted ways, individually and collectively, biographically and critically, in contexts ranging from the local and regional to the national and international, from the artistic locus of intimate literary coteries and small magazines to book publication and international festivals, from the public intellectual milieux of emergent media such as radio and television to academic and political institutional engagements. How does this important and necessary revision of our literary genealogy alter our understanding of women's cultural history, and of the modernist movement as such? The women writers represented in this anthology did not, for example, subscribe to models of aestheticism divorced from social and political engagement; they were teachers, mothers, wives, social workers, public intellectuals, and holders of political office, as well as innovative writers and mentors to colleagues and students. They resisted binary oppositions between domestic and public interests, and indeed between regional, national, and internationalist concerns, practising a wide range of fluid identifications that crossed numerous conventional categorizations and boundaries. They seized in linguistic experimentation the opportunity to revise their own civic and personal responsibilities and liberties. They practised in this way radically experimental collective and individual subjectivities and cultural expressions that paved the way for contemporary women's lives and altered the shape of the culture generally, in profound and lasting ways. Their refusal to accept the masculinist model of aestheticism divorced from the challenges and obligations of personal life brought experimental innovation and political involvement much closer together, and caused a revolution in cultural values and opportunities for both sexes.

Dorothy Livesay's poem "We Are Alone" suggests that the ambivalence the poet feels about the revolutionary cultural project she shares with unnamed "comrades" is not because she doubts its aims, but rather because she feels discouraged by the many political obstacles the movement has encountered. Let us remember that women in Canada did not receive the vote in Canada until 1917 and then under racialized conditions; women in Quebec received the provincial vote in 1940, and Aboriginal women across the country in 1960. Canadian women were forced by law to choose between public careers and marriage until 1955, and by social convention for another decade after that. The monumental struggle—acquiring the right to have a public career; the right to have intellectual opinions; the right to expect family and community support for artistic, activist, and professional work; the right to maintain domestic interests and sexual relationships while pursuing a public career—left its indelible mark on the work of all modernist women, though it has not yet been adequately acknowledged and appreciated by those of us who follow in their footsteps and benefit from the fruits of their labour. The two world wars and the Great Depression were extremely traumatic for the whole culture, especially men, who were sent to their deaths in great numbers; many of the stunned survivors of World War One were disenfranchised by a faltering economy soon after. Despair over the loss of connection to the traditions of the past and over the failure of rationalism and positivism to prevent the horrors of mass violence has often been cited as the grounds for modernist revision (e.g., Friedman 97), though as Shari Benstock points out, such an interpretation belies the hugely optimistic, creative, revolutionary impulse evident in the movement. Much of this impulse came from the rising up of previously disenfranchised groups, including Blacks and homosexuals, the jobless, and most prominently, women, especially those of privileged enough backgrounds to have access to education and especially travel, which allowed them to escape conventional definitions of sociality and develop "new" definitions of individuality and community. As many of the essays in this volume demonstrate, the cultural activism engaged in by modernist women writers and artists was a complex negotiation, as they learned to juggle their own personal and professional aspirations and new, experimental social engagements with domestic and public forms of support for disenfranchised individuals and groups, including men, while at the same time resisting the seductions of male mentors and colleagues into revised servant roles, as secretaries, "stenographers" (to quote Page's famous poem by that title), and extramarital mistresses. There is much still to be said on the subject.

The new urban landscape, with its concentrated pockets of impoverishment, newly devastated industrialized environments, and shattered local traditions, lifestyles, and communities, was also of great concern to the modernists, as eloquently epitomized in Eliot's canonic *The Waste Land*. Many White male artists responded to this devastation by championing a techno-scientific, "impersonal" futurism that might offer optimistic new vistas of exploration and imagination despite these problems, as evident in the manifestoes and productions of the Futurists and Vorticists, for example, and in the ironic materialist imagism of Ezra Pound and William Carlos Williams; others responded by championing the irrational, the absurd, the spiritual, and the dreamlike, pushing the limits of language and human expressiveness to new levels, most extremely in Dadaism and Surrealism. Women artists, even when participating in similar kinds of artistic experiments, tended to focus more on their practical aspect, in the nurturance of the new subjectivities, communities, and social actions made necessary and possible by the dislocations of capitalist expansion and industrialism, and on a more fluid, transpersonal, and often spiritually inflected sensibility that focussed on survival and harmony with the non-human world, rather than championing further territorialization and conquest. We can, for example, contrast Pound's ironic imagism with H.D.'s, which was much more interested in celebrating natural, psychic, and cosmic energies and connections, her starry, magical flowers refusing the violent yoking together of "petals on a wet black bough" with human crowds in the dirty urban metro (as in H.D.'s oft-cited "Stars Wheel in Purple" and Pound's canonical "In a Station of the Metro"). In Canada, F.R. Scott's "Trans Canada" is an enthusiastic poetic celebration of "steel" and the airplane, and A.J.M. Smith's vivid description of a river's rushing narrows as "sharpness cutting sharpness, / arrows of direction, / spears of speed" in "Swift Current" (8–10) deftly erases the distinction between the natural, primitive tools and contemporary technologies, implying direct unmediated continuity between them. These poems can be contrasted with Livesay's "Green Rain" and "Fire and Reason," and Page's "Stories of Snow" and "After Rain," among numerous other poetic examples. These latter poems focus rather on the predominance of the natural world and the surrounding cosmos over our human activities, and plead for greater environmental respect and gratitude for our relatively small place in this great web of life, employing imagist and surreal techniques to enact harmonious imaginative engagements between the human and natural.

Diana Relke has offered an extended meditation on the ecopoetic aspect of Livesay's, Page's, and Webb's writing in her study, *Greenwor(l)ds: Ecocritical Readings of Canadian Women's Poetry* (1999), which she places in a women's genealogy going back to nineteenth-century poets Marjorie Pickthall, Constance Lindsay Skinner, and E. Pauline Johnson ("Tekahionwake"), and forward to such contemporary writers as Margaret Atwood, Daphne Marlatt, Jeanette Armstrong, and Marilyn Dumont. Relke's point is that the nineteenth-century shift toward ever greater technological interventions and domestic displacements had direct implications for women's lives in all industrialized countries, radically interrupting and undermining their traditional domestic powers and reproductive responsibilities, which sharpened their critique of increasing technologization and militaristic nation building. Disagreeing radically with their male colleagues' sense of what Northrop Frye famously typified as a "deep terror in regard to nature" and resulting "garrison mentality," Canadian modernist women poets tended to favour more holistic, fluid, and sustainable relations with the natural world, and new forms of self-expression and community building. These included extensive dialogues across traditional cultural boundaries, which contributed actively to the building of new multicultural communities such as have come to characterize the postmodern. Patricia Smart, writing about the emergence of the feminine in the Quebec literary tradition, observed a similar dynamic in French-speaking Canada: male writers clinging to a "dream of enduring forever," a fortress-like identity erected "against all it perceives as 'other,' including and especially woman"; women, in contrast, seemed more "capable of imagining a country in movement and with ever-expanding borders, a house open to diversity and offering solidarity to all those— female or male [and, we would add, non-human]—who are struggling for justice within it" (*Writing in the Father's House* 18–19).

The socialist aims we hear echoed in Livesay's poetic lament, "We Are Alone," trying to gather together the fragmented pieces of a shattered holistic vision, therefore represent an agenda of radical cultural reform that was widely shared among artists and intellectuals of the modernist era, but that found specific, additional recognitions and aims among women writers, in diverse but interconnected ways. The essays that follow attempt to explore and spell out these connections, while inviting further investigations on these themes. Livesay's poetic lament for the widespread failure of her cause, at least in the moment, is tempered by a breathtaking leap into the future, where hopefully the collective labours of the movement can bear great fruit, despite the difficulties of the moment. We can respond both positively and negatively to this point from the vantage point of our own time and situation. On the one hand, things have only become much worse; the lives of young women and men, trying to juggle personal, professional, and artistic aspirations with the demands of an increasingly relentless hyper-capitalist global economy, have not gotten easier; our prospects for the future, economically and environmentally speaking, are bleaker than ever. On the other hand, the poetic hope for greater communal support for the project of radical cultural reform, in a way that opens up new opportunities for women and people of formerly oppressed and dispossessed homelands, has indeed borne glorious fruit in the proliferation of stylistic expression and feminist and multicultural access to artistic and intellectual opportunity, no doubt far beyond what our literary foremothers dreamed of for us. Environmental awareness and a multifaceted critique of fascist appropriations of regional and national agendas—the problem that bedevils the modern moment, in the absence of traditional religious and cultural practices to limit their aspirations to power—have also multiplied in creative ways that would have delighted and astonished Livesay and her colleagues. It has taken a long time for us to turn around and thank our modernist literary foremothers properly for their forward-looking cultural labours. We could also say that it's possible to measure the stature of these courageous artists' achievement and talent in part by how many decades it took for their vision to bear appreciative critical fruit: that is how large their project was.

Wider Boundaries of Daring: The Modernist Impulse in Canadian Women's Poetry aims, then, to complicate previous genealogies and critical analyses of the modernist period in anglophone Canada by highlighting the rich legacy of our women poets and their contribution to the modernist movement in both its social and its aesthetic aspects, and to enact critical reading strategies that might serve to rewrite the making of modernism in Canada and beyond. In so doing, we wish more accurately to reflect the enlarged scope of subjectivities, the proliferation of experimental linguistic and perceptual strategies, and the emergence of new environmental, social, and political concerns that define the period, and further, to highlight women's central contribution to their development in extensive innovative activist gestures and production of exciting literary and artistic texts. Our collection features sixteen essays by some of Canada's best established and emerging scholars, adopting a diverse range of approaches in their assessment of the achievement and legacy of Canada's modernist women poets. The project began as a public dialogue at the conference/festival "Wider Boundaries of Daring: The Modernist Impulse in Canadian Women's Poetry," held in 1991 at the University of Windsor, the Art Gallery of Windsor, and the Scarab Club, Detroit; it has expanded considerably in several directions since then, including an ongoing conversation among the contributors represented here. We hope, in presenting these essays to the public, to foster further enquiries into the under-studied accomplishments of these important women writers and their part in the creation of Canadian literary modernism, and to take up their challenge to future generations, to expand the imaginative possibilities of our cultural expressions, in order to open up new, life-giving, life-enhancing opportunities for our children and our beloved earth, as we face our own ecologically and politically uncertain future.

The essays in the first half of our anthology, titled "The Making of Canadian Literary Modernism," explore the complex and diverse influences at work in the birthing and development of Canadian literary modernism. Ann Martin, in "The Writing Livesays: Connecting Generations of Canadian Modernism," takes up the challenge issued by Arnason, Godard, and Gerson, to affirm and investigate further the origins of the movement in Livesay's early poetic experiments and relationship with her poet and cultural activist mother Florence Randal Livesay. Livesay's experiments with imagism, and her exploration of the new "rural–urban split" and the public role of women in the modern world, were nurtured by similar motifs in her mother F.R. Livesay's writing and cultural activism, according to Martin, even though their aesthetic styles differed considerably according to their times. Martin's essay confirms the existence of a female genealogy in the development of modernist writing in Canada. Christine Kim significantly revises the role of small magazines in the making of Canadian modernism in her essay, "Feminist and Regionalist Modernisms in *Contemporary Verse, CV/II*, and *CV2*," positing the primacy of *Contemporary Verse*, established by Dorothy Livesay and several colleagues in Vancouver in 1941, over the often cited originary significance of *Preview* and *First Statement*. If we acknowledge gender and multiple points of view as significant modernist concerns, then the definitions of the movement proposed by these latter magazines appear more narrowly biased in favour of centrist, masculinist, and nationalist interests, rather than the cosmopolitan and universalist interests they claimed to promote. *CV/II*, established by Livesay in 1975 in Winnipeg as a regionally representative poetry review journal, and later renamed *CV2* by its new feminist editorial collective, has experienced grave difficulties over the years in sustaining a national feminist public forum in Canada, for numerous financial and political reasons; *CV2* has survived much the way its predecessor *CV* did, by privileging difference and multiplicity over synthesis and unity.

Sandra Djwa examines early intellectual and artistic influences on Page in her essay, "P.K. Page: Discovering a Modern Sensibility," such as Virginia Woolf and Katherine Mansfield, thus broadening the notion of a women's genealogy in the creation of Canadian literary modernism to the international context. Page chose, at age seventeen, to travel abroad for a year in lieu of a college education, and she spent an impressionable year in London, visiting galleries and bookstores, and trying her hand at writing and art. She therefore did not arrive in the *Preview* group in Montreal in 1942 as a naïve and uneducated writer waiting to be taught by male mentors, as is often implied, but rather, as a woman with cosmopolitan experience and an already developed modernist and woman-centred sensibility and artistic practice. Bina Toledo Freiwald, in "Tradition, Individual Talent, and 'a young woman / From backwoods New Brunswick': Modernism and Elizabeth Brewster's (Auto) Poetics of the Subject," theorizes that Brewster's considerable poetic oeuvre has been overlooked because the literary establishment has lacked a critical idiom to examine her project. Freiwald proposes a Foucauldian exploration of the "technologies of the self" as a suitable frame for examining Brewster's poetics, recognizing subjectivity as a deliberate act, a "willed performance," the staking of a claim, whether "territorial, epistemic, or aesthetic." Reading Brewster's poetry in this way highlights the numerous existential and formal risks she, and modernist women writers generally, had to take in their life and writing, resulting in "multiple and shifting" identifications and affiliations.

Kathy Mezei, in "'And we are homesick still': Home, the Unhomely, and the Everyday in Anne Wilkinson," examines the domestic aspect of Wilkinson's poetry, and demonstrates a dialogism at work in her poetics, whereby the personal, the quotidian, and the everyday are put into dynamic oscillation with the mythopoetic and universalist interests for which she has been recognized. Domestic space and women's bodies in this decimated though once powerful female domain are often figured in women's writing of the modernist era in "macabre images of dissection, drowning, disfigurement and dismemberment," but also in images of "metamorphosis and reincarnation," indicating the depth of the renegotiation of women's spaces that occurred in this period.

Marilyn J. Rose analyzes Anne Marriott's lack of critical attention despite a substantial body of poetry that is "haunting and evocative, spare and laconic" in the high modernist style, and despite great early success, in her essay, "Anne Marriott: Modernist on the Periphery." By literalizing Marriott's peripherality as geographical and ideological, that is, located on the West Coast far from the centres of Canadian literary power and dedicated to a "discourse of locality," Rose rehabilitates Marriott's choice of short lyrics of place and personal experience after her early success as the writer of long poems in the more fashionable cosmopolitan style, as "ex/centric," in the positive sense of deliberately challenging established, centrist views and practices. Her long periods of silence, Rose argues, must be understood as indicative of her lack of cultural support as a woman artist, working against prevailing social norms in a relatively isolated context.

Lianne Moyes's essay on literary influence, "Discontinuity, Intertextuality, and Literary History: Gail Scott's Reading of Gertrude Stein," concludes the first section of our anthology. Moyes's reading of Scott's contemporary texts in modernist terms derives from Scott's identification with the French and American feminist avant-garde rather than English-Canadian literary writing. Moyes finds Gail Scott's modernité, particularly in her recent poetic travel narrative, *My Paris* (1999), to be multiply inflected with feminist, transnational, modernist, and postmodernist concerns, in a context that is Canadian and European (as well as global), English and French, and in a genre that is both poetry and prose, documentary and fiction. The example of Scott complicates any simple genealogical—or even generic—reading of Canadian literary modernism by challenging its defining categories; Moyes's essay thus foregrounds principles of complexity, discontinuity and multiplicity of identifications that are implicit in our collection as a whole, and that invite further investigations in numerous directions.

The second half of our anthology, "Literary Modernism as Cultural Act," further highlights the complex negotiations that Canadian women writers enacted in their poetics and social activism in the modernist period, in the struggle to fashion a more open-ended, experimental, woman-centred cultural space. Modernism is often characterized as detached from the world of everyday affairs, but the work of the women writers featured here profoundly contradicts that view. Not only were they deeply involved in the cultural issues of their time, as their passionate and complex poetics amply demonstrates, but many of them also spent long hours working as public intellectuals—in addition to their domestic responsibilities—participating fully in the opportunities presented by the new media, newspapers, and radio, joining political parties and demonstrations, and taking up academic positions as critics and teachers. Dorothy Livesay, trained as a social worker, briefly lived and worked in New Jersey in the 1930s, where she encountered the shocking legacy of American slavery and racism face to face. Pamela McCallum demonstrates, in "'They cut him down': Race, Class, and Cultural Memory in Dorothy Livesay's 'Day and Night,'" how Livesay's communist-inflected social politics served as a model for the development of an evocative rhythm- and repetition-based poetics that enacted a devastating critique of American racism and the industrial enslavement of labour, while simultaneously envisioning "a transformed world where new social relations might emerge." Peggy Kelly documents the productive and sometimes fraught relationship Livesay had with CBC Radio in the forties and fifites in her study, "Dorothy Livesay and CBC Radio: The Politics of Modernist Aesthetics, Gender, and Regionalism." Livesay's relationship with the CBC was complicated by its masculinist and regionalist biases, and the extensive correspondence she carried on with editors at the CBC highlights both the experimental and fiercely political aspects of her literary practice. Livesay was a fiercer fighter than most women writers; one can only imagine how many times other, less combative women writers backed down in the face of similar masculinist opposition in their careers. Kelly's essay also foregrounds the complicated place that public radio occupied during those years in Canada, as an important internationalist intellectual forum, rapidly developing into what it has since become, a popular mass medium.

Phyllis Webb served as CBC Radio's founding director of the new program, *Ideas*, in the mid-sixties, when its gender restrictions had evidently become much less severe. Pauline Butling examines "Phyllis Webb as Public Intellectual" in Webb's work at the CBC and its relation to her poetic accomplishments. Butling concludes that, even though it was exhausting and left no time or energy for poetry, the position was productive for Webb the poet, giving her an influential and prestigious public forum in which to explore social and political ideas such as nationalism and modernism, which would become important to her own poetics later on. The experience also highlighted for her the overwhelmingly male character of cultural institutions and galvanized her to seek a more feminist-inflected community and writing practice. Miriam Waddington was perhaps Canada's most prolific and perceptive modernist woman critic, publishing extensively and influentially in the areas of poetry and criticism, in newspapers and radio. Candida Rifkind examines Waddington's under-recognized critical writing from the 1950s to the 1970s in her essay, "'A Collection of Solitary Fragments': Miriam Waddington as Critic," finding that Waddington consistently articulated cultural dissension from a Jewish and feminist minority point of view, which gave her also an understanding of other communities of alterity and difference, and fuelled an extensive discussion about Canadian nation building in a context of rich cultural multiplicity. Waddington consistently challenged women writers by both example and exhortation to be more "aggressive" in their feminist interventions in the public arena. A significant portion of her criticism grappled with the aesthetic and social potential of the new electronic media. Her concern was the failure of radio and television to realize their dynamic intellectual potential under pressure from the commercializing status quo, disagreeing in this way with Marshall McLuhan, whom Waddington charged with being too politically detached.

Genre was another area that required extensive and complex negotiations for modernist women writers intent on not giving over their subjectivity and independence to masculinist conventions. Sara Jamieson, in "'Our hearts both leapt / in love with metaphor': P.K. Page's Professional Elegies," shows how Page successfully refashioned the elegy as a form of feminist expression in her poetry. The convention was fraught with peril for young women writers, who risked falling into the Victorian stereotype of the "sympathetic poetess" weeping over the personal loss of friendships, and Page judiciously avoided elegies in her early writing. In later writing, however, she used the elegaic convention with great sophistication and ambivalence, reflecting the complexity of the sexual politics involved in negotiating her place as a woman writer in a male-dominated tradition. Elizabeth Smart, by contrast, did battle with the conventions and pitfalls of conventional romance by embracing a reckless and extravagant poetics of excess. In her essay exploring "The Passionate and Sublime Modernism of Elizabeth Smart," Anne Quéma asserts that Smart developed an emotionally suffused "poetics of the subjective and suffering personality" in her writing, which dramatically challenged Eliot's creed of impersonality yet fully participated in the modernist project of inventing new experimental subjectivities and relations. She famously and dramatically lived her idea of independence suffused with romance as the long-time mistress of the married poet George Barker, bearing five of his children and raising them on her own. Quéma, citing Barbara Godard's "Ex-centrique" argument, observes that Smart's poetic prose represents the kind of literary experimentalism that was typical of Canadian women's prose writing of the 1940s, and included fiction by Watson and Roy, in contrast to the social realist fiction by male writers often cited as characteristic of the period.

Miriam Nichols gives a nuanced reading of Jay Macpherson's modernist poetics in her essay, "Jay Macpherson's Modernism." While Macpherson's imagery is traditional-sounding in its evocation of a conventional quest motif, it is thoroughly modern in its skepticism and woman-centred perspective. Macpherson's mythopoetic vision speaks eloquently to both the modernist age and our own, initiating "an intricate dance of disenchantment and possibility," thereby envisioning the dynamics of renewal for not just women but an entire culture that urgently needs "to face what it has repressed and so reinvent itself." Macpherson's valorization of flood-like temporalities such as wasteland, ark, umbrella, and teddy bear resonates eerily with the catastrophic resonances of the contemporary environmental crisis. Margaret Avison is also drawn to motifs of transformation, but in her case, with an enthusiastic embrace of religious belief. Katherine Quinsey, in "Word, I, and Other in Margaret Avison's Poetry," describes Avison's writing as straddling both modernism and postmodernism in its aesthetic and existential concerns, her oeuvre straddling both periods—as is true of many of the women writers featured in this volume. Quinsey identifies Avison's articulation of human alienation, fragmented subjectivity, and linguistic economy as recognizably modernist, while the breaking open of conventional definitions of self and Other, and the undermining of the primacy of rationalist ways of knowing in favour of the regenerative insubjectivity and heightened perceptiveness of the "optic heart," can be called postmodern—though in the genealogy we have been tracing here, Avison's strategies evoke also the modernist visionary experiments of H.D. and Virginia Woolf, and the early ecopoetic and surreal poetics of Livesay and Page.

Elena Basile's essay, "Reading P.K. Page in English/Italian; or, On the Politics of Translating Modernist Gender," concludes our volume, throwing open the parameters of our study of Canadian literary modernism by offering an example of the foreign reception of the writing from this period in other languages and cultures and times. Basile finds the translation of Page's modernist poetry in the contemporary Italian context to be, unsurprisingly, a complicated venture. She observes that Page's highly ambiguous gender identifications in the text under question, a bilingual selected edition, *Rosa dei Venti / Compass Rose* (translated by Franscesca Valenti, illustrated by Italian artist Mimmo Paladino, and published by Longo Editore in 1998 as one of a series of Canadian poetry collections in translation), are rendered, somewhat reductively, as unambiguous and masculinist in the Italian version. Likewise, the metapoetic and inclusive implications of Page's imagist metaphors are often elided in favour of more realist psychological and referentially oriented interpretations. Basile finds that bilingual editions like Longo Editore's highlight the failure of "domesticating" translations such as this one to accurately render the complexities of original texts, but she praises them nonetheless for encouraging "semantic drift" beyond the texts themselves, cultivating, in this way, the kind of "transnational literacy" that Gayatri Chakravorty Spivak has championed as a necessary critique against the hegemonic assumptions of the permeability of languages under anglophone dominance.

In these multiple ways, we wish to challenge and augment existing histories of the modernist period, by positing a broad international context for the study of Canadian literary modernism, but with diverse regional and local inflections and concerns, and a strong focus on the aesthetic and political interests of women. Engaging deeply with the political, social, and aesthetic issues of their period, the women writers featured in this volume gave us numerous gifts of creative expression, revisionary thinking, and exemplary action to guide and inspire us in the present, when many of the rights and privileges they fought for have become the norm, and transversely, many of the problems they foresaw and tackled have become augmented to extreme proportions. Individually and together, the Canadian modernist women poets featured in this volume created a spectacular poetic legacy that has inspired a century of writers and readers of both genders, across Canada and around the world, and that stands among the best poetic writing of all time, anywhere. In sum, their works redefine the literary meaning of modernism and reshape its history in ways that we are delighted to celebrate.

Notes

We thank the University of Windsor, York University, the Art Gallery of Windsor, the Scarab Club (Detroit), the Social Sciences and Humanities Research Council of Canada, the Canada Council for the Arts, the Writers' Union of Canada, the League of Canadian Poets, and the Laidlaw Foundation for generously supporting the international conference/festival "Wider Boundaries of Daring: The Modernist Impulse in Canadian Women's Poetry" in October 2001. The dialogues that inspired the essays in this collection first took place at that conference. Thank you to Christine Kim for inputting the manuscript and to Lisa Quinn at Wilfrid Laurier University Press for excellent editorial advice. Thank you to Brandon University and the Canada Research Chair Council for research time, and to York University for financial assistance in the preparation of the manuscript for publication. The companion volume to this collection is *Re:Generations: Canadian Women Poets in Conversation* (Windsor, ON: Black Moss, 2005), which features poetry, interviews, testimonials, reflections, photographic reproductions of paintings, and musical scores by poets and scholars who attended and were featured at the "Wider Boundaries of Daring" conference/festival. The anthology highlights the interdisciplinary, transgenerational, and multimedia aspects of Canada's modernist women's poetry, and their inspiring influence upon succeeding generations of women writers, artists, and composers. *Awakenings* is a one-hour poem–song cycle in four voices, with poetry by Di Brandt and Dorothy Livesay, and music by Rebecca Campbell and Carol Ann Weaver, commissioned for and premiered at "Wider Boundaries" and produced as a CD audio recording in 2003 (c/o caweaver@uwaterloo.ca). A second poetry-music audio recording is forthcoming, titled *Planet Earth,* featuring Canadian women's poetry set to music for soprano and piano, and including Jana Skarecky's setting of three poems by P.K. Page, two of which were commissioned for and premiered at the conference/festival.

Dorothy Livesay's poem, "We Are Alone," was probably written in the 1930s but was first published in the posthumous collection, *Archive for Our Times*, edited by Dean Irvine (1988), and appears here by permission of the Livesay Estate.

1 See Linda Rogers's edited collection *P.K. Page: Essays on Her Works* (2001) and the special issue of *Malahat Review* on Page, edited by Jay Ruzesky.
2 Trehearne doesn't mention Rosemary Sullivan's essay on Page's friendship with both Leona Carrington and Remedios Varo in Mexico, "Meeting in Mexico," which first appeared in *Brick* in 1996, then in Sullivan's essay collection *Memory-Making*, in 2001, and again in *Re:Generations: Canadian Women Poets in Conversation*, in 2005, though of course artistic influence doesn't depend on personal meetings, as Trehearne seems to imply.

Works Cited

Arnason, David. "Dorothy Livesay and the Rise of Modernism in Canada." Dorney, Noonan, and Tiessen 5–18.

Atwood, Margaret, ed. *The New Oxford Book of Canadian Verse in English.* Toronto: Oxford UP, 1982.

Benstock, Shari. *Women of the Left Bank.* Austin: U of Texas P, 1986.

Brandt, Di, and Barbara Godard, eds. *Re:Generations: Canadian Women Poets in Conversation.* Introd. Di Brandt. Windsor, ON: Black Moss, 2005.

Butling, Pauline. *Seeing in the Dark: The Poetry of Phyllis Webb*. Waterloo: Wilfrid Laurier UP, 1997.

———, guest ed. *"You Devise. We Devise": A Festschrift for Phyllis Webb*. Spec. issue of *West Coast Line* 6, 25/3, 1991–1992: 14–17.

Campbell, Wanda. "Moonlight and Morning: Women's Early Contribution to Modernism." Irvine, *Canadian Modernists Meet*. Ottawa: U of Ottawa P, 2005. 79–99.

Dorney, Lindsay, Gerald Noonan, and Paul Tiessen, eds. *A Public and Private Voice: Essays on the Life and Work of Dorothy Livesay*. Waterloo: U of Waterloo P, 1986.

Dudek, Louis, and Michael Gnarowski, eds. *The Making of Modern Poetry in Canada: Essential Articles on Contemporary Canadian Poetry in English*. Toronto: Ryerson P, 1967.

Friedman, Susan Stanford. *Psyche Reborn: The Emergence of H.D.* Bloomington: Indiana UP, 1981.

Geddes, Gary, ed. *15 Poets x 3*. Toronto: Oxford UP, 2001.

———, ed. *20th-Century Poetry and Poetics*. 5th ed. Toronto: Oxford UP, 2006.

Geddes, Gary, and Phyllis Bruce, ed. *15 Canadian Poets*. Toronto: Oxford UP, 1970.

Gerson, Carol. "Sarah Binks and Edna Jacques: Parody, Gender and the Construction of Literary Value." *Canadian Literature* 134 (1992): 62–73.

Gilbert, Sandra M., and Susan Gubar. *No Man's Land: The Place of the Woman Writer in the Twentieth Century*. 2 vols. New Haven, CT: Yale UP, 1988–89.

Godard, Barbara. "Between One Cliché and Another: Language in *The Double Hook*." *Studies in Canadian Literature* 4.1 (Summer 1978): 114–65. Rpt. in *Sheila Watson and the Double Hook*. Ed. George Bowering. Ottawa: Golden Dog, 1985. 159–76.

———. "Ex-centriques, Eccentric, Avant-Garde: Women and Modernism in the Literatures of Canada." *Tessera* 1 / *Room of One's Own: A Feminist Journal* 8.4 (1984): 57–75.

———. "Kinds of Osmosis." Pollock 65–75.

———. "Transgressions." *Fireweed* 5 (1979–80): 120–29. Rpt. as "Trangressions." Trans. Lori St. Martin. *L'autre lecture: Critiques au féminin de textes québécois*. Montreal: XYZ, 1992. 2:85–95.

Irvine, Dean, ed. *Archive for Our Times: Previously Uncollected and Unpublished Poems of Dorothy Livesay*. Vancouver: Arsenal Pulp, 1998.

———, ed. *The Canadian Modernists Meet*. Ottawa: U Ottawa P, 2005.

———, ed. *Heresies: The Complete Poems of Anne Wilkinson, 1924–1961*. Toronto: Signal, 2003.

———. Introduction. *The Canadian Modernists Meet*. Ed. D. Irvine. Ottawa: U of Ottawa P, 2005.

———. "The Two Giovannis: P.K. Page's Two Modernisms." Pollock 23–45.

Kroetsch, Robert. "A Canadian Issue." *Boundary 2* 3.1 (Autumn 1974): 1–2.

Lecker, Robert, and Jack David, eds. *The New Canadian Anthology: Poetry and Short Fiction in English*. Toronto: Nelson, 1988.

Lister, Rota Herzberg. "From Confrontation to Conciliation: The Growth of Dorothy Livesay as a Political Dramatist." Dorney, Noonan, and Tiessen 53–70.

Livesay, Dorothy. "Day and Night." *Day and Night: Poems*. Toronto: Ryerson, 1944.

———. "Decadence in Modern Bourgeois Poetry." *Right Hand, Left Hand: A True Life of the Thirties; Paris, Toronto, Montreal, the West, and Vancouver; Love, Politics, the Depression, and Feminism*. Ed. David Arnason. Erin, ON: Porcépic, 1977. 61–67.

———. *Green Pitcher*. Toronto: Macmillan of Canada, 1928.

———. *Signpost*. Toronto: Macmillan of Canada, 1932.

———. "We Are Alone." *Archive for Our Times: Previously Uncollected and Unpublished Poems of Dorothy Livesay*. Ed. Dean Irvine. Foreword by Miriam Waddington. Afterword by Di Brandt. Vancouver: Arsenal Pulp, 1998.

McInnis, Nadine. *Dorothy Livesay's Poetics of Desire*. Winnipeg: Turnstone, 1994.

Miki, Roy, ed. Notes on Contributors. *"You Devise. We Devise": A Festschrift for Phyllis Webb*. Spec. issue of *West Coast Line* 6, 25/3 (1991–1992): n.p.

Pierce, Jonathan C. "A Tale of Two Generations: The Public and Private Voices of Dorothy Livesay." Dorney, Noonan, and Tiessen 19–32.

Pollock, Zailig, ed. *Extraordinary Presence: The Worlds of P. K. Page / Une présence extraordinarie: Les univers de P.K. Page*. Spec. issue of *Journal of Canadian Studies / Revue d'études canadiennes* 38.1 (2004).

Rado, Lisa. "Lost and Found: Remembering Modernism, Rethinking Feminism." *Rereading Modernism: New Directions in Feminist Criticism*. Ed. Lisa Rado. New York: Garland, 1994. 137–58.

Relke, Diana. *Greenwor(l)ds: Ecocritical Readings of Canadian Women's Poetry*. Calgary: U of Calgary P, 1999.

Rogers, Linda, ed. *P.K. Page: Essays on her Works*. Toronto: Guernica, 2001.

Ruzesky, Jay, ed. *P.K. Page*. Spec. issue of *Malahat Review* 117 (1996).

Scott, Bonnie Kime, ed. *The Gender of Modernism*. Bloomington: Indiana UP, 1990.

Scott, F.R. "The Canadian Authors Meet." *McGill Fortnightly Review*, 25 March 1927, 62.

———. *New Provinces: Poems of Several Authors*. Ed. F.R. Scott. Toronto: Macmillan, 1936.

———. "Trans Canada." Lecker and David 66–67.

Smart, Patricia. *Les femmes du Refus Global*. Montreal: Boréal, 1998.

———. *Writing in the Father's House: The Emergence of the Feminine in the Quebec Literary Tradition*. Toronto: U of Toronto P, 1991.

Smith, A.J.M. "Swift Current." Lecker and David 66–67.

Stevens, Peter. *Dorothy Livesay: Patterns in a Poetic Life*. Toronto: ECW, 1992.

———. *The McGill Movement: A.J.M. Smith, F.R. Scott and Leo Kennedy*. Toronto: Ryerson, 1969.

Sullivan, Rosemary. "Meeting in Mexico." *Memory-Making: Selected Essays*. Windsor, ON: Black Moss P, 2001. 25–37. Orig. published in *Brick: A Literary Journal* 55 (1996): 25–30. Rpt. with photographic reproductions of paintings by Remedios Varo, Leona Carrington, and P.K. Irwin in Brandt and Godard 50–60.

Thompson, Lee. *Dorothy Livesay*. Boston: Twayne, 1987.

Trehearne, Brian. *Aestheticism and the Canadian Modernists: Aspects of a Poetic Influence*. Montreal: McGill-Queen's UP, 1989.

———. *The Montreal Forties: Modernist Poetry in Transition*. Toronto: U of Toronto P, 1999.

———. "P.K. Page and Surrealism." Pollock 46–64.

Willmott, Glenn. *Unreal Country: Modernity in the Canadian Novel in English*. Montreal: McGill-Queen's UP, 2002.

THE MAKING OF
CANADIAN LITERARY
MODERNISM

The Writing Livesays
Connecting Generations of Canadian Modernism
ANN MARTIN

Dorothy Livesay states in *Right Hand Left Hand* that her poetic contemporaries were mainly men born "soon after the turn of the century," and that

> No companion women poets were born until the end of the First World War: P.K. Page, Miriam Waddington, Ann Wilkinson, Anne Marriott, Margaret Avison and Phyllis Webb. So until they began to make their mark in the forties, I always had the feeling I was struggling alone to make a woman's voice heard. (19)

Livesay's comments offer an interesting perspective on the position of women in the Canadian literary circles of the early twentieth century; but they are particularly revealing in terms of Livesay's apparent dismissal of her mother, Florence Randal Livesay. If Dorothy Livesay is Canada's first modernist woman poet, how do we read the poetry that F.R. Livesay published in the 1920s, especially as it responds to Canadian experiences of urban modernity? How might an acknowledgement of F.R. Livesay's life and work trouble Dorothy Livesay's depiction of her isolated struggle, and thus complicate the generational tensions that have come to define modernism? Could a reading of the connections rather than the differences between the two authors shift our gaze to the social and cultural situations that prompt both Livesays' experimentations with form and content?

To address these questions, I want to link Dorothy Livesay's relationship with her mother to early twentieth-century literary movements. At the heart of my exploration of their respective places in the modernist canon is Dorothy Livesay's emphasis—whether in poetry, prose fiction, biographies, or interviews—on the disconnection between the two women. As a number of critics have argued, Dorothy Livesay's ambivalence towards F.R. Livesay derives in part from a complicated family dynamic in which the daughter felt compelled to choose between the rather different influences of mother and father, who are often characterized as practitioners of poetry and prose respectively. Reading Dorothy Livesay's work through this writerly family triangle, especially in relation to the difficulties involved in her assertion of a female authorial voice, has been productive. However, the "writing Livesays" (Weekes 33) represent not just two genders or genres, but two generations, and in most depictions of their relationship, Dorothy Livesay's rejection of her literary and literal foremother comes to symbolize her rejection of a previous era's formal and social limitations. The mother's literary reputation is thus overshadowed, perhaps understandably, by her daughter's, and the significance of F.R. Livesay's work—and by extension, the work of her contemporaries—is downplayed and contrasted to Dorothy Livesay's later, higher modernism.

A vision of modernism as the avant-garde's rejection of inherited forms may suggest the ways in which Dorothy Livesay's poetry differs from her mother's. However, reading Canadian modernism according to a model of literary progress does not fully explain the striking similarities of their work and their feminist projects. An alternate approach may be to view the poetry of the two Livesays according to the influence of lived modernity, and not just in terms of the influence of literary tradition.[1] Indeed, F.R. Livesay's responses to the rise of the modern metropolis, changing gender roles, and the effects of technological innovation indicate a perspective on social and artistic concerns that is reflected, even as it is inflected, in Dorothy Livesay's own writing. Instead of being read for what it is not, then, I suggest that F.R. Livesay's poetry needs to be read in terms of what it is: a negotiation not just with the techniques of modernism, but with the demands of modernity at the level of both content and form. It is this negotiation that we find in Dorothy Livesay's own explorations, in her earlier poetry, of the rural–urban split in Canadian society, of "the conflict between culture and nature" (Relke 17), and of the changing place of women in the society. Dorothy Livesay's ambivalence towards F.R. Livesay may thus betray her recognition of her mother's similar reactions to and literary constructions of this era of social and cultural change. More importantly, her ambivalence indicates the limitations of our received vision of Canadian modernism as a primarily aesthetic form of experimentation, influenced by artistic movements from abroad. Through these two figures, then, I suggest that writers from the 1910s and 1920s such as F.R. Livesay are indeed "more with the 'moderns' than against them" and not "more against them than we have cared to admit" (Trehearne 74). The connection rests, however, not on a shared aesthetic but rather on a shared response to the material experience of urban modernity.

Both F.R. and Dorothy Livesay witnessed the increasing industrialization and urbanization of Canadian society in the first half of the twentieth century. They experienced firsthand the shattering of traditional and communal institutions that led to the typically modernist sense of the "futility and anarchy which is contemporary history" (Eliot, "*Ulysses*" 177). Widespread cultural anxiety was, however, accompanied by an increased sense of autonomy (see Simmel 418), and an awareness of the possibilities of social reformation. Thus, while for Eliot "April is the cruellest month" (*Waste Land* 63), Dorothy Livesay writes "the spring is ours" in "Broadcast" (*Archive* 42). Of course, the cultural contexts of F.R. Livesay and Dorothy Livesay contain significant differences, and their responses to modernity reflect the variety of modernisms that emerge from their times. Nevertheless, their work indicates a shared interest in and engagement with their respective contemporary moments, especially in relation to the rise of the city and a new social order. Where Florence Randal Livesay experiences the suffrage movement, the Boer War, and World War One, Dorothy Livesay sees the effects of the Winnipeg General Strike, the Great Depression, and the Spanish Civil War. Where F.R. Livesay's journalism and literature provide a direct and continuing commentary on her society from the turn of the century onwards, Dorothy Livesay's poetry and documentary work indicate the pressures of social change after 1920.

Born Florence Hamilton Randal in 1874, Florence Randal Livesay became a governess and a teacher after her father's death in 1888, and submitted poetry and short stories to *Massey's Magazine* (Gerson, "Florence" 205–6; Gwyn 372). In the mid-1890s, she became the editor of the society page of the *Ottawa Evening Journal*. When she went to South Africa in 1902 to teach in Boer concentration camps, she sent fortnightly letters to the *Journal* and also described her experiences for the *Winnipeg Telegram*. At the same time, she was submitting creative pieces to *Saturday Night* (Gwyn 374; Thompson, "More Public Voice" 44). Upon her return to Canada, she relocated to Winnipeg, and in 1906 became the editor of the women's page for the *Telegram* (Gerson, "Florence" 206). She then joined the *Winnipeg Free Press*, addressing a range of feminist issues in her journalism, such as suffrage and the career opportunities that were becoming available to women (Gwyn 385). In 1908, she married one of the eventual co-founders of the Canadian Press, John Frederick Bligh Livesay. They had three children: Dorothy, Sophie, and Arthur, who died shortly after his birth. In 1920, the Livesays moved from Winnipeg to their rural home near Clarkson, just west of Toronto, where they became increasingly involved in the Canadian literary scene. After her husband's death in 1944, Florence Randal Livesay moved to Toronto and then to Grimsby, where she died in 1953 (Gerson, "Florence" 206–7).

F.R. Livesay's newspaper and magazine work was, as this brief summary of her life suggests, extensive, as was her range of styles, subjects, and media. Her short stories and her verse appeared in the major Canadian journals of the day, such as *Saturday Night* and *Canadian Poetry*. Her work was also featured in international publications such as the *Outlook*, the *Dial*, and *Poetry* (Chicago), which was perhaps the most influential magazine in terms of "the international development of modernism in English-language poetry" (Doyle 38). She was also anthologized in a number of Canadian collections, where her work indicates not just her participation in the Imagist movement, but also the vitality of the national literary scene in the early twentieth century. Her adaptations of Ukrainian, or Ruthenian, poetry were published as *Songs of Ukraina* in 1916 and established her reputation as a poet.[2] She issued another collection of verse, *Shepherd's Purse*, in 1923, and her novel *Savour of Salt* followed in 1927. In 1947, she edited and published her husband's unfinished autobiography, *The Making of a Canadian: J.F.B. Livesay*, and by 1951, she had completed a rough draft of a historical novel, "The Moon and the Morning Star."[3]

Like other early twentieth-century Canadian writers, the extent to which F.R. Livesay was published in her own time differs greatly from the extent to which she has been anthologized in ours. Carole Gerson observes that, of forty-five anthologies of Canadian poetry and/or prose published between 1916 and 1986, Livesay is present in seven. Those seven appeared between 1916, the year in which *Songs of Ukraina* was published, and 1954, the year after F.R. Livesay's death ("Anthologies" 71–74). As Gerson suggests, one reason for the decrease in attention is that the broad and inclusive anthologies of the first part of the twentieth century yielded to more selective collections (60). F.R. Livesay's poetry does not fit into a clear literary trend or category that might epitomize a specific movement in Canadian literature. It does not, for example, represent a particular regional or national identity, since she addresses both urban and rural landscapes, and draws upon a range of cultural influences (British, French, Irish, Native Canadian, and Ukrainian); nor does it represent a specific style of writing, since she invokes a number of different forms as well. In *Shepherd's Purse*, for instance, strictly metered and rhymed verse is juxtaposed with imagist and found poetry. A three-stanza "Rondel" in strict iambic trimeter appears alongside the free verse of "Windows," and rhymed sentimental poems based in pastoral landscapes are paired with works of modernist irony set in the city. In terms of Canadian understandings of literary movements, then, she is not that "rather lewd and most ungodly poet" that F.R. Scott identifies as the coming modernist in "The Canadian Authors Meet"; but neither is she entirely the nineteenth-century "poetess" he critiques for her conservatism (348). Like other poets of the 1910s and 1920s, such as Frank Oliver Call, Arthur Stringer, and, as Wanda Campbell has argued, Louise Morey Bowman and Katherine Hale (80), F.R. Livesay's work represents a response to changing artistic and social imperatives, and seems to fall between the cracks.

F.R. Livesay's muted place in Canadian literature is, in this sense, a symptom of critical constructions and definitions of Canadian modernism. As James Doyle suggests, the split sensibility reflected in the poetry of F.R. Livesay, Arthur Stringer, Arthur Phelps, and Louise Morey Bowman indicates "how relative the qualities of modernism were" at this time, and "how grey the areas of distinction between the new poetry and the poetry of Victorianism" (40–41). According to Doyle, only after 1929 does Harriet Monroe, the editor of *Poetry* (Chicago), acknowledge the "genuinely new angles of vision and innovative rhetoric" displayed in the works of A.J.M. Smith and W.W.E. Ross (45). With Monroe's delayed recognition of this apparently pure literary form, Canadian modernism truly begins. The voices of later modernists are thus distinguished from those of earlier poets, where the latter's verse is often too "firmly rooted in the technical and emotional attitudes deriving from poetry of the late nineteenth century" to be considered fully modern (Trehearne 73). In such a reading, modernism represents a primarily aesthetic reaction against "poetry weighted down by a transplanted Victorian tradition living out a protracted decadence in Canada" (Norris 59). It represents also a rejection of that "strain in Imagism (particularly under the guidance of Amy Lowell) that tended towards the pretty and the delicate" (Trehearne 35). Later modernist poets, such as Ross and

Raymond Knister thus mark a return to the "original stimulating Imagism of 1912 to 1914," which had "more muscle and sinew and also had the courage to reject much late nineteenth-century sentimentalism" (35).

Here, the role of gender is perhaps only slightly less central to definitions of modernism than is the role of generation, though both are invoked in order to distinguish earlier from later twentieth-century writing. Either way, F.R. Livesay and her contemporaries—delicate females or decadent aesthetes—are emblematic of those poets whose works fail to reach a high modernism.[4] Dorothy Livesay, in contrast, seems to have cracked the glass ceiling, despite her exclusion from *New Provinces*, and her poetry, politics, and status in literary circles quickly overshadowed the reputation of earlier women writers, including her mother. Dorothy Livesay is the better-known and more prolific author, as well as the more accomplished poet; and if F.R. Livesay is known today, she is known mainly as Dorothy Livesay's parent. In fact, in several versions of their relationship, Dorothy Livesay is depicted as having rejected entirely the influence of her mother in order to establish her own more politically engaged and aesthetically challenging poetry.

The result is that in many accounts of the writing Livesays, family politics and literary politics converge in the overdetermined figure of the mother. While Dorothy Livesay's father, J.F.B. Livesay, is characterized as "a freethinker," her mother is the figure most often associated with "the constraints of [Dorothy Livesay's] somewhat Edwardian upbringing" (Wayne and Mackinnon 35). F.R. Livesay is not just the politically conservative and repressive parent, however; she is also portrayed as the poetically conservative and repressed writer, whose "increasing rigidity and bias" speaks to both her personal and her professional drawbacks (Thompson, *Dorothy Livesay* 53). Unfortunately, such a view of F.R. Livesay's character and literature has led to some questionable readings of both her life and work. For instance, in identifying her primarily as a mother, and as one who struggled to overcome her "authoritarian background," Peter Stevens states erroneously that she "published no more books after 1923" and became primarily "her husband's helpmate" (24). His focus on F.R. Livesay's limitations also seems to cause a bit of a glitch when Stevens suggests that Dorothy Livesay's "emerging sense of feminist concerns" was, "*ironically*, perhaps fostered by her mother" (25; emphasis mine). There should be no irony here unless we have already situated the mother as a political non-entity, and thus only a foil to her daughter's success.

The main issue betrayed by these textual moments is, of course, the tremendous influence Dorothy Livesay and her conflicted views of her mother and of her mother's work had on such criticism. Obviously, Dorothy Livesay is a valuable source of information. Her generosity is cited in almost every academic account of F.R. Livesay's life, and, as a witness, she was consistently willing to revisit and reexamine previous opinions, troubling the assertion of any singular view.[5] However, Dorothy Livesay's ambivalence towards and even resentment of her mother's career and her parents' marriage become evident in many of her depictions of F.R. Livesay. Because Dorothy Livesay was and remains the primary source of information regarding F.R. Livesay's work and life, we need to contextualize existing portraits of their relationship in terms of writing as well as mothering. We need to re-evaluate especially those views of F.R. Livesay that indicate a division between the mother and daughter that is consistently linked to and prompted by literary production. Such moments indicate not just Livesay family politics but also the generational and gendered politics of literary modernism: a politics related to the avant-garde, which necessitates a rejection of the precursor's work.

Dorothy Livesay's short story collection *A Winnipeg Childhood* involves an explicit link between writing and the tensions between mother and daughter. In the stories, the protagonist, Elizabeth Longstaffe, identifies primarily with her father and with the phallic power signified by his patronymic. She must search, however, for positive and powerful maternal figures who might compensate for what she perceives as her female parent's lack. The main substitute is Aunt Maudie, a spinster who embodies, ironically, those domestic traits of selflessness and comforting contact that the mother does not provide. Indeed, in "The Uprooting," Elizabeth realizes "long afterwards that Aunt Maudie had been a mother after all; for she had taught Elizabeth what mothering was like" (194). In contrast, Mrs. Longstaffe is "always busy in the dining-room at her typewriter, with sheafs of green foolscap brought home from the newspaper office, and piles of scribbled notes wandering this way and that across a page" (53). Livesay suggests through this description of a woman without a study of her own the pressures that face the working mother caught between the demands of the domestic and office worlds. However, the story depicts more forcefully the effects of the woman's career on the daughter, who feels that she is less important to the mother than is the mother's writing. The child has been replaced by "wandering" "scribble[s]" on "foolscap"; the description of the mother's work reduces her writing to random scrawls on a page. The diction of the passage suggests the foolishness of both the prose and the parent who fulfills her personal and her professional obligations inadequately.

Dorothy Livesay touches upon such tensions again in "The Halloweens" from 1969, as the speaker tries to come to terms with her "mother's wilful / short-sighted love" (*Collected Poems* 352). The poem depicts a Hallowe'en in which the speaker's mother has dressed her in an "authentic Ukrainian costume" (351). Read in the context of F.R. Livesay's *Songs of Ukraina*, the scene crystallizes the parent's attempt to combine mothering and writing. However, the costume itself signals the pressure that the daughter experiences: she has been turned into an embodiment of her mother's work, subsumed or replaced by the poems her mother has adapted. Little wonder that once the daughter is with her contemporaries, she changes her costume and becomes a ghost in a white sheet, bowing, as Lee Thompson suggests, to the "prejudice" of her peers (*Dorothy Livesay* 53). When the speaker thinks of her choice later, she expresses shame at rejecting the diversity represented by "the gay Ukrainian skirt" in favour of a generic White identity (D. Livesay, *Collected Poems* 352), but this feeling is coupled with the speaker's frustration at the mother's inability to see her own daughter uncostumed, to see her daughter's own identity. The "sheet" (351) that the speaker wears becomes highly evocative here. On one level, it resonates with the disturbing symbolism of the Ku Klux Klan, pointing to the daughter's sense of guilt for remaining "White" instead of embracing ethnic or racial difference, and indicating the kind of social issues that Dorothy Livesay critiques and condemns throughout her career. On another level, the double meaning of the word "sheet" also suggests that the daughter's capitulation to her peers stems from her conflicted rejection of the mother's work. The "sheet" is what allows the author to cover over and redress her mother's vision of her identity, as the daughter replaces the original costume and its associations with a fresh, blank page. As the signifier of both her mother's career and the poet's own response, the sheet allows the speaker to displace her mother's words and vision, to assert her own voice, and to re-explore this moment in time from another perspective.

"The Halloweens" demonstrates Dorothy Livesay's typically doubled vision of her mother and her mother's writing, where the influence of F.R. Livesay is admitted but, as importantly, disavowed. Sandra Gwyn has pointed out that Dorothy Livesay was "estranged" from her mother "for most of her life" (387), and Livesay herself acknowledges that "in later years, I felt very hostile to my mother" ("Interview" 89). Dorothy Livesay's poetry and prose fiction indicate this tension, but the extent of the daughter's sense of alienation takes its most striking public form in Dorothy Livesay's discussions of her mother's career. In an interview with Doug Beardsley and Rosemary Sullivan published in 1978, for instance, Livesay actually states that she was unaware her mother was anything but a newspaper columnist until well after F.R. Livesay's death: "She died in 1953 and I'd never known about her poetry. I always thought she was a journalist" (87). This assertion is undercut, however, by other statements in the interview. For example, Dorothy Livesay recalls her mother's work on and publication of *Songs of Ukraina*: "she got a Ukrainian Baptist minister (who had been a socialist) to come and translate the songs that she liked, in rough prose. She then rendered them into English verse" (88). Livesay also indicates that her mother, being "very adept" at formal poetry, tried to "persuade" her to experiment with different techniques, an attempt against which she "revolted" (90). There is an almost disingenuous profession of ignorance regarding her mother's creative writing in these inconsistent anecdotes. Through her doubled vision, Dorothy Livesay seems to acknowledge her mother's influence, but almost as frequently, she implies its insignificance.

Pamela Banting places these tensions in a Freudian context and argues that the triangle formed by the three writers in the family—Dorothy, F.R., and J.F.B. Livesay—reflected the problems of Florence and Fred Livesay's marriage, as well as the conflict between genres and traditions that the parents represented for the child. Thompson has argued that Dorothy's father thought of fiction "as a more elevated genre than poetry" ("More Public Voice" 45–46). Stevens suggests that the parents actually symbolized for Dorothy "the two sides of Livesay's literary personality: father as mentor on the prose and fiction side, and mother on the side of poetry and song" (18). Dorothy Livesay herself certainly struggled with these influences, stating that "Each parent sought to reign over me" (*Journey* 55), and, in "The Origin of the Family," describing her position as "the wishbone's centre / made of their two-pronged / rivalries" (*Self-Completing* 104). For Banting, her choice was to select the father's social power rather than the limitations of the mother's position, and thereby to situate herself as an author within "an almost exclusively patriarchal literary tradition" (12). By "forsaking her mother and allying herself with her father" (14), Dorothy Livesay attempted both to seize the father's power and to move beyond the influence of either parent. In this scenario, "the family romance overlapped with the

Bloomian intra-poetic romance of the family of literary precursors" (19), which led to a persistent sense of anxiety. The result was her "ongoing exploration of and dialogue with her antecedents" (19), as well as her recognition of the marginalization of a female literary tradition.

Banting's reading of the Livesays according to an Oedipal model of influence addresses the gendered tensions that existed amongst the family's writers. Her argument does not, however, account for why Dorothy Livesay consistently acknowledges the importance of her mother's role in her artistic development, an acknowledgement that troubles the clear distinctions between genders and traditions. Dorothy Livesay not only chooses her mother's genre; she also states that "in a very real sense Florence Randal Livesay made me a poet" (Preface 12). What Dorothy Livesay's doubled vision of her mother may indicate more specifically, then, is the ambiguity that female precursors involve and the complicated process of precursor selection that is seemingly necessary in her assertion of a modern voice. As Sandra Gilbert and Susan Gubar suggest, since the woman poet can only dream of struggling with a strong, authentic precursor, she faces not the "anxiety of influence" (Bloom 30) experienced by the male author, but instead an "'anxiety of authorship'" (*Madwoman* 49). The attempt to "think back through our mothers if we are women" (Woolf 69) is thus an attempt on the woman writer's part to find a female role model who "legitimize[s] her own rebellious endeavors" in picking up the pen (Gilbert and Gubar, *Madwoman* 50). However, in order to identify with the precursor's power, the modern writer must reject inappropriate female role models that are not as successful. The choice is not just between the male and the female traditions, then, but within the latter, between the "empowering ancestress" and the woman artist whose work is only "trivial" (Gilbert and Gubar, *No Man's Land* 203).

F.R. Livesay seems to embody for Dorothy Livesay the inferior precursor whose limitations must be overcome if the modern poet is to succeed: she is significant, but mainly in relation to the more accomplished successor. Dorothy Livesay may acknowledge her mother's influence, but she cannot affiliate herself with it if she is to be a modernist author. She thus distances herself consistently from F.R. Livesay's poetry and politics. She emphasizes her mother's inferiority as a poet by citing her father's opinion: "Your poor mother never had an aspiration beyond pretty-pretty" (*Journey* 37). She suggests the conservatism of F.R. Livesay's work and life by quoting Gina or Jim (Watts) Lawson: "And the mother, while she wrote, it is true, I would think she was a very minor writer. The main thing about her was that she was extremely traditionally religious" (*Right Hand* 45; *Journey* 61). Dorothy Livesay celebrates female writers, but writes her tribute to "The Three Emilys"—Emily Brontë, Emily Dickinson, and Emily Carr—rather than to F.R. Livesay (*Self-Completing* 83). She lists the imagists whose poetry she admires, including Louise Morey Bowman, Arthur Stringer, Amy Lowell, and H.D., but not F.R. Livesay, who was published alongside them (*Journey* 90).[6] In this schema, then, F.R. Livesay is depicted as being neither a good mother, nor a good writer, nor a real poet, nor a politicized woman, nor, most importantly, a modernist. Dorothy Livesay's literary identity seems, in fact, to depend upon the mother's position as Other—that is, as the precursor who must be rejected if the modern artist is to establish her own position in the avant-garde.

Geometric metaphors of literary movements, whether based on the family triangle or on a line of literary inheritance, allow critics to sum up key divisions between genders, genres, and generations. Of course, there are significant distinctions to be made between the poets and their projects; this becomes evident in F.R. Livesay's *Shepherd's Purse*. In "On the White Keys," for instance, F.R. Livesay participates in a Victorian sentimentality that saturates the diction, the subject, and the rhyme scheme of the poem:

> Nay, sweetheart, your sad music stay!
> It hath too subtly strong a sway
> Over my heart. Is true love slain?
> You sigh "Yes!" in that old refrain
>   On the white keys. (*Shepherd's Purse* 17)

Compared to her daughter's "Day and Night" of 1936 (*Collected Poems* 120–25), the difference between the two poets is, well, like night and day. Dorothy Livesay's juxtaposition of styles, voices, and rhythms, and her exploration of class and racial tensions, are clearly at odds with F.R. Livesay's bourgeois, "White," and highly traditional love poem. Where the daughter's work plays with the sounds of machines, dance music, and African-American spirituals, and is clearly influenced by Stephen Spender, W.H. Auden, and Cecil Day-Lewis (Irvine 253), the mother relies on the "old refrain" inspired by a highly structured, European piano piece. Here, Dorothy Livesay's modernism can indeed be viewed as her "rejection of conventional nineteenth-century poetic structure" (Arnason 6). However, as David Arnason and other critics suggest, the Canadian imagists were themselves divided between tradition and experimentation (7). F.R. Livesay's *Shepherd's Purse* includes styles and subject matter that signal changes in formal trends and thus trouble clear-cut divisions between moments of literary history. While influenced by the previous century's poetry, the book has been read also as a collection of "terse modernist verses" (Gerson, "Florence" 206), examples of *vers libre* that indicate a distinct vision of modernist poetry as an incisive portrayal of modern life. As such, the collection signals a shift not just in style, but also in subject matter and in its treatment.

It is F.R. Livesay's expression and construction of modernity in her writing that make the verse terse, as her engagement with the realities of her time necessitates the change not just in content but also in form. As indicated by a range of writers from the 1910s and 1920s, the experience of modernity—of industrialization, urbanization, shifting gender roles, increased class mobility, and varied immigration—had dramatic effects on the substance and the style of modernist poetry. F.O. Call's foreword to *Acanthus and Wild Grape* is one piece that indicates this connection, especially where he suggests that *vers libre* echoes the movement and sensibilities of "the motor-car and aeroplane" (10). The mention of mechanical innovation is clearly a reference to modernist formal experimentation; but the analogy connects the poetry with the new technologies that dramatically shifted the viewer's perspective on space, time, and subjectivity. The fluidity of identity that arises from being in a car or from being part of a metropolitan crowd has a significant influence on the form and the content of both Dorothy Livesay's and F.R. Livesay's verse. Images from nature are still mainstays in some of the Livesays' poems—testimonies to the influence of the Canadian rural landscape on the popular imagination—but urban images of cars, pavement, classed neighbourhoods, and gendered infrastructures and power structures signal a rather different sensibility. It is the common ground of modernity that may lead us, then, to recognize connections between the Livesays' poetry written in the 1920s and in the early 1930s. Such connections may trouble the generational distinctions that have arisen from critics' focus primarily on the aesthetics of modernism, rather than on the Canadian spaces and experiences to which those aesthetics respond. They may also challenge our reading of Dorothy Livesay's distance from her mother and her mother's writing, since there are significant overlaps in both the subjects and politics that the two writers address.

For F.R. Livesay, modernity's power structures and the freedom that becomes associated with city settings are explored through women's experiences in both private and public spaces. The thematic patterns of *Shepherd's Purse* contrast the relative anonymity of the individual in an urban environment with the pressures of insular rural communities, as personal relationships are determined by the ground upon which they occur. In the country setting of "Short-Cuts," for example, the "fierce virago" down the road yells at the speaker to "Get off my land," and the poem ends with the speaker's choice to follow "the shorter, better way that leads to town" (*Shepherd's Purse* 13). In contrast, the characters of "Time" do not meet in the mapped and marked spaces of the rural landscape, but instead collide randomly on the public street: "Caught in an eddy of a crowd / I heard one call my name aloud" (42). It is not just time that leads to reconciliation between the old rivals in the poem; it is space. They have achieved a distance from their traditional identities and enmities by virtue of the crowd and the changing social dynamics of the new setting.

We see depictions of specifically metropolitan moments in Dorothy Livesay's early poetry as well. In "Old Man Dozing," originally published in *Signpost*, the feet on the pavement signal the diversity of the metropolis and convey the sense of movement and shifts in perspective that speak to Canadian urban modernity. The poem also suggests the power of the crowd. In comparing the citizens to "ants / And other such small, determined creatures" (*Collected Poems* 53), the speaker emphasizes the futility, the anonymity, and the alienation of the city experience, as well as the industry of this community, in which the individual represents part of a larger whole. The isolation of the individual in the city is both asserted and undercut in this compact poem. While the old man is separate within the crowd, the people around him suggest the network of social relationships in the city that seems to resist division. The same emphasis on varied perspectives and on the nature of the individual's relationship to his or her social and physical environment is expressed in "City Wife." The split subjectivity of this woman from an urban centre arises from her uncanny experience of the country, which she has not even "half understood"—or rather, has understood in a radically different way than has her rural husband (*Collected Poems* 42). Here, too, perspective and community are emphasized: the farmhouse, and "the meal and the quietness" (43) it represents for the farmer, seem to constrain the identity of the woman. The house signals the same "threat of domestic isolation and entrapment" that we see in poems such as "Threshold" and "Staccato" (Relke 31). The house fixes the city wife's identity. However, her perception of the landscape signals an imaginative escape: her "mind" becomes "a little open space / Free for all varying winds to stop and rest" (D. Livesay, *Collected Poems* 43). The singularity of the house is contrasted here to the image of the countryside, where the wind can stop and then continue like a pedestrian on a city street.

Interestingly, this tension between imprisonment and free movement is reflected in Dorothy Livesay's "Journey," but in a city landscape, in which the speaker feels that the "street-car," rather than the house or room, "is a cage" (*Collected Poems* 48). The car is placed in contrast to the street and the "night air" that echoes the "varying winds" of "City Wife." This air signals the city's possibilities and the speaker's sense of release when the streetcar stops and she gets out. In "Monition," the opposition between the individual and the mechanized society becomes even more pronounced: "The soft, silken rush of a car over wet pavements" makes the speaker start. Because she is waiting for "some footfall / The rush of a motor is too sudden a wind / In [her] mind" (*Collected Poems* 26). The city is still a place of possibility and freedom, but this "too sudden" gust emphasizes not so much the autonomy of the individual as her vulnerability to strangers and technology. The threat is possible because the space is not mapped in the same traditional way: with possibility comes a new sense of anxiety, representing the complicated dynamics of the city.

The urban spaces that are depicted in both F.R. and Dorothy Livesay's works speak to the social structures that can restrict or constrain the individual, but that can also be traversed and resisted by the subjects whom the writers depict. The plot of F.R. Livesay's novel *Savour of Salt*, for instance, revolves around a country girl's arrival in Toronto and the changes in identity she experiences while living there. F.R. Livesay's poem "Her Evening Out" presents a related topic, where the speaker is a domestic servant who anticipates a more temporary spatial shift that will free her from the restricted areas of the master's house: "Of course they lingered over dinner! / In the hot stifling kitchen where / She washes up, she sighs in her despair" (*Shepherd's Purse* 25). The poem is subtitled "(In the brief day of the Jitney)," and the freedom of the night off becomes aligned with the means of transportation that will take her away from the kitchen and into the city. There, she

> Is free of women and of men,
> Of doing what they like. She's her own mistress
> In her own auto with a friend or so—
> "O ain't it hot!" She smiles into his face,
> And moves a trifle to give him more space. (25)

The Jitney, speeding towards the city, becomes a metaphor for the excitement of modernity and for the possibilities it involves, especially for women who, once outside the home, have the opportunity to meet with men in public spaces—traditionally coded masculine. Such poetry speaks to the increasingly public presence of women and their experiences of the city. In "Romance," too, lovers are not associated with the parlour, but instead with public transit. On this new meeting-ground, the sexed bodies of the city come into contact according to a new and different rhythm: "The street-car bangs and clatters over curves / And men and women sway as the car swerves" (*Shepherd's Purse* 39). Here, the movement of the streetcar is expressed by the alliteration of the lines and by the uneven pattern of emphasis. The experience of the modern city is expressed in an urban poetry, where F.R. Livesay's free verse echoes the freedom of the metropolis and her experimentations with form and subject echo her characters' experimentations with modern identity.

Interestingly, F.R. Livesay's focus on the hierarchical spaces in which domestic servants work, and from which they free themselves, is echoed in Dorothy Livesay's poem from the early 1930s, "In Green Solariums." Again, we see an overt contrast between the master's house and the less organized space of the city, through the opposition between the green solariums that enclose and protect the family, and the more vulnerable snow-covered neighbourhoods below (*Collected Poems* 72). However, there is a significant difference between the kinds of resistance performed by the women depicted by the two Livesays. F.R. Livesay's work signals the constant movement of bodies through such spaces, where the hierarchical social system is not necessarily overturned but rather resisted and negotiated on an individual basis. In contrast, Dorothy Livesay signals the revolutionary potential of the city as a whole, where the individuals of the metropolis are inevitably connected through economic structures of exploitation, even though neighbourhoods and houses are divided according to classed, gendered, and racialized roles.

At the beginning of "In Green Solariums," for instance, the speaker works and lives within the master's house, and is having an affair with the master's son. His "hunger" is thus satiated not only by the speaker's labour in the kitchen but also by her body in the bedroom (D. Livesay, *Collected Poems* 72). The sense of emotional and sexual escape she finds in his body, the sense of "otherwhere" that echoes the green solarium in the midst of winter, is contrasted, however, to the punishment of exile and homelessness that she experiences when she becomes pregnant.[7] Only the "well brought up" women who offer charity and hard "kindliness" seem able to bridge the two worlds: "They live useful lives / And even see the city, look at it" (73). Unlike the speaker, they have the resources to "clamber back to green solariums" without experiencing the pain of the pleasure for which they condemn the women they aid. Instead of returning to "the unreal town, the paper roofs" (74) that house such hypocrisy, the speaker and her son move to the harbour area, a liminal space of movement, change, and social unrest. There, the speaker sees another side of the city, and through her knowledge of domestic service, is able to compare the exploitation of women by the men of the house to the exploitation of workers by the men of business. This perspective enables her to become involved in a larger movement, based not on "one lone rebel" but rather on "solidarity"—that is, on a different kind of social structure in which artificial divisions are truly bridged (74). By the end of the poem, the speaker sees the city as a corporate entity, seething with life, when she awakes in the morning. She prophesies a day when the "snow will be bloody in the alley-ways" and when she and her army will "march up past green solariums / With no more fear, with no more words of scorn" (75). In this portrayal of class divisions within the metropolis, the revolution arises from the connections between the various systemic injustices of the city; the goal of revolution is to supplant the existing structures with a new order that leads into a new world: "the International's born!" (75).

F.R. Livesay's reaction against tradition—both literary and political—is obviously not as pronounced as her daughter's reaction is in her own socialist and Marxist writings. However, F.R. Livesay's subtle critique of social and literary conventions signals her larger challenge to authority and established gender roles, which strikes a chord with many of the issues that are implicit in *Signpost* and explicit in Dorothy Livesay's works from the 1930s. F.R. Livesay's "In the Public Ward," for instance, involves her presentation of a doubled perspective on a single mother. She undercuts the medical and moral authority of a male doctor in the poem, whose judgement of a dead woman who has stepped outside social conventions is contrasted to the female nurse's more compassionate, individual view (*Shepherd's Purse* 33). Similarly, in "Drugs: Vacation Requirements," the male doctor's advice to the speaker—"You take a rest! You'll be a long time dead" (24)—becomes estranged from its original context when it is repeated as the refrain of the poem. Through repetition, the doctor's statement of knowledge and authority becomes an absurd cliché, and the chorus that should reassert his supremacy indicates instead the poet's power to manipulate language. Where

Dorothy Livesay's poetry suggests a call for community, solidarity, and revolution that would overturn the inequities of existing social structures, then, F.R. Livesay suggests the individual's resistance to authority through local tactics and transgressions. For both writers, however, urban space is the ground upon which such resistance is possible.

What F.R. Livesay and Dorothy Livesay represent, then, are versions of a Canadian modernism in which an increasingly urban society is reacted to and reflected upon in the early 1920s as well as in the 1930s. While F.R. Livesay's poetry is not Canada's version of high modernism, it represents a response to modernity in which new technologies, shifting gender roles, and increasing urbanization lead to a change in perception that is signalled in the form and content of her verse. Her exploration of cityscapes and her reaction against authority in the forms of poetic and social traditions are echoed and expanded upon in the work of her daughter. Poetry is thus a means through which both authors express varied experiences of modern urban space, especially in their depictions of the power structures that women, working class and otherwise, must negotiate. These points of intersection suggest that modernism is not necessarily a sudden paradigm shift based upon an untroubled rejection of earlier writers, literary forms, images, and themes. Rather, the similarities between these two poets and the two generations they represent suggest a common bond amongst different writers of the early twentieth century, linked as they are by their responses to a rapidly changing social and physical landscape. In the works of the writing Livesays, such responses to modern cultural contexts signal connections rather than differences, and indicate the complexities involved in mapping literary traditions, family politics, and modernity itself.

NOTES

1 See also Candida Rifkind's reading of Miriam Waddington's prose in this volume, and her emphasis on the material conditions of modernity, and not only the aesthetics of modernism.
2 See Marilyn Rose's consideration of F.R. Livesay's translation of Ukrainian poetry, and of "the larger cultural narratives" that affect the poetry's reception, if not its actual uses by Livesay herself (154).
3 The manuscript of this novel is in the Fisher Rare Book Library at the University of Toronto.
4 In an article for *Poetry* (Chicago) published in October 1925, F.R. Livesay lists many prominent Canadian women poets of her day, beginning with Marjorie Pickthall, "Canada's most famous woman poet" (38), and moving on to her own contemporaries: Bowman, Anne Elizabeth Wilson, Cecilia Mackinnon, and Katherine Hale.

5 In writing of "a" childhood in Winnipeg, in examining both the "left and right hands," and in considering her "selves," Dorothy Livesay acknowledged throughout her life a range of perspectives in her autobiographies, critical works, and poetry. As Nadine McInnis writes in her Acknowledgements to *Dorothy Livesay's Poetics of Desire*, Livesay was committed to "an ongoing universe" (n.p.).

6 Dorothy Livesay does, however, indicate that she was made aware of such poets through her mother (*Journey* 90).

7 In a fascinating echo of F.R. Livesay's novel *Savour of Salt*, in which the protagonist Aine is suspected of sexual misconduct and sent off with a matron from the Salvation Army, the respectable household in Dorothy Livesay's poem also places the servant, Annie, in the custody of the Sally Ann.

Works Cited

Arnason, David. "Dorothy Livesay and the Rise of Modernism in Canada." *A Public and Private Voice: Essays on the Life and Work of Dorothy Livesay*. Ed. Lindsay Dorney, Gerald Noonan, and Paul Tiessen. Waterloo: U of Waterloo P, 1986. 5–18.

Banting, Pamela. "Daddy's Girl: Dorothy Livesay's Correspondence with Her Father." *Canadian Poetry* 22 (1988): 10–21.

Bloom, Harold. *The Anxiety of Influence: A Theory of Poetry*. 2nd ed. New York: Oxford UP, 1997.

Call, F[rank] O[liver]. Foreword. *Acanthus and Wild Grape*. Toronto: McClelland and Stewart, 1920. 9–13.

Campbell, Wanda. "Moonlight and Morning: Women's Early Contribution to Canadian Modernism." *The Canadian Modernists Meet*. Ed. Dean Irvine. Ottawa: U of Ottawa P, 2005. 79–99.

Doyle, James. "Harriet Monroe's *Poetry* and Canadian Poetry." *Canadian Poetry* 25 (1989): 38–48.

Eliot, T.S. "*Ulysses*, Order, and Myth." *Selected Prose of T.S. Eliot*. Ed. Frank Kermode. San Diego: Harcourt Brace, 1975. 175–78.

———. *The Waste Land*: *Collected Poems, 1909–1962*. London: Faber and Faber, 1974. 61–86.

Gerson, Carole. "Anthologies and the Canon of Early Canadian Women Writers." *Re(Dis)covering Our Foremothers: Nineteenth-Century Canadian Women Writers*. Ed. Lorraine McMullen. Ottawa: U of Ottawa P, 1990. 55–76.

———. "Florence Randal Livesay." *Dictionary of Literary Biography: Canadian Writers, 1890–1920*. Ed. W.H. New. Detroit: Gale, 1990. 205–8.

Gilbert, Sandra M., and Susan Gubar. *The Madwoman in the Attic: The Woman Writer and the Nineteenth-Century Literary Imagination*. New Haven: Yale UP, 1979.

———. *No Man's Land: The Place of the Woman Writer in the Twentieth Century*. Vol. 1, *The War of the Words*. New Haven: Yale UP, 1987.

Gwyn, Sandra. *The Private Capital: Ambition and Love in the Age of Macdonald and Laurier*. 1984. Toronto: McClelland and Stewart, 1986.

Irvine, Dean J. "Editorial Postscript." Livesay, *Archive for Our Times*. 250–72.
Livesay, Dorothy. *Archive for Our Times: Previously Uncollected and Unpublished Poems of Dorothy Livesay*. Ed. Dean J. Irvine. Vancouver: Arsenal Pulp, 1998.
———. *Collected Poems: The Two Seasons*. Toronto: McGraw-Hill, 1972.
———. "An Interview with Dorothy Livesay." By Doug Beardsley and Rosemary Sullivan. *Canadian Poetry* 3 (1978): 87–97.
———. *Journey with My Selves: A Memoir, 1909–1963*. Vancouver: Douglas and McIntyre, 1991.
———. Preface. *Down Singing Centuries: Folk Literature of the Ukraine*. Trans. Florence Randal Livesay. Ed. Louisa Loeb and Dorothy Livesay. Winnipeg: Hyperion, 1981. 11–12.
———. *Right Hand, Left Hand*. Erin, ON: Press Porcépic, 1977.
———. *The Self-Completing Tree: Selected Poems*. Victoria: Press Porcépic, 1986.
———. *A Winnipeg Childhood*. Winnipeg: Peguis, 1973.
Livesay, Florence Randal. "Canadian Poetry Today." *Poetry* (Chicago) 27.1 (1925): 36–40.
———. *Savour of Salt*. London: J.M. Dent, 1927.
———. *Shepherd's Purse*. Toronto: Macmillan, 1923.
———, ed. *The Making of a Canadian: J.F.B. Livesay*. Toronto: Ryerson, 1947.
McInnis, Nadine. *Dorothy Livesay's Poetics of Desire*. Winnipeg: Turnstone, 1994.
Norris, Ken. "The Beginnings of Canadian Modernism." *Canadian Poetry* 11 (1982): 56–66.
Relke, Diana M.A. "The Task of Poetic Mediation: Dorothy Livesay's Early Poetry." *Ariel* 17.4 (1986): 17–36.
Rose, Marilyn J. "Translating/Transliterating the Ethnic: Florence Livesay's *Songs of Ukraina* and Keibo Oiwa's *Stone Voices*." *Canadian Issues / Thèmes Canadiens* 18 (1996): 145–57.
Scott, F.R. "The Canadian Authors Meet." *An Anthology of Canadian Literature*. Ed. Russell Brown and Donna Bennett. Vol. 1. Toronto: Oxford UP, 1982. 348.
Simmel, Georg. "The Metropolis and Mental Life." 1903. *The Sociology of Georg Simmel*. Trans. and ed. Kurt H. Wolff. New York: Free Press, 1950. 409–24.
Stevens, Peter. *Dorothy Livesay: Patterns in a Poetic Life*. Toronto: ECW, 1992.
Thompson, Lee. *Dorothy Livesay*. Boston: Twayne, 1987.
———. "A More Public Voice: Poet as Journalist." *A Private and a Public Voice: Essays on the Life and Work of Dorothy Livesay*. Ed. Lindsay Dorney, Gerald Noonan, and Paul Tiessen. Waterloo: U of Waterloo P, 1986. 42–52.
Trehearne, Brian. *Aestheticism and the Canadian Modernists: Aspects of a Poetic Influence*. Kingston: McGill-Queen's UP, 1989.
Wayne, Joyce, and Stuart Mackinnon. "Dorothy Livesay: A Literary Life on the Left." *A Private and a Public Voice: Essays on the Life and Work of Dorothy Livesay*. Ed. Lindsay Dorney, Gerald Noonan, and Paul Tiessen. Waterloo: U of Waterloo P, 1986. 33–41.

Weekes, Mary. "An Afternoon with the Livesays at Their Home in Clarkson." *Saturday Night* 60 September 1944: 33.

Woolf, Virginia. *A Room of One's Own*. 1929. *A Room of One's Own* and *Three Guineas*. Ed. Michèle Barrett. London: Penguin, 1993. 1–103.

Feminist and Regionalist Modernisms in *Contemporary Verse*, *CV/II*, and *CV2*

CHRISTINE KIM

Contemporary Verse (1941–52)

The important work that small poetry magazines did in circulating and so developing modernist poetry in Canada is well documented. Literary histories have focussed on the significance of little magazines such as the *McGill Fortnightly Review*, which was largely the work of the Montreal poets Leo Kennedy, F.R. Scott, and A.J.M. Smith in the 1920s; and on *Preview* and *First Statement,* which, going into print in the 1940s, merged in 1945 to form *Northern Review*. Within discussions of magazine culture and Canadian modernism, *Contemporary Verse* also usually receives a nod: a small West Coast literary magazine devoted exclusively to Canadian poetry, *Contemporary Verse* was founded by Doris Ferne, Dorothy Livesay, Anne Marriott, and Floris Clark McLaren in 1941, and edited by Alan Crawley until 1952. However, while *Contemporary Verse* is acknowledged as a magazine that printed good poetry, it is rarely regarded as having been a primary force in the shaping of Canadian modernism proper. Instead, studies about this period remap the field of literary production in a fashion reminiscent of colonialist territorialism: numerous complicated exchanges between writers, readers, and editors are repressed so that neat lines can be drawn between the various Montreal coteries.[1] While room is given to accommodate the conflicts between and within these various collectives, there is often little critical space left over to discuss the ways in which magazines like *Contemporary Verse* contest this project of institutionalizing modernism within the Canadian literary canon.[2] The general tendency has been to link polemical periodicals like *Preview* and *First Statement* with modernism while more aesthetically inclusive and regionally dispersed periodicals like *Contemporary Verse* are not connected to modernism. In the initial section of my essay, I want to locate *Contemporary Verse* within the field of Canadian modernist magazine publishing and the cultural milieu of the 1940s to demonstrate that subsequent periodizations have often been less concerned with modernist poetic production than with the production of a modernism whose logic conforms to that of nationalism, since both operate by overlooking specific contradictions in order to make broader generalizations. Moreover, both modernism and nationalism as ideological movements attempt a similar erasure of gender.[3] Subsequent sections of this paper take up the legacy of *Contemporary Verse* by situating *CV/II* and *CV2* within discussions of contemporary nationalism and feminist politics.[4]

While the thirty-nine-issue run of *Contemporary Verse* preceded the publications of *Preview* and *First Statement* by a year and outlasted both of them, the critical work of canonizing modernism in the 1960s, which located the origins of Canadian modernism in small magazine production, largely excluded *Contemporary Verse*. However, more recent critics like Pauline Butling and Dean Irvine, attentive to different critical paradigms, examine *Contemporary Verse* by considering its differences from the Montreal magazines in terms of gender, regionalism, and editorial approach. A notable exception to this distinction between earlier and more recent criticism is Joan McCullagh's book, *Alan Crawley and* Contemporary Verse.[5] In it, she notes that "there are polite, usually respectful references to it in the literary histories" (xx). She cites Desmond Pacey as praising Crawley's "almost impeccable taste in the choice of good poetry and … [his] sympathetic and perceptive reviews of the current output of verse" (xx). However, Pacey's *Creative Writing in Canada* covers the contribution made by *Contemporary Verse* in one paragraph, and then spends the next five pages examining the literary output of *Preview* and *First Statement*; he forgets about *Contemporary Verse*'s "impeccable taste" and "perceptive review[ing]" (Pacey qtd. in McCullough 154). Pacey's cursory approach to the magazine is symptomatic of the general treatment it has received in Canadian criticism in the past. *Contemporary Verse* is a West Coast production, and most considerations of Canadian modernism locate its centre in Montreal. Both geographically and symbolically, the distance between the West and the East coasts is difficult to overcome. Michael Gnarowski claims, "the vortex of literary action in Canada has chosen to spin in Montreal," a view echoed by other critics ("Role" 213). The contrast between the minimal space devoted to *Contemporary Verse* and the extended discussion of *Preview* and *First Statement* in Louis Dudek's "The Role of Little Magazines in Canada" suggests that Dudek shares Gnarowski's opinion (208).[6] Similar sentiments are articulated by Robert K. Martin, who uses the Montreal scene to contextualize his discussion of Patrick Anderson. Martin's first paragraph opens: "In June 1943, a quarrel erupted between two leaders of Canada's emergent national literary movement, then centred in Montreal, a quarrel that would come to be seen as defining the future course of the national literature" (110). Again, the implication is that acts of significance occurred in Montreal and acts that occurred elsewhere were of lesser influence on the Canadian cultural scene. Such literary histories suggest that Montreal was the cultural capital of the modernist movement, and Vancouver and Victoria its suburbs—distant and dependent on the urban centre for creative sustenance. As Peggy Kelly notes in this volume, Dorothy Livesay, one of the editors of *Contemporary Verse*, struggled against this regionalized hierarchy of literary value.

Contemporary Verse's position is further complicated because editorial policies and mandates locate themselves within the field of literary production by alternately invoking and denying gender. *Preview*, *First Statement*, and *New Provinces*, the anthology that consisted of poetry by Robert Finch, Leo Kennedy, A.M. Klein, E.J. Pratt, Scott, and Smith (but excluded other key poets like Livesay) are similar to each other for their polemical editorial policies and, not coincidentally, for the critical attention that they have garnered from the literary institution. These positions suggest that Jayne Marek's observations, made specifically of the American modernist magazine scene, that "men have been expected to be bold or experimental ... [and that] post hoc discussions of the bravado that is obvious in much modernist writing will be pitched a certain way" (8), is also applicable to the Canadian context. Not only do cultural expectations demand firm editorial policies from male publications, but subsequent rewritings of these contributions also typically focus on, and often even exaggerate, editors' courage and vision. Consequently, despite the six years and various ideological chasms that separate the publication of *New Provinces* from *Preview* and *First Statement*, the publications are comparable because all advertised their positions through programmatic statements that are often returned to during discussions of Canadian modernism. It is also not a coincidence that writings about these publications often perceive the texts as extensions of masculine personalities: *First Statement* is equated with John Sutherland, *Preview* with Patrick Anderson, and *New Provinces* most often with A.J.M. Smith. Ken Norris is able to make the somewhat reductive claim that "behind each stood a single personality who shaped the magazine" because masculine icons function as metaphors of modernity within this symbolic economy, giving the "man" in manifesto a particular resonance (27). This logic then precludes inclusion in the modernist corpus of a magazine like *Contemporary Verse* because its editor, Alan Crawley, is not a militant personality and cannot act as a metonymical substitute for the magazine in the same way Sutherland, Anderson, and Smith can signify their publications' visions of the modernist movement. While Anderson and Sutherland are often characterized as heroic, or what Ethel Wilson calls "splendid and tragic," Crawley is represented in radically different terms (33). References to Crawley and his work with *Contemporary Verse* constantly refer to his blindness.[7] Although literary histories often write Anderson and Sutherland as dominant forces that influenced the production of poetry because of their strengths, such histories perceive Crawley as making his mark on the modernist poetry scene in spite of his disability. For instance, Wilson's discussion of Crawley's contributions "beg[s] [us] to believe and remember, that the editor of *Contemporary Verse* was blind" (34). These references to Crawley's blindness imply that he is an imperfect man and so not a militant modernist.

New Provinces, begun in 1934 but not published until 1936, is often referred to as a significant marker in modernism, or as Munro Beattie phrases it in *The Literary History of Canada*, "a literary milestone," even though very few copies of the anthology sold when it was first published (753). The anthology has two prefaces: one by Smith, which was rejected, and a much shorter one by Scott and Kennedy, which was actually published. The former was rejected by Finch and Pratt because of its tone and "the general impression which will be left on the public mind," not because they fundamentally disagreed with his point of view (Gnarowski, Introduction xix). The rejected preface frames the poems in terms of their radical difference from the Romantic verse of earlier poets whose "two great themes are nature and love—nature humanized, endowed with feeling, and made sentimental; love idealized, sanctified, and inflated" (Smith xxvii).[8] The poems in *New Provinces* are valued, in part, because "there is certainly nothing specially Canadian about more than one or two poems" (Smith xxix). In other words, they are worthy because the poems speak to universal rather than local, or as Smith phrases it, "cosmopolitan" rather than "native" readers. Smith's preface advocates a radical break from Canadian literary tradition; this is a somewhat masculine and elitist solution as it simplifies past and ongoing negotiations, institutionalized values, and competing discourses into a unified and hermetically sealed tradition. His article dismisses Canada's Confederation poets and their influence on new writing, but does not problematize English and American traditions of modernist poets like Eliot and Pound or even acknowledge a tradition of Canadian women writers that included poets such as Pauline Johnson or Isabella Valency Crawford. Smith's demand for a rupture with the past needs to be questioned because it is only those local influences that prevent Canadian modernism from becoming cosmopolitan or distinct from a transnational brand of modernism that he perceives as negative. Smith's paradigm attempts to contain cultural production during this period within a masculine avant-garde poetics, thus indicating a desire to regulate both the producer and reader of poetry according to an international literary standard. Somewhat paradoxically, the logic of containment that Smith articulates is in turn used by others involved in *New Provinces* to keep what Scott in a letter to Smith terms his "greater radicalism" in line (Gnarowski xiii). Political and aesthetic values are used to patrol even the limits of Smith's program.

Preview and *First Statement* also issued programmatic statements about the function of poetry, but these differ from Smith's because they locate themselves within a nationalist frame.[9] The first issue of *Preview* takes a militant stance and proclaims itself as "five Montreal writers who recently formed themselves into a group for the purposes of mutual discussion and criticism and who hope, through these selections to try out their work before a somewhat larger public" (1). The magazine further defined its work as having "the capacity to 'sting' with social content and criticism" (1). *First Statement* differs from *Preview* in that it mythologizes itself as more working-class, anti-intellectual, American rather than British in inspiration, and more radically socialist. These different interests are often used to explain what has become a "celebrated rivalry" between the magazines (Fisher 7). Wynne Francis notes that the poets of *First Statement* "prided themselves on writing a masculine, virile 'poetry of experience'" (27). What is consistent about *New Provinces*, *First Statement*, and *Preview* is that they were what Dorothy Livesay called "cliques" (McCullagh 13). While *First Statement* published a wider range of writers than *Preview* and obviously *New Provinces*, all three forums were largely inaccessible to the majority of Canadian writers.[10] These sites are not public places to experiment with poetry, but rather sources of manifestoes and programmatic statements that attempt to define a modernist movement. That academic critics have embraced these three publications and written a dominant narrative of modernism around them suggests that these programmatic statements are used symbolically to represent a complex and contested field that otherwise resists the referential aspect of language. They are useful for institutional purposes because these statements mark literary production in the 1930s and 1940s as what Pierre Bourdieu calls "a field of position-takings" (34). The clearly staked ideological positions of these groups act as the parameters for discussions of modernism as a movement. Additional parties can then be located within this field because it has already been organized according to key players and significant conflicts; it is no longer a messy series of debates and cross-debates but a system of discourses.

These two Montreal magazines are interesting, in part, because their various conflicts have been so well documented. Francis, for one, notes that the tension between them "generated much of the poetic activity that went on in Montreal and made the Forties Canada's most exciting literary decade"; Francis considers this rivalry to be a force that pushed boundaries and drove writers to experiment creatively with language, a narrative that privileges competition rather than nuanced poetic criticism (23). The magazines' distinct identities are useful for critics who later classify poets and editorial collectives into political camps and consider poetic development to be the product of conflict and debate; it is most often these clearly demarcated groups that are written into narratives about this period precisely because they make such stories possible. Norris's *The Little Magazine in Canada* positions the 1920s Montreal magazines at the beginning of its cultural history and claims that the "*First Statement* poets began the second wave of Canadian Modernism" (41). *Contemporary Verse* is located on the margins of such projects because it undermines the authoritative stance of such periodizations by implicitly questioning their internal logic; if, as Norris's study intimates, the accepted narrative of modernism is organized around antagonism and conflict, whether it be with other magazines or preceding generations, then *Contemporary Verse*'s deliberate refusal to participate in such debates writes it out of modernist metanarratives.

It was presumably in response to *Preview*'s editorial statement, which declared its political program and presented it as a coterie, that *Contemporary Verse* issued in its fourth issue what can be taken as a counter-statement. Crawley's "Editor's Note" claims that

> *Contemporary Verse* is not the chapbook of a limited or local group of writers. The contents of each number will at once dispel any charge that it exists to press political propaganda, particular social readjustment or literary trend. The aims of *Contemporary Verse* are simple and direct and seem worthy and worthwhile. These aims are to entice and stimulate the writing and reading of poetry and to provide means for its publication free from restraint of politics, prejudices and placations, and to keep open its pages to poetry that is sincere in thought and expression and contemporary in theme and treatment and technique. (3–4)

Contemporary Verse resists a logic of avant-gardism by making a concerted effort to be inclusive rather than exclusive, thus soliciting contributions throughout the country and publishing poems of varying aesthetic modes. By opening its pages to those other than the vanguard, *Contemporary Verse* resists equating modernism with only the avant-garde. In this way, ironically, *Contemporary Verse* is less local and parochial than the "internationalist" and "cosmopolitan" cliques of Scott and Smith. The magazine's explicit but vague desire for "contemporary" poetry suggests that it went to great lengths to avoid favouring specific regions or types of poetry. *Contemporary Verse* is also unique in that while it was most clearly not a women's magazine, it is one in which women played active roles and contributed by writing, editing, and circulating poetry that articulated their modern social realities.[11] This inclusive logic is taken up again in Livesay's *CV/II*, her journal dedicated to Canadian poetry criticism published out of the University of Manitoba, throughout whose history women's literary labour is visible.

That the original *Contemporary Verse* emerged and remained in existence for eleven years, despite shortages of money and labour that were exacerbated by the war, suggests that its board, subscribers, and poets felt a considerable need for a non-partisan forum that circulated and edited poetry rather than regulated it. *Contemporary Verse*'s emphasis on the contemporary makes it clear that certain social visions and perceptions of reality as well as particular poetic modes dominated. The magazine countered this tendency by publishing poetry diverse in terms of subject and mode; various issues feature the work of more established poets like Birney, Livesay, and Smith, alongside newer voices like Jay Macpherson and Anne Wilkinson, and older poets like Audrey Alexandra Brown. McCullagh has noted that MacPherson and Wilkinson appreciated the editorial guidance and encouraging atmosphere *Contemporary Verse* provided when they were first emerging as poets and looking for a place to publish their work.[12] *Contemporary Verse* might then be regarded as a magazine that made the limitations of modernist publications apparent and attempted to rectify them by acting as a space that legitimated other types of cultural production and approaches, as well as regional and women's modernisms, and helped make future feminist interventions possible.

However, this commitment to a nebulous "good" rather than more sharply defined criteria made *Contemporary Verse* vulnerable to barbs. *First Statement*'s Louis Dudek remarked that although the magazine printed "good poetry,… it was not a fighting magazine with a policy" ("Role" 208). Presumably because *Contemporary Verse* did not respond to the cultural moment with manifestoes like those of *Preview* or *First Statement*, or programmatic statements like Smith's, its contemporaries as well as later critics have dismissed it. Programmatic statements make publications' identities clear by inscribing political lines around them; in other words, they act as strategies of containment and dissemination. *Contemporary Verse*'s resolve not to declare a political or aesthetic position might then be read as a refusal of such strategies; such a reading of the magazine's editorial strategy transforms editorial inclusiveness into a statement of sorts, or at the very least, a negation of other statements. While Dudek criticized the eclecticism of *Contemporary Verse*'s poetry as apolitical and for not "work[ing] out any program of ideas," it is precisely this eclecticism that appears in fact to be the magazine's policy, legacy, and approach to tradition (208). Discourse such as Dudek's is implicitly masculine and suggests that the little magazines are to be, following on the military metaphors, hard-hitting and iconoclastic. Such rhetoric implicitly excludes the feminine and the more open borders of *Contemporary Verse*. That such a possibility has not been taken up within dominant narratives of modernism raises questions about the premise of those narratives as they have been institutionalized. Precisely how does modernism then presume to challenge the strictures of tradition? What place does multiplicity occupy in modernist visions?

Acknowledging that *Contemporary Verse* is a poetry magazine with a distinct identity that addressed a pressing need in modernist literary production is one way of historicizing Canadian modernism and making it apparent that narratives about poetic production in the 1940s are embedded within larger narratives of nationalism, aesthetics, and gender. *Contemporary Verse*'s devaluation has been essential to the project of writing modernist literary histories because it complicates the simple, dogmatic lines that currently map out this period. By testifying to the complexity of the field, the broad range of poetry published in *Contemporary Verse* delegitimizes narratives that naturalize modernism's origins in masculine figures and texts. The absence of an explicitly political editorial platform suggests that poems speak to and from various positions rather than support specific aesthetic theories or social movements. At the very least, the absence of a declared program suggests that the magazine lacked the impulse to break with history because its relationships with traditions are multiple, varied, and necessary. As *Contemporary Verse* is inextricably located within the same modernist field as the Montreal coteries, its attempt at neutrality is ideologically impossible. Consequently, its own position is defined in part through what it is not, namely a Montreal coterie, as well as what it is unwilling to do, which is break with the past absolutely.

It is precisely this sense of identity and non-identity that complicates narratives of modernism and challenges how cultural institutions write literary histories. The current understanding of Canadian modernism is useful to the institution because it provides a reasonable map of events that transpired to bring about modernism, and it is also one that neatly coincides with the end of colonialism and the rise of capitalism, two other events that have often been used to proclaim Canada a modern nation. These narrative intersections indicate that Canadian literary modernism as it has been institutionalized enables the social reproduction of dominant orders by legitimating a certain logic of homogeneity. While arguing for a strong line of innovation in poetics, Canadian little magazines like *Preview* and *First Statement*, in their taking up of this rhetoric of the avant-garde, are socially conservative. They reinforced gender hierarchies just as the feminist movement was making major changes in the public sphere. *Contemporary Verse* is thus a telling cultural document because it makes it apparent that while texts can circulate and share meaning, they can also be used to inscribe circles and demarcate centres that exclude meanings. The exclusion of this magazine from most literary histories is a symbolic violence that prevents the recognition of much work that resists assimilation within institutional narratives. This is problematic not only for *Contemporary Verse* and narratives around its contributions, but for all cultural production that sits on the margins of institutional narratives. If, as Bourdieu has claimed, "works of art exist as symbolic objects only if they are known and recognized, that is, socially instituted as works of art and received by spectators capable of knowing and recognizing them as such," the consequences are dire for much experimental artistic production that draws upon discourses of gender, "race," class, and queer sexuality that offend the sensibilities of dominant culture (37). How are such projects to be recognized as art and valued if the discourses that support such works are themselves discredited?

CV/II (1975–84)

While analyses of collectives like that of *Contemporary Verse* do much to draw attention to the relations between institutionalized narratives of modernism, modernist women's cultural production, and little magazines during the modernist era, much work remains to be done in reshaping the genre of literary histories. More than two decades after *Contemporary Verse* stopped publishing, its mantle was taken up again by Dorothy Livesay when she started *CV/II*, a journal of poetry criticism. First published in May 1975, *CV/II* is a site in which multiple contemporary political and aesthetic discourses intersected and developed. The work accomplished by *CV/II* makes evident the value of tracing the various contributions of the modernist period and the manner in which they continue to influence the contemporary moment. Here I propose to locate *CV/II* within the field of contemporary cultural production to examine the negotiation of a field both constituted and complicated by issues of feminism, women's writing, regional and national politics, and avant-garde aesthetics. In part, *CV/II* staked out its position within the field of poetics by drawing upon the eclectic mandate of *Contemporary Verse*; these choices generated possibilities for reading the overlap between modernist and contemporary literary production.

In her initial editorial, Livesay declares the contemporary moment to be a time of "growth into maturity of the arts in Canada" (2). She suggests that since the 1950s of *Contemporary Verse* the needs of both the arts and artists in Canada have shifted significantly: unlike the modernist period, a time of poetic "drought" because of a shortage of periodicals in which established and younger poets could publish their creative works, the problem with the 1970s scene is that there is a critical drought. *CV/II* proposes to remedy this problem by functioning as a forum for the critical discussion of poetry from all regions in Canada. *CV/II* uses *Contemporary Verse*'s title as an abbreviated prefix to write itself into a genealogy that positions its work as a logical and teleological extension or even reincarnation of its predecessors, foreshadowed by Phyllis Webb's description of *Contemporary Verse* in 1953 as "an incipient phoenix." The implicit suggestion made by *CV/II* is that the creation and criticism of poetry are complementary elements that constitute a poetic whole. Collectively, poetry and its criticism foster a poetry that "best expresses our craving for confrontation with the real, with direct, day-to-day living" (Livesay, "Editorial" 2). *CV/II* draws upon *Contemporary Verse* in particular, and the semiotics of Canadian modernism in general, to distinguish itself from other periodicals and to gain recognition within a contested field. It generates its field of possibilities by invoking the historical to ground the terms of both its similarity and its difference. In this situation, *Contemporary Verse* occupies the position of what Bourdieu refers to as "the consecrated avant-garde" given its "social ageing" (59). *CV/II*'s strategic return to *Contemporary Verse* legitimates its operations, but is complicated by its need to also distinguish itself from this consecrated avant-garde. In *The Field of Cultural Production*, Bourdieu makes the following useful observation about the struggle between consecrated and new avant-garde positions: "a work or an aesthetic movement is irreducible to any other situated elsewhere in the series; and *returns* to past styles ... are never 'the same thing,' since they are separated from what they return to by negative reference to something which was itself the negation of it" (60). *CV/II*'s return to *Contemporary Verse* is similarly a struggle between the old and the new that seeks to open up dialogue through the multiplication of new positions, a process that to some extent depends on the recognition of former positions. The movement between the language of modernism and contemporary discourse is comparable to the translation between national languages. In this sense, *CV/II*'s positioning of itself in relation to *Contemporary Verse* encourages a reading strategy similar to the "shuttle reading movement" that Elena Basile's contribution to this volume describes in its discussion of a bilingual edition of P.K. Page's poetry. The spaces between languages, whether temporal or national, are valuable sites from which the limitations of each can be critiqued.

A similar principle of negation and affirmation is at work when Livesay qualifies her assertion that criticism is necessary to supplement the creation of poetry. Unlike *Contemporary Verse*, in which the first issue sought broadly to publish "writers of our own times who can speak to us in words and images and forms that interest and appeal" (Crawley 2), Livesay's editorial imposes stricter parameters around the kinds of criticism that are suitable for such a project. While Livesay echoes Crawley's vision in her call for poetry "that best expresses our craving for confrontation with the real, with direct, day-to-day living," she also identifies a series of ideological positions that contemporary criticism needs to recognize if it is to serve that function

("Editorial" 2). This mandate is articulated though a language of inclusivity, one that seeks criticism that focusses on poetry that speaks with

> the authority of experience and action from all levels of society: the deprived, the enslaved, the sheltered, the brainwashed; as well as the fat, sleek, jaded. It must spring from all ethnic (and immigrant) sources, whose roots will nourish us. Where necessary, as with the literature of Quebec, we must translate and expound. And especially from all parts of the country we would like to explore the true feelings of women. (2)

The editorial's emphasis on the word "all" demonstrates a commitment to rectifying the historic neglect of regionalism, women's writing, ethnic production, and Québécois poetry in a way that distinguishes itself from "elitist quarterlies" (2). This vision of contemporary poetry and poetic criticism is, like that of *Contemporary Verse*, multiple, eclectic, and in some senses, impossibly inclusive[13] given that its rhetoric discreetly signals the presence of aesthetic, albeit ambivalent, criteria (2). From the outset, in this editorial, *CV/II* configures itself as a utopian journal whose horizon is always visible, yet always slightly beyond reach. Inclusivity again operates as a mandate of sorts, but one that is more difficult to implement than the exclusivity of more specifically focussed publications.

While Livesay and *Contemporary Verse* remained considerable influences on *CV/II*, her departure after a brief three-year term as editor "left open the possibility for the editorial transformation of *CV/II*" (Irvine 71). Even though Livesay's inaugural editorial expressed an interest in multiple kinds of criticism, following her exit in the late 1970s, *CV/II* became primarily a journal of poetry reviews that focussed on Canadian cultural geography. A series of special issues gave attention to regional differences: each issue investigated the poetic production of a particular region. Many writers queried how regional distinctiveness was to be judged and how the regional identity of a particular work or poet was to be defined. For instance, John Steffler's editorial in the special *Newfoundland Poetry* issue (6.3)[14] grapples with feeling that "the time ... was ripe for a new collection of current Newfoundland poetry" but does not know "how to identify a *Newfoundland* poet" (3). Steffler's problem stems from his believing that, on the one hand, there is a distinct quality to Newfoundland and its poets, but that on the other hand, "having to classify people and their work according to rigid territorial or genealogical criteria" is unsettling (2). Reading poetry in regional terms involves drawing explicit links between land, cultural products, and genealogy that are deeply problematic. Drawing further attention to the difficulty of settling questions of land, culture, and belonging, Adrian Fowler's article in the same issue, "Newfoundland Poetry in the 70s: The Context," investigates the origins of Newfoundland poetry through specific reference to E.J. Pratt. Pratt's heroic poetry is contrasted with other poetic visions that focus on the everyday, such as Michael Harrington's, in order to query questions of authenticity and regional voice. Fowler notes almost in passing that Pratt left Newfoundland "in 1907 at the age of 25, long before his career as a poet had begun," as if to underline the intricacy of an issue like belonging, which involves much more than residence (5).

In addition to the special issues, in 1982 *CV/II* introduced a short-lived series of regional reports that were to provide "information and reflection which our regional editors believe should be shared across the country" (6.4: 2). While the commitment to keeping readers apprised of developments across Canada is laudable, it is a project whose execution is riddled with problems, as the first line of the Maritimes and Newfoundland regional report makes clear:

> The Maritimes and Newfoundland are no more a single region than the Prairies or Ontario. In fact, they are probably less so when one considers the difficulties of getting from one to another of these provinces, their sparse, scattered populations, their lack of a single metropolitan centre. Reporting from here I realize will not be easy, possible even, unless those I'm reporting on send me their news. (Gibbs 9)

Similar difficulties are noted in b.p. Nichol's "Ontario Report," published in the following issue, which complains that such a regional column requires "covering a hell of a lot of ground" (7). These difficulties result from the competing fictions that constitute both the local and the national, and the differing emphases on detail or generalization that each requires. The underlying principle governing the magazine's editorial process is that bodies of local poetry can be organized into a national whole because relationships between particular regions already exist. Robert Foster signals this in a 1981 editorial when he diagnoses Canadian "demons" (2). Foster discusses this particular problem through a rhetoric of progress: "movements beyond modernism," "seeds of hope ... to move beyond our traditional superficial optimism and our deep national despair" (2). The list of demons that are responsible for Canadian inertia, according to Foster, includes the American demon and a national fear of risk (2). His solution is to advocate poetry inspired by love that "cares for the beauty and the suffering of the land with a passion" (2).

I draw attention to this editorial not to take issue with Robert Foster's proposed solutions, but to query the ways in which he constructs the category of national aesthetics. Foster's editorial suggests that tradition and national identity can be written in monolithic terms, even as other contributions to the magazine repeatedly flag problems with such a project. By yoking together regional literary productions and consolidating them under a larger umbrella of national aesthetics, he overlooks, for instance, the ways in which these sites are gendered. Foster's strategy indicates a desire to reshape Canadian literary production according to a dominant narrative of nationalism. This logic suggests that even if Livesay was right in claiming that in Canada there was now poetry "pushing up from every crack and cranny" ("Editorial" 2), Canadian literature as a whole had not received institutional recognition. *CV/II* attempts to legitimize this literature through the construction of a Canadian poetic identity able to circulate throughout the cultural field because its narrative has been simplified into a form that can be repeatedly retold, much like the dominant narratives of modernism. This erasure of the multiplicity of discourses in favour of a single overarching narrative explains in part why, despite Livesay's emphasis on the journal's openness to women's writing, Foster's 1982 editorial in issue 6.4 notes "the decrease in contributions to *CV/II* from and about women," a change he justifies in part by claiming that "other magazines report the same problem" (2). This reorganization of the larger cultural field around positions of nation and region, art and culture, largely excluded women's poetry and criticism that came into conflict with these dominant national narratives. Barbara Godard suggests that "a high-point in the recognition of feminist culture in Canada appears now to have been 1985–1986," the years in which the editorship of *CV/II* changed hands ("Feminist Periodicals" 209).

CV2 (1985–)

Three years later, in 1985, the priorities of the magazine were reconsidered when outgoing editor Robert Foster was replaced by an editorial collective composed of four women: Pamela Banting, Di Brandt, Jane Casey, and Jan Horner. Their introductory editorial in issue 8.4, signed by Pamela Banting, articulates a commitment to "women and men in dialogue, *re*interpreting Dorothy Livesay's original vision for a national poetry magazine" (4). This ideological transformation, telegraphed by the renaming of the magazine *CV2*, ruptures the genealogical line by demonstrating its difference from the interests and priorities of *CV/II*. While *CV2*'s initial editorial professes a continued commitment to Livesay's vision, subsequent editorials perform acts of double displacement as they often advocate moving beyond Livesay's original goals.[15] These manoeuvres, which break with and affirm the genealogy, are at work when the collective credits the "Women and Words" conference as the immediate impetus for its new focus on feminist poetics.[16] It justifies this contemporary feminist slant as both a return to and a recontextualization of the magazine's "roots," in part by reinvoking the narrative of how *Contemporary Verse* was founded (Banting, "Editorial: Blurred Mirrors" 6). *CV2* frames its difference from *Contemporary Verse* by prioritizing "the writing of difference and of différance," and it signals its difference from *CV/II* by locating itself within a field of women's rather than Canadian writing (6). The symbolic shifts *CV2* underwent are, however, mediated by economic constraints since the magazine was not able to remodel itself completely given market pressures and limited funding. For instance, while *CV2* distinguished itself from *CV/II* in later issues by devoting itself primarily to poetry rather than criticism, it later published fiction as well, a decision influenced by the economic advantages of prose's wider readership and the financial struggles of the collective.[17] Nonetheless, the transformation from *CV/II* to *CV2* marks the difference between a women's and a theoretically conceived "feminist" writing project. Furthermore, the shifts in *CV2*'s mandates, for instance from issues 17.1 to 24.1 to 24.3, signal additional ways in which the proliferation of difference occurs within the magazine between issues.[18] While the title *CV2* remains consistent between issues, its subheadings signify affinity with both *Contemporary Verse* and *CV/II* and the fragmentation of the field into multiple positions.

The distance from each other imposed by various editorial boards of *CV/II* and *CV2* is similar to some modernists' desire to distance themselves from the Confederation poets. While the particular circumstances and the ways in which they were executed differ, this rupturing of past and present is common to both and suggests the necessity as well as the impossibility of razing the cultural field. In the case of *CV2*, this strategy suggests a current incompatibility between the politics of the nation and the politics of women's writing and feminist writing. Godard suggests the reasons for this friction when she argues that gendered economies operate according to different principles. Following Bourdieu, she notes that symbolic capital is accrued through the disavowal of economic profits ("Feminist Periodicals" 211); yet this system of recognition through refusal is often absent from a feminist "economy of debt not surplus or profit" (212). The consequences of such a lack of cultural and economic capital are evident in a periodical like *CV2*, which has "hovered on the near brink of extinction," and demonstrate why these issues of gendered economies are pertinent for readings of both modernist and contemporary cultural production (C. Foster 5).

The feminism of *CV2* has been challenged on numerous occasions by having to negotiate the politics of representation, a balancing act similar to that attempted by *CV/II* with respect to local and national poetry. The challenge for *CV2* is to represent the concerns of Canadian feminists and women, a utopian ideal given the possibility of publishing only representative selections. This act of selection politicizes the relations between periods through the ways in which the semiotics of modernism are deployed. *CV2* also returns to Livesay and *Contemporary Verse* as signs that make possible certain narratives of modernism, women's writing, and the contemporary in order to legitimize its own position.[19] Not only does the legacy of *Contemporary Verse* influence the shape of *CV2*, but also the ways in which *CV2* is read are determined in part by the position *Contemporary Verse* occupies in the cultural field. Livesay's return to *Contemporary Verse* not only provided a means to establish *CV/II*, but it also became a means to consolidate *Contemporary Verse*'s authority within the masculine practices of consecration. Earlier influential literary histories and surveys of Canadian literature minimized the impact of *Contemporary Verse*. However, more recent returns to examine it as a fruitful point of departure by other publishing enterprises question the institution's neglect of the periodical and so reshape reading practices for both the past and present.[20]

Another key difference that distinguishes *CV2* from its predecessors is that it explicitly acknowledges the various strands that complicate its dominant logic, in this case, feminism. The issue of *Tessera* hosted by *CV2* in 1988 makes visible numerous divisions within Canadian feminist thought and self-reflexively problematizes the terms of its discussion.[21] The focus of this particular issue of *Tessera* was "a look at the state of current feminist critical theory in Quebec and English Canada" (Marlatt and Mezei 5). This issue distinguishes itself from most others published by *CV2* through the dialogue between its two editorials: one by Jane Casey, and one by Barbara Godard. Following a foreword by Daphne Marlatt and Kathy Mezei, Jane Casey's editorial outlines some of the discrepancies between her feminist politics and those in *Tessera*. The variety of feminist positions and the debates they make possible becomes, according to this editorial, a way to "change the way we think" (Casey 7). This collision of "contemporary versus contemporary" involves not only the positions that these feminists take on, but also the language in which they are articulated (6). While Godard's editorial targets the need to "rewrite both the product and process of representation and self-representation" if ideologies of gender are to be contested (12), Casey argues that "the highly specialized language they [these *Tessera* contributors] use precludes the possibility for dialogue among a wide base of feminist readers" (8). Aside from raising familiar problems of inclusivity and exclusivity, the dialogue between editorials demonstrates sociological and theoretical tendencies that characterize differing strands of feminist thought. The numerous complicated lines and feminist genealogies explain in part the often radically divergent understandings of feminism, feminist, and women's cultural production. Unlike *CV/II*'s practice of reading local poetic production as part of a larger national literary whole, this issue of *Tessera* organizes these feminist discourses into conversations and privileges difference and multiplicity rather than synthesis.

While the connections of the magazine, whether in its *CV/II* or its *CV2* form, influenced the position it staked out within various discussions of culture, its ability to remain within the field depended on factors such as technology and institutionalization. The serial production of periodicals suggests an ephemeral nature that is always changing, replaceable, and fleeting.[22] The numerous revisions to *CV/II*'s and *CV2*'s ideological positions, editorial boards, and genres do not counteract this impression. What does, however, challenge the status of magazines as "sites of cultural impermanence, always subject to change" is another change, this time made by *CV2* to its appearance (Irvine 71). In issue 8.4, the incoming editorial board announced that, "with the next issue, *CV/II* will have a new look. It will come out in smaller, journal form with better quality paper" (Banting 4). The decision to use sturdier materials and change its size has made *CV2* easier to use but harder to damage, two advantages for feminist archives. *CV2*'s use of technological advances in magazine publishing mediates constructions of gender in additional ways. Godard's editorial in the *CV2*-hosted issue of *Tessera* argues that "literature, a technology of gender like other cultural signifying practices, offers a privileged terrain for the binding of the individual subject into representation and so is an important area of investigation for feminist inquiry" (13–14). The durable and convenient appearance of the magazine signals the lasting nature of the intervention that feminist thought has made in the academy, critical circles, and creative work in discussions of Canadian culture.[23]

CV/II and *CV2* stake out separate positions within the field of contemporary poetic production, and even within the confines of the same magazine, by taking up divergent possibilities laid out in the eclecticism of the original magazine's modernism. As *Contemporary Verse* provides the conditions of possibility for two radically different articulations of contemporary poetic production, it is possible to read these tendencies towards the national and the feminist as two separate interests that dominate this specific cultural space at various moments. *CV/II* and *CV2* set up the criticism of contemporary poetry according to particular cultural, political, and aesthetic criteria to influence the circulation and constitution of Canadian cultural production. The impetus in these quarterlies is to consider poetry in certain local, global, and transnational movements and politics, and unlike their predecessor *Contemporary Verse*, to make the ideological explicit. Despite the consistent commitment to poetry and criticism of poetry produced in Canada, the different focusses of *CV/II* and *CV2* have meant that they have written dissimilar kinds of social and literary histories. While the magazine has already revised literary history, its utopian visions require that it continue its efforts as it seeks to solve problems of representation.

Notes

I would like to thank the participants in this volume, especially Di Brandt and Barbara Godard, for their generous comments and suggestions on this paper.

1 For instance, Munro Beattie's entry in *Literary History of Canada* reads *Contemporary Verse* as "mainly the creation of a devoted and gifted editor, Alan Crawley, assiduously aided by four poetesses: Doris Ferne, Dorothy Livesay, Anne Marriott, and Floris Clarke McLaren" (766). Beattie quickly praises Crawley before moving on to the relationship between *Preview* and *First Statement*. These two magazines are read entirely in terms of their "literary and political convictions" because, according to Beattie, their interests in cosmopolitanism, native achievements, colonialism, and social protest dominated them (767). These publications are classified through their opposing approaches to literature and by reference to key figures such as P.K. Page, "who contributed to *Preview*" (770). This use of well-known figures to map out positions ignores any traffic between the three magazines or ways in which their interests overlapped. Desmond Pacey's *Creative Writing in Canada* limits its discussion of *Contemporary Verse* to a brief mention. Unlike Beattie's history, Pacey edits out the contributions of Ferne, Livesay, Marriott, and McLaren altogether and instead credits Crawley with having "founded *Contemporary Verse* in 1941 with the specific object of encouraging the new poetry in Canada" (154). Ken Norris's *The Little Magazine in Canada, 1925–80* sets out the ideological differences that separate the various publications; *Contemporary Verse* is briefly discussed and then left behind as Norris maps out the trajectories of *Preview* and *First Statement*. Norris retells the magazines' stories of origins largely according to their oppositions: Anderson vs. Sutherland,

cosmopolitanism vs. nativism, British vs. American influence. This teleological narrative of conflict culminates with the merge into *Northern Review* (40). The structure of Louis Dudek's and Michael Gnarowski's *The Making of Modern Poetry in Canada* differs from the previous texts in the sense that it is not a literary history written by the authors, but rather a compilation of "essays and documents intimately involved in the literary history of the period" (n.p.). While the collection claims not to contain "the exemplary or autotelic showpieces of criticism," it nonetheless includes documents such as Smith's "A Rejected Preface," Sutherland's "Review of *Poems* by Robert Finch," and the resignations of *Northern Review* editors, which map out conflicts between well-known players. Wynne Francis's influential history of the 1940s writes a similar narrative of conflict between *Preview* and *First Statement*, thus framing it in terms of a generational overthrow of the former by the latter. Francis also traces the differences between the factions and meditates on the editors' personalities before concluding that the merger of the two magazines "seemed most practical" (31). All these literary histories repeatedly return to the conflicts and ideological differences between *Preview* and *First Statement* to retell a dominant narrative of competition that excludes the contributions of *Contemporary Verse* and of women and simplifies the exchanges between players.

2 One well-documented example is that of the breakup of the *Northern Review* editorial board over Sutherland's review of Robert Finch's Governor General's Award–winning book of poetry. The resignations of several editors appeared in *Northern Review* in the October–November 1947 issue (Editors 38). As well, Page's letter of resignation, republished in Gnarowski and Dudek's *The Making of Modern Poetry in Canada*, is the only text by a woman included in that canonical anthology of position pieces on modernism.

3 Resistance to this erasure of gender is explored in Sandra Djwa's and Lianne Moyes's essays in this volume, which refer to writers such as Katherine Mansfield, Gertrude Stein, and Virginia Woolf. Djwa and Moyes note that the works of these modernist women are referred to by other writers, such as Page and later Gail Scott, and thus offer alternatives to the dominant masculine models of writing. Approaching this problem of gender and erasure from a slightly different angle, Marilyn Rose's recent essay on archives and Anne Marriott attributes the marginalization of Marriott, a recipient of the Governor General's Award for Poetry in 1941, in part to issues of gender. Rose describes, for instance, Marriott's heavy domestic responsibilities as well as creative conflicts she had with her masculine mentors.

4 *Contemporary Verse*, *Contemporary Verse II* (*CV/II*), and *Contemporary Verse 2* (*CV2*) are three different incarnations of a small Canadian poetry magazine. The first version, *Contemporary Verse*, ran from 1941 to 1952 and devoted itself to publishing Canadian poetry. Dorothy Livesay, one of the original founders of *Contemporary Verse*, later resurrected the magazine as *CV/II* in 1975. This version of the magazine, under the stewardship of multiple different editors (with Livesay moving into the background after the first few issues and remaining there as the magazine's publisher), published both poetry and poetry criticism and remained in existence until 1984. In 1985 the magazine changed hands again, this time becoming *CV2*, and was run by a feminist collective. For a brief period the magazine also published short fiction, but it has since returned to publishing primarily poetry and criticism.

5 Correspondence in the Alan Crawley archives indicates that such critical attention was unusual but welcomed by Crawley. McCullagh's project "was originally a dissertation at the University of British Columbia" (Cogswell 16).

6 Gnarowski and Dudek's anthology did much to establish the canonical narrative of modernism in Canadian literature. Both were poets from Montreal and influential professors, and this gave them and their narrative of modernism certain kinds of cultural capital. That their version of modernist history focusses largely on *First Statement* is interesting; as Francis notes, "Sutherland, Layton and Dudek, different as they were in many ways, formed the hard core of the 'First Statement Group'" (23).

7 For instance, Dorothy Livesay's foreword to Joan McCullagh's *Alan Crawley and Contemporary Verse* gives a brief overview of Crawley's association with the magazine. She discusses his problems with his eyesight and the difficulties and opportunities afforded to him by his subsequent blindness. Perhaps most interestingly, early in her foreword, Livesay offers the following description of Crawley: "After a careful scrutiny of the long narrow face, the hawk-like Roman nose, the *blind eyes* still seeming alive as they look downward at a book, the high, thoughtful, furrowed forehead, the fine white hair, there emerges a Renaissance man, one who could have held forth with Shakespeare in a tavern or posed with Leonardo in a sunny Italian street" (vii; emphasis mine). McCullagh's introduction also raises Crawley's blindness, citing Louis Dudek's dismissive comment that "Crawley was 'handicapped by blindness and cornered in the far west'" (qtd. in McCullagh xxi). In his interview with Crawley, Livesay, McLaren, and Page, George Robertson's opening comments begin with "a man and a young girl are walking by Second Beach in Vancouver. The time is the beginning of the war, and the man is *blind*, the girl is a poet" (87; emphasis mine). Ethel Wilson's "Of Alan Crawley" also spends time discussing "the shock and disaster of *total blindness* [that] came upon Alan" (36; emphasis mine).

8 The contrast between Romantic verse and its theme, and poetry by younger modernists is also taken up in Ann Martin's "The Writing Livesays" in this volume. Martin explores the similar negotiations of gender, literary traditions, and modernity by Dorothy and Florence Livesay despite their very different literary styles and generational gap.

9 Norris discusses *Preview*'s nationalism through its patriotism. He notes that Anderson believed in the "literary task of the Canadian writer during times of war" as a way to influence the outcome of the war (28). Beattie frames *First Statement*'s nationalism in terms of "native achievements and possibilities" (279). He cites the magazine's first editorial in which they dedicate themselves to Canadian writing.

10 Livesay's exclusion from *New Provinces*, for instance, which Sandra Djwa briefly explains in her chapter in this volume as the consequence of political differences between Livesay and Smith, is an example of the inaccessible nature of the anthology. As well, Livesay notes that "in Canada we've been rifled by cliques, and we still are you know ... I mean the Montreal group around *First Statement* was a fascinating group, but it was a clique. For instance, I never got into any Montreal magazine, but anyone from there could and did write for *Contemporary Verse* and get published" (qtd. in Robertson 92).

11 Jean Crawley, Alan Crawley's wife, is one example of a woman whose labour was invaluable in the production of *Contemporary Verse*. While her contributions are not often publicly acknowledged, P.K. Page notes in a letter to Ethel Wilson on 13 July 1963 that "it was Jean, you know as much as Alan who helped create this '*ambiente*.' But I needn't tell you. You will know all that."

12 Correspondence between Alan Crawley and Floris Clark McLaren indicates that she, Anne Marriott, and Doris Ferne encouraged Crawley's practice of sending poets critiques of their works instead of rejection slips. McLaren's position that "in a non-

commercial venture such as this half the use and reason would be lost if your contact with writers who wish to contribute is reduced to form-letters" suggests the board intended to promote ongoing dialogue between the poets and the magazine (McLaren to Crawley, Friday evening, 1942; Dorothy Livesay fonds, box 3, file 30).

13   While *Contemporary Verse* boasted that it was not a coterie, it nevertheless had to contend with the problems of inclusion and exclusion that plague any publication. Fred Cogswell's review of Joan McCullagh's *Alan Crawley and* Contemporary Verse acknowledges that Crawley did much to foster the talent of poets such as Livesay, Page, and Webb; he also notes that "time spent on a few poets, however, does not leave much time for many others" (16). Cogswell suggests that while *Contemporary Verse* was not a clique, Crawley did rely on a "stable of poets" (16). Crawley's decision to nurture certain poets rather than others meant that his position in the field of Canadian poetry was constituted through what was negated as well as what was advocated. Cogswell's review is itself a position-taking and implicitly draws attention to the predicament of *Fiddlehead*, which in its first issue articulates a need to negotiate tradition and experimentation. The magazine interprets this to mean that "tradition must be forever unfolding by means of constant experimentation" (Bailey 1). However, this same statement also notes that "the poems contained herein are not 'published,' but are brought together in this form as a record largely for private circulation among members of the Society and their friends" (1). *Fiddlehead*'s pages are dominated by a few poets such as Elizabeth Brewster, Fred Cogswell, A.G. Bailey, and A. Eleanor Belyea. Desmond Pacey, A.J.M. Smith, and Bliss Carman appeared occasionally, as did less well-known poets such as Frederick Boyle and Linden Peebles. The notes at the end of issue 15 indicate that most poets published in *Fiddlehead* had some sort of institutional affiliation, often as professors or librarians, with University of New Brunswick. *Preview* tended to publish the poetry of F.R. Scott, Patrick Anderson, P.K. Page, Neufville Shaw, and Bruce Ruddick. It also often included work by Miriam Waddington, Anne Marriott, James Wreford, and less frequently material by A.J.M. Smith and A.M. Klein. While both *Fiddlehead* and *Preview* tended to publish the work of a select group, the former included poets outside of its stable on a more frequent basis than the latter and worked to counter the privileging of the Montreal poets by publishing those from New Brunswick. However, *Contemporary Verse* included poets outside of its core group more frequently than either *Fiddlehead* or *Preview*. While *Contemporary Verse* tended to rely on the work of Livesay, Page, Waddington, Marriott, and McLaren, it also included new talent in most issues, such as Hermia Harris Fraser and Marya Fiamengo. As well, it published poets associated with other little magazines, such as Elizabeth Brewster, Fred Cogswell, Louis Dudek, Irving Layton, and John Sutherland.

14   In the body of the paper, issues of the magazine will be identified using MLA format (e.g., 6.4 is volume 6, issue 4).

15   Sharon Caseburg's editorial in a recent issue of *CV2*, a special issue entitled *The Feminism of Our Discontent*, makes this ongoing process of negotiation explicit when she writes "up until our recent shift in mandate and return to our roots (two issues ago), *CV2* was, for many years, recognizable as one of Canada's feminist literary journals. That said, consider this issue a fusion of the *Contemporary Verse 2* of old and the new *CV2*; acknowledging our past and addressing our feminist concerns while looking towards the future" (4).

16   The conference proceedings of "Women and Words," published as *In the Feminine: Women and Words* (1985), are marked by the complex politics of representation involved

in feminist cultural production. The papers note the different perspectives of women who identify, for instance, as Québécois, anglophone, lesbian, Native, and of colour, and the impact this has on feminist dialogue.

17 In issue 18.2, Clarise Foster and Judith Kearns's editorial notes that "*CV2* has recently survived a financial threat to its continuing existence, and it has been necessary for the magazine to make yet another transformation: as you can see, *CV2* is no longer solely a poetry magazine but has been enhanced by the inclusion of prose" (6). The publication of prose, however, was a decision that the journal reversed on a few occasions, and it now currently does not publish fiction.

18 In 17.1, the magazine defines itself as "a feminist poetry journal that strives to promote, strengthen and unify women. We publish work by women and men. *CV2* is a forum for social action and change. We publish feminist writing: poetry, prose poems, criticism, reviews, columns, interviews, artwork and letters. We will not print sexist, homophobic or racist material" (n.p.). In 24.1, the mandate, signed by Catherine Hunter, reads "*Contemporary Verse 2* is a quarterly literary journal which promotes accomplished writing by both emerging and established writers. We encourage writing which in its diversity represents a range of social and cultural experience, with a particular focus on the experience of women. We publish poetry, prose, reviews, essays, interviews and artwork by women and men." By 24.2, the description of its activities has been considerably shortened and states "*Contemporary Verse 2* is a quarterly literary journal which publishes poetry and critical writing about poetry. Critical writing about poetry includes interviews, articles, essays, and reviews" (Clarise Foster).

19 For instance, Clarise Foster and Judith Kearns's 1995 editorial begins by referring back to Livesay's first editorial in *CV/II*. Foster and Kearns write that "then, as now, the magazine was intended to respond to the felt needs of a particular time and place, to provide a forum for the expression of many voices, to be inclusive of region, ethnicity, and gender" (5). As well, in 1999, *CV2* devoted an entire issue to Livesay: the front cover of issue 21.3 reads, "The Early Years of *CV2*: A Special Issue on Dorothy Livesay." Furthermore, the phrase "Founded by Dorothy Livesay (1909–1996)" appears on the first page of a few issues of *CV2* (19.4).

20 The tenuous and complicated relationship of *CV/II* and *CV2* to dominant cultural institutions and literary histories is influenced by the explicit resistance to institutional affiliations that the early issues under Livesay's editorship proclaimed. The magazine's resistance to institutionalization is tempered by its awareness of the extent to which the Canadian literary scene depends on its universities and government subsidies. This is perhaps most evident in the "Notes on Little Mags" section, in which other magazines are listed and commented on. Barry Chamish's annotations range from "ANTIGONISH REVIEW—English Dept., St. Francis Xavier University, Antigonish, N.S. A boring university journal" to "THE FIDDLEHEAD—The Observatory, University of New Brunswick, Fredericton, N.B. A tough cookie to crumble, nut to crack and all that. Been in business the longest, has a certain reputation for literary fineness and tries to keep it. Succeeds somewhat" to "OTHER VOICES—100 Duchess St., London, Ont. Nice mimeo job" (48–49). The column often reserves its highest praise for independent magazines and its harshest comments for those with university affiliations, yet reports on both and pointedly notes where they are published. The column, a three-part series, indirectly offers a means of assessing *CV/II*'s position through its refusal to participate in the type of work that other magazines did. As Ken Norris notes about the status of magazine publishing in Canada in the 1970s, "Many of the eclectic magazines were attached to Canadian universities, and were

caught up in the trappings of academia. The universities provided the magazines with credibility, offices, and funds. The typical university magazine did not pioneer new territories, but echoed the accepted norms of the day. Most magazines coming out of the universities are of minor interest, not involved with the true revolutionary spirit of the fighting little magazine" (176). *CV/II* was itself housed during this period at the University of Manitoba and funded in part by the Canada Council. Livesay's comment that "there has been scant room for serious criticism except for reports in the elitist quarterlies (with a few honourable exceptions)" suggests, however, that it is nonetheless committed to creating alternate publishing forums (2). At the same time, *CV/II*'s use of *Contemporary Verse* as its point of departure suggests that it sought to establish a space, but not necessarily as a "fighting little magazine" like either *Preview* or *First Statement*. My aim is not to imply that Livesay was not as polemical a thinker as, for instance, the editors of *Preview* or *First Statement*. I do, however, want to suggest that by the 1970s, the scene had changed in a number of ways and thus invited different kinds of interventions.

21 See also Lianne Moyes's contribution to this volume.

22 This perception is articulated by Pacey who writes, "Much of the poetry of the war period, undoubtedly, was ephemeral, and much of it already seems dated. To reread *Preview* now, with its naïve talk of making poetry a weapon, is a disillusioning process" (155–56).

23 While *CV2*'s position on the margins of cultural institutions provides it with a degree of aesthetic and political liberty, it is precisely this location that makes its existence radically unstable. The danger of *CV2* disappearing entirely is signaled in 17.4 by the change in the appearance of the magazine's cover. Guilbert notes that the "cover has been transformed (temporarily and perhaps permanently) into a less expensive format" because of increasing costs and decreasing subsidies (6). Despite the advantages of employing technological advantages to making *CV2* more accessible and durable, these modifications are accompanied by financial costs that are often difficult to maintain. The need to incorporate technology and the difficulty of financing such innovations are part of the challenge faced by the magazine. Similarly, although feminism occupies a fairly stable position in contemporary critical discussions of cultural practices, individual feminist projects like *CV2* are much more vulnerable given their lack of institutional support and governmental funding.

Works Cited

Bailey, A.G. "The Fiddlehead." *Fiddlehead* 1.1 (1945): 1.

Banting, Pamela. Editorial. *CV/II* 8.4 (1985): 4.

———. "Editorial: Blurred Mirrors and the Archaeology of Masks." *CV2* 9.1 (1985): 5–8.

Beattie, Munro. "Poetry (1935–1950)." *Literary History of Canada: Canadian Literature in English*. Ed. Carl F. Klinck. Toronto: U of Toronto P, 1965. Rpt. with corrections 1966. 751–84.

Bourdieu, Pierre. *The Field of Cultural Production*. New York: Columbia UP, 1993.

Butling, Pauline. "Re/righting Literary History: Women and B.C. Little Magazines." *Open Letter* 7.8 (1990): 60–76.

Caseburg, Sharon. "Editor's Notes." *The Feminism of Our Discontent*. Spec. issue of *CV2* 24.4 (2002): 4–5.
Casey, Jane. "Editorial: Writing in Response." *Tessera* 4 / *CV2* 11.2–3 (1988): 6–9.
Chamish, Barry. "Notes on Little Mags." *CV/II* 1.2 (1975): 48–49.
———. "Notes on Little Mags." *CV/II* 2.1 (1976): 33.
Cogswell, Fred. "Review: The Sage of Caulfield." *CV/II* 2.3 (1976): 16.
Crawley, Alan. Alan Crawley fonds. A. Arch 2010. Queen's University Archives, Kathleen Ryan Hall, Queen's University, Kingston, ON.
———. "Editor's Note." *Contemporary Verse* 1.1 (1941): 2.
———. "Editor's Note." *Contemporary Verse* 1.4 (1942): 3–4.
Dudek, Louis. "The Role of Little Magazines in Canada." *The Making of Modern Poetry in Canada*. Ed. Louis Dudek and Michael Gnarowski. Toronto: Ryerson, 1967. 205–11.
Dudek, Louis, and Michael Gnarowski. Preface. *The Making of Modern Poetry in Canada*. Ed. L. Dudek and M. Gnarowski. Toronto: Ryerson Press, 1967. N.p.
Dybikowski, Ann, Victoria Freeman, Daphne Marlatt, Barbara Pulling, and Betsy Warland, eds. *In the Feminine: Women and Words / les femmes et les mots. Conference Proceedings*. Edmonton: Longspoon Press, 1985.
Editors of *Northern Review*. "Notices of Resignation." *Northern Review* 2.1 (1947): 38.
Fisher, Neil H. *First Statement, 1942–1945: An Assessment and An Index*. Ottawa: Golden Dog, 1974.
Foster, Clarise. "Editor's Notes." *CV2* 24.2 (2001): 4–6.
Foster, Clarise, and Judith Kearns. "Editorial." *CV2* 18.2 (Fall 1995): 5–7.
Foster, Robert. Editorial. *CV/II* 5.3 (1981): 2.
———. Editorial. *CV/II* 6.4 (1982): 2.
———. Editorial. *CV/II* 8.4 (1985): 2.
Fowler, Adrian. "Newfoundland Poetry in the 70s: The Context." *CV/II* (1982): 5–8.
Francis, Wynne. "Montreal Poets of the Forties." *Canadian Literature* 14 (1962): 21–34.
Gibbs, Robert. "Maritimes and Newfoundland Report." *CV/II* 6.4 (1982): 9.
Gnarowski, Michael. Introduction. *New Provinces: Poems of Several Authors*. Toronto: U of Toronto P, 1974. vii–xxxii.
———. "The Role of 'Little Magazines' in the Development of Poetry in English in Montreal." *The Making of Modern Poetry in Canada*. Ed. L. Dudek and M. Gnarowski. Toronto: Ryerson Press, 1967. 212–21.
Godard, Barbara. "Editorial: Feminist Critical Theory in English Canada and Quebec: Present State and Future Directions." *Tessera* 4 / *CV2* 11.2–3 (1988): 10–14.
———. "Feminist Periodicals and the Production of Cultural Value: The Canadian Context." *Women's Studies International Forum* 25.2 (2002): 209–23.

Guilbert, Naomi. "Editorial." *CV2* 17.4 (1995): 6–7.
Hunter, Catherine. "Editor's Notes." *CV2* 24.1 (2001): 5–6.
Irvine, Dean J. "Dorothy Livesay's Perspectives, Retrospectives, and Prospectives: 'A Putting Down of Roots' in *CV/II*." *The Early Years of CV2: A Special Issue on Dorothy Livesay*. Spec. issue of *CV2* 21.3 (1999): 65–78.
Livesay, Dorothy. Dorothy Livesay fonds. A. Arch. 2024. Queen's University Archives, Queen's University, Kingston, ON (Queen's).
———. "Editorial: A Putting Down of Roots." *CV/II* 1.1 (1975): 2.
———. Foreword. *Alan Crawley and* Contemporary Verse. By Joan McCullagh. Vancouver: UBC P, 1976. vii–xvii.
Marek, Jayne. *Women Editing Modernism: "Little" Magazines and Literary History*. Lexington: UP of Kentucky, 1995.
Marlatt, Daphne, and Kathy Mezei. Foreword. *Tessera* 4 / *CV2* 11.2–3 (1988): 5.
Martin, Robert K. "Sex and Politics in Wartime Canada: The Attack on Patrick Anderson." *Essays on Canadian Writing* 44 (1991): 110–25.
McCullagh, Joan. *Alan Crawley and* Contemporary Verse. Vancouver: UBC P, 1976.
Nichol, b.p. "Ontario Report." *CV/II* 7.1 (1982): 6–7.
Norris, Ken. *The Little Magazine in Canada 1925–80*. Toronto: ECW, 1984.
Pacey, Desmond. *Creative Writing in Canada*. 2nd ed. Toronto: Ryerson, 1952. Rpt. 1961.
Page, P.K. Letter to Ethel Wilson. 13 July 1963. Alan Crawley fonds, box 1, file 20.
Robertson, George. "Alan Crawley and *Contemporary Verse*." *Canadian Literature* 41 (1969): 87–96.
Rose, Marilyn J. "The Literary Archive and the Telling of Modernist Lives: Retrieving Anne Marriott." *The Canadian Modernists Meet*. Ed. Dean Irvine. Ottawa: U of Ottawa P, 2005. 231–49.
Smith, A.J.M. "A Rejected Preface." *New Provinces: Poems of Several Authors*. Toronto: U of Toronto P, 1974. xxvii–xxxii.
Steffler, John. Introduction. *Newfoundland Poetry*. Spec. issue of *CV/II* 6.3 (1982): 3–4.
Webb, Phyllis. Letter to Alan Crawley. 4 April 1953. Alan Crawley fonds, box 1, file 34.
Wilson, Ethel. "Of Alan Crawley." *Canadian Literature* 19 (1964): 33–42.

P.K. Page
Discovering a Modern Sensibility
SANDRA DJWA

In 1943, when preparing a preface for his anthology *The Book of Canadian Poetry*, the poet-critic A.J.M. Smith divided modern Canadian poetry into two groups. To one, he assigned "native" poets like E.J. Pratt (1882–1964), Earle Birney (1904–95), Dorothy Livesay (1909–96), W.W.E. Ross (1894–1966), and Anne Marriott (1913–97). In a second group, he placed "cosmopolitan" poets like F.R. Scott (1899–1985), P.K. Page (1916–), Margaret Avison (1918–), and Patrick Anderson (1915–79) (Smith 29–30). The natives he viewed as attempting "to describe and interpret what is essentially and distinctively Canadian and thus come to terms with an environment that is only now ceasing to be colonial." The cosmopolitans he characterized as metaphysical, not directly concerned with nature, making a "heroic attempt to transcend colonialism by entering into the universal, civilizing culture of ideas" (5). This second group, which Smith clearly favoured, was characterized by intelligence, direct speech, and allusive imagery—all qualities that he had recognized in T.S. Eliot's criticism, notably in the essays on "The Metaphysical Poets" and "Tradition and the Individual Talent."

As a striking example of the new cosmopolitan poetry, Smith cited Page's poem "The Stenographers," referring to its "vivid concluding image":

> In their eyes I have seen
> the pin-men of madness in marathon trim
> race round the track of the stadium pupil. (qtd. in Smith 30)

Not surprisingly, both W.H. Auden and Roy Daniells, the Chicago publisher's readers for *The Book of Canadian Poetry*, objected to Smith's division on the grounds that poets in both groups exhibited the same qualities, but he refused to change his categories.[1] He may have wished to give primacy of place to his own generation by assigning to it alone those qualities that Eliot had praised. However, there was a rationale for Smith's schemata. Many of the poets he assigned to the native stream were older poets, publishing in the twenties and preoccupied with nationalist topics, whereas many of the poets in the cosmopolitan stream were younger poets of the forties, more concerned with technique than with content, and looking towards contemporary English and American writers for direction.

In this semi-biographical essay, I will attempt to situate P.K. Page in relation to both Canadian and international modernism. She was a little younger than her predecessors Livesay[2] and Marriott,[3] who had read Canadian women poets of the twenties (especially Marjorie Pickthall); Page did not know these poets because they rarely appeared on the curriculum of St. Hilda's, a private school she had attended in Calgary. Although she published in periodicals like the *Canadian Poetry Magazine* from the late thirties onwards, she found little there to stimulate her own writing.[4] Her response to Pratt, the primary poet between the wars, was simply that she found his poems "too masculine."[5] Towards the end of the thirties, she read *New Provinces* (1936), the first anthology of modern Canadian poetry, and admired the poems of A.M. Klein (1909–72), Scott, and Smith (1902–80). Livesay was omitted from this anthology (Smith disliked her socialist verse), however, and Page had no pervasive sense of a Canadian women's tradition,[6] although she very much liked Marriott's *The Wind Our Enemy* (1939). She did not read the poems of Livesay or Avison until approximately 1944.

Where, then, in the Canadian thirties, was a young woman writer to find poetic nourishment? Indeed, was there a sustaining tradition for any Canadian poet, male or female, writing between 1920 and 1950? Pratt had followed D.C. Scott's long narrative poems, and Smith, Livesay, and F.R. Scott all began their writing careers with finger exercises on Pan derivative of Bliss Carman's *The Pipes of Pan*. However, all looked abroad for further direction: Pratt to John Masefield, Roy Campbell, and Eliot; Smith to W.B. Yeats, Eliot, and Edith Sitwell; and Livesay to Edna St. Vincent Millay, Katherine Mansfield, Virginia Woolf, and the British social poets of the thirties. Furthermore, although Canadian critics have historically referred to modernism as gender neutral, it is clear that women writers of the thirties adhered to a different tradition than did their male counterparts. Although they shared the common post–World War One disillusionment (for which Eliot's *The Waste Land,* 1922, was the chief expression), women writers also fell heir to the suffrage movement and new expectations regarding the role of women in society. Consequently, they gravitated towards English and American women writers of the late twenties and early thirties, particularly Woolf (1882–1941) and Mansfield (1888–1923), who spoke candidly of the woman artist and of the changing relations between women and men. Because Page, like the older Livesay and the younger Elizabeth Brewster (1922–), read such writers closely, I will, like Lianne Moyes in this volume, be primarily tracing "intertextual relationships among women writers of different generations and different national identifications, women writers who, in many cases, have never met."

Page's modernism, identified as "cosmopolitan" by Smith, has been most frequently ascribed to the influence of the *Preview* group of the Montreal forties (Patrick Anderson, Scott, Neufville Shaw) and their mentors, Stephen Spender, Auden and Cecil Day-Lewis. Thus, discussions of her poetic career are often tripartite, as in George Woodcock's 1973 analysis: he finds a formative early forties period of social protest influenced by the English poets of the thirties; a middle period of psychological portraits or "inner landscapes"; and a later period of "mystical concern" (240–41). This structure, however, requires a special explanation for some of Page's most important middle poems like "After Rain," where she clearly reflects upon the use of a feminine persona in poetry.[7] Most importantly, this hypothesis does not acknowledge Page's actual formative influences in the thirties, concerns that resurfaced in the late forties and fifties. These influences have not been immediately apparent, partly because Page's early writing history has not been known and partly because they were overlaid in the forties by the dominant poetics of the *Preview* group.

Nonetheless, the evidence of Page's early poetry and prose suggests that by the mid-to-late thirties, before her first contact with *Preview* in March 1942, she had developed a modern sensibility and a sense of herself as a practicing woman artist. By "modern," I do not mean international high modernism, gendered masculine, as associated with the later Eliot, Auden, and Ezra Pound, but rather the early modernism of imagism and *vers libre,* especially as practised by H.D., Pound, D.H. Lawrence, and the imagists in Harold Monro's *Twentieth Century Poetry: An Anthology* (1929) and in the worldly wise quatrains of Edna St. Vincent Millay in *A Few Figs from*

Thistles. In prose it is represented by the minutely detailed realism of Mansfield's short stories such as "At the Bay" (1922) and the suprarealism (including stream-of-consciousness) of Woolf's *The Waves* (1931). In visual art it is to be seen in the exaggerated realism, sometimes surrealism, of much art of the London Group in the thirties. This is a modernism that tended towards myth and symbol in verbal and visual structures, and included synesthesia and self-reflexivity in verse.

My focus, then, is the development of Page's modern and feminine aesthetic consciousness. The strongest influences on this aspect of her early work appear to have been generated by her readings in a number of poetry anthologies, by the visual arts, and by the women writers of the twenties and thirties. This modern sensibility in her writing can be traced over a seven-year period from 1934 to 1941 in the process by which the Georgian form and imagery of an early poem, "The Moth" (1935), gives way to a more disjunctive and modern expression in "Ecce Homo" (1941). How did a young woman, a Calgary high school graduate with a flair for verse, develop a contemporary poetic voice in less than seven years? This question continues to intrigue us today. The answer, perhaps, had much to do with a pivotal year in London, which led Page to believe that she could become a writer, a discovery consolidated on her return to Canada in 1935. During the next six years, through her own agency, she learned to interpret modern art, literature, and psychology, and began to write a recognizably modern poetry.

In July 1934, at the age of seventeen, Patricia Page took passage for England alone. Her parents had offered her the choice of either attending university or spending a year in England with her mother's sister, Beatrice Whitehouse. She chose London without hesitation. Like so many of Henry James's North American protagonists bound for Europe, Page was "affronting her destiny" (James 8). She longed to be a writer—specifically, a journalist.[8] Delivered to the ship, just before she left Halifax in July, was a letter from her father, Lieutenant Colonel Lionel Page, a career officer in the Canadian Army. He wrote, acknowledging her high ambition, "this is going to be your first real step in life. I have every confidence in you." Nonetheless, he advised his daughter to try to be open-minded and to keep a tight rein on her ambition, which, as he said, "can become a headstrong hardmouthed horse if given his way."

When Page arrived in England, she settled in Purley on the outskirts of London with her aunt, a bluestocking who had attended Cambridge in the 1890s. Women were not then permitted to receive degrees, and "Aunt Bibbi," as she was known, had developed a successful career in the Ministry of Health while retaining a great love of literature. She provided the young woman with a special membership in Boots (the chemist's) Book Lovers Library, which meant that Page could request any published book that she wanted to read. She also enrolled her niece for a course in journalism with Sir Philip Gibbs, the English war journalist and novelist, and bought Page a season's pass on British Rail, so that she could independently travel from Purley to London.

Page, who took Gibbs's classes for several months, did not find that he offered what she wanted, but it is possible that his practical instructions on how to make one's living through writing encouraged her to submit her own work to newspapers and journals. Five months after her arrival in England, in December 1934, she submitted a brief poem, "The Moth," to the London *Observer* and signed it "P.K. Page":

I caught a moth,
A silver moth
That fluttered in my hair;
And when I peeped within my hand
I found but star-dust there. (35)

The sentiments are conventional and the form Georgian; nonetheless, "The Moth" was accepted and published next to a poem by Rainer Maria Rilke.[9] Page later recalled that she hid behind her initials when submitting the poem because she did not want friends and classmates to know that she was publishing poetry.[10] It was acceptable to publish in a high school yearbook but somehow "not quite decent" to publish professionally.

During this year abroad, Page seems to have set up a schedule, a Cook's Tour for one, in which she went up to London by train nearly every day and found her way around the city by bus or underground. She was delighted with "the elegant architecture of London, the beautiful paintings," the ballet and the theatre.[11] During that year, much of her spare money went to pay for cheap seats at the back of the theatre for performances such as John Gielgud's *Hamlet* and George Bernard Shaw's *Major Barbara*. She visited art galleries, especially the Tate, where she loved the Blake room and the paintings of the Pre-Raphaelite Brotherhood, with Millais' drowned Ophelia bedecked with flowers. When Maxwell Bates, the Canadian artist and family friend studying art in England, provided her with a list of the best painters in London, Page began to seek out a number of smaller avant-garde galleries, such as the Wertheim. Many of the painters and sculptors that she liked best were members of the London Group: Jacob Epstein, Paul and John Nash, Ben Nicolson, and Stanley Spencer. The paintings that intrigued Page were either mystical or very modern: she particularly liked Paul Nash's surrealistic landscape paintings, influenced by Blake, and Spencer's elongated, El Greco–like *Saint Francis and the Birds* (1935).

One of these visits to the Leicester Galleries took place in the spring of 1935. An older woman, a friend of a former teacher in Calgary, had taken her to lunch in Soho. Page found the woman's conversation radical and astonishing: she spoke of polygamy, then of Rima, the birdlike figure of W.H. Hudson's *Green Mansions* that Epstein had sculpted. Page knew something of Epstein; she and her close friend, Elizabeth Carlile, had borrowed art books from the Calgary library and studied his sculptures. After lunch, the older woman suggested that they go to view Epstein's new sculpture, *Ecce Homo*. The sculpture was a *cause célèbre* in London in March 1935 because many critics condemned Epstein's rendering of Christ—an eleven-foot, squared, roughly chiselled sculpture—as primitive and savage (Gardiner 340–41). For Page, whose family was not conventionally religious, the experience of seeing the statue was a revelation of the power of the Old Testament Jehovah. More importantly, it was an intellectual breakthrough later described in the poem "Ecce Homo." The youthful narrator in this poem (whom I equate with Page) recognizes an "unexpected entry / into the door of my mind," acknowledging not only the enormous power of visual art and sculpture, but also its liberating effect upon her own creative faculties (17).

This year, 1935, was a time when Page was conscious of many doors opening. She was reading the moderns: Woolf, Vera Brittain, Winifred Holtby, Mansfield, Lawrence's *Letters*, and Monro's *Twentieth Century Poetry*, which offered excerpts from the major poets.[12] However, the writer who had the most impact on Page's evolving consciousness was Woolf, whom she discovered in the Boots Lending Library in Purley:

> I can remember ... just browsing on the shelves, and coming across *The Waves*. I had never heard of Virginia Woolf. Why my hands went up, I can see where it was on the shelf, and my hand went up and picked it off the shelf, and I opened it up and started reading it, and I burst into tears. It was such a relief to me to find that people wrote that way. I had never read anything but pretty linear stuff before. And it seemed to me that she opened a whole new world to me that was most magical. And then I started to read her with great enthusiasm, and I remember her *Three Guineas* [1938].

Page found the arresting monologues of the opening passages of *The Waves* staged, totally unrealistic: it was as if the characters existed in another dimension. She also sensed a loss of self, an almost mystical merger with a greater unity. Page seems to have responded both to Woolf's technique—her avant-garde language and structure—and to her metaphysics.

By 1935, Page had read several books about the writing life, including Frances Winwar's *Poor Splendid Wings: The Rossettis and Their Circle* (1933), with its vivid evocations of the life of the artist, and Woolf's manifesto, *A Room of One's Own* (1928). Although the young Page longed to be a writer, she found it difficult to think of herself as one. In provincial New Brunswick of the late 1930s, where her father was the senior military commander, who could imagine that an attractive young woman of good social standing would want to be a writer? It is almost impossible today to appreciate the situation of such a young woman, still unsure of her capabilities, with few examples in the English literary tradition to follow. To be sure there were Woolf and Mansfield, but even they did not figure large in the English literary world of the thirties, dominated as it was by Thomas Hardy, Yeats, Lawrence, Eliot, and Auden.[13] Nonetheless, Page was conscious of a "very personal relationship" with Woolf.[14] At first it was the language of *The Waves*—the shock of aesthetic discovery—and the sense of a larger vision. Then *A Room of One's Own* seems to have helped the young Page clarify her determination to become a writer. She may have been absorbing the fact, without being overly conscious of it, that a woman did not need university training to become a writer. In any event, an older Page recalls that she was getting "food" from Woolf,[15] and "food" is the word used twice by Woolf in *A Room of One's Own* as shorthand for the "knowledge, adventure, art" required by a woman who wishes to become a writer (84).

More significantly, the older Page associates *A Room of One's Own* with what she calls "the hidden room," a phrase that she used in 1997 as the title of her *Collected Poems*. Page recalls, "I suppose I was reacting ... [to Woolf's encouragement of the woman writer]. But I don't remember that. I just remember the hidden room. I just remember the relief of it."[16] Woolf does not specifically mention a hidden room in *A Room of One's Own*; yet, in retrospect, we can see that this term is a microcosm of the creative process that Woolf describes. Although *A Room of One's Own* stresses the material conditions that make it possible for a woman to write, Woolf's metaphors focus on the *space* in which a woman's artistic creativity can take place.

Woolf, as narrator, introduces her book with an exemplary tale in which she is engaged in the process of creating while sitting by a peaceful stream at "Oxbridge" and gazing at trees: "On the further bank the willows wept in perpetual lamentation, their hair about their shoulders ... Thought ... had let its line down into the stream" (7). However, the "little fish," or idea, that the narrator catches so stimulates her mind that, unthinkingly, she treads on the grass of the college. Immediately, she is expelled by an officer of the college because "he was a Beadle; I was a woman. This was the turf; there was the path. Only the Fellows and Scholars are allowed here; the gravel is the place for me" (8).

The larger message is that the restrictions that bar women from education at Oxford or Cambridge also impede their creativity. Halfway through the book, the narrator returns to this incident to declare, "Literature is open to everybody. I refuse to allow you, Beadle though you are, to turn me off the grass. Lock up your libraries if you like; but there is no gate, no lock, no bolt that you can set upon the freedom of my mind" (76). Near the end of *A Room of One's Own*, Woolf boldly resituates the place of artistic creation in a woman's consciousness. She describes a small room, where the curtains are "close drawn," a private place in the mind where the marriage of the opposites in the self, male and female, is consummated (103). Here, in this hidden room, where the mind is wide open to all experience, creation takes place.

In the largest sense, this microcosm of "a room of one's own" can be seen as a metaphor for the creative feminine consciousness. Given this reading, we might speculate that this is "the hidden room" that Page associates with Woolf, and the "relief" that she intuits but does not explain is the recognition that this internal psychological space is the place where a woman artist can create. We do know that the young Page internalized this text because Woolf's description of the river trees and the little fish of thought is echoed in the imagery of Page's first novel, *The Sun and the Moon*, written a few years later.[17]

Moreover the designation of "the hidden room" as the place where creation happens recurs in the title poem of Page's *Collected Poems*, where she describes her own creative process:

I have been coming here since I was born ...
It is in a house
deeply hidden in my head ...

    a hidden place
    in cellar or attic
    matrix of evil and good (*The Hidden Room* 1.11)

For Page, as for Woolf, the hidden room is found in the mind, and it is a place where opposites meet and creation takes place. For Page, it is also "a prism," "a magic square," and "a child's bolt-hole" because, years before, in 1933 in Calgary, she and Elizabeth Carlile had built a little room, a "bolt-hole," in a stairwell in order to paint and write poetry and talk of their hopes to become artists. She describes this space in "The Hidden Room." Unlike Woolf, Page gives primacy to creative inspiration: she can reach this hidden room "only when it permits me" (11). Nonetheless, the older Page confirms her vocation as a writer by assimilating her early creative experience to Woolf's metaphor for creativity: this suggests that Woolf occupied a similar position for the young Page.

Woolf had also urged the readers of *A Room of One's Own* to escape from the common sitting room to see humans "in relation to reality; and the sky, too, and the trees ... if we face the fact ... there is no arm to cling to, but that we go alone and that our relation is to the world of reality" (112). By "reality," Woolf means not just nature in the widest sense but those inner "moments of being" that constitute mystical experience. As Woolf says elsewhere, "we are sealed vessels afloat upon what is convenient to call reality; at some moments, without a reason, without an effort, the sealing matter cracks; in floods reality" (qtd. in Kane 332). Page's own later poems and short stories like "Unless the Eye Catch Fire" express a similar view of this larger reality.

In 1935, when Page was reading Woolf's views on a woman's creativity, these ideas were reinforced by the new Freudian psychology in *A Life of One's Own* (1934), a book written by one of Woolf's younger contemporaries, Marion Milner, who wrote under the pseudonym "Joanna Field." Milner's book appears to have been written in response to Woolf's question in *A Room of One's Own*: "Where shall I find that elaborate study of the psychology of women by a woman?" (78). Field's aim is to help young women take control of their creative lives, and for several years the young Page read and reread her book. Field, like Woolf, sees the mind as made up of a male and female side, and she offers practical exercises for developing aesthetic consciousness. She explains that she had unthinkingly assumed that the desirable way to live was the male life of "objective" understanding and action; but when she questioned her own experience, Field began to discover impulses that led her to explore the meaning of her own femininity. Her first perception had come when she was still a young girl: "It had begun, I remembered quite clearly, one day at the age of twelve, when I found myself lying quite still in the sun, being aware in some new way of a feeling of the hot sand against my body, and wondering why I had never felt like that before" (233).

She had experienced such great joy during these moments of discovery that she had attempted to re-create them. She set out a program of practical exercises for herself (and for her readers) to develop perception by moving the centre of awareness from the narrow perception of the head to a wider focus that involved the whole body. In one exercise, for example, Field describes her attempt at "putting herself out" into one of the chairs in the room: "at once the chair seemed to take on a new reality, I 'felt' its proportions and could say at once whether I liked its shape" (64). Field, later a distinguished British Freudian psychologist, also speaks of the importance of self-knowledge and provides her readers with suggestions to help tap unconscious feelings.

Page, who could afford few books, brought both Woolf's *A Room of One's Own* and Field's *A Life of One's Own* back to Halifax and then to Saint John, New Brunswick, in the fall of 1935. There, through the Saint John Public Library, she added Mansfield and Lawrence to her reading. If Woolf helped Page to see herself as a potential artist, and Field stimulated states of aesthetic consciousness, Mansfield seems to have been, above all, a woman writer with whom Page could personally identify. This sense of identification was so strong that Page's close friend Erica Deichmann, a potter in Rothesay, New Brunswick, recalled that Page, then about twenty-three, had told her that she sometimes felt that she *was* Katherine Mansfield.[18]

Page, who had started to read Mansfield in London, was given both volumes of *The Letters of Katherine Mansfield* in 1937 as a birthday present. She soon acquired Mansfield's *Stories,* the *Journal* and the *Scrapbook*. Mansfield's writings had a similar function to Page's earlier reading in books such as Winwar's *Poor Splendid Wings*: she wanted to know more about the life of the artist and remembered herself trying to find out more about this life but not quite sure how to do so.[19] Rothesay, where the Pages now lived, was a rich man's village where young people were expected to follow conventional lives, largely social. Except for the occasional kindred spirit like poet Kay Smith, Page felt very much alone with her books.

She had seen a great deal of art in London but felt unguided in her seeing and reading, and she knew no English artists or writers. What Mansfield offered was both insight and intellectual company—"I felt I was feeling what she was feeling, yearning to write, to create," she recalls.[20] Page may have been comforted by the thought that Mansfield, also a colonial, had become a fine writer. Not surprisingly, the passages in Mansfield's *Letters* that Page has marked, or commented upon in the margins, are largely descriptions of the artistic life. She marks, for example, the following passage in Mansfield's letter to Murry: "I believe the only way to *live* as artists under these new conditions in art and life is to put everything to the test for ourselves. We've got, in the long run, to be our own teachers" (*Letters* 1:91). What is really striking when reading Page's marginal annotations is the extent to which she is now becoming her own teacher, carrying on a critical dialogue with Mansfield, just as Mansfield, when learning her own craft, had carried on a dialogue with Chekhov.[21] For much of this time, Page was not aware that Mansfield was not a living artist: she did not discover that Mansfield had died in 1923 until the late thirties, when she came across this fact in a preface Murry wrote to one of Mansfield's works.

Page responded especially to the descriptions of nature found in Woolf and Mansfield. She pencilled a note by a paragraph in which Mansfield wrote to S.S. Koteliansky of a wharf where the sand barges unload: "Do you know the smell of wet sand? Does it make you think of going down to the beach in the evening light after a rainy day and gathering the damp drift wood ... and picking up for a moment the long branches of sea weed that the waves have tossed?" (*Letters* 2:27). Page has written in the margin "the wetness, the saltiness, the tang in this paragraph," indicating that it is Mansfield's technique—the expressive realism of her diction—that she most admires. She also adapted one of Mansfield's primary images, the tree that in Mansfield's letters and short stories is a symbol of life and creativity. In another letter to J.M. Murry, Mansfield comments, "The trees on the island are in full leaf ... I had quite forgotten the life that goes on *within* a tree—how it flutters and almost plumes itself, and how the topmost branches tremble and the lowest branches of all swing lazy" (22). Beside this paragraph, Page has written, "Does she feel everything as intensely as the tree experience?"

A similar allusion recurs in Page's annotations to Ezra Pound's poem "A Girl," collected in *Twentieth Century Poetry*, where Page has pencilled in the margin, "Since my tree experience, E.P. vaguely makes sense to me."[22] The lines of Pound's poem read,

> The tree has entered my hands,
> The sap has ascended my arms,
> The tree has grown in my breast—
> Downward,
> The branches grow out of me, like arms. (230)

Page's marginal note suggests not only that she is responding to Pound's use of the Daphne metaphor of girl-into-tree but also that she has undergone a similar "tree experience." This implies that she was following another of the exercises in *A Life of One's Own*, where Field writes about projecting her own consciousness into the larger reality of a tree: "I remember to spread the arms of my awareness towards the trees, letting myself flow round them and feed on the delicacy of their patterns till their intricacies became part of my being" (67–68).

By 1939, Page had written both a short story and a poem about metamorphosis and the Daphne myth. The poem, "Reflection," appears to allude to Page's own personal "tree experience":

> In the noon of yesterday I saw a tree
> pretending it was a woman,
> bending over a stream,...
> And I bent over the water beside it ...
> and I was a tree ...
> In the reflection I saw
> a tree and a woman bending,
> merged in the water
> and knew not whether I was the woman or tree. (23)

Diana Relke, in a discussion of ecocriticism and the feminist psychoanalysis of Jessica Benjamin, has noted the connection between this poem and Page's subsequent novel, *The Sun and the Moon* (22–23). In fact, Page had been reading about metamorphosis throughout the thirties in a series of post-war novels that dealt with changes in human consciousness and reincarnation. Now, in the late thirties, she read John Cowper Powys's novel *Wolf Solent* (1929), with its curious emphasis on individuals who experience striking changes in consciousness by identifying with external objects. Page recalls an intense experience from this period in which she imagined herself within the atoms, the molecular dance of a chair, an exercise also described by Field (7). Some of these experiments in consciousness seem to have found their way into a short story, now lost, about a young woman who is metamorphosed into a tree. Kay Smith, Page's closest poet friend during these early days in Saint John, recalls encouraging Page to try her hand at developing the story into a novel.[23]

The Sun and the Moon, which Page began to write during the summers of 1939–40 at New River Beach near Saint John, New Brunswick, is a kind of Künstlerroman in which Page's protagonist is now a young woman artist rather than a young man.[24] It is the story of Kristin, whose birth coincided with an eclipse of the moon, giving her supernatural powers. She is a "moon-child,"[25] the victim of her innate ability to project her consciousness into material objects so that she can become one with the inanimate objects like the beach rocks or a chair. The apprentice Page is now applying her reading to her writing; there are traces of Woolf and Mansfield in her metaphors, of Lawrence in her presentation of the relations between men and women, and of Ibsen in comments on a hypocritical social order. The following passage suggests both Powys and Field in her description of changing consciousness:

> Lying there unmoving [on a rock on the sand], Kristin felt something she had never felt before. A change came over her. Slowly she stiffened and became hard and still ... Then suddenly there was movement somewhere and voices talking. But she knew without hearing, for her ears were stone; she knew only as a rock can know, by the vibrations of sound striking an inanimate thing. Then, as gradually as she had stiffened from flesh to stone she melted from stone to flesh. (6)

Kristin is seventeen—Page's age when she began her own voyage of discovery—and a passive observer of the world when she falls in love with Carl, an established artist and an older man.[26] The two become engaged to marry, but Kristin is devastated when she discovers that she has the power to "eclipse" Carl's "sun," his talent as an artist. Ultimately, she allows herself to metamorphose into a tree during a climactic storm, losing human consciousness and with it the power to harm the man she loves. The novel winds down with reference to their brief marriage and separation; it concludes with the omniscient narrator's sharp focus on the natural landscape which seems to contain Kristen. Atwood, who later edited this novella in 1973, found the conclusion "utterly chilling."[27]

As Atwood recognized,[28] this is a romance in which Page uses myth, symbol, and psychology to give resonance to story. The male and the female figures of this novel are associated with the sun and the moon respectively; but the novel is also exploring prevailing stereotypes about the social roles of men and women in relation to perception and art:

> He [*The Boy* in Carl's painting] looked strong and virile and masculine against the pale femininity of her bedroom. Here we have it, [Kristin] said to herself, the sun and the moon together, and she looked from the painting and felt secure. Carl will predominate, she thought, as he does here. (Page, *Sun and the Moon* 82)

Page is clearly intrigued by the modernist debate about the nature of the creative consciousness (although she might not describe it as such) and its relation to gender. Carl says to Kristin at one point, "you almost take the words out of my mouth. It's as if you know me from the inside—an empathetic knowledge of me." He later defines "empathetic" as "a psychic term really. An inner knowledge resulting from the projection of the mind of the observer into the thing observed" (107). As both Constance Rooke and Rosemary Sullivan have noted, the term is not too different from Keats's "chameleon poet" who has no identity of his own and becomes what he perceives.[29] It is clear that Keats's vision and Field's exercises could be extraordinarily useful to the apprentice writer because through both the poet enters into a wider sphere of art-making relationships; but the danger, as both Rooke and Sullivan emphasize, is that the poet can be invaded by her surroundings or dissipated into them.[30] In *The Sun and the Moon*, the reader's attention is drawn to the "chameleon" metaphor when Kristin questions whether she has a personality of her own or whether she is simply "a chameleon ... absorbing the colours about me" (119). If this were the case, she speculates, pushing the metaphor a little further, and she and Carl married, "it will mean the obliteration of two personalities" (119).

This statement carries overtones of some of the twenties and thirties commentary on gender and its relationship to art. Woolf had suggested that the truly creative mind is fertilized by both male and female, but Lawrence had reflected in his letters (which Page was reading in the late thirties) on the fearful possession of the male by the female that he saw as death (565). Field's position in *A Life of One's Own* was more complex. She accepts the human psyche as bisexual but recognizes that human beings are governed by unconscious forces: consequently, she speculates on "the fear of surrender" of one part of the psyche to another:

> Was it that to my blind thinking ... the satisfaction of the female meant the wiping out of the male forever? To satisfy the feminine to the full without the loss of one's individuality, perhaps this was an idea beyond the powers of blind thinking to grasp ... And in its terror of losing the male in the female it had in fact lost both. (Field 238)

There is a similar associative leap in the actions of Page's characters. It is also suggested in her title, which seems to be derived from Blake's "Auguries of Innocence": "If the Sun & Moon should doubt, / They'd immediately Go out" (599). It is the modernist gender debate, however, that seems to be enacted in *The Sun and the Moon*, where there is finally an eclipse of the male sun by the female moon.

The reading of the novel that I offered when introducing *The Sun and the Moon* suggests that Kristin, an embryo artist, upholds the conventional mores of the period and sacrifices herself for Carl's art. Nonetheless, at that point in the novel where the climactic metamorphosis takes place, Page's text does allow a second and underlying reading:

> [Kristin] could hear the wind again, pulling at the trees ... And she felt part of it, like a branch torn off and carried by the wind ... She knew only an instinctive desire to stay standing, to battle with the wind and so remain upright and invincible, to dig her roots into the earth ... She was pitting her strength against the wind in a battle for existence and she was winning ...
>
> Graceful, swaying slightly, she faced the calm of the day and drank from the rich, wet earth—steady in the security of her fibre and bark; content in the sweet uprising form of her growth, holding her branches up to the sky in the simple, generous gesture of the victor who knows victory to be within. (120–21)

This final metaphor of woman-as-tree, ultimately perhaps the feminine life force, is strong and self-assured. Moreover, after Page has explored in fiction the dilemma of the female protagonist who sacrifices herself for the male's art, in real life she determines to take up the role of the female artist in a dominantly male world. In this sense, the tale can be seen as a medium through which the young Page begins to explore—both consciously and unconsciously—some of the issues to be faced by a woman artist.

The period from 1934 to 1941, then, was a time of active experimentation in which Page tried out a number of conflicting roles and concepts, performing some of them in her own life and work. Throughout this decade, she sought out the latest in modern art, literature, and psychology, responding to all. In 1941, in the first issue of *Contemporary Verse,* she published a new poem, "Ecce Homo," which recapitulated some of these experiences, notably the powerful intellectual and emotional encounter, some six years earlier, with Epstein's giant sculpture:

> I looked and the little room was filled with might,
> with the might of fear in stone,
> immense and shackled ...
> the God of Death,
> in a little room in a gallery in Leicester Square,
> silently standing there.
>
> "There is much we do not know,"
> you turned to me.
> (Behold the Man, Rima, polygamy!)
> "I think we should find somewhere nice and quiet for tea,
> To think," you said.
> I nodded my head. "To think," I said.
> And like a young tree I put out a timid shoot
> and prayed for the day, the wonderful day when it bore its fruit.
> And suddenly we were out in the air again. (1:18)

This poem reflects the modernist movement in its free verse and elliptical construction, in its use of disjointed commentary and allusion, and above all, in the narrator's self-reflexive statement about her own development as an artist. Furthermore, the autobiographical "I" and the employment of the tree metaphor (because of its previous associations in Page's work) suggest a female artist: "like a young tree, I put out a timid shoot" (18).

In October 1941, shortly after finishing this poem and a draft of *The Sun and the Moon,* Page left the Maritimes with the intention of becoming a writer. She recalled later how her father had read the manuscript of her novel and recognized that his ambitious and talented daughter deserved support.[31] He offered her sufficient funds to live on—$85.00 a month—to rent a room of her own to practice her craft in Montreal. There she kept regular office hours, writing short stories and poems, and sending them out to various little magazines and publishers. Some five months later, in February–March 1942, Page met a young English poet, Patrick Anderson. He had seen and admired her poems in *Contemporary Verse,* and suggested she meet a group of poets associated with a little magazine called *Preview.*[32] As Anderson recognized, Page was already cognizant of much that was modern in contemporary English and American writing; however, her sense of a largely female thirties modernism was now to be overpowered by *Preview* and the group's concept of the role of the artist in wartime (Vanteste 16–17).[33]

Moreover, from *Preview*'s discussion of Eliot's criticism, especially his use of metaphor and the "objective correlative," Page concluded that she must find larger and more impersonal metaphors for her social poetry. She began to develop a number of personae, some male. One of these, "Cullen," who describes some of the odyssey of the forties generation, is borrowed from the name of a contemporary American Black poet, Countee Cullen. To Cullen as persona, Page attributes incidents from her own life: her journey to Montreal, her trips to the theatre in England, and her observations as a shopgirl in Saint John. Significantly, the poem concludes with the war, the most important social upheaval that Page the poet had yet experienced:

> [Cullen] discovered it was nineteen thirty-nine
> and volunteered at once and went to war
> wondering what on earth he was fighting for.
> He knew there was a reason but couldn't find it
> and marched to battle half an inch behind it. (*Hidden Room* 1:129)

Cullen, like the Romantic heroes of Tennyson's *Maud* and Mann's *The Magic Mountain*, is an idealist who, when thwarted, goes to war. If there is any gender distinction to be made perhaps it can be said that idealistic young men of Page's generation went to war; idealistic young women like Page ("half an inch behind it") went to Montreal and attempted, through their early social poetry, to support the war effort.

Notes

1. Roy Daniells, Reader's Report to the University of Chicago Press (1942). W.H. Auden, Reader's Report to the University of Chicago Press (1942). Each appears to have pointed out that all of the poets that Smith had anthologized shared native and cosmopolitan qualities.
2. In *Right Hand Left Hand: A True Life of the Thirties* (1977), Livesay suggests that in the twenties she stood alone without female contemporaries: "No companion women poets were born until the end of the First World War" (19). However, in a 1974 interview with the author, Livesay stated that she came to know contemporary Canadian women poets through an anthology that her mother, Florence Randall Livesay, was editing with Florence Black. This projected anthology included male poets like Robert Finch and Raymond Knister, but emphasized women poets like Louise

Morey Bowman, Marjorie Pickthall, and Gertrude MacGregor Moffatt. Livesay, who admired Bowman, spoke highly of Moffatt and said of Pickthall, "I read and memorized almost all of her poems: her rhythms, her music entranced me."

3 In a 1974 interview with the author, Anne Marriott spoke of reading E.J. Pratt, Nellie McClung, and Audrey Alexandra Brown. Alan Crawley introduced her to T.S. Eliot, and she read both *The Waste Land* and the choruses from *The Rock*. Dorothy Livesay's father, J.F.B. Livesay, helped Marriott by bringing her manuscript, *The Wind Our Enemy* (1939), to the attention of Lorne Pierce, publisher of Ryerson Press. However, Marriott had not read any of Dorothy Livesay's poetry until after its publication.

4 A youthful Page was submitting poems to the Canadian Authors Association by 1935–36 and, together with the poet Kay Smith, she organized a branch of this association in Saint John in 1941. Through this organization, Page was to influence the younger poet, Elizabeth Brewster.

5 P.K. Page to S.D., interview, 24 February 2003.

6 For example, P.K. Page did not know Isabella Valancy Crawford (1850–87) had read only one poem of Marjorie Pickthall, which she did not care for, and did not know twenties imagist Louise Morey Bowman (1882–1944).

7 Both Constance Rooke (171–72) and Rosemary Sullivan (33–34) have commented on the importance of this poem in Page's canon.

8 "Next year [Pat Page] hopes to study journalism in England, and we know she will do well in this sphere of life" (*Ammonite* 1934, 11).

9 The Rilke poem was "Autumn Day." Curiously, Page was later to write a glosa, "Autumn," on this poem for *Hologram* (1994), forgetting her earliest encounter with "Autumn Day."

10 P.K. Page to S.D., interview, May 1996.

11 P.K. Page to S.D., interview, November 1997.

12 P.K. Page to S.D., interview, September 1997.

13 Virginia Woolf, in *A Writer's Diary* (1953), wishes to separate herself from Katherine Mansfield, her chief rival; yet she admits that it is only with Mansfield that she can talk intimately about fiction.

14 P.K. Page to S.D., interview, September 1997.

15 P.K. Page to S.D., interview, September 1997.

16 P.K. Page to S.D., interview, February 2001.

17 "'Look,' he cried, jumping up suddenly, 'I'm going to do a painting—of the river—this part of it where it's deep and the trees bend down to meet themselves ... His brush moved to the palette; her mind moved with his hands—back and forth ... until thought dissolved in motion and swam like a fish in the current of a stream'" (Page, *Sun and the Moon* 97).

18 Anneke Deichmann Gichuru wrote in her diary on 17 May 1955: "I read some of Katherine Mansfield's stories in evening. Erica [Deichmann] said that Pat Page used to feel that she looked like Katherine Mansfield—*was* her" (P.K. Page fonds, University of New Brunswick Archives).

19 P.K. Page to S.D., interview, October 2001.

20 P.K. Page to S.D., interview, October 2001.

21 In the unpublished poem "To Katherine Mansfield," Page wrote, "Are you bound to the earth again in some new shape? / Are you perhaps encased in form less frail, ... / I like to think you mingle in a world / with Checkhov, whom you loved, but never knew." P.K. Page fonds, Library and National Archives Canada, MG30, D311.

22 Also included in *Twentieth Century Poetry* is another poem on mythic metamorphosis, "Daphne—An Adaptation from John Milton," by Sacheverell Sitwell (Monro 224).
23 Letter from Kay Smith to S. Djwa, 24 June 1997.
24 See my further development of this analysis of *The Sun and the Moon* in Djwa, "P.K. Page: A Portrait of the Artist as Woman," and Djwa, "P.K. Page and Margaret Atwood: Continuity in Canadian Writing."
25 See the earlier Page poem, "The Moon-Child," in *Canadian Poems*. I am grateful to Dean Irvine for bringing this reference to my attention.
26 In Page's first published version of *The Sun and the Moon*, Carl is spelled Karl, the alliteration emphasizing the affinity between Karl and Kristin.
27 Letter from Margaret Atwood to Jim Polk and Shirley Gibson, circa fall of 1973. Margaret Atwood fonds, University of Toronto Archives, Coll. 200, Box 162.
28 Introduction, *The Sun and the Moon*, n.p.
29 Keats writes, "The Poetical Character is everything and nothing—It has no character—it enjoys light and shade; it lives in gusto, be it foul or fair, high or low, rich or poor, mean or elevated—It has as much delight in conceiving an Iago as an Imogen. What shocks the virtuous philosopher, delights the chameleon Poet" (1:387). See also Rooke and Sullivan.
30 Both Rooke and Sullivan also raise the interesting question of loss of autonomy by the perceiving poet. Rooke suggests that "the fear expressed in [P.K. Page's] poetry ... is that one might enter ... another form of being and never be released" (171). Sullivan emphasizes the alternative rhythm "where the self is invaded, and becomes the receptacle of external objects" (33).
31 P.K. Page to S.D., interview, November 1998.
32 See a transcription of a taped discussion of *Preview* by F.R. Scott, Bruce Ruddick, Neufville Shaw, and Margaret Surrey in "Four of the Former *Preview* Editors: A Discussion," wherein Margaret Surrey says that Patrick Anderson met P.K. Page at Bill Fraser's flat. Fraser was a Scotchman living in the Grosvenor Apartments. Scott also states that Anderson read *Contemporary Verse* and found a poem that he liked. The girl (P.K. Page) then turned up in Montreal (98).
33 The editorial in the first issue of *Preview* declares, "All anti-fascists, we feel that the existence of a war between democratic culture and the paralysing forces of dictatorship only intensifies the writer's obligation to work ... Secondly, the poets among us look forward, perhaps optimistically, to a possible fusion between the lyric and didactic elements in modern verse, a combination of vivid, arresting imagery and the capacity to 'sing' with social content and criticisms" ("Statement," *Preview*, March 1942).

Works Cited

Atwood, Margaret. Introduction. *The Sun and the Moon*. By P.K. Page. 1944. Toronto: Anansi, 1973.

———. Letter to Jim Polk and Shirley Gibson. Fall 1973. Margaret Atwood fonds, University of Toronto Archives, Coll. 200, Box 162.

Blake, William. "Auguries of Innocence." *The Complete Poetry and Selected Prose of John Donne and The Complete Poetry of William Blake*. Ed. and intro. Robert Silliman Hillyer. New York: Random House, 1941. 597–600.

Djwa, Sandra. "P.K. Page: A Portrait of the Artist as Woman." *Journal of Canadian Studies / Revue d'études canadiennes* 38.1 (2004): 9–22.

———. "P.K. Page and Margaret Atwood: Continuity in Canadian Writing." *Margaret Atwood: The Open Eye.* Ed. John Moss and Tobi Kozakewich. Ottawa: U of Ottawa P, 2006. 81–93.

Editorial. *Preview* (March 1942): 1.

Field, Joanna [Marion Milner]. *A Life of One's Own.* 1934. London: Chatto and Windus, 1935.

Gardiner, Stephen. *Epstein: Artist Against the Establishment.* London: Michael Joseph, Penguin Group, 1992.

Gichuru, Anneke Deichmann. Unpublished diary.

Heilbrun, Carolyn. *Writing a Woman's Life.* New York: Norton, 1988.

Hudson, W.H. *Green Mansions.* New York: G.P. Putnam, 1904.

James, Henry. *Portrait of a Lady.* Ed. Leon Edel. New York: Houghton Mifflin, 1956.

Kane, Julie. "Varieties of Mystical Experience in the Writings of Virginia Woolf." *Twentieth-Century Literature* 41.4 (Winter 1995): 328–49.

Keats, John. *The Letters of John Keats 1814–1821.* Vol. 1. Ed. Hyder Edward Rollins, 1958.

Lawrence, D.H. Letter to Katherine Mansfield. 21 November 1918. *The Collected Letters of D.H. Lawrence.* Vol. 1. Ed. and intro. Harry T. Moore. New York: Viking, 1962. 565.

Livesay, Dorothy. Personal interview with S. Djwa. 15 December 1974.

———. *Right Hand Left Hand.* Erin: Press Porcépic, 1977.

Mansfield, Katherine. "At the Bay." *The Garden Party and Other Stories.* New York: Knopf, 1922. 1–58.

———. *Bliss and Other Stories.* London: Constable, 1920.

———. *The Journal of Katherine Mansfield.* Ed. J. Middleton Murry. London: Constable, 1927.

———. *The Letters of Katherine Mansfield.* Ed. J. Middleton Murry. 2 vols. London: Constable, 1928.

———. *The Scrapbook of Katherine Mansfield.* Ed. J. Middleton Murry. London: Constable, 1939.

Marriott, Anne. Personal interview with S. Djwa. 15 December 1974.

Millay, Edna St. Vincent. *A Few Figs from Thistles: Poems and Four Sonnets.* New York: Frank Shay, 1920.

Monro, Harold. *Twentieth Century Poetry: An Anthology.* London: Chatto and Windus, 1929.

Page, Lionel F. Letter to P.K. Page. 1 July 1934.

Page, P.K. "Cullen." *The Hidden Room: Collected Poems.* Erin: Porcupine's Quill, 1997. 1: 127.

———. "Ecce Homo." *The Hidden Room: Collected Poems* 1: 17–18.

———. "The Hidden Room." *The Hidden Room: Collected Poems* 1: 11.
———. *Hologram: A Book of Glosas*. London, ON: Brick Books, 1994.
———. "The Moon-Child." *Canadian Poems*. Calgary: Canadian Authors Association, 1937.
———. "The Moth." *Observer* 2 December 1934: 35.
———. Personal interview with S. Djwa. 21 May 1996.
———. Personal interview with S. Djwa. 30 September 1997.
———. Personal interview with S. Djwa. 2–3 November 1997.
———. Personal interview with S. Djwa. 9 November 1998.
———. Personal interview with S. Djwa. 21 February 2001.
———. Personal interview with S. Djwa. 3 October 2001.
———. Personal interview with S. Djwa. 24 February 2003.
———. "Reflection." *Canadian Poetry Magazine* July 1939: 23.
———. *The Sun and the Moon*. 1944. Intro. Margaret Atwood. Toronto: Anansi, 1973. n.p.
———. "Unless the Eye Catch Fire." *Evening Dance of the Grey Flies*. Toronto: Oxford UP, 1981. 38–60.
Pound, Ezra. "A Girl." *Twentieth Century Poetry: An Anthology*. Ed. Harold Monro. London: Chatto and Windus, 1929. 230.
Powys, John Cowper. *Wolf Solent*. London: Simon and Schuster, 1929.
Relke, Diana. "Tracing a Terrestrial Vision in the Early Work of P.K. Page." *Canadian Poetry* 35 (Winter 1994): 11–30.
Rollins, Hyder Edward, ed. *The Letters of John Keats, 1814–1821*. 2 vols. Cambridge: Harvard UP, 1958.
Rooke, Constance. "P.K. Page: The Chameleon and the Centre." *Malahat Review* 45 (January 1978): 169–95.
Scott, F.R. "Lakeshore." *The Collected Poems of F.R. Scott*. Toronto: McClelland and Stewart, 1981. 50–51.
Scott, F.R., Bruce Ruddick, Neufville Shaw, and Margaret Surrey. "Four of the Former *Preview* Editors: A Discussion." *Canadian Poetry* 4 (Spring/Summer 1979): 98–119.
Smith, A.J.M., ed. *The Book of Canadian Poetry: A Critical and Historical Anthology*. Introd. A.J.M. Smith. Chicago: U of Chicago P, 1943.
Smith, Kay. Letter to S. Djwa. 24 June 1997.
Sullivan, Rosemary. "A Size Larger Than Seeing: The Poetry of P.K. Page." *Canadian Literature* 79 (Winter 1978): 32–42.
Vanteste, Hilda M.C. *Northern Review, 1945–56: A History and an Index*. Ottawa: Tecumseh, 1982.
Winwar, Frances. *Poor Splendid Wings: The Rossettis and Their Circle*. Boston: Little, Brown, 1933.
Woodcock, George. "Page, P.K." *Supplement to the Oxford Companion to Canadian History and Literature*. Ed. William Toye. Toronto: Oxford UP, 1973. 240–41.

Woolf, Virginia. *A Room of One's Own*. 1928. Harmondsworth, Middlesex: Penguin, 1945.
———. *The Waves*. London: Hogarth, 1931.
———. *A Writer's Diary: Being Extracts from the Diary of Virginia Woolf*. Ed. Leonard Wolf. London: Hogarth, 1953.

Tradition, Individual Talent, and "a young woman / From backwoods New Brunswick"
Modernism and Elizabeth Brewster's (Auto)Poetics of the Subject

BINA TOLEDO FREIWALD

Although Elizabeth Brewster (1922–) has had a long and prolific writing career as a poet, short story writer, and novelist, and while her work has often received favourable reviews, we have yet to see any sustained critical engagement with her poetry or prose. To date, Brewster has published close to twenty volumes of poetry: her first chapbook, *East Coast*, was published by Ryerson in 1951, and her most recent volume, *Bright Centre*, came out in 2005 from Oberon (her principal publisher), which has also issued her *Collected Poems I* (2003) and *Collected Poems II* (2004). There have also been three short story collections, two novels, and two mixed-genre autobiographical volumes, suggestively entitled *The Invention of Truth* (1991) and *Away from Home* (1995). As a recent review of *Collected Poems I* notes, "Brewster has long been denied the level of critical and public attention her work deserves" (Webb 37), and it will be my argument in the present essay that this critical neglect has been in part due to a failure to find a critical idiom with which to fruitfully engage the terms of Brewster's poetics. I will further suggest that an examination of Brewster's own explorations—over a lifetime of writing across different genres—of what Michel Foucault has called "technologies of the self" can offer a productive critical framework within which to read her oeuvre and place it in relation to both modernists like Virginia Woolf and Dorothy Livesay, and ongoing post/modern(ist) interrogations of subjectivity.

The Scene

In 2001, Brewster was appointed to the Order of Canada, but she had won her first literary prize, awarded by a jury that included P.K. Page (only six years Brewster's senior), over sixty years earlier, when still a teenager.[1] As the connection with Page reminds us, and as Bruce Whitman has noted, Brewster's roots are in the forties and fifties. To Robert Gibbs's astute observation, in a review of *In Search of Eros*, that "always she keeps her own distance" (83), I want to add the broader recognition that as a woman, a Canadian, and a New Brunswicker from the poverty-stricken "backwoods," distance from the centre was the very condition of Brewster's entry into the modernist scene. This is the sentiment captured in the poem I allude to in my title, "Harvard-Radcliffe Daze" (Brewster was a graduate student at Radcliffe in 1946–47), from the autobiographical sequence "Poems for Seven Decades" (occasioned by the poet turning seventy). In the poem, Brewster recalls—with a characteristic irony directed as much at the self as at inflated notions of grandeur, artistic or other—the time in 1946 when "T.S. Eliot came to read" and was introduced "As Our Greatest Living Poet"; the poem concludes,

> I too planned to be a poet—
> Maybe even (such is youthful arrogance)
> The Greatest Living
>
> Though how could a young woman
> From backwoods New Brunswick
> Be so uppity
> As to place her individual talent
> next to all that tradition? (*Wheel of Change* 71–72)

Speaking of this estrangement in a letter written shortly after arriving at Radcliffe, Brewster's tone is markedly less playful, her critique of privilege sharper, her sense of exclusion as a gendered and classed subject painfully visceral. In the letter, dated 1 February 1947, Brewster tells Desmond Pacey, her former professor at the University of New Brunswick, about her reaction to one of her Harvard professors: "when I look at him I feel suffocated by the presence of all the past, present, and future Harvard graduates, all with precisely the same expression—an expression which I am inclined to think of as the mark of 'a scholar and a gentleman' and which, in my plebeian way, I heartily detest" (Pacey–Brewster correspondence). There were other reminders of the suffocating weight of "all that tradition" for this aspiring young poet and scholar: as a woman, she was not eligible for the undergraduate Lord Beaverbrook scholarships at the University of New Brunswick that made higher education possible for many of her male peers; although eligible for an overseas graduate Lord Beaverbrook scholarship, she was refused the first time she applied (she would win one a couple of years later), because, as Desmond Pacey wrote to her at the time,[2] while only one woman had placed higher than her on the list of twenty finalists, the university president thought "it quite likely that Lord Beaverbrook will only recommend one woman candidate, in which case Miss Brewster will be disappointed"; and then there was the incident at the Harvard Widener Library, reminiscent of the Oxbridge library episode in Woolf's *A Room of One's Own*, in which Brewster, a graduate student at the time, was asked to leave the Reading Room, reserved exclusively for men (Brewster, Interview).

By the 1940s, of course, "all that tradition" would also include the weight of modernist thought proclaimed in essays like Eliot's "Tradition and the Individual Talent."[3] As Sandra Gilbert and Susan Gubar, Florence Howe, and Bonnie Kime Scott, among others, have demonstrated, this modernist doxa—motivated, in part, by male anxiety over women's successful entrance into the literary marketplace—constructed "an implicitly masculine aesthetic of hard, abstract, learned verse [in opposition to] the aesthetic of soft, effusive personal verse supposedly written by women and Romantics" (Gilbert and Gubar 154). While Eliot's call for an escape from emotion and personality might have served his personal and aesthetic ends well, it was ill suited for writers differently positioned in relation to the centre.[4] Bonnie Kime Scott urges us to consider the ways in which

> Eliot's invalidation of "personal" emotion undermines a potential focus of the isolated writer. His skepticism over "new" emotion denies validity to the artist who writes of experience that has not been taken up adequately in literary monuments—women's experience ... for example. Finally, Eliot's theoretical image of literary "monuments" and his living role as the great modernist created awe and a fear of exclusion in any but the most self-assured newcomer. (*Refiguring Modernism* 128)

Brian Trehearne has suggested in *The Montreal Forties* that the aesthetics of impersonality had its uses for those 1940s poets "whose marginality—by today's scales of cultural significance—was most marked," arguing that "the articulation of difference at mid-century was easier in the impersonalist mode" (313). Trehearne gives the example of P.K. Page, whose use of that modernist technique allowed her, he writes, to "set the terms of her proto-feminist aesthetics in a cultural period in which their candid declamation could have denied her her appreciative readership, if not publication itself" (313). That may be so, but resistance through indirection, dissimulation, or suppression exacts its own heavy price. A sobering reminder of this awaits us every time we turn to that canonical modernist archive that is Louis Dudek and Michael Gnarowski's *The Making of Modern Poetry in Canada* (1967). Symptomatically, the only female voice in this collection of "Essential Articles on Contemporary Canadian Poetry in English," as its subtitle declares, is an apologetic P.K. Page in her brief letter to the editors of the *Northern Review* on the Sutherland–Finch affair; here is an exquisite poet reduced to a whimper: "I very much regret"; "[I] am sorry"; "I would be grateful" (110).

Brewster herself has been rather discreet on the politics of gender and region[5] that have shaped her professional and literary fortunes. Her contemporary and fellow insider/outsider Miriam Waddington (1917–2004), however, has been more outspoken. Waddington offers an interesting corrective to the narrative that presented "'poet' and 'woman' ... as incompatible concepts" (Gerson 92), a narrative canonized through anthologists' enduring fondness for the F.R. Scott poem that also inspired the title of the recent "The Canadian Modernists Meet" conference.[6] Here is Waddington's take on "The Canadian Modernists Meet," complete with a little sketch of the versifier who, oh so cleverly, rhymed Miss Crotchet's virginal passion with fashion while reserving for himself the trendier modernist attributes of being "The very picture of disconsolation, / A rather lewd and most ungodly poet / Writing these verses, for his soul's salvation";[7] Waddington is cutting in her indictment of an ethnocentric, colonialist, classist, and sexist modernist scene:

> Much has been written about the so-called cosmopolitanism of the Preview group ... What did the Preview cosmopolitanism consist of? If to be British or American, or to have been educated in either of those countries, or to believe it is more worldly to be middle-class British than middle-class Maritimes or middle-class Jewish or middle-class Polish, then the Previewites were cosmopolitan. My own word for it is not cosmopolitan but colonial ... In this respect I cannot help remembering F.R. Scott, whom I always found intimidating ... He shone with an icy composure that always made me feel like a pre–World War I Russian immigrant fresh off

the boat. We never really had a conversation until one day when he was old and we were seated beside each other at dinner ... I felt he had never paid attention to or been interested in what women thought, and that if you were a woman you could never really engage him intellectually. And it was not just a matter of my own perception. It was definitely an attitude on his part—unconscious though it may have been—and on the part of the Previewites and many of their subsequent chroniclers. (31–32)

Distanced from "all that tradition," then, Brewster's poetic trajectory has not been one driven by the kind of dynamic tension between impersonality and subjective expression that Trehearne finds in his forties poets.[8] Nor has it been characterized by an eventual turn, found in the later poetry of P.K. Page, towards "constructing a healed and whole poetic self" (Killian 102). Stephen Scobie has suggested that "The impersonality of modernism, the judicious self-effacement of T.S. Eliot, for instance, still implied that there was a unitary self, present but hidden, in the figure of the elided artist" (65). Interrogating the very premise of a unitary self, Brewster's rejection of Eliot's ideal of "escape from personality" (Eliot 1096) has thus been motivated by an interest not in the *expression* of personality, but in what she calls in a 1980 interview with Paul Denham "the creation of personality ... the creation of a self" (Brewster, "Speeding" 155–56). In a 1970 manifesto-like essay written to counter criticisms of her first substantial poetry collection, *Passage of Summer* (1969), Brewster embraces some precursors and disavows others: "I was not much influenced by T.S. Eliot, the dominant figure of the period, or by Ezra Pound, although of course I had read them" ("Chronology of Summer" 34). It is to one of the modernists Brewster counts among her "favourite writers" (37) that we need to turn to gain a better understanding of the epistemological and affective logic that underlies their shared interrogation of the terms of subjectivity itself.[9] "If one is a woman," Woolf writes in *A Room of One's Own* (1929), "one is often surprised by a sudden splitting off of consciousness, say in walking down Whitehall, when from being the natural inheritor of that civilization, she becomes, on the contrary, outside of it, alien and critical" (88). In Woolf, Brewster finds a modernist subject who, unlike Pound's, seeks to tell not the epic "tale of the tribe" (qtd. in Bernstein 7), but the stories that emerge when the tribe is seen through the double consciousness of its insider-Others.

The poetic persona that inhabits some of Brewster's earliest poems—such as the untitled poem opening the inaugural issue of the *Fiddlehead* (1945), "East Coast—Canada" (written in 1947), and "In the Library" (written in 1946)[10]—is such a subject: a geographically, politically, culturally, and ultimately ontologically liminal subject. The speaker in the untitled *Fiddlehead* poem wonders,

> If I should meet myself
> Ten years or twenty from today,
> Would I still know myself
> Or turn unrecognized away?

The speaker in "East Coast—Canada" is "poised between sleep and waking/ Here on the continent's edge" (*Collected Poems* [*CP*] 1:139). Her house is shaken by a wind that blows from the "fabulous mountain ranges" and "the prairies," from "England over swelling seas" and "the populous south"; and she is both of a "civilization" and critically distanced from it: "Pretend we belong to a civilization, even a dying one. / Pretend. Pretend" (1:139).[11] "In the Library" is another early foray into the problematics of subjectivity and the relations that constitute it: self and/as Other; the poet and the traditions that claim and are claimed by her; the porous boundaries between experience and representation, between corporeality and textuality. The poetic persona challenges the framed portrait on the library wall,[12] stating, "Believe me, oh believe me, you are not I," and asserting, "But of course I am myself" and "This is I, not Byron or Vanessa." While insisting on a corporeality whose lessons are that "I must differentiate my body from all other bodies, / Realizing the mole on my neck, the scar on my hand," the speaker also recognizes the impossibility of maintaining such differentiation or containing the flux of subjectivities:

> But I know I am not convinced, feel uneasily the lie.
> Because actually I am Byron, I am Vanessa,
> I am the pictured man with the frigid smile.
>
> I am the girl at the next table, raising vague eyes,
> Flicking the ash from her cigarette, the thoughts from her mind.
> (*CP* 1:23)

Already in the early poetry, Brewster's speaker is a subject both intimately familiar with, and split off from, the hegemonic subject: she is female, rural, and poor; Canadian and not British or American; set off and to the east side of the nation. This is a subject who enters the library from the frozen spaces where "Vast tracts of Arctic ice enclose our adjectives," as Brewster writes in "East Coast—Canada" (*CP* 1:139), and thus knows better than to claim either culture or nature as her true home. It is a subject who knows that for many—for the itinerant worker or the poor farmer trying to protect themselves from the encroaching "snow and darkness outside" with an "old overcoat/ [laid] in front of the door to keep the draught out"—the roads are many, "Leading home and leading away from home, / But mostly *leading nowhere*" in her 1957 "Roads" (*CP* 1:140; emphasis mine).[13] Such liminality, in turn, produces what P.K. Page describes in her fictionalized portrait of Brewster as a "willingness to be observer" ("Victoria" 83). As an observer—fully present but also ex-centric—Brewster's poetic persona can see through accepted and naturalized meanings; can question familiar notions of space, time, and identity (personal, collective, or national); and can interrogate the commonplace binaries of experience/art, self/Other, outside/inside, centre/periphery, conscious/unconscious. Perhaps most importantly, such a liminal position allows her to see the staking of any claim—be it territorial, epistemic, or aesthetic—as just that, a willed (and self-serving, in the broadest sense) performance: "Pretend we belong to a civilization … / Pretend. Pretend."

The critics, or at least many of them, will fail or pretend not to see any of it.

The Critics

Although Brewster's large and varied body of writing has been regularly, and often favourably, reviewed, and while her poems have been included in important anthologies,[14] her writing has received almost no sustained critical attention. I want to start outlining here the terms of its initial critical reception, as a gesture towards the kind of critical literary history that many contributors to this volume have been actively pursuing. The beginning, for Brewster, was rather auspicious. Reviewing her chapbook *East Coast* in the 1952 *University of Toronto Quarterly*'s "Letters in Canada" (a review that would unfortunately be omitted from *The Bush Garden*), Frye notes that "Miss Brewster writes poetry because she thinks poetically; she is aware of the triviality in the love of mere poeticizing, 'the poet baying the familiar moon' [the line is from Brewster's "City Street"], and her own images are sharp and crisp, her ideas wrapped around them [an allusion to another poem in the collection, "The Loneliness That Wrapped Her Round"] with great dexterity and precision" (256). Milton Wilson's review in *Canadian Forum* (July 1952) is equally positive, insightfully noting (even on the basis of the small sample in the chapbook) that Brewster's "work falls into two clearly distinguishable parts: objective sketches of people and scenes, and carefully polished personal statements, reminiscent of Emily Dickinson"; the latter mode is captured by a poem like "Granite Is Not Enough," where Brewster writes, "Sharper blade must divide / To make me one" (Wilson 95). Considering Brewster's first three chapbooks—*East Coast* (1951), *Lillooet* (1954), and *Roads and Other Poems* (1957)—in the *Canadian Forum* (October 1958), the reviewer notes Brewster's sustained exploration of "person as place" and "place as made up of personalities," and bemoans the limiting chapbook format which leaves out too much (M[acpherson] 163). In these chapbooks and poems published elsewhere (in periodical publications), the reviewer glimpses a broad and promising artistic vision: "Faith, doubt and dream seem equal components of Miss Brewster's world, and we may look forward to a book in which they are all brought together" (164). Munro Beattie's assessment of Brewster's first three chapbooks in the 1965 *Literary History of Canada* (2nd ed., 1977) praises her ability to "speak with the authentic voices of the region and its people," notes her exploration of experiences of "isolation—geographical, cultural, and personal," and favourably comments on a tone that "combines affection, entirely devoid of sentimentality, with amusement entirely without bitterness" (312). Beattie concludes his discussion with what will prove to be a particularly insightful prediction: these early volumes, he notes, also include another kind of poem, represented in *East Coast* by "In the Library," and in *Roads* by "Supposition." These "subjective, non-representational poems," and their evocation of moments of "doubt about self-identity," suggest that "the next phase of Elizabeth Brewster's development may be towards a less local point of view, a tendency to look out over a larger world of people and ideas, or into the even vaster world of the self" (312).

Although Brewster will indeed go on to probe this "even vaster world of the self" in an impressive range of works in a number of genres, George Woodcock's ill-informed characterization of her poetry in the 1977 *Literary History of Canada* will unfortunately stick. Reviewing Brewster's first retrospective collection, *Passage of Summer: Selected Poems* (1969), and *Sunrise North* (1972), Woodcock places Brewster in a cohort that includes Leonard Cohen, Milton Acorn, James Reaney, Eli Mandel, and Phyllis Webb, only to dismiss her in a short paragraph as "the least complex of these poets, reminiscent in many ways of the writers of the Maritimes, where her origins lay," and "one of our few naturally direct poets" whose writing is marked by a mood of "kindness" (313). It is hard to reconcile this judgement—in which poet and poetry are devalued through associations with simplistic realism, a narrow regionalism, and femininity—with any number of poems in these two collections. Poems that draw on the landscape of dreams and a sequence like "Poems for Psychoanalysis" (in *Sunrise North*) invite comparison with another modernist poet Brewster will pay tribute to, H.D. Other poems in these two collections continue to elaborate an idiom of self-creation, in which the speaker seeks to understand what it means "to be one's own wholly," as in "Self-Reliance: To Ralph Waldo Emerson" (*CP* 1:198), or, in "November Sunday," fears that in love "[I] might forget the boundaries / of my own selfhood" (*CP* 1:200), or, in "Shock," observes how "I split from myself like a husk" (*CP* 1:248).

Although Robert Gibbs's 1974 essay in *Canadian Literature* would offer a nuanced and suggestive reading of Brewster's work, it is Desmond Pacey's 1973 article in *Ariel* that anticipates the tenor of the reception of her work in the decades to come. The essay is instructive as it crystallizes the key tropes that would become associated with Brewster as a woman and an artist, often through a conflation of the two. Pacey rises to Brewster's defence, implicitly responding to reviews such as Len Gasparini's with their echoes of F.R. Scott's caricaturing of women poets: "If Emily Dickinson were alive today she'd be a librarian with a blue-nose background ... [the poems in *Passage of Summer*] are stilted, self-conscious and conservative—the same stuff the C.A.A. is made of" (Gasparini 91). Pacey retorts, "as her poems rely very heavily upon memory, and as I have known Miss Brewster ever since she first became a student of mine in 1944, I feel it is my duty to say something about her life and personality. Reviewers have often sought to dismiss her as a merely regional poet, or as a typical spinster librarian of limited experience and weak feeling" ("Poetry" 59). Pacey then proceeds to defend her on each of these counts. Against the charge of regionalism, he offers Brewster's already impressive curriculum vitae: she is no mere regionalist in either literary formation or life experience, having studied at Radcliffe, the University of London, and Indiana where her PhD thesis was on George Crabbe; she has thus lived in the United States, in England, and across Canada. Against the double charge of the feebleness and bloodlessness of the spinster-librarian he declares her to possess the kind of "complex sensibility" that draws on "personal memories" but is not nostalgic (61). Yes, Pacey concedes, she writes of loneliness, but with stoic self-assurance to counter it, and with empathy for others to supplement it, all of which "give the lie to charges that Miss Brewster is self-absorbed" (67). Ultimately, it is the terms of the attack—the familiar double bind that sees "woman" and "artist" as mutually exclusive—that determine the terms of the praise. Anxious to prove Brewster both feminine (against the spinster-librarian-of-weak-feeling charge) and not-feminine (against charges of sentimentality and lack of formal sophistication), Pacey fails to register any of the poetry's modernist, exploratory qualities; Brewster's, he writes, is an art "which is disciplined but which controls very strong reserves of feeling. The style is classical in its simplicity, dignity and balance, but the substance has much in it of romantic passion and intensity" (69). A similarly well-intentioned but equally ambivalent assessment comes from the pen of another Brewster supporter, Tom Marshall, who would later provide the introduction to Brewster's 1985 *Selected Poems*. Marshall's review of *Passage of Summer* is rather favourable: he calls the poetry "deceptively quiet," and "contemplative, wise." His concluding observations, however, betray an inability to think outside the gendered terms of a binary paradigm that always-already marks the woman poet as "feminine," repeating the familiar "dual, hierarchical oppositions" that align "man/woman" with "Superior/Inferior" and "Activity/passivity" (Cixous and Clément 63–64). Reviewing Brewster's volume alongside Jay Macpherson's *The Boatman* and Daphne Marlatt's *Frames of a Story*, Marshall writes, "How come Canada has so many good women poets?... Perhaps feminine qualities of patience, wise passivity, acceptance, toughness and practicality are especially relevant to survival in this physical and emotional environment" (295).

At times, the critics themselves seem aware of a failure to find an adequate idiom with which to approach the poetry, of being literally at a loss for words. Reviewing *Passage of Summer*, Michael Hornyansky registers a very positive impression of the collection: "I remember a full world loved and understood, immense sympathy and a calm assured mastery of word and image, line and rhythm." However, he concludes, "I could not think how to find words for [her poems] ... I still cannot" (334). A similar stunned silence seems to afflict Rosemary Sullivan, as she chooses to include three of Brewster's poems in her 1989 anthology *Poetry by Canadian Women* but passes her over in her introductory remarks on the poets. This oversight, in turn, appears symptomatic of what has been a virtual silence on Brewster's writing in Canadian feminist literary criticism. While an exhaustive examination of the reception of Brewster's predominantly woman-centred poetry and prose fiction lies outside the scope of this essay, I would venture here to suggest two likely factors for such a neglect: Brewster's reluctance, in person or persona, to ally herself with a particular ideological stance; and the persistence of a gendered idiom (the legacy of the earlier generation of critics discussed above) that continues to read "Miss Brewster" as a "peculiarly feminine" writer (Thompson 81), whose voice is "kindly, spinsterish, cautious" (Pell 170) and whose wisdom is "domestic" (Vaisius 115).

Towards a Different Web

As Bonnie Kime Scott makes clear in her introductory remarks to *The Gender of Modernism*, outlining a "new scope for modernism" does not mean "fitting neglected figures into what is now seen as a limited definition [of modernism]" (Introduction 4). It does involve considering a much broader literary scene than the one allowed for by the canonical narrative. One result of such an opening up—strikingly illustrated by Scott's "Tangled Mesh of Modernists" (10), which was itself inspired by Virginia Woolf's figure of the "golden mesh" (9)—is a fuller appreciation of the connections that emerge among the various writers. In Brewster's case, a particular interest in the making of a self suggests clear affinities with other modernist women writers.

Brewster opens *The Invention of Truth* with an interrogation of the terms of her life-long creative project: "One friend of mine tells me that I have been writing autobiography all my life. In some senses this is true, but then what is autobiography?... and what is the self anyway?" (5–6). For Brewster, then, the originary question is not the traditional autobiographer's "who am I?" but its necessary modernist/postmodernist antecedent, "what is the self anyway?" Shirley Neuman has suggested that it might be more helpful to see postmodernism not as opposed to modernism, but as continuous with certain strands of modernism that foreground "self-reflexivity;... an acknowledgment of the impossibilities of origin; strategies of deferral and discontinuity;... formal, rhetorical, and generic eclecticism; intertextuality; a conception of language as inescapably mediating our knowledge or perception of the real; and *a repudiation of holistic notions of the self* ... [so that] *disjunctures in the self multiply*" (66; emphasis mine). This has also been the territory Brewster has been relentlessly exploring, in a variety of genres, for over half a century: the nature of subjectivity and the exigencies of self-representation.

"Back in those early days," Brewster writes in "Marching Feet,"

> When I first wrote verses
> I wanted couplets, quatrains, villanelles,
> sonnets, Spenserians, everything difficult,
> rhymed mostly, but at least a good blank verse:
> iambic, trochee, dactyl, anapest;
> forms with a long tradition: ode, elegy,
> epic, mock epic, satire (*Wheel of Change* 50)

In time, she continues, she "Escaped, made my own line" (50). The narrative of this trajectory invites us to ask: escaped from what? And with whose help? The escape, I have been suggesting, was, among other things, from the doctrine of impersonality central to what D.M.R. Bentley has characterized as the "abstracting and universalizing programme of high Modernism" (270). As Brewster reiterated in a 1980 interview with Paul Denham, "I read Pound and Eliot, of course, but they didn't appeal to me as much as some others" (154). Part of the answer to the second question—escaped with whose help?—can be found in "Beginning the Fifties," the poem that immediately follows "Harvard-Radcliffe Daze" (about Eliot's reading at Harvard) in the autobiographical sequence "Poems for Seven Decades." The poem suggests the kind of tradition that could nourish this poet. The speaker remembers a decade that "began for me in London," where she would "read in the BM reading room (unheated) / [thinking] of its famous ghosts / Karl Marx or Freud or Virginia Woolf" (*Wheel of Change* 73). The enabling presence of Freud is evident in Brewster's enduring interest in "the language of dreams," in, for instance, "Hilda Doolittle Analyzes Sigmund Freud" (*Entertaining Angels* 21). It also appears in Brewster's fascination with the intersubjective dynamics of psychoanalysis, as when the speaker in "Psychoanalyst" wonders, "Is the psychoanalyst herself neurotic / to need all this love and hate? / I don't know; it is hard for a patient to tell" (*Collected* 1:250). The influence of Freud can also be seen in "Poem about a Summer," in the speaker's understanding of the self as layered and subject to a different, psychic, temporality:

> Time does not end. Past is as real as present,
> perhaps more real because solidified;
> present is past and future all at once,
> and so is nothing. (*Digging In* 46)

Brewster's dialogue with Woolf dates back, by her own account, to the summer before the Eliot appearance at Harvard, and her reading of the poetic novel she would fall in love with, *The Waves*. Particularly resonant for Brewster's own interrogation of the nature of selfhood is Woolf's "'poetics'—of persons" (Schroeder 160), her presentation, in the novel, of self-identity as "never fixed once and for all ... a continuous intermixture, a dispersal and reassembly of diverse elements" (Minow-Pinkney 157).

It is with Woolf and Bernard in *The Waves* that Brewster is directly or indirectly carrying on a dialogue in that early poem "In the Library." In a 1996 essay entitled "Time and Tide," Brewster reflects on a fascination with the novel that has not diminished over the years. What has attracted her to Woolf is a questioning that has been central to her own writing. In the essay, Brewster turns and returns to Bernard's recurring question in *The Waves*, "Who am I?" and his answers: "This? No, I am that ... I am not one and simple but complex and many"; "I do not altogether know who I am"; and finally, in old age, "This difference we make so much of, this identity we so feverishly cherish, was overcome" (quoted in Brewster 14, 21, 22). Like Bernard, Brewster conceives of the self-reflexive turn as drawing her not away from, but closer to a shared humanity and a sense of "belonging to the great family of Nobody," as she expresses it in "Woman Talk" (*Spring Again* 41).

The self, under different guises, has perhaps always been a contentious entity; but for some subjects—for those who are, in Brewster's words, "exile[s] of some sort" (*Away from Home* 129), the repressed and oppressed subjects to whom Marx, Freud, and Woolf sought to give a voice—the stakes in selfhood are particularly high. Dorothy Livesay, to whom Brewster's 1982 volume *The Way Home* is dedicated, writes in her memoir *Journey with My Selves* (1991): "This is my truth ... I had worn four hoods: childhood, girlhood, womanhood and motherhood. Now there were two more waiting: widowhood and selfhood" (15, 197). The self is but another hood, not an essence, Livesay suggests, so there is much to be gained by closely scrutinizing the patterns (scripts)—gendered and other—on which it comes to be modelled, the better to fashion a hood of one's own. Livesay, a daughter of a particular time and place, comes to recognize that, for her, widowhood was a necessary precondition for selfhood. In Virginia Woolf's *Orlando*, too, it is specifically through the consciousness of Orlando as a middle-aged *woman* that the novel's climactic insights about the nature of selfhood are delivered. What Orlando has learned from her three-hundred-year literary and cross-cultural romp, first as a man then a woman, is that, to echo Luce Irigaray, this self is not one. A self is made up of "a great variety of selves," each with its own set of "difficult terms"; "these selves," *Orlando*'s biographer-narrator muses, "of which we are built up, one on top of another, as plates are piled on a waiter's hand, have attachments elsewhere, sympathies, little constitutions, and rights of their own" (294). Woolf's palimpsestic model of identity recognizes both the driving desire of the "conscious self" to be "nothing but one self," and the plural and contingent processes that constitute subjectivity as a continuously unfolding narrative written on the body. The novel ends, however, on a cautionary note, warning against capitulation to the desire for a unitary self. When Orlando's wish is finally granted and she feels like "a single self, a real self," she also falls utterly silent (299).

The resonance of Woolf's and Livesay's modernist interrogations of subjectivity for Brewster's autopoetic project is captured by a fragment from "Victorian Interlude," a collage-like text (previously published as a short story) included in *The Invention of Truth*. Here the autobiographical narrator tells of a dream with echoes of both Woolf's *Orlando* and the tragic tale of the imagined Judith Shakespeare in *A Room of One's Own*:

> Long ago, when I was a student at university, I had a dream of a young man who had the disconcerting habit of turning into his mother. His life was ruined. Young, brilliant, ambitious, he wished to enter public life, to attain a commanding position. But, just as he was about to make a speech or assume authority, his mother would take over. He would disappear, her skirts would sweep the ground. The voice and the words would be hers. (*Invention of Truth* 69)

Seeking to understand the dream, the narrator identifies both gendered and familial scripts as part of that grid with and against which a nascent subject defines itself: "Did I object to being a woman? Or did I simply fear that I was overwhelmed by the power of my mother's personality? Swallowed up in her?" (69). In another recurrent dream, she is smothered by the mother's close embrace (63); but the father's embrace is no less suffocating: wishing for a son whom he was going to name James, he names her "for two ghosts"—his dying mother, and the daughter of his commanding officer in the war, a young girl who had died of tuberculosis (41). Brewster's persona, like Woolf's Orlando, survives these potentially deadly blows to the female subject by refusing their monologic grip and embracing a heteroglossic selfhood. Her mother's ghost, she recognizes, will always "speak from my depths. But *the others are in me too*: the cool observer, the Muse who is husband and father, the voice of Athena's owl, crying out, 'Who, who?'" (69; emphasis mine).

An Autopoetics of the Subject

I am calling Brewster's project an autopoetics of the subject because at the centre of her writing has been a sustained probing of those acts of self-making through which, she has maintained, everything else passes. Hers is an interrogation that never presumes to know more than the "I" can conjure up, borrow from others, imagine, dream of: "Is[n't] everything any author writes autobiographical," Brewster invites us to ask, "since (even if she wishes) she cannot go totally beyond the boundaries of her experience and observation[?]" (*Invention of Truth* 5). Anything else would be pretense, posturing—all too apparent to the one who is kept at a distance, and quickly learns the benefits of staying there. Brewster's critical essay on F.R. Scott, "The I of the Observer," demonstrates a keen eye for the ways in which the "I," that inescapably singular voice behind any utterance, can be made to pass for a "godlike vision" (28). She is not fooled by the appearance of an "eye [that] seems remarkably detached" (23); looking closer, she finds that the many assumed voices—the "didactic 'we'" (23), "the god-like narrator" (27), the removed third person, the adopted "'I' of another author" (30), as well as the "solitary, sardonic, observant 'I'" (25)—are but the clever guises of "I."

Particularly helpful for a reading of Brewster's autopoetic project is the work of auto/biography theorist Leigh Gilmore, who has drawn on Foucault, Louis Althusser, and Teresa de Lauretis, among others, to develop a critical idiom with which to rethink the broader project of "becoming a person" (*Limits* 103). Of particular relevance to Brewster's work is Gilmore's understanding of the subject as "multiply coded in a range of discourses" that cut across the divide autobiography/fiction, history/story (*Autobiographics* 42), and her focus on writers who are less invested in the certainties of traditional autobiography and more interested in asking "what the self is that it could be the subject of its own representation" (*Limits* 9). Autobiographics, Gilmore suggests, is not a metaphoric but a metonymic practice: "insofar as autobiography represents the real, it does so through metonymy, that is, through the claims of contiguity wherein the person who writes extends the self in the writing, and puts her in another place" (*Limits* 101). Such a practice becomes further foregrounded in serial autobiography, where the return to the scene of self-narration demonstrates the ongoing project through which "a subject-in-process is constructed" (97). Brewster's entire oeuvre can be seen as engaged in such a serial narrative of self-construction, and in the remainder of this essay I would like to suggest some of the ways in which her two explicitly (serial) autobiographical volumes, *The Invention of Truth* and *Away from Home*, both construct a palimpsestic self/text and allow us to explore the ends to which such representations can be put. Through such a reading of the autobiographical volumes, in which I see Brewster as both performing and reflecting on an autopoetics of the subject, I seek to begin an articulation of a critical idiom with which to approach her considerable oeuvre.

Tellingly, the figure of a palimpsestic self/text appears in a specifically modernist context in a poem from Brewster's 1990 collection *Spring Again*. The poem, part of the sequence "Garden Cantos: A Month of Poems," draws on Pound's use of the figure of the palimpsest in Canto 116 to articulate the poet's own vision in "12. Magpie":

> Pound's just an excuse, of course,
> I have to admit.
>   My poem is mine.
> As Pound (magpie or Phoenix)
> gathered straw and gems
> from a hundred sources
>
> made them cohere
> (failed to make them cohere?)
> with his eye's glue
>
> so I this palimpsest (22)

Through syntactic economy, the "I" of the last (one-line) stanza both *is* "this palimpsest," and has just created a thematically and formally palimpsestic poem. Similarly, Brewster's two autobiographical volumes both thematize as palimpsestic a range of experiences that define and constitute the autobiographical subject—the experience of time and place, for example, and the way memory and dreams work—and are narratively constructed as palimpsests. Subject formation is seen as thoroughly palimpsestic, as earlier, often violent, experiences both fictional and lived resurface in the present in unforeseen ways, following the (Freudian) logic of a traumatic wound that is "not available to consciousness until it imposes itself again, repeatedly" (Caruth 4). A brief passage from *The Invention of Truth* serves to illustrate. The section starts with the autobiographical narrator pondering the question "whether it was ever possible to make a change in one's life" (130). The question makes her think of Jane, the narrator-protagonist of her autobiographical novel, *The Sisters*. This train of thought leads her to link and superimpose two incidents: a violent childhood experience she had fictionalized in *The Sisters* and a recent encounter with a lover she here calls Adrian. The resulting palimpsest yields an insight into the formation of the subject's affective life: "Nothing is ever quite erased. The other night with Adrian, just for a minute, I thought of Jane and Roger Harrigan [the boy who molests Jane in the novel]. Adrian was holding my throat between his hands—so—and I was suddenly glad I knew so much about him. When you have been raped as a child, you don't want violence again, ever" (131).

Palimpsestic practices also inform every narrative level of the *The Invention of Truth* and *Away from Home*, forcing us, as Raylene Ramsay has observed in connection with the French new autobiographies, "to accept multiplicity, nonexclusive contradiction and uncertainty" as constitutive of the subject (34). At the microtextual level, the smallest unit of recollection starts in the present and involves calling up memories, examining dreams, and then "tack[ing] them together, layer on layer" (*Invention of Truth* 55). At the macrotextual level, there is, within each of these two autobiographical volumes, an extensive interweaving and layering of previously published short fiction and poetry into and onto a personal narrative that includes diary entries, excerpts from letters, and self-reflexive commentary interpreting and revising the autobiographical content of the stories and poems. There are intertextual palimpsestic relations with earlier works. Within both *The Invention of Truth* and *Away from Home,* the layering of traditional autobiographical narrative with more experimental strategies of self-narration produces an intrageneric palimpsest, in which the postmodern narrative places "the territories of old autobiographies ... 'under erasure' so that they are never fully erased, only struck out and so still perceptible" (Ramsay 24).

Finally, a particularly significant palimpsestic interplay is enacted *between* the two volumes, as *Away from Home* revisits the years 1946 to 1951. Brewster comments on its relation to the first volume, *The Invention of Truth*: "Beginnings and endings are the most difficult parts of a book to compose. That's why I have written the middle first, and must now double back and begin again" (*Away from Home* 5). The deferred beginning of *Away from Home* foregrounds the constructed nature of origins, asking, rather than affirming: what/where is home? Home is a polysemic signifier in *Away from Home*, involving experiences of belonging and alienation embedded in many identity-contexts, including the familial, regional, and national. The volume interrogates the many inflections of being at home or away from home:

the tension "between the desire for change and the yearning to be rooted to one sheltered spot" (6); the small details, like the familiar dishes and a few shelves of books, that create a sense of home even when "home itself was rather fluid and uncertain" (7); the fear of not "feel[ing] at home anywhere" (113); the experience of leaving home, then returning, only to find, "that 'home' had moved" (6). With respect to collective identity, there are the insights born of contacts with the Other, the experience of "'not being the same' as" (18)—in Brewster's case, being a Canadian and a New Brunswicker in the States and then in England (17–18). These experiences, in turn, lead Brewster to reflect on what keeps a nation together on the occasion of Newfoundland joining Confederation; to reflect on the price of secession (73); and to query the very condition of collective belonging: "[are] Canadians, or North Americans in general, ... only birds of passage?" (129). It is perhaps this sense of difference that defamiliarizes for Brewster the very notion of identity and belonging.

A second reason for the need to double back and begin again has to do with the need to represent what had been unrepresentable. *Away from Home*, Brewster tells us, "fills in a gap of some consequence in my life" (6). As we find out, the book's climactic ending involves an incident left out of the earlier volume: the autobiographer's suicide attempt at age twenty-nine. This ending also constitutes the proper beginning of the story of the self, for it is in the aftermath of the attempted suicide that a self, having survived, presents itself, demanding articulation. In a recent poem, "Winter Trying to Become Spring," Brewster muses, "Yet it's death—the thought of death—/ that makes my living self most real" (*Burning Bush* 31).

Finally, I want to reflect briefly on another aspect of Brewster's palimpsestic practice, one that relates to the ends of the autobiographical as a site for both continuous becoming and ongoing interrogation of the terms of such self-making. From this vantage point, the question to bring to bear on the autobiographical is not what it "is an interpretation *of*," but what "is it *for*?" (Kerbrat 33; my translation). These, as I see, are some of the answers suggested by Brewster's exploratory, speculative, autobiographical volumes. They can, in turn, serve as a grid with which to reread her poetry and prose.

Why autobiography? Because the knowledge that the reality of the self is not a given provokes an unbearable and debilitating anxiety. An embedded fragment of a story features a character who is plagued by a sense of "lack of identity" (*Away from Home* 34) and tormented by doubt: "what, after all,... is reality? And what is the present?... Here I am ... [ellipsis in original] ...

But am I? am I?" (32). Brewster writes in *The Invention of Truth*, "I thought I didn't have any personality ... But if I acted I could invent a personality for myself. I think maybe I write for the same reason" (112).

Why autobiography? Because the invented self is multiple and shifting, presenting its creator with a series of questions demanding, if not an answer, at least a response. Brewster writes, "what is my own person? ... Am I still the same person (or persons) I was in 1949? Partly yes, partly no" (*Away from Home* 70). Such a view of the self—as invented and plural—necessitates a revision of the narrative of the self's origins. Brewster reflects, "Now I may feel that I'm almost as much the child of William Wordsworth or Jane Austen as of my parents, so how important is blood parentage?" (71).

Why autobiography? Because none of the available fictional paradigms seems to provide the right narrative model for the life story of the self. Four paragraphs into *The Invention of Truth*, Brewster recognizes that she is replicating the structure of Wordsworth's *The Prelude*, and decides she is "going in too straight a line" (7). In the autobiography's concluding section, she similarly rejects another narrative paradigm, that of the novel, because "it formalizes life too much" (109).

Why autobiography? Not because of the uniqueness of the self, but because of its commonness. One of the autofictional narrators in *The Invention of Truth* comments, "I have often painted my own portrait, not so much from any great narcissism as from the realization that I look like so many other people I know" (92).

Why autobiography? Because the present can know the past in ways that the past could not have known itself. In the autobiographical story "Essence of Marigold"—written in counterpoint to P.K. Page's rendition of the same event (the occasion of their first meeting) in her story "Victoria"—the narrator considers the best way to represent a particular moment in the past: "I have a diary dating from the time I met Marguerite. I have a bundle of letters from her ... I have clippings about exhibitions, a few sketches. I could look them up, I could document this account, but I don't intend to this time. I'll try to get at the essence" (*Invention of Truth* 89). Discursive recreation is the only way "to bring back the past" (127), and there are many reasons for wishing or needing to do so. The past, it turns out, is often the unfinished business of the present. Brewster reflects, "Is this what I really want to do in this story: to do penance for being ashamed of my father?" (47). Although the logic of mortality is an irrevocable linearity, some relationships survive the demise of the body and continue to demand attention.

Brewster writes of her now-dead parents, "I could never choose between them. Sometimes I think I'm still trying to choose" (30). The flip side of the same coin is that some relationships that have never materialized in the flesh might be made to live on paper. Brewster imagines the daughter she does not have: "If I had a daughter, she would probably argue with me now, say angrily, 'Life isn't just something to put up with'" (42).

Why autobiography? Since neither the meaning of a life nor its value are a given, they need to be invented or purposefully uncovered for one's existence to be validated. "I've wasted so much of my life," Brewster comments at the conclusion of *The Invention of Truth* (131), and she opens *Away from Home* with the determination "to find a clearness, a coherence in my life" (11). In searching for such coherence, however, one comes up against others' interpellations of the self, and one's own internalization of them—another reason for self-writing.

Finally, this last one: why autobiography? So that as a writer, Brewster can invoke a life and say, see this, flesh, not mere paper. Also, so that, being mere flesh, she could comfort herself: "nothing lasts" (*Invention of Truth* 46)—except perhaps this, paper.

Coda

If I were to choose a signature Brewster poem, it would be that untitled poem in the first issue of *Fiddlehead* cited earlier, a poem that playfully yet earnestly stages the self's unsettling encounters with its ever proliferating avatars:

> If I should meet myself
> ten years or twenty from today,
> would I still know myself
> or turn unrecognized away?
>
> Would I still like myself
> or would myself not then like me?
> little enough I care
> for the self that then will be.
>
> Little enough I'll care
> in twenty years from now, or ten,
> for the distant, dusty thoughts
> of a self not living then. (n.p.)

Fittingly, the poem's publication history and the initial elision of its title mirror the very condition of elusive liminality that Brewster here suggests is the very mark of self. Accorded pride of place on the first page of the inaugural issue of the magazine, the poem remained uncollected until its recent inclusion, sixty years later, in *Bright Centre* (with the first line used as title). In the intervening years, like some ur-text, it would disappear only to surface and resurface with amplified resonance: it is the last poem in Brewster's earliest Manuscript Notebook, dated "c. 1943/1944," and again the last poem in the Manuscript Notebook dated "1955–59, 1980" (Elizabeth Brewster fonds, vol. 1); it is the poem Brewster turned to in a 1977 interview with Jon Pearce when trying to explain her view of the "I" as multiple and shifting, since "every human being is many persons" (11); and it was this poem that Brewster chose to recite from memory as we were settling down for an interview in 2004 (Brewster, Interview). It was possibly our ensuing conversation that prompted Brewster to include the poem in her latest collection, *Bright Centre*, where it is followed by "By the River Again," a recent poem that carries on the self's conversations with its selves and characteristically ends on an interrogatory note:

> What would I say to her
> if I met my twenty-year-old self
> in her cheap little red coat from Eaton's catalogue
> and her black handbag from Woolworth's,
> and the question in her eyes? (72)

Such questions reverberate throughout the corpus of Brewster's writing. In the 1987 short story "Visitations," the first-person narrator, browsing through old diaries, reflects, "Are they evidence for me or against me? How true are they? Am I still the same person who wrote them?" (*Visitations* 5). In "Taking Stock," from the 1998 volume *Garden of Sculpture*, the speaker wonders,

> At seventy-four
> (nearly seventy-five)
> am I still the same self
> that I was at twelve or twenty
> or even at fifty? (90)

In the sequence "Mosaic of Dreams" from *Burning Bush* (2000), the speaker's dream unfolds in a classroom or a lecture hall in which she is "about to read poems to an audience": "I decide to read from my book, / but these poems too are unfamiliar. / I wonder if I have become / someone else" (114). This essay has been an attempt to outline a framework within which such post/modern(ist) interrogations of the subject could be more fruitfully engaged.

Notes

This essay draws on and expands work I initially presented at two conferences: "'Wider Boundaries of Daring': The Modernist Impulse in Canadian Women's Poetry" (University of Windsor, October 2001) and "The Canadian Modernists Meet: A Symposium" (University of Ottawa, May 2003). My research was supported by a SSHRC Standard Research Grant.

1. Both Page and Brewster have written short stories about that first encounter: Page's "Victoria" (first appeared in *Tamarack Review* 1976, then collected in *A Kind of Fiction* in 2001), and Brewster's response, "Essence of Marigold" (first published in the 1983 *A House Full of Women*, then included in *The Invention of Truth* in 1991). These stories circle around questions of memory, identity, and representation, but also playfully capture the personal and aesthetic tensions that have been part of their long-standing friendship. A later interchange between the writers occasioned Brewster's "On P.K. Irwin's *Bright Centre*," a poem in response to Page's drawing, which Brewster had purchased, first published in *Re:Generations: Canadian Women Poets in Conversation* (Brandt and Godard 2005, 98), a volume of creative dialogues initiated at the "Wider Boundaries of Daring" conference.
2. This information was likely in a copy of Pacey's letter to George Sherburn, chairman of the English department at Harvard (dated 6 March 1947), forwarded to Brewster at Radcliffe (Pacey–Brewster correspondence).
3. Florence Howe writes, "For my generation of women and men born in the late 1920s and '30s—Eliot was the star in both the literary and critical firmaments" (3).
4. It is quite telling that, as Eliot himself reportedly noted, while at Harvard he "left the Woolf lectures to his assistant ... though he did the Joyce himself" (Scott, *Refiguring Modernism* 1:137).
5. Although a consideration of the role of region in literary reception and canonization lies outside the scope of this essay, I would like to suggest that an important factor affecting Brewster's literary fortunes has been the marginalization of the poetry magazine she helped found in Fredericton in 1945, as a member of the Bliss Carman Society at the University of New Brunswick, and in which her early poetry regularly appeared. Like *Contemporary Verse* (discussed in Christine Kim's contribution to the present volume), the *Fiddlehead*, broadly inclusive rather than polemical or programmatic in its approach—A.G. Bailey's editorial in the first issue, drawing on T.S. Eliot, called for an understanding of tradition as "forever unfolding by means of constant experimentation"—has been left out of the normative, Montreal-centred, and conflict-oriented account of the place of little magazines in Canadian modernism.
6. This conference took place at University of Ottawa, May 2003.
7. This is from the last stanza (subsequently dropped) of F.R. Scott's "The Canadian Authors Meet," as it originally appeared in the *McGill Fortnightly Review*, 27 April 1927.

8   Three essays in a section of *The Canadian Modernists Meet* (ed. Dean Irvine) entitled "Beyond Impersonality" (the essays by Anne Quéma, Medrie Purham, and Shelly Hulan) explore responses by Canadian modernist writers and artists to impersonalist aesthetics.
9   See Sandra Djwa's essay in this volume for the role Woolf's writing played in the artistic development of P.K. Page.
10 Both "East Coast—Canada" and "In the Library" appeared in Brewster's first chapbook, *East Coast* (1951). The poems are dated in Brewster's Manuscript Notebooks: Manuscript Notebook 1944–46 includes "In the Library," and Manuscript Notebook 1946–48 includes "East Coast—Canada" (Elizabeth Brewster fonds, vol. 1).
11 Since Brewster's early publications are out of print, all subsequent references to *East Coast, Lillooet, Roads and Other Poems, Passage of Summer,* and *Sunrise North* will refer to the recent *Collected Poems*, vol. 1.
12 The painting is likely Charles MacGregor's portrait of Sir Charles G.D. Roberts, in the Arts library at the University of New Brunswick.
13 "Roads" is the title poem of Brewster's third chapbook, *Roads, and Other Poems* (1957).
14 Margery Fee's *Canadian Poetry in Selected English-Language Anthologies: An Index and Guide* (1985) cites thirty-nine entries for Brewster in fourteen anthologies. As Fee notes in her introduction, these are "mainstream" anthologies, and include *Canadian Poems 1850–1952* (1953; ed. Louis Dudek and Irving Layton), *The Oxford Book of Canadian Verse in English and French* (1960; ed. A.J.M. Smith), *Canadian Anthology* (1974; ed. Carl F. Klinck and Reginald E. Watters), *The Penguin Book of Canadian Verse* (1975; ed. Ralph Gustafson), *Literature in Canada* (1978; ed. Douglas Raymond and Leslie Monkman), and *The New Oxford Book of Canadian Verse in English* (1982; ed. Margaret Atwood).

Works Cited

Atwood, Margaret, ed. *The New Oxford Book of Canadian Verse in English*. Toronto: Oxford UP, 1982.

Bailey, A.G. Editorial. *The Fiddlehead*. 1 (1945): n.p.

Beattie, Munro. "Poetry 1950–1960." *Literary History of Canada: Canadian Literature in English*. Ed. Carl F. Klinck et al. Toronto: U of Toronto P, 1977. 2:297–329.

Bentley, D. M. R. *The Gay/Grey Moose: Essays on the Ecologies and Mythologies of Canadian Poetry, 1690–1990*. Ottawa: Ottawa UP, 1992.

Bernstein, Michael André. *The Tale of the Tribe: Ezra Pound and the Modern Verse Epic*. Princeton: Princeton UP, 1980.

Bliss Carman Society of Fredericton. *Minutes of the Bliss Carman Society of Fredericton, founded December, 1940*. Fredericton, NB, 1940–44.

Brandt, Di, and Barbara Godard, eds. *Re:Generations: Canadian Women Poets in Conversation*. Windsor: Black Moss, 2005.

Brewster, Elizabeth. *A House Full of Women*. Ottawa: Oberon, 1983.

———. *Away from Home*. Ottawa: Oberon, 1995.

———. *Bright Centre*. Ottawa: Oberon, 2005.

———. *Burning Bush*. Ottawa: Oberon, 2000.

———. "Chronology of Summer." *Humanities Association Bulletin* 21.1 (Winter 1970): 34–39.

———. *Collected Poems of Elizabeth Brewster*. Vol. 1. Ottawa: Oberon, 2003.
———. *Digging In: New Poems*. Ottawa: Oberon, 1982.
———. *East Coast*. Toronto: Ryerson, 1951.
———. Elizabeth Brewster fonds. MG30 D370. Library and Archives Canada, Ottawa, ON.
———. *Entertaining Angels*. Ottawa: Oberon, 1988.
———. "Essence of Marigold." *A House Full of Women* 17–27; *The Invention of Truth* 87–97.
———. *Garden of Sculpture*. Ottawa: Oberon, 1998.
———. "The I of the Observer." *Canadian Literature* 79 (Winter 1978): 23–30.
———. ["If I should meet myself"] Untitled poem. *The Fiddlehead* 1 (1945): n.p.
———. Interview with Bina Freiwald (taped). Victoria, BC. 22–23 March 2004.
———. *The Invention of Truth*. Ottawa: Oberon, 1991.
———. *Jacob's Dream*. Ottawa: Oberon, 2002.
———. *Lillooet*. Toronto: Ryerson, 1954.
———. *Passage of Summer*. Toronto: Ryerson, 1969.
———. *Roads and Other Poems*. Toronto: Ryerson, 1957.
———. "Speeding Towards Strange Destinations: A Conversation with Elizabeth Brewster." Interviewed by Paul Denham. *Essays on Canadian Writing* 18–19 (Summer/Fall 1980): 149–60.
———. *Spring Again*. Ottawa: Oberon, 1990.
———. *Sunrise North*. Toronto: Clarke Irwin, 1972.
———. "Time and Tide." *Wascana Review of Contemporary Short Fiction* 31.1 (Spring 1996): 11–24.
———. *Visitations*. Ottawa: Oberon Press, 1987.
———. *The Way Home*. Ottawa: Oberon, 1982.
———. *Wheel of Change*. Ottawa: Oberon Press, 1993.
Caruth, Cathy. *Unclaimed Experience: Trauma, Narrative, and History*. Baltimore: Johns Hopkins UP, 1996.
Cixous, Hélène, and Catherine Clément. *The Newly Born Woman*. Trans. Betsy Wing. Minneapolis: U of Minnesota P, 1986.
Dudek, Louis, and Michael Gnarowski, eds. *The Making of Modern Poetry in Canada*. Toronto: Ryerson, 1967.
Dudek, Louis, and Irving Layton, eds. *Canadian Poems 1850-1952*. 2nd ed. Toronto: Contact, 1953.
Eliot, T.S. "Tradition and the Individual Talent." *The Norton Anthology of Theory and Criticism*. Ed. Vincent B. Leitch et al. New York: Norton, 2001. 1092–98.
Fee, Margery. *Canadian Poetry in Selected English-Language Anthologies: An Index and Guide*. Halifax: Dalhousie University Libraries, 1985.
Foucault, Michel. "Technologies of the Self." *Technologies of the Self: A Seminar with Michel Foucault*. Ed. Luther H. Martin, Huck Gutman, Patrick H. Hutton. Amherst: U of Massachusetts P, 1988. 16–49.

Frye, Northrop. "Letters in Canada: English-Canadian Letters." *University of Toronto Quarterly* 21.3 (April 1952): 252–58.
Gasparini, Len. Rev. of *Passage of Summer*, by Elizabeth Brewster. *Canadian Forum* 49 (July 1969): 91.
Gerson, Carole. "'The Most Canadian of all Canadian Poets': Pauline Johnson and the Construction of a National Literature." *Canadian Literature* 158 (Autumn 1998): 90–107.
Gibbs, Robert. "Next Time from a Different Country." *Canadian Literature* 62 (Autumn 1974): 17–32.
———. Rev. of *In Search of Eros*, by Elizabeth Brewster. *Canadian Literature* 72 (1977): 83–84.
Gilbert, Sandra M., and Susan Gubar. *No Man's Land: The Place of the Woman Writer in the Twentieth Century*. Vol. 1, *The War of the Words*. New Haven: Yale UP, 1987.
Gilmore, Leigh. *Autobiographics: A Feminist Theory of Women's Self-Representation*. Ithaca: Cornell UP, 1994.
———. *The Limits of Autobiography: Trauma and Testimony*. Ithaca: Cornell UP, 2001.
Gustafson, Ralph, ed. *The Penguin Book of Canadian Verse*. 2nd rev. ed. Markham, ON: Penguin, 1975.
Hornyansky, Michael. Rev. of *Passage of Summer*, by Elizabeth Brewster. *University of Toronto Quarterly* 39 (July 1970): 334.
Howe, Florence. "Introduction: T.S. Eliot, Virginia Woolf, and the Future of 'Tradition.'" *Tradition and the Talents of Women*. Ed. Florence Howe. Urbana: U of Illinois P, 1991. 1–33.
Irvine, Dean, ed. *The Canadian Modernists Meet*. Ottawa: U of Ottawa P, 2005.
Kerbrat, Marie-Claire. *Leçon littéraire sur l'écriture de soi*. Paris: Press Universitaires de France, 1996.
Killian, Laura. "Poetry and the Modern Woman: P.K. Page and the Gender of Impersonality." *Canadian Literature* 150 (Autumn 1996): 86–105.
Klinck, Carl F., and Reginald E. Watters, ed. *Canadian Anthology*. Toronto: Gage, 1974.
Livesay, Dorothy. *Journey with My Selves: A Memoir, 1901–1963*. Vancouver: Douglas and McIntyre, 1991.
M[acpherson], J[ay]. Rev. of *Roads and Other Poems*, by Elizabeth Brewster, and *Dazzle*, by Dorothy Roberts. *Canadian Forum* (October 1958): 163–64.
Marshall, Tom. Rev. of *Passage of Summer*, by Elizabeth Brewster. *Queen's Quarterly* 77 (Summer 1970): 295.
Minow-Pinkney, Makiko. *Virginia Woolf and the Problem of the Subject*. Brighton: Harvester, 1987.
Neuman, Shirley. "After Modernism: English-Canadian Poetry Since 1960." *Studies on Canadian Literature: Introductory and Critical Essays*. Ed. Arnold E. Davidson. New York: Modern Language Association of America, 1990. 54–73.

Pacey, Desmond. Desmond Pacey–Elizabeth Brewster correspondence. Pacey fonds. MG L1, series 2.1, case 7. University of New Brunswick Archives, Fredericton, NB.

———. "The Poetry of Elizabeth Brewster." *Ariel* 4 (July 1973): 58–69.

Page, P. K. "Letter to *Northern Review*." *The Making of Modern Poetry in Canada*. Ed. Louis Dudek and Michael Gnarowski. Toronto: Ryerson Press, 110.

———. "Victoria." *A Kind of Fiction*. Erin: Porcupine's Quill, 2001. 81–85.

Pearce, Jon. "A Particular Image of the Self: Elizabeth Brewster." *Twelve Voices: Interviews with Canadian Poets*. Ottawa: Borealis, 1980. 7–23.

Pell, Barbara. Rev. of *Visitations*, by Elizabeth Brewster. *Canadian Literature* 118 (Autumn 1988): 169–71.

Ramsay, Raylene L. *The French New Autobiographies: Sarraute, Duras, and Robbe-Grillet*. Gainesville: UP of Florida, 1996.

Raymond, Douglas, and Leslie Monkman, eds. *Literature in Canada*. Toronto: Gage, 1978.

Schroeder, Steven. *Virginia Woolf's Subject and the Subject of Ethics: Notes Towards a Poetics of Persons*. Lewiston: Edwin Mellen, 1996.

Scobie, Stephen. "Leonard Cohen, Phyllis Webb, and the End(s) of Modernism." *Canadian Canons: Essays in Literary Value*. Ed. Robert Lecker. Toronto: U of Toronto P, 1991. 57–70.

Scott, Bonnie Kime. Introduction. *The Gender of Modernism*. Ed. Bonnie Kime Scott. Bloomington: Indiana UP, 1990. 1–18.

———. *Refiguring Modernism*. Vol. 1. Bloomington: Indiana UP, 1995.

———. "A Tangled Mesh of Modernists." Ed. Bonnie Kime Scott. *The Gender of Modernism: A Critical Anthology*. Bloomington: Indiana UP, 1990. 10.

Scott, F.R. "The Canadian Authors Meet." *An Anthology of Canadian Literature*. Ed. Russell Brown and Donna Bennett. Vol 1. Toronto: Oxford UP, 1982. 348.

Smith, A.J.M., ed. *The Oxford Book of Canadian Verse in English and French*. Toronto: Oxford UP, 1960.

Sullivan, Rosemary. Introduction. *Poetry by Canadian Women*. Ed. Rosemary Sullivan. Don Mills, ON: Oxford UP, 1989. x–xiv.

Thompson, M.A. Rev. of *Visitations*, by Elizabeth Brewster. *Quarry* 36.3 (Summer 1987): 80–82.

Trehearne, Brian. *The Montreal Forties: Modernist Poetry in Transition*. Toronto: U of Toronto P, 1999.

Vaisius, Andrew. "All Sorts of Things—The Wisdom of Elizabeth Brewster." Rev. of *Entertaining Angels*, by Elizabeth Brewster. *Event* 18.2 (Summer 1989): 113–16.

Waddington, Miriam. *Apartment Seven: Essays Selected and New*. Toronto: Oxford UP, 1989.

Webb, Peter. Rev. of *Collected Poems I*, by Elizabeth Brewster, *To Be Now: New and Selected Poems, 1989–2003*, by Marty Gervais, and *An Island in the Sky: Selected Poetry of Al Pittman*. *Journal of Canadian Poetry* 20 (2006): 34–41.

Whitman, Bruce. "Chosen Words." Rev. of *Away From Home*, by Elizabeth Brewster. *Canadian Forum* 75 (January–February 1997): 46–47.

Wilson, Milton. Rev. of *East Coast*, by Elizabeth Brewster and other Ryerson chapbooks. *Canadian Forum* July 1952: 95–96.

Woodcock, George. "Poetry." *Literary History of Canada: Canadian Literature in English*. Ed. Carl F. Klinck et al. Toronto: U of Toronto P, 1977. 3:284–317.

Woolf, Virginia. *A Room of One's Own* and *Three Guineas*. Ed. Michèle Barrett. London: Penguin, 1993.

———. *Orlando*. Oxford: Oxford UP, 1998.

———. *The Waves*. New York: Harcourt-Brace, 1931.

Wordsworth, William. *The Thirteen-book Prelude*. 1850. Ed. Mark L. Reed. Ithaca: Cornell UP, 1991.

"And we are homesick still"
Home, the Unhomely, and the Everyday in Anne Wilkinson
KATHY MEZEI

Locating Home

Houses, home, homesickness, and homelessness reverberate through Anne Wilkinson's poetry, prose, and autobiographical writing. Born into the privileged Osler family and raised amid stately mansions and large summer estates in southern Ontario, she is obsessed by houses, the unhomely, and a pervasive sense of dislocation. Although Wilkinson probably never washed a dish or held a duster in her life (Coldwell, "Walking the Tightrope" 10), her journals and letters are preoccupied with domestic affairs, and her poetry is playfully infiltrated by a language of dailiness.

Like other modernist women poets, however, her poetry at times appears to waver between the language and subject of domesticity, the everyday, and the decorative, on the one hand, and the mythic, symbolic, abstract, historic, and monumental, on the other. Her ambivalence towards the domestic and the everyday reflects that of modernism, for as Christopher Reed notes, "the domestic, perpetually invoked in order to be denied, remains throughout the course of modernism, a crucial site of anxiety and subversion" (16); yet the domestic is also a site of creative tension for writers like Virginia Woolf, particularly when inflected by gender issues, such as the role of women in public and private spheres, the construction of the subject(s), or the evolution of an individual or feminine modernist language, voice, and poetic. These contradictory impulses surface in Wilkinson's poetry and prose, the contradictions themselves constituting an ongoing philosophical and poetic inquiry. In the opening lines of her best-known poem, "Lens," "The poet's daily chore / Is my long duty" (*Heresies* 82): the everyday (daily chore, duty, milk) merges with an aesthetic inquiry, what makes a poet? Dean Irvine astutely points out that "the labour of making a poem is feminized" ("Heresies" 4), but this poem, like most of Wilkinson's work, walks an aesthetic tightrope between the language and experience of the everyday, and a highly intertextual and allusive language, as in the clever image in "Lens" of "Eve and Adam, pearled / With sweat, staring at an apple core" (84).[1]

What Robert Lecker and other critics[2] have signalled as a pattern of "polar oppositions" (35) between the quick and the dead, red and green, a poet's lens and a woman's eye could be read instead as a pattern of the between or third space of uncertainty, questions, ambiguity, and contradiction: "I wish a poem to be technically finished, but spiritually to have a question mark at the end," wrote Wilkinson in her journal in December 1952 (*Tightrope Walker* 110). We might read Wilkinson's "ands" as amplifying and conjoining rather than as oppositional, keeping in mind Gilles Deleuze and Félix Guattari's image of the rhizome with its "logic of the AND" (Forlini 25) and its acentric, non-hierarchical, non-signifying system (Forlini 21). Wilkinson's "and," like the rhizome with its "logic of the AND," is characterized simultaneously and paradoxically by connection and heterogeneity, by stable configurations and the possibility of destabilizing lines of flight (Forlini 27). For example, although many poems seem to propose a binary—"Black and White" (61), "Theme and Variation" (62), "The Red and the Green" (94)—Wilkinson appears more interested in the play of contradiction, polysemy, and connection, and in destabilizing hierarchies and presuppositions, than in simple opposition. Thus, in the latter poem, the red blood of her heart is "confused" with the green world in her "new green arteries" and her blood "sings green" (95). Metaphysical questioning is transformed into literal question marks, which repeatedly close her poems. In "One or Three or Two," a title that, like the privileging of Eve in the reference to "Eve and Adam" in "Lens," disrupts our sense of order and presuppositions, Wilkinson concludes with a question and sphinx-like riddle, asking "if one joined to one / Makes ONE or three or two?" (79).

Wilkinson, like P.K. Page, Margaret Avison, Dorothy Livesay, and Phyllis Webb, struggled for recognition of the validity of her specific experience of the world and for a way to negotiate her place within the international modernist movement. How among her male mentors F.R. Scott, A.J.M.

Smith, Kildare Dobbs, Louis Dudek, Alan Crawley, and John Sutherland, some of whom were her lovers, could she carve out her own poetic voice and her own poetic forms? How best could she inscribe her pleasure in and her resistance to the role of mother, daughter, housewife, ornament, and muse poet? How could the descendant of such a wealthy, proper, and established family play the part of the bohemian, the socialist, or the sexual adventurer?

In her poems, prose, and journals, we find Wilkinson frequently querying gender roles, the position of women, and the construction of feminine subjectivity in relation to house and home since, as Marjorie Garber points out, "the longstanding symbolic association between houses and women is partly an extension of the cult of domesticity and partly a 'literal' reading of women's sexuality as something enclosed and interior" (58). In "Lens," for example, Wilkinson sets out the "contradictions in a proof" (*Heresies* 83) between her weak woman's eye and her muscled working poetic eye, while in her journals she wishes she were "a woman with female interests, a woman with a genius for making a home and soothing a man, instead of a creature with a passion for hieroglyphics" (*Tightrope Walker* 96). Amid the postwar cult of domesticity, her dedication to her art must have seemed illicit; yet, although she protests the inequitable situation of women in society and the anomalous position of the female poet in her journals, and although she complicates the "and" that both joins and opposes the *weak* woman's eye to the *muscled* working eye, in her poetry Wilkinson regularly resorts to male personae and voices, and cannot be said to feminize or subvert traditional images like the tower or the stairs in any consistent way.

Erasing the Domestic Everyday

Critical attention has focussed on the natural world, the elemental, the metaphysical, and the mythic in Wilkinson's poetry, ignoring the significance of home, belonging, and the everyday; yet we continually encounter the domestic and the everyday—particularly in her "Poems from the Copy-Books" (*Heresies* 163–203), unpublished poems, and autobiographical writings. Although they are often concealed or relegated to a casual, flippant interjection, a pun, or the surprise of the everyday amid the noumenal and green order of her poetics, the domestic and the everyday perform a vital role in the unfolding of Wilkinson's poetics, voice, and modernity.[3] House objects and the everyday leave recognizable traces, but precisely because of their banality may elude even the attentive reader. Interestingly, A.J.M. Smith, in the introduction to his 1968 collection of her work, observes that her "radiance of mind" is "cast often on small, familiar things, or things overlooked before" (xiii), but he does not subsequently dwell on these "things" in his discussion of her poetry. Perhaps this is because, as Henri Lefebvre reminds us, while the everyday is the most universal, unique, and social condition, it is also the most obvious and most hidden (34).[4]

By means of their thorough research into Wilkinson's manuscripts and unpublished writing, Joan Coldwell and Irvine alert us to A.J.M. Smith's (and others') construction of Wilkinson as a metaphysical, cosmopolitan poet. Through his elegaic reading of her life and works, and his choice of material to include in the 1968 *Collected Poems of Anne Wilkinson and a Prose Memoir*, Smith reinforces the view of Wilkinson as a poet in his own metaphysical image, a view that influenced subsequent readers.[5] In her account of editing Wilkinson's journals and autobiography, *The Tightrope Walker*, Coldwell relates some choice examples of several male mentors' domestication of Wilkinson. For example, Kildare Dobbs, her editor at Macmillan, concludes his evaluation of her manuscript, *The Hangman Ties the Holly*, by observing, "she seems to be no more than humming as she does the dishes" (qtd. in Coldwell, "Walking the Tightrope" 9). In another example, Earle Birney's card index of contributors to *Canadian Poetry* characterizes Wilkinson as a Toronto housewife without a university education (Coldwell, "Walking the Tightrope" 9). Irvine carefully traces the suppression of Wilkinson's leftist, socialist, anti-McCarthy, and anti-religious views—her heresies—by Smith, Dobbs, and John Sutherland ("Heresies"). Poems that refer to the quotidian, the banal, or the home, and resonate with a quirky, colloquial voice, were often excluded by others from Wilkinson's publications. According to Irvine, the satirical, unruly, and strikingly contemporary "Notes on Suburbia" was removed from *The Hangman Ties the Holly* by Dobbs (Irvine, Email). The opening lines of "Notes on Suburbia" reveal how she incorporates and satirizes the suburban everyday:

> 1. A BETTER HOME FOR THE EXECUTIVE TYPE
> In treeless fields, row on row
> Burgeons the ranch-style bungalow,
> Thermapane the windows yawn
> On unexecutive underpants
> Waving amputations at
> Nylons in a neighbour's lot. (191)[6]

Omissions, constructions, and suppressions by editors and publishers can be tracked through her manuscripts, published volumes, and publications in small magazines such as *Contemporary Verse*. Apparently Wilkinson deferred to her male editors and mentors, and acquiesced to their suggestions and revisions (Irvine, Introduction, *Heresies* 29–36). More difficult to trace is Wilkinson's self-censorship, which seems to manifest itself in a self-deprecatory, flippant tone—a form of distancing and defamiliarization—that permeates her work and suggests a mind and body not entirely at home. It is also possible that she resorted to the everyday, the colloquial, and the conversational precisely in order to mock and discomfit the pretensions of highbrow culture and the oppressive power of patriarchy, capitalism, and conservative politics. It is certainly striking that a number of poems that invoke the everyday and a colloquial, derisive voice were omitted from her published collections, lacunae that Irvine has corrected and documented in editing the collection, *Heresies: The Complete Poems of Anne Wilkinson, 1924–1961*.

Whereas Henri Lefevbre's concept of the everyday is that it is "simply 'real life'" (13), Gayatri Spivak redefines "the everyday, not as lived experience, some 'real' underlying consensus, but as the ongoing deconstruction of that illusion of experience" (qtd. in Langbauer 33). Since, as Lefebvre recognizes, "the 'real' is precisely what cannot be represented," everyday life may elude metaphor and "the grip of forms"; "'writing can only show an everyday life inscribed and prescribed' because 'everyday insignificance can only become meaningful when transformed into something other than everyday life'" (qtd. in Langbauer 19). The transformation of the everyday into the mythopoetic and the mythopoetic into the everyday, the juxtaposition of the decorative and the monumental, and the inscription of the everyday through pastiche, quotation, nursery rhymes, and riddles are the ways in which Wilkinson, in the modernist vein of Eliot and Pound, grapples with the "real" (Fiorindi).

Wilkinson's repeated invocation of witches, a green order, birth, death, amniotic seas of origin, underwater worlds, seasons, colours, trees, flowers, unicorns, lions, tigers, stones, sleep, and time through a "poet's eye view" (59) join representations of home and the everyday to constitute what Gaston Bachelard would call phenomenological reverberations (xxii). Out of this bricolage of elements and carefully contrived dissonance Wilkinson constructs a dwelling place for her poetic imagination: "Who has the cunning to apprehend / Even everyday easy things / Like air and wind and a fool / Or the structure and colour of a simple soul?" she queries in "One or Three or Two" (79), setting out what she perceives to be the poet's task. In her idiosyncratic fashion, Wilkinson alters our common understanding of "everyday, easy things" to involve the intangible and the metaphysical—air, wind, structure and colour of a soul. Dislocation and unhomeliness are frequently reflected in witticisms, couched in the banal and the everyday, which interrupt the poems: "In milk and curd of cheese / Guess the whey and whyfore / Of our interval need of peace" ("Letter to My Children" 190).

Symbolic Houses

For Wilkinson, house and home and their interior spaces—doors, stairs, windows, halls, and walls (and daily routines and rituals)—serve as tropes of the conflicting pleasure and difficulty of dwelling poetically in the world. In her poetics of space, houses stand as monuments, spectacles, and performances, symbolizing the historical time of family genealogies and ancestries, and furnishing the site of family romance and its unhomely aftermath. They return again and again as uncanny personifications of the sick, traumatized, or dying body, of the erotic and gendered body, and of the psyche. As Steven Harris remarks, "Potential sites for an architecture of the everyday begin with the body. Secretive and intimate, it is marked by the routine, the repetitive, and the cyclical; as the locus of desire, it is often home to the transgressive, the perverse and the abject" (4). Wilkinson's symbolic houses paradoxically shelter and disturb the construction of her self and subjectivity as woman and as poet, while also mirroring her struggle with a teleological but skeptical longing for a spiritual, edenic, or originary home, often depicted in images of a maternal, semiotic home: "Home is no longer a place, but a mother, Sukey [nurse-housekeeper], Wilson [chauffeur], even Yee [cook]. Or is it Roches Point?" (*Tightrope Walker* 181).

The oft-lamented absence of house and home reinforces her posture as a nomadic figure of modernity, a homeless, dislocated self: "I put on my body and go forth / To seek my blood," she writes in "The Red and the Green" (94). Like many other authors, she writes to make a home for herself. On 2 November 1954, in a letter to Dobbs, she complains about the task of writing *Lions in the Way*, her history of the Osler family: "My need to go back to poetry is like the acute homesickness of someone who has been, for a long time, away from his native land" (Anne Wilkinson fonds). Her desire for home—ancestral, maternal, or originary—is an echo of Heidegger's concept of poetry as a "letting-dwelling, as a—perhaps even *the*—

distinctive kind of building" (111). In "I was born a boy, and a maiden, a plant …," she writes,

> I live in only one of innumerable rooms
> When I damp the fire with purposeful breath,
> Stare at ash, sharpen
> My pencil on stone at a cold hearth (*Heresies* 80)

Wilkinson is a restless house dweller, however, and she both yearns for and resists the nostalgia of house and home. Indeed, as J. Douglas Porteous has pointed out, home cannot be understood except in terms of journey (387). Wilkinson explores this paradox in relation to an image of an enduring home. The "home" at the centre of this journey is the cottage at Roches Point, the one enduring home and the place where she did much of her writing.

> The body still goes back
> For of necessity
> It makes strange journeys,
> I, my being,
> Shut the door against return
> And in the attic pack
> One hundred summers (*Heresies* 201)

Here as elsewhere she evokes the correspondence between body, house, and psyche, yoking the everyday together with the metaphysical and elemental into her poetics of space.[7] The body metamorphoses into the elements of the green world or the interior spaces of the house through whose acres or corners the poetic persona travels and searches.[8]

For Wilkinson, the home and the body, and their unhomeliness or ugliness, reflect a postwar modernity and malaise, as well as her anxieties over her daily chore as a woman and a poet. In her contradictory presentations of home, homelessness, and the unhomely, Wilkinson exhibits a "disquieting slippage" between "what seems homely and what is definitively unhomely" (Vidler ix–x). The tropes of house, home, domesticity, the *heimlich* and the *unheimlich*—the "architectural uncanny"—open up "problems of identity around the self, the other, the body and its absence," and become a force "in interpreting the relations between the psyche and the dwelling, the body and the house, the individual and the metropolis" (Vidler x).[9] The uncanny domestic spaces in Wilkinson's poems may well reflect a "quintessential bourgeois kind of fear" best expressed and experienced "in the privacy of the interior" of the home (Vidler 4). In "After Reading Kafka," the interiority of home and self metamorphoses into the *unheimlich*, as the wounded speaker, menaced by death and lost love, feels the seeping walls with blistered fingers:

> Delicate as ears, fingers fest
> (Walls are seeping)
> Weeping blisters cry out from their tips,
> ...
> Can the wounded walk the voyage back?
> Feel their door distinct from a hundred doors? (*Heresies* 67)

In a heresy of home, Wilkinson's poems affirm dislocation and nostalgia (sickness for home); her lost poetic persona positions itself as the barred observing eye, the photograph, the windows of the house gazing out upon the world, or the lost speaker under the sea or stone, wandering through the halls of the house, mounting or tumbling down stairs, searching out the secret corners and closing doors behind her. Thus, Wilkinson recognizes how poems and houses—both constituting built forms—endeavour to make sense of the world, to imagine and create ways of being at home in a world where we do not feel at home, and to express our alienation and homesickness (Vidler 7–8). The poem turns into a desired but uneasy dwelling place, replicating the search and longing for home, rather than belonging or being at home.

Four Corners of My World

> For our house is our corner of the world. (Bachelard 4)

> Memory is inscribed not only in narratives, but in gestures, in the body's mannerisms. And the narratives are like gestures, related to gestures, places, proper names. The stories speak themselves on their own. They are language honouring the house, and the house serving language. (Lyotard, "Domus and the Megalopolis" 272)

When Wilkinson opens her prose memoir, "Four Corners of My World,"[10] with the observation that "three houses dominated our London (Ontario) world: Lornehurst, Eldon, and our own" (Smith 1968, 181), she draws us into a Bachelardian poetics of domestic space where imagination, intimacy, and subjectivity are mediated by houses redolent with personality and atmosphere, which leave their traces upon a highly sensitive child and "where the trees and the family are temples" ("Summer Acres," *Heresies* 52). Wilkinson's writings instantiate Gaston Bachelard's famous dictum that the "house image would appear to have become the topography of our intimate being" (xxxvi). Bachelard's *haut bourgeois* background resonates with Wilkinson's own privileged, Edwardian, eccentric upbringing within an Upper Canadian moneyed and propertied family of distinguished lineage.[11] Both Bachelard and Wilkinson spent their childhoods in spacious city and country houses whose hidden corners, winding stairs, towers, attics, and pastoral settings invoke nostalgic spaces for privacy, intimacy, and reverie. We must remember, therefore, as we wander through Wilkinson's unhomely, that her abiding sense of house and home and her experience of domestic space and life emerged out of a socially prominent and wealthy milieu, cushioned by a bevy of servants—cooks, gardeners, housekeepers, nannies. Washing dishes and preparing meals—"the daily chore" ("Lens," *Heresies* 82)—were beyond the scope of her experience. Servants carried out domestic chores and minded her children, giving her the time and space and privacy for reading and writing denied most of her contemporary women writers. When, in remembering "houses" and "rooms," she tries to "abide" within herself (Bachelard xxxvii), the remembered houses and rooms of time past have an affinity with the celebrated and privileged houses that fanned the imaginations of Virginia Woolf, Henry James, Marcel Proust, T.S. Eliot, and Emily Dickinson.[12]

The four corners of Wilkinson's world are located in four houses of her childhood: London (Eldon House), Toronto (Craigleigh), California (Bambooland), and Roches Point, Lake Simcoe (the Lodge and Lakeside Cottage). Comparing this memoir with the unfinished but more extensive autobiography she edited for *The Tightrope Walker,* Coldwell protests that the memoir domesticates Anne, that the focus shifts from associations with the mother to places and family connections, and that the voice is "that of a well-informed docent leading a tour of historic houses" ("Walking the Tightrope" 17). However, it is important to acknowledge that in the memoir Wilkinson is mapping out the topography of her imagination in the fertile ground of recollected houses and landscapes; house and home are warmly identified with the mother, and the voice initiates us into the house image as a site of intimacy and reverie. For example, the playful substitution of "world" for "room" indicates the centrality of the correspondence between self and domestic space for Wilkinson.

There are many houses, more than four, in the mansion of childhood, and in different ways they all assume importance in her poetic imaginary. On the paternal Gibbons side there are the homes in London: Lornehurst, Eldon, their own, and later, the "dark Victorian house with two acres of old-fashioned garden" in Goderich where her father lay dying (Wilkinson, *Tightrope Walker* 199). The sunlit Bambooland in California symbolizes seemingly carefree, vagabond childhood days spent with her mother and siblings. Then, on the maternal Osler side are the thirteen-acre Osler estate, Craigleigh, in Rosedale, and her most cherished home, Roches Point on Lake Simcoe. This vast eighty-acre Osler property, originally landscaped by Frederick Olmsted of Central Park fame, had been acquired in 1885. Sir Edmund Osler then distributed the summer houses on the property to his children: Beechcroft to his son; the Lodge to Mary, Anne Wilkinson's mother, where the "lakeside cottage" was later added; and a portion of the property to his other daughter, Annabel, on which she and her husband built Cottage-in-the-Field. It is here at Roches Point where Anne wrote most freely, and where a number of poems—"Summer Acres," "Roches Point," "Lake Song," " A Sorrow of Stones"—are discernibly situated. There were also temporary homes in London and New York, and then several Toronto homes in the wealthy Rosedale area during and after marriage to her physician husband, Robert Wilkinson.

Wilkinson's spirited history of the Osler family, *Lions in the Way*, is narrated through the different family houses, and she describes the homes and home lives of family members in lavish detail: Cornwall, England, in the early nineteenth century; settler life in Upper Canada in the 1830s, which ranged from a vermin-infested one-room shack to the parish-built Parsonage House in Tecumseh, Ontario; and England again with Sir William Osler's house in Oxford. The book closes with an epilogue, which is a house biography of Craigleigh from 1919 to 1924, the period when Anne and her family moved in with Edmund Osler, her grandfather, following her father's death.

With their anglophile names and anthropomorphic features, these venerable houses, "visible histories of personal and collective life" (Chandler 11), are simultaneously sites for reverie and prisons of an extended family life. In imitation of the European tradition of family estates and manor houses signifying patriarchal lineage, social status, and class, the Oslers and the Gibbons were defined by their homes. Successive generations manipulated and were manipulated by the tyranny of the family house. Within the houses, a rigid social order and set routines and conventions were prescribed and perpetuated. In her journal, Wilkinson writes of a visit to her estranged husband: "I got up to leave, saying it was lunch time. [Dr.] Bill Mustard was to arrive shortly and he [her husband] wanted me to stay. I told him I couldn't keep my mother's staff waiting for dinner" (*Tightrope Walker* 97).

The outside façades of these impressive houses registered a personality and demeanour, synedoche of the family and the body of the family, while their domestic interiors, decorations, and furnishings supplied an abode for the imagination—a confusing hybrid of nostalgia, entrapment, longing, and comfort. "It is impossible," writes Lyotard, "to think or write without some façade of a house at least rising up, a phantom, to receive and to make a work of our peregrinations" (275). Throughout her prose writing—memoir, autobiography, family history—Wilkinson turns the narrative around the pivotal trope of the house, which embodies and personifies the family and family history. In "The Autobiography," Wilkinson reminisces,

> Eldon ... is a house of many faces, a storeroom with layer upon layer of memories; the open house of childhood and of youth; later the sombre one that contained my aunt and her illness ... We loved [Lornehurst] for its size, the dark halls and elaborate ugliness, which didn't seem ugly to us, only strange and exotic ... a door led to a stair that led to the top of the tower. But the door was locked. Years ago someone had fallen; we did not know who, or if the fall had ended in death. We only knew that it would never be opened again, that the tower, our heart's desire, was forbidden us. (*Tightrope Walker* 192–93)

Both Freud and Jung analyze the representation of the human figure and psyche as a house in dreams. However, highly evocative objects like towers, locked doors, windows, keys, and stairs are not only metaphors of a collective unconscious or repressed desire, but, as Bachelard insists, the inspiration for reverie and poetry. Wilkinson was certainly well versed in Freud and Jung, and references to uncanny domestic spaces, locked doors, staircases (up to attics or down to cellars) leading to death, dark halls, towers, and keys are captured from childhood memories and resonate with literary echoes; these images recur, sometimes ironically, throughout her poems, as in "Tower Lullaby":

> Climb, as a child easy with circles
> Spins to the tower
> ...

> The stair is soft;
> . . .
> The stair is bare-faced stone;
> So creak on curv-
> Ing rock or leap
> From turf to the top, to the turret.
> Then, panting, lean
> The moment, prop
> It on the parapet
> Before it tumbles
> Over and old again
> Climb again
> Young again
> Sleep. (*Heresies* 64–65)

Here is a Wilkinsonian mix of the archaic, the old world (turret, parapet), the colloquial echoing childhood songs and rhymes, the allusions to nineteenth-century poems (Lord Tennyson's "The Lady of Shalott," Robert Browning's "Childe Roland to the Dark Tower Came," and W.B. Yeats's "The Tower"), the shock of defamiliarization ("over and old again"), and the grounding in the visceral and the concrete ("bare-faced stone") (*Heresies* 65). The structure of the poem itself is architectural, replicating the long, narrow, tapering tower; inevitably the tower is suggestive of a transcendental signifier, the phallus, the forbidden, and the plunge to death, as well as the ascent to the poetic imagination, idealism, and aloofness from the ground world of experience.[13] Wilkinson domesticates an old world symbol and repackages it in an imagist mode. Her poetry, like her prose, often revolves around domestic spaces and objects such as windows, towers, doors, stairs, but their function in the poems as interface between body, psyche, and the material world resonates not only with Wilkinson's childhood memories but also with mythic and literary echoes, often deployed whimsically, parodically, or self-deprecatorily, a not unfamiliar feminine strategy.

The symbolic domestic space of windows is presented in Wilkinson's description of Craigleigh in *Lions in the Way*:

> The Craigleigh nursery had four barred windows. The two facing south gave us a distant view of street life. We knew our elders lied when they told us how lucky we were, with thirteen acres at our disposal, while the Nanton Avenue children were confined to city sidewalks. But they lied in

innocence for they believed that by having too much we had everything. (226–27)

Although barred windows were customary in nurseries, the contradiction represented in this oxymoron—the view or gaze upon that which is forbidden, the separation between inner protected and privileged space and the plebian but seductive outer space—reverberates with contradictions invoked throughout the poems. As Georg Simmel remarks, "the teleological emotion with respect to the window is directed almost exclusively from inside to outside: it is there for looking out, not for looking in" (68). The window "creates the connection between the inner and the outer chronically and continually, as it were, by virtue of its transparency" but the connection is in a one-sided direction "just like the limitation upon it to be a path merely for the eye" (68).

In the physiognomy of houses, windows are eyes: they are the means by which those inside engage in surveillance of the public outside world; they are also openings upon the interior of the house, the soul of the body. If, as Freud suggests, windows and doors stand for openings in the body, the Craigleigh windows, as remembered by Wilkinson, offer a contradictory message of a restricted opening (Chandler 11). This barred window, view, or eye reflects Wilkinson's recurring image of the lens, the poet's eye view, or the one good eye, and her theme of vision that, following her practice of dwelling in contradiction, is sometimes blurred, sometimes visionary. As Wilkinson reflects in her journal on 31 May 1951, "The artist, as much or more than anyone, is shaken by the bats and witches flapping about in the attic of his solitude… To see *anything* clearly you have to have seen it with the inaccurate organ of the eye and then again and again when the eye is shut and the imagination supplies the meaning that the eye has missed" (*Tightrope Walker* 88). By means of this paradox of blinded vision or imprisoning privilege, Wilkinson opens up an in-between space, a third space, a question.

Another form of embodiment of houses occurs when death enters: the house as site of family romance, ritual, and heritage turns unhomely in both Bhabha's and Freud's sense. When the family romance is shattered, the house, in a form of domestic fallacy, mourns and sickens. Home sick. Sick home. Body and buildings are dismembered, fractured, and diseased; they weep, seep, and blister. Wilkinson remembers the Goderich house as an incarnation of her father's death: "This clumsy brooding house with its twisted pictures of dragons, its elaborate engravings of hell, becomes a symbol of everyone's despair … we never go back to London at all, except to visit, later, when we are older" (*Tightrope Walker* 199). London, Ontario, is ever after tinged with grey by death. More than forty years later, Wilkinson laments her homesickness: "Children transplant happily enough if it is done as a family, intact. But we were uprooted by storm and not bedded back in our own earth. And we are homesick still" (*Tightrope Walker* 200). From the time of relocation to Toronto and Craigleigh, Wilkinson speaks of her psychic and physical dislocation, of herself as homeless and longing for a home, as a DP (displaced person), a kind of Benjaminian rootless modern artist (Bhabha 449).

Writing Home

During the years of the dissolution of her marriage and her divorce in 1954, when her own family romance disintegrates, the idea/l of the house as sanctuary is undone. The connection between home and writing is undeniable. Writing in her journal after the divorce, she insists, "I hate my room, the house, the smell, the endless ugly furniture ... No new poetry for months. I knew I wouldn't write in this house" (*Tightrope Walker* 99). A few months later, on 7 July 1952 from the Lodge at Roches Point, she observes, "Caged in a bedroom ... Somehow, somewhere, I will find a house where I can grow and put down roots—or better still, slip beyond the point of needing my own possessions, garden ... I think that every poem I've written in the last year has had the word "home" in it at least once. A displaced person must be acutely conscious of the psychological dangers" (*Tightrope Walker* 106). The unease occasioned by her experience of the *unheimlich*, coiled wormlike within the homeplace, also inspires and shapes her poetry, furnishing it with wit, edge, and ironic distance; and it is during these difficult years that she began writing in earnest, perturbed by an escalating apprehension of the unhomely as reflected in the closing image of "the home sweet hearth of hell" in "A Folk Tale: With a Warning to Lovers" (*Heresies* 53). In her journal, she ponders the effects of the unhomely on her writing: "During the last year I have moved away from my old mystical moods of identification with earth and animals and plants to a more human situation ... But, at odd moments, I am homesick, as an adolescent mourns her childhood, for the peaceful intoxication of fusion with the green growing world, although I came to see it as a dead end, an escape from being a person" (*Tightrope Walker* 93). Thus, writing about Roches Point in "Summer Acres," she concedes that, although "My eyes are wired to the willow / ... My ears are tied to the tattle of water," and "Here, in my body's home my heart dyes red" (*Heresies* 51–52).

Although she could not write in *that* house (4 Cluny Drive), through her writing she continually seeks to build a habitable space. From the safe space of Roches Point, she advises herself, "Plan a long poem. Keep notebook of ideas and lines. Decide on theme then play the variations, each thing going a step further from the original; conclude by bringing the whole thing [like the voyaging Ulysses] *home*" (*Tightrope Walker* 89).[14] She had attempted to construct a mythopoetic, elemental world (Irvine, "Poetics") out of a green order with exotic and mythical creatures, bringing the foreign and the monstrous into the domestic, and letting them clash—lions, tigers, unicorns—in the hope of giving birth to a home in the world. Her domestication of mythical, magical, exotic *foreign* creatures—the Other—and their reincarnation into the everyday indicate a subversion of master narratives and authoritative voices. In the poem "Unicorn," when the speaker opens the "black door" and "[shakes] the rain / From my good eye," the unicorn runs down her "tumbling stair" (*Heresies* 133). In another fragment from the notebooks, she pushes the juxtaposition of the everyday and the exotic through playful images, a domestic voice, and sexual innuendo and puns (trunk, key) further into flippancy, when an "elephant" lover visits her home and amuses her children, but confounds her with his "trunk":

> An elephant came to stay with us
> For a week or two
> The children were glad to see him
> But
> *I* didn't know what to do with his trunk.
> When I murmured "shall I unpack for you?"
> He blushed (it turns an elephant blue)
> Replying in sorrow
> "Perhaps tomorrow
> I'll find the key." (*Heresies* 164)

Often her search for a primeval home signifies an amniotic womb world, an underwater world, a maternal body, a Kristevan semiotic *chora*. Each section of "Four Corners of My World" begins with the association of Wilkinson's mother with the house in question (Coldwell, Introduction xi). In "Lake Song," the first love poem she wrote (*Tightrope Walker* 18), she concludes, "The arms of my lover will carry me home to the sea" (*Heresies* 63).

In "Amphibian Shores" she calls from the bottom of the sea, "We cry 'A house!,' choke, / A thatch of sea-weed is green-growing roof" (*Heresies* 175). In "The Great Winds," she narrates, "Once upon a briny while ago / The sea was home" (*Heresies* 69).

Wilkinson represents her sense of self in terms of mental and physical dislocation, "a naked snail lost without a towering shell" (*Tightrope Walker* 95). This body/house is at times ridden with guilt (at her divorce) or anxiety, and flayed by malady; at other times, it is gleeful, erotic, and rooted in earth, air, water, and fire. It is subjected to dissection, drowning, disfigurement, dismemberment, metamorphosis, and reincarnation: "I'd love this body more / If graved in rigid wood," she observes in "Still Life" (60). In "After Reading Kafka," she writes,

> Here at my door I swing between obsessions:
> Hall by day, corridor by night.
> I am obsessed with exits ...
> I tear my foot ... but if it bleeds
> I do not know (*Heresies* 65–67)

In "Nature Be Damned," she claims, "I was a witch and I could be / Bird or leaf / Or branch and bark of tree" (121). In "Virginia Woolf, "Her coral remnants lie / Where fishes keep their watch by night" (113); and in "Fishwife,"

> Down you dive
> ...
> And quick with jumping silver knife
> You slit my tail, that we may love
> Without impediment (*Heresies* 197)

"Summer Storm" emphasizes the body's permeability: "Skull's skin is paper thin/ Migraine is seeping in" (*Heresies* 163). The body, however, seems an unhomely home, for Wilkinson continually suffered and wrote about illness: hers, her children's, and her extended family's.

Metaphysical Maladies

Sick home. Home sick.

In her prose and poetry, the ailing psyche and the disease stricken body are manifested in the walls and rooms of the house, which is represented as a working, organic body. As she remarks with relief in her journal on 4 February 1948, "the hustle and bustle of acute illness subsides into convalescence. It is in the house itself, in the walls, floating down from ceilings and rising from floors" (*Tightrope Walker* 6). In "After Reading Kafka," she transmits a Kafkaesque malaise onto the door, hall, and walls of the house:

>   —Signal
> If you touch an opening in the line to home!
> Delicate as ears, fingers fest
> (Walls are seeping)
> Weeping blisters cry out from their tips. (*Heresies* 67)

The house, like the body, is traumatized.

Unlike Emily Dickinson, whose persona "I" repeatedly spoke from a concealed position, and whom Wilkinson admired (Fuss 1–46), Wilkinson's own poetic self is nomadic, a time–space traveller, swimming under the sea, tumbling down stairs, rooting in gardens, a self who crosses genders and assumes multiple voices and masks: puritan, Kafka, boy, maiden, plant, witch, tightrope walker, mermaid, Virginia Woolf, to name a few.

In one of the early (1946) notebook poems, "Claustrophobia," omitted from the 1968 *Collected Poems*, the room transforms into an analogy of the poet's skull, body, psyche, and the world. It seems to be a migraine poem, like "Summer Storm," quoted above, and the later "Dissection,"

> We crawl though craniums, stare
> Beneath the bone at spasms …
> And while we squint to focus microscopes,
> Dissect each bleeding head,
> Sun bursts in splendour from the attic skull (*Heresies* 71).[15]

The room takes on the topography of a disturbed, entrapped inner being and an ailing body. The four walls are a manifestation of the quaternity she expresses in the four elements (wind, air, water, earth), four corners, and four houses.[16] The blind window, like the "barred windows" described earlier, presents the poet's eye view (positioned here in a liminal domestic space between inside and out and between mind and world) as limited, inward gazing, self-deceiving, and blind—but also as visionary. Imprisoned in this enclosed space, which is also that of the body and mind, the subject's position is one of immobility:

> I do not know if I can move
> Inside this little room
> It has four walls,
> Four seem enough
> But they enclose a square
> And any way I walk
> Is equi-distant there.
> It has a blind square window
> With an endless view
> Of four square walls—
> I beat my head
> To see if pain's the clue. ("Claustrophobia," *Heresies* 169)

Oddly, earlier variants of the last two lines offer more lyrical and less pedestrian concluding images: "Walls without / A shadow for a clue"; "Walls and a window / No shadow for a clue"; "Walls within / A room devoid of view" (*Heresies* 294). Why did Wilkinson settle for the less evocative, more colloquial and literal ending? Was it a desire to ground the poem even further in the everyday and the body? Or was this another of her habitual turns to flippancy and mockery? Or was it an attempt to escape from the terrors of the uncanny within home and self?

It may be that, as Lyotard suggests, "the domestic world does not cease to operate on our possibility to writing, right up to the disaster of the houses ... Thought cannot want its house. But the house haunts it" (277). It may be that the everyday provided the scaffolding but also the nemesis for Wilkinson's life and poetry. She was indeed haunted by the idea of home.

Notes

An earlier version of this essay appeared in *Studies in Canadian Literature* 30.1 (2005) and is reprinted here with the journal's permission. I would like to thank Dean Irvine for his generosity in sharing ideas and materials on Anne Wilkinson and in sending me poems and information on the domestic in Anne Wilkinson. I would also like to thank and acknowledge Chiara Briganti, who is working with me on a project on domestic space, and Barbara Godard for her invaluable support and comments. My thanks also to the Special Collections of the Thomas Fisher Rare Book Room of the University of Toronto. Despite recent interest in modernism in Canada, such as the conference and collection *The Canadian Modernists Meet* (2005), as yet little attention has been paid to Wilkinson's work. All quotations from Wilkinson's poetry are from *Heresies: The Complete Poems of Anne Wilkinson, 1924–1961*, unless otherwise noted.

1. Note how Eve precedes Adam.
2. See, for example, Robert Lecker, "Better Quick Than Dead: Anne Wilkinson's Poetry," Douglas Barbour, "Day Thoughts on Anne Wilkinson's Poetry"; and Wendy Keitner, "Canadian Women Poets and the Syndrome of the Female Man: A Note on the Poetry of Audrey Alexandra Brown and Anne Wilkinson."
3. I like Homi Bhabha's take on Freud's unhomely, which he perceives as capturing "something of the estranging sense of the relocation of the home and the world in an unhallowed place ... the shock of recognition of the world-in the-home, the home-in-the-world" (445).
4. We should remember that although Lefebvre admits that the everyday weighs heaviest on women, yet it provides them realms for fantasy, desire, rebellion, and assertion (McLeod 18). He also felt that because of their ambiguous position in everyday life, women were incapable of understanding it (Langbauer 21).
5. See Smith's "Introduction: A Reading of Anne Wilkinson" in the 1968 *Collected Poems* and an earlier version of this essay, "A Reading of Anne Wilkinson," in *Canadian Literature*.
6. In a letter to Wilkinson on 16 February 1955, Louis Dudek writes that her not-to-be-published poems are all excellent, if more or less crazy, and that he would run "Suburbia" right away (in *CIV/n*) if she weren't so possessive about them (Anne Wilkinson fonds).
7. See Dean Irvine's description: "Wilkinson's 'imaginal attic' is filled with both elemental and memorial images; it is an imaginal house, a dwelling-place for archetypal images of her family's lived body and world. But the attic is moreover resonant of death: it is a place where relics of past lives and of dead relatives are stored ... [It] is the home of her 'elemental being'—a corner of her family's life, and death, detached from her 'body's home'" ("Poetics" 47). However, for Bachelard and Jung, the attic is a privileged site of spirituality, the intellect, and reverie, one suggesting opening of the boundaries of the self; it is opposite to the cellar, which represents the unconscious and enclosure, forces that may contain and constrain the creative self. Rather than a place of death, the attic has now become a storage place, holding the treasure house of memories of a family; these memories could lock the dreamer into the past instead of allowing the mind to roam among the elements.
8. For example, "stanza" is Italian for room. Frederic Jameson, in thinking about built space as a kind of language, deliberates whether "words of built space, or at least its substantives, would seem to be rooms, categories which are syntactically or syncategorematically related and articulated by the various spatial verbs and adverbs—corridors, doorways and staircases, for example, modified in turn by adjectives in the form of paint and furnishings, decoration and ornament ... these 'sentences'—if that indeed is what a building can be said to 'be'—are read by readers whose bodies fill the various shifter-slots and subject-positions; while the larger text into which such units are inserted can be assigned to the text-grammar of the urban" (261).
9. Vidler also goes onto to say that "the uncanny has been interpreted as a dominant constituent of modern nostalgia, with a corresponding spatiality that touches all aspects of social life" (x).
10. This fragment was first published in *Tamarack Review* 20 in 1961 (pp. 28–52) and reprinted by Smith in *The Collected Poems of Anne Wilkinson and a Prose Memoir* (1968 181–207), and by Coldwell in *The Tightrope Walker: Autobiographical Writings of Anne Wilkinson* (1992 163–247).

11 Her uncle was Sir William Osler, the famous physician; her grandfather, Sir Edmund Osler, was the president of the Dominion Bank, member of Parliament, and a patron of the Royal Ontario Museum and the Art Gallery of Ontario.
12 As Bachelard so eloquently puts it, "Of course, thanks to the house, a great many of our memories are housed, and if the house is a bit elaborate, if it has a cellar and a garret, nooks and corridors, our memories have refuges that are all the more clearly delineated ... All our lives we come back to them in our daydreams" (8).
13 Bettina Knapp suggests that Jung's tower is an architectural metaphor for an inner psychic climate (vi).
14 In a comment to me, Barbara Godard noted that it's interesting that Wilkinson identifies with voyaging Ulysses rather than with Penelope at home, weaving and waiting.
15 An early variation is "bloody skull"; it is interesting to note that she brings in the house image to render her phrase more tangible and concrete (*Heresies* 219).
16 See Joan Coldwell, "Wilkinson, Anne," and Dean Irvine, "A Poetics of the Elemental Imagination," for an analysis of Wilkinson's quaternity.

Works Cited

Bachelard, Gaston. *The Poetics of Space*. Trans. M. Jolas. Boston: Beacon, 1994.
Barbour, Douglas. "Day Thoughts on Anne Wilkinson's Poetry." *A Mazing Space: Writing Canadian Women Writing*. Ed. Shirley Neuman and Smaro Kamboureli. Edmonton: Longspoon/Newest, 1986. 179–90.
Bhabha, Homi K. "The World and the Home," *Dangerous Liaisons: Gender, Nation, and Postcolonial Perspectives*. Ed. Anne McClintock, Aamir Mufti, Ellen Shohat. Minneapolis: U of Minnesota P, 1997. 445–55.
Chandler, Marilyn R. *Dwelling in the Text: Houses in American Fiction*. Berkeley: U of California P, 1991.
Coldwell, Joan. "Introduction." *The Tightrope Walker: Autobiographical Writings of Anne Wilkinson*. Ed. Joan Coldwell. Toronto: U of Toronto P, 1992. vii–xvii.
———. "Walking the Tightrope with Anne Wilkinson." *Editing Women*. Ed. Ann M. Hutchison. Toronto: U of Toronto P, 1995. 3–25.
———. "Wilkinson, Anne." *The Oxford Companion to Canadian Literature*. Toronto: Oxford UP, 1983. 831–32.
Deleuze, Gilles, and Félix Guattari. *A Thousand Plateaus: Capitalism and Schizophrenia*. Trans. Brian Massumi. Minneapolis: U of Minnesota P, 1987.
Dudek, Louis. Letter to A. Wilkinson. 16 February 1955. Wilkinson Papers.
Fiorindi, Lisa. "Into the 'Curd and Why of Memory': The Use and Subversion of the Nursery Rhyme in the Poetry of Anne Wilkinson." Paper presented at "'Wider Boundaries of Daring': The Modernist Impulse in Canadian Women's Poetry." Conf. held at University of Windsor, Windsor, ON. 25–28 October 2001.
Forlini, Stefania. "Learning to Read Literary Machines." Unpublished paper. 2002.
Freud, Sigmund. "The Uncanny." *The Standard Edition of the Complete Psychological Works of Sigmund Freud*. 24 vols. London: Hogarth, 1955. 17:217–52.

Fuss, Diana. "Interior Chambers: The Emily Dickinson Homestead." *Differences: A Journal of Feminist Cultural Studies* 10.5 (1998): 1–46.
Garber, Marjorie. *Sex and Real Estate: Why We Love Houses*. New York: Pantheon, 2000.
Harris, Steven. "Everyday Architecture." *Architecture of the Everyday*. Eds. Steven Harris and Deborah Berke. New York: Princeton UP, 1997. 1–8.
Heidegger, Martin. "… Poetically Man Dwells …" *Rethinking Architecture: A Reader in Cultural Theory*. Ed. Neil Leach. London: Routledge, 1997. 109–19.
Irvine, Dean, ed. *The Canadian Modernists Meet*. Ottawa: U of Ottawa P, 2005.
———. Email to K. Mezei. 14 June 2001.
———. "Heresies and Other Poems: An Editorial Postscript to Anne Wilkinson." Unpublished paper presented at the Association of Canadian College and University Teachers of English annual conference, Congress of the Social Sciences and Humanities, Université Laval. May 2001.
———. "A Poetics of the Elemental Imagination: Anne Wilkinson's Poetry and Autobiographical Writings." MA thesis. University of Calgary, 1996.
———. Introduction. *Heresies: The Complete Poems of Anne Wilkinson, 1924–1961*. Ed. Dean Irvine. Montreal: Signal Editions, 2003. 19–47.
Jameson, Frederic. "Is Space Political?" *Rethinking Architecture: A Reader in Cultural Theory*. Ed. Neil Leach. London: Routledge, 1997. 255–69.
Jung, C.G. *Memories, Dreams, Reflections*. Trans. Richard Winston and Clara Winston. New York: Pantheon Books, 1963.
Keitner, Wendy. "Canadian Women Poets and the Syndrome of the Female Man: A Note on the Poetry of Audrey Alexandra Brown and Anne Wilkinson." *Tessera* 1 / *Room of One's Own: A Feminist Journal* 8.4 (1984): 76–81.
Knapp, Bettina L. *Archetype, Architecture, and the Writer*. Bloomington: Indiana UP, 1986.
Langbauer, Laurie. *Novels of Everyday Life: The Series in English Fiction, 1850–1930*. Ithaca: Cornell UP, 1999.
Lecker, Robert. "Better Quick Than Dead: Anne Wilkinson's Poetry." *Studies in Canadian Literature* 3 (1978): 35–36.
Lefebvre, Henri. "The Everyday and Everydayness." *Architecture of the Everyday*. Ed. Steven Harris and Deborah Berke. New York: Princeton UP, 1997. 32–37.
Lyotard, Jean-François. "*Domus* and the Megalopolis." *Rethinking Architecture: A Reader in Cultural Theory*. Ed. Neil Leach. London: Routledge, 1997. 271–79.
McLeod, Mary. "Henri Lefebvre's Critique of Everyday Life: An Introduction." *Architecture of the Everyday*. Ed. Steven Harris and Deborah Berke. New York: Princeton UP, 1997. 9–29.
Porteous, J. Douglas. "Home: The Territorial Core." *Geographical Review* 66.4 (1976): 383–90.
Reed, Christopher. Introduction. *Not at Home: The Suppression of Domesticity in Modern Art and Architecture*. Ed. C. Reed. London: Thames and Hudson, 1996. 7–17.

Simmel, Georg. "Bridge and Door." *Rethinking Architecture: A Reader in Cultural Theory.* Ed. Neil Leach. London: Routledge, 1997. 66–69.

Smith, A.J.M. "Introduction: A Reading of Anne Wilkinson." *The Collected Poems of Anne Wilkinson and a Prose Memoir.* By A. Wilkinson. Ed. A.J.M. Smith. Toronto: Macmillan, 1968.

———. "A Reading of Anne Wilkinson." *Canadian Literature* 10 (Autumn 1961): 32–39.

Vidler, Anthony. *The Architectural Uncanny: Essays in the Modern Unhomely.* Cambridge: MIT P, 1996.

Wilkinson, Anne. Anne Wilkinson fonds. MS Coll. 29. Thomas Fisher Rare Book Library, University of Toronto, Toronto, ON.

———. *The Collected Poems of Anne Wilkinson and a Prose Memoir.* Ed. A.J.M. Smith. Toronto: Macmillan, 1968.

———. "Four Corners of My World." *Tamarack Review* 20 (1961): 28–52. Rpt. in Wilkinson, *Collected Poems,* and *Poetry of Anne Wilkinson and a Prose Memoir.*

———. *Heresies: The Complete Poems of Anne Wilkinson, 1924–1961.* Ed. Dean Irvine. Montreal: Véhicule, 2003.

———. *Lions in the Way: A Discursive History of the Oslers.* Toronto: Macmillan, 1956.

———. *The Poetry of Anne Wilkinson and a Prose Memoir.* Ed. Joan Coldwell. Toronto: Exile Editions, 1990.

———. *The Tightrope Walker: Autobiographical Writings of Anne Wilkinson.* Ed. Joan Coldwell. Toronto: U of Toronto P, 1992.

Anne Marriott
Modernist on the Periphery
MARILYN J. ROSE

Anne Marriott (1913–97) is a little-known Canadian poet of the modernist period, despite having produced seven books of poetry, beginning with *The Wind Our Enemy* (1939) and ending with her last collection, *Aqua* (1991), published almost a half-century later. She also left a substantial body of poetry that appeared in literary periodicals but has never been collected. Much of her work is haunting and evocative, spare and laconic, utterly in tune with the aesthetics of the great modernist women poets of the twentieth century—the "quiet objectiveness" advocated by Marianne Moore, for example, or the hard, clear "concentration" advocated by Amy Lowell. However, Marriott's oeuvre, the substantial work of a lifetime, has not been collected, and a critical biography has yet to be written. That Anne Marriott has virtually disappeared from view is mysterious, given her long writing life and the fact that she was still publishing poetry into the 1990s. Her contemporaries, P.K. Page, Dorothy Livesay, and Elizabeth Brewster, are all better remembered, while Marriott appears to have slid from critical view at some crucial point during the development of the Canadian modernist canon.

Poets who "disappear" in this way do so by critical edict. In "editing out" some at the expense of others, editors, anthologists, historians, and literary critics govern as much by acts of omission as by acts of inclusion, and those whom they "marginalize" deserve reconsideration if one seeks to investigate the whole cloth from which certain aesthetic sails have been trimmed over a period of time. At the same time, however, the question of a poet's having been relegated to cultural margins is a complex one. To what extent can a poet be said to have been "relegated" to ostensible "margins," and to what extent is exile from "the centre" a demonstrable handicap, in the long run, given the complications and permutations of a long working life?

In Marriott's case, the question of marginalization is indeed complicated. Her geographic isolation and familial circumstances need to be considered, as does her publishing history, her relationship with her early mentors, her long period of poetic silence between the publication of *Sandstone and Other Poems* (1945) and *Countries* (1971), and her subsequent fate at the hands of the modernist anthologists who shaped the Canadian literature teaching canon that persists, in large measure, into our own time. At the same time, it must be acknowledged that Marriott had certain advantages, particularly at the beginning of her career, that militate against reading her simplistically as a hapless victim of hostile cultural forces. In the end, the cumulative effect of marginalization on Anne Marriott's voice and vision invites critical scrutiny. In reconstructing Marriott's life (as imperfect as that process is) and attempting to tell her story (as interested as such telling always is), issues of critical gatekeeping and exclusionary practices surface, but so does a sense of the way in which marginalization ultimately may have served this lyric poet well, given Marriott's own aesthetic responses to peripherality—which is to say her fascination with edges, margins, borders, restraints, and enclosures of various kinds, and ultimately their recessiveness, their "unbreachability." Would Marriott have been other than a poet of peripherality, even if embraced by the metropolitan centre, as she was not, except in earliest days? Such a question, while not easily answerable, offers fruitful ground for critical exploration.

Anne Marriott is quite literally a poet of Canada's margins. Born in Victoria in 1913 and educated in private schools there, she lived virtually all of her life in British Columbia—Victoria, Prince George, and Vancouver. While often characterized as a "prairie writer," because most famous for having written the spectacular long poem *The Wind Our Enemy* while in her twenties (a poem she actually wrote after visiting relatives in Saskatchewan for a few weeks in 1937, during the Great Depression), Marriott was fundamentally a west coast writer, with significant literary connections there. She was a founder with Dorothy Livesay, Floris McLaren, Doris Ferne, and Alan Crawley of the literary magazine *Contemporary Verse* in Victoria in 1941. For a time in the 1940s, she was the poetry columnist for the Victoria *Daily Times* (1943–44). While she worked briefly as a scriptwriter for the National Film

Board of Canada in Ottawa and produced more than seventy-five broadcast scripts for CBC radio, by 1947 Marriott had married and returned to British Columbia for good. There she would spend the rest of her life caring for a family of three adopted children and an almost blind father, under often difficult circumstances, while working as a journalist, broadcaster, and teacher of writing workshops in order to pay the bills. Clearly, the demands of family and the need for establishing a writerly livelihood far from Canada's economic centre blunted Marriott's impetus as a creative writer in significant ways. In her case, as in that of many other women poets with complicated family lives, the conditions of daily life contributed significantly to an unevenness and intermittency of poetic output.

Initially, Marriott's geographic peripherality was not a serious barrier to publication. While located far from the ostensible centre of incipient Canadian modernism in her early days—which is to say the Montreal–Toronto publishing axis associated with editors E.J. Pratt, Lorne Pierce, and A.J.M. Smith, amongst others, during the first half of the twentieth century—the writing community in British Columbia was quite highly developed during the 1930s and 1940s, and influential with respect to little magazine culture in Canada. As Dean Irvine notes in his unpublished thesis on the role of little magazines and women writers between 1926 and 1956,[1] two poetry journals of considerable influence during this period, *Canadian Poetry Magazine* (the official organ of the Canadian Authors Association [CAA]) and *Contemporary Verse* (1941–52), had close connections with West Coast branches of the CAA, particularly in Victoria in the 1940s. *Canadian Poetry Magazine*, for which Annie Marriott served as associate editor under Earle Birney's editorship, was published by the CAA and homed in Toronto, but was edited by Birney from the University of British Columbia between 1946 and 1948. *Contemporary Verse*, the more significant publication of the two in terms of Canadian modernism, was founded by four women poets, McLaren, Livesay, Ferne, and Marriott, as members of the CAA's Victoria branch; they wished to move beyond the too often romantic and Georgian overtones of that branch's annual publication, *The Victoria Poetry Chapbook*. Their choice of Alan Crawley as editor and Crawley's agreement to edit the magazine sought to ensure that *Contemporary Verse* would be published out of Victoria, and that it would emulate and uphold the standards of *Poetry* (Chicago), edited by Harriet Monroe.

Hence it must be recognized that while she was situated geographically at the perceived margins of Canadian modernism, Anne Marriott's connections to the *Contemporary Verse* poets and to Alan Crawley ensured her the attention of the most rigorous of Canadian modernist editors and access to a most respected Canadian modernist journal, *CV*. Indeed, Marriott's poetic output during the period from 1936 to 1953 was prodigious, in response, one might argue, to the invigorating West Coast cultural climate of which she was an important part. Her early chapbooks brought her much acclaim, as *The Wind Our Enemy* (1939) was quickly followed by her Governor General's Award–winning collection, *Calling Adventurers!* (1941). The latter is based on choruses she had written originally for *Payload*, a documentary radio drama produced by the CBC, an indication of her access to radio as well as magazine outlets for her verse during this period. Additionally, Marriott published more than two hundred poems in periodicals before 1945, and another twenty-seven between 1945 and 1953 (Irvine 96). Given her productive association with a Toronto publisher (the influential Ryerson Press), then, as well as her CBC radio work, and her success in magazine publishing during the 1940s, Anne Marriott cannot be read as seriously marginalized at this time, but instead appears to have been very well situated as a young poet emerging onto the national stage.

After 1945, however, Marriott's rate of publication fell off sharply. The two collections that followed *Calling Adventurers!*, *Salt Marsh* (1942) and *Sandstone and Other Poems* (1945), were published to little fanfare. She managed to place very few poems in literary magazines after 1945, and she produced nothing at all in monograph form until the appearance of *Countries* (1971), followed by *The Circular Coast* (1981), *Letters from Some Islands* (1986), and *Aqua* (1991), none of which generated anything like the attention paid to her earliest works, those of a young woman embraced by male patrons. Indeed Marriott's sharp withdrawal into poetic silence at mid-century and her failure to re-emerge upon the national stage until 1971 raise questions about women poets of the modern period, their writing lives and the effects of literary reception upon them at the point when powerful anthologists were beginning to define the contours of contemporary Canadian literature in particular narratives.[2]

One might attempt to lay Marriott's "silencing" at the door of her loss of male mentorship during a period when Canadian publishing was a male bastion and male sponsorship an essential ticket to publishing success. Certainly men in positions of cultural power had been crucial to Anne Marriott's early success, and her period of decline corresponds to a time when she no longer felt she could produce according to their standards. *The Wind Our*

Enemy appeared as a Ryerson chapbook under the prestigious editorship of Lorne Pierce in 1939 when Marriott was a virtual unknown, only twenty-six years of age and writing out of presumably staid Victoria. It had been brought to Pierce's attention by J.F.B. (Fred) Livesay, Dorothy Livesay's father and general manager of the Canadian Press, who chanced to hear the sequence at a poetry reading sponsored by the Victoria branch of the CAA, and urged Pierce to take it up (Philp 11). Pierce himself had long been known for his sponsorship of young women poets (such as Marjorie Pickthall and Audrey Alexandra Brown), though his advocacy in these cases was always something of a two-edged sword. Pierce preferred women poets to be traditional and "feminine" in theme and craft, and his support for Marriott and *The Wind Our Enemy* may be read as a mark of his conservatism. While modernist in its reliance upon imagery and plain speech, the poem performs appropriately feminine cultural work in documenting human suffering on the Prairies during the Great Depression. Moreover, it is altruistic in nature.

The acquisition of a distinguished Toronto mentor by a little known West Coast woman poet was an enormous coup for Anne Marriott at the time. It was Pierce, for instance, who entered *Calling Adventurers!* into the Governor General's stakes under his imprint in 1941, knowing that the literary climate would likely be favourable towards Marriott because of the widespread critical attention that had been paid to *The Wind Our Enemy* over the previous two years. However, it is clear from Marriott's archive that her pace and poetic direction after *Calling Adventurers!* was disappointing, both to herself, as she began to fear that her muse had deserted her, and to Pierce, who characterized her work, particularly in the case of *Sandstone and Other Poems* (1945), as slow in coming and uneven in quality.

Nor was Marriott able to continue to please her West Coast mentor, Alan Crawley, who had done much to encourage her to experiment with the modernist long poem, a form that brought her much success in the case of *The Wind Our Enemy*, whose imagistic sequencing is thought by such critics as David Bentley and Anne Geddes Bailey to owe much to Eliot's *The Waste Land*. By the mid-1940s, however, Marriott had turned away from the extended poem, for the most part, choosing to include only shorter, more imagistic lyrics in her two later collections in the 1940s, and thereby betraying, in effect, the long poem standard she had set for herself and Crawley had endorsed in *The Wind Our Enemy* and *Calling Adventurers!* One could argue that Marriott, in turning to the short lyric, and particularly the personal "place lyric," rejects the long poem expectations on which her reputation had been founded, thereby forfeiting the golden opportunity to retain the position in the modernist pantheon that her early success had afforded her. I would rather argue that, in publishing short, impressionistic lyrics reflecting personal place and space, she was choosing to enter into a discourse of locality that cosmopolitan modernism, with its emphasis on objectivity, impersonality, and universality, could not endorse and would quickly reject as slight, as turned out to be the case.

In any case, Marriott's increasing unorthodoxy in terms of the high modernist project represents only part of the picture. A larger issue (though it is difficult to distinguish cause and effect in this matter) was the decline in Marriott's poetic output during this period. Archival records betray a great crisis of faith on her part during the late 1940s and 1950s, a growing fear that the poetic muse had deserted her, perhaps permanently.[3] Certainly her creative energies were being deployed in many directions, and she can be said to have spread herself too thin during the years of her married life, which also entailed moving to northern British Columbia and to West Vancouver, and thus separating herself from her writing community in Vancouver for long periods of time. In any case, writing for the National Film Board, CBC radio, local newspapers, and local radio broadcasts, and simultaneously undertaking considerable work as a visiting writer in the schools, left Marriott with little time for writing poetry. Dorothy Livesay, who understood the complexities of family life and the need to earn a livelihood in the absence of a powerful husband-patron, attributes Marriott's slowdown after the mid-forties to twin factors: the intensity of the wartime work Marriott undertook for the CBC, producing dozens of broadcast scripts as part of the war effort; and her need, according to Livesay, to "sacrifice" her "creative" side to the "economics of living" (90). However, Livesay's assessment also falls short of fully explaining Marriott's increasing separation from the poetic mainstream in Canada, a process exacerbated by the cessation of the publication of *CV* as of 1953, by unfavourable reviews of *Salt Marsh* and *Sandstone* (including Livesay's own), and, perhaps most significantly, by the fact that a new literary establishment was firmly in place in central Canada by mid-century, and it was one unlikely to respond to Anne Marriott and the direction that her work had begun to take.

By the mid-1930s, A.J.M. Smith had clearly emerged as the voice of "cosmopolitan modernism" in Canada, and as a trendsetting anthologist who stood in opposition to literary tastes and values of the men of the previous generation (John Garvin and Vernon Rhodenizer, as well as Lorne Pierce), a role he would sustain throughout his academic life. As the main "theoretician of the new poetry" (Norris 13), Smith, along with his principal colleague F.R. Scott, had produced their groundbreaking anthology *New Provinces* (1936), followed by Smith's second anthology, *The Book of Canadian Poetry* in 1943, the same year in which E.K. Brown's *On Canadian Poetry* appeared. Despite modest challenges from other contenders such as John Sutherland's *Other Canadians* (1947), Smith's modernism would dominate Canada for decades, largely because of its entrenched connections with the Toronto literary establishment—first through Smith's contacts with conservative publishing elements there, such as elder poet E.J. Pratt and editor Hugh Eayrs of Macmillan, and later through spinoff connections with the University of Toronto. As Desmond Pacey observes in the *Literary History of Canada*, by the early 1940s Smith and Brown effectively "controlled" the critical atmosphere in Canada—Smith through the virtual monopoly and high prestige that his verse anthologies enjoyed, and Brown because of the influence of his critical study and his annual surveys of Canadian poetry in the *University of Toronto Quarterly* (21).

Theirs was a long reach indeed, for they quite literally shaped the next generation of literary critics. Pacey notes that, just as Lorne Pierce dominated the critical landscape before Smith and Northrop Frye after, it was Smith who influenced those in the space between, namely Malcolm Ross, A.G. Bailey, Roy Daniells, Carl Klinck, Claude Bissell, Hugo McPherson, Milton Wilson, and Pacey himself, whom he sees as all "undoubtedly willing" to acknowledge their debt to Smith. He goes on to note, without remarking at all on the hegemonic nature of this confluence, that these are the very scholars called upon to put together the massive *Literary History of Canada* starting in 1965, all of whom had come together through their connections with the University of Toronto (22).

The chief dynastic instrument in Canadian letters, moreover, is not the little magazine, the place of beginnings in Canadian literary culture, and the site of Marriott's sporadic publishing during the 1950s and 1960s, or literary histories, but the literary anthology, the chief mechanism by which the Canadian literary canon was established and imported into the schools during the period of the "invention" of Canadian literary studies as a separate academic discipline, beginning in the 1970s. Through a series of well-connected "national" anthologies, these modernist adjudicators constructed and defended a literary pantheon from which "magazine poets" like Anne

Marriott were progressively excluded. Marriott's own exile persists to this day. The pre-eminent teaching anthologies of our times, *The Anthology of Canadian Literature in English* series, first edited by Russell Brown and Donna Bennett in 1982,[4] omit Marriott's work entirely, as do *15 Canadian Poets X 3*, edited by Gary Geddes (2001), *The New Canadian Anthology*, edited by Robert Lecker and Jack David (1988), and the earlier *Oxford Anthology of Canadian Literature*, edited by Robert Weaver and William Toye (1973). Women editors have tended to nod in her direction, as in Atwood's *New Oxford Book of Canadian Verse* in 1982 and Rosemary Sullivan's *Poetry by Canadian Women* (1989), as does Daniel Lenoski's western collection, *A/long Prairie Lines* (1989). None of these collections features more than a few of her poems, however, and the same three are habitually selected: "The Wind Our Enemy," "Prairie Graveyard," and "Countries." Her poetry collections are all out of print, with the nominal exception of *Aqua* (1991), although I have not been able to track down a copy.

What the record with respect to Marriott's poetry suggests is the degree to which Canadian anthologies of the twentieth and twenty-first centuries are genealogical. Having fallen from modernist view as early as 1945, Marriott continues to be unacknowledged as part of Canada's "anthological canon" as late as 2002, despite having produced a substantial body of lyric poetry over her lifetime. Accounting for such concerted anthological neglect is itself a complex matter. Linda Hutcheon's notion of "ex/centricity" is of some use. Despite the liveliness of *CV* and the indomitability of West Coast literary culture over the years, Smith and his centrist canon-making editorial descendants were certainly demonstrably inhospitable to "ex/centrics," to writers working beyond a centralized and urban literary-geographic circle. *New Provinces* (1936), for example, featured the work of six male poets, all from Toronto or Montreal (Scott, Smith, A.M. Klein, Leo Kennedy, Robert Finch, and E.J. Pratt), but deliberately excluded the West's Dorothy Livesay, although she had by 1932 published two poetry collections, *Green Pitcher* (1928) and *Signpost* (1932). Smith's early critical work failed to acknowledge certain harbingers of Canadian modernism who had preceded him, notably Arthur Stringer (from Chatham, and later the Prairies) whose *Open Water* (1914) was radically written in free verse, or W.W.E. Ross (from Peterborough), who had published two collections of poetry by 1932, and who had been contributing imagist poetry to *Dial* and *Poetry* (Chicago) since 1923 (Dudek and Gnarowski 4). Nor did he recognize the Quebec Eastern Township's Franklin Oliver Call and his colleague, Louise Morey

Bowman, whose work had been praised by such adjudicators of modern poetry as Harriet Monroe and Amy Lowell, as had been the work of Dorothy Livesay's mother, Florence Randall Livesay, who (though hardly a groundbreaking modernist) had also been published in Monroe's *Poetry* (Malus et al. 60). Another "absentee" is Constance Lindsay Skinner, who had the misfortune to be a truly "unconnected" West Coast poet during this period of central Canadian literary hegemony; nor are Alan Crawley's *Contemporary Verse* founders (as of 1941) recognized by Smith: of these four West Coast women poets, Dorothy Livesay, Floris McLaren, Doris Ferne, and Anne Marriott, only Livesay ever received any significant attention from Smith and his cohort.

The problem of geographic ex/centricity was exacerbated, moreover, if one were both "provincial" and female, as is evident in the case of Anne Marriott. Smith's own *Book of Canadian Poetry* appeared in three successive editions (1943, 1948, 1957) and culminated in his 1960 *Oxford Book of Canadian Verse in English and French*, none of which was particularly hospitable to women poets. Between 1943 and 1960, his Marriott selections were reduced from two to one, and by the time of his 1967 edition of *Modern Canadian Verse in English and French*, she had disappeared altogether. Carole Gerson has traced what she calls a further "narrowing process" during the period 1970–86, when (she says) Smith and his successor, Ralph Gustafson, successfully "purg[ed] Canadian literature" of all that did not "suit their taste" and "their network of literary acquaintances" (Gerson, *Anthologies* 61). Gustafson's *Penguin Book of Canadian Verse* (1967) omits Marriott as well. Gerson's contention, argued in a number of articles, that women poets with local interests of various kinds[5] were particularly disadvantaged by an entire critical dynasty cut from the Smith cloth, is supported, in fact, by the most substantial book-length discussion of modernism in Canada, Brian Trehearne's *Aestheticism and the Canadian Modernists* (1989), which deals with Raymond Knister, W.W.E. Ross, Finch, Kennedy, Scott, John Glassco, Smith, Call, Louis Mackay, and Neil Tracy (3–4)—men, one and all.[6]

However, "ex/centricity," with its inclination to think in terms of concerted gatekeeping (the exclusion of whole classes of individuals) seems less compelling to me in examining the neglect of Anne Marriott than another way of looking at "the politics of space" in the world of Canadian publishing, and that is cosmopolitan modernism's dismissal of anything smacking of regionalism (a better word, I think, than "nativism" in describing cosmopolitanism's obverse). That which is regional is imbued with the local and with emotion tied to the specifics of place and space, contrary to the demands for "objectivity," impartiality, and cool distance that mark Smith's own brand of modernism. In the study of Canadian literature, appreciation of place in the geographical sense (a matter of landforms, climate, and political boundaries) has been firmly entrenched, indeed privileged, as closely connected to questions of identity, authenticity, and legitimacy on the part of the "place-speaker." However, it is also true that such regional writing, like the "local colour" writing from which it is seen as having descended, has tended to be arbitrarily dismissed by writers and critics of modernism as significantly lesser than writing seen to be of "cosmopolitan" stature and vision.

I would propose that Anne Marriott's poetry be read, and read positively, as regional discourse. Regionalism is a concept currently undergoing critical renovation in the academy and is now largely seen as a discourse of marginalization. In *New World Regionalism* (1994), David M. Jordan observes that "because a region is by definition a small part of a larger whole, regionalism necessarily precedes from a decentred world-view, and this decentred world-view distinguishes regionalism from other place-based literature, such as nature writing or travel writing" (8–9). Inherent in the concept of "regionalism" is the notion of "place-based" writing as provincial, since, as Jordan argues, region is always by definition "on the periphery" of something or somewhere else. Its "locality" consists in its existence as a non-metropolitan, hence lesser cultural nexus, which is likely to be underprivileged in direct proportion to the strength of "the centre" at any given cultural moment. Certain cultural periods may actually celebrate margins and localities of various kinds; contemporary postmodernism, for example, is vitally interested in diversity and difference, including the local as a "rich" site of "thick" difference. For Marriott, however, a turn from documentary to lyric poetry—in particular to the place-based personal lyric, her métier of choice as a mature poet—so frustrated expectations (both her own and those of her early mentors) that it could only contribute to the modernist anthologist's conviction that her writing was provincial, minor, and undeserving of attention.

What interests me, however, is the way in which Anne Marriott's later lyric poetry is regional in both senses of that term. It embodies the local, in inscribing place and space particular to her own lived experience (which is to say the West Coast region where she lived almost her entire life); but it also participates in the discourse of marginalization that David Jordan argues inheres in regionalism, for her poems consistently explore borders and edges, margins and shores, and champion their embrace, whatever the cost of exercising that allegiance.

Andrew Stubbs and Jeannette Seim see Anne Marriott as a "frontier poet," wherein a "frontier" or "border" represents a point of paradoxical separation and concomitant interaction (49), a shifting, transformative sphere. Their focus on her work highlights the sheer number of its references to borders, coasts, shores, beaches, and promontories, or in Marriott's own words, the "mysterious edge where all things meet and merge," and Stubbs and Seim characterize Marriott ultimately as a language poet, one focussed on margins or verges as if in pursuit of "the vanishing point of language, the extreme limit of articulation" (49). My own interest is less in Marriott's ostensible dialogue with language and its limits, however, than in her lyric expression of the experience of liminality, which I see as central to her sense of herself as a writer. In life, she frequently noted her outsider status, her difficulty in being heard, read, and promoted.[7] In the art of her later years, it is clear that a part of her, at least, has accepted her position "on the margins"—indeed, has embraced the liminal as a site of both resistance and originality, as can be seen, for example, in her poems of sea and shore.

With regularity, the speakers of Marriott's poems seek out the sea and haunt its verges, as if to resist all calls to face in the opposite direction, towards endless land, which is construed in her poetry as a broad "meadow" more comfortable to others than herself. To choose beach over grassland is to accept a necessary isolation: the speaker in "Two Poems of Wall," for example, construes herself as a "dark lonely dweller" (*Circular Coast* 33); and in "Oregon," that isolation is accepted as a prerequisite to progress:

> The rest of the part
> take the Other Route
> through the wide meadow.
> But I know for me
> this lonely dark walk is the only walk ...
> And I shall learn how good I am
> at maps
> when I reach the border
> where the trees thin out. (*Letters from Some Islands* 87)

The word "maps" gives pause: to map is to inscribe borders, and a border—myth that it always is, a mere gesture, a line drawn in sand—comes into existence only in its own breaching.

Marriott's speakers seek out border states. It is not always easy to get there: in "Barriers," she writes that "every sea road has the sign DETOUR" and "(each night in dreams I find they've put another barrier up)" (*Circular Coast* 24). To be at the verge, and especially at the edge of the sea, however, is to be able to transgress, to cross desirable borders, to submerge oneself in water, and come back transformed;[8] and Marriott's speakers are limp with desire for the sea. "On the promontory south," she writes in "Full Circle," "Roads open to the sea." At its margin, her speaker gives herself over ritualistically to "the tomb / the womb" of the sand (*Circular Coast* 21). In "Living under Water," she enters the ocean only to be rebuffed, and while immersed, she is battered, chafed, encroached upon, resurfaced:

> there's the endless itch
> as sin corrodes
> and thickens into scales.
> Never ignore the crabs!
> The tiniest still
> has pincers
> seeking the tender spots
> where new grey skin
> hasn't quite closed over.
> Even anemones
> so flowery, soft
> sprout murderous tentacles.
> Limpets begin to grow
> rooting in one's face like warts. (*Aqua* 14–15)

To be tossed back ashore is to be alone again, "beached" with pictures half-forgotten behind one's "watery eyes"—but, oh, the lingering transformative "phosphorescence" of the drowned moment!

Truly, for Anne Marriott, the local involves inscribing the liminality that she associates with British Columbia, that province bordering the sea and separated from Canada's centre by barely penetrable mountains; the mode, local and lyrical, best suited to rendering it lies at the heart of her poetic enterprise. To resist the siren call of the centre, to cover her ears with "summer seashells," to occupy her place and space wholly, is essential. If "from coasts you came," as she did, then "to coasts you must return," as she writes in a poem of that name (*Circular Coast* 19). The margin is the message; the centre be damned.

Notes

1 I am grateful to Dean Irvine for his generosity in letting me read his unpublished PhD dissertation, "Little Histories: Modernist and Leftist Women Poets and Magazine Editors in Canada, 1926–56." His insights into the life and work of Anne Marriott have been valuable and contribute much to our understanding of the working life of this neglected Canadian poet.
2 While my own emphasis is on the role of anthologists in narrowing the postwar Canadian literary canon to the detriment of writers like Anne Marriott, Sharon H. Nelson refers in "Anne Marriott: Treading Water" to the broader "cultural phenomenon of silencing" that overtook women writers like Marriott after World War Two. As Western governments made a "determined effort" to redefine gender roles for women after the war, Nelson argues—pressuring them to adhere more rigidly to specific gender roles within the nuclear family as part of an evolving "consumer society and consumerist culture"—women writers grew increasingly more isolated and found it substantially more difficult to achieve book publication (35).
3 In "The Literary Archive and the Telling of Modernist Lives: Retrieving Anne Marriott," I examine the ways in which literary archives complicate as much as they resolve biographical questions in exploring the lives of modernist writers. In the case of Anne Marriott, the archive includes statements by Marriott that attest to her lack of confidence in herself as a poet during the postwar period. It also includes a great deal of detail attesting to the disparate duties that characterized her domestic life and her growing feelings of cultural marginalization as the postwar years passed. In short, the archive attests to the myriad factors contributing to what I see as a "fallow" period for Marriott, out of which a somewhat altered voice and vision would emerge, reflecting her lifelong feelings of liminality in productive ways.
4 A two-volume edition came out in 1982, it was abridged to a single volume in 1990, and a revised edition was produced in 2002.
5 "Local interests" is my phrase, not hers.
6 Trehearne's bibliography makes reference to not one female poet of the period. He says of the male poets he considers, "we have paid too little attention to their journals, manuscripts, and private papers; and we have regularly failed to see in ... critical prose an important measure of the poet's work and thought"—and yet he pays no attention to the private and working papers of *women* poets who might have fallen under his critical gaze as "imagists" and other kinds of modernists (5).
7 Marriott's unpublished letters, held in the Anne Marriott fonds at the University of British Columbia, record her sense of being an outsider, unable to cross boundaries that sever her understanding and recognition. In 1978, she writes of being ignored by the "literary mafia" in Canadian publishing (folder 6). In a 1984 letter to Geoff Hancock, she states that she has never felt other than "on the fringe of [the *CV*] group" but always seems to exist on the edges, "a lifetime position" she fears (box 4). In 1985, she bristles when Seymour Mayne, editor of *Mosaic*, asks her to "cut out a lot of the Queen Charlotte poems and make [the submission] more universal rather than 'merely particular and personal'" (box 8).

8   One is reminded in Marriott's "sea fetish" of other modernist poems: the sea as medium of creative transformation from which Eliot's Prufrock hears the mermaids singing (though not for him); the sea that P.K. Page's "Marina," who ought to have been a "water woman rich with bells," has come to fear to enter, to her own creative detriment; or the "Lakeshore" of F.R. Scott's poem of that title, from which one emerges, fecund, only to drown in the "sea of air" that floods our infant gills upon our return.

Works Cited

Atwood, Margaret, ed. *The New Oxford Book of Canadian Verse in English*. Toronto: Oxford UP, 1982.

Bailey, Anne Geddes. "Re-visioning Documentary Readings of Anne Marriott's *The Wind Our Enemy*." *Canadian Poetry: Studies, Documents, Reviews* 31 (1992): 55–67.

Bentley, D.M.R. *The Gay/Grey Moose: Essays on the Ecologies and Mythologies of Canadian Poetry, 1690–1990*. Ottawa: U of Ottawa P, 1992.

Brown, Russell, and Donna Bennett, eds. *A New Anthology of Canadian Literature in English*. Toronto: Oxford UP, 2002.

———. *An Anthology of Canadian Literature in English*. 2 vols. Toronto: Oxford UP, 1982.

Brown, Russell, Donna Bennett, and Nathalie Cooke, eds. *An Anthology of Canadian Literature in English*. Rev. and abridged ed. Toronto: Oxford UP, 1990.

Dudek, Louis, and Michael Gnarowski, eds. *The Making of Modern Poetry in Canada: Essential Articles on Contemporary Canadian Poetry in English*. Toronto: Ryerson, 1967.

Gerson, Carole. "Anthologies and the Canon of Early Canadian Women Writers." *Re(Dis)covering Our Foremothers: Nineteenth-Century Women Writers*. Ed. and intro. Lorraine McMullen. Ottawa: U of Ottawa P, 1990. 55–76.

———. "The Canon Between the Wars: Field-notes of a Feminist Literary Archaeologist." *Canadian Canons: Essays in Literary Value*. Ed. Robert Lecker. Toronto: U of Toronto P, 1991. 46–56.

Gustafson, Ralph. *The Penguin Book of Canadian Verse*. Rev. ed. Toronto: Penguin, 1967.

Irvine, Dean. "Little Histories: Modernist and Leftist Women Poets and Magazine Editors in Canada, 1926–56." PhD dissertation, McGill University, 2001.

Jordan, David M. *New World Regionalism: Literature in the Americas*. Toronto: U of Toronto P, 1994.

Lane, Travis. "Contemporary Canadian Verse: The View Here." *University of Toronto Quarterly* 52.2 (Winter 1982-3): 179–90.

Lecker, Robert, and Jack David, eds. *The New Canadian Anthology*. Toronto: Nelson, 1989.

Lenoski, Daniel S, ed. *A/long Prairie Lines*. Winnipeg: Turnstone, 1989.
Livesay, Dorothy. *Green Pitcher*. Toronto: Macmillan, 1928.
———. "The Poetry of Anne Marriott." *Educational Record* 87–90. Dorothy Livesay fonds. Mss. 37. Department of Archives and Special Collections, Elizabeth Dafoe Library, University of Manitoba, Winnipeg, MB.
———. *Signpost*. Toronto: Macmillan, 1932.
Malus, Avrum, Diane Allard, and Maria van Sundert. "Frank Oliver Call, Eastern Townships Poetry, and the Modernist Movement." *Canadian Literature* 107 (Winter 1985): 60–69.
Marriott, Anne. Anne Marriott fonds. University of British Columbia Library, Rare Books and Special Collections, Vancouver, BC.
———. *Aqua*. Toronto: Wolsak and Wynn, 1991.
———. *Calling Adventurers!* Toronto: Ryerson, 1941.
———. *The Circular Coast*. Oakville: Mosaic, 1981.
———. *Countries*. Fredericton: F. Cogswell, 1971.
———. *Letters from Some Islands*. Oakville: Mosaic, 1986.
———. *Salt Marsh*. Toronto: Ryerson, 1942.
———. *Sandstone and Other Poems*. Toronto: Ryerson, 1945.
———. *The Wind Our Enemy*. Toronto: Ryerson, 1939.
Nelson, Sharon H. "Anne Marriott: Treading Water." *Re:Generations: Canadian Women Poets in Conversation*. Ed. Di Brandt and Barbara Godard. Windsor, ON: Black Moss, 2005. 34–49.
Norris, Ken. *The Little Magazine in Canada, 1925–80: Its Role in the Development of Modernism and Post-Modernism in Canadian Poetry*. Toronto: ECW, 1984.
Pacey, Desmond. "The Course of Canadian Criticism." *The Literary History of Canada: Canadian Literature in English*. Ed. Carl Klinck. 2nd ed., vol. 3. Toronto: U of Toronto P, 1976. 16–31.
Page, P.K. "Portrait of Marina." *The Hidden Room: Collected Poems*. Erin, ON: Porcupine's Quill, 1997. 72–73.
Philp, Ruth Scott. "Anne Marriott: Poet of Prairie and Coast." *Canadian Author and Bookman* 58.3 (1983): 11–12.
Rose, Marilyn J. "The Literary Archive and the Telling of Modernist Lives: Retrieving Anne Marriott." *The Canadian Modernists Meet*. Ed. Dean Irvine. Ottawa: U of Ottawa P, 2005. 231–49.
Scott, F.R. "Lakeshore." *Selected Poems*. Toronto: Oxford University Press, 1966. 12–13.
Smith, A.J.M. *The Book of Canadian Poetry*. Toronto: Oxford UP, 1943. Rev. ed. 1948; 3rd ed. 1957.
———. *Modern Canadian Verse in English and French*. Toronto: Oxford UP, 1967.
———. *New Provinces*. Toronto: Macmillan, 1936.
———. *The Oxford Book of Canadian Verse in English and French*. Toronto: Oxford UP, 1960.

———. "A Rejected Preface." *The Making of Modern Poetry in Canada: Essential Articles on Contemporary Canadian Poetry in English*. Ed. Louis Dudek and Michael Gnarowski. Toronto: Ryerson, 1967. 38–41.

Stringer, Arthur. *Open Water*. New York: John Lane, 1914.

Sullivan, Rosemary, ed. *Poetry by Canadian Women*. Toronto: Oxford UP, 1989.

Sutherland, John. *Other Canadians*. Montreal: First Statement, 1947.

Trehearne, Brian. *Aestheticism and the Canadian Modernists*. Kingston: McGill-Queen's UP, 1989.

Weaver, Robert, and William Toye, eds. *The Oxford Anthology of Canadian Literature*. Toronto: Oxford UP, 1973.

Dicontinuity, Intertextuality, and Literary History
Gail Scott's Reading of Gertrude Stein
LIANNE MOYES

Literary history does not favour misfits. Writers whose texts fall outside period boundaries or between national literatures, whose texts write the oversights of their day, or disturb widely held views about the evolution of a given movement or national literature are particularly vulnerable. Such writers would be better served by a literary history more tolerant of difference and disjunction. Dorothy Livesay's poem "We Are Alone" (66) points toward such a reconceptualization of literary history. Writers, artists, activists, and intellectuals, the poem reminds us, frequently labour alone, separated from one another by region, nation, or generation. In the context of Canadian women's poetry, this relative isolation has important effects, including the coexistence in the mid-twentieth century of disparate modernist impulses and influences, which resurface in disparate ways—sometimes in prose, sometimes in poetry—later in the twentieth century. In this sense, the field of Canadian women's poetry and experimental writing knows many misfits. The work of a writer such as Gail Scott, who is not of the generation of the majority of writers discussed in this collection of essays, becomes relevant here as an indicator both of the persistence of what the editors of the collection call the "modernist impulse" and of important discontinuities (as well as continuities) in lines of literary affiliation among Canadian women writers. Scott is not a poet, but her use of language is far from prosaic: it hits her readers "like mud in the eye" ("My Montréal" 5).[1] She is not a modernist, but, like Sheila Watson, she is very interested in the writing of American expatriates such as Gertrude Stein.

Juxtaposed with the theme of isolation in Livesay's poem is the collectivity implied by the repetition of the pronoun "we." This repeated use of "we" reinforces the idea in the final lines that "we are *not* alone" and that something more may come of a writer's work than can immediately be seen or imagined. Livesay's "we" is an alternative collectivity that operates in the absence of actual meetings and beyond the parameters of a single lifetime. For the purposes of my essay, I imagine this "we" as a network of writers and readers, a network that includes Scott, as well as an even younger generation of women writers who look to Scott (among others) for their connection to the modernist impulse in Canadian women's poetry. A network is not a "tradition"; it is a weave of readings and writings that allows threads to be dropped, even broken, and then picked up years later in other readings and writings. Scott has a place in that network in spite of the fact that she looked not to the generation of Livesay or P.K. Page or Sheila Watson for inspiration but rather to writers beyond the borders of Canada. In this, she is not unlike the generation of Livesay, Page, and Watson.

The critical gesture of giving Scott a place in the networks of the present collection involves rethinking the temporality of literary history. Once again, Livesay's poem anticipates the critical challenge. In the final lines, "Neither one alive to see / In wider boundaries of daring / What the recompense might be" (66), Livesay's speaker both looks to the future and imagines or projects a look back from a point in the future. As Barbara Godard and Di Brandt point out in the "Call for Papers" for this volume, the poem "announces a bold project and expresses curiosity about its future reception." This mobile perspective, this possibility of opening representational spaces for women of future generations and, at the same time, returning to earlier writing through the texts of future generations, is crucial to women's literary history. I am reminded of Teresa de Lauretis's explanation of reading and history in an article on lesbian representation:

> Representation is related to experience by codes that change historically and, significantly, reach in both directions: the writer struggles to inscribe experience in historically available forms of representation, the reader accedes to representation through her own historical and experiential context; each reading is a rewriting of the text, each writing a rereading of (one's) experience. (23)

Processes of writing and reading open productive relations between texts from different moments in history, relations that are potentially achronological insofar as texts can be read outside the order in which they were written. The "wider boundaries of daring" enjoyed, for example, by women writers at the turn of the twenty-first century exist thanks to the literary and other strivings of women like Livesay. What is more, those wider boundaries allow readings of Livesay and other women that their contemporaries could not have produced and that received histories of Canadian modernism have resisted.

In what follows, I theorize literary history as a network of intertextual relationships that function in and through discontinuity. My focus is intertextual relationships among women writers of different generations and different national identifications, women writers who, in many cases, have never met.[2] I qualify these relationships as "intertextual" to underline my sense that any text is traversed by many others, and that any text is, in the terms of Julia Kristeva, "the result of the intersection of a number of voices, of a number of textual interventions, which are combined in the semantic field, but also in the syntactic and phonic fields" (281). As Kristeva further explains, intertextuality entails "a specific dynamics of the subject of the utterance" (281). To read or to write, she suggests, is to place the self at the intersection of the text's plurality, to put the self into process (281–82). In thinking about literary history, I am particularly drawn to women writers whose texts foreground intertextuality and thereby signal the subjective processes involved in their writings, readings, and literary affiliations.[3]

Given intertextuality, it is very difficult to police the "Canadianness" of what I am calling "literary history." The institutional processes that claim writers for a national literature and the identificatory processes through which writers position themselves in terms of national literatures represent temporary stops in the intertextual traffic, stops that provide them with important kinds of recognition and support, including awards and grants from governments. Many women writers locate themselves *between* national literatures, however, and find interpretive communities for their work among international groups of writers and artists. Insofar as national institutions and narratives have a tendency to short-circuit women's literary culture and to forget women's roles in literary history, women writers often have reason to position themselves otherwise: to affiliate locally or regionally, to affiliate with a diasporic community, and/or to affiliate according to sexual orientation, political identification, or aesthetic project. Whatever the lines of affiliation—and they are often multiple and contradictory—drawing attention to the intertextual traces they leave in women's writing helps make legible the movement across borders that is part of literary history in Canada.

In this essay, I offer my reflections on intertextuality and literary history as they have developed through reading Gail Scott. Although Scott's work is somewhat eccentric to a discussion of "The Modernist Impulse in Canadian Women's Poetry," it is nevertheless relevant insofar as it challenges the limits of categories such as "poetry," "modernism," and "Canadian." Scott is a writer of experimental prose more than a writer of poetry, and her writing is associated with *la modernité*, postmodernism, and the international avant-garde more than with the movements of Canadian literary modernism. Writing from a space that is in between the literatures of Canada and Quebec, she traces her principal lines of literary affiliation to women in Quebec (among them France Théoret and Nicole Brossard), in France (among them Kristeva, Luce Irigaray, and Hélène Cixous), and in the United States (among them Carla Harryman and Kathy Acker) more than to those in English-speaking Canada. When she looks back to women of an earlier generation, it is to French writers Colette, Marguerite Duras, and Anaïs Nin, to British-born Virginia Woolf and Leonora Carrington, or to expatriate Americans Gertrude Stein, Djuna Barnes, and Jane Bowles.

This is not to say that Canadian women writers of Livesay's generation have not played a role in Scott's writing career. Her first collection of short stories, *Spare Parts*, was published in 1981 at Coach House Press, a Toronto publishing house that brought her into contact with the writing of women such as Livesay, Phyllis Webb, and Sheila Watson. Scott does not explicitly affiliate her writing with these women, but there are nevertheless connections. In 1988, the fourth issue of *Tessera*, a feminist magazine of which Gail Scott was a co-founder in 1982, appeared as an issue of *CV2*, a magazine founded by Livesay in 1975. This connection was made possible by the feminist editorial collective that took over *CV2* in the mid-1980s (Brandt 247),[4] but it was nonetheless Livesay who opened the space in practical as well as conceptual terms. Scott knows Watson's work through Montreal writer France Théoret and through writers associated with Coach House. Théoret, who knew Watson at the Canada Council (where both women served on peer assessment committees in the early 1980s), remembers Watson's support for Scott's first book, *Spare Parts*.[5] Moreover, in 1981, while Scott and Théoret were co-editors of the Quebec cultural magazine *Spirale*, Scott published a review of Watson's *Four Stories*, and in *Spaces Like Stairs* (1989) she comments on Watson's "theoretical sophistication" (69).

Scott also shares with some women writers of Livesay's generation an interest in the more experimental practices of literary modernism. As Godard points out, literary history in Canada has been relatively silent on the influence of such practices on Canadian modernism. There is a tendency, she suggests, to associate linguistic and other forms of innovation with postmodernism ("Ex-centriques, Eccentric, Avant-Garde" 62–65; "El Greco in Canada" 55–56; "Re: post" 134). Godard traces connections between the texts of writers such as Watson and Elizabeth Smart, and those of the Symbolists and Surrealists ("Ex-centriques" 62–65). Although Scott knows Watson's writing, the connection between the two writers is not a direct one. Indeed, the principal link between Scott and Watson lies in a shared link back to Stein and other English-language writers strongly influenced by early and mid-century continental literary movements. Watson, for example, wrote a dissertation at University of Toronto in the 1950s on Wyndham Lewis, a writer influenced by Cubism and Futurism. She also published an essay in the mid-1970s entitled "Gertrude Stein: The Style Is the Machine," an essay to which Godard returns in her article "'Between One Cliché and Another': Language in *The Double Hook*" on the gender specificity of Watson's project. However, instead of reading Watson reading Stein, Scott reads Stein. In other words, instead of reading Canadian modernists, she turns directly to the most experimental of an international group of modernist writers—or to contemporary writers in Quebec, France, Canada, and the United States who respond to the international writers. As Scott explains to an American friend in her essay "My Montréal," "As a young woman writer, I gained confidence by listening to the best women writers, and the edgiest poets of both genders" (7).

Scott's essays foreground her engagement with the discourses and practices of Surrealism, feminism, *la modernité*, postmodernism, and new narrative; these discourses and practices take distinctive forms in particular places at particular moments. The essay "The Virgin Denotes," for example, has Scott reading the Surrealist Manifestos, analyzing dreams, and "going around the city putting up mad broadsheets" (12) with several other Montreal artists in the late 1970s. "Miroirs inconstants" mentions Claude Gauvreau, a writer associated with *les automatistes*, the surrealist-influenced group of Quebec writers and painters of the late 1940s and 1950s whose non-figurative use of words and paint paved the way for the experimental writing and counter-culture of Brossard, Scott, Théoret, and other young artists in the 1960s and 1970s.[6] "What We Talk about on Sundays" represents the project of a group of feminist writers—Louky Bersianik, Brossard, Louise Cotnoir, Louise Dupré, Scott, and Théoret—who brought about a sea-change within literary modernity in Quebec by insisting upon the (gendered) writing subject. A number of Gail Scott's essays acknowledge George Bowering, Michael Ondaatje ("The Virgin Denotes" 16), and Leonard Cohen ("My Montréal" 7; "Miroirs Inconstants" 23), men whose writing practices are associated with postmodernism in English-speaking Canada. Canadian feminist responses to postmodernism are in evidence in "Theorizing Fiction Theory," a conversation among co-editors at *Tessera* that foregrounds the relationship between prevailing economies of representation and their gender-specific oversights. Finally, written for the web-based magazine *Narrativity*, "Bottom's Up" speaks of dialogue with Americans Robert Glück, Carla Harryman, Camille Roy, Sarah Schulman, and Barrett Watten, all of whom are associated with new narrative movements of the 1980s and 1990s, movements whose language-sensitive prose crosses theory with fiction, politics with autobiography, and writing with other media in ways that interrogate narrativity and foreground (queer urban) subjectivity.[7]

In thinking about Scott's interest in writers beyond the borders of Canada, it is worth remembering the international and cosmopolitan character of modernism and its offshoots: "Flourishing contemporaneously in San Francisco, New York, Calgary, Montreal ... and in pockets in Ontario and British Columbia" ("My Montréal" 7), new narrative is one such offshoot. Its centres of activity are multiple and marked by the coexistence of subjects with different national and cultural identifications. Scott clearly thrives in spaces of heterogeneous, contradictory, often contestatory subjectivities. As an Anglo-Quebec writer living in Montreal, a cultural space that is sufficiently politicized to foster radical breaks in literary practice (*Spaces Like Stairs* 38; "The Porous Text" 202–3), Scott understands the possibilities early twentieth-century Paris provided writers such as Stein and Barnes. In the relative absence of such radicalizing literary culture in early and mid-century Canada, Canadian women writers, too, looked to international cosmopolitan centres. That new narrative and other forms of experimental culture thrive in various places across Canada at the turn of the twenty-first century suggests that the situation is changing. If, in spite of such change, Scott remains more strongly identified with the literary scene in Quebec than with that of English Canada, it has to do with the link in Quebec between artistic experimentation and social change, as well as with the failure she has often found among English Canadians to imagine that a minority culture such as Quebec might have "the vitality to operate as a sphere of influence on those 'minorities' (anglophones) that live within its parameters"

(*Spaces Like Stairs* 48). If, especially in the writing of the 1990s and early 2000s, she looks to writers in the United States, it is not because they are any more able to make such a leap of imagination but because they allow her to situate her writing in relationship to centres of activity such as San Francisco where queer culture is strong and where "politics and literature meet, combust" as they do in Montreal ("My Montréal" 8).

In a discussion of the ways in which the French-language literature of Quebec informs certain currents of Anglo-Quebec writing, Scott asserts that "toute intertextualité a un côté matériel, concret, c'est-à-dire qu'elle ... est forcément enracinée dans le 'local'" ("Miroirs inconstants" 25). Scott's investment in writing from "elsewhere" and the kinds of discourses and practices she draws from that writing, then, are also an effect of the specificity of her relationship to Montreal; that is, they are an effect of the desire to render what it means to write from a space between languages or to listen for the heteroglossia of the city, for the productive friction between its official and unofficial discourses. Scott's relationship to Montreal has a substantial effect on how she reads Gertrude Stein, and on how she reads Stein's relationship to Paris, questions to which I return in the final section of the essay.

Gertrude Stein is the modernist woman writer discussed most frequently and at greatest length in Scott's recent essays, interviews, and fiction. Like Scott, Stein is a writer who problematizes identity (including sexual and gender identity), who focusses on the sentence, who sets specific compositional limits for herself, who insists upon the present tense, who resists sentimentality and anecdote, who confounds genre distinctions, and who writes in English in a French-speaking milieu. Stein provides a literary precedent for Scott's experiments with grammar, subjectivity, and narrative. One has only to flip the pages of journals such as $L=A=N=G=U=A=G=E$, *Open Letter*, *La nouvelle barre du jour*, *Tessera*, *HOW(ever)*, and *Chain* to see that Stein's work is crucial to experimental writing in North America. In engaging with Stein, Scott locates her writing within this field. At the same time, as Sherry Simon and Dianne Chisholm both note, she registers her difference from Stein, especially from the postures Stein adopts as an expatriate American living in Paris (Simon, "Paris Arcades" 144–45; Chisholm 168–69). In other words, if Scott's reading of Stein is, in part, made possible by Stein's experiments, that reading also takes Stein in directions the latter could not have imagined. As the relations between the texts of Scott and Stein make clear, literary history is structured by discontinuity as well as by continuity. In this section, I address the implications of discontinuity for the writing of women's literary history, as well as the broader question of how to address the mechanisms by which women's writing is misread, misplaced, and written out of literary histories.[8] In the final section, I consider the suggestiveness of Scott's reading practice for an intertexual understanding of literary history. Tracing Scott's reconceptualization of the writing subject back through Stein's portrait writing, I foreground some of the continuities in their views of subjectivity.

Scott's intertextual relationships beyond Canada's borders, along with her troubled national affiliation ("My Montréal" 8), complicate the model of a nationally based tradition in literature in which a writer inherits from literary predecessors of the same country. The idea of locating Scott's writing within a tradition of women's writing is equally problematical. As Margaret Ezell points out, "The use of the term 'tradition' implies the existence of common ground and continuity in literary works—in terms of subject, genre, style—and in the authors' lives, their education, social class, and literary activity" (19). Interested in the ways in which women's literary histories have misrepresented or excluded women's writing before 1700, Ezell questions the tendency "to investigate using a linear cause and effect analysis, either to start in the past and work forward in time, looking for development and searching for patterns of influence, or to read backward, starting with the present and looking for predecessors, a sort of literary genealogy" (19). Ezell's critique of linear models of literary history is genuinely productive, yet her study is ultimately more interested in finding a place for specific women writers *within* the tradition than in exploring alternative models.[9]

The intertextual relations between Scott and Stein that I read here pose a challenge to the concepts of temporality and textuality taken for granted in linear models. Literary history is not a sequence into which the texts of Stein and Scott can be slotted; nor is it something a critic can stand outside, an object susceptible to study. A reader has a certain writerly agency in relationship to literary history, but she is nevertheless imbricated in its practices. Literary history, in this sense, is constituted by work with texts. It is a complex set of relations in which a writer such as Stein opens possibilities for subsequent generations of women writers and in which various historical and practical contingencies allow a writer such as Scott to read Stein innovatively, in ways that signal both the discontinuities and the continuities in their work. My own reading, achronological in the sense that it begins with Scott, holds the texts of Stein and Scott together across national and generational differences. In this it takes its cue from Scott's own work. Casting forward and backward simultaneously, Scott's texts speak of a "wish to gather everything, including the past, into an imperfect present" ("My Montréal" 204). This strategy of splicing together past and present, a strategy borrowed from materialist thinker Walter Benjamin, thwarts evolutionary or progress-oriented narratives and makes legible the breaks and disjunctions ushering change in literary history. It also asks readers to look for the differences between texts, particularly the differences in the relationships of those texts to the material conditions in which they are produced and received. For example, in *My Paris*, the text I address in the final section of this paper, Scott's writing subject engages with Stein not only as an experimental writer but also as an American in Paris whose texts give little sense of her everyday practice of the city that allows her to write.

Rather than think of Canadian writing or of women's writing as traditions, I would like to think of them as heterogeneous practices of reading and writing. If they are understood in this way, then it becomes easier to allow for traffic across borders, generational discontinuities, and differences in cultural affiliation and literary sensibility. It becomes possible, for example, to imagine that although Scott does not affiliate strongly with her Canadian literary predecessors, her writing might have an important influence on a younger generation of Canadian women writers interested in international as well as Québécois currents of literary experiment.

The literary history I have in mind reads for discontinuity as much as continuity. Such a history could accommodate, for example, writers who seem not to belong within their moment or within received narratives of literary inheritance, periodization, or literary evolution. Discontinuity, disjunction, and contradiction tend not to be foregrounded in women's literary history, perhaps because they are taken to be the mechanisms by which women's writing has been, or will continue to be, excluded from prevailing accounts. According to this logic—and it is a logic I can understand—women's literary history needs a chance to cohere before it falls to pieces; yet it is also possible to argue that if literary history were more able to accommodate discontinuity—both through time and at a given moment—then women writers, minority writers, or experimental writers might be better received and remembered—and, significantly, it would be for their difference, for their conflictual or emergent status, for their radical continuity with others (before, during, or after their time), that they would be remembered. Think, for example, of Stein's wish in "Composition as Explanation" that people "would realise that beauty is beauty even when it is irritating and stimulating not only when it is accepted and classic"—in other words, that texts might be given cultural value while they are still "irritating annoying stimulating" (515). Stein's writing, of course, waited half a century before it receives readings that investigate its discontinuities with its moment (Friedman and Fuchs 8) or its radical continuities with writers such as T.S. Eliot (Perloff 44–76).

Writing literary history is often thought of as a diachronic activity; but literary history is as much a question of synchronic relations as of diachronic relations, as much a question of reading the web of literary discourses and practices that exist at a given moment as one of tracing relationships through time. Bonnie Kime Scott's graphic, "A Tangled Mesh of Modernists" (10) generates such a web by drawing lines of affiliation among well-known and lesser-known modernist writers, among women and men. In mixing "major" and "minor" figures, Bonnie Kime Scott draws attention to the connections among writers in a given period, connections that are often lost in diachronic accounts that focus on relations among a few major figures through time. "A Tangled Mesh" reminds us that to draw a single line of descent and to locate writers along it is to produce a particular representation of literary history, a representation that is both selective and retrospective. To draw a line between Stein and Scott, for example, is selective in the sense that it focusses on connections to one writer at the expense of others (both historical and contemporary), and retrospective in the sense that such a line is not available when one is in the thick of reading or writing. For this reason, I try to indicate both the range of literary intertexts in Scott's writing and the way in which Scott's emphasis on discontinuity fractures any line of descent from Stein to Scott.

"Intertextuality" is not the only term that has been used in the wake of poststructuralism to theorize literary history.[10] "Genealogy" is the term Godard uses to account for discontinuity in her history of *Tessera*. Recognizing her tendency to reconstitute *Tessera* "within a historical narrative," to present issues chronologically, she pursues "other ways to remember these texts by moving sideways and tracking particular 'topics,'" topics such as feminist activism, racial difference, and problems of cultural translation that are "interwoven" with questions of writing in the pages of the magazine ("Women of Letters [Reprise]" 300). The term "genealogy" surfaces again in the pages of Ann Vickery's history of language writing:

> Rather than proposing an organic model of growth or a model of equivalence, a genealogy explores the shifting "mess" that encapsulates actual poetic practice through the traces it leaves. It maps out the interweaving, multiple lines of affiliation as well as the debates arising out of difference, whether these be regional, aesthetic, cultural or ideological. (13)

For Vickery, "feminist genealogy becomes a mode of intervention that may reveal otherwise hidden or elided differences as well as unpredictable relationships" (15); it is "a way of reading texts and their contexts against each other, and in ways that mediate cultural knowledge with textuality" (16). Godard's and Vickery's use of the term "genealogy" is different from that of Ezell. Drawn from Michel Foucault, it understands origins, cause–effect relations, and literary inheritance as retrospective constructions, as fabrications that attempt to conceal disparate and unequal forces. Relying upon "a vast accumulation of source material" (Foucault 140), a genealogy is constructed from "'discreet and apparently insignificant truths'" (Nietzsche, qtd. in Foucault 140); it offers no suprahistorical perspective, no totalizing or sovereign view.

With its critique of teleology and its displacement of origins, genealogy allows a reconceptualization of literary origins and of temporal relations among texts. Perhaps even more importantly, it attends to the heterogeneous assemblage of discourses and practices that are part of the history of literary texts. Without questioning the value of genealogical projects such as Godard's or Vickery's, I give preference here to the term intertextuality. Insofar as this term has its intellectual and conceptual roots in Kristeva's reading of Mikhail Bakhtin and her exchanges with Roland Barthes (Kristeva 280), it allows—and, to my mind, requires—an examination of the problematics of the enunciation and its imbrication in subjectivity. As Godard points out, intertextuality has acquired conflictual definitions since the 1970s ("Intertextuality" 569). As I am using it, intertextuality is not limited to a sense of pure textuality or to a study of sources. The term interests me because of its capacity to hold in tension questions of subjectivity, textuality, literary history, and social discourse. Intertextuality allows a reconceptualization of the writing subject by locating her enunciation at the juncture of the text's mix of voices, languages, textual fragments, structures, and discursive rules. It is this reconceptualization of the writing subject—as an agent and an effect of intertextual relations—that preoccupies me in the final section of the essay.

As I suggested earlier, Scott's essays are extraordinary for the range and number of lines of affiliation they draw. In the 1998 essay, "What If the Writer Were in Bed? On Narrative," these lines of affiliation take the form of citations from various writers, among them Harryman, Théoret, Gayatri Spivak, Maurice Blanchot, Walter Benjamin, and Jean-Luc Godard. The line from Godard that opens the essay and serves as its refrain, "only the hand which erases everything can write" (3), speaks of a productive tension within Scott's writing between the gesture of emptying the text of identity, making it extremely porous to other texts, and the gesture of constituting an "I" and making the text one's own. "What If the Writer Were in Bed?" is almost entirely composed of citations (including excerpts from Scott's own writings), intercalated with the meditations of the essay's writing subject. Citation is not in itself intertextuality. However, when there are so many citations that it is difficult to discern what is "new" from what has already been said, what is proper to Scott and what is proper to others, a text can be said to insist upon its intertextuality. Pieced together from fragments of various texts, shifting between bits of narrative (regarding the weather, her lover, her anguish, her inability to get out of bed) and aphorisms (about writing, desire, truth, the feminine), Scott's essay is generically heterogeneous.

Another recent essay, "The Virgin Denotes," links the explicit intertextuality of Scott's texts to their poetic quality and hints at what might be gained from reading Scott's prose the way one reads poetry:

> But what impetus, exactly, gave "story" the rush of something new: these written ghosts of subjects, fragile substantives, compiled from public text, experience, and facing the world obliquely?... Precisely those elements that trope the vaguely comic autobiographical conjunction of semiotics, semantics, gossip, what she now thinks of as prose; "experimental" inasmuch as implying failure to represent the universal, linked to class, gender, sometimes race, but also to the pleasure of sounding out, a kin to poetry. Sometimes, she watches, regretfully, as her little tales float, textured, suggestive, by the averted eyes of certain poets she admires. Who, along with lovers of more conventional fiction, persist in reading "experimental" prose for content or "voice" alone. As if a subject redistributed across hazardous abutments, torqued by inner syntax in dissonance with outer, or the reverse, can be absorbed as passively as a drugstore novel. (13)

For Scott, sentences organized in prose lines can be read for rhythm and texture in the same way that poetry can: "A sentence, after all, is a device, like any other" ("Virgin Denotes" 18). In this sense, it is difficult to secure the border between poetry and prose in Scott's writing. What is more, in the passage cited above, poetry becomes a way of understanding the intertextuality of the writing subject, the fact that she is "compiled from public text, experience," that she is a "vaguely comic autobiographical conjunction of semiotics, semantics, gossip." This writing subject is radically continuous with the city she reads, writes, and apprehends. At the same time, "redistributed across hazardous abutments, torqued by inner syntax in dissonance with outer," she signals a certain disjunction between the discourses of city and self.

In "The Porous Text, or the Ecology of the Small Subject," Scott elaborates upon the project of "putting self in abeyance in favour of listening" and "constructing the writing subject out of the heteroglossia of voices surrounding [her]" (203). Intertextuality, here, is an effect of translating in several directions at once and of writing across disparate cultural discourses. In a place such as Montreal, where narratives, languages, institutions, and codes fracture and collide, Scott's writing subject hears poetry; she hears "constant doomed-to-failure attempts at explanation, interpretation" (204); she hears "a soundscape from which melodies emerge ... in the form, for example, of female patrons" (205). Scott needs a writing subject small enough to take in this heteroglossia and to register the moments in which language becomes music. At the same time, she needs a writing subject big enough to take the risk of extreme porosity, a risk that can only be taken, in her view, because she has an interpretive community of women readers and writers (203): "Bowing two or more ways at once ... [,] absorb[ing] paradoxes like a pin cushion, then regurgitat[ing] them as if she were *someone*" (204). In postures reminiscent of the narrative voice in Djuna Barnes or in Jane Bowles, the writing subject becomes, for Scott, clown-like. This writing subject has simultaneously to assume identity and to erase identity, to claim her text and to acknowledge it as derivative, to situate her text within a field of (literary) discourse and to situate the field of (literary) discourse within her text.

As an English-language writer who seeks "to locate, semiotically, the unique sounds of a French-dominant multi-linguistic city" ("Virgin Denotes" 14), Scott is interested in Stein's relationship to the French-language milieu of Paris. She hears in Stein's writing the influence of French grammar, especially the way in which that grammar centres on the verb ("Porous Text" 205; "Intertexts" 116; *My Paris* 35); yet Stein, who attributes her preoccupation with verbs to their capacity to be "so mistaken" ("Poetry and Grammar" 211), maintains that in her work she has no ears for any language other than English. She writes, "It does not make any difference to me what language I hear ... there is for me only one language and that is English" (*Autobiography of Alice B. Toklas* 65–66). This is not an assertion Scott could make. In "My Montréal," Scott rejects the suggestion that she lives in exile like Stein and Hemingway, and explains that French language and culture are "part of her cultural background" (5). Furthermore, as Sherry Simon observes, Scott's 1999 novel *My Paris* foregrounds contact between languages by including words in French followed by a comma and an English translation ("Paris Arcades" 143). Scott does not share Stein's sense that commas are of no use ("Poetry and Grammar" 219). In the words of *My Paris*, "But if comma of translation disappearing. What of French-speaking America remaining" (*My Paris* 49). Scott's "comma of translation" effectively undermines the universality of Stein's statements regarding commas—and regarding America. Scott, far more than Stein, has a stake in acknowledging the impact of French language culture on her English language texts.

Throughout *My Paris*, the writing subject, "in search of contemporaneous literary avant-garde" (112), finds only the ghosts of writers and artists who walked the same streets earlier in the century. She is haunted, in particular, by Stein's reflections on grammar ("Poetry and Grammar"), portraiture ("Portraits and Repetition"), Americans inventing the twentieth century ("How Writing Is Written"), and Paris (*Paris France*). Her response is to inhabit Stein's words and her streets differently:

> Below on boulevard—green-clad worker from "south." Vacuuming up dog shit. Followed by another green-clad guy. Green broom and matching refuse bag. Against backdrop of that fine men's store opposite. Windows of exquisitely stitched collars. Reflecting meridian strip. Where Gertrude Stein's poodle Basket used to shit. With other rich expatriate puppies. Thinking Paris belonging to them. Turn on some Arab music. Low. (22)

In a second passage, later in the book, she writes,

> Passing jellied trout. In traiteur window. Near Gertrude Stein's. Whose genius. Being American. Interested in gathering what ordinary (common). In all of "**us**." While loving Paris as refuge. Of individuals (artists). Traces of winter. In air. Ankle-high in pamphlets. From yet another unemployment demonstration. Man. Writing Je suis sans travail. Sans abri, I am jobless. Homeless. Rewinding long scarf around neck. Waving complicitly at marchers. (135–36)

Whereas Stein's texts rarely mention ordinary Parisians, *My Paris* juxtaposes the situation of the writing subject with that of others in the streets. Fragments of her life as a writer from abroad are collocated, for example, with the abjection of the unemployed, homeless, and sick, with the deportation of a Kenyan without papers, with the suicide of another man of African origin, with the harassment of North Africans, and with the experience of women in Sarajevo. Such a strategy of juxtaposing and superimposing disparate points of view, moments, fragments of syntax, and so forth is not unlike the collage poetics one finds in Stein and other modernists. As Dianne Chisholm argues, it is specifically indebted to the montage technique of Walter Benjamin, another figure who haunts Scott's Paris. *My Paris* makes a number of references to Benjamin's *The Arcades Project*, a text it describes as "**Not** a real history. Rather—vast collection of 19th-century quotes and anecdotes. Initially seeming huge pile of detritus. But—on looking closer. More like montage. Possibly assembled using old surrealist trick. Of free association" (18). The two short passages cited above cannot do justice to the radical "dream analysis" (Chisholm 160) that subtends Scott's practice of montage in *My Paris*, but they do give a sense of the disjunctive images selected by the writing subject, images that affront readers with the disparate and conflictual histories hidden by the narratives of fine cuisine, haute couture, bohemian culture, cosmopolitanism, modernity, and so forth that constitute Paris. The images of workers "from south" vacuuming dog shit and of Stein's poodle shitting in the streets of Paris would seem to be unrelated. However, held together in Scott's text, they speak of various interlocking histories of colonialism, imperialism, and migration, and of different ways in which groups occupy the land of another.

Both passages locate Stein in relation to subjects who fall outside the purview of her texts. The "foreigners" of *Paris France*, for example, are not immigrants; they are not akin to those who, later in the century, clean the streets and number heavily among the unemployed. Rather, Stein's foreigners are expatriate writers and artists who experience their foreignness as productive insofar as it alters their relationship to their own language and culture. Scott's writing subject is ambivalent about counting herself among Stein's expatriates, an ambivalence that is registered graphically in the quotation marks and bold typeface on "**us**" in the second passage. Lacking the right documents to show the French immigration authorities or the kind of wealth that many expatriates enjoyed, and living as she does "with foreign queen on dollars" (83), she identifies with the disenfranchised. At the same time, her situation is clearly not the same as those from Africa and the Maghreb (12). That she waves "complicitly" at the protestors suggests that she is both sympathetic to their cause and painfully aware of her relative privilege. Indeed, throughout the novel, she struggles with the contradictions of a city that suppresses as it celebrates and glorifies proletarian revolution.

Although *My Paris* is not a portrait of Stein, the references to Stein's highly unconventional portraits make it possible to read sequences such as those cited above as oblique portraits of her. In fact, insofar as Scott's "portraits" approach Stein through her dog Basket or through condensations of her words, postures, and practices, they are not unlike Stein's portraits. Stein's portraits do not describe their subjects. Instead, using various compositional strategies, among them the patterns of three words that Scott's writing subject comments on in *My Paris* (49, 65), they convey a sense of the process of perceiving the portrait subject, her patterns of thought, and her ways of relating to others. Scott's text, too, uses grammar to suggest the processes of perception and to diagram relationships, including her own troubled relationship to Stein.

There are, however, substantial differences between the sentences of *My Paris* and those of Stein's portraits. Sentences in *My Paris* are often fragments—that is, syntactic units that may or may not belong together, separated by periods. Think, for example, of the "portrait" of Stein in the second passage from *My Paris* cited above: "Near Gertrude Stein's. Whose genius. Being American. Interested in gathering what ordinary (common). In all of '**us**.' While loving Paris as refuge. Of individuals (artists)." Such sequences of clipped sentences—part of Scott's practice of Benjaminian montage—often serve to foreground the contradictions of Paris or to evoke the rhythms of the writing subject's movement through the city (Chisholm 156, 167–68). Here, they highlight the presumption behind Stein's claims. By minimizing syntactic connections, Scott's text questions the self-evidence of the relationships between "Stein," "genius," and "being American," and troubles the coherence of Stein's expatriate "we" (Stein, *Paris France* 15). Scott's writing subject, like Stein's, includes her own subject position within the portrait—"all of '**us**'"—but she does so in order to mark her difference from Stein.

Compare Scott's "portrait" to Stein's 1910 portrait of Alice Toklas, "Ada":

> She was telling some one, who was loving every story that was charming. Some one who was living was almost always listening. Some one who was loving was almost always listening. That one who was loving was

almost always listening. That one who was loving was telling about being one then listening ... Trembling was all living, living was all loving, someone was then the other one. Certainly this one was loving Ada then. (16)

Working with minimal vocabulary, Stein's sentences create strings of simple syntactic units through a form of "insistence" that differs from simple repetition. If, as I argued earlier, Scott is intrigued by what Stein does with verbs, she is also troubled by it. In *My Paris*, the writing subject comments that the multiplication of predicates has the effect of "soaking up surroundings. Until mysteriously inflating subject (narrator). Into huge transparent shadow" (36). Although the comments of Scott's writing subject refer more to texts such as *Paris France* or "How Writing Is Written" than to the portrait cited here, they are nevertheless relevant. It is Stein as much as Toklas who is revealed by these lines from "Ada." The combination of pronouns and progressive verbs has the effect of aggrandizing Stein as portrait writer, as one who "was telling about being one then listening." At the same time, of course, this combination works to confound—and thereby diffuse—the identities of the two women and to capture their becoming lovers (Burke 232). One might further argue that, at least in texts such as "Ada," Stein is as interested in rendering the process of listening and the porosity of the subject as Scott is. Perhaps because of the desire to distinguish "*My Paris*" from Stein's Paris, a desire that is clear from Scott's interview with Corey Frost ("Intertexts" 106–7), *My Paris* focusses on texts in which Stein promotes and explains her work. As a result, the novel says very little about the writers' shared view of the subject as a dynamic process.

Scott's compositional strategies in *My Paris* resist Stein's strong sense of American identity. In "My Montréal," Scott's writing subject recounts how she crosses out the "I" in the "false diary" that would become *My Paris* in order to "reduce it to the smallest possible entity. The eye of a clown. A female-sexed clown" (8).[11] At the same time, she recognizes in "The Porous Text" that "behind this small clownlike figure speaking its porous text lurks a huge shadow. The shadow of western culture. Her own. Speaking through and against her" (205). In other words, Scott finds in her own writing practice the tension I have identified in Stein's.

Just as Stein's predicates work simultaneously to generate and to dissipate ego, Scott's writing subject both claims Paris and disappears into its streets. Both writers are caught between losing the self in the process of writing and being a "someone," that is, a writer with a history, a project, and an interpretive community (Scott, *My Paris* 147; Stein, "Portraits and

Repetition" 175–76). Stein frames this tension in terms of the difference between writing and remembering: "The thing one gradually comes to find out is that one has no identity that is when one is in the act of doing anything. Identity is recognition, you know who you are because you and others remember anything about yourself but essentially you are not that when you are doing anything" ("What Are Master-pieces?" 496). In contrast, Scott frames the tension in terms of the interface between the writing subject and the colloquies of history and place, an interface generated (among other things) by participles in *My Paris*. For her, "The present participle does not go straightforward. The movement is gestural, swings forward and back, extending the writing subject into its environment. And the reverse! It links within to without" ("Porous Text" 205). Whereas Stein uses progressive verb forms to render the process of perception and the intersubjectivity of portraiture, Scott uses them to locate a subject in history and to expose the contradictory relationship of the writing subject to specific histories made legible by her visit to Paris.

Scott's writing brings the historical and material to bear upon the exploration of grammar and subjectivity that she finds in Stein's texts. If *My Paris* engages the question of what it means to write "while identity is not" ("What Are Master-pieces?" 499), it does so in ways that emphasize the porous interface between city and subject. Whether she is circulating in the streets or reclining on her divan, Scott's writing subject is alive to quotidian details such as the name of a given street and the kinds of living, working, shopping, and protesting carried out there; she is alive to the experiences of her body (movement, lethargy, intoxication, pleasure, abjection), and alive to what is going on elsewhere in the world (wars, migrations, national elections), as well as to what is going on—unacknowledged—in Paris (discrimination, suicide, poverty, subterranean existences, lesbian sex). The writing subject of *My Paris* is both an agent and an effect of an intertextual weave of discourses and practices that include music, visual art, media, immigration, war, literature, travel, postcolonial theory, labour history, culinary arts, politics, urbanism, and film.

Stein's writing is less interested in foregrounding intertextuality. Where it does acknowledge other discourses and practices—for example, in *The Autobiography of Alice B. Toklas* or in "How Writing Is Written"—the acknowledgement serves to locate Stein's writing on the cutting edge of early twentieth-century technology and artistic practice; that is, it serves to highlight Stein's genius, her originality. Of course, Scott's "small subject," as much a performance as Stein's "ego," locates her writing on the cutting edge of artistic practice at the turn of the twenty-first century. Scott admits as much in "The Porous Text" (203–5). This is precisely the difference between the two. Scott admits to the performance, to the contingencies of the performance (the need for an interpretive community of women readers and writers), and to the contradictions of the performance (the "shadow of western culture"). "The Porous Text," for example, concludes its reflections on the small subject with the words, "Walter Benjamin, commenting on his own revolutionary montage-style history method, stated truth was ultimately dependent on analysing where the self-interest lay. Ditto for the porous *I* of my porous text" (205–6).

There are many ways of accounting for the differences between Stein's writing and Scott's writing—including the historical interventions of feminism, poststructuralism, and postcolonialism, all of which allow Scott to read the oversights of modernism.[12] The difference is also attributable to Scott's reading of Walter Benjamin. Benjamin is one of the figures to whom Scott turns again and again in *My Paris*, as well as in recent essays, and it is arguably through the lens of Benjamin's Paris—the Paris of *The Arcades Project* and "On Some Motifs in Baudelaire"—that Scott reads Stein's Paris. Benjamin's oeuvre is as important an intertext in *My Paris* as Stein's oeuvre. In my discussion, I have focussed primarily on Scott's reading of Stein, partly because other readings, notably those of Simon and Chisholm, have focussed on Benjamin, and partly because I am interested in intertextual relationships between women writers. Simon and Chisholm acknowledge Scott's debt to Stein but tend to emphasize Scott's departures from her predecessor. In many ways, Scott's text does the same. These departures are crucial; indeed, they motivate my reading of *My Paris*, as well as my sense of the need to allow for discontinuity within literary history. As I have suggested in this section, however, the continuities also deserve attention, especially the continuities in the writers' treatment of subjectivity and the enunciation. Although the posture of the writing subject in Stein's lectures and interviews can hardly be described as one of listening, as one of a "small" subject, there is nevertheless in the portrait writing of both women an interest in the enunciative drift between subject and object, in the porosity of the "I" (Chisholm 168).

Throughout this essay, I have addressed the specificity of women's relationships to literary history and the kinds of readings made available by holding women's texts together across national, generational, and other differences. Scott's return to Stein reminds us of the role of international connections in the history of Canadian modernism, connections that are especially crucial for women writers such as Scott whose experiments are difficult to locate within the paradigms of a national literature. Scott's return makes legible not only the assumptions and oversights of Stein's expatriate American "I," but also what is at stake for a woman writer in the contradiction between losing her self in the process of writing and presenting herself as a "someone," a "female-sexed" "someone." Whereas Stein was unable to present herself this way, Scott is able—thanks to an international community of women writers and readers—to "lose herself" in writing, to dwell in the enunciative drift as a woman, without utterly compromising her place in literary history. Gender is a key element in Scott's sense of literary affiliation and belonging. It is not, of course, the only one and, in this sense, Scott's writing, like that of Stein, cannot be contained by my inscription of it within a feminist history of women's writing. The intertexts abound.

Notes

I would like to thank Di Brandt, Barbara Godard, Andrew Miller, and Gail Scott for their dialogue during the writing of this essay. Research for the project was enabled by funding from the Social Sciences and Humanities Research Council of Canada.

1. As Sherry Simon observes, "Creative interference becomes the basis of a transcultural poetics ... built on a history of friction and divisiveness" (*Translating Montreal* 125).
2. Throughout this essay, there is a slippage between what is attributed to writers and what is attributed to their texts. This slippage is symptomatic of a tension between poststructuralist understandings of the writing subject as an effect of the text and feminist understandings of the text as an effect of the meanings, desires, identifications, investments, locations, movements, and histories of specific subjects. I read Scott's discourse—whether in her fictions, her essays, her interviews, or her conversations with me—as a text. At the same time, I allow what she says in essays and interviews (for example, about her relationship to Montreal or Paris, about reading Gertrude Stein or Walter Benjamin, or about the compositional limits she sets herself) to bear upon my reading of her fiction. Not to do so would be to ignore the ways in which Scott's texts work to break down absolute borders between writer and narrator, between the fictional and the real, between the realm of literary criticism and that of representation, and between the moment of reading and that of writing.
3. For a discussion of these subjective processes in the context of Virginia Woolf's practices of literary history, see Beth Carole Rosenberg, especially the observation, "In traditional literary history it is the role of the writer that is the focus; in Woolf's history the audience is given equal emphasis, and it is through the audience that the identity of the author is determined" (1119). Also relevant, in the context of Woolf's response to Jane Austen, is the point that "*A Room [of One's Own]* becomes self-reflexive, and it tells us more about Woolf and her own subjective historical moment—what her literary values and goals are as an early twentieth-century writer—than it does about any objective history from which she allegedly comes" (1122).

4 The new collective comprised Pamela Banting, Di Brandt, Jane Casey, and Jan Horner. For a more detailed analysis of the history of *Contemporary Verse* and the changes in editorial policy between Livesay's *CV/II* and the collective's *CV2*, see Christine Kim's "Feminist and Regionalist Modernisms in *Contemporary Verse, CV/II* and *CV2*" in this volume.
5 In a private conversation with the author, Scott indicated that Théoret had told her of Watson's support for her early work.
6 See Patricia Smart's *Les femmes du Refus global* for insight into the work of the women who participated in this movement but who, for various reasons, fall outside the histories.
7 See the articles of Gregory W. Bredbeck, Dianne Chisholm (204n1), and Robert Glück for further discussion of new narrative. See also *Biting the Error: Writers Explore Narrative*, edited by Mary Burger, Glück, Camille Roy, and Scott.
8 Kathleen Fraser discusses the latter mechanisms as they function within American literature (30, 34, 38). Fraser's sense of her project as a reconstruction of a pre-existing tradition, as a "'dig' for a female tradition of linguistic intervention" (38), is nonetheless different from my understanding of literary history as a process in which readings and writings have an ongoing productivity. On the subject of misreading, specifically the "re-writing" of Gabrielle Roy, Anne Hébert, and Marie-Claire Blais within the English-Canadian literary field, see Godard's "Une littérature en devenir: La réécriture textuelle et le dynamisme du champ littéraire; Les écrivaines québécoises au Canada anglais."
9 Rosenberg observes that "Ezell's analysis frames Woolf's *A Room* in the same terms as those she criticizes—she views this work as actual history, as an attempt to create a definitive, linear progression in women's writing. *A Room* must be viewed in the same light as Woolf's other so-called literary histories to understand her project as one that is ultimately concerned with the processes of reading and writing" (1113).
10 Jonathan Monroe uses the term "cross-generational intertextuality" in conjunction with "interorality" in an essay on the poetry of Muscogee writer Joy Harjo. He does so advisedly, noting that such terms "risk obscuring the fact that Native American traditions involved such interweavings long before modernism" (95). Intertextuality, in Harjo's poetry, is akin to "'Tribal Memory,' a collective 'autobiographical' sense that has less to do with individual identity than with the 'web' of shared histories and relations" (95). Also significant for a consideration of literary history is Monroe's comment that "for Harjo, the value of innovation cannot be measured in and of itself, but only in terms of the value of what gets preserved and what gets lost in the ever-changing 'web'" (93).
11 Note the insistence in Scott's text upon the fact that the writing subject is a woman, something that is signalled only very obliquely in one or two of Stein's texts. For the most part, Stein refers to writers and artists as men. My essay "Sex of a Clown: Gail Scott's *My Paris*" addresses at length questions of sex and gender in Scott's text.
12 As Godard notes in "Re: post" (134), Andreas Huyssen qualifies this form of reading as "postmodern" (209).

Works Cited

Benjamin, Walter. *The Arcades Project*. Trans. Howard Eiland and Kevin McLaughlin. Boston: Harvard UP, 1999.

———. "On Some Motifs in Baudelaire." *Illuminations: Essays and Reflections*. Ed. Hannah Arendt. Trans. Harry Zohn. New York: Shocken, 1968. 155–200.

Brandt, Di. Afterword. *Archive for Our Times: Previously Uncollected and Unpublished Poems of Dorothy Livesay*. Ed. Dean J. Irvine. Vancouver: Arsenal Pulp, 1998. 246–49.

Bredbeck, Gregory W. "The New Queer Narrative: Intervention and Critique." *Textual Practice* 9.3 (1995): 477–502.

Burger, Mary, Robert Glück, Camille Roy, and Gail Scott, eds. *Biting the Error: Writers Explore Narrative*. Toronto: Coach House, 2004.

Burke, Carolyn. "Gertrude Stein, the Cone Sisters, and the Puzzle of Female Friendship." *Writing and Sexual Difference*. Ed. Elizabeth Abel. Chicago: U of Chicago P, 1982. 221–42.

Chisholm, Dianne. "Paris, *Mon Amour*, My Catastrophe, or Flâneries through Benjaminian Space." *Gail Scott: Essays on Her Works*. Ed. Lianne Moyes. Toronto: Guernica, 2002. 153–207.

de Lauretis, Teresa. "Sexual Indifference and Lesbian Representation." *Performing Feminisms: Feminist Critical Theory and Theatre*. Ed. Sue-Ellen Case. Baltimore: Johns Hopkins UP, 1990. 17–39.

Ezell, Margaret J.M. *Writing Women's Literary History*. Baltimore: Johns Hopkins UP, 1993.

Foucault, Michel. "Nietzsche, Genealogy, History." *Language, Counter-memory, Practice: Selected Essays and Interviews*. Ed. Donald F. Bouchard. Trans. Donald F. Bouchard and Sherry Simon. Ithaca: Cornell UP, 1977. 139–64.

Fraser, Kathleen. "The Tradition of Marginality ... and the Emergence of *HOW(ever)*." *Translating the Unspeakable: Poetry and the Innovative Necessity; Essays*. Tuscaloosa: U of Alabama P, 2000. 25–38.

Friedman, Ellen G., and Miriam Fuchs. Introduction. *Breaking the Sequence: Women's Experimental Fiction*. Ed. E.G. Friedman and M. Fuchs. Princeton: Princeton UP, 1989. 3–51.

Glück, Robert. "Long Note on New Narrative." *Narrativity*. Ed. Mary Burger, Robert Glück, Camille Roy, and Gail Scott. 1 (n.d.), <www.sfsu.edu/~newlit/narrativity/home.html>.

Godard, Barbara. "'Between One Cliché and Another': Language in *The Double Hook*." *Studies in Canadian Literature* 3.2 (Summer 1978): 149–65.

———. "El Greco in Canada: Sinclair Ross's *As for Me and My House*." *Mosaic* 14.2 (1981): 55–75.

———. "Ex-centriques, Eccentric, Avant-Garde: Women and Modernism in the Literatures of Canada." *Tessera* 1 / *Room of One's Own: A Feminist Journal* 8.4 (January 1984): 57–75.

———. "Intertextuality." *Encyclopedia of Contemporary Literary Theory: Approaches, Scholars, Terms*. Ed. Irena Makaryk. Toronto: U of Toronto P, 1993. 568–72.

———. "Une littérature en devenir: La réécriture textuelle et le dynamisme du champ littéraire; Les écrivaines québécoises au Canada anglais." *Voix et images* 72 (1999): 495–527.

———. "Re: post." *Quebec Studies* 9 (1989–90): 131–43.

———. "Women of Letters (Reprise)." *Collaboration in the Feminine: Writings on Women and Culture from Tessera*. Ed. Barbara Godard. Toronto: Second Story, 1994. 258–306.

Godard, Barbara, and Di Brandt. "Call for Papers: 'Wider Boundaries of Daring': The Modernist Impulse in Canadian Women's Poetry [conference]." University of Windsor, Windsor, ON. 25–28 October 2001. <www.uwindsor.ca/poetry conference>.

Huyssen, Andreas. *After the Great Divide: Modernism, Mass Culture, Postmodernism*. Bloomington: Indiana UP, 1986.

Kristeva, Julia. "An Interview with Julia Kristeva." By Margaret Waller. Trans. Richard Macksey. *Intertextuality and Contemporary American Fiction*. Ed. Patrick O'Donnell and Robert Con Davis. Baltimore: Johns Hopkins UP, 1989. 280–93.

Livesay, Dorothy. *Archive for Our Times: Previously Uncollected and Unpublished Poems of Dorothy Livesay*. Ed. Dean J. Irvine. Vancouver: Arsenal Pulp, 1998.

Monroe, Jonathan. "Untranslatable Communities, Productive Translation, and Public Transport: Rosmarie Waldrop's *A Key into the Language of America* and Joy Harjo's *The Woman Who Fell from the Sky*." *We Who Love to Be Astonished: Experimental Women's Writing and Performance Poetics*. Ed. Laura Hinton and Cynthia Hogue. Tuscaloosa: U of Alabama P, 2002. 90–102.

Moyes, Lianne. "Sex of a Clown: Gail Scott's *My Paris*." *Un certain genre malgré tout: Pour une réflexion sur la différence sexuelle à l'oeuvre dans l'écriture*. Ed. Catherine Mavrikakis and Patrick Poirier. Montreal: Nota Bene, 2006. 157–73.

Perloff, Marjorie. *21st-Century Modernism: The "New" Poetics*. Oxford: Blackwell, 2002.

Rosenberg, Beth Carole. "Virginia Woolf's Postmodern Literary History." *Modern Language Notes* 115 (2000): 1112–30.

Scott, Bonnie Kime. "A Tangled Mesh of Modernists." *The Gender of Modernism: A Critical Anthology*. Ed. Bonnie Kime Scott. Bloomington: Indiana UP, 1990. 10.

Scott, Gail. "Bottoms Up." *Narrativity*. Ed. Mary Burger, Robert Glück, Camille Roy and Gail Scott. 1 (n.d.), <www.sfsu.edu/~newlit/narrativity/home.html>. Rpt. in *Spare Parts Plus Two*. 1981. Toronto: Coach House, 2002. 83–89.

———. "Elixir for Thinking: Carla Harryman's *There Never Was Rose Without a Thorn*." *West Coast Line* 31.2 (Autumn 1997): 144–48.

———. "*Four Stories* de Sheila Watson." *Spirale* (March 1981): 5.

———. *Heroine*. Toronto: Coach House, 1987; Vancouver: Talonbooks, 1999.
———. "Intertexts." Interview with Corey Frost. *The Matrix Interviews*. Ed. R.E.N. Allen and Angela Carr. Montreal: DC, 2001. 103–26.
———. "Miroirs inconstants." In dossier "Écrire en anglais au Québec: Un devenir minoritaire?" Ed. Lianne Moyes. *Quebec Studies* 26 (Fall 1998–Winter 1999): 23–25.
———. "My Montréal: Notes of an Anglo-Québécois Writer." *Brick* 59 (Spring 1998): 4–9.
———. *My Paris: A Novel*. Toronto: Mercury, 1999.
———. "The Porous Text, or the Ecology of the Small Subject, Take 2." *Different Languages*. Ed. Jena Osman and Juliana Spahr. Spec. issue of *Chain* 5 (1998): 202–6, <www.temple.edu/chain/archives/index.html>.
———. *Spaces Like Stairs: Essays*. Toronto: Women's Press, 1989.
———. "Theorizing Fiction Theory." With Barbara Godard, Daphne Marlatt, and Kathy Mezei. *Collaboration in the Feminine*. Toronto: Second Story, 1994. 53–62.
———. "The Virgin Denotes, Or The Unreliability of Adverbs, To Do with Time." *Spare Parts Plus Two*. 1981. Toronto: Coach House, 2002. 7–18.
———. "What If the Writer Were in Bed? On Narrative." *Matrix* 48 (1996): 3–6.
———. "What We Talk About on Sundays." With Nicole Brossard, Louky Bersianik, Louise Cotnoir, Louise Dupré, and France Théoret. Trans. Barbara Godard. *Collaboration in the Feminine*. Toronto: Second Story, 1994. 127–35.
Simon, Sherry. "The Paris Arcades, the Ponte Vecchio and the Comma of Translation." *Gail Scott: Essays on Her Works*. Ed. Lianne Moyes. Toronto: Guernica, 2002. 142–52.
———. *Translating Montreal: Episodes in the Life of a Divided City*. Montreal: McGill-Queen's UP, 2006.
Smart, Patricia. *Les femmes du Refus global*. Montréal: Boréal, 1998.
Stein, Gertrude. "Ada." *Geography and Plays*. 1922. New York: Haskell House, 1967. 14–16.
———. *The Autobiography of Alice B. Toklas*. 1933. *The Selected Writings of Gertrude Stein*. New York: Vintage, 1990. 1–237.
———. "Composition as Explanation." 1926. *The Selected Writings of Gertrude Stein*. New York: Vintage, 1990. 513–23.
———. "How Writing Is Written." 1974. *The Gender of Modernism*. Ed. Bonnie Kime Scott. Bloomington: Indiana UP, 1990. 488–95.
———. *Paris France*. 1940. New York: Liveright, 1970.
———. "Poetry and Grammar." 1935. *Lectures in America*. Boston: Beacon, 1957. 209–46.
———. "Portraits and Repetition." 1935. *Lectures in America*. Boston: Beacon, 1957. 165–206.

———. "A Transatlantic Interview 1946." By Robert Bartlett Haas. *The Gender of Modernism*. Ed. Bonnie Kime Scott. Bloomington: Indiana UP, 1990. 502–16.

———. "What Are Master-pieces and Why Are There So Few of Them?" 1940. *The Gender of Modernism*. Ed. Bonnie Kime Scott. Bloomington: Indiana UP, 1990. 495–501.

Vickery, Ann. *Leaving Lines of Gender: A Feminist Genealogy of Language Writing*. Hanover, NH: Wesleyan UP-UPNE, 2000.

Warren, Joyce W., and Margaret Dickie, eds. *Challenging Boundaries: Gender and Periodization*. Athens: U of Georgia P, 2000.

Watson, Sheila. "Gertrude Stein: The Style Is the Machine." *Open Letter* 3.1 (Winter 1974–1975): 167–78.

LITERARY MODERNISM
AS CULTURAL ACT

"They cut him down"
Race, Class, and Cultural Memory in Dorothy Livesay's "Day and Night"

PAMELA MCCALLUM

On a cool urban winter evening in the early 1970s, I went with two friends to hear the poet Dorothy Livesay read at York University. Over thirty years later, a particular moment of that reading remains vivid in my mind. One of the poems that Livesay chose to read was "Day and Night," her long documentary lyric written in the mid-1930s after her year's residence in New Jersey (*Collected Poems* 120–25). The poem begins with an account of factory labour, almost hypnotically repeating the phrase "one step forward, two steps back," and as she read, she stepped forward and back, miming the movements her words described. It was this embodied performance of the repeated motions of factory workers—a few minutes while the poem was read—that challenged her audience to imagine those actions stretched out to thirty minutes, to an hour, to several hours, to the eight hours of a shift, and to engage, if only in their minds, the world of those she described: muscles aching from the resistance of materials, arms pressed close to machinery, breath stifled by the fumes of fire and molten metal, the human body marked by wearying work. It was a powerful reminder within the class-marked space of a poetry reading in a university setting not to forget another world of repetitious and exhausting labour.

There are, however, other resonances in the phrase "one step forward, two steps back": it is the title of a pamphlet written by Vladimir Lenin in 1904 during the early debates about the direction of the exiled Russian left opposition. In "One Step Forward, Two Steps Back," Lenin argues for the strong central organization and concentration of authority in a disciplined political party and its leaders, a structure that later would come to characterize the Bolsheviks in their successful revolution against the czarist state. Lenin's "democratic centralism," a strategy that stressed unity at the expense of dissent, was intended to challenge the idea that history was locked into a largely unchangeable evolutionist process by interjecting the flexibility necessary for "discontinuous acts of revolution" (Carr 49), the unexpected moment of insurrection that might alter the course of history. Although the Bolshevik model of revolution, like its French Jacobin inspiration, ended up in a rigid, intransigent party structure, it is important to historicize Lenin's arguments and to stress that democratic centralism attempted to open a space for a spontaneous, transformative intervention. How do these two apparently contradictory concepts figured in "Day and Night"—arduous, exhausting, repetitive labour and the exhilarating instant of historical change—work together in Livesay's poem? In what ways does her text negotiate the requirements for realism implicit in the documentary form and the very different demands of imagining a transformation of what is? How does the specific historical conjuncture of mid-1930s politics offer her unique resources for lyric composition?

In the fall of 1934, Livesay left Canada to work in the United States, quickly finding a job as a social worker at an agency in Englewood, New Jersey, across the Hudson River from New York City. She was particularly impressed by the social democratic projects of Roosevelt's National Reconstruction Administration and the Works Progress Administration: instead of the demeaning work camps for the unemployed that the Bennett government had set up in Canada, the NRA and the WPA had embarked on a wide range of economic, social, and cultural initiatives that empowered local communities and created employment, including projects for artists, writers, actors, and musicians (*Journey* 145–46). In contrast to the bleak hopelessness of the Depression in Canada, the United States represented, Livesay would recall many years later, "a place to breathe in" (*Right Hand* 130). The agency she worked with served both an impoverished Black population and more affluent Whites who had been declassed by the Depression, but employed Black and White social workers for the respective populations and stressed that the two groups were not to socialize together. This rule, however, was regularly broken. Livesay writes, for instance, about an evening across the river in Harlem where an interracial group of five friends visited a jazz bar, something they could not do in Englewood: there "we could never be seen together in a car, three whites and two Blacks" (*Journey* 146–47).

Such negotiations of the complex "race" politics of everyday life in the United States drew Livesay's attention to the tensions and overdeterminations of racialization and class, and impelled her to think through the intersections of these different but overlapping modes of domination. Livesay has repeatedly commented that the time she spent living in the United States introduced her to the injustices of racism (*Journey* 146–49; *Right Hand* 129–30). She was made aware of grinding poverty: "housing, overcrowding, unemployment—all affect[ed] the hundreds of Black people who were moving or had moved from the south into small towns around New York" (*Journey* 146). She also learned of the injustices and exclusions faced by her three Black co-workers, two women and one man, a Harvard-educated lawyer whose persona Livesay later depicted as the determined but psychologically damaged Paul in her radio play "The Times Were Different." "From these three," she writes, "I got to know how stifled and impoverished was the Black population" (*Journey* 146). Nor was she inattentive to the tensions of racialization and gender within leftist movements. Her short story "Herbie" (*Right Hand* 150–52) represents, in the classic modernist style of interiorized subjective narrative, the thoughts and reactions of an angry man whose advances towards a young Black woman working in the CP bookstore are rejected: "nigger bitch," "coloured flashes" (*Right Hand* 151). In Canada, she had been very active in the Progressive Arts Club working with agit-prop theatre, writing for *Masses* and later for *New Frontier* (Irvine, "Editorial" 252–53; Lister 53–64).[1] Contemplating her experiences four decades later, she drew attention to her ignorance of racism and utter lack of experience with Black people during her youth and young adulthood in Canada: "My only relationship with Negros had been on trains—with friendly coloured porters—and in Canada; even in Montreal, I had not encountered the racial antagonisms or thought they existed" (*Right Hand* 129).[2] She went on to connect her awakening to the oppressions of racism with her earlier understanding of anti-Semitism: "I knew all about the Jewish problem of course and was always out in defence of the Jew as underdog" (129). If Livesay's coupling of these oppressions seems somewhat naïve now, following more recent conflicts between Black and Jewish communities in New York City and elsewhere, it is important to situate her reaction in its historical moment, a brief time when the Communist Party and the Popular Front brought together divergent leftist struggles.

In a 1944 review of Livesay's poetry collection *Day and Night*, F.R. Scott drew attention to her aesthetics of social commitment; she was "a contemporary of the growing number of Canadian poets on whom the impact of the present age is direct and not derivative" (qtd. in Kelly 57). Indeed, living in the United States during the mid-1930s provided an unusual opportunity to experience a historical conjuncture within which innovative social and cultural resistance to racism and other modes of social domination took shape. When Livesay moved to New Jersey, she was accepted, on the strength of her Canadian Communist Party card, into a Communist Party USA (CPUSA) group in the nearby town of Hackensack. In 1928, the Sixth World Congress of the Comintern had taken the position that African-Americans were an "oppressed nation" in the South and a "national minority in northern cities" (Smethurst 18). The effect of such a declaration was to bring the question of "race" into far more prominence than it had previously held and to release it from subordination to class. During a few years in the early-to-mid-1930s, "race" and class were understood within the CPUSA as complementary and inseparable in a way that previously had not been possible. As James Smethurst describes in his study *The New Red Negro: The Literary Left and African American Poetry, 1930–1946*, what distinguished "the CPUSA most sharply from other Left organizations was the degree to which it elevated the struggle against racism and what it called 'Negro liberation' to the center of its work, particularly after the Comintern's Sixth Congress, which linked 'Negro liberation' to anticolonial struggles around the world" (22). Within such a context, the cultural energies of leftist writers produced a startling body of work. Writers as diverse as Sterling Brown, Langston Hughes, Zora Neale Hurston, and Countee Cullen retrieved and developed forms of Black folk culture—music, storytelling, preaching, dance, humour—into new aesthetic practices. Innovative and unforeseen forms of collaboration were taken up by Black cultural figures: Richard Wright, for example, wrote lyrics to a song about the boxer Joe Louis ("King Joe") that was recorded by Paul Robeson and the Count Basie Orchestra (Smethurst 32). In addition, leftist and CPUSA journals—*New Masses*, the *Daily Worker*, the *Southern Worker*, the *Anvil*, *Dynamo*, and *Contempo*—provided forums for the publication of experimental Black writing (Smethurst 33–35). When Livesay lived in New Jersey during the mid-1930s, therefore, she encountered a uniquely critical moment in the construction of an emergent oppositional political aesthetic. "It was," she reflected more than forty years later, "an extraordinarily stimulating experience to be there" (*Right Hand* 130).

What is especially significant about "Day and Night," I will argue, is the reworking of her encounter with Black culture into powerful figurations of harsh oppression and, conversely, of an imagined collective response to modes of domination. Cultural memories of the distant past of slavery intersect with contemporary images of racism, converging in the ferocious violence of lynching. In a parallel manner, the rhythms of Livesay's poem evoke the relentless motion of men and machines patterning factory labour, constructing, in Marvin Gilman's phrase, "a radical snapshot of industrial depersonalization" (28). At the same time, from Black cultural traditions counter-discursive figurations of solidarity and collectivity work their way out of the ruthless brutality to provide a vision of other possibilities.

Livesay's engagement with Black culture in "Day and Night" inevitably raises the vexing issue of cultural appropriation. How might readers who have been sensitized in the twenty-first century to issues of appropriation assess her use of Black culture in this poem? It is crucial to situate Livesay's textual practice in the historical moment of the mid-1930s, and especially in the cultural politics of the Communist Party and the Popular Front. Writing in *Borrowed Power: Essays on Cultural Appropriation*, Kwame Dawes has commented that the interaction and sharing of culture "whether it be exploitative or that of mutual respect and sharing—is something that is arguably inherent in human behaviour" (117–18). Dawes goes on to suggest that the crucial question to be asked about cultural appropriation is the extent to which such representations arise out of disregard and exploitation or out of respect and shared possibilities (119). Within leftist cultural politics in the 1930s, exchanges between groups were conceived less as a ground where the individual attributes of an identity politics might be appropriated than as a space of collective opposition to common oppressions. Livesay's use of fragments drawn from Black culture and cultural memories, I will argue, is part of a shared emancipatory project.

"Day and Night," published in the inaugural issue of E.J. Pratt's *Canadian Poetry Magazine* in 1936, bears the structural markings of a radio documentary verse in its six sections and shifting voices. Paul Denham characterizes the poem's organization as "separate scenes, spoken by different voices," representing a technique "closer to cinema than narrative" (93). Using a similar figure, Caren Irr describes the poem's movement in terms of "the famous image of the dancing camera and tripod" in Ziga Vertov's classic film *Man with a Movie Camera* (229). Livesay opens "Day and Night" with a third-person voice that, like those of Walt Whitman and Carl Sandburg, portrays the dehumanization of the individual by machinery: "Men in a stream, a moving human belt / Move into sockets, every one a bolt" (1.5–6).[3] The slippage of organic metaphor (men as a human stream) into a metonymic fission of mechanistic human sockets and bolts aptly represents the subordination of the workers to the vast impersonal organization of factory labour. In the second section, the poem draws closer, much like the focussing of a documentary camera lens, on the repetitive movements of the men on the factory floor (the hypnotic chorus of "One step forward / Two steps back"). The words of the third section provide a more interiorized, first-person reflection on the psychological violence of factory labour: "We move as through sleep's revolving memories," this voice tells the reader, "Piling up hatred, stealing the remnants" (3.6–7). The speaker poignantly asks, "On what agenda / will you set love down? Who knows of peace?" (3.9–10). In the fourth section, this gentle, questioning voice is elided into another first-person voice that narrates the unjust treatment of a Black worker, and trails off into the words of a gospel song. At this point in the poem, it is difficult to distinguish the individual voices.[4] Just as the workers disappear into the relentless transpersonal structures of factory production, so Livesay's text represents a merging of the individual voice into a social collectivity. Are the words in the fourth section spoken by the same voice as that in the previous section? Is the haunting spiritual song sung by the White worker, who tells of his Black friend's demotion, a remembrance of shared Black culture, or are the words the trace of the Black man's voice, which persists over the deafening factory noise? While the poem raises these questions, it does not seem to require an answer; rather, it is more important to recognize the collectivity embodied in the shifting transindividual voices. In the two final sections, the voice becomes more confident, asserting the factory's inability to break the workers' spirits: "Into thy maw I commend my body / But the soul shines without" (4.1–2). The daily indignities suffered in the steel mills may harm the body, but not the persistence of the soul.

Read in this way, "Day and Night" seems to be a teleological progression from a state of grinding oppression through to a hopeful recognition of the resilience of the human spirit; yet crisscrossing this trajectory are powerful figurations of cultural memories of slavery and abjection that work to intertwine different pasts with the present, and to layer past oppressions onto the present. When Livesay's text begins to evoke the repetitive movements of "one step forward / two steps back" labour, the factory is represented through one of the most culturally significant and brutalizing images of slavery: the whip. In the third verse of the second section, Livesay writes,

> One step forward
> Hear it crack
> Smashing rhythm
> Two steps back (2.9–12)

In another quatrain, she continues,

> Across the way
> A writhing whack
> Sets you spinning
> Two steps back—(2.17–20)

In these metaphors and others—"Set your voice resounding / Above the steel's whip crack" (3.21–22)—Livesay draws out the connections between the back-breaking labour of cotton or sugar-cane fields, under the implacable gaze of the overseer and the constant threat of the whip, and the workplaces of the Northern factories where poverty and necessity became whips, just as real, of a new kind. The relentless repetition of "two steps back" suggests that migration to the industrial North has not unproblematically opened up opportunities for the Black population. The past reaches into the present both with its cultural memory of slavery and with the continuation of oppression.

The shift in voice in the fourth section introduces a more familiar, direct tone as one worker speaks of his friendship with a Black colleague, born out of the shared labour in front of the steel furnaces. In the blunt, clipped phrasing of working-class speech, rhetorically posed to counter the reader's disbelief—"we were like buddies, see?"—Livesay both establishes the men's friendship and the transgression of racial barriers that it implies:

> We were like buddies, see? Until they said
> That nigger is too smart the way he smiles
> And sauces back the foreman; he might say
> Too much one day, to others changing shifts.
> Therefore they cut him down, who flowered at night
> And raised me up, day hanging over night—
> So furnaces could still consume our withered skin. (4.7–13)

On the level of direct description, this short narrative relates an incident where the management of the factory demotes the Black worker and promotes the White man above him, thereby attempting to break their friendship with the anger and resentment generated. On another level, however, Livesay's diction projects cultural memories of the most gruesome and horrifying force exerted onto the body of the Black man. If slaves existed in a world shot through with fear of the master's violent and often capricious reprisals, their descendants lived with the threat of one punishment that surpassed the whip in its sheer brutality—the act of lynching. When Livesay writes, "they cut him down, who flowered at night," she evokes not only the gestures of lowering a hanged man, but also the unforgettable image of the lifeless body on the tree branch in the photograph and song "Strange Fruit."[5] She continues to draw out this gestural repertoire in the figuration of the White worker—"raised ... up, day hanging over night"—who becomes the next victim.

To begin to assess this unforgettable tableau of torture and death, it is necessary to underscore the fact that lynching was still common in the United States when Livesay lived in New Jersey. A book characterized by an "emphasis on protest" (Young 117), Nancy Cunard's *Negro: Anthology,* counts forty-eight lynchings in 1933 (iii), and contains an extensive section—some thirty pages by various writers—telling the stories of lynchings (163–97).[6] In *Exorcising Blackness: Historical and Literary Lynching and Burning Rituals,* Trudier Harris points out that between 1882 and 1927 as many as 4,951 people were lynched in the United States, the vast majority of them Black men (7). *Exorcising Blackness* draws attention to the dramatic increase in lynching as the "economic disasters" of the Depression took hold: in 1930, the number of lynchings rose almost two hundred percent over those in 1929 (96). Harris continues, "increased idleness and irritability were probably additional factors. Blacks, who had always been an irritation to whites, now found themselves in an even more precarious position for receiving the effects of white frustration" (96). Indeed, the history of lynching demonstrates an increasing focus on the punishment of the Black body. Developed initially as a strategy of terrorizing Loyalists during the American War of Independence, Captain William Lynch's law came in the early nineteenth century to mean summary justice administered without the legal institution of a court hearing. Normally, lynching did not involve capital punishment: being run out of town or being tarred and feathered were far more common punitive measures (Harris 5–11). Following the Civil War, however, deadly lynching was appropriated as a widespread tactic to discipline the large population of freed slaves. In his ground-breaking 1905 study, *Lynch-Law: An Investigation into the History of Lynching in the United States,* James E. Cutler comments that after 1865 "the negro had ceased to be valuable as property and was looked upon as a dangerous political factor in the community; to take his life was thought to be the easiest and quickest way to dispose of him" (qtd. in Harris 7). In other words, the practice of lynching was mobilized to maintain the social conditions of slavery after emancipation.

Acts of lynching seem to reach back into history to earlier centuries when slaveholding was legal, and when, as Michel Foucault has argued in *Discipline and Punish*, public executions functioned as an inscription of power onto the body of the condemned. The purpose of the public execution was, he writes, "to make everyone aware, through the body of the criminal, of the unrestrained presence of the sovereign. The public execution did not reestablish justice; it reactivated power … Its ruthlessness, its spectacle, its physical violence, its unbalanced play of forces, its meticulous ceremonial, its entire apparatus were inscribed in the political functioning of the penal system" (33). Foucault goes on to describe how the excessive public demonstrations of power involved in executions in the absolute monarchies of the eighteenth century gradually gave way to the more subtle internalizations of power within systems of imprisonment and within wider carceral institutions of civil society in Western democratic states. Viewed from this perspective, lynching appears to be a social anomaly: the courts and legal institutions of the United States offered ample redress for the charges of theft, assault, and rape with which the (often innocent) victims of lynching were accused. Why did public execution exist well into the twentieth century in a country that characterized itself as a developed Western democracy? A possible answer can be found in the ways in which lynching functions to establish a circulation of White terror by inflicting an excess of power over the body of the Black man (though we ought to note here that Black women were also lynched). By taking a body that cultural discourses and social beliefs endowed with physical and sexual prowess and reducing that body to suffering, inert flesh—I am aware of the oxymoronic adjectives; one might more accurately say "suffering and then inert" flesh—White power reproduces itself in a surplus superabundance. As a social practice to elaborate and establish White power outside the legal penal systems, the "stylized violence" (Harris 2) of lynching usually mobilized whole communities, unfolded in processions that lasted several hours, and often involved beatings, burnings, and other tortures before the victim was eventually hanged. It is no wonder, then, that lynching remained a haunting presence in Livesay's writings about her experiences in New Jersey and New York. In her radio drama "The Times Were Different," lynching functions as a kind of persistent trace that sets boundaries and draws limits between experiences. No character is confronted with lynching; no extended discussion of it occurs; yet lynching continues to be an unwavering spectre within the text. References to lynching in conversations (*Right Hand* 140, 144) function as a social boundary to separate the cultural memories of the two national histories.

It comes as no surprise, therefore, that the sheer brutality of lynching in the twentieth century became an emblem for the violence of oppression that demonstrated such tenacity in the democratic civil institutions of the United States. The path-breaking collection *Negro: Anthology* published a striking collage image of a Black man's body hanging from the Liberty Bell (Cunard 33). As the symbol of American freedom and democracy becomes the scaffold from which the hanged body is suspended, the hollowness in "liberty" is unmistakable. At the same time, the immediacy of the visual depiction, whose collage structure announces itself as a construction, raises crucial questions about representation and the Real. The placement of the image on the page, at the right margin, comes to signify the failure of the written word, the brute materiality of unnecessary death before which the letters are brought to a halt. Like the overfamiliar phrasings characterizing American democracy ("all men are created equal," "government by the people for the people," and so on), whose institutions have failed to prevent this violent death, the abstract signification of words trails off when confronted by the sheer impact of the visual image. The juxtaposition of the two constructions—language and collage—gives powerful figuration to a space where the strategies of representation are confronted by the grim cruelty of the material.

The art and literature of the 1930s also examined the persistence of lynching by foregrounding contradictions that existed within a nation that claimed to be founded on Christian principles ("In God we trust") and by developing allegorical interpretations that Christian gospels, stories, and traditions readily suggested for the victims of lynching. *Negro: Anthology* (1934) includes an article by Black commentator William Pickens for whom lynching was a "sadistic carnival which has become approved and established ritual in the South" (29). He goes on to describe a horrific incident in Rome, Mississippi, where a Black man, Henry Lowry, was tortured for several hours, his legs burnt in bonfires, before being killed. The title of Pickens's article, "A Roman Holiday," ironically underscores the "pastimes" of a Southern summer; it also evokes the bloody gladiatorial fighting of ancient Rome and the sacrifice of early Christian martyrs to gruesome deaths, underlining the contradiction of such brutality in a democratic nation with a legal system supposedly committed to human rights, and at the same time aligning the Black victims with Christ and his followers, who were also victims of state or mob executions. Black writers on the left—Langston Hughes in "Christ in Alabama" and Countee Cullen in "The Black Christ," for example—explored the implications of these contradictions in their poetry (Nelson 68–75). When Hughes's first line announces "Christ is a Nigger," the poem opens up what Cary Nelson calls "a new vista on American history" in which "cast out, vilified and crucified, the historical Christ returns to Earth in serial fashion—in the person of every Black man 'beaten and black,' every slave, every lynching victim, every post–Civil War Black denied the full rights of citizenship" (70). The Black Christ, like the Black body suspended from the Liberty Bell, powerfully underscores moments where utopian visions of equality, both political and Christian, fall into material histories of divisive social oppression.

In a similar fashion, Black culture worked a complex process of allegorizing on the Biblical stories of the Judeo-Christian traditions, which proved to be the site of powerful social and historical resonances: the stories of Israel's enslavement in Egypt and Babylon offered readily recognizable narratives of suffering, lamentation, and hope for freedom. W.E.B. Du Bois, in a well-known passage from *The Souls of Black Folk*, describes the interconnections of the miseries of slavery and the yearnings for deliverance in the Black sorrow songs: "they tell of death and suffering and unvoiced longing toward a truer world, of misty wanderings and hidden ways" (267). Echoing Du Bois, Eugene Genovese writes in *Roll Jordan Roll: The World the Slaves Made* that "the spirituals vibrated with the message: God will deliver us if we have faith in Him. And they emphasized the idea of collective deliverance of the slaves as a people by their choice of such heroes as Moses, Jonah, and Daniel" (245). However, the spirituals were never merely expressions of longing for freedom; they were also part of concrete political resistance to slavery. In his important study *Culture on the Margins: The Black Spiritual and the Rise of American Cultural Interpretation*, Jon Cruz points out that, especially after the Nat Turner rebellion, Black spirituals were often interpreted by White authorities as calls for slave revolts; the chorus of a gospel hymn, "There's a better day a coming," was taken to be an incitement to rebellion (79). Indeed, White suspicions were not unfounded: Genovese notes an ex-slave's report that secret meetings were announced by a strategy of singing

"Steal Away to Jesus" at work (236) and Maud Cuney-Hare describes how "O Canaan, Sweet Canaan, I am bound for the land of Canaan" could signify slaves' determination to run away to Canada, an anagram of Canaan (67–68). The allegorizing in Black spirituals traversed and evoked a history of political and social agency. Like Walter Benjamin's materialist historian, the anonymous Black collectivity that "wrote" the spirituals seized a memory [the captivity of Israel] as it flashed up in a moment of danger [slavery in America] (Genovese 255). The layers of meanings in the gospel songs represent, in Genovese's words, "a necessary and intrinsic ambiguity that reflects a view of the world in which the spiritual and the material merge" (249). Songs such as "Go Down, Moses" or "Didn't My Lord Deliver Daniel?" mobilize the distant memories of the stories of Israel to construct a continuing cultural memory of emancipation from slavery. In Genovese's view, the words of the spirituals "do not necessarily refer to deliverance in this world or in the other, for they might easily mean either or both" (249).

Livesay draws on this culture of resistance, shifting from brutalization and injustice to defiance, when she inserts fragments of a Black spiritual into "Day and Night" following the references to lynching:

> Shadrach, Meshach and Abednego
> Turn in the furnace, whirling slow.
> > Lord, I'm burnin' in the fire
> > Lord, I'm steppin' on the coals
> > Lord, I'm Blacker than my brother
> > Blow your breath down here. (4.14–19)

The scraps of song, like Livesay's memory of her co-worker Luella's "haunting voice singing spirituals" (*Journey* 151), function to embody concretely the speech and cultural traditions of the Black workers.[7] The chiaroscuro of the dark human figures within the flames of the fiery furnace seems particularly apt for the image of the steel factory with the shadowy bodies of the workers illuminated against the flames of furnaces. At the same time, the images of the song—"burnin' in the fire," "steppin' on the coals"—stress the ache and suffering of exhausting labour. When smoke, soot, and sweat blacken all the workers' faces, it is difficult to distinguish whether the repeated line, "Lord, I'm Blacker than my brother," refers to skin colour or to the sheer exertion of labour (working closer to the steel furnaces).

This is not all, for the story the spiritual tells has resonances that reach deeply into cultural memories of slavery and the allegorizing of Bible stories in Black history in America. As recounted in the *Book of Daniel* (4:4–27), Shadrach, Meshach, and Abednego are three young Hebrew men, enslaved in Babylon, and renamed so that they are positioned within the ideological configurations of Nebuchadnezzar's sovereignty. Shadrach means "in the command of Aku, the moon god" (Clow 349), Meshach means "who is Aku"(Clow 254), and Abednego means "a worshipper of Nego or Nebo, another Assyrian god" (Clow 5). Just as slaves in America were given Christian names to further dissever connections with their African roots, Shadrach, Meshach, and Abednego are interpellated within the enslaving nation, and it is only by a collective act of will—a refusal to worship Nebuchadnezzar's golden idol—that they retrieve and enact who they are. It is as punishment for this collective act of spiritual and cultural resistance that they are thrown into the fiery furnace.

In his perceptive reading of Livesay's poem, Dennis Cooley describes the tone of "Day and Night" as "communal song whose voice comes with the power of tribal chant, declaring purpose and solidarity" (256). Collectivity and group formation lie at the heart of the Black spiritual tradition. Writing in *Negro: Anthology* in 1934, Zora Neale Hurston sought to distinguish the improvisational and unpredictable character of spirituals sung in Black churches from the more formal, harmonized versions being popularized in mass-marketed recordings. The marketing of spirituals as part of the development of the music industry formalizes the songs into cultural artifacts that sever connections with the ongoing process of collective remaking in the act of singing. Hurston argues, "The spirituals are being made and forgotten every day … These songs, even the printed ones, do not remain long in their original form. Every congregation that takes it up alters it considerably" (359). Stressing the disharmony of the spiritual—"the shifting keys and broken time" (360)—she argues that spirituals are collective creations of a group at a particular moment, with spontaneous and diverse interventions by individuals as the song unfolds:

> The various parts break in at any old time. Falsetto also takes the place of regular voices for short periods. Keys change. Moreover, each singing of the piece is a new creation. The congregation is bound by no rules. No two times singing is alike, so that we must consider the singing of a song not as a final thing, but as a mood. It won't be the same thing next Sunday. (360)

Building from Hurston's observations, I want to suggest that in the peculiar combination of the familiar (the words, the story the song tells) and spontaneity (the jagged harmony, changing keys, falsetto voices) the spiritual offers a Black cultural alternative to the "day and night" rigidity of the routinized and mechanized labour in the "fiery furnace" of the steel mill. In its collective form, the spiritual stands as an alternative to the mechanically constructed assemblage of workers in the factory where each one becomes a part of a steel production line, a proverbial "cog in the machine." If Livesay gestures towards the well-known leftist figuring of the labourers as "wage slaves" in the Babylon of the steel factory, the traces of Black music preserve and extend the difficult cultural work of keeping alive the imagination of anticipation and resistance.

This is undoubtedly the place to inquire about the effects of such an appropriation of Black culture. What are the implications of Livesay's insertion of traces of Black voices into "Day and Night"? How does the fragment of the spiritual song, drawn from the collective cultural memory of slavery, perform political work within a mid-twentieth-century poem? In *Culture on the Margins*, Jon Cruz analyzes how the movement to study folklore, emergent in the mid-nineteenth century and later institutionalized in the disciplines of cultural anthropology and sociology, created an ethnological interest in Black culture that brought the values of modernity—rationalism and scienticism—to the investigation of Black culture. Black music was separated from the communities in which it was produced and became a cultural artifact or object to be investigated. In Cruz's words, "fractured, dissected, sorted, and reclassified into more discrete and knowable parcels, Black expressivity was objectified and pulled into modern rationalized interpretation" (162). From his point of view, the process had a double-edged effect: on the one hand, ethnological studies of Black music were "a long overdue embrace of culture on the margins"; on the other hand, in the process of institutionalization, "Black music began to be severed from its crucial social domain" (163). Black spirituals had emerged from cultural practices of resistance where the religion of the enslaving society was refunctioned by a dominated group to express their grief, their sufferings, and their yearnings for freedom. Such a recognition ought not merely to interpret culture as a site of utopian longing, although the imagination of different ways of being in the world remains crucial to political transformation. Rather, culture is one aspect of the complex social interactions that work together with political commitment and organization to effect transformation. When Black spirituals became the object of analysis for ethnological studies and the new social science disciplines, however, the music was subjected to ideological strategies of containment that dissevered it from the communities and politics that had been crucial to its formation. In ways that parallel the concerns Hurston articulated about the commodification of spirituals by the music industry, folkloric studies and the ethnosciences emptied Black music of its collective politics.

Does Livesay's use of the Shadrach, Meshach, and Abednego fragment participate in this process of political containment? Does the insertion of the spiritual into "Day and Night" slip into what Michael Thurston, writing about 1930s political poetry, has designated as "sympathetic borrowings" that slide all too quickly into an unpalatable condescension ("Documentary Modernism" 69)? There is no doubt that the words and rhythms of the spiritual are semiotic indicators of an unfamiliar voice, both in the context of the factory labour depicted and in the context of the poem's first publication in a Canadian poetry magazine; they therefore cannot escape signifying, to a certain extent, exoticism and Otherness. Livesay's interjection of the lines of the song, however, also works to reinsert the spiritual into political struggles against new forms of domination within the Northern factories to which many Southern Blacks had migrated seeking employment. "Day and Night" remobilizes the images of the spiritual into a finely drawn emphasis on the exhausting labour of steel production: the factory workers are "smothered in the darkness" and "shrivellin' in the flames" (4. 20–21), allegorically positioned as the suffering chosen people. Moreover, the blurring of racialized groups in the soot-darkened skin of the men represents a new collectivity emerging from shared labour and shared exploitation, a group formation that undercuts the management's attempt to use racial tensions to divide the workforce of the factory. If the previous section depicted the two men as lynching victims ("And raised me up, day hanging overnight" iv.12), the fragment of the spiritual—"Lord, I'm burnin' in the fire / Lord, I'm steppin' on the coals"—reaffirms a collectivity of voice that asserts the importance of Black culture at the same time that it situates the potential emergence of a new group formation. In this way, Livesay's writing strategies connect with the cultural memories and contemporary practices of Black communities to imagine a politics of possibility and the shaping of new collectivities.

In the final sections of "Day and Night," the poem returns to the confused longings for love that might soothe the harshness of the workday at night and hatred of workplace oppressions that insidiously persist into personal life:

> We bear the burden home to bed
> The furnace glows within our hearts:
> Our bodies hammered through the night
> Are welded into bitter bread. (5.13–16)

The raw bitterness of the factory—"labour's ache" (5.42)—which projects itself into the life-world of the workers, proved to be a site of lingering dissatisfaction for Livesay. Later, she returned to this space in the poem, composing and inserting new lines that underscored another affective pull in distinct tension with the emotional negativity of hate.[8] With a resonant simile that figures the healing tenderness of touch, much like folk medicine might apply a compress of arnica or aloe to relieve a painful wound, and with a calming evocation of sheltering natural growth, the poem shifts to emotions of resilience, hope, and resistance:

> A child's hands as a leaf are tender
> And draw the poison out.
>
> Green of new leaf shall deck my spirit
> Laughter's roots will spread:
> Though I am overalled and silent
> Boss, I'm far from dead! (6.3–8)

The contradictory oscillation between emotions of hate and love—both in their own way empowering and disabling—dynamically articulates the tensions that constituted the lived experience of leftist activists. From one perspective, it is critically necessary to despise capitalism and the immense suffering, both personal and social, caused by daily conditions of work and the disastrous effects of the Depression. From another perspective, that very hatred hardens and shapes consciousness in ways that prevent the imagination of potential social transformation and other possibilities of living. Similarly, from one perspective, the tender warmth of love in the touch of a child, in shared laughter and affection, is crucially necessary to counteract the deadening harshness of a world shot through with oppressive social relations. From another perspective, the same gentleness opened up by offering and returning love creates a vulnerability that has the potential to disable resistance to modes of social domination. Like Brecht's moving condensation of this still urgent conflict in "An die Nachgeborenen" [To Those Born Later]—"Hatred, even of meanness / Contorts the features / Anger, even against injustice / Makes the voice grow hoarse" (318–20)—Livesay's documentary poetics negotiates the contradictory emotions that provoke and sustain radical dissent. Put in a somewhat different way, politically committed leftist poets mobilized the modernist lyric "in an effort simultaneously to represent the suffering of individuals and to overcome the atomization sustained by a cultural insistence on individual experience" (Thurston, *Making Something Happen* 44). Poetry could be a space for articulating mute pain and for reaching towards the collectivity that promises a different lived experience.

In the final section of the poem, the choral repetition of "one step forward, two steps back" recurs, but with a significant slippage of meaning:

> One step forward
> Two steps back
> Will soon be over:
> Hear it crack! (6.9–12)

As a verb, "crack" no longer seems to designate the sound of the whip snaking out over the backs of workers, either in the distant cultural memory of slavery or in the present of back-breaking factory labour. Instead, the meaning has shifted to signify the fissures, rifts, and fractures that expose capitalist society to the possibility of transformation, and that promise capitalism itself will "crack," will be broken apart. At this point, the final lines of the poem raise pressing questions for a twenty-first-century reader. How is the triumphalism of a poem from the 1930s to be interpreted and assessed? If, from our historical moment at the beginning of the next century, we are all too familiar with the resilience of capitalism, which recovered from the Depression during the war years, spectacularly instigated a postwar growth in consumerism, and subsequently expanded to a remarkable global scope, how are we to react to a confidence that now seems misleading and naïve?

Cary Nelson's *Revolutionary Memory* maps out an innovative reading strategy for the political poetry of the 1930s. Nelson begins by retracing the historical constructions of modernist poetry within academic institutions. In the critical theories of John Crowe Ransom, Allen Tate, and Cleanth Brooks, the valuation of poetry was based on the writings of T.S. Eliot and Ezra Pound, with an emphasis on dense symbolization, intricate texture, and ironic structure. By the mid-1950s, these New Critical approaches (to which can be added the English Practical Criticism of F.R. Leavis and I.A. Richards) began to be entrenched within university teaching practices. Even when the poststructuralist criticism of the late 1970s and 1980s offered new readings, valorizing allegory over symbolism and instability over unity, few critical practices within North American institutions seemed adequate to address the politically and historically situated leftist poetry of the 1930s. Drawing on the concrete conditions of composition and reception in the leftist writing communities of the 1930s, Nelson proposes a tactic of reading that retrieves and reworks specific configurations of the historical moment in which the poetry was composed. In particular, he stresses the collectivity at the heart of the lived experience of 1930s poetry. Rooted in both the extraordinary suffering of the Depression and in political longings for transformation, a poem participated in a process of exchange within leftist communities, "engag[ing] in a continuing dialogue both with other poetry and with the other discourses and institutions of its day" (157). A poem might be read at a cultural or political event, used on posters and leaflets; it might be the catalyst for response by other writers; it might develop and reflect on figures or tropes circulated in other leftist writings. Most importantly, as Nelson comments, "there is thus a continual dialogue taking place in the effort both to describe social conditions and to invent ways for poetry to intervene in them" (157). Reading and interpreting the political poetry of the 1930s, therefore, require a recognition of the poem as a collective political gesture and a willing suspension of the assumption that a poem is an autonomous, self-contained literary artifact, a presupposition itself founded on a certain version of imagist modernism.

Nothing perhaps illustrates this dialogue between poetry and history more concretely than Livesay's late revisions of "Day and Night." In the 1960s, inspired by the civil rights movement and the growing opposition to the Vietnam war, she added verses alluding to Martin Luther King Jr.'s dream of a non-violent transformation of racist society:

> Are you waiting?
> Wait with us
> Hand in hand
> We'll walk in peace.
>
> Deep in our hearts
> We're not afraid.
> We'll overcome
> The barriers laid. (qtd. in Boylan 31)

Like Hurston's comments on the fluidity of singing by Black congregations, and like the quotation of the Black spiritual in the original version of

"Day and Night," the insertion of the popular chorus of "We Shall Overcome" reinforces the impressions of collectivity: the song, which was used in union struggles, in the Civil Rights movement, and in rallies and demonstrations against the Vietnam war, takes apart the illusion that the poem, as published, is a completed aesthetic object.[9] Instead, it is reinvented as a dialogic conversation with contemporary politics in which the earlier antiracist struggles of the 1930s are interconnected with the resurgent demands for social justice of the 1960s.

"Day and Night" undertakes the aesthetic and social task of representing the hardship of arduous factory labour and the psychological suffering of the workplace's numbing of affect; it also strives to envision a transformed world where new social relations might emerge. In this critical work of cultural imagination and cultural memory, resistances to slavery in Black history, awareness of contemporary racist oppressions, and the shared narratives of the Judeo-Christian traditions are linked with struggles to live differently. Socialist traditions are similarly reworked in the poem's echoes of Lenin's title "one step forward, two steps back," in its description of the exhausting repetition of factory labour, implying a dialectical movement in which advancement (one step forward) will only be discovered as the layers of the past (two steps back) are unravelled and reconfigured into new patterns. Livesay's encounter with Black culture and forms of Black expressivity in the politically charged moment of the mid-1930s interconnected with her passion for social justice to produce a poem of unique intensity and imagination.

Notes

I would like to thank Barbara Godard, Dean Irvine, Barbara McCarthy, Christian Olbey, and Apollonia Steele for helpful advice when I was researching this paper.

1. Irvine, in "Among Masses," offers a trenchant analysis of Livesay's later self-construction in *Right Hand Left Hand*. My own focus here is concerned with the dynamics of social class and racialization that she encountered in the mid-1930s; for a complementary analysis of more personal and familial tensions expressed in her writing, see Ann Martin's essay in this volume. Irvine's collection *Canadian Modernists Meet* offers an extensive reassessment of modernism in Canada and is an important resource for the context of Livesay's poetry. It does not, however, include a discussion of the representation of "race" in her writing.
2. It is important to stress that Livesay's statement ought not to imply an absence of Black cultural politics in Montreal in the 1930s. *Free Lance*, a weekly newspaper that at one time was as large as the mainstream Montreal paper *La Presse*, was directed towards Black workers, primarily in the railway industry. Inspired by Marcus Garvey's ideas, it published a wide range of articles on international (Mussolini's invasion of Ethiopia; the Scottsboro case) and national (segregation and its effects in Canada; local protests against the refusal of the Montreal Forum to serve beer to a Black customer) issues.

See Dorothy W. Williams, *The Road to Now* (74–82) and her interview on CBC's *Morningside*. In addition to "Day and Night," Livesay also explored her growing awareness of racism in a direct, poignant poem, "New Jersey: 1935," that describes two young friends—one White, one Black—who spend a quiet evening and dinner together. In the garden, their skin colours seem to merge with the shadows and fading light ("we walked entwined in moonlight ... tree and shadow of tree" (*Right Hand* 131). This idyllic moment is shattered when the landlady confronts her tenant, strenuously objecting to the presence of a Black woman in her house.

3 This and subsequent references to "Day and Night" will refer to the part of the poem and the line number.

4 Writing in 1965, at the height of New Criticism, in the canon-constructing *Literary History of Canada: Canadian Literature in English*, Munro Beattie complains of the inconsistency of voice in "Day and Night." On the one hand, he praises the poem: it "powerfully evokes the violence and oppressiveness of industrial labour; anguish and aspiration are expressed in two-stress lines in quatrain, strain in passages in free pentameter" (741). On the other hand, he argues that Livesay does not accurately convey a worker's expressivity: "At the emotional centre of 'Day and Night' there speaks a gentle suffering spirit which is clearly the poet's and not the factory-worker's" (741). It is true that Beattie draws attention to the impossibility of any poem, mediated through language and formal structures, as well as the author's situated subjectivity, to represent directly workers' (or any others') lived experiences. It is also true that Livesay's intonation and rhythm are sometimes close to the high modernism of T.S. Eliot: "We move as through sleep's revolving memories" ("Day and Night" 3.6). However, Beattie's comments underscore the reading strategies by which the institutions of New Criticism judged the social poetry of the 1930s, in this case by pointing out that the author has not adequately distanced her own emotions in an objective correlative. Significant too are class assumptions that workers are insensitive, hardened, and incapable of tenderness. See Boylan's discussion in "The Social and Lyric Voices of Dorothy Livesay" (27–28). In this context, see also the portrait of a welder at the Montreal shipyards, reproduced in *Right Hand Left Hand* (156). The sketch by Louis Muhlstock, Livesay's artist friend and neighbour when she worked in Montreal in the early 1930s (*Right Hand* 73–74), depicts a calm, wearied man whose gaze seems filled with aching sadness (156).

5 The most famous version of "Strange Fruit" was recorded by Billie Holiday and Frank Newton at the Commodore Music Shop of New York (Denning 323–25).

6 Young points out that Hugh Ford's abridged version of *Negro* (1970) removes much of the discussions and reportage on lynchings (114).

7 Livesay has also commented that she had the rhythms of the popular Cole Porter song "Night and Day" in her mind when she began to compose "Day and Night" (*Journey* 151).

8 See Irr (233–34). Livesay's *Collected Poems* publishes the revised version.

9 Livesay seems never to have published these new lines for "Day and Night." Her hesitation might be read both as a recognition of the poem's roots in the 1930s and as an awareness that the new oppositional politics of the mid-1960s were provisional and changing. A year after she read the expanded version of the poem, Martin Luther King Jr. was assassinated, underlining the persistence of racial violence in the United States and the continuation of new forms of "lynching" (the murder of Medgar Evers and other civil rights activists, the bombing of a church that killed young children, the shooting of Malcolm X, and the assaults by police in the early 1970s on the Black Panther leadership).

Works Cited

Beattie, Munro. "Poetry, 1920–1935." *Literary History of Canada*. Ed. Carl. F. Klinck. Toronto: U of Toronto P, 1965. 723–41.
Benjamin, Walter. *Illuminations*. Ed. Hannah Arendt. Trans. Harry Zohn. New York: Schocken, 1969.
Boylan, Charles Robert. "The Social and Lyric Voices of Dorothy Livesay." Diss. U of British Columbia, 1969.
Brecht, Bertold. *Brecht: Poems; Part Two, 1929–1938*. Ed. John Willett and Ralph Manheim. London: Eyre Methuen, 1976.
Carr, E.H. *The Bolshevik Revolution, 1917–1923*. Vol. 1. Harmondsworth: Penguin, 1966.
Clow, W.M. *The Bible Reader's Encyclopaedia and Concordance*. London: Collins, n.d.
Cooley, Dennis. *The Vernacular Muse: The Eye and Ear in Contemporary Literature*. Winnipeg: Turnstone, 1987.
Cruz, Jon. *Culture on the Margins: The Black Spiritual and the Rise of American Cultural Interpretation*. Princeton: Princeton UP, 1999.
Cullen, Countee. "The Black Christ." *My Soul's High Song: The Collected Writings of Countee Cullen*. Ed. Gerald Early. New York: Doubleday 1991. 207–36.
Cunard, Nancy, ed. *Negro: Anthology*. London: Wishart, 1934.
Cuney-Hare, Maud. *Negro Musicians and Their Music*. New York: Da Capo, 1974.
Dawes, Kwame. "Re-appropriating Cultural Appropriation." *Borrowed Power: Essays on Cultural Appropriation*. Ed. Bruce Ziff and Pratima V. Rao. New Brunswick: Rutgers UP, 1997. 109–21.
Denham, Paul. "Lyric and Documentary in the Poetry of Dorothy Livesay." Dorney et al. 87–106.
Denning, Michael. *The Cultural Front: The Labouring of American Culture in the Twentieth Century*. London: Verso, 1996.
Dorney, Lindsay, Gerald Noonan, and Paul Tiessen, eds. *A Public and Private Voice: Essays on the Life and Work of Dorothy Livesay*. Waterloo: U of Waterloo P, 1986.
Du Bois, W.E.B. *The Souls of Black Folk*. New York: Signet, 1982.
Foucault, Michel. *Discipline and Punish: The Birth of the Prison*. Trans. Alan Sheridan. New York: Vintage, 1979.
Genovese, Eugene D. *Roll Jordan Roll: The World the Slaves Made*. New York: Pantheon, 1974.
Gilman, Marvin. "Lines of Intersection: The Two Dorothys and Marxism." *New Literatures Review* 28–29 (1994–95): 23–32.
Harris, Trudier. *Exorcising Blackness: Historical and Literary Lynching and Burning Rituals*. Bloomington: Indiana UP, 1984.
Holiday, Billie. "Strange Fruit." Rec. 20 April 1939. *The Complete Billie Holiday*, vol. 1. Columbia, 2004.
Hughes, Langston. "Christ in Alabama." *The Collected Work of Langston Hughes*, vol. 3. Ed. Arnold Rampersad. New York: Columbia UP, 2001. 155.

Hurston, Zora Neale. "Spirituals and Neo-Spirituals." Cunard 359–61.
Irr, Caren. *The Suburb of Dissent: Cultural Politics in the United States and Canada during the 1930s.* Durham, NC: Duke UP, 1998.
Irvine, Dean J. "Among Masses: Dorothy Livesay and English Canadian Leftist Magazine Culture of the Early 1930s." *Essays on Canadian Writing* 68 (1999): 183–212.
———, ed. *The Canadian Modernists Meet.* Ottawa: U of Ottawa P, 2005.
———. "Editorial postscript: 'A poem is an archive for our times'; Selecting and Editing Dorothy Livesay." *Archive for Our Times.* Vancouver: Arsenal Pulp, 1998. 250–72.
Kelly, Peggy. "Politics, Gender and *New Provinces*: Dorothy Livesay and F.R. Scott." *Canadian Poetry* 53 (Fall–Winter 2003): 54–70.
Lenin, Vladimir. *Essentials of Lenin.* London: Lawrence and Wishart, 1947.
Lister, Rota Hertzberg. "From Confrontation to Conciliation: The Growth of Dorothy Livesay as a Political Dramatist." Dorney et al. 53–70.
Livesay, Dorothy. *Archive for Our Times.* Ed. Dean J. Irvine. Vancouver: Arsenal Pulp, 1998.
———. *Collected Poems: The Two Seasons.* Toronto: McGraw-Hill Ryerson, 1972.
———. "Day and Night." Livesay, *Collected Poems* 120–25.
———. *Day and Night Poems.* Toronto: Ryerson, 1944.
———. *Journey with My Selves: A Memoir, 1909–1963.* Vancouver: Douglas and McIntyre, 1991.
———. *Right Hand Left Hand: A True Life of the Thirties.* Erin: Press Porcépic, 1977.
Nelson, Cary. *Revolutionary Memory: Recovering the Poetry of the American Left.* New York: Routledge, 2001.
Pickens, William. "A Roman Holiday." Cunard 29–35.
Porter, Cole. "Night and Day." Rec. 1932. *The Very Best of Cole Porter.* Hip-O Records, 2004.
Smethurst, James Edward. *The New Red Negro: The Literary Left and African American Poetry, 1930–1946.* New York: Oxford UP, 1999.
Thurston, Michael. "Documentary Modernism as Popular Front Poetics: Muriel Rukeyser's 'Book of the Dead.'" *Modern Language Quarterly* 60.1 (1999): 59–83.
———. *Making Something Happen: American Political Poetry Between the World Wars.* Chapel Hill: U of North Carolina P, 2001.
Williams, Dorothy W. Interview. *Morningside.* CBC Radio. Toronto. 4 July 2002.
———. *The Road to Now: A History of Blacks in Montreal.* Montreal: Véhicule, 1997.
Young, Tory. "The Reception of Nancy Cunard's *Negro* Anthology." *Women Writers of the 1930s: Gender, Politics and History.* Ed. Maroula Joannou. Edinburgh: U of Edinburgh P, 1999. 113–22.

Dorothy Livesay and CBC Radio
The Politics of Modernist Aesthetics, Gender, and Regionalism

PEGGY LYNN KELLY

Dorothy Livesay had a long relationship with CBC Radio, as a writer, broadcaster, and critical listener. In *Dorothy Livesay and the CBC*, Paul and Hildi Tiessen discuss Livesay's work of the 1930s and 1940s. In addition, Livesay's papers show that, between 1939 and 1959, she submitted hundreds of poems, short stories, book reviews, scripts, talks, outlines, and ideas, mainly to the Vancouver radio station, CBR, where she was known as an established member of the Canadian literary field.[1] Livesay was a mentor to the women of British Columbia on *A Life of My Own*, a women's discussion group on radio.[2] She wrote literary biographies of writers and other cultural producers,[3] and she spoke back to the CBC both publicly, in lectures on *Critically Speaking*, and privately, in correspondence with CBC radio producers (Tiessen and Tiessen 3–17).[4] In some cases, she worked as a cross-media journalist, a strategy which is commonly followed by journalists today.[5] Her engagement with contemporary political issues is evident in her dramas about racism and in the talks she proposed on disarmament and on Canadian writers' global responsibilities.[6] Although Livesay wrote original and historical drama for radio, in both prose and poetic forms, most of the talks and scripts published in *Dorothy Livesay and the CBC* were never produced. As critics, we must ask why.

Part of the answer lies in the difficulties all freelance radio writers in Canada, men and women, encountered with the CBC administration. As an example, consider the case of Livesay's radio play, "Momatkum."[7] On 9 April 1951, G. Kristjanson, a script editor at CBC Radio's Toronto offices, faced a humbling task: to write a letter of apology to Livesay.[8] Kristjanson apologized for sending an earlier letter that acknowledged receipt of "Momatkum." An apology was in order because "Momatkum" had already been produced and broadcast, on 23 February 1951, on CBR Vancouver's *Opening Night* series. A copy of Livesay's script was misfiled for three months. Kristjanson made light of the error by writing to Livesay, "our right hand was unaware of what our left was doing."[9] Furthermore, Livesay had to chase the CBC for payment. Alice Frick, editorial assistant to the drama producer Andrew Allan and a powerful gatekeeper in her own right, explains that lack of communication between herself and the *Opening Night* producer caused the missed payment.[10] This letter was not the first contact between the two women; their working relationship began on a rocky footing in 1946, when Livesay wrote to Frick concerning two scripts: "Saguenay's Job" and "Flags for Canada." Livesay was submitting "Flags for Canada" for the first time, whereas "Saguenay's Job" had already been submitted five months earlier, without response. Livesay states,

> As an established writer, I find it incomprehensible that there should be such delay in making a decision. You were out here [Vancouver] last year, apparently anxious to find new writers and themes for the radio. But how can a writer interested in topical questions ever be encouraged when material definitely suited for B.C. and definitely timely last winter does not even receive the courtesy of comment?[11]

Kristjanson's and Frick's letters are a small part of the massive correspondence between Livesay and the CBC, but they are significant because they represent the kind of bureaucratic nightmare facing writers who ventured to deal with a huge institution like the CBC, especially the way it was organized in 1951. Until 1953, when the script bureau opened, the CBC had no central office to receive manuscripts from writers. The results were lost submissions, delayed payments, and time wasted searching for the appropriate producer or programming officer.

Many radio writers were frustrated by their working relations with the CBC. In 1951, the Association of Canadian Radio Artists (ACRA) presented the CBC with a list of demands for streamlining and legalizing the script submission process.[12] A standardized payment scale; payment on acceptance (rather than on broadcast date); extra pay for rewrites, outlines, auditions, and research; and observation of copyright rules were among ACRA's demands.[13] The association could not fix everything, however. Writers' negotiations with CBC producers and editors, like any human interaction, were (and are) subject to the biases, differing world views, political positions, and personal aesthetics of the people involved—in other words, subject to their ideological interpellations and social constructions. My reading of Livesay's correspondence with CBC Radio producers and editors suggests four reasons for her slight representation on Canadian radio in the 1940s and 1950s: disagreements over style and process between Livesay and the CBC, internal power struggles within the CBC, the politics of gender, and the politics of regionalism.

Livesay's modernist writing challenged CBC Radio, which had a complex relationship with literature, modernism, and female cultural producers. As a new technology, radio fulfilled at least two modernist criteria: the development of new forms of communication and the expansion of public discourse from local to international spaces. However, as a mass medium, radio belonged to the popular end of the low/high cultural continuum, and the tension between these two is evident in CBC programming. Nevertheless, in the late 1930s, CBC Radio was perceived as a site of high culture modernism by young Canadian writers in private radio, such as Harry Boyle, who writes, "All of us working in private radio at that time had our eyes opened to the fact that broadcasting wasn't just a parochial thing in a small town or even a large city. It was a national and international thing and that's what attracted many of us away from private radio to the CBC" (qtd. in McNeil and Wolfe 252).[14] Livesay, too, was interested in "global conversations": she wanted Canadian audiences to communicate nationally and internationally and she often submitted work to CBC's International Service (Tiessen and Tiessen 1).[15]

Although internationalism was highly valued by modernist cultural producers, it was only one of many criteria defining modernism, and many different positions were taken by writers along the modernist continuum.[16] Furthermore, the spectrum of modernist categories is complicated by its articulation with other perspectives on literature, such as the low/high continuum. Literary historians use low and high modernism to distinguish among differing aesthetics, content, and periods of modernism. For instance, the artistic autonomy claimed by high modernism—that is, its isolation from material contexts—turned the high modernist gaze away from political topics; yet low modernists like Livesay addressed material and political issues. Maria DiBattista defines low modernist literature as realistic, non-experimental, popular, and information-oriented (9). Where does this leave politically radical modernists who integrated their politics into their formally experimental writing? Livesay's low modernist poetry and radio drama address state and class politics, as Pamela McCallum shows elsewhere in this volume. My use of low modernism encompasses both socially conscious modernist writing and modernist popular literature. I believe that popular literature deserves consideration, along with high art and political strands of modernism, in formulations of the modernist literary field. Writers of popular literature drew on high modernist literary strategies, such as stream-of-consciousness narration, psychological preoccupations, or open endings, for their own work.[17] As a result, the canonized high modernisms of A.J.M. Smith or Sheila Watson did not monopolize the Canadian modernist arena of this period.[18] The complexity of this arena impacts our discussion of the intersection of popular media, such as CBC Radio, with modernisms. Furthermore, the prominence of regionalism in all areas of Canadian culture complicates CBC Radio's relationship to modernisms and to lowbrow/highbrow cultures. For example, regionalism's challenge to internationalism has the potential to make it an anti-modernist impulse.[19] Christine Kim explains elsewhere in this volume that Canadian regionalism is one of two "dominant national narratives" that tend to function as exclusionary paradigms. As we shall see, regionalism underlies and defines the organizational structure of CBC Radio in this period.

CBC Radio is a site of intersecting genres, politics, movements, binaries, and hierarchies. Instituted in 1936 as an antidote to the Americanization of Canadian airwaves, CBC continued its two predecessors' mandates to unite Canada. The first predecessor, the Canadian National Railway's Radio Department (CNR), began providing radio programs to its passengers in 1924, and the Broadcasting Act of 1932 created its successor, the Canadian Radio Broadcasting Commission (CRBC), a public institution directly responsible to Parliament. The CRBC was reorganized into the more independent CBC in 1936.[20] Today, CBC Radio programming is composed of a multiplicity of genres designed to appeal to a wide range of audiences: lowbrow, highbrow, and avant-garde. However, in the forties, a mandate to educate listeners motivated the institution of school broadcasts, and high culture reigned in radio drama. For instance, a deliberate effort was made by Andrew Allan, in 1939, to develop a national theatre of the air (New 932; Fink 1983, 12–14).

Moreover, World War Two had a profound influence on the corporation's structure and cultural policy. Development of an already bifurcated radio system began when the federal government found radio to be very useful "in furthering the war-effort" (Weir 234). News and public interest programs dominated prime time during the war, and private radio stations, which were regulated by CBC, found themselves restricted to 35% of prime time.[21] The problem was so severe that audiences in some regions heard the same program simultaneously on all local stations. Private radio stations, which were dependent on commercial sponsors for income, clamoured for a separate network so they could get access to evening programs. Partly to satisfy its private commercial affiliates, the CBC started the Dominion Network, which initially broadcast only in the evenings (Weir 233–36).[22] At the same time, the established National Network became the Trans-Canada Network, a commercial-free network that broadcast all day. This low/high distinction between private or public radio and between commercial or commercial-free radio was the foundation of Canadian radio policy in the forties and fifties. Consequently, differences developed in each network's programming and audiences. Sponsors wanted their commercials to appear in programs that garnered high audience ratings, such as soap operas, comedies, mysteries, or popular music.[23] Mystery series, such as *Design for Murder*, and nationalist documentaries, such as *It Happened Here*, were broadcast on the Dominion Network,[24] while the Trans-Canada Network boasted Andrew Allan's showcase for original drama, *Stage*, and the CBC's "grand experiment in highbrow radio," *Wednesday Night* (Rutherford 1539).[25] In 1962, the Dominion and Trans-Canada Networks merged, as a result of television's domination of mass media and capture of CBC Radio's audiences (Rutherford 1540; Weir 236). CBC Radio's highly dichotomous and hierarchical broadcasting structure in the 1940s and 1950s, when Livesay was active in the field of radio, make these decades unique in Canadian radio history.[26]

Acknowledging the high/low divide inherent in the field of culture, poet Earle Birney wrote to Livesay, his friend and colleague, that he wasn't "above working for radio" (Cameron 289). Livesay was one of many freelance writers who turned to radio for another source of income, and she was disappointed that so little of her radio drama and poetry was produced and broadcast by the CBC. In her 1986 collection of poetry, *The Self-Completing Tree*, she points out that two "poems about the Depression," and "three post-war [World War Two] documentaries" were "definitely written with radio in mind," but were never broadcast (155).[27] She adds, "This has been a source of regret for me because I think, as I have written recently, a poem is an archive for our times" (155). To understand why Livesay's writing did not appear more frequently in the program listings of *CBC Times*, let us briefly examine the question of style in relation to "Saguenay's Job," one of her unproduced submissions (Tiessen and Tiessen 61–79). "Saguenay's Job" is a short drama about a fictional Canadian veteran, Grant Gordon, and his struggle to find a place in postwar society. Grieving for a lost comrade named Saguenay Stuart, Grant is persuaded by Saguenay's sister, Sally Stuart, to take on Saguenay's leadership role in a small northern community. Before World War Two, Saguenay had planned to build a community centre for local youth. Andrew Allan rejected "Saguenay's Job" with this explanation:

> Although I feel you have a good theme, I cannot feel that you have written a play. There is no real conflict to hold the listener's interest, nor is the idea of the community center as part of rehabilitation plans treated thoroughly and specifically enough to make the piece a good documentary. You have vacillated somewhat between handling the subject poetically and handling it naturalistically. The result is to embarrass the listener in the poetic passages and shock him in the naturalistic passages.
>
> I feel that in future our plays are going to need fuller content and more dramatic treatment. It seems to me that the public is unwilling now to listen to a mere idea. There is a need to represent the idea in the midst of action and conflict.[28]

In this script, conflict exists within the main character, the veteran Grant Gordon, but the dramatic conflict consists merely of an argument between Sally and Grant. Allan's critique represents radio as a medium for the narrative form, a representation that contradicts histories of radio drama, many of which describe Allan's productions as part of the "Golden Age of Radio" (Fink, *Canadian National Theatre* 3) as "highbrow radio" and as designed for "discriminating listeners" (Rutherford 1539).[29] In his correspondence with Livesay, in contrast, Allan shows his valuation of the popular literature tradition of "action and conflict" over the modernist tendency to psychological analysis, which is evident in Livesay's characterization of Grant and his inner conflict.

Allan was not the only CBC producer who looked for strong plots in radio drama. Livesay's episodic poem "Ontario Story" was rejected by James R. Scott in 1948 because it wasn't narrative enough. Scott, who later reviewed books for Toronto's *Telegram*, gave Birney's "David" as an example of a poem that, in his words, "has a strong story to carry it along."[30] Fragmentation, a modernist literary strategy used by Livesay in "Ontario Story," was considered undesirable by some CBC Radio producers. Livesay persisted in submitting her writing to CBC Radio because, like Harry Boyle, she saw that institution as a potential site of modernist cultural production. She wanted the corporation "to inject into CBC drama the same qualities of experimentation and admirable restraint that we find in the documentaries," and to provide "a higher standard of programming" (qtd. in Tiessen and Tiessen 14, 8).[31] Nonetheless, as Paul Tiessen argues, Livesay's practice of listening critically to CBC programs overturned modernists' claims that new media, such as radio, disembodied and disempowered audiences. Tiessen outlines the fears expressed by writers Wyndham Lewis, Malcolm Lowry, and Marshall McLuhan concerning the passivity demanded of audiences by the new media and the potential power held by mass media to destroy modernist aesthetic standards. However, like earlier modernist women writers Virginia Woolf, Dorothy Richardson, and Hilda Doolittle, Livesay both engaged with popular culture and maintained modernist literary standards (Tiessen 208).

Livesay wanted to write modernist programs, but she faced an uneven cohort of creative thinkers and readers at CBC Radio. A good example of the lack of uniformity among CBC producers' responses to submissions can be seen in two different assessments of Livesay's script "Legendary Land,"[32] one by Alice Frick, another by Raymond Whitehouse. In 1948, two years after Andrew Allan's comments on "Saguenay's Job," Frick rejected Livesay's script, "Legendary Land," for lack of a strong narrative. She writes in her letter, "while your subject is interesting and unusual, your script lacks shape. Your various scenes are very loosely put together and there is no strong theme connecting various episodes which will compel and hold attention."[33] On the other hand, Raymond Whitehouse, CBC supervisor of the English Language Service in Montreal, postponed acceptance of the same script not because it lacked shape, as Frick claimed, but because it was shaped by "the narration and chorus technique."[34] He had already scheduled other plays structured by the same form and was searching for balance in his program. Whitehouse's respect for Livesay's work is evident in their correspondence; he once described her radio writing as "tone poems" and was very enthusiastic about working with her.[35] Livesay recognized Whitehouse as an ally. In an undated letter, she wrote, "I know you are interested in experimentation so I would be pleased to know which of the above themes interest you the most."[36] The wide range of CBC Radio producers' evaluations reveals differences in literary aesthetics arising from both regional differences in a large country, and differing positions on the modernist and popular continuum. In these early years, Whitehouse, a western Canadian whose name has been dropped from Canada's cultural history, exhibits more interest in and support for modernist poetry than does Robert Weaver, a native of central Canada who has been canonized in Canadian literary history. In the correspondence, Whitehouse stands out as a modernist experimenter; the majority of CBC producers of this period wanted non-episodic scripts with strong narratives.

In addition to aesthetic disagreements, gender is a prominent element in Livesay's relationship with the CBC. She faced discrimination on the basis of sex in CBC's infrastructure and in personal relationships with CBC management. Like all federal government institutions in the first half of the twentieth century, the CBC adopted discriminatory employment practices. From 1921, married Canadian women were not permitted to work full-time in Canadian government institutions. This widely accepted discriminatory labour practice was instituted by Arthur Meighen's Conservative federal government as a means of cutting back on civil service staff, and it was adopted by all levels of government (Strong-Boag 62). Livesay feared that she would be laid off from her social work position in a Vancouver social service agency, when she married the unemployed Duncan Macnair in 1937, but her female supervisor allowed her to remain until Duncan found employment. The federal government discontinued this practice in 1955, but the CBC did not comply until 1961 (*Women in the CBC* 133). For example, Margaret Stevens, CBC news editor, and Jean Finlay, CBC drama script editor, both left their jobs when they married, shortly after World War Two (Frick 42–43). In fact, the World War Two veteran who corresponded with Livesay about the misplaced "Momatkum" script, G. Kristjanson, was hired in Finlay's place. Pauline Butling points out that Phyllis Webb criticized CBC for "its sexist hiring policies," which persisted through the 1960s (1205).

The ideology underlying such systemic discrimination is reflected in CBC Radio's program content. For example, the guidelines for *A Life of My Own*, sent by producer Ada McGeer to Livesay, required the writer to "picture what she gained from 'A Life of My Own' to enrich the lives of her own family circle." This guideline suggests that the family is a woman's first responsibility, and that any time she spends away from family life must be productive for family members, as well as for herself. The declared purpose of *A Life of My Own*, to show postwar women how to make time for personal development, is contradicted by gender role assumptions underlying the guidelines. "The object," wrote McGeer, "will be to encourage other women to extend their interests and activities beyond their domestic circle, and also to suggest working techniques by which this may be achieved."[37] Although McGeer and Livesay may have felt that "A Life of My Own" intervened in patriarchal social arrangements, the program also served to interpellate women into the entrenchment of patriarchal social structures. The acquiescence of Canadian housewives to discrimination on the basis of sex, in the workforce and in the family, is exchanged for a qualified freedom from "home responsibility."[38]

Cultural expectations surrounding gender also arise in characters found in CBC drama productions. Len Peterson's radio play "Maybe in a Thousand Years"[39] shows major differences in gender representation from Livesay's "If the World Were Mine,"[40] although both plays deal with the issues of racism and miscegenation in North America. In 1946, Len Peterson was described in a *Canadian Author and Bookman* article as "an advanced thinker" and "one of the best radio dramatists on the North American continent" (Kemp 25, 24). Peterson had a long career with CBC from 1939 on, and he worked closely with Andrew Allan (Goodwin 242, 244). Peterson's "Maybe in a Thousand Years," which was first broadcast in 1944, dramatizes the ostracization faced by a married couple whose backgrounds are differently racialized (a White Anglo-Celt woman, Nancy, and a Chinese-Canadian man, Frank). The couple is evicted from their apartment because neighbours object to Frank's "race"; furthermore, Frank is forced to use a pseudonym to get his writing published. As the marriage deteriorates, Frank's masculinist gender construction becomes evident in his assumption that, because marriage is a woman's career, Nancy can solve her income problem after their impending divorce by remarrying. At the same time, Nancy's enactment of the traditional feminine role is seen in her assumption that the marriage's failure is her personal failure. In contrast, Livesay's play on racism in the United States and Canada, "If the World Were Mine," is structured as the autobiography of a strong protagonist, Margaret, who strives to overcome racism both in personal relations and social arrangements. The play deals with anti-Semitism in Canada and the semi-apartheid social relations practiced in the northern United States in the early 1930s. Through personal love relationships with a Jewish-Canadian and an African-American, as well as less personal relationships with clients and co-workers, Margaret comes to terms with the confining structures of racism and patriarchy in American and Canadian societies.[41] Although Peterson wrote modernist, Brechtian radio drama critical of the class system and the established social order, such as "Burlap Bags" and "They're All Afraid," his work does not question patriarchy. For example, a character in "They're All Afraid" describes gender-inclusive language as fascist "literalism" (35). Livesay's work, in contrast, challenges patriarchy, as well as social divisions based on class, "race," ethnicity, and religion. The comprehensiveness of her challenges to the status quo contributed to the difficulties Livesay experienced with CBC producers, most of whom were male.

Livesay's belief that her sex was a factor in her working relationship with CBC producers has been corroborated by the historical record. Her sense of unequal treatment is evident in her self-comparison to Birney, canonized modernist poet, UBC professor, and World War Two veteran. In 1951, when Livesay was challenging the CBC to develop "a clear-cut policy" on the role of the writer in the production process, she complained to Doug Nixon that "other script writers like Earle Birney work very closely with producers, and insist on so doing." Nixon replied that "in a few cases producers and writers have formed such a close association that for their shows the problem [of writer–producer cooperation] has been eliminated."[42] Livesay's interest in learning production technology was never fulfilled, a fact which resonates with the systemic exclusion of women from science and new technology, long deemed to be masculine terrains.[43]

Fourteen years later, Livesay was still concerned about her record of radio appearances in comparison to Birney. She wrote to Allan Campbell on 1 March 1965, "The CBC gave me an opportunity to give five talks last summer, for which I was grateful. But Earle Birney, who is also a Vancouver poet, has had some 10 talks on the air, as well as long interviews and commentaries; and this fairly continuously within six months. It therefore seems to me reasonable that I should be heard, at some point."[44] Livesay was aware that she and Birney shared age, place, politics, literary standards, and career paths. However, she often pointed out that her longevity as a writer was evident in the publication record: her first volume of poetry, *Green Pitcher* (1928), was published fourteen years before Birney's first volume, *David and Other Poems* (1942). Nevertheless, Birney was called on by CBC personnel more often. In the 1940s and 1950s, the CBC was run by a network of male colleagues, a network which persisted to the late 1970s.[45] For instance, the majority of works on CBC's *Wednesday Night* were by male authors (Frick 57–60). Birney's *Four to the Queen* (a series), "Gawain and the Green Knight," "The Duel," and "The Damnation of Vancouver" all appeared on *Wednesday Night* (Fink, "Earle Birney's Radio Dramas" 56). In addition, dramas were sometimes developed through an informal network of male friends. In 1945, "Hot Afternoon on Malta" was produced for CBC's *Stage* through such a process. Alice Frick notes that CBC playwright "Fletcher Markle introduced one of his fellow-officers in the RCAF who talked to Andrew Allan about his experiences during the siege of Malta" (43). As we have seen, Allan disliked the episodic nature of Livesay's modernist writing.[46] According to Howard Fink, "Earle Birney's dramatic output, not by accident, spans just this period [The Golden Age of CBC Radio Drama]—to be exact, from 1946 to 1957" ("Earle Birney's Radio Drama" 5). Several of Birney's contributions to CBC Radio, such as "Beowulf," "Gawain and the Green Knight," and "Piers Plowman," were adaptations from a masculine literary canon. Livesay, in contrast, wrote original scripts, many of them Canadian historical dramas, a genre CBC claimed to value highly. Scholars of Livesay's oeuvre are indebted to those CBC producers, such as Doug Nixon, Ira Dilworth, and Raymond Whitehouse, who admired and praised her radio writing.

In addition to aesthetic disagreements and systemic gender discrimination, Livesay's poor showing in CBC Radio's production history can be traced to the politics of regionalism. The regional structure of the CBC, intended to reflect Canadian geography, articulates with regional differences in important ways. In addition to the Dominion and Trans-Canada networks, representing low and high culture respectively, CBC Radio programming was organized and produced regionally, by staff on the Pacific, Western, Central, and Eastern networks. For example, *Prairie Playhouse* and *Vancouver Theatre* were two drama series on the Trans-Canada network. Livesay was instructed to send her scripts to her local production staff, in Vancouver. In many cases, her work was passed around and read by producers in Vancouver, Winnipeg, and Toronto, before any decision was made. However, the CBC was centralized in Toronto in 1939, as a wartime cost-cutting measure, and all CBC radio stations had to wait for approval from headquarters before producing or broadcasting a show locally or regionally. The new centralization policy gave control over all radio drama in Canada to the CBC's national drama department, led by Allan (Fink and Jackson, "Introduction" ix). According to Frick, centralization also deprived the regions of talented people who moved to Toronto to work in the central drama department (11). The corollary to this regional deprivation is found in the negative career impact on those regional writers, such as Livesay and Elsie Park Gowan, who were unable to move to Toronto for family reasons (Day 22).[47] As Livesay implies in her complaint to Frick about "material definitely suited for B.C.," Toronto executive producers could not be well informed about all topics relevant to all regions of Canada. The disadvantages attached to centralization, from the writer's point of view, were compounded by programming directors' tendency to ignore advice from regional offices.

The control by the central programming office in Toronto is evident. In 1949, Nora Gibson of the Programme Division at CBR Vancouver wrote to Livesay, "I have just had confirmation from the East of your talk on the book "Human Destiny" for our series *A Book I Like*.[48] The regions' lack of autonomy also led to inefficiencies, as seen when, in September 1964, Livesay sent a copy of her poetry volume *The Colour of God's Face* to CBC Toronto producer Robert McCormack, requesting a radio review. When she did not hear from McCormack, she wrote to Allan Campbell, Public Affairs producer in Vancouver, on 23 February the next year, and asked him to intervene on her behalf; Campbell did. From his office in Toronto, McCormack apologized for the delay and gave Campbell the go-ahead for the review.[49]

The hegemony of the CBC's central office, evident in the onerous approval process, is also reflected in CBC producers' practice. Consider Robert Weaver's first extant letter to Livesay, written on 8 April 1949, one year after he started working at CBC. Weaver rejected Livesay's verse drama about the Japanese-Canadian internment, "Call My People Home," which she had submitted for broadcast on the Trans-Canada Network, because "a shorter version has already been done on the western network. In a sense," he added, "that was the best place for it."[50] In this situation, the gatekeeping power of CBC producers is clear. The internment of Japanese Canadians in 1942, presumed to be a regional event by a central Canadian producer, is barred from national broadcast by the same producer in 1949. The element of competition among producers may also have motivated Weaver, a young producer working his way to the top of a national cultural corporation. George Woodcock describes Weaver as "a kind of impresario in the Canadian literary world" for his later productions of Mordecai Richler's and Alice Munro's works on *Canadian Short Stories*, for example (1172). However, at this point in his long and productive radio career, Weaver's rejection of Livesay's "Call My People Home" was a major mistake, in my view. "Call My People Home" represents, in a long poem, an important event in Canadian history: the racism, physical hardships, and emotional and material losses experienced by Japanese Canadians during World War Two are treated poetically and metaphorically in Livesay's verse drama. It was produced by Whitehouse in Montreal and was broadcast on the Trans-Canada Network once, in 1949. In 1954, it was produced once again by Emrys Jones of Winnipeg and broadcast regionally, on the Eastern Network.

The process through which "Call My People Home" came to be broadcast on the Trans-Canada Network in 1949 illustrates the CBC's position as a huge, unwieldy bureaucracy, difficult even for established writers like Livesay to access. In February 1949, two different producers, at opposite ends of the country, were reading and considering "Call My People Home": Doug Nixon, production manager of CBR Vancouver, and Weaver, who was then with Talks and Public Affairs, in Toronto. In early March, Nixon wrote to Livesay on 7 March that he was unable to get the play on *CBC Wednesday Night*, adding that he would look elsewhere because he had "considerable confidence in the worth of the material."[51] He showed Livesay's script to Ira Dilworth, International Service Supervisor, who wrote two letters to Livesay in mid-March, full of praise for her verse-drama.[52] Meanwhile, Nixon produced an abridged, fifteen-minute version of "Call My People Home" for the Pacific Network. Four days after the broadcast of 28 March 1949, Nixon told Livesay about the enthusiastic audience response. "I, personally, have been very gratified at the comments I have heard about the broadcast," he wrote. "I feel you did a very moving piece of writing ... I only regret that we were unable to get it into our *Wednesday Night* series."[53] *Wednesday Night* was a "cultural flagship" with "hundreds of thousands of listeners," and both Livesay and Nixon were well aware of the cultural capital that would have been theirs if "Call My People Home" had been produced on it, rather than on a program that received only regional dissemination (Woodcock 1172; Fink and Jackson xi). Livesay wrote to Dilworth on 25 March about the importance of having a full-length version of her long poem broadcast nationally during the week of 31 March because that date would be "a significant moment for the Japanese-Canadians."[54] On 31 March 1949, the federal orders-in-council which removed Canadian Japanese from the west coast were finally lifted (Adachi 39).

Dilworth had been lobbying for the broadcast of "Call My People Home" on the highbrow Trans-Canada Network. He gave a copy of the script to three different programming supervisors and managers in Toronto, including Whitehouse, but he was unaware of Nixon's broadcast in Vancouver and had no idea whether that broadcast would "make any difference to the decision of the National Office."[55] Toronto producers were concerned about being upstaged by the Pacific Network production. Whitehouse was also subject to the cultural producer's code that new material was more valuable than broadcast material. He wrote to Livesay on 21 April 1949, saying that he was "very eager to do this script this summer on the Trans-Canada Network," but he also asked her for "other half-hour dramas which have not been aired."[56] His admiration for Livesay's long poem overcame concerns over cultural capital and career promotion. It is significant, however, that "Call My People Home" did not appear on Allan's *Stage* series, which has been described by radio historian Howard Fink as "on the leading edge of contemporary social analysis and commentary" (Fink and Jackson x). In *Canadian National Theatre on the Air, 1925–1961*, Fink writes that "the *Stage* series was launched with the conscious intention of creating a showcase for original Canadian drama in an original Canadian medium" (14). *Stage* was the logical place for "Call My People Home," yet Livesay struggled to find a producer for this important radio drama, and she was dependent on Dilworth's networking efforts.

Livesay suspected that the pressure of national public politics prevented some CBC producers from taking on "Call My People Home," and she addressed this possibility by seeking print publication and giving "a private reading of the poem for members of the Civil Liberties Union" in Vancouver.[57] Present at that meeting was Professor G.G. Sedgewick of the University of British Columbia's English department, who suggested that "there might be some political reason for the CBC getting cold feet over the poem which is of course, in BC at least, a controversial issue at this time."[58] Exemplifying socially critical low modernism, "Call My People Home" is a site where national politics intersects with literature, an intersection that occurred internationally.[59] Radio analyst Graham Murdock claims that "BBC turned down [Howard Brenton's] radio play, 'Government Property,' because it dealt with the internment policy in Northern Ireland and its effect on the British Army and public life" (146). "Call My People Home's" trajectory on CBC Radio illustrates the influence of location on writers' topics and on producers' careers. Moreover, the fact that regional considerations affected radio production so profoundly resonates with the anti-modernist nature of mass media.

Livesay's interest in writing for the radio was a logical development, deriving partly from her long-standing commitment to poetry as a spoken art closely related to music. She felt strongly about the importance of her personal "speech rhythms" to the performance of her poetry.[60] When Robert Weaver proposed hiring "a professional reader" to read poems from *The Unquiet Bed* on *Anthology*, she adamantly refused. "I am exploring new techniques with the voice and the breath in relation to the poetic line," she wrote. "For instance, in a poem like 'Soccer Game,' only the particular dramatic and dance effect, and the timing can be expressed most effectively through my own voice [*sic*]."[61] In "Song and Dance," Livesay commented publicly on the place of rhythm and melody in her writing process: "I don't know how it is with other poets, but as far as I am concerned I am always hearing this other *beat* behind the ordinary spoken language and I'm always hearing the melody" (41; emphasis in original). Livesay ascribes this musicality to her childhood environment: Florence Livesay played nursery rhymes and songs on the piano, and Ukrainian domestics sang folksongs in the Livesay home. Livesay writes, "as a small child I felt words as being linked with music. In my mind a poem was a tune" ("Song and Dance" 41). In 1951, she collaborated with composer Barbara Pentland to produce a chamber opera based on the memoirs of Susan Allison, a BC pioneer. Like her mother, Livesay played piano, a useful skill during this collaboration, which resulted in CBC's production of "The Lake" in 1954. In 1976, Pentland set Livesay's poem series "Disasters of the Sun" (1971) to music; it was produced on radio in 1983 (Tiessen and Tiessen xxiii). Pioneer female Canadian composer Violet Archer was also inspired to work with Livesay's poetry. In the late 1970s, Archer created a program of songs and piano music from poems by Livesay, e.e. cummings, Arthur Bourinot, and Amy Bissett. It includes several poems from Livesay's *Signpost* (1932) and *Plainsongs* (1977).[62]

Livesay's decision to write for radio also relates to her politics: she saw the CBC as a developer of a Canadian national identity through its production and dissemination of culture. In 1969, two years after Canada's centenary celebration, which initiated a new phase of Anglo-Canadian nationalism, Livesay wrote to CBC's director, George Davidson, to protest the cancellation of the *CBC Times*: "Canadian newspapers and Canadian critics have utterly failed to appreciate radio and the marvellous job that has been done for forty years in making us aware of our music, our art, our poetry and fiction, drama and films."[63] Livesay knew that the ability of radio to reach a large audience made it a very useful medium for didactic purposes.[64] On 7 June 1946, she wrote to Alice Frick, "In the U.S. and England, people are learning their country's history for the first time—on the air. It seems highly urgent to some Canadian writers that the same opportunity be given our own people, and by the CBC."[65] As proponents of Romantic nationalism have held since at least the eighteenth century, the widespread knowledge of a nation's history among its people contributes to the development of a national identity and, therefore, to national unity (Fee 36, 63). Livesay's vision for radio was corroborated by some CBC Radio program officers, such as Art Sager, who wanted to develop "a series of broadcasts on books, a series which will emphasize the great importance of our Canadian authors."[66] Literature has always been seen by nationalists as central to the development of a national identity, and the rise of CBC Radio in the first half of the twentieth century was understood to be a means to that end.

In the late 1940s and early 1950s, Livesay was building a network of like-minded, supportive, and receptive colleagues at CBC Radio. She broke ground for the following generation of modernist/activist women poets, such as Phyllis Webb, whose work for CBC Radio is analyzed by Pauline Butling in this volume.[67] Livesay and Webb were both internationalists who joined the CCF party; they both integrated their political beliefs into their literary work; they both saw the CBC as a site for public discussion in Canada; and they both faced not only the systemic discriminatory practices of a large bureaucracy, but also the rejection of their work by producer Robert Weaver. The negotiations of freelance contributors, such as Livesay and Webb, with CBC staff were vulnerable to assumptions surrounding gender, ethnicity, racialization, age, class, sexual orientation, and position on the continuum of literary values. The narrative of private struggles revealed to us in the correspondence between Livesay and CBC Radio producers develops our understanding of the foundations of systemic discrimination in the cultural sectors of Canadian society. These private struggles accumulate to produce entrenched cultural effects, yet the importance of this process is seldom addressed, either by writers or critics. Understanding how Livesay negotiated systemic assumptions and hierarchies in the Canadian cultural field of the 1940s and 1950s sheds more light on the articulation of modernist aesthetics with respect to gender and location. It also highlights the extent of Livesay's determination and struggle to resist professional discrimination and underscores the multiple aspects of her long-term literary success.

Notes

The conference paper on which this essay is based was written during a Canada Research Chair Postdoctoral Fellowship at the University of Alberta. The essay was revised during a SSHRC Postdoctoral Fellowship at the University of Ottawa. I am grateful to both universities, to their departments of English, and to the Social Sciences and Humanities Research Council of Canada for their support. Thanks to the archivists and librarians at the Bruce Peel Special Collections Library of the University of Alberta (BPSC), the Elizabeth Dafoe Library of the University of Manitoba (EDL), and the Archives of

Queen's University (Queen's) for their efficiency and for the many kindnesses extended to me during the research for this essay.

1 For example, in 1939, she gave a lecture on the program "Canadian Poetry Today." In 1944, "Morning Visit" profiled her literary career, and in 1947, she was interviewed by Ellen Harris about her writing (Livesay Collection, BPSC, Queen's box 1, Correspondence CBC, January 1939–October 1949, letters of 18 January 1939, 16 April 1944, and 11 February 1947). Throughout the 1950s, Livesay's short stories appeared on Robert Weaver's program *Canadian Short Stories*. During the 1960s, her poetry was read on *Anthology* and *Wednesday Night* (Livesay Collection, BPSC, Queen's box 1, Correspondence CBC, May 1960–9 September 1970, Livesay-Weaver correspondence of April and May 1967; "The Poetry of Dorothy Livesay Read by John Drainie").

2 See the letters of 19 March and 14 April 1947 from Ada A. McGeer to Livesay (Livesay Collection, BPSC, Queen's box 1, Correspondence CBC, January 1939–October 1949).

3 In 1946, she wrote "Our Painters, Writers and Musicians" for CBC's *Panorama* and, between 1954 and 1960, she developed several scripts about other writers, such as Charlotte Brontë, Emily Dickinson, Edwin Muir, and Edith Sitwell, for the *Wednesday Night* and *Letters and Journals* programs. Some of these scripts were never broadcast (Emily Dickinson and Edwin Muir). The Edwin Muir program was cancelled in 1960 (see Robert Weaver's letter to Livesay, 30 May 1960, Livesay Collection, BPSC, Queen's box 1, Correspondence CBC, January 1950–May 1959). The Brontë show was broadcast twice in 1957, and the Edith Sitwell program was broadcast in 1954.

4 Long after her *Critically Speaking* broadcasts of 1950–52, she wrote to various CBC producers to suggest programming ideas and experimentation in production methods, or simply to complain about omissions or errors in radio programs. For instance, see Livesay's letters of 20 and 22 April 1964 to Dorothea Cox, program organizer for Public Affairs, concerning "an out and out apologist for the reactionary white apartheid-minded minority" in South Africa on *Speaking Personally* (Livesay Collection, BPSC, Queen's box 1, Correspondence CBC, May 1960–9 September 1970).

5 Cross-media writing is not a recent innovation. Bill McNeil and Morris Wolfe point out that many early radio announcers also worked as newspaper reporters (92). For example, in early 1947, Livesay proposed a series of radio talks on postwar reconstruction efforts in England and Europe (Livesay Collection, BPSC, Queen's box 1, Correspondence CBC, January 1939–October 1949, Nixon-Livesay correspondence of 11 January and 11 March 1947). The series was based on the research she did for several articles published in the *Toronto Star* (Livesay Collection BPSC, Queen's box 2, file 21: Correspondence *Star Weekly*, May 1944–June 1949, 7 June 1946, from H.C. Hindmarsh). Livesay was paid $75 per week plus expenses for her research trip to England and France.

6 Livesay's dramas about racism, "Call My People Home" and "If the World Were Mine," were broadcast in 1949 and 1950 (Fink 1983, 1925–1961, fiche 8, section E-755). See also Livesay's "Statement for New Year's Day" (1953) (Tiessen and Tiessen, *Dorothy Livesay*, 18–19) and her talk on *Town Meeting* in 1951, "What Is the True Approach to Peace?" (Livesay fonds, EDL, mss37, box 106, folder 19).

7 "Momatkum," a metaphor for Native peoples' modernization, is the story of a Native community's decision to divert a spring for irrigation. Livesay did the research in 1947 (Stevens 55) and wrote the radio play in 1950 (Thompson 131). To current readers, the play draws on stereotypes, binaries, and the appropriation of voice. In her senior years, Livesay felt distanced from this work.

8   The letter is signed G. Kristjanson. Howard Fink identifies one of *Prairie Playhouse*'s regional drama directors as Guy Kristjanson ("Sponsor's vs. the Nation's" 235). Alice Frick identifies a script editor in her Toronto drama office as Gustaf Kristjanson, who "became the drama producer in Winnipeg [in the early fifties]" (43).
9   Kristjanson's words are ironic in view of Livesay's later publication of *Right Hand Left Hand: A True Life of the Thirties* (Livesay Collection, BPSC, Queen's box 1, file: January 1950–May 1959).
10 Frick was writing on 6 April 1951 (Livesay Collection, BPSC, Queen's box 1, file: Correspondence CBC, January 1950–May 1959).
11 Livesay was writing on 7 June 1946 (Livesay Collection, BPSC, Queen's box 1, file: Correspondence CBC, January 1939–October 1949). "Saguenay's Job" was timely because it dealt with a World War Two veteran's reintegration into the community, and "Flags for Canada" was timely because, in postwar Canada, "there was considerable agitation in the country to establish a Canadian flag" (Tiessen and Tiessen 81).
12 ACRA was the precursor to ACTRA, the Alliance of Canadian Cinema, Television and Radio Artists.
13 A copy of ACRA's national council's "Submission to the CBC Regarding Script Writers' Grievances" is in the Dorothy Livesay Collection at BPSC (Queen's box 1, file: Correspondence CBC, January 1950–May 1959), suggesting her involvement. ACRA's success is immediately evident in Livesay's correspondence with Robert Weaver, who wrote on 29 March 1951 that he was accepting Livesay's story, "The Other Side of the Street," and sending "a voucher" to the accounts department; he added that Livesay would receive payment in two or three weeks (Livesay Collection, BPSC, Queen's box 1, file: Correspondence CBC, January 1950–May 1959).
14 Writer–broadcaster Boyle was responsible for starting *CBC Wednesday Night* in 1947. He was later an active print journalist and author. In the field of radio, CBC was highbrow in comparison to lowbrow private radio.
15 For example, on 25 June 1946, Livesay submitted a short story, "The Green Jacket," about a female radio announcer, to CBC International Service (Livesay Collection, BPSC, Queen's box 1, Correspondence CBC, January 1939–1949).
16 Historians and theorists of modernism vary in their adherence to one or more of the following descriptors of modernist art or literature: scientific, intellectual, experimental, fragmented, objective, anonymous, efficient, individualistic, dislocated, internationalist, non-decorative, functionalist, urban, masculine, sexually liberated. Few artists or writers draw on all these aspects of modernism in one work.
17 See, for example, the open ending of Madge Macbeth's modernist fiction, *Shackles* (1926).
18 For example, see Lawren Harris's "The Evangelist" in *Contrasts* (1922), which David Arnason rightly points out is prescient of poetics in the 1960s (Arnason 30).
19 At the same time, as editors Di Brandt and Barbara Godard point out, some modernist poets, such as William Carlos Williams and Raymond Souster, celebrate the local (email to Peggy Kelly, 19 July 2003).
20 The Broadcasting Act of 1958 gave the CBC's "regulatory role" to the newly created Board of Broadcast Governors (Eaman 271). The board lasted ten years, until the Canadian Radio and Television Commission was set up in 1968.
21 Prime time is defined as 7:00 to 11:00 PM.
22 Sources disagree over the date for the introduction of the Dominion Network, but 1944 is given most frequently. Paul Rutherford avoids giving a specific date. Alice Frick gives January 1944 (26). Howard Fink also gives 1944 in *Canadian National Theatre on*

the Air, 1925–1961 (33); however, in "The Sponsor's vs. the Nation's Choice: North American Radio Drama," Fink gives 1943 (228).
23 Some popular shows: *Ma Perkins, Wayne and Schuster, Don Messer and the Islanders, Maggie Muggins, Jake and the Kid*, Hockey broadcasts with Foster Hewitt.
24 One episode of *Design for Murder*, titled "The House on Torture Hill," described as a "gothic ghost story," was broadcast on 31 October 1947 on the Dominion Network. "The Making of a Scientist," by Ted Allan, about Frederick Banting, appeared on the Dominion Network's *It Happened Here* on March 19, 1952. "Against All Odds," also on *It Happened Here*, explains the 1942 discovery in Montreal of how adrenal hormones could cure infected babies (Fink, *Canadian National Theatre* fiche 1).
25 *Stage* was launched in 1944 and *CBC Wednesday Night* in 1947. Although both appeared on the highbrow Trans-Canada Network, from the literary field's perspective, *Stage*'s dedication to drama and privileging of original drama over adaptations made it more culturally valuable than *Wednesday Night*, which had a variety show format, broadcasting documentaries, music, and drama, which were often adaptations from the literary canon.
26 In 1971, CBC Radio returned to two networks when the FM stereo network started, and advertisements were dropped from both networks in 1975. In 1997, these networks were renamed Radio 1 and Radio 2. In the 1990s, the proliferation of radio stations and cell phone usage forced CBC Radio to disregard the FM/AM distinction and use whatever wavelength was available locally. However, the high/low distinction is less prominent between Radio 1 and Radio 2 than it was between the Dominion and Trans-Canada networks because funding cutbacks have led to these latest English networks, Radio 1 and Radio 2, sharing programs. Nevertheless, Radio 2 definitely emphasizes high culture. For example, *Saturday Afternoon at the Opera* appears on Radio 2, while *Definitely Not the Opera*, on Radio 1 every Saturday afternoon, self-consciously distinguishes itself from the perceived formality of the other network.
27 The two "poems about the Depression" are "Day and Night," and "West Coast: 1943" and the "three post-war [World War Two] documentaries" are "Zambia," "Prophet of the New World," and "The Raw Edges."
28 Allan's letter, dated 5 July 1946, is held in the Livesay fonds (Queen's).
29 Norman Newton takes issue with this historiography.
30 Scott's letter is dated 6 February 1948 (Livesay Collection, BPSC, Queen's box 1, Correspondence CBC, January 1939–October 1949). By 1951, Scott was the book editor of Toronto's *Telegram* and his response to Livesay's and Birney's defence of radio as a site of culture suggests that he left the CBC due to a disagreement with the CBC's self-appointed role as a "guardian of national culture" ("Radio and Writers West Coast Replies," *Telegram* 27 Jan. 1951: 4).
31 The last quotation is from a talk broadcast on 14 January 1951: see Ross McLean's letter to Livesay dated 16 January 1951 (Livesay Collection, BPSC, Queen's box 1, file: Correspondence CBC, January 1950–May 1959). McLean, on staff at CBR Vancouver, commented on Livesay's talk and agreed that CBC programming sometimes juxtaposed "culture and corn." It is notable that Miriam Waddington, who, like Livesay, was educated for social work, encouraged CBC Television to experiment and to provide highbrow programming (see Candida Rifkind's essay in this volume).
32 "Legendary Land" revolves around Ogopogo, the mythic sea-serpent of Okanagan Lake, in the BC interior (Vernon, Kelowna, Penticton area). In an undated letter to Whitehouse (possibly December 1951), Livesay describes "Legendary Land" as

"humorous, gay and musical" (Livesay Collection, BPSC, Queen's box 1, Correspondence CBC, January 1950–May 1959; Tiessen and Tiessen, Introduction xvi).

33 The letter is dated 24 February 1948 (Livesay Collection, BPSC, Queen's box 1, Correspondence CBC, January 1939–October 1949).

34 Whitehouse's letter postponing acceptance is dated 20 May 1949 (Livesay Collection, BPSC, Queen's box 1, Correspondence CBC, January 1939–October 1949; Queen's, box 1, Correspondence CBC, January 1939–October 1949, item 65).

35 Whitehouse's letter is dated 19 July 1949 (Livesay Collection BPSC, Queen's box 1, Correspondence CBC, January 1939–October 1949). In another letter, on 4 April of the the next year, he writes that he's "tremendously excited" about Livesay's "idea of a documentary on the Indian people" (Livesay Collection, BPSC, Queen's box 1, Correspondence CBC, January 1950–May 1959).

36 The letter may have been written in December 1951 (Livesay Collection, BPSC, Queen's box 1, Correspondence CBC, January 1950–May 1959).

37 McGeer's letter and the guidelines were sent on 14 April 1947 (Livesay Collection, BPSC, Queen's box 1, Correspondence CBC, January 1939–October 1949); the guidelines are held in Queen's University Archives (Livesay Collection, Queen's box 1, Correspondence CBC, January 1939–October 1949, item 37).

38 There is also the question of class: patronization of the uneducated housewife by the professional woman.

39 A production script is held in the Morris Surdin Collection at the University of Calgary Archives, Calgary. Surdin (1914–80) composed the music for the 1961 CBC production of Peterson's play. He also worked with W.O. Mitchell on the famous *Jake and the Kid* series. Surdin worked for the CBC on both an in-house staff and a freelance basis from 1939.

40 This play has three versions with different titles. In correspondence between Whitehouse and Livesay on 16 March and 24 April 1950, it is called "Personal History," before its radio production (Livesay Collection, BPSC, Queen's box 1, Correspondence CBC, January 1950–May 1959). The produced play is called "If the World Were Mine" (Broadcasting Archives, Concordia University). The title of the same play in Livesay's *Right Hand, Left Hand* is "The Times Were Different" (132–50).

41 Six years after Peterson's play appeared, Whitehouse produced "If the World Were Mine" for *CBC Summer Theatre* in August 1950. He requested revisions and Livesay complied. For instance, she rewrote the original ending, the version that appears in *Right Hand Left Hand*, and the radio audience's response was very good. Charlotte Sergay of Detroit wrote on 8 August, "I felt that it was a very original and extremely impressive production ... I certainly hope that we will be hearing more broadcasts of this high quality." Whitehouse sent a copy of this fan letter to Livesay (Livesay Collection, BPSC, Queen's box 1, Correspondence CBC, January 1950–May 1959).

42 See the Nixon–Livesay correspondence of 14 and 25 September 1951 (Livesay Collection, BPSC, Queen's box 1, Correspondence CBC, January 1950–May 1959).

43 See the work of Geraldine Finn, Evelyn Fox Keller, Cynthia Cockburn, Joan Rothschild, and Wendy Faulkner.

44 Livesay Collection, BPSC, Queen's box 1, Correspondence CBC, May 1960–9 September 1970.

45 *Women in the CBC*, a 1975 report on the sexual division of labour within the corporation, shows that the male network continued to disadvantage female applicants and employees. See also Dorothy Smith's work on "the stag circle" in the social sciences. Thanks to Barbara Godard for this reference.

46 The feeling was mutual. In a fragment from her *Critically Speaking* series, Livesay criticizes Allan's "comedies of manners from three centuries," saying, "These plays I could not swallow. They were too superficial altogether for their verbal power to have any effect" (*Dorothy Livesay and the CBC* 13).
47 Gowan worked in Edmonton. Her CBC salary was kept artificially low; the assumption appears to have been that her marriage to a university professor exempted the CBC from paying her a salary equivalent to that of other (male) radio writers.
48 Her letter is dated 27 April 1949 (Livesay Collection, BPSC, Queen's box 1, Correspondence CBC, January 1939–October 1949).
49 See the correspondence of 23 February and 1 March 1965 (Livesay Collection, BPSC, Queen's box 1, Correspondence CBC, May 1960–9 September 1970). Campbell's letter of 1 March 1965 suggests that he declined to review Livesay's book on air.
50 Livesay Collection, BPSC, Queen's box 1, Correspondence CBC, January 1939–October 1949.
51 Livesay Collection, BPSC, Queen's box 1, Correspondence CBC, January 1939–October 1949.
52 Dilworth (1894–1962) was a native of BC who taught and administered in the Victoria secondary school system (1920–38) before working for CBC (1938–60). Neighbour, friend, and literary executor to Emily Carr (1871–1945), Dilworth wrote the foreword to a second edition of Carr's *The Book of Small* (1951), and edited her journals and other works after her death (*Hundreds and Thousands: The Journals of an Artist* [1966], *Pause* [1953], and *The Heart of a Peacock* [1953]). He also edited literary anthologies for schools; see his *Nineteenth-Century Poetry* (1931) and *Twentieth-Century Verse: An Anthology* (1945). His letters to Livesay from 10 and 14 March 1949 are held in the Dorothy Livesay Collection at BPSC (Queen's box 1, Correspondence CBC, January 1939–October 1949). The following year, Dilworth became "national director of programming" for CBC English Radio (New 2002).
53 Livesay Collection, BPSC, Queen's box 1, Correspondence CBC, January 1939–October 1949.
54 Livesay Collection, BPSC, Queen's box 1, Correspondence CBC, January 1939–October 1949.
55 Dilworth's letter is dated 29 March 1949 (Livesay Collection, BPSC, Queen's box 1, Correspondence CBC, January 1939–October 1949).
56 Livesay Collection, BPSC, Queen's box 1, Correspondence CBC, January 1939–October 1949.
57 Livesay contacted B.K. Sandwell, editor of *Saturday Night*, offering the poem for publication on 31 March 1949, and Birney also wrote Sandwell on her behalf. See Livesay's letter to B.K. Sandwell, 28 February 1949 (Livesay Collection, BPSC, Queen's box 2, file 25, Personal Correspondence 1949–60).
58 Graham Murdock points out that BBC producers also practised self-censorship by avoiding "politically contentious material" (*Radio Drama* 146).
59 As Zailig Pollock pointed out on 11 May 2003, at "The Canadian Modernists Meet: A Symposium," held at the University of Ottawa, some modernist scholars consider the oppositional element to be essential to the definition of modernism.
60 See her letter dated 13 April 1967 (Livesay Collection, BPSC, Queen's box 1, Correspondence CBC, May 1960–9 September 1970). See also Paul Gerard Tiessen and Hildi Froese Tiessen's article "Dorothy Livesay and the Politics of Radio" (78).
61 Livesay, letter to Weaver, 13 April 1967, Livesay Collection, BPSC, Queen's box 1, Correspondence CBC, May 1960–9 September 1970.

62 On 28 February 1978, Archer's program was performed in concert in Edmonton, by mezzo-contralto June Hunt and pianist Albert Krywolt. See "A Programme of Songs and Piano Music" by Violet Archer and "Violet Archer, A Bio-bibliography" in the Music Library, University of Alberta. Archer's settings of Livesay's poems were performed by mezzo-soprano Melinda Enns and pianist Paul McIntyre in a concert at "Wider Boundaries of Daring: The Modernist Impulse in Canadian Women's Poetry," University of Windsor, October 2001.
63 Her letter is dated 28 October 1969 (Livesay Collection, BPSC, Queen's box 1, Correspondence CBC, May 1960–9 September 1970).
64 Didacticism was anathema to high modernism, another factor in the perception of mass media as anti-modernist.
65 Livesay Collection, BPSC, Queen's box 1, Correspondence CBC, January 1939–October 1949.
66 Livesay Collection, BPSC, Queen's box 1, Correspondence CBC, January 1939–October 1949, letter from Sager to Livesay, Sept. 8, 1947.
67 Webb did freelance radio writing in the 1950s and was on staff at CBC Radio in Toronto for five years (1964–69); during this period she produced *Ideas*. In 1966–67, during her employment at CBC, Webb corresponded with Livesay about her appearance on Webb's program, to read her own work (Livesay Collection, BPSC, Queen's box 1, Correspondence CBC, May 1960–9 September 1970).

Works Cited

Adachi, Ken. "A History of the Japanese Canadians in [British] Columbia, 1877–1958." *Two Monographs on Japanese Canadians*. Toronto: Arno, 1978. 1–43.

Arnason, David. "Canadian Poetry: The Interregnum." *CV/II: A Quarterly of Canadian Poetry Criticism* 1.1 (Spring 1975): 28–32.

Bourdieu, Pierre. *The Field of Cultural Production: Essays on Art and Literature*. Ed. Randal Johnson. New York: Columbia UP, 1993.

Brandt, Di, and Barbara Godard. Email to Peggy Kelly. 19 July 2003.

Burckhardt-Qureshi, Regula, Albert LaFrance, and Brenda Dalen, eds. *Voices of Women: Essays in Honour of Violet Archer*. Spec. issue of *Canadian University Music Review* 16.1 (1995).

Butling, Pauline. "Phyllis Webb." *Encyclopedia of Literature in Canada*. Ed. W.H. New. Toronto: U of Toronto P, 2000. 1204–6.

Cameron, Elspeth. *Earle Birney: A Life*. Toronto: Viking, 1994.

Canadian Radio Broadcasting Act, 1932, S.C. 1932, C51.

Carr, Emily. *The Book of Small*. Foreword by Ira Dilworth. Toronto: Clarke, Irwin, 1951.

———. *The Heart of a Peacock*. Ed. Ira Dilworth. Toronto: Oxford UP, 1953.

———. *Growing Pains: The Autobiography of Emily Carr*. Foreword Ira Dilworth. Introduction Robin Laurence. Vancouver: Douglas & McIntyre, 2005.

———. *Klee Wyck*. Foreword by Ira Dilworth. Toronto: Clarke, Irwin, 1951.

———. *Pause: A Sketch Book*. Toronto: Clarke, Irwin, 1953.

Day, Moira, ed. *The Hungry Spirit: Selected Plays and Prose by Elsie Park Gowan*. Edmonton: NeWest, 1992.

DiBattista, Maria. "Introduction." *High and Low Moderns: Literature and Culture, 1889–1939*. Ed. Maria DiBattista and Lucy McDiarmid. New York: Oxford UP, 1996. 3–19.

Dilworth, Ira, ed. *Nineteenth-Century Poetry*. Preface G.G. Sedgewick. Toronto: Copp Clark, 1931.

———. *Twentieth-Century Verse: An Anthology*. Toronto: Clarke, Irwin, 1945.

Eaman, Ross. "Canadian Broadcasting Corporation." *Canadian Encyclopedia*. Edmonton: Hurtig, 1985.

Fee, Margery. "English-Canadian Literary Criticism, 1890–1950: Defining and Establishing a National Literature." Diss. U of Toronto, 1981.

Fink, Howard. *Canadian National Theatre on the Air, 1925–1961: CBC–CRBC–CNR Radio Drama in English, A Descriptive Bibliography and Union List*. Toronto: U of Toronto P, 1983.

———. "Earle Birney's Radio Dramas." *Essays in Canadian Writing* 21 (Spring 1981): 53–72.

———. "The Sponsor's vs. the Nation's Choice: North American Radio Drama." *Radio Drama*. Ed. Peter Lewis. Essex, UK: Longman, 1981. 185–243.

Fink, Howard, and John Jackson, eds. *All the Bright Company: Radio Drama Produced by Andrew Allan*. Toronto: CBC and Quarry, 1987.

Frick, Alice. *Image in the Mind: CBC Radio Drama, 1944–1954*. Toronto: Canadian Stage and Arts Publications, 1987.

Goodwin, Jill Tomasson. "Len Peterson." *Dictionary of Literary Biography*. Vol. 88, *Canadian Writers, 1920–1959*. 2nd series. Ed. W.H. New. Detroit: Gale, 1989. 240–46.

Kemp, Hugh. "Len Peterson: A Portrait." *Canadian Author and Bookman* June 1946: 24–25.

Livesay, Dorothy. *Dorothy Livesay and the CBC: Early Texts for Radio by Dorothy Livesay*. Ed. and introd. Paul Gerard Tiessen and Hildi Froese Tiessen. Waterloo: mlr editions canada, 1994.

———. Dorothy Livesay Collection. 96–69. Bruce Peel Special Collections Library, University of Alberta, Edmonton, AB (BPSC).

———. Dorothy Livesay fonds. Mss. 37. Department of Archives and Special Collections, Elizabeth Dafoe Library, University of Manitoba, Winnipeg, MB (EDL).

———. Dorothy Livesay fonds. 2024. Queen's University Archives, Queen's University, Kingston, ON (Queen's).

———. "If the World Were Mine." Broadcasting Archives, Concordia Centre for Broadcasting Studies, CCBS Bibliography, Vol. 1, Microfilm #000101, E-755-4.

———. *Journey with My Selves: A Memoir, 1909–1963*. Vancouver: Douglas and McIntyre, 1991.

———. *Right Hand Left Hand: A True Life of the Thirties*. Erin, ON: Press Porcépic, 1977.

———. *The Self-Completing Tree: Selected Poems*. Victoria: Press Porcépic, 1986.
———. "Song and Dance." *Canadian Literature* 41 (Summer 1969): 40–48.
Macbeth, Madge. *Shackles*. Ottawa: Graphic, 1926.
McNeil, Bill, and Morris Wolfe. *Signing On: The Birth of Radio in Canada*. Toronto: Doubleday, 1982.
Murdock. Graham. "Organising the Imagination: Sociological Perspectives on Radio Drama." *Radio Drama*. Ed. Peter Lewis. London: Longman, 1981. 143–63.
New, W. H., ed. *Encyclopedia of Literature in Canada*. Toronto: U of Toronto P, 2000.
Newton, Norman. "Malcolm Lowry and the Radiophonic Imagination." *Malcolm Lowry Review* 36 (Spring 1995): 56–95.
Peterson, Leonard. *Burlap Bags: A Play in One Act*. Toronto: Playwrights Co-op, 1945.
———. "Maybe in a Thousand Years." Production Script. Morris Surdin Collection, University of Calgary Archives, Calgary, AB.
———. *They're All Afraid*. Agincourt: Book Society of Canada, 1981.
———. "Under the Feet of the CBC's Stampeding Bureaucracy." *Globe and Mail* 27 November 1976: 35.
"The Poetry of Dorothy Livesay Read by John Drainie." *CBC Wednesday Night*. ISN 229608. Library and Archives Canada, Ottawa, ON.
Rutherford, Paul. "Radio Programming." *The Canadian Encyclopedia*. Edmonton: Hurtig, 1985.
Scott, F.R. "Radio and Writers West Coast Replies." *Telegram*, 27 January 1951: 4.
Stevens, Peter. *Dorothy Livesay: Patterns in a Poetic Life*. Toronto: ECW, 1992.
Strong-Boag, Veronica. *The New Day Recalled: Lives of Girls and Women in English Canada, 1919–1939*. Toronto: Copp Clark, 1988.
Thompson, Lee Briscoe. *Dorothy Livesay*. Boston: G.K. Hall, 1987.
Tiessen, Paul. "Dorothy Livesay, the 'Housewife,' and the Radio in 1951: Modernist Embodiments of Audience." *The Canadian Modernists Meet*. Ed. Dean Irvine. Ottawa: U of Ottawa P, 2005. 205–28.
Tiessen, Paul Gerard, and Hildi Froese Tiessen. Introduction. *Dorothy Livesay and the CBC: Early Texts for Radio by Dorothy Livesay*. Waterloo: mlr editions canada, 1994. xi–xxviii.
———. "Dorothy Livesay and the Politics of Radio." *A Public and Private Voice: Essays on the Life and Work of Dorothy Livesay*. Eds. Lindsay Dorney, Gerald Noonan, and Paul Tiessen. Waterloo: U of Waterloo P, 1988. 71–86.
Weir, E. Austin. *The Struggle for National Broadcasting in Canada*. Toronto: McClelland and Stewart, 1965.
Women in the CBC: Report of the CBC Task Force on the Status of Women. Toronto: Canadian Broadcasting Corporation, 1975.
Woodcock, George. "Robert Weaver." *The Oxford Companion to Canadian Literature*. 2nd ed. Toronto: Oxford UP, 1997. 1172.

Phyllis Webb as Public Intellectual
PAULINE BUTLING

In the spring of 1964, Phyllis Webb took a full-time job at CBC Radio in the Public Affairs Department as program organizer for *University of the Air*, an adult education program that was broadcast on the FM network. Her qualifications for the job included a BA in philosophy and English (UBC, 1949), previous experience at CBC Radio as a freelance writer, and, more generally, an inquiring and eclectic intelligence. Her intellectual interests ranged from philosophy to Zen Buddhism, visual art, poetry, anarchism, left-wing politics, and minority rights. Personal attributes included an edgy humour, acute intelligence, an adventurous spirit, a resonant voice, and a stunning appearance. Nevertheless, given the fact that Webb was first and foremost a poet—indeed she was recognized as one of the best young poets of the day, with two poetry books[1] and numerous magazine publications to her credit—CBC's choice seems at first glance somewhat surprising. Why would the CBC want to hire a poet?[2]

Webb's decision to work full-time at CBC Radio for what turned into five intensive, exhausting years is also somewhat surprising. To that point she had lived a poet's life of intermittent travel (in Montreal, Vancouver, London, Paris, Toronto, and San Francisco), supporting herself with secretarial jobs, freelance radio work, sessional teaching, and the occasional grant. In the year prior to taking the CBC job, Webb's poetry-first agenda seemed as strong as ever. In the summer of 1963, she did extensive interviews with Charles Olson, Robert Duncan, Robert Creeley, Denise Levertov, and Allen Ginsberg about the experimental American poetry and poetics.[3] She was also experimenting with new poetic forms herself. In an application for a Canada Council travel grant for the fall of 1963, she outlined two ambitious poetry projects: "The first, probably to be titled NAKED POEMS, will be a small volume of small poems." A second, tentatively titled "SCORPION AND BULL," she describes as "a book of big poems" that would offer "social satire," "a critique of language," and "serious poetry of somewhat cosmic proportions" (Phyllis Webb fonds). *Naked Poems* was published in 1965, but the second project was shelved when she took the CBC job.

Instead, Webb gave the job her full attention. No sooner had she begun than she suggested to co-worker William A. Young, who ran another adult education program called *The Learning Stage,* that they merge their respective programs into an "ideas" program aimed at a wider audience. At first called *The Best Ideas You'll Hear Tonight* (later shortened to *Ideas*), the program was launched in 1965 on FM radio, with selected portions carried on the AM network. Thus began one of CBC's most long-lived and successful programs. Over the next few years, Webb, Young, Janet Sommerville, and other members of the production team, established the program's characteristic signature of cutting-edge, educational, critical, socially conscious, and sometimes quixotic programming. Webb was program organizer from 1965 to '67 and executive producer from 1967 to '69, except for a six-month leave of absence in 1967.

You may well ask—as I did, and that's what started me on this research—what accounts for this co-joining of two seemingly very different trajectories? Not only why did CBC hire a poet, but also why was Webb willing to put her writing life on hold to devote five intensive, exhausting years to the program?[4] Finally, why do so few people know about this? Given the contribution of the *Ideas* programs to the political and philosophical debates of the 1960s, together with Webb's continuing exploration of philosophical and social issues in her subsequent poetry, Webb should be celebrated as one of Canada's major public intellectuals. She fits the profile in most respects. Defined as writer/critics who offer incisive analysis of current issues, public intellectuals are typically well-educated, socially responsible, left-leaning, independent thinkers. They seek an audience of similarly thoughtful people. Indeed, they often help to create and shape the views of such an audience.[5] In Canada, examples might include John Ralston Saul, M. Nourbese Philip, Marshall McLuhan, Jane Jacobs, Jeannette Armstrong, Patrick Watson, Laurier Lapierre, or Paul Kennedy. Webb fits the profile, except for one important point—her lack of a public presence.

One reason for her invisibility is very straightforward: Webb produced but did not host the broadcasts, unlike the current host of *Ideas*, Paul Kennedy. Webb's voice is heard only occasionally as an interviewer or as an unidentified reader, and her name is mentioned only in the program credits. However, I suspect gender bias is at work in Webb's invisibility in the sense that women, especially women poets, have rarely been valued for their intellectuality. Like Dorothy Livesay or Miriam Waddington before her, Webb was praised more for her sensitivity and emotional depth than for her incisive wit, intellectual range, or social activism. As many of the essays in this volume demonstrate, the intellectual labour of women poets was often undervalued, if not ignored, for the generation that immediately preceded Webb. The gender of modernist intellectual work was overwhelmingly male. Candida Rifkind and Paula Kelly offer a critical revaluation of two modernist female public intellectuals, Mariam Waddington and Dorothy Livesay. My discussion of Webb's work participates in the same project: I outline Webb's *Ideas* programming in some detail to show its social and intellectual range, as well as to explore its relation to a social critique in her poetry.

First, from a personal standpoint, *Ideas* not only provided Webb with a much-needed job, but also furthered her work in poetry in that it served as a site to develop the social critique first proposed in her "Scorpion and Bull" project—to expand her intellectual and critical range. More generally, *Ideas* also fed her love of intellectual inquiry, always a central feature of her poetry. Webb describes this life-long passion in "The Question as an Instrument of Torture":

> The thirst for knowledge, that cliché, rightly refers to a bodily hunger. We would drink in the life-giving nourishment, or eat what is food for thought. There is, I suggest, an element of lust in the desire to know … We are hunters stalking abstractions, numbers, the bright-eyed doe in the forest. (*Talking* 35)

Webb's "thirst for knowledge" was matched by an equally intense passion for social justice. Raised as a modernist with a social conscience by mentors ranging from F.R. Scott, Earle Birney, and Louis Dudek to Virginia Woolf,[6] Webb's activism had already taken several forms. In the late 1940s, she joined the CCF party[7] and ran for election in the 1949 British Columbia provincial election on a platform that advocated improved social programs for workers and equality for minority groups. In the 1950s, she turned her attention to cultural politics. She did a survey, gave talks, and wrote articles on the problems in Canadian literary publishing.[8] In her *Ideas* programming, she continued to advocate for minority rights and to offer critiques of established ideas and practices. Program guests included some of the most radical thinkers and innovative artists of the decade. Austin Clarke, R.D. Laing, Norman O. Brown, Stokely Carmichael, Northrop Frye, Marshall McLuhan, Paul Goodman, Daniel Berrigan, Leonard Cohen, Martin Luther King, Lester B. Pearson, Louis Dudek, Leonard Cohen, Robert Duncan, Earle Birney, and Glenn Gould were some of the better known guests. These and many other philosophers, anarchists, poets, artists, and politicians inhabit Webb's subsequent poetry as much as they inhabited her *Ideas* program. Throughout her writing life, she continued to explore the nature of social responsibility, to ask what constitutes effective revolutionary action, and to critique power and dominance. Webb's sojourn at *Ideas* served her well in that it helped her to develop the intellectual and ethical discourses necessary for the social critique that she had envisioned, but failed to realize, in 1963.

In addition, Webb's *Ideas* work helped her break a dependency on literary and cultural fathers that had plagued her life as a poet. As Webb has explained on several occasions, her own father left the family when she was a young girl, and she spent many years attaching herself to father figures, from a high school history teacher, to F.R. Scott, Louis Dudek, Earle Birney, and other male friends and mentors, as well as to cultural fathers ranging from Yeats, Pound, and Shakespeare, to Socrates and the Russian anarchist Prince Kropotkin. It took her a "very long time," she explained in a 1993 interview with Janice Williamson, "to start thinking about where some of ... [her] difficulties in writing were coming from, like the silences and the difficulty in carrying off a programmed poem or book." She continues, "Finally I had this overbearing sense that there had been too many fathers, literary and otherwise. I know by 1969 it was conscious, and I wrote a little prose piece in which I dispatched the fathers to the river Lethe, and I saw them sail away" ("Read the Poems" 322). Certainly Webb's *Ideas* programming was male-dominated, with some 80% of the speakers being men. By putting the cultural "dads" on stage as it were, she perhaps began to *see* their dominant role in her psyche. It is surely no accident that recognizing her dependency and quitting the CBC go hand in hand.

Breaking away from the fathers proved to be a life-long process, however.[9] "Oh dear," she exclaims as recently as 1990 when Hermes pops up in an essay she is writing on the role of gender: "why has old psyche thrown up yet another male figure ...?" ("Message Machine" 293–94). From her recognition of the problem in 1969, it would take more than a decade for an active and assertive I/eye to emerge in Webb's poems. Indeed, her poetry of the late 1960s and early 1970s belies the 1969 liberating moment altogether. She titles one group of poems from this period "Poems of Failure" (*Wilson's Bowl* 13–21).[10] In her foreword to *Wilson's Bowl* (1980), she emphasizes her failures and silences, and apologizes for "the domination of a male power culture in my educational and emotional formation so overpowering that I have, up to now, been denied access to inspiration from the female figures of my intellectual life, my heart, my imagination" (n.p.). Her failure, she explains, shows up not only in the "Poems of Failure," where she fails to complete a poetic project on Prince Kropotkin ("the infantile ego could not solicit that beautiful anarchist dream poem"), but also in the eight "Portraits" that follow.[11] Seven of these are about men—"Socrates," "Kropotkin," "Dostoevsky," "Ezra Pound," "Rilke," "Vasarely," and "Father." The one portrait of a woman ("Letters to Margaret Atwood"), Webb explains, was not the result of a conscious choice on her part: she only wrote it because "she was *asked* to write on the subject of women" (Foreword n.p.; emphasis in original).

Webb's "Letters to Margaret Atwood" are complimentary to Atwood, but very hard on Webb. The "I" of the poems speaks in an ironic, self-deprecating tone, emphasizing her silence, inaction, and failure. While the poet's anguish is palpable and personal, "cross-hatched" on the body, its causes are in part cultural and institutional:

> I refuse to publish because I refuse to write. What I've written I hoard, hoping the poems will eventually turn into satisfactory failures. I've been preparing the model *in vitro* for years. There's some chance of success ... So I'll leave a legacy of buried verbs, a tight-mouthed treasure. Someday when you require more evidence you can dig them up, my bones crosshatched with grim messages. I even give permission for them to be displayed under glass in the National Museum in Ottawa, otherwise known as the Great Canadian Coffin. (*Wilson's Bowl* 37)

Buried in "the Great Canadian Coffin"—all but erased by the weight of tradition—the woman poet's despair comes not from the classic modernist lament over the loss of tradition, but rather from feeling buried by its oppressive presence.

What Webb fails to note here are her successes: she in fact breaks her poetic silence of several years, albeit in ways that fall short of her expectations. Also, her "study of power" (Foreword n.p.) in the Kropotkin poems facilitates liberation in the sense that understanding how power works is crucial to changing power relations. By the late 1970s, in "Imperfect Sestina," the poet still struggles to overcome her silencing, but at least she speaks her anger and frustration:

> Can I really say I found even two cents at the crossing?
> There I was stabbed and pecked by spirit Raven.
> There in that marriage I turned into stone,
> and did not understand he carved me at his mirror. (*Wilson's Bowl* 73)

Also, in the "Portraits" of the cultural fathers that follow the "Poems of Failure," the poet becomes defiant. She often mocks, criticizes, and/or talks back. She criticizes Ezra Pound for his "fixed obsessions" (*Wilson's Bowl* 31). To Rilke she says, "I speak your name I throw it away" (32). In "Vasarley," she declares, "I shift my gaze from the abode of adoration" (34). Finally, she posits a new, embryonic self in "Letters to Margaret Atwood," albeit with an irony that almost completely undercuts its potential. She can only offer "buried verbs" and "grim messages," but nevertheless the potential for growth is there, "*in vitro.*" That potential quickly materialized. The next fifteen years would be Webb's most productive, with four outstanding books appearing in quick succession in the early 1980s (*Wilson's Bowl*, *The Vision Tree: Selected Poems*, *Water and Light*, and *Talking*), followed by her stunning, final poetry collection, *Hanging Fire*, in 1990.[12]

For the CBC, its five-year relationship with Phyllis Webb was also empowering. As an arm of the nation, it too was involved in asserting independence from father figures—in this case, independence from the Imperial fathers. From its inception in 1936, the CBC's mandate has been to define and affirm an independent *Canadian* identity. Politicians and artists alike have long argued that developing a distinct Canadian culture would bring an end to Canada's colonial period, while also protecting a fragile national identity from US influence and dominance. Along with other Canadian cultural institutions such as the National Gallery (1880) and the Canada Council for the Arts (1957), the CBC is a cornerstone of cultural nationalism. As stated in the report of the Royal Commission on Canadian Broadcasting in 1929, by "fostering a national spirit and interpreting national citizenship" the CBC would strengthen the nation (qtd. in Bonikowsky 365). Not until global capitalism demanded more porous cultural boundaries did this ideological bedrock start to crumble, as, for instance, in the erosion of cultural sovereignty that began with the North American Free Trade Agreement (NAFTA) in 1989.

While the mandate of the CBC and other national cultural institutions has been to strengthen the nation, its methods appear to contradict that goal. For the nation to prove that it has shed its colonial past, its cultural production must be modernist, which is to say anti-national, critical, radical, internationalist, and/or avant-garde. The outcome of this modernist insistence on revolutionizing culture is a state-sponsored resistance to and critique of itself. In an excellent article on "Canada's Modernist Legacy," Jody Berland provides a succinct summary of these combined nationalist and modernist tenets, as articulated by the benchmark Massey Commission *Report* on the state of the arts in Canada in 1951. They include

> antipathy to the dominance of American commercial and popular culture ...; an agreement that art and artistic works would inhabit an autonomous professional world, accountable only to juries of professional peers who could judge artistic value in its own terms; the belief that national subjects were ... united by shared cultural beliefs and values, nurtured by the country's art; [and] the arguably countering belief that art ought to be disengaged and free from local traditions, community standards, politically motivated strategies of representation or other "idiosyncrasies." (Berland 17–18)

The structural challenges and contradictory ideologies in this position are obvious. Culture must be avant-garde, autonomous, and progressive to be modernist; but it must be managed by government in order to serve the nationalist project of identity formation. The structural challenge is to find ways to support cultural production when that production must, by definition, be autonomous, radical, and internationalist. The solution in part is a structural sleight of hand, an arm's-length relationship between government and its cultural institutions. The federal government formulates general policy but leaves implementation and interpretation to the cultural institutions and/or to independent peer juries. The arm's-length mechanisms enable national cultural institutions such as CBC radio to support innovative, cutting-edge, and seemingly autonomous critical and cultural work. Anything less would confirm Canada's continuing colonial status. Driven by the twin engines of nationalism and modernism, then, the CBC promotes an identifiable Canadian culture with programming that is critical of that very identity.

By the time Webb entered the picture, the CBC's reputation for innovative arts and public affairs programming was well established. In the post–World War Two period, Morley Callaghan chaired *Of Things to Come: An Inquiry into the Post-War World*, which evolved into another successful 1950s program called *Citizens' Forum*. Both programs addressed current and often controversial topics. In the heydays of 1960s radicalism, the CBC further established its pivotal role in providing public space for controversial people and ideas. Indeed, many of Canada's most creative people earned some or all of their living working for the CBC. Often characterized as Canada's coming-of-age decade, which culminated in the Centennial celebrations of 1967, the 1960s firmly established Canada's status as a "modern" nation.

To return to my opening question: Webb's credentials were in fact ideal for the CBC job. A poet with a degree in English and philosophy who was in touch with both national and international avant-garde writers and intellectuals, Webb was just the sort of person CBC Radio wanted and needed to further its reputation for "modern," cutting-edge programming. Indeed, on its current website, CBC still boasts about the innovative and eclectic nature of *Ideas* at its inception: "The first three programs featured a discussion of Darwin's theory of evolution and an interview with members of the CBC Galapagos Expedition, a series called Peace on Earth, the music of Villa-Lobos, and a talk by Earle Birney about poetry and creativity" (*Ideas*).

Webb's personal imperatives were also intertwined with the twin engines of nationalism and modernism, albeit with a gendered twist. Her despair comes from her inability to escape male dominance; but experimenting with new forms, sending the fathers to Lethe, challenging authority, and developing a social critique are all modernist impulses. Simultaneously, she shared the nationalist project of developing a distinctive Canadian culture, as seen in her research and writing in the 1950s on the state of Canadian literary publishing. Finally, the CBC provided a public forum for Webb to explore ideas and issues that were crucial to her work in poetry.

Having traced the trajectories that produced this productive intersection of individual and institutional agendas, I want now to describe some of the outstanding results of this "marriage." In 1967, Canada's Centennial, the year Webb became executive producer, *Ideas* began without nationalist fanfare or flag waving. The first series, titled "Money and Power," was internationalist in scope and subversive in content. It included an interview by Austin Clarke with the US Black activist Stokely Carmichael (chair of the

Student Nonviolent Coordinating Committee). Clarke and Carmichael discuss such revolutionary topics as the role of guerilla warfare in the Black revolution and the importance of Black culture as a "cohesive force" in the work of James Brown, James Baldwin, and others. Also included in the broadcast is an excerpt from a speech by Carmichael on Black Power and the inspiration to be gained from Franz Fanon's *The Wretched of the Earth*. Webb's choice for the 1967 Massey lectures was the equally controversial figure Dr. Martin Luther King. King gave five talks titled "Tradition and Revolution," in which he delivered his radical message that equality and justice for Black people can only be achieved through major systemic changes.

Webb's choice of a Black American civil rights activist for the premier *Ideas* series in Canada's centennial year served several agendas. The fact that neither the speaker nor the topic is even remotely nationalist, yet the series takes place within one of Canada's major cultural institutions, foregrounds the salutary autonomy of the CBC and thereby affirms Canada's "mature" nation status. At the same time, Webb had long been interested in minority rights and power issues. Her cutting-edge programming became mutually beneficial, simultaneously fulfilling the CBC's mandate and her own creative and critical interests.

Webb eventually did a Centennial project of sorts, but it was characteristically idiosyncratic. A docu-drama titled "The Idea of North" and produced by the eccentric Glenn Gould, the project focusses on the theme of isolation. The program was innovative in form as well as content. Voices of a geographer, a sociologist, a Department of Northern Affairs official, a Canadian Northern Railway surveyor, and a nurse who live in the North are montaged together with musical motifs in a "soundscape," a form that Gould pioneered in this and other CBC *Ideas* programs. The program ends with a montage of voices and music that represent a variety of perspectives on and experiences of the North. It was Canadian, yes, but about a relatively unknown part of Canada and produced by a maverick artist-intellectual. Other maverick artist/intellectuals on the 1967 roster included Webb's old friend from her Vancouver and San Francisco days, the poet Robert Duncan, talking about "The Poet as Celebrant," and the quixotic US critic Leslie Fiedler, whose discussion abandons traditional literary scholarship to speak about US popular culture and contemporary nihilism.

Webb's 1968 programming continued to address current political issues with a two-part series on "Tradition and Revolution." In one part, Norman Endicott, the son of a Canadian missionary to China, presents the unusual (and then unpopular) view that the Chinese communist revolution was regenerative and productive for the Chinese people. In part two of the same series, subtitled "The Viability of Democracy in the United States," an eclectic group of panelists discusses democratic processes and the seeming inevitability of violence in the confrontational climate of the late sixties. Panelists included novelist Norman Mailer, politician Arthur Schlesinger (who served in the Kennedy administration), and sociologist Herbert Marcuse. Philosophical dimensions of 1960s counter-cultural activism were addressed in another series featuring Henry David Aiken from the London School of Economics[13] speaking on Karl Marx and Jean-Paul Sartre, two of Webb's favourite thinkers from her undergraduate days at UBC.[14] Aiken explains Sartre's critique of the Enlightenment and positivist philosophers for their "Utopian socialism," the belief that you can change the world through changing ideas. Aiken argues that for Sartre the *idea* of freedom is insufficient: "real freedom is more than a feeling, more than an enjoyment, or an idea—it is the achievement of groups working together, it is people working, creating a world for themselves." Idealism deceives "because it implies that the *idea* of freedom is sufficient" (Aiken). The value of both Marx and Sartre, in Aiken's view, is that they advocate social transformation through direct action. All of these speakers and programs directly pertain to the hotly debated issues of the 1960s, as well as to Webb's own poetic and political concerns about how to achieve social change.

Webb's final year as executive producer (1969) was truly a grand finale, with a stunning array of programs dealing with the now and the new. Topics included structuralism, the neo-anarchist youth movements, the new linguistics, experimental theatre, international politics, and love poetry. Webb's internationalism showed up again in a series titled "Peace in the Family of Man." In one episode, Lester B. Pearson, former Canadian prime minister and a staunch internationalist, addresses topics ranging from the importance of the United Nations, to the challenges presented by the pan-African movement, to how international organizations such as the World Bank, the United Nations, and NATO erode national sovereignty. In the same series, Father Daniel Berrigan—poet, pacifist, political radical, and professor at Cornell University—leads a panel discussion about effective forms of resistance to the Vietnam war and reads some of his poetry reflecting on the war (Berrigan in Pearson, "The United States of the World"). On another current topic, 1960s student radicalism, Canadian writer/critic George Woodcock talks about the current popularity of classic anarchist principles in Europe and the US. He notes the importance of the US writer Paul Goodman and Britain's Sir Herbert Read as contemporary anarchist philosophers and then discusses "Holland's radicals, the 'Committee of 1000' in England, and those French students who flew the black flag, the anarchists' banner, over the Sorbonne during the student strike." In the same series, the associate editor of the *Village Voice* and a New York drama critic debate the merits of classical versus contemporary, experimental theatre (Wetzsteon and Simon).

On a more philosophical note, Professor Maurice Cranston of the London School of Economics gave six talks on language and philosophy. Cranston describes Wittgenstein's revolutionary notion that philosophy is the study of meaning rather than the study of truth ("Wittgenstein's *Tractatus*") and explains Wittgenstein's innovative ideas about language games ("Wittgenstein's Later Theories"). In his last two talks, Cranston presents the groundbreaking ideas of Lévi-Strauss, in particular Lévi-Straus's articulation of the interconnections between language and culture ("Structuralism"). As in all Webb's programming, the arts were also well represented in the 1969 season, with an intriguing series on "The Unnatural History of Love." Topics ranged from the courtly love tradition, to incest, mystical love, romantic love, Urdu love poetry, and the *Ghazals of Ghalib*.[15]

Clearly, Webb's five-year association with CBC Radio proved to be one of those fortuitous intersections where institutional and individual agendas temporarily converge to produce more than the sum of their parts. Questions remain as to whether Webb quit only for health and other personal reasons (Hulcoop 7; Webb, "Intimations of Mortality" 9) or whether she also became disenchanted with the nationalist/modernist agenda. Did she recognize her own co-optation in the nationalist project? Her contradictory role in that project? I wonder if her explanation of health problems and "too many fathers" (Webb, "Read the Poems") tells the whole story. Her description of the National Museum as "the Great Canadian Coffin," cited above ("Letters to Margaret Atwood" 37), suggests a stultifying institutional effect. Did the CBC prove to be the biggest daddy of them all?

In any case, *Ideas* served Webb well in at least three crucial ways: it provided a public forum to explore her political and social interests, it helped her to recognize "the domination of male power culture in ... [her] educational and emotional formation" (Foreword 9), and it left her with starting points for much of her later work in poetry. Certainly the CBC benefitted from the partnership in that Webb's programming more than satisfied its modernist nationalist mandate. Webb's readers, as well as those interested in Canadian culture generally, have also been well served by this fortuitous intersection. Webb provided a role model of a highly intellectual, socially conscious woman poet taking action in the public domain—one who also challenged male dominance both in her own "educational and emotional formation" (9) and within the cultural institutions that shaped and sustained her.

NOTES

1. *Even Your Right Eye* (1956) and *The Sea Is Also a Garden* (1962).
2. Compare Webb's credentials, for instance, with those of the current *Ideas* host and producer, Paul Kennedy: "Paul Kennedy is a veteran broadcaster and award-winning documentarist. He is well-known to CBC Radio listeners as a regular replacement host on such flagship programs as *Morningside, Stereo Morning* and *Arts National*. He has produced and presented close to 100 documentaries for IDEAS over the past 24 years ... Paul has a BA from Queen's University, an MLitt from the University of Edinburgh, Scotland. He's done post-graduate work at the University of Toronto where he studied with Marshall McLuhan" (*Ideas*).
3. Creeley, Olson, Duncan, and Ginsberg were in Vancouver to teach a Summer Poetry Workshop at the University of British Columbia. The interviews were intended for broadcast on CBC Radio, but in a letter to Webb on 27 January 1964, Robert Weaver (CBC Radio special programmes officer) vetoed the project, claiming that the interviews were mostly "fatuous nonsense" (Phyllis Webb fonds). Typescripts of the interviews are available in the Phyllis Webb fonds at Library and Archives Canada in Ottawa.
4. In a 1983 interview with Eleanor Wachtel, Webb explains that she did very little writing during those years and that she was exhausted by the time she quit ("Intimations of Mortality" 9).
5. In twentieth-century North America, the concept of a public intellectual originated in the United States in the 1930s with the social/cultural critics associated with the *Partisan Review* in New York. They provided independent analyses and critiques of current issues (Jacoby, *The Last Intellectuals*). Intellectual was first used as a noun to describe the intervention of Emile Zola in the Dreyfus affair at the end of the nineteenth century in France.
6. Woolf was a mentor in the sense that Webb studied her work avidly as an undergraduate at UBC in the late 1940s. The archives of the UBC Letters Club include a copy of a paper that Webb presented on Woolf as a member of the Letters Club. UBC Letters Club fonds: 1920–1957. University of British Columbia Archives. Box 7, vol. 40 (1948/49).
7. CCF stands for Cooperative Commonwealth Federation. It was the forerunner of the New Democratic Party.
8. Webb wrote three essays on "The Poet and the Publisher." The first one, published in *Queen's Quarterly* 61 (Winter 1954–55) was a summary of the results of her survey on the state of publishing in Canada; the second was a "brief account of a similar survey that she had recently completed in England" (Whalley xi), which she delivered at the Canadian Writers' Conference on "The Poet, His Media, and the Public" at

Queen's University in July 1955. A third version was published in the conference proceedings in 1956. This version was also broadcast on CBC Radio in November 1955. For more discussion of this project, see Lorna Knight, "'With all best wishes, high hopes, and thanks': Phyllis Webb, Canadian Poetry, and publishing in the Early 1950s," and Butling, *Seeing in the Dark* (131–32).
9   It was a slow process partly because it was more complex than the traditional male model, where the son "kills off" the father. In my book on Webb, I suggest that she developed an intersubjective/intertextual model of resistance, one that combines identification *and* separation (Butling, *Seeing in the Dark* 89–108).
10 See Collis (122–27) for an excellent discussion of the complexities of "failure."
11 *Wilson's Bowl* was not published until 1980, but the "Portraits" of Ezra Pound and Kropotkin were first published in 1970, corroborating Webb's comment that by 1969 she had initiated a transformative process. For details about publication dates and places, see Cecelia Frey's annotated bibliography in the *Annotated Bibliography of Canada's Major Authors*, vol. 6.
12 Webb's writing life appears to be complete. In the early 1990s, she stopped writing and turned to collage and painting as her creative media. After *Hanging Fire* (1990), she has published only the essay collection, *Nothing but Brush Strokes* (1995).
13 Webb worked briefly as a secretary at the London School of Economics while living in London in 1954–55. Presumably she met Professor Aiken then.
14 Webb studied existential philosophy as an undergraduate at the University of British Columbia. She was self-educated in Marx because the professor in her course on government refused to include Marx in the course syllabus.
15 Some fifteen years later, Webb returned to the *Ghazals of Ghalib* as the starting point for *Water and Light: Ghazals and Anti Ghazals* (1984).

Works Cited

Aiken, Henry David. "Chance and Novelty: The Revolt Against Necessity." Selections from the 5 part series *Best of Ideas*, 19 August 1968. Exec. prod. Phyllis Webb. Accession no. 680819–02. CBC Radio Archive, Toronto, ON.

Berland, Jody. "Nationalism and the Modernist Legacy: Dialogues with Innis." *Capital Culture: A Reader on Modernist Legacies, State Institutions, and the Value(s) of Art*. Ed. Jody Berland and Shelley Hornstein. Montreal: McGill-Queen's UP, 2000. 14–38.

Berrigan, Daniel David. In Pearson, "The United States of the World." *Peace in the Family of Man* series. *Ideas*, 8 January 1969. Exec. prod. Phyllis Webb. Accession no. 690108–05–00. CBC Radio Archive, Toronto, ON.

Bonikowsky, Laura Neilson. "Founding of the CBC." *The Canadian Encyclopedia*. 2000 ed. 365.

Butling, Pauline. *Seeing in the Dark: The Poetry of Phyllis Webb*. Waterloo, ON: Wilfrid Laurier UP, 1997.

Carmichael, Stokely, and Austin Clarke. "Minorities of Power." *Ideas*, 27 March 1967. Exec. prod. Phyllis Webb. Accession no. 670327–05–00. CBC Radio Archive, Toronto, ON. 10 September 2002 <http://radio.cbc.ca/programs/ideas/history.html>.

Collis, Stephen. *Phyllis Webb and the Common Good: Poetry, Anarchy, Abstraction.* Vancouver: Talonbooks, 2007.

Cranston, Maurice. "The Structuralism of Claude Lévi-Strauss." *Ideas.* 26 March 1969. Exec. prod. Phyllis Webb. Accession no. 690326–05–01. CBC Radio Archive, Toronto, ON.

———. "Wittgenstein's Later Theories: Analysis as Therapy." *Ideas.* 12 March 1969. Exec. prod. Phyllis Webb. Accession no. 690312–01–01. CBC Radio Archive, Toronto, ON.

———. "Wittgenstein's *Tractatus* on Language as a Picture of Reality." *Ideas.* 26 February 1968. Exec. prod. Phyllis Webb. Accession no. 690226–01–01. CBC Radio Archive, Toronto, ON.

Duncan, Robert. "The Poet as Celebrant." *Ideas.* 10 May 1967. Exec. prod. Phyllis Webb. Accession no. 670510–09–00. CBC Radio Archive, Toronto, ON.

Endicott, Norman. "Tradition and Revolution." Part 1. *Ideas.* 17 June 1968. Exec. prod. Phyllis Webb. Accession no. 680617–06–00. CBC Radio Archive, Toronto, ON.

Fiedler, Leslie. "The Tradition of the New and the Tradition of the End." *Ideas.* 30 October, 6 November, and 13 November 1967. Exec. prod. Phyllis Webb. Accession no. 671030–06/00, 671106–03–00. CBC Radio Archive, Toronto, ON.

Frey, Cecelia. "Phyllis Webb: An Annotated Bibliography." *The Annotated Bibliography of Canada's Major Authors.* Ed. Robert Lecker and Jack David. Toronto: ECW, 1985. 6:389–448.

Goodman, Paul. *Like a Conquered Province: The Moral Ambiguity of America.* Massey Lectures. Toronto: CBC Publications, 1966. Accession no. 661107–03–00. CBC Radio Archive, Toronto, ON.

Gould, Glenn. "The Idea of North." *Ideas.* 28 December 1967. Exec. prod. Phyllis Webb. Accession no. 671228–06–00. CBC Radio Archive, Toronto, ON.

Hulcoop, John. Introduction. *Selected Poems, 1954–1965 by Phyllis Webb.* Vancouver: Talonbooks, 1971. n.p.

Ideas. CBC.ca. Canadian Broadcasting Corporation. 26 July 2008 <www.cbc.ca/ideas/host.html>.

Jacoby, Russell. *The Last Intellectuals.* New York: Noonday, Farrar, Straus and Giroux, 1987.

King, Martin Luther. "Tradition and Revolution." Massey Lectures. *Ideas.* 20, 27 November, 4, 18, 24 December 1967. Exec. prod. Phyllis Webb. Accession no. 671120–05, 671127–03, 671204–06, 671218–04, 671224–02. CBC Radio Archive, Toronto, ON.

Knight, Lorna. "'With all best wishes, high hopes and thanks': Phyllis Webb, Canadian Poetry and Publishing in the Early 1950s." *West Coast Line* 25.3 (1991–92): 43–53.

Mailer, Norman, Herbert Marcuse, and Arthur Schlesinger. "The Viability of Democracy in the United States." Panel discussion. *Ideas.* 17 June 1968. Exec.

prod. Phyllis Webb. Accession no. 680617-06-00. CBC Radio Archive, Toronto, ON.

Pearson, Lester B. *Peace in the Family of Man*. Reith Lecture Series of six lectures: Lecture #3, "The United States of the World." *Ideas*. 8 January 1969. Executive Producer, Phyllis Webb. Toronto: CBC Radio archive. Accession #690108-05-00.

———. Lecture #5, "A Poor Thing but Our Own." *Ideas*, 22 January 1969. Executive Producer, Phyllis Webb. Toronto: CBC Radio archive. Accession #690122-03-00.

Royal Commission on National Development in the Arts, Letters and Sciences. *Report*. Chair Vincent Massey. Ottawa: King's Printer, 1951.

Weaver, Robert. Letter to Phyllis Webb. 27 January 1964. Phyllis Webb fonds.

Webb, Phyllis. *Even Your Right Eye*. Toronto: McClelland and Stewart, 1956.

———. Foreword. *Wilson's Bowl*. Toronto: Coach House, 1980. 9.

———. *Hanging Fire*. Toronto: Coach House, 1990.

———. "Imperfect Sestina." *Wilson's Bowl*. Toronto: Coach House, 1980. 73.

———. "Intimations of Mortality." Interview with Eleanor Wachtel. *Books in Canada* November 1983: 8–15.

———. Letter to Robert Stanton. 16 June 1970. Phyllis Webb fonds.

———. "Letters to Margaret Atwood." *Wilson's Bowl*. Toronto: Coach House, 1980. 36–38.

———. "Message Machine." *Language in Her Eye: Views on Writing and Gender by Canadian Women Writing in English*. Ed. Libby Scheier, Sarah Sheard, and Eleanor Wachtel. Toronto: Coach House, 1990. 293–96. Rpt. in Webb, *Nothing but Brush Strokes* 136–42.

———. *Naked Poems*. Vancouver: Periwinkle, 1965.

———. *Nothing but Brush Strokes: Selected Prose*. Ed. Smaro Kamboureli. Edmonton: NeWest, 1995.

———. Phyllis Webb fonds. LMS-0098. Literary Archives, Library and Archives Canada, Ottawa, ON.

———. "Poems of Failure." *Wilson's Bowl*. Toronto: Coach House, 1980. 13–21.

———. "The Poet and the Publisher." *Queen's Quarterly* 61 (Winter 1954–55): 498–512. Rev. ed. *Writing in Canada: Proceedings of the Canadian Writers Conference, Queen's University, 28–31 July, 1955*. Ed. George Whalley. Intro. F.R. Scott. Toronto: Macmillan, 1956. 78–89.

———. "Portraits." *Wilson's Bowl*. Toronto: Coach House, 1980. 25–38.

———. "Read the Poems, Read the Poems. All Right?" Interview by Janice Williamson. *Sounding Differences: Conversations with Seventeen Canadian Women Writers*. Toronto: U of Toronto P, 1993. 321–39.

———. *The Sea Is Also a Garden*. Toronto: Ryerson, 1962.

———. *Talking*. Montreal: Quadrant, 1982.

———. *Water and Light: Ghazals and Anti-Ghazals*. Toronto: Coach House, 1984.

Wetzsteon, Ross, and John Simon. "Disappearing Boundaries." *Ideas*. 5 February 1969. Exec. prod. Phyllis Webb. Accession no. 690205–03–00. CBC Radio Archive, Toronto, ON.

Whalley, George. Preface. *Writing in Canada: Proceedings of the Canadian Writers Conference, Queen's University, 28–31 July, 1955*. Ed. George Whalley. Intro. by F.R. Scott. Toronto: Macmillan, 1956. vii–xii.

Woodcock, George. "Neo-anarchism in the Late 1960s." Series "Disappearing Boundaries." *Ideas*. 5 February 1969. Exec. prod. Phyllis Webb. Accession no. 690205–03–00. CBC Radio Archive, Toronto, ON.

"A Collection of Solitary Fragments"
Miriam Waddington as Critic
CANDIDA RIFKIND

Miriam Waddington is and will be an important figure in feminist reconceptualizations of Canadian literary modernism. She is clearly important because of her poetry, which spans from the 1930s to the 1990s and has been widely anthologized, but also for her less studied work as an essayist, commentator, and critic. This essay deliberately sets aside Waddington's poetry, although it is in need of greater critical attention, to discuss examples of her prose as sites of cultural and literary interventions that are at risk of being designated ephemeral and lost to Canadian intellectual history. I am particularly interested in the criticism Waddington first published in periodicals between the 1950s and 1970s. Some of this material appears in her 1989 collection of essays, *Apartment Seven*, but much remains uncollected. These essays were written at the tail end of the period now identified with literary modernism in Canada, and they meditate in different ways on the cultural consequences of modernity. To read her criticism is to enter into Waddington's ongoing investigation of her own and others' artistic practice, which also interrogates many of the ideas about identity and history, the nation and art, that have formed—to borrow one of her favourite phrases from John Stuart Mill—"the received opinion" (Mill 65).

In what follows, I tease out the ways in which Waddington's criticism voices the experiences and politics of a dissenting minority in Canadian culture. Just as her poetry is concerned with difference in all its forms, so is her prose a decades-long meditation on relationships between the individual and the collective, the word and the world. Part of the project of the "Wider Boundaries of Daring" conference was to raise the issues for literary history and feminist theory surrounding the retrieval of modernist women's writing in Canada. In keeping with the revisionary spirit of the conference, as well as the dissenting thrust of Waddington's writing itself, I want to focus on her literary and cultural criticism to dislodge not only the prevailing narrative that the gender of modernism is male but also the assumption that the genre of modernism is poetry.

The significance of poetry to Canadian women's modernist writing cannot be underestimated, but, like their male counterparts, numerous women writers, including Dorothy Livesay, Phyllis Webb, and Waddington, intervened in Canadian cultural politics from both inside and outside the academy. Existing scholarship often introduces female poets as supplements to a masculinist narrative of literary modernism, just as Canadian intellectual history tends to celebrate the critical production of poets Louis Dudek, D.G. Jones, Eli Mandel, and James Reaney, among others, and public intellectuals Northrop Frye, George Grant, and Marshall McLuhan.[1] Between these poets and academics of modern Canada, however, there stands the intellectual labour of a group of female poet-critics.

In this volume, Pamela McCallum explores how the historical and geographic conjunctures of 1930s radical politics work, and are worked upon, in Livesay's "Day and Night." Pauline Butling's essay on Webb foregrounds the intersections between Webb's poetry and her full-time job as a producer for the CBC radio program *Ideas*. Although these poets were interested in the public life of the nation, their intellectual and political contributions have often been overshadowed by several factors, including masculinist definitions of the modern poet as cultural authority and the literary institution's preference for academy-based liberalism over community-based leftism. Another factor at work in the broader society has been a celebration of writers as distinct from, and better than, intellectuals. Edward Said explains this difference:

> In the language of everyday use, a writer in the languages and cultures that I am familiar with is a person who produces literature, that is, a novelist, a poet, a dramatist. I think it is generally true that in all cultures writers have a separate, perhaps even more honorific, place than do intellectuals; the aura of creativity and an almost sanctified capacity for originality (often vatic in its scope and quality) accrues to them as it doesn't

at all to intellectuals, who with regard to literature belong to the slightly debased and parasitic class of critics. (25)

Said does note that, in the final decades of the twentieth century, these two categories became increasingly blurred. Writers began to assume "the intellectual's adversarial attributes in such activities as speaking the truth to power, being a witness to persecution and suffering, supplying a dissenting voice in conflicts with authority" (25). Said maps this crossroads of literary and intellectual labour onto the postmodern era. However, his comments can also be applied to one stream of Canadian modernism in which a group of female poets went public to cross boundaries between the aesthetic and the social. They switched from poetry to essays and literary criticism in order to register dissenting positions in the newly formed institutions of English-Canadian literary criticism. As well, Livesay, Webb, and Waddington took an interest in radio and television as a means to address a national public. In so doing, they used their positions as writers to intervene in the form and content of the broadcasting institutions of the modern Canadian state.

Waddington produced a body of criticism that may have been out of sync with the particular aesthetic concerns of her male contemporaries, but that nonetheless participates in an older national tradition of cultural criticism written from and about the social margins. In the 1920s, Barker and Margaret Fairley transformed the Toronto student journal the *Rebel* into the *Canadian Forum*, and it became by the 1930s an important venue for a range of socialist and modernist criticism. Historians, artists, economists, and social scientists joined poets and novelists to form an interwar circle of social democratic critics. Included in this circle were Jean Burton, Morley Callaghan, Margaret Gould, Leo Kennedy, A.M. Klein, Livesay, F.R. Scott, A.J.M. Smith, and, towards the end of the 1930s, Earle Birney and Waddington herself. In her later criticism, just as in her poetry, Waddington displays a familiarity with this national progressive tradition and seeks new ways to bring it into postwar literary and public discourse. To read what Waddington thought about other Canadian writers and writing, the nation and the state, the arts and the media, to mention only a few of her recurrent subjects, is to gain insight into this particular modernist woman writer's aesthetic philosophy and to expand current boundaries of cultural knowledge about the intersections between aesthetics and politics, literary modernism and cultural modernity.

The Past in the Present: Reading A.M. Klein

In her literary criticism, Waddington returns often to the poetry of A.M. Klein, that passionate and difficult poet, critic, intellectual, and activist whose premature silence leaves a scar on both of his progeny, modernist poetry and Jewish writing in Canada. Waddington, along with Livesay and other writer-critics, has explicated Klein's poetry to celebrate his complex plays with language and his evocation of multiple cultural places, moments, and stories. She draws on her familiarity with Yiddish folklore and Hebrew texts, English and European literature, linguistics and poetics, to contextualize and critique Klein's writing. However, Waddington's readings of Klein must themselves be read as conversations with more than a single interlocutor. As she reads Klein's poetry and prose, Waddington intervenes in the dialogues between celebrated Canadian literary critics whose maleness, Englishness, and Christianity may only seem visible to those outside these subject positions.

Waddington's affiliation with Klein has been observed in studies of Jewish-Canadian literature, which tend to position Klein as the father of Jewish-Canadian writing, but has received scant notice in more general studies of Canadian modernism or feminism. Michael Greenstein describes Klein's innovation of an *"avant-garde* of solitude" (4) as fundamental to Jewish-Canadian poetry and fiction in the twentieth century, but he also laments the paucity of criticism on his work both during Klein's lifetime and today. One "tributary" he does note, however, is Waddington's recognition of Klein as a source of poetic tradition. He reads her 1969 poem "Breaking with Tradition" as an allusion to Klein, the literary father represented as an "old master," "walking forward but speaking to [his] followers with backward glances" (Greenstein 7). Ancestors and their descendents are caught here in typically Kleinian dialectics of negation and affirmation, severance and incorporation, past and future (7). Greenstein emphasizes a particularly Jewish feature of Waddington's affiliation with Klein since he implies it is an affinity located in a shared history, literature, culture, and folklore. In her criticism, Waddington insists that this shared Jewish heritage must be understood as a diverse tradition that includes a secular humanism she locates in some of Klein's writing. As Jewish-Canadian writers and modernists, Waddington and Klein share, paradoxically, an avant-garde solitude. Moreover, this exilic consciousness inspires the recognition of other communal identities structured by difference and alterity.

Their shared cultural tradition is only a starting point from which Waddington develops her larger ideological affiliations with Klein around questions of identity and tradition, justice and the nation. Following Klein, her appeal to the past makes visible histories, events, and people largely invisible in official culture and dominant poetics. When she comments in 1979 on Klein's late shift from Jewish to Québecois folklore as one source of his images, Waddington describes these symbols of French Canada as referring back, within collective history as well as the individual history of the poet, to earlier Judaic symbols: a Québecois grain elevator symbolizes the "spiritual nourishment and human fellowship" of bread in a way that "evokes memories" of the Old Testament; Judaic and French-Canadian folklore images thus proliferate through each other ("Function of Folklore" 16). It is when she summarizes his exploration of quintessentially Canadian folk objects such as rocking chairs, spinning wheels, and skis, however, that Waddington best articulates her theory of cultural temporality: "Even if Klein's objects do not qualify as Canadian folklore, we can still perceive in them and in the poet's use of them, the beginnings of the long slow process through which the future will transform the elements of the present into the symbols of the past" (17).

Folkloric objects are those small things in which Klein found a wealth of meaning. This focus resonates with T.E. Hulme's proclamation that, for writers of the modernist age, "it is essential to prove that beauty may be in small, dry things" (131). The smallness of Klein's folk objects betrays to Waddington the largeness of his vision when she writes that "sometimes a poem uses a folklore image as the basis for a metaphor for the psychological trait of a whole group" ("Function of Folklore" 16). Folklore binds the poet to multiple pasts, presents, and futures just as it binds the individual to a collective. Although folklore may fold the individual into a community, these communities themselves may be internally fractured and externally marginalized.

In her article on Klein's 1930s radical poems, "The Cloudless Day," Waddington writes that these under-recognized works based in experiences of Depression poverty and social injustice are "rooted in Klein's double tradition, Jewish and Canadian" (*Apartment Seven* 121). What Klein often called this "twinship of his thought" can be as disorienting as it is invigorating because each element in this duality is itself divisible (qtd. in Waddington, Introduction ix). In her 1965 analysis of Klein's *The Second Scroll*, Waddington takes the time to explain the novel's cultural, historical, and religious consciousness but insists that "once you go beyond the manifest content of *The Second Scroll*, the theme turns out to be secular and humanist, and not, as first appears, doctrinal in Judaic terms" ("Signs" 26). Here, as elsewhere, Waddington complicates the notion of Jewishness as a singular religious identity or image. Instead, throughout her poetry and prose, Waddington unfolds the sign of Judaism to display its polysemic possibilities of ethnic, linguistic, cultural, intellectual, religious, and secular ways of being.

Similarly, Waddington refutes received notions of nationalism when she argues that Canada, its histories, and its traditions exist only through its conflicts and its contradictions. In her 1969 article "Canadian Tradition and Canadian Literature," Waddington resists state definitions of the nation to declare that what some call a "mosaic" she would call "a collection of solitary fragments" (140). She refutes the centennial optimism of the Canadian mosaic when she invokes colonial history to argue that there is no guarantee "that the collisions between opposites will be constructive and energizing. Such collisions, as we have seen, may as easily result in hatred and destruction as in unity and growth" (141). Her status as outsider (as a European, a Jew, a Western Canadian, a woman, a writer) tempers Waddington's differentiated subject and vision of a harmoniously diverse nation. The despair of her historically informed vision is then countered by her hope for redemption through art.

The complexities of traditions that exclude as much as they include the artist consequently dovetail with Waddington's ideas of the nation. Greenstein asserts that, for Jewish-Canadian writers, Frye's famous query of "where is here?" frequently becomes "where was there?" (12). The temporal shapes the spatial as memory underwrites a poetics of exile. For Waddington, the poet works Janus-faced, with one eye to the future and one to the past.[2] Likewise, the nation and the construction of a national literary tradition are constantly pulled between what has been and what might be. Canada and Canadian literature become categories bounded by history, but they may open up into a more just future. Tradition is defined as much by a potential based on the past as it is on the past itself. This potential, however, is by no means necessarily positive. As she considers her own initially negative response to *The Second Scroll*, Waddington describes how reading Emmanuel Ringelblum's *Notes from the Warsaw Ghetto* in 1958 reshaped her understanding, so that she now sees "the broad range of possible values in Jewish Ghetto society, and what was possible, was not all good" ("Signs" 22). Specifically, Waddington describes recognizing for the first time what she calls "the threat from within" that has for so long been overshadowed for Jews by the "threat from without" (22). This insight leads her to see the relatively new state of Israel as more than "a political entity; it became a symbol of rescue and recognition, the concrete expression of what was best in the ethos of a whole culture. And, from the artist's point of view, is any nationalism ever more or less than this?" (22). I am interested here in the grammar of this statement: nationalism, for the artist, is "the concrete expression of what *was* best in the ethos of a whole culture" (22; my emphasis). The present of the nation is the articulation of a selective past and the hope for its achievement in the future.

In one sense, this theory of the modern poet's relationship to tradition upholds T.S. Eliot's famous dictum that the poet must achieve a historical sense "not only of the pastness of the past, but of its presence" (38). Modern poetic achievement must be measured aesthetically against the tradition of valuable works of which the conscious poet is always aware (39). To modernist Canadian critic E.K. Brown, Klein's poetry resembles Eliot's despite their different social and geographic locations (50–52). For Waddington, however, Klein's poetic and political differences from Eliot and the canon of British "high" modernism allow her to articulate an alternate theory of tradition. Whereas Eliot insists that the poet "must be aware that the mind of Europe—the mind of his own country" is "much more important than his own private mind" (39), Waddington's accumulation of exilic positions compels her to challenge the authority of any national "mind" or dominant tradition. Although Waddington's poet looks backwards and forwards in time, what she sees there is multiple. Competing and contentious interpretations of the nation and a national literature are key to Waddington's sense of tradition.

This collision of competing ideas of nationhood is registered and worked through in poetic language itself. Waddington looks to Klein to see how a poet can play with traditional poetic, linguistic, and semiotic materials, but also how the poet can represent the social achievements of modernity. As much as Klein loved to play with language and inflection, Waddington observes that, on visiting Israel, he was thrilled by the ways modern Hebrew mutated and developed to accommodate political upheaval: "The Hebrew language and speech was in a feverish process of renewal in 1949; it was responding to and reflecting all the new experiences of the people who were then arriving in Israel. The figurative language of its advertisements and daily transactions constituted the real miracle for Klein" ("Signs" 26). The diversity of Jews arriving in Israel opens the language up just as commodity culture demands a new lexicon of daily life. This collision of tradition and innovation, art and commerce, yielded new forms of a language, a grammar and poetics of the present day through which glimpses of an ancient past and desires for a future are visible. As well, innovations in the Hebrew language signify the mutual dependence of artistic modernism and the cultural conditions of modernity. If the former is an aesthetic movement and the latter a social, political, and economic one, then the "real miracle" Klein felt in Israel may have been the ways that language works to represent but also to suture the lived experiences of an often violent modernity.

"Public Principle over Private Expediency": The Canadian Forum *Columns*

Waddington's attention to Klein's modernism in her literary criticism is thus as interested in the conditions of modernity as it is an interrogation of the formal aesthetics of modernism. In her less celebrated role as a public intellectual, she engaged with the socio-political and cultural conditions of modernity and, particularly, with the complex relations between modern media, technology, and the state. Between July 1956 and October 1958, Waddington wrote nineteen "Radio and Television" columns on broadcasting for *Canadian Forum*. A long-standing contributor of poetry to the left-leaning *Forum*, Waddington was one of only a few regular media critics in Canada at this time. She differed from her counterparts at *Saturday Night* and in the daily press by not merely providing summaries of individual programs but analyzing the political and social functions of the media; and she upheld a leftist intellectual tradition begun a generation earlier to advocate state sponsorship of public broadcasting and oppose the powerful private industry lobby. These columns testify to her engagement with broad political and cultural debates about the arts, the state, and technological determinism from within a national tradition of leftist cultural critique.

Whereas radio had arrived in Canada in the early 1920s and its programming was frequently reviewed in newspapers and magazines, the advent of Canadian television in 1952 brought with it relatively little critical commentary. At the end of the 1950s in English Canada, the magazines *Saturday Night* and *Canadian Forum* were unique in their commitment to a regular television column.[3] However, the viewing public was growing rapidly. About ten per cent of homes had television sets when Canadian transmissions began in 1952, but by the decade's end this number reached over eighty per cent (Rutherford 49). The social transformation of the home through the acquisition of television sets is matched at the end of the 1950s by political transformations taking place in the regulation of broadcasting. Waddington wrote her columns in the midst of fervent debates over state control of the media arising from the release of the report of the Fowler Commission (the Royal Commission on Broadcasting, 1955–57). Since the creation of the CBC radio network in 1936, the public broadcaster had been assigned the authority to regulate and set policies for both itself and private broadcasters. The Fowler Commission was struck in 1955 with the mandate to review CBC policies, finances, and regulatory powers (Peers 67–68). At a moment when influential Canadian poets were staking positions in university departments and the intellectual sphere was becoming increasingly garrisoned, Waddington remained a public intellectual interested in radio and television as art forms with greater potential to achieve formal innovation, provide social critique, and reach mass audiences than traditional live theatre, concerts, or readings.[4]

When the Fowler Commission began to hear testimonies from interest groups across the country, Waddington used her *Forum* column of September 1956 to generate greater public interest in the debate. In her column, she anticipates readers' resistance to getting involved by conceding, "in the past it has been customary to apply Royal Commissions like leeches to the sick places of the body politic, and if a cure was not immediately effected, the patient and his family were at least temporarily placated" (134). Despite this skepticism, she goes on to declare that she places "radio and television media in the realm of the arts," and that they play "a powerful role ... in transmitting moral and cultural values"; therefore, "the pervasive reach of these instruments should make us curious to know just what are the matters at issue in the present inquiry of the Fowler Commission" (134). She explains that the main argument against maintaining the current system is that it allows the CBC to control the highest and most powerful frequencies through which they transmit educational programs perceived as dull (135). While Waddington is open to a diversity of programming, her defence of the CBC opposes calls for increased privatization in the language of enlightened social democracy:

> No one grudges their advertisers their profits, but it should be pointed out that a public service is not a financial investment, but an expenditure. Its earnings cannot be measured in dollars and cents, but must be calculated in terms of enrichment of public taste—and thus, of individual lives— the wider dissemination of knowledge, and other benefits which may not yet be discernible. (135)

If the phrase "enrichment of public taste" rankles today because of its elitist and Arnoldian overtones, it is also important to recognize the ways in which this statement envisions a national community unified through a new medium whose fate Waddington refuses to see determined solely by technology or the market. Throughout her *Forum* columns, she insists that the public maintain an interest in the medium and laments the potential for its total seizure by private interests. In so doing, she enters a thicket of issues far greater than just the regulation of broadcasting. Waddington's columns anticipate Raymond Williams's observation "that many of the contradictions of capitalist democracy have indeed come out in the argument about television control" (132). What seems to be an anti-authoritarian, free, and easily accessed medium is in fact a controlled operation of limited choices in the hands of a few powerful interests (133). Waddington's broadcasting columns thus assert a dual identity: she is at once an artist invested in the ways a new medium could be used by her creative peers, and a member of the Canadian viewing public anxious about how broadcasting mediates relations between the state, business, and the public interest.

When the report of the Fowler Commission was finally released, Waddington read it in its entirety and devoted her May 1957 column to its analysis. She praises the report for following in the tradition of the best Royal Commissions to represent "a triumph of the general over the particular, and of public principle over private expediency" (39). Although the report's recommendations were open to favourable interpretation by both sides, Waddington reads it as a positive endorsement of the CBC as a necessary public expenditure and of the need to establish a separate government entity to regulate private stations. Most gratifying to her, however, is the fact that the report champions programming "for such minority groups as farmers, children, and music-lovers," as well as the socially minded forms of documentary and news programming that "the private broadcasters are apt to call egg-head stuff" and cancel due to low ratings (40). For Waddington, this recommendation is crucial because it upholds her belief that "public taste develops upwards" when it is exposed to programming with political and aesthetic substance (40).

Later that year, in her October 1957 column, Waddington encourages the CBC to implement some of the Fowler Commission recommendations to produce "experimental programs" and forego the "lively vulgarity" of variety shows (161). That Waddington felt the CBC had the power to improve the public's aesthetic taste is evident in her position on the level of state funding required by the CBC to replace dwindling commercial sponsorship of shows with poor ratings: "As long as the program in question aims to educate or extend the viewer's consciousness of his humanity, the expenditure of public money is justified" (161). Perhaps it is these articulations of the need for broadcasting to improve and elevate public taste that lead other readers of her columns to brand her a cultural elitist. For instance, Waddington's *Forum* columns garner numerous citations in Paul Rutherford's study of Canadian television history, but she is usually denigrated as a "highbrow" too interested in "the High Arts" to understand that most viewers cared less about the cultural and educational content of programs than she did (85). When he cites her complaint that popular variety shows fail to reflect the harsher realities of daily life, Rutherford comments that "what Waddington failed to realize was that viewers wanted exactly the kind of escape into a dream world offered by these apparently superficial and syrupy shows" (197). However, Waddington's critique of vapid fare originates less in any high-minded ideal of aesthetic purism than it does in a social critique of the way television programming's static and even exploitative representations of Canadian daily life operate through exclusion.

Unlike her fellow reviewers, Waddington analyzes both the content and the form of television productions. In her February 1958 column, she critiques television for not living up to one of the "chief functions of art" to provide "criticism and protest" of social injustices (255). Reviewing a CBC *Close-Up* interview of an unemployed family in Windsor, she invokes her training as a social worker to observe that the interview may have brought a harsh reality home to viewers across the country, but that it may also have humiliated and exploited the interviewees. She asks, "What did it do to the family, and how did the *Close-Up* producers make it right for them?" to indicate that her vision of documentary realism extends beyond the representation of suffering to its alleviation (255). It is not sufficient to meet the liberal welfare state's mandate to expose social problems: instead the public broadcaster should intervene to propose and enact their solutions.[5]

If social protest needs to be one of the functions of art, and television is an art form, then Waddington's critique of television seems less founded in what Rutherford identifies as her status in the cultural elite than in her position as a voice of cultural dissent. In a humorous column of February 1957, Waddington quotes a poem from L.A. MacKay's 1948 collection, *The Ill-Tempered Lover*, that satirizes her magazine's commitment to critique. The poem begins with a description of a world full of joy and song and then concludes with a biting couplet: "All sang as one, all but one only thing, / For the *Canadian Forum* would not sing" (251). Waddington then writes that her magazine "would not sing then, and judging by recent television drama, there is nothing to sing about now" (251). True to the tradition of the *Forum*, she asserts, the critic must complain, but not "because I am hard to satisfy, nor do I believe I am setting too high a standard" (251). Instead, Waddington's complaint is that television drama fails the viewer in subject matter and form: "they have studiously avoided picturing real life or dealing with serious human issues" and even when they manage the latter, "they have failed to accept the limitations of the medium" as different from the stage (251–52). She develops this idea further in September 1957 when she contends that "the urgent need for television drama now is to *get out of the studio*" so that the full possibilities of camera movement and perspective can be mobilized (135). In objection to the static staginess of television drama, Waddington demands that it mobilize the realist possibilities of moving from indoor sets to outdoor locations, from artistic conservatism to formal experimentation with the new media.

Rutherford foregrounds Waddington's status as a poet and intellectual in his characterization of her columns as the products of a snob who is out of step with the will of the masses. In so doing, he glosses over her articulation of leftist positions on media–state relations to reposition her as a cultural conservative in relation to populist producers and advertisers. Diminishing a leftist intellectual's commentaries on cultural affairs by reconfiguring the political spectrum—business becomes closer to the imagined community of the masses than are intellectuals, artists, or government—is not uncommon in the broadcasting literature of modern Canada. The movement for public broadcasting led by Graham Spry and Alan Plaunt's Canadian Radio League in the late twenties and early thirties was characterized by its opponents in the private broadcasting lobby as a group of "middle-class do-gooders" trying to impose BBC-style educational programming on a commercial market primarily consisting of enjoyable light entertainment (Vipond 284). Like Waddington after him, Spry certainly did endorse a vision of broadcasting as the medium to unify and educate the national community, but, also like Waddington, he balanced this idealism with the recognition that light entertainment can be part of the pleasures of listening and learning. In his 1931 *Queen's Quarterly* manifesto, "A Case for Nationalized Broadcasting," Spry insists that "broadcasting, primarily, is an instrument of education in its widest significance, ranging from play to learning, from recreation to the cultivation of public opinion, and it concerns and influences not any single element in the community, but the community as a whole" (153). When Waddington articulates a similar ideology three decades later, then, her criticisms must be read as part of this dissenting intellectual tradition and not simply as an immediate response to the increasingly privatized conditions of cultural production in the late 1950s.

Waddington's vision of the CBC was not only different from that of private broadcasters and advertisers; it was also opposed to the powerful media statements of Marshall McLuhan. In competition with her *Forum* columns, *Saturday Night* ran an article by McLuhan in February 1957, titled "Why the CBC Must Be Dull." McLuhan wades into the debate over public ownership of broadcasting to reveal a mistrust of the federal government quite contrary to Waddington's and more in keeping with the Cold War politics of the era. McLuhan argues that the CBC not only is, but must always be, dull: "When the government owns a medium of expression, that medium becomes consciously an instrument of power. To disguise power one must be dull. Dullness is the only form which makes power acceptable or tolerable" (13). To prove his argument, he refers to the liberating effects of private radio in oppressed regions, such as "the Soviet area" and Indonesia, where the government-run radio stations are far less popular than the American-run stations and films through which subjugated populations glimpse the material comforts available to middle-class Americans (13). The CBC cannot possibly compete with these attractive, privately owned American broadcasters, and so it must not try to disguise itself as entertainment. Moreover, McLuhan blames "Canadian book culture" (14) as conspiring with the government to "adopt a condescending attitude to the new media and its audiences" (14). As a result, television professionals are forced out of the CBC because they cannot conform to a "government imposed policy of bureaucratic dullness and mediocrity" (14).

If McLuhan's reading of broadcasting sides with the commercial lobby to argue for the privatization of the airwaves to meet public demand, it also refuses to enter into the question of the public interest that he characterizes as the domain of a literary elite hostile to popular fare. A member of this "book culture," Waddington's growing concern about television content is born not of hostility to the medium but of disillusion about its endorsement of the status quo. Although she may question much of the mindless fare taking over the airwaves, Waddington remains by September of 1957 "a lover of the television medium" and its possibilities for aesthetic innovation and social change (135). Indeed, it is because she loves the medium that she critiques its developments so harshly: "the truth is that over the past year I have been transformed from the type who is irresistibly captured by the set to the type who can hardly bring himself to sit through yet another half hour play" (135). In her columns she does not address McLuhan's growing influence on media criticism, but a decade later she registers her ambivalence to his ideas. In her 1971 review of Donald Theall's book about McLuhan, she writes that "McLuhan has remained socially detached, and because of it, his esthetic [sic] theories can be used to support social positions that are reactionary" ("Falling for a Magic Pot?" 16). His distrust of government-funded media and his faith in the market are some of the ways in which McLuhan fails to meet Waddington's expectations of the engaged media critic. As a dissenting voice that resists the increasingly powerful business lobby and its supporters in the late 1950s, Waddington's *Forum* columns testify to the range of opinions articulated in a crucial national debate, the outcome of which may seem inevitable today. As the Cold War contributed to an English-Canadian culture of political conservatism and resistance to government intervention in mass media, Waddington used a public forum to insist that the social, technological, and national consequences of capitalist modernity are as much in need of criticism as are the literary and artistic developments of modernism.

"An Awareness of Difference": Canadian Literary Criticism

Although by the 1970s she was a full professor in the Department of English at York University, in her critical writing Waddington continued to position herself on the margins. From this peripheral position, she insisted on the connections between the conditions of social and literary production. Waddington's *Apartment Seven* essay "Outsider: Growing Up in Canada" describes the reluctance of established literary critics in Canadian departments of English, the majority of whom "came from the British Isles or the United States," to teach Canadian literature (42). When confronted in the 1970s by a "polite amused silence" towards her proposals to teach Canadian literature courses, Waddington realized the extent to which being Canadian was just as important to her poetic identity as was being a woman or being Jewish (42). In this essay, she dates her identification with a national identity, albeit one that can never be rigidly or completely defined, to her entry into the academy. Waddington's dialogue with academic criticism takes the form of a series of interventions that seek to disrupt the dominant narrative of the nation and its literary tradition. She asserts in her 1969 essay "Canadian Tradition and Canadian Literature" that "there is no such thing as a single tradition in Canadian literature. There are numerous traditions, both culturally and politically. I use the word 'numerous' because I hope to avoid imposing unworkable theoretical dichotomies in the way Professor Smith and Professor Matthews have already done" (128).

Waddington intervenes in critical debates with this pointed ad hominem comment that maps the history of Canadian literary criticism as a bifurcated tradition in which tenured male academics take sides. To this female poet and critic, for whom gender has so long been central, the Canadian critical tradition reads like a battle of Titans, beginning with the mid-1920s debate between Archibald MacMechan and Lionel Stevenson. The first of two critical schools Waddington identifies begins with MacMechan's 1924 *Headwaters of Canadian Literature* and is followed by such influential men as E.K. Brown, John Sutherland, Carl Klinck, Desmond Pacey, and A.M. Klein. This is the "historical-social" school of Canadian criticism. The second school, initiated in 1926 by Lionel Stevenson's *Appraisals of Canadian Literature*, is the "apocalyptic-mythic" group, amongst whom rank Northrop Frye, Malcolm Ross, and James Reaney ("Canadian Tradition" 129).[6] This is the dominant group, she argues, for two reasons: "it is a well-known fact that aesthetic categories blend more easily with mythopoeic interpretations of literature than do historical or political ones. There is therefore less risk of change, and less necessity for political action in adopting the apocalyptic approach to Canadian tradition, rather than the historic one" (137). In a 1985 interview, Waddington suggests a related further reason for what she sees as the "Christian" and "theological" terms of Canadian criticism: the dominance of Northrop Frye and the marginalization of critics working as public intellectuals outside the academy, such as John Sutherland ("Miriam Waddington" 8).

Waddington aligns herself with the historical-social school, home of her two mentors Sutherland and Klein, because, as she states at the close of the essay, "there is, in fact, no real Canadian literary tradition but only a social matrix, an accumulation of historical events, full of contradictions, forces, and counter-forces; we live in a sort of vast cultural chaos upon which all are free to draw" ("Canadian Tradition" 140). She calls to poets to "reclaim and bring to the surface the cast-off and denied elements in our national life" (141), those that she earlier describes as "still buried in the suppressed radical tradition ... the story of the long struggle of the dissenting minority against the forces of colonial conservatism" (140). One poet who has begun to tell these stories is Klein, who "made a beginning when he showed that there is more depth and human suffering in the Canadian tradition than can be ascribed to the mere power of place or the longing for the motherland" (141). Another is Earle Birney, whom Waddington describes in a 1966 *Globe Magazine* review as an anti-nostalgic chronicler of Canadian experiences: "Birney should not be read for his sweetness, he should be read for northness, to find out what the Canadian spirit is really like. And it isn't all likeable, as Birney's group of poems titled 'Canada: Case History' shows" (13). The Canadian writer, Waddington suggests, has a responsibility to work towards justice in current national life through a poetic recuperation of forgotten cadences, rhythms, and stories.

For Waddington, the artistic work is a bridge between the inner and outer lives of the artist: "in the poem it is the act of *writing* that relocates the inner feelings and outer experience" (*Apartment Seven* 159). Writers have multiple ideologies and forms from which to choose, but, in turn, "the shape, texture, and sound of the outer world imprint themselves on the artist's psyche, and his selection of elements is seldom either voluntary or conscious" (159). In refutation of theories of the artist as autonomous genius, she thus locates artistic production firmly within the social in ways that often lead to a contradiction between the pleasures of the aesthetic and the pains of experience (158). She also foregrounded this interaction between literary and social experiences in her approach to teaching Canadian literature. Like other poet-critics, Waddington mobilized her position in the classroom to install a particular history and literary legacy of modernism in the Canadian university curriculum.

The reading list for a course in the graduate program in English at York University in 1975 illustrates her attempts to bridge the social and the textual for a younger generation of scholars and writers. The title of the course itself, "English 649: Social Issues and Literary Interactions in Canadian Literature, 1920–1950," situates literature as an encounter with the everyday. In this way, her pedagogy seeks to correct Canadian criticism because it minimizes "the importance of this outside world, which includes historical events and economic facts" (*Apartment Seven* 162). As well, Waddington encourages students to read texts in relation to other arts, government reports, and works from other countries. Twenty years prior to the formation of a Canadian Cultural Studies Association (August 2002),

Waddington's course demands that students read modernist literature and works about the modernist period as cultural products to raise questions about history, class, knowledge, and cosmopolitanism as well as beauty and the role of the artist in society ("English 649"). Waddington's reading list includes relatively canonical writers of the period (Morley Callaghan, E.J. Pratt, Sinclair Ross, and F.R. Scott) but also the less consecrated authors Irene Baird, Louis MacKay, Anne Marriott, and Adele Wiseman. Students were required to read prose by visual artists Emily Carr and Lawren Harris and a lengthy list of background material in history, geography, literary theory, aesthetic criticism, Marxist criticism, political economy, and religion. Finally, students were encouraged to read through nearly twenty runs of periodicals from the modernist period until the present, including the celebrated little magazines of modernism *Canadian Mercury* and *Canadian Poetry*, but also the communist magazine *Masses* and the anti-fascist *New Frontier*, not to mention such popular fare as *Saturday Night* and *Maclean's*. Whether or not the students were able to locate and absorb all of this material, the course description nonetheless attests to Waddington's desire to achieve a diverse social and literary history of the period that straddles high-, middle-, and low-brow cultural production.

This pedagogical approach enacts the point Waddington makes when she argues that "part of the problem of modernism is to accept that not everything can be unified, or even should be" (*Apartment Seven* 160). Just as she resists singular narratives of a triumphant nation, so does Waddington embrace the ambiguities of aesthetic modernism. The "vast cultural chaos" that characterizes the Canadian literary tradition is echoed in her description of the conditions of modernity:

> My own problem in poetry has always been how to create meaning in language without destroying the shimmer of ambiguity; perhaps even how to see the ambiguity more clearly and to face the chaos, for chaos is still another condition of modernity. It is important to remember that chaos contains not only nothingness and what is negative; it also contains hope and the possibility of new discoveries. (160)

It is the writer and critic's task, then, to navigate these oppositions in ways that confront the complexities of the modern experience and its representation in modernist cultural forms. Waddington thus gestures in her thinking and teaching towards the centrality of the writer as a privileged identity that overshadows but does not erase completely identities of gender, nationality, and religion.

Indeed, in "Women and Writing" Waddington suggests that female artists may be particularly able to represent the cacophony of experiences that comprise the national tradition as well as modernity: "Women artists can make known what has been—and still is—unknown" (*Apartment Seven* 200). Although her critical essays include detailed analyses of feminist icons Mary Wollstonecraft and Simone de Beauvoir, Waddington's feminist vision extends beyond these specific figures to prove her claim that "every woman who was an artist and who wrote out of herself, her life, and her values was a feminist whether she knew it or not" (201). Consequently, her essay "Canadian Tradition and Canadian Literature" should be received as a feminist critical touchstone not because Waddington recuperates or interprets female Canadian writers, but because she describes a tradition of male academic dialogue only to interrupt and expose its lacunae. Her critical practice exemplifies Waddington's belief that female writers should not retreat "into feminist criticism where they don't have to challenge the men on masculine territory. They should be out there being more aggressive, writing reviews using feminist theory" ("Miriam Waddington" 8). Feminist criticism, she implies, must take on "received opinion" both from within and without: it must look forward as it looks backward, and it must turn its gaze on the centre as well as the margins. Most importantly, Waddington's readings of the literary products of modernism and the cultural politics of modernity serve as reminders that feminist reconceptualizations of Canadian modernism must pay attention to modern women writers' multiple affiliations and varied contributions, through which they at once bracket and assert the importance of gender.

Notes

I am grateful to the participants of the conference "'Wider Boundaries of Daring': The Modernist Impulse in Canadian Women's Poetry," and especially to Di Brandt and Barbara Godard for their feedback on an earlier version of this paper. I would also like to thank Jan Pearson of the Graduate Programme in English at York University for providing copies of Waddington's course descriptions.

1. Recent and forthcoming scholarship on Canadian women writers in the modern period is overturning this critical tradition. See the essays on women writers in *The Canadian Modernists Meet*, edited by Dean Irvine, Colin Hill's critical introduction to the new edition of Irene Baird's *Waste Heritage*, Irvine's *Editing Modernity: Women and Little Magazine Cultures in Canada, 1916–1956* (which includes discussion of Waddington), and my own *Comrades and Critics: Women, Literature and the Left in 1930s Canada*.
2. Waddington's summation of a national ideal chimes with the provocative theories of nationalism of Scottish public intellectual Tom Nairn. In his influential work in the 1970s, Nairn describes twentieth-century nationalism as "The Modern Janus."

Nairn sees the dual perspectives of nationalism arising from an "underlying dilemma of modernisation, which compelled one population after another to desire progress" (71). In the intervening years, Nairn has modified his earlier premise of the two faces of nationalism to acknowledge that it actually has many visages. The past and the future are always multiplying in the national imagination: they are deep wells, "much richer and more heterogeneous than most nationalist, and counter-nationalist, ideology ever admitted" (72).

3 Although a few newspapers, including Toronto's *Globe and Mail*, employed a television critic, the media beat was disdained by most serious journalists and intellectuals as "a kind of graveyard, somewhere between the obituary column and the service clubs" (Gwyn, qtd. in Rutherford 84). The *Saturday Night* columns written by Mary Lowrey Ross in the late 1950s ran under the title "The Lively Arts" and included film as well as radio and television commentary, but were limited to strict summaries of the programs rather than their critical evaluation or discussions of the media in general.

4 In "Privacy, Publicity, and the Discourse of Canadian Criticism," Robert Lecker argues that the 1950s inaugurated a shift away from public literary criticism towards an increasingly private and "industrialized" discourse of Canadian literature (32–35). Lecker maintains that by the sixties and seventies the formerly public nature of Canadian criticism was threatened by the dominance of Frygian mythopoeic theories of literature (45). He refers to Frye's influential "Conclusion to *A Literary History of Canada*" to observe that the notion of a garrison mentality can apply equally well to Canadian criticism as it does to Canadian literature: "the major effect of Frye's conclusion—such an ostensibly public document—was to bring the study of Canadian Literature further indoors" (46). The field of Canadian literature became at once professionalized and exclusive as its criticism became the territory of an increasingly privatized membership.

5 Waddington's suggestion that television documentary has an obligation to ameliorate social conditions has much in common with Livesay's vision of the role of documentary poetry articulated in her landmark essay, "Documentary Poetry and the Canadian Tradition" (1969). In turn, Livesay is indebted to the theories of documentary advanced by social democrat John Grierson, founder of the National Film Board of Canada. All three critics envision documentary art as a modern form particularly well suited to improving the conditions of Canadian life. The implicit and explicit cross-referencing of their ideas also points to the fertilization of modernist aesthetic and social theories across the arts, from poetry to film to television.

6 Waddington admits that A.J.M. Smith is hard to place in this dichotomy because "his method is historical; but his attitudes are Christian–mythic, so on the whole he belongs to the apocalyptic group" (129).

Works Cited

Brown, E.K. "The Immediate Present in Canadian Literature." *Sewanee Review* 41 (1933): 430–42. Rpt. in *Responses and Evaluations on Canada*. Toronto: McClelland and Stewart, 1977. 43–56.

Canada. Royal Commission on Broadcasting. *Report*. Chair Robert Fowler. Ottawa: Queen's Printer, 1957.

Eliot, T.S. "Tradition and the Individual Talent." 1919. *Selected Prose of T.S. Eliot*. Ed. Frank Kermode. New York: Harcourt Brace, 1975. 37–44.

Greenstein, Michael. *Third Solitudes: Tradition and Discontinuity in Jewish-Canadian Literature*. Kingston: McGill-Queen's UP, 1989.
Hill, Colin. Introduction. *Waste Heritage*. By Irene Baird. 1939. Ottawa: U of Ottawa P, 2007. ix–lvii.
Hulme, T.E. "Romanticism and Classicism." *Speculations: Essays on Humanism and the Philosophy of Art*. Ed. Herbert Read. New York: Harcourt Brace, 1924. 111–40.
Irvine, Dean, ed. *The Canadian Modernists Meet*. Ottawa: U of Ottawa P, 2005.
———. *Editing Modernity: Women and Little Magazine Cultures in Canada, 1916–1956*. Studies in Book and Print Culture. Toronto: U of Toronto P, 2008.
Klein, A.M. *The Second Scroll*. Ed. Elizabeth Popham and Zailig Pollock. Toronto: U of Toronto P, 2000.
Lecker, Robert. "Privacy, Publicity, and the Discourse of Canadian Criticism." *Essays on Canadian Writing* 51–52 (1993–94): 32–82.
Livesay, Dorothy. "The Documentary Poem: A Canadian Genre." *Contexts of Canadian Criticism*. Ed. Eli Mandel. Toronto: U of Toronto P, 1971. 267–81.
MacKay, L.A. *The Ill-Tempered Lover, and Other Poems*. Toronto: Macmillan, 1948.
MacMechan, Archibald. *Headwaters of Canadian Literature*. 1924. Toronto: McClelland and Stewart, 1974.
McLuhan, Marshall. "Why the CBC Must Be Dull." *Saturday Night* 16 February 1957: 13–14.
Mill, John Stuart. *On Liberty*. 1859. Ed. Edward Alexander. Peterborough, ON: Broadview, 1999.
Nairn, Tom. *Faces of Nationalism: Janus Revisited*. London: Verso, 1997.
Peers, Frank W. *The Public Eye: Television and the Politics of Canadian Broadcasting, 1952–1968*. Toronto: U of Toronto P, 1979.
Rifkind, Candida. *Comrades and Critics: Women, Literature and the Left in 1930s Canada*. Toronto: U of Toronto P, 2009.
Rutherford, Paul. *When Television Was Young: Primetime Canada, 1952–1967*. Toronto: U of Toronto P, 1990.
Said, Edward. "The Public Role of Writers and Intellectuals." *The Public Intellectual*. Ed. Helen Small. Oxford: Blackwell, 2002. 19–39.
Spry, Graham. "A Case for Nationalized Broadcasting." *Queen's Quarterly* 38.1 (1931): 151–69.
Stevenson, Lionel. *Appraisals of Canadian Literature*. Toronto: Macmillan, 1926.
Vipond, Mary. *Listening In: The First Decade of Canadian Broadcasting, 1922–1932*. Montreal: McGill-Queen's UP, 1992.
Waddington, Miriam. *Apartment Seven: Essays Selected and New*. Toronto: Oxford UP, 1989.
———. "Canadian Tradition and Canadian Literature." *Journal of Commonwealth Literature* 8 (1969): 125–41.

———. "English 649: Social Issues and Literary Interactions in Canadian Literature 1920–1950." Course Description. Toronto: Graduate Programme in English, York University, 1975.

———. "Falling for a Magic Pot?" Rev. of *The Medium Is the Rear-View Mirror: Understanding McLuhan*, by Donald F. Theall. *Globe Magazine* 20 February 1971: 16.

———. "The Function of Folklore in the Poetry of A.M. Klein." *Ariel* 10.3 (1979): 5–19.

———. Introduction. *The Collected Poems of A.M. Klein*. Ed. Miriam Waddington. Toronto: McGraw-Hill Ryerson, 1974. vi–x.

———. "Miriam Waddington: An Afternoon." Interview by Marvyne Jenoff. *Waves* 14.1–2 (1985): 5–12.

———. "Poetry of a Frontier World." Rev. of *Selected Poems 1940–66*, by Earle Birney. *Globe Magazine* 21 May 1966: 13.

———. "Radio and Television." *Canadian Forum* July 1956: 83.

———. "Radio and Television." *Canadian Forum* September 1956: 134–35.

———. "Radio and Television." *Canadian Forum* February 1957: 251–52.

———. "Radio and Television." *Canadian Forum* May 1957: 39–40.

———. "Radio and Television." *Canadian Forum* September 1957: 135.

———. "Radio and Television." *Canadian Forum* October 1957: 161.

———. "Radio and Television." *Canadian Forum* February 1958: 254–55.

———. "Signs on a White Field: Klein's *Second Scroll*." *Canadian Literature* 25 (1965): 21–32.

Williams, Raymond. *Television: Technology and Cultural Form*. London: Fontana, 1974.

"Our hearts both leapt / in love with metaphor"
P.K. Page's Professional Elegies

SARA JAMIESON

Despite the increasing preoccupation with questions of death in P.K. Page's later poetry, the number of poems that may be termed elegies in the strict sense is relatively small. It is therefore significant that there should be so many poets among the dead whom Page chooses to memorialize in this way. "Ours" (1979) is an elegy for Patrick Anderson; the death of Dorothy Livesay in 1996 is the occasion for the elegy "But We Rhyme in Heaven." In *Hologram*, Page devotes the bulk of an entire collection to commemorating the favourite poets of her youth. Blending the words of dead and living poets, the glosas of *Hologram* "generate voice out of the silence left by a predecessor," thus fulfilling "the very purpose of the classical elegy" (Schenck, *Mourning and Panegyric* 179).[1] These poems may or may not be occasioned by the sudden absence of a specific person from the poet's life, but they all involve some consideration of how language is passed from poet to poet and carried into the future.

By focussing on Page's elegies, this essay participates in a scholarly dialogue that addresses the complexity of her relationship to Canadian literary modernism. Marilyn J. Rose has shown how the high modernist critical values that governed the production of Canadian anthologies between 1940 and 1970 have produced a lingering misconception of Page as a poet chiefly concerned with maintaining a stance of emotional detachment and objectivity. Rose contends that the inclusion of the same few Page poems from anthology to anthology has caused readers to overlook aspects of Page's work such as the domestic and, I would add, the elegiac, since these do not easily accord with the high modernist code of impersonality. Like the domestic, the elegiac occupies a complex position within modernism generally. Modernism is ostensibly founded upon a rejection of traditional poetic forms, and the privileging of virile wit and irony over the feminine expression of mournful emotion. As Jahan Ramazani points out, however, elegy is one of the most important genres implicated in high modernist poetry (25). Think, for example, of the "murmur of maternal lamentation" that pervades *The Waste Land* (Eliot 5.368). While a male poet like Eliot can evoke female mourning and hold it at a safe distance from himself, it is much more difficult for modernist women poets to separate themselves from the elegy's negative associations with the sentimentality of a feminized literary past. Cheryl Walker observes that, during the nineteenth century, the note of lament so frequently sounded in the work of Felicia Hemans, Lydia Sigourney, and other so-called "nightingale" poets caused the elegy to be associated particularly with women writers (23). In view of the widespread modernist bias against the figure of the "sentimental poetess," it is not surprising that, as a young woman trying to make a name for herself as a modernist writer, P.K. Page wrote very few elegies.[2] The elegies that I will discuss in this paper were written after the modernist period came to an end, and they are direct and straightforward in expressing the sadness of loss. They also provide some insight into how Page positions herself in relation to other modernist poets, both colleagues and precursors, as she reflects on creative achievements, friendships, and tensions from an earlier time in her life. In an essay included in this collection, Ann Martin examines the complex play of dependence and distance with which a poet like Dorothy Livesay represents her relationships to other modernist women writers, most notably her mother. As I will show, a similar ambivalence characterizes Page's articulation of her own place among modernist poets both female and male, as she negotiates the complicated sexual politics of the elegy in order express her affiliation with and her difference from her mentors and colleagues.

The subgenre of the professional elegy traditionally foregrounds an ambivalent relationship between poet and predecessor. As critics such as Ramazani, Peter Sacks, and Celeste M. Schenck have pointed out, the elegist's praise of a forebear or fellow poet very often masks a fierce competitiveness.[3] Leisurely pastoral singing contests like those depicted in Theocritus's first idyll and Virgil's fifth eclogue in part represent the elegist's earnest attempts to surpass the efforts of previous poets. The seriousness of what is at stake in the poet's elegy for a predecessor is articulated by Lawrence Lipking when he says that "such elegies are the heart of literary history" (138). Ben Jonson on Shakespeare, William Collins on James Thomson, W.H. Auden on W.B. Yeats: mixing criticism with praise, each of these elegists finds something in the work of a predecessor upon which he can improve, and so represents himself as the latest in a series of great poets.[4]

While the elegy's enactment of mourning has traditionally been codified as feminine, its emphasis on poetic rivalry has been interpreted as an exclusively masculine preoccupation. As Lipking's assemblage of poets indicates, the English elegiac canon constructs a literary history that is founded upon a male line of succession. The degree of success with which women poets have participated in this tradition by writing their own elegies for poets continues to be a site for critical debate. Schenck, for example, attributes the "notable absence" of women poets from the tradition of pastoral elegy in general to the fact that the form offers no satisfactory roles for a speaking woman, but relegates female nymphs and muses to the periphery of a central scene in which poetic potency is passed from male to male in rituals of initiation and inheritance (*Mourning and Panegyric* 169). When women poets do attempt to elegize a male poet forebear, she argues, their efforts often register their sense of unfitness for the work, as when Anne Bradstreet, in her elegy for Sir Philip Sidney, is grateful when the muses take away her "scribbling pen," thus relieving her of a task she feels unworthy to carry out (Schenck, "Feminism and Deconstruction" 14).[5] Ramazani contests Schenck's insistence that women writers' historical lack of literary mentors leads them to shy away from elegizing predecessor poets by pointing to "hundreds of professional elegies" written by women poets from the seventeenth to the nineteenth centuries (297). Interestingly, however, when he looks closely at the work of women elegists in his landmark study *Poetry of Mourning*, he ignores these poems to focus exclusively on family elegies instead, thus reinforcing Schenck's contention that women are more comfortable in mourning their "personal dead" than their professional rivals and forebears (Schenck, "Feminism and Deconstruction" 15).

Page's professional elegies complicate this debate: they may be relatively few in number, but since most of the elegies she writes are for poets, they do contradict the assumption that women's elegies tend to foreground personal relationships over professional ones. In this essay, I will trace the varying degrees of assurance and uncertainty with which Page uses elegiac conventions to represent herself in relation to other poets, first by looking briefly at *Hologram*, and then in more detailed readings of her elegies for

Patrick Anderson and Dorothy Livesay. While these poems do register some of the difficulties she faces as a woman poet writing in an overwhelmingly masculine genre, Page nonetheless recognizes her indebtedness to elegiac conventions and uses those conventions in ways that ultimately enable her to insert herself successfully into scenes of poetic inheritance. As I will show, these poems exhibit a range of responses to elegiac tradition, and point to the problems inherent in previous attempts, notably Schenck's, to isolate a stable set of characteristics that differentiate women's elegies from the masculine elegiac canon. Finally, in emphasizing the varied and particular circumstances in which some of Page's elegies were produced, I will focus especially on age as an important factor that inflects her approach to elegiac conventions. These poems are all products of relatively late phases of Page's career, and my readings will suggest how an approach to elegy that is attentive to issues of aging reveals the complexities of the dialogue between women's poems and the mainstream elegiac tradition more effectively than past approaches based on gender alone.

In the foreword to *Hologram*, Page describes the process by which the collection came to be written, a process that led her to retrace the reading habits of her youth, and returned her to an elegiac scene of instruction[6] at the hands of the poets whose work inspired and guided her "when, falteringly, [she] was searching for [her] own voice" (*Hologram* 12). If Page's language here suggests that she experienced something akin to an "anxiety of authorship"[7] in the presence of "the giants of [her] youth" (12), the poems themselves bear no trace of this: on the contrary, her choice of the glosa form, which demands that she seamlessly integrate her own lines with those of some of the world's most revered poets, bespeaks a considerable amount of confidence in her abilities. As Rosemary Sullivan observes, "rarely has the female voice found such authority among the great modernists" (125). In her account of her relationship to favourite predecessor poets, Page emphasizes the idea of an "affinity" between poets over that of the "influence" of one poet upon another (*Hologram* 12). Page's choice of terms here converts the implicitly hierarchical relationship between a poet and her "masters" into a more lateral relationship, furthering the impression of confidence by diminishing the undercurrent of anxiety often implicit in a poet's confrontation with past masters. In the poems themselves, "affinity" is most clearly conveyed through the glosa form, which requires that Page incorporate the work of her mentors into the fabric of her own verse, ending her stanzas with their lines and rhyming with their words.

Page's substitution of a communal affinity for the more agonistic concept of influence foregrounds the dynamics of attachment and separation that characterize elegiac consolation: this substitution is central to attempts to identify a specifically female elegiac poetics. Reading elegy as an expression of a Bloomian narrative of sons violently replacing their poetic fathers, Schenck finds in the consolatory convention of apotheosis the defining element of the "masculine elegiac": by celebrating "the deification of the dead one in a process that lifts him out of nature, out of the poem, and out of [the] way" ("Feminism and Deconstruction" 14–15), the elegist "presents himself as heir to the tradition" (13). She argues that this particular consolatory strategy inscribes an Oedipal "act of identity" that is dependent upon the severing of attachments to others, and she seeks to differentiate women's elegies from this tradition by drawing on Nancy Chodorow's model of a female psychosexual development that is "characterized by continuity with the mother and an attenuated separation" (Schenck, "Feminism and Deconstruction" 16). Marshalling examples of elegies by women in which the poets "seem unwilling to render up their dead," Schenck posits a counter-tradition of women's elegy characterized by the refusal of the separative thrust of traditional consolations in favour of a "continuous mourning" through which the woman poet sustains an ongoing connection to the dead (15, 20).

Schenck rightly draws attention to the elegy as a site wherein a patriarchal literary history is constituted. While she gestures toward a reading of elegy as the production of a culture in which women have been denied access to the more privileged forms of representing loss, however, she ultimately accounts for this by turning to essentializing descriptions of women's internal experience of loss. Her response to the historical exclusion of women from the rewards of elegiac consolation is to conclude that women do not really value those rewards anyway. She goes so far as to give women elegists the moral high ground over their male counterparts by insisting that they regularly privilege mourning the dead over reaping the rewards of poetic production. As Melissa F. Zeiger points out, Schenck's theory that women elegists reject consolation in favour of a prolonged attachment to the dead is disturbingly compliant with a patriarchal construction of woman as a site of death, loss, and silence that threatens to exclude women from participation in elegiac production. In contrast to Schenck's vision of an ongoing "connectedness" between the woman poet and the dead that is problematically based on the rejection of the genre's opportunities for claiming a place in a poetic tradition, Zeiger insists that the elegy has been and will remain, for women, "a way of organizing, or reorganizing poetic agendas, and of claiming creative entitlement" (63).

Page's glosas clearly demonstrate that this so-called "careerist" aspect of elegy is not necessarily incompatible with the maintenance of an ongoing sense of connection to the "loved dead" (Sullivan 121). In *Hologram*, rather than draw attention to any displacement of her predecessors, she welcomes their words into the space of her own poems; however, as Robert Stacey observes, Page's linguistic mergings with the voices of those predecessors are also consistently accompanied by reflections on the development of her own career from its earliest beginnings, and these poems of homage to favourite poets are laced with echoes of some of Page's own most acclaimed and frequently anthologized poems (Stacey 110).[8] Declaring affinities between herself and her forebears enables Page to envision unabashedly her own initiation into a select group of "master" poets.

For Page, the merging of two poets' voices in a glosa results in something she calls "a curious marriage" (*Hologram* 9). Coming from a woman poet, this choice of metaphors is intriguing, since it is often in the inclusion of epithalamic elements that the homosocial poetics of elegy can be most clearly discerned. Several critics of elegy have addressed the way in which the genre signifies the exclusion of the feminine from elegiac production by deploying wedding imagery in ways that simultaneously evoke and erase the presence of women. Bruce Boehrer, for example, shows how the "unexpressive nuptial song" that accompanies Lycidas's climactic entry into paradise functions as "a mystical wedding rite that doubles and yet denies the institution of earthly marriage" (232–33) and imparts a paradoxically disembodied homoerotic charge to "Milton's attempts to imagine the company of the elect in heaven—and the company of poets on earth" (231).[9] In *Hologram*, Page envisions her own inclusion into an elect company of poets through textual "marriages" that are similarly disembodied. She writes glosas to both male and female poets, and it would be difficult to identify anything intrinsically masculine or feminine about the two voices that comprise each poem. Thus, while Page does position herself within elegiac tradition by gesturing toward conjunctions of elegy and epithalamium, she does not do this by invoking the idea of marriage as a heteronormative union based on any essentialized gender opposition. Rather, these poems suggest how the elegy's possible range of sexual subject positions can be broadened to include a woman poet who celebrates her own sense of artistic achievement through the figuration of indissoluble unions with predecessor poets, both male and female.

Page's use of the marriage metaphor is an example of how she is able to work within the parameters of elegiac convention in order to position herself as the inheritor of the voices of her predecessors. Combining a focus on personal achievement with an acknowledgment of ties to an instructive community of predecessor poets, Page's elegiac glosas draw attention to the reductiveness of approaching the poems that comprise the masculine elegiac tradition as nothing more than individualistic "gesture[s] of aspiring careerism" (Schenck, "Feminism and Deconstruction" 14). When we turn from *Hologram* to poems that are more immediately recognizable as elegies in a strict sense—that is, poems written on the deaths of poets whom Page knew personally—her responses to a full range of elegiac issues including friendship and rivalry, love and loss, and the gendering of poetic production come into sharper focus. In contrast to the confidence with which Page includes herself among her favourite poets in *Hologram*, "Ours," a poem written after Patrick Anderson's death, more clearly manifests the kinds of anxieties that Schenck identifies as characteristic of women poets' attempts to elegize their male predecessors. In a way that anticipates the impetus behind the *Hologram* poems, Page looks back to the beginning of her career, but here, she represents the relationship between her youthful self and a male mentor as a gendered hierarchy that threatens to stop her voice. Patrick Anderson was an important figure in Page's life during the years when she was first coming to prominence as a poet. It was he who invited her to join the *Preview* group, an experience that Page remembers in interviews as an "earthquake," a crucial rite of passage in her early career ("'That's me'" 47). Sandra Djwa, in her contribution to this collection, provides persuasive evidence that Page was already writing in a modernist idiom before she met Anderson. Page herself stresses the importance of her meeting with him by describing her acceptance into the *Preview* group as a scene of initiation: she represents herself as an "inarticulate" ingenue ("'That's me'" 48) introduced to contemporary literature by Anderson and the *Preview* poets, who impart new knowledge that "[breaks] her head wide open" ("Conversation" 70). Anderson himself appears as a revered and charismatic figure, a "driving force" whose facility with language Page recalls as "a kind of fire which enveloped [her]" ("'That's me'" 49). In these reminiscences, her contact with him takes on something of the character of a ritual purification by fire from which she emerges into a new stage of her life.

Dean Irvine suggests that Page's relationship to the Montreal little magazine culture of the 1940s that included *Preview* was perhaps more complex than these reminiscences would have it. The *Preview* poets favoured adherence to an implicitly masculinist code of modernist impersonality that, according to Irvine, Page was already beginning to question even as she practiced it. "Ours" is an overtly personal and subjective poem about Page's experience in a poetic environment in which these very qualities were discouraged. The occasion of Anderson's death sparks recollections of a scene of poetic initiation that is fraught with tensions not apparent in the interviews quoted above: "At something over sixty he is dead / and I, a friend of his twenties, / I am still—tentatively—here" (*Hidden Room* 1:181). Page's tentativeness mimics the polite hesitation often adopted by the elegist at the grave of a forebear whom he seeks to supplant.[10] In this case, such a pose considerately obscures the fact that at the time when the poem was written, Page enjoyed a far more prominent reputation in Canadian letters than did Anderson. This attitude of studied respectfulness, however, clashes with the apparent *dis*respectfulness of the first line, which creates the impression that Page cannot remember how old Anderson was when he died.

As the poem continues, this tension between the poet's memories of the deceased and her commission as a eulogist to speak nothing but good of him becomes more profound:

> "Friend." Were we friends?
> Our alliance something less:
> acquaintances who knew each other well
> and met each other often,
> warmed by the same blaze.
>
> Sparked by his singular talent
> my small fires
> angered him.
>
> He wished me near,
> appreciative of his skills,
> *aficionada* of good writing.
> *His* good writing.
> Not to write well.
>
> Hard to be friends. (*Hidden Room* 1: 181)

In the poem, Page tells a different story about her relationship with Anderson than she does in interviews. Anderson's anger in the poem does not correspond to Page's recollections of *Preview* meetings as "light-hearted romps" marked by "good-natured tensions," but "no rancour" ("'That's me'" 48). It was Anderson who, on discovering that she "wrote" (47), invited Page to join the group, but in these lines he paradoxically appears as someone who desires to prevent her from writing. Page claims that she cannot remember suffering any discrimination as the only woman on the editorial board of *Preview* (48), yet there is much in the poem to suggest that she has difficulty in trying to insert herself into a scene of elegiac inheritance that traditionally offers no place for the woman poet as creator. She identifies Anderson as an inspiration for her own writing, but he refuses the role of mentor, becoming angry at the work she produces after his example, and relegating her to the role of appreciative audience, which the word *aficionada* defines as female. That this word derives from one that originally designated a devotee of bullfighting also serves to characterize his view of writing as an exclusively male activity. With her "small fires," the poet appears to be trying to placate an angry god with burnt offerings, an impression reinforced by the capital letters on "He" and "*His*." This mock deification of an Anderson imbued with exaggeratedly masculine qualities contributes to a scene of elegiac instruction in which the implicit power imbalance between mentor and pupil is exacerbated by gender difference. The poet's sense that she does not fit into the scenario of elegiac succession produces some apparent confusion as to how she ought to represent her relationship to her resistant mentor. In contrast to Schenck's assertion that female elegists foreground personal relationships over professional ones, Page's poem suggests that the two are not always easily separated. Her vacillation as to whether or not she can call Anderson her "friend" intriguingly echoes Ben Jonson's "praise" of Michael Drayton:

> It hath been question'd, Michael, if I bee
> A Friend at all; or, if at all, to thee:
> . . .
> And till I worthy am to wish I were,
> I call the world that envies mee, to see
> If I can be a Friend, and Friend to thee. (lines 1–2, 92–95)

As an ironic echo of the upper hand that Jonson displays in judgement of his fellow poet's work, Page's statement that it was "hard to be friends" with

Anderson serves to emphasize the woman poet's exclusion from the professional rivalries through which literary history has been constituted.[11] In place of the serene pastoral surroundings in which the scene of elegiac instruction customarily takes place, in "Ours" the poets occupy a landscape in which they are separated by "ditches and hedges," the implication being that, for the woman writer, the path to literary prestige is not the gentle slope of the *locus amoenus*, but an obstacle course (*Hidden Room* 1:181).[12]

Despite the difficulty she experiences in finding a place for herself in this scenario, ultimately it is the professional elegy's complex play of praise and criticism, attachment and distancing, that enables Page to express—certainly more clearly than she does in interviews—the ambivalence of her feelings toward Anderson. While she is implicitly critical of the way in which the professional elegy has traditionally defined the relationship between mentor and initiate as a relationship between men, the ambivalence implicit in that traditional relationship is something that enables her to honour Anderson as a valued mentor who profoundly influenced her writing in the early days of her career, and also to stress how her voice has continued to develop beyond that influence. She eases the tension that has characterized the gendered hierarchy of this particular mentor–initiate relationship by turning to the poets' shared love of language:

> And yet, at times
> our hearts both leapt
> in love with metaphor,
> or we laughed, played verbal handball,
> eyes locked. We were friends. (*Hidden Room* 1: 181)

Here, the love that both poets bear toward language is extended to include the poets themselves. The image of their locked eyes is reminiscent of the lovers in John Donne's poetry who see themselves reflected in one another's eyes,[13] but underlying this intimacy is the suggestion that something is being *locked* away and kept secret. This is a glance in which much is being shared, but something is also being withheld. Earlier in the poem, inequalities between mentor and initiate, aggravated by gender difference, inhibited the transmission of voice from one poet to another. With the admission that "nothing pass[es] for love" between the poets, Page not only gestures toward Anderson's homosexuality, but also draws attention to her exclusion from the homoerotic relations between poets that characterize the classical elegy. By insisting that "something" nonetheless does pass between herself and Anderson, she ultimately claims a place for herself that is both inside and outside the parameters of elegiac tradition.[14] By converting the eroticism of elegy from love between poets to the love that poets bear toward language, Page transforms a difficult initiation, in which an angry, autocratic mentor threatens to stop her voice, into something more cooperative, in which the poets' skills are mutually nurtured by jokes and word games.

In "Ours," Page's insertion of herself into an elegiac scene of poetic inheritance by emphasizing love over conflict anticipates her substitution of affinity for influence in *Hologram*, but there is one important difference. In the *Hologram* poems, affinity is conveyed through the glosa form, which requires that the poet approximate the style of a mentor in a sustained manner; "Ours," in contrast, bears no trace of Anderson's style. Its short lines and simple diction are studiously different from the virtuosic complexity that distinguishes Anderson's poems. Page makes no attempt to reproduce the "density of image[ry]" that she identifies as Anderson's primary influence on her early work ("Conversation" 70). Instead, in traditional elegiac fashion, she represents her transcendence of a style associated with her apprenticeship as a poet. Through her emphasis on their shared love of language, Page acknowledges her debt to Anderson, but she also exposes the limits of that debt by writing about it in a style that has evolved beyond what she learned from him. Her affirmation of their friendship is not, therefore, a rejection of professional concerns in favour of defining her relationship with Anderson in exclusively personal terms; rather, it is precisely because of the assurance with which she measures how far her own voice has developed since their time together that she is able to declare that "[they] were friends," and mourn him as such.

As an elegy for a woman poet, "But We Rhyme in Heaven," more than "Ours," deviates from the classical elegiac tradition of a man mourning the death of an older male mentor. Even though Dorothy Livesay was born before both Anderson and Page, she did not exert the same kind of immediate influence over Page's career as Anderson did, so her role in Page's life was closer to that of a peer than an acknowledged teacher. The affinities that might be expected to arise from the poem's grounding in a sisterly relationship as opposed to one between a teacher and a learner, however, are complicated by the evocations of animosity and conflict that pervade much of the poem:[15]

> The moment we meet
> tangles and snares spring up
> on the asphalt street.
> At airports and theatres
> magnets pull us together
> and we go for each other. (*Hidden Room* 2:231)

Recalling the "air-ports" and "instruments" of Auden's elegy for W.B. Yeats (80), Page's evocation of an anti-pastoral urban landscape registers points of connection and conflict between two poets. At "the moment [they met]" (in the mid-1940s) both Page and Livesay were committed to an overtly political kind of modernist poetry that often explored the alienation of modern urban life. In Page's elegy, however, the hostile urban environment, rather than appearing as a subject of common interest between the two poets, instead registers their personal differences and disagreements. Letters written from Page to Livesay do indeed provide evidence of tensions that existed between them at the time.[16]

Rather than using these differences as the basis for the kind of narrative of contest and surpassal that characterizes many professional elegies, Page instead interrogates such narratives along with the source of her own personal conflict with Livesay in a series of questions:

> It is so irrational
> What is the bloody bone
> we struggle and fight for?
> Not my bone. Not hers.
> An astrological quirk?
> Or grit in the oil of the works
> that set us in motion—some
> meddlesome tamperer's mischief? (*Hidden Room* 2: 231)

The struggling and fighting pictured in these lines encompasses not only the personal conflict that existed between Page and Livesay, but also the kind of literary struggle through which elegists have often represented themselves as surpassing and replacing their predecessors. Here, Page's attitude toward this aspect of the genre is, at least initially, an ambivalent one. While she calls this struggle "irrational," she cannot entirely dismiss it. After all, the prize that is at stake in elegiac contests is the poet's chance to assert his place in literary history by positioning himself in relation to fellow poets and predecessors. Calling this prize a "bloody bone," Page seems to emphasize its primal importance, even as she shows some impatience with the divisiveness of the struggle through which it is gained, a divisiveness that she ultimately rejects. Right from the beginning of the poem, she consistently attributes the friction between herself and Livesay to forces outside of them and beyond their control: the city, the stars, a "meddlesome tamperer." The second stanza ends with the decisive statement that the antagonism implicit within their personal relationship and within the professional elegy is "No part of us."

With this statement, Page would appear to be distancing herself and Livesay as women from one of the central features of the masculine elegiac tradition, an impression that becomes clearer in the final stanza. Here, the title phrase, borrowed from Livesay herself, enables a resolution of all the conflict that has dominated the poem up to this point:

> But her anguished, defiant phrase—
> "we rhyme in heaven!"
> is like a balloon
> that carries our anger up
> to a rarefied air
> where rancour is blown away,
> and remedial stars appear,
> and Venus is kissing the moon
> as the Spanish say. (*Hidden Room* 2: 231)

This sudden upward rush to the stars recalls the apotheosis through which Lycidas is "mounted high" near the end of Milton's elegy (line 172). In contrast to the all-male paradise that Lycidas enters, however, the image of Venus kissing the moon echoes the eroticism of the "nuptial song" that accompanies that entry, but in an implicitly female context (Milton line 176).[17] Inspired by Livesay's "phrase," this is a vision that affirms bonds between writing women and asserts a female poetic lineage alongside the male line of succession that elegy habitually celebrates. Rather than draw attention to herself as a poet who has survived or in any way surpassed her contemporary, Page ends her elegy by deferring to some of the central preoccupations of Livesay's own work: the kissing at the end recalls the lesbian eroticism of some of Livesay's late love poems; the suggestion that the image is drawn from a Spanish proverb echoes Livesay's (and Page's) earlier poems dealing with the Spanish Civil War. In some ways, then, this poem exemplifies Barbara Godard's conception of how women's elegies for other women can privilege "overlapping" interests and "interconnection" over succession and transcendence (50).

On the whole, however, Page's elegy for Livesay raises the kinds of problems that have attended critical attempts to place Page among her female colleagues and predecessors. For example, the use of Livesay's phrase as the basis for a vision of a female writerly community seems highly significant in view of Page's habitual reticence in claiming kinship with literary sisters and foremothers.[18] The significance of Page's willingness to do so here is perhaps undermined, however, by the fact that she seemingly cannot envision this community as something that is possible on earth, but can only locate it in "heaven." Then again, the division between heaven and earth in the poem is something that enables Page to represent her relationship with another writing woman as marked by both co-operation and conflict, and signals her refusal to represent a community of women writers as an entirely untroubled space. Another potential stumbling block to reading the poem as a straightforward celebration of community between women writers is the implication that Page can only celebrate a sense of community with Livesay after Livesay has died. Writing an occasional poem on Livesay's death is what enables Page to articulate a sense of her association with Livesay, while at the same time it is the fact of Livesay's death that threatens to dissolve the association. No less than in "Ours," elegiac convention enables Page in "But We Rhyme in Heaven" to represent her relationship to a fellow poet as a complex play of closeness and distance.

The occasional aspect of elegy draws attention to how the timing of the poem's appearance introduces factors such as age, which, in addition to gender, adds to the complexity with which Page represents her relationship to Livesay. The harmonious spirit of the final stanza suggests a re-evaluation of whatever antagonism once existed between the two women when they were younger.[19] At the same time, Page's use of the present tense throughout the entire poem indicates her unwillingness to locate the potential for conflict and disagreement strictly in the past. "But We Rhyme in Heaven" is a late poem in which Page pays tribute to a colleague in a way that nonetheless shows her ongoing readiness to engage in debate and criticism.

By contrast, "Ours" was written when Page was just entering old age, and in its final stanzas, her past differences with a fellow poet are assessed somewhat more poignantly. Having reviewed everything that she has gained from her association with Patrick Anderson, Page turns to what she has lost:

> Now he is dead.
> And I think of the breath
> he breathed into his poems
> and of how
> with nothing passing for love between us
> something passed
> something memorable and alive—
> a kind of walking bird
> which, when we least expected,
> would suddenly take flight.
>
> His and mine, that bird. Ours.
> Now
> unable to fly. (*Hidden Room* 1: 182)

While the style of the poem represents the opportunities for self-renewal and longevity that poetry can offer, the conclusion reminds us that it cannot fully compensate for loss. The assurance with which Page is able to celebrate the survival of her own voice is curtailed by the obscurity into which Anderson's has fallen.[20] She thinks not of his poems, but of his breath, which, now that he is dead, no longer exists. It is as if the poems cannot survive the loss of his energizing presence. Moreover, the walking bird that is unable to fly at the end suggests that, now that Anderson is no longer alive, Page's own vision is somehow diminished. Page's ending of the poem with the image of the grounded bird signifying the diminishment of her own powers might be interpreted as a privileging of loss over consolation, one which indicates a distrust of the rewards of poetic achievement, if not the refusal that Schenck attributes to female elegists. Ultimately, however, I suspect that the poet's inability to celebrate unequivocally the survival of her own voice has less to do with gender than with age. In the very first line of the poem, the apparent carelessness with which Page fails to divulge Anderson's exact age can also be read as a deliberate refusal to reveal her own, as she herself is also "something over sixty" as she writes (*Hidden Room* 1:181). His death impels her to look ahead to her own, a necessity that marks the limit of the extent to which she is able to transform and renew herself by adopting new styles of writing. This, combined with the fading of Anderson's reputation, signified by the absence of his voice from the poem, casts some doubt upon the ability of poetry to compensate for the losses sustained in aging.

By reading the consolation reached in "Ours" as recognizably that of an aging and accomplished poet looking back on a youthful friendship, I wish to suggest that the category of gender is, on its own, insufficient for approaching all of the nuances of women poets' dialogue with elegiac tradition. As an aging woman, Page is, after all, at a double remove from an elegiac tradition that is customarily the preserve of *young* men. The pastoral elegy is traditionally a song sung near the beginning of a poet's career.[21] Theocritus's Thyrsis and Virgil's Mopsus are young poets who sing at the request of their elders, who afterwards reward them with gifts signifying their initiation into mature poetic status. Their symbolic vanquishing of older poets through the fiction of the singing contest promises a reassuring outcome to young poets troubled by anxieties about their relationships to rivals and predecessors, and their chances for fame. A poet like Page, however, who is closer to the end of her career than the beginning, might be expected to approach these issues from a different perspective. Indeed, her substitution of affinity for influence in *Hologram* can be interpreted as something that modifies the potentially unstable power dynamics of the relationship between young poets and their predecessors, making the elegiac scene of instruction more amenable to an older, more experienced poet who feels herself capable of meeting the "giants" of her youth on something of an equal footing. Rather than let herself be excluded by the elegy's traditional focus on the problems of the youthful poet, Page instead shows the form to be particularly conducive to late life creativity: paying tribute to the poets whose work has inspired her own returns Page to the scene of her beginnings as a poet, enabling her to capture a renewed confidence in her creativity that is abetted by a consoling review of past accomplishments and achieved fame, a privilege not always available to young, apprentice poets.

Grouping herself among a very prestigious company of poets, repeatedly evoking the symbols of royalty,[22] Page perhaps intended, like Eliot in "Little Gidding," to fashion in *Hologram* "a crown to set upon [her] lifetime's effort" (*Four Quartets* 44). In contrast, however, to Eliot's pessimistic assessment of "the gifts reserved for age" (45), Page in her poem "Autumn" portrays a time of "bounty," albeit one whose rarest gifts are available only to a select few, a time wherein "that sharp sweetness in the tea-stained air / is reserved for those who have made a straw / fine as a hair to suck it through / fine as a golden hair" (*Hidden Room* 2:194). With this emblem of a very finely honed craftsmanship, the kind it takes years to accomplish, Page affirms the possibility of self-renewal through late-life creativity, suggesting that while it cannot restore one's golden hair in a literal sense, it can offer a consoling access to something of the promise and potential of youth. Page's suggestion of the practice and discipline required to sustain a long literary career characterizes the aging poet as one who, however accomplished, continues to strive after seemingly impossible goals: is it possible to suck air through a straw as fine as a hair, any more than to reverse the progression of time and death? In this way, Page registers her resistance to the roles that society assigns to the elderly, and to aging writers in particular. She has been referred to as the *grande dame* of Canadian poetry,[23] but such a title, while respectfully intended, hints darkly at the fate of the aging poet as Eliot describes it, the fate of "becoming dignified, of becoming a public figure with only a public existence" from whom nothing new is to be expected ("Yeats" 257). Page's emphasis on the importance of an ongoing commitment to the *craft* of poetry-making alerts us to the ways in which the elegy's customary focus on professional concerns encompasses far more than a narrowly "careerist" desire for advancement and fame. Imagining different kinds of relationships to her poetic predecessors than the professional elegy so often represents, Page shows herself to be open to everything she still can learn from them, celebrating at the same time her own past accomplishments and ongoing creative potential.

NOTES

1. As Page explains in the foreword to *Hologram*, the glosa is a Spanish form of courtly verse dating back to the late fourteenth and early fifteenth centuries. The form consists of an opening quatrain, or *cabeza*, written by another poet, followed by ten four-line stanzas, "their concluding lines taken consecutively from the quatrain; their sixth and ninth lines rhyming with the borrowed tenth" (9).
2. For a detailed reading of Page's evolving response to the figure of the "sentimental poetess," see Laura Killian, "Poetry and the Modern Woman" (1996); an example of the modernist bias against the direct expression of grief in poetry occurs in T.S. Eliot's 1936 essay on Tennyson's *In Memoriam*, in which Eliot approves of the depth and sincerity of Tennyson's feelings, which are only to be discerned "a good way below the surface" (294)—the implication being that, among high modernists, for grief to be meaningful, it had to be indirectly expressed. Critical statements by Canadian modernists sometimes evince a similar distrust of poetic mourning. In his rejected preface to *New Provinces*, for example, A.J.M. Smith self-deprecatingly apologizes for the "melancholy" strain of his own contributions, which he compares unfavourably with the "healthier robustness" of F.R. Scott's satires (41).
3. On contests and rivalry in elegy, see Sacks, *The English Elegy* (36–37) and Ramazani, *Poetry of Mourning* (241–43). Schenck writes extensively on this aspect of the genre; see especially "Feminism and Deconstruction" (1986).

4 In chapter 3 of *The Life of the Poet*, Lipking borrows the term *tombeau* from Mallarmé in order to designate a type of professional elegy marked by a palpable tension between "the eulogist's respect" and "the critic's animus" (145). As classic examples of English *tombeaux*, he includes Ben Jonson's "To the Memory of my Beloved, the Author Mr. William Shakespeare: and What He Hath Left Us" (1623), William Collins's "Ode Occasion'd by the Death of Mr. Thomson" (1749), and W.H. Auden's "In Memory of W.B. Yeats" (1939).

5 For Schenck's reading of the poem, see "Feminism and Deconstruction" (13–14). Nancy E. Wright offers a very different reading of Bradstreet's professional elegies. Where Schenck sees an anxiety of authorship, Wright sees Bradstreet's deliberate use of a topos of humility through which she displays her knowledge of classical forms and asserts her "worthiness to write poetry" (244–45).

6 I borrow this term from Schenck, who herself borrows it from Harold Bloom and adapts it to describe what she sees as the central drama of pastoral elegy: an initiatory scenario in which a young man "is treated to arcane lore and welcomed to mature poetic stature" by an elder (*Mourning and Panegyric* 169). Schenck locates the roots of such elegiac initiation scenes in Plato's pastoral dialogue, the *Phaedrus*, and traces its continuance in a variety of English poems from the sixteenth to the twentieth centuries. Page's self-conscious return to her beginnings as a poet in *Hologram* suggest a further dimension to what Rosemary Sullivan has already identified as the elegiac aspect of the collection. Sullivan locates this elegiac quality primarily in Page's recovery of the voices of the dead (127).

7 This term, coined by Sandra Gilbert and Susan Gubar, designates the anxiety that can result from the woman writer's sense of exclusion from a patriarchally determined literary canon that includes few female precursors on whom she can model herself (47–49).

8 For example, in "Hologram," the colour of the sea is compared with that of the "breast of a slain peacock" (*Hidden Room* 2: 190) and pierces the speaker in a way that recalls the union of peacock and poet's eye in "Arras" (*Hidden Room* 1: 46–47). In "The Gold Sun," a white sky against which "no swan / is visible, and no least feather falling / could possibly or impossibly be seen" (*Hidden Room* 2: 191) is a curious inversion of the falling swans and feathers in "Stories of Snow" (*Hidden Room* 1: 53–54).

9 Richard Dellamora also addresses the homosocial poetics of elegy by placing Tennyson's *In Memoriam* within a "tradition of erotic male pastoral" (19). His discussion shows how Tennyson's use of marriage imagery conveys a homosocial eroticism that is ultimately subordinated to marriage in the conventional sense. On the varied implications of marriage imagery in contemporary AIDS elegies, see Zeiger (109–10, 115).

10 See, for example, the classic lament for Bion, in which the poet is at first hesitant to take up the flute of his master (Harrison 38, lines 50–56).

11 Jonson's poem appeared as a commendatory preface to a collection of some of Drayton's works, published in 1627. From the beginning, some readers have interpreted it as a covert satire (Lipking 141).

12 On the landscape of the pastoral scene of instruction, see Schenck (*Mourning and Panegyric* 28–30).

13 See, for example, "The Ecstasy." My reading of this moment in the poem is assisted by the references to Donne scattered throughout *Evening Dance of the Grey Flies*, the collection in which "Ours" was published. "The Flower Bed" similarly evokes those

moments when "human eye can lock with human eye / and find within its ever-widening core, / such vastnesses of space / one's whole self tumbles in" (*Hidden Room* 1:159).

14 An example of a woman poet's elegy for a male mentor contemporary with Page's is Elizabeth Bishop's "North Haven," an elegy for Robert Lowell, published in 1978. Like Page, Bishop recognizes her inevitable indebtedness to elegiac convention, yet uses convention in such a way as to articulate a sense of connection to Lowell that still registers her distance from his own elegiac aesthetic and the rivalries of his (mostly male) circle of colleagues (Zeiger 75–79). In Anne Sexton's elegy for John Holmes, "Somewhere in Africa" (1962), the woman poet mourns her modernist mentor while asserting her devotion to an aesthetic very different from his (Schenck, "Feminism and Deconstruction" 21–22).

15 In a conversation with Mary di Michele about Bronwen Wallace, Barbara Godard suggests that by situating relationships between poets "among friends rather than between a teacher and a taught," both di Michele and Wallace write elegies that violate the norms of a masculine elegiac tradition that stresses the elegist's transcendence over the other poet (50).

16 Letters written during this period show that the two poets were in disagreement over who should be included in the proposed federation of Canadian writers: Page also accuses Livesay of lacking sympathy as a critic and takes issue with statements Livesay made in reviews of her own and other poets' work. See Page's letters to Dorothy Livesay, 1944–70, in the Dorothy Livesay fonds. I am grateful to Dean Irvine for informing me of possible connections between these letters and Page's elegy for Livesay.

17 Boehrer traces Milton's evocation of paradise in "Lycidas" to classical and Christian sources that celebrate the repudiation of contact with women (226–31).

18 Laura Killian observes that, in the early days of her career, "P.K. Page could have laid claim to a women's modernist tradition, in which her literary mothers and sisters would be Woolf, H.D., Amy Lowell, Mina Loy, Marianne Moore and certainly Dorothy Livesay. If she did feel herself to be working within just such a tradition, however, she failed to acknowledge it openly" (90). The elegy to Livesay thus constitutes a break in Page's silence concerning her relationship to other women writers, and, insofar as it is dedicated to Livesay, functions as a response in a dialogue initiated by Livesay herself in her 1975 poem "The Other Side of the Wall," which is dedicated to Page.

19 Letters written from Page to Livesay in 1969–70 are more cordial than the ones from the 1940s, and suggest that their relationship had by this time become more amicable (Dorothy Livesay fonds).

20 In 1986, Patricia Whitney addressed the obscurity into which Anderson's reputation in Canada had fallen, describing him as the subject of "fading memories, vague recollections," and "anecdotes dredged up from forty-odd years ago" (26). On the neglect of Anderson's work among Canadian critics, and the more recent revival of his work in a gay studies context, see Brian Trehearne, *The Montreal Forties* (1–40).

21 The pastoral elegy is traditionally an apprenticeship genre. In the much-imitated model of the poetic career outlined in the alternate beginning to Virgil's *Aeneid*, pastoral comes first, serving as the mode wherein the aspiring poet tests his powers before attempting the subsequent levels of georgic, and, finally, epic (Lipking 69).

22 In "Presences," the speaker is accepted "new-born, royal" into a company of "extraordinary" beings (*Hidden Room* 2: 201–2); the speaker of "The Answer" imagines a

surrender of identity through a love that clothes her in "coronation cloth" (*Hidden Room* 2: 213–14). In "A Bagatelle," the fanciful description of "princess hibiscus" enthroned among fawning courtier-flowers characterizes the poet as one who moves freely in royal circles, perhaps as an attempt to compensate for poets' lack of status in a society in which poetry is not very visible (*Hidden Room* 2: 209–10).

23 Shelagh Rogers introduced her as such for a CBC Radio interview in May 2001 (Page, Interview).

Works Cited

Auden, W.H. "In Memory of W.B. Yeats." *Selected Poems*. Ed. Edward Mendelson. New York: Vintage, 1989. 80–83.

Boehrer, Bruce. "'Lycidas': The Pastoral Elegy as Same-Sex Epithalamium." *PMLA* 117.2 (2002): 222–36.

Dellamora, Richard. *Masculine Desire: The Sexual Politics of Victorian Aestheticism*. Chapel Hill: U of North Carolina P, 1990.

Eliot, T.S. *Four Quartets*. London: Faber and Faber, 1944.

———. "In Memoriam." *Selected Essays*. 1950. London: Faber and Faber, 1960. 286–95.

———. *The Waste Land*: *Selected Poems*. 1954. London: Faber and Faber, 1990. 51–74.

———. "Yeats." *On Poetry and Poets*. London: Faber and Faber, 1957. 252–62.

Gilbert, Sandra M., and Susan Gubar. *The Madwoman in the Attic: The Woman Writer and the Nineteenth-Century Literary Imagination*. New Haven: Yale UP, 1979.

Godard, Barbara, and Mary di Michele. "'Patterns of their own particular ceremonies': A Conversation in an Elegiac Mode, Between Mary di Michele and Barbara Godard." *Open Letter* 7.9 (1990): 36–59.

Harrison, Thomas Perrin. *The Pastoral Elegy: An Anthology*. Austin: U of Texas P, 1939.

Irvine, Dean. "The Two Giovannis: P.K. Page's Two Modernisms." *Journal of Canadian Studies / Revue d'études canadiennes* 38.1 (2004): 23–45.

Jonson, Ben. "The Vision of Ben Jonson, on the Muses of his Friend M. Drayton." *Poems of Ben Jonson*. Ed. and intro. George Burke Johnston. London: Routledge and Kegan Paul, 1980. 292–94.

Killian, Laura. "Poetry and the Modern Woman: P.K. Page and the Gender of Impersonality." *Canadian Literature* 150 (1996): 86–105.

Lipking, Lawrence. *The Life of the Poet: Beginning and Ending Poetic Careers*. Chicago: U of Chicago P, 1981.

Livesay, Dorothy. Dorothy Livesay fonds. 2024. Queen's University Archives, Queen's University, Kingston, ON.

Milton, John. "Lycidas." *Complete Poems and Major Prose*. Ed. Merritt Y. Hughes. New York: Macmillan, 1957. 116–25.

Page, P.K. "A Conversation with P.K. Page." Interview with John Orange. *Canadian Poetry: Studies, Documents, Reviews* 22 (1988): 68–77.

———. *Evening Dance of the Grey Flies*. Don Mills, ON: Oxford UP, 1981.

———. *The Hidden Room: Collected Poems*. 2 vols. Erin, ON: Porcupine's Quill, 1997.

———. *Hologram: A Book of Glosas*. London, ON: Brick, 1994.

———. Interview with Shelagh Rogers. *This Morning*. CBC Radio One. 21 May 2001.

———. "'That's me, firing Salvador': An Interview with P.K. Page." By Eleanor Wachtel. *West Coast Review* 22.2 (1987): 42–64.

Ramazani, Jahan. *Poetry of Mourning: The Modern Elegy from Hardy to Heaney*. Chicago: U of Chicago P, 1994.

Rose, Marilyn J. "Anthologizing P.K. Page: The Case of a Protean Poet." *Journal of Canadian Studies / Revue d'études canadiennes* 38.1 (2004): 154–65.

Sacks, Peter M. *The English Elegy: Studies in the Genre from Spenser to Yeats*. Baltimore: Johns Hopkins UP, 1985.

Schenck, Celeste M. "Feminism and Deconstruction: Re-Constructing the Elegy." *Tulsa Studies in Women's Literature* 5.1 (1986): 13–27.

———. *Mourning and Panegyric: The Poetics of Pastoral Ceremony*. University Park: Pennsylvania State UP, 1988.

Smith, A.J.M. "A Rejected Preface." *The Making of Modern Poetry in Canada: Essential Articles on Contemporary Canadian Poetry in English*. Ed. Louis Dudek and Michael Gnarowski. Toronto: Ryerson, 1967. 38–41.

Stacey, Robert David. "Looking at 'The Gold Sun'; or, The Glosa's Glasses." *Journal of Canadian Studie / Revue d'études canadiennes* 38.1 (2004): 108–17.

Sullivan, Rosemary. "Hologram." *Malahat Review* 117 (1996): 121–28.

Trehearne, Brian. *The Montreal Forties: Modernist Poetry in Transition*. Toronto: U of Toronto P, 1999.

Walker, Cheryl. *The Nightingale's Burden: Women Poets and American Culture Before 1900*. Bloomington: Indiana UP, 1982.

Whitney, Patricia. "From Oxford to Montreal: Patrick Anderson's Political Development."*Canadian Poetry: Studies, Documents, Reviews* 19 (1986): 26–48.

Wright, Nancy E. "Epitaphic Conventions and the Reception of Anne Bradstreet's Public Voice." *Early American Literature* 31.3 (1996): 243–63.

Zeiger, Melissa F. *Beyond Consolation: Death, Sexuality, and the Changing Shapes of Elegy*. Ithaca: Cornell UP, 1997.

The Passionate and Sublime Modernism of Elizabeth Smart

ANNE QUÉMA

> Under the redwood tree my grave was laid, and I beguiled my true love to lie down. The stream of our kiss put a waterway around the world, where love like a refugee sailed in the last ship. My hair made a shroud, and kept the coyotes at bay while we wrote our ciphers with anatomy. The winds boomed triumph, our spines seemed overburdened, and our bones groaned like old trees, but a smile like a cobweb was fastened across the mouth of the cave of fate. (*By Grand Central Station I Sat Down and Wept* 34)

The reappraisal of Elizabeth Smart's writings began in the late seventies, swelled in the eighties and the nineties, and has since come to a trickle.[1] The reader of this literature of reappraisal ends up with a composite if not paradoxical picture of an author who is both hailed as a genius producing a mature piece of work and chided as a helplessly romantic woman spawning a narrative of masochistic slavery to man. These two assessments may ultimately expose a fundamental fissure running through Smart's texts, but an analysis of her production in the modernist context may also help us grasp the historical and artistic specificity of her writings. What have often been identified as signs of victimization and lip-service to phallogocentrism in Smart's writings may well take on a different shade of meaning when one examines them in the light of the modernist movement in its plural manifestations.

Smart was first identified as a modernist two decades ago when, in "Excentriques, Eccentric, Avant-Garde," Barbara Godard boldly argued that, in ignoring the writings of Smart, Thérèse Tardif, Sheila Watson, and Gabrielle Roy, historians had edited Canadian modernism so that "the only mode of writing in the forties [appeared] to be that of social realism" (64).[2] Pasting these writings back into the main text of Canadian literary history has the effect of revealing the presence of a modernist tradition and its linguistic experimentalism. Godard goes on to note that with their repetitiveness, lack of plot, syntactic disruption, and focus on epiphanies, female modernist writings are located on the margins of a male modernist pantheon.[3] It is the eccentric and liminal position of Smart's modernist journals and poetic narrative, *By Grand Central Station I Sat Down and Wept* (1945), that I shall explore in the course of this essay.[4] More specifically, I argue that Smart's writing should be regarded both as a practice and a critique of modernism. While struggling with and suffering from the gender politics of modernist culture, she produced an oblique critique of the impact of this politics on writing and creativity. Her critique eventually led her to adopt a position antithetic to Eliot's poetics of impersonality by developing a poetics of the subjective and suffering personality in her poetic narrative. In this regard, Smart's writing exemplifies Christine Kim's argument elsewhere in this volume, where, she argues, a revision of Canadian modernism in the light of regional and women's writing leads to the reassessment of what has been often perceived as a cultural and homogeneous institution.

The co-presence of modernist practice and critique of modernism can also be deciphered in Smart's creation of a new subjectivity for modern times. Her writings participate in the great modernist reflection on time. In particular, she shares with modernist writers and thinkers such as Gertrude Stein, Martin Heidegger, and D.H. Lawrence a rejection of time as teleological development, which in a novel would translate as an Aristotelian chronology of plot with a beginning, middle, and end. However, her conception of a new temporality for a new self is unique. Her poetic narrative, which reads like the distillation of a process already initiated in her journals, should be regarded not only as part of a well-established tradition of feminine writing, but also as a gendered, modernist attempt to checkmate realistic metonymy with metaphors of the sublime that expand linear time. Smart is also known, perhaps too well known, for her representation of passionate love and transgression. I propose to explore this representation as a modernist critique of humanism from the standpoint of a gendered reflection on the role of passion, which Smart interpreted not only as erotic love but also as mystical gateway to reality. It is tempting to interpret this vision in romantic terms, but it is also possible to see in it a critique of modernist nihilism.

Locating Elizabeth Smart's Writing in Modernism

The analysis of Canadian modernism has resulted in two critical trends. One consists in defining the literature in relation to the milieu it stems from. Critics such as A.J.M. Smith and George Woodcock have defined the development of Canadian modernist poetry in terms of a search for the language that would best render the perceptual, phenomenological aspects of Canadian culture and landscape.[5] The other trend consists in defining Canadian modernism in relation to international modernism and avant-gardism. For instance, Barbara Godard points to the colonial connotations that international modernism held from a Canadian viewpoint, and argues that Canadian modernism could only locate itself in the margins of the movement, hence its unique position and composition. Already in 1989, Brian Trehearne argued that "we have arrived at a point of cultural security at which we will not be afraid to discover the influences that have shaped us, a point at which we can seek and take pride in the ways in which our artists have seized upon, and adapted with their own efforts, the traditions of other countries and of foreign artists" (*Aestheticism* 9). More recently, Susan Rudy and Lianne Moyes have argued for an international perspective on Canadian modernism.[6]

I do not see a necessary contradiction between these two trends, which can be read as two faces of the same coin: Canadian modernism has to be studied in the international context of Canada's colonial links with British culture and the country's struggle to differentiate itself from American culture, and this double predicament has in turn led Canada to define itself through its various regionalisms and relationship to Aboriginal society and culture. Smart's writing practice should be located within the cultural field that Christine Kim identifies in her discussion of Canadian feminist and regionalist modernisms in this volume. Kim draws a distinction between, on the one hand, A.J.M. Smith's support of a Canadian modernism tailored along international lines, and on the other hand, the kind of nationalist militancy the programmatic statements of the magazines *Preview* and *First Statement* advocated. In her attempt to establish a dialogue between what she perceived as Canadian culture and international culture, Smart's position is situated beyond the binary oppositions that the holders of national and international modernisms generated.

British and American imperialism, regionalism, and Aboriginal culture constitute the main elements of Canada's postcolonial history, which, as Glenn Willmott argues, "begins in close synchrony with the fin-de-siècle origins of modernity as well as modernism in Anglo-American culture. Hence the simple need for a theoretical discourse concerning modernity which aligns rather than opposes modernist expression with postcolonial experience" (44). The historical, cultural, and economic tensions between global and regional spaces are fundamental to Smart's poetic narrative, which is associated with references to Ottawa and its surroundings as well as to the Pacific coast of British Columbia. Her adherence to a local and Canadian culture implies the cosmopolitan and historical supplement of Willmott's description: "No great neon face has been superimposed over [Canadians'] minor but memorable history. Nor has the blood of the early settlers, spilt in feud and heroism, yet been bottled by a Coca-cola firm and sold as ten-cent tradition" (Smart, *By Grand Central Station* 57). Both neons and Coca-Cola act as signs of an economic and historical context that conditions Smart's endeavour to create a text on the periphery of British and American cultures.

At the same time, the traces of the cosmopolitan and modernist supplement, to use Willmott's Derridean terminology, are conspicuous throughout Smart's intertextual writings, which, as both Elizabeth Podnieks (66) and Alice Van Wart note, are characterized by "allusion" or "metalepsis" (Van Wart, 41). Critics such as Brigitta Johansson have also demonstrated Smart's dexterous and dazzling use of intertextuality (2001). Similarly, Smart's journals are peppered with literary references that bespeak a wide, varied, and international knowledge of her contemporaries, and this before she began writing her poetic narrative. The most recognizable modernist references include Katherine Mansfield, Virginia Woolf, Ernest Hemingway, James Joyce, Rainer Maria Rilke, Marcel Proust, André Gide, T.S. Eliot, D.H. Lawrence, E.M. Forster, Aldous Huxley, Stephen Spender, Archibald McLeish, Roger Fry, W.B. Yeats, W.H. Auden, Oscar Wilde, George Bernard Shaw, Lawrence Durrell, Anaïs Nin, and Henry Miller.[7] Her participation in the great tradition of intertextual modernism should not be seen in purely linguistic or autotelic terms; instead, her intertextual experimentalism creates a writerly space where Canadian culture and history are positioned in relation to international and cosmopolitan culture.

Smart's poetic novel or narrative poem remains stubbornly refractory to established and new definitions of modernist fiction and poetry. For instance, Willmott argues that formal and innovative features function in Canadian modernist fiction "without the openly alternative or aggressive relationship to conventional form characteristic of canonical texts" (41) as Canadian authors did not have access to a local elite market. This definition of Canadian modernism does not apply to Smart's text, which stands out as being more akin to European than Anglo-Saxon modernism in its uncompromising and difficult contract with the reader.

However, Smart's writing presents more ambiguity than meets the eye. While in *By Grand Central Station* the intertextual references could lead to the categorization of her work as an elitist piece of writing, the writing process of her journals produces a poetics of the demotic word. This poetics remains for the most part invisible in the various editions of her journals because mundane and material references to things such as daily events and shopping lists have been excised. Van Wart describes the way Smart's original journals consist of a collage of manuscripts like "My Lover John," lists of books Smart had read, as well as "poems, stories, sketches, lists, drawings, quotations." However, the collage effect is lost on the reader of the versions edited by Van Wart, who presents the following editing rationale: "if there is a bias in my selections, it is towards the literary. I have tried … to reveal the evolution of the romantic sensibility at the root of all Elizabeth Smart's writing" ("Textual Matters" n.p.). By leaving out the mundane and privileging the literary, Van Wart reinstates a generic and cultural hierarchy that Smart's experimental writing aimed at subverting.[8] In addition, what Willmott refers to as Canada's "bourgeois commercial and consumer culture" (51) actually acts as a subtext to Smart's narrative, which is treated both through literary intertextuality and references to popular culture such as Dorothy Dix's column, published during World War Two, offering advice on marriage and love to her readers. Smart's text refers to Dix in the following terms:

> As I sat down in the swivel chair in my father's office, with his desk massively symbolic between us, I realized that I could never defend myself. What was my defence but one small word which I dared not utter, because jazz singers and hypocritical preachers and Dorothy Dix had so maligned it. (*By Grand Central Station* 61)

Ironically, Dorothy Dix's rules were entitled "Dictates for a Happy Life."[9]

We can also try to assess Smart's role with regard to Canadian modernist poetry. In his accounts of its development, Brian Trehearne gives a central role to poetic practices of imagism grounded in the phenomenological representations of visual stimuli (*Aestheticism* 31–69). His account of the influence of imagism indicates that the fragmentary and static quality of the Poundian image proved problematic to Canadian modernist poets. In *The Montreal Forties*, Trehearne argues that Page's poetry of the forties tends to be characterized by an accumulation of such imagist metaphors, which deprived her poems of what he refers to as *integritas* or structure and coherence. Brigid Brophy, however, has celebrated Smart's metaphorical style and, in this sense, one can argue that Smart's text participates in the formalist experiments of the forties. My sense of the novel is that the experiment is successful, and this can be ascribed to Smart's modernist exploration of time as flux, which I shall examine.

Trehearne further associates the structuring of poems around the accumulation of metaphors with the doctrine of impersonality. *By Grand Central Station I Sat Down and Wept*, in contrast, is renowned for its emotional intensity. This discrepancy is worth noticing and requires our attention. I shall analyze the complexity of Smart's modernist poetics in the following section by focussing on the relationship between genre and gender in her poetic narrative.

Wrestling with the Modernist Angel

Like H.D., Joyce, Stein, Eliot, Ezra Pound, and others, Smart was a writer who chose to live in exile; this exile makes it difficult for the historian to decide whether she should be seen as a major participant in Canadian modernism, or whether she should be recorded as a bleep of Canadian origin on the international modernist radar screen. Smart's modernism is peculiarly decentred when compared to the likes of Eliot and Pound, who were almost fatally drawn into nationalistic politics. In both her journal and her poetic narrative, Smart offers the family psychological plot as the primary motivation for exile: "Parents' imaginations build frameworks out of their own hopes and regrets into which children seldom grow, but instead, contrary as trees, lean sideways out of the architecture, blown by a fatal wind their parents never envisaged" (*By Grand Central Station* 55). However, the term "family" has wider connotations and, in her case, it connoted both class structure and gender identity. Smart's parents belonged to the upper crust of Ottawa's political elite, with which Elizabeth Smart and her sisters were familiar through receptions and social connections. Smart also developed her sense of identity contending with her mother, Louie Smart, whom she perceived and experienced as a conservative and authoritarian woman.[10]

This family plot seems to support Willmott's argument that a significant number of Canadian modernist novels tend to belong to the genre of the bildungsroman. Willmott identifies Smart's novel as a bildungsroman (17), but I suggest we are also dealing with a künstlerroman. The novel represents the activity of writing in at least two ways. Towards the beginning of the narrative, the narrator briefly describes a scene in which she types her lover's manuscript and is seduced by him. In addition, and on account of its highly wrought prose and self-referential character, the text constantly signals its own textuality to the reader. The creative process is therefore at the heart of the narrative. It could be counter-argued that the narrator never identifies herself as a writer and that therefore the novel does not qualify as a künstlerroman. There are, however, two reasons for looking at this novel with fresh eyes. To begin with, the novel exists in a paratextual relation to Smart's early journals, which retrace her development as a young writer. A comparison of the novel and the journals reveals that passages of the novel originated in the journals. Furthermore, we need to pause on the fact that the narrator remains anonymous throughout the narrative. Critics have noted the anonymity of the lover, but the same comment applies to the narrator.

I suggest that the anonymity of the novel's narrator, Elizabeth Smart's exile in England, the reference to World War Two in the novel, and the representation of maternity are all part of the same problem, which can be stated in the following terms: anonymity and exile are both expressions of dispossession that the subject tries to control through representation or reenactment. What both the narrator and Smart are dispossessed of is their identity as creative and artistic women, which resulted from a patriarchal and historical situation. Like H.D., Djuna Barnes, and Jean Rhys, Smart struggled to define herself as a writer in a masculine context. The story of *By Grand Central Station* concerns the passion, in the Christian sense of the term, that the female protagonist has to undergo in her struggle to become an artist in a society historically defined in patriarchal terms. Thus the novel can be read as a künstlerroman in the making, whose metaphor of the birth process is inevitably associated with the process of creativity and artistic self-creation. The convergence between maternity and creativity occurs with poignancy in Smart's creation of craft-like books that are devoted to the births of her children and that combine the poetry of origins with the pragmatism of birth weight and vaccination (*Autobiographies* 81–102).

Lianne Moyes has analyzed the historical specificity of Canadian cultural patriarchy by showing that women of Smart's generation, such as Sheila Watson, who felt excluded from the Canadian literary field tended to get involved in international culture in order to escape local gender strictures ("Discontinuity, Intertextuality, and Literary History"). The texts Peter Stevens anthologized in *The McGill Movement* reflect the extent to which literary and non-literary writing were part of a masculine culture in Montreal. Christine Kim, also in this volume, points out the masculinist culture associated with modernist magazines such as *First Statement* and *Preview*, and the anthology *New Provinces*, which are perceived as "extensions of masculine personalities." Thus one can recognize in Smart's early peregrinations an attempt to escape from her cultural matrix, and this escape solidified in the late forties when she moved from Canada and settled in England for most of her life. Podnieks argues that Smart chose the genre of the diary in the way that women of the modernist period sought recognition without exposing themselves to judgement, stereotyping, and sarcasm. The diary, "constructed as a literary work," was the initial solution to that problem (57).

The other form gender conflict took in Smart's life and career was her relation to George Barker. Her lover and the father of her children, Barker identified with and received advice from T.S. Eliot, and in interacting with him and other artists such as the French painter Jean Varda, Smart was undoubtedly aware of the discourse surrounding the development of literary and visual modernism in Europe and Britain. In 1987, Christina Burridge incorporated Barker's sharp criticism of Smart's narrative in her edition of *Autobiographies* and described it as a "generous, but apt, critique" (71). However, I tend to see this critique as the kind of gender stricture Smart had to contend with as a writer. Barker is quick to identify and praise the modernist, metafictional character of her narrative, which "is just as much written about all the objects you bring in as illustrations as about the objects these metaphors are supposed to illustrate" (qtd. in *Autobiographies* 73). However, he adds that her style is so glutted with metaphors that the reader tends to get lost in the ambiguities of the connotations and to lose track of the "legitimate object" (74) to which the metaphor is applied. After analyzing an example, he states, "it's a helluva metaphorical mêlée in which as spectator I am completely lost. Clear it up, dearie, please" (75). I think this kind of statement speaks to the annoyance that readers might experience with some of the narrative's passages. The question, however, is this: Is Smart's style the reflection of artistic immaturity or is it the sign of a conception of language that aims at an effect Barker is hard put to grasp? The terminology he uses is revealing. He jeers at her writing when "the passion goes whoring after exhibitionism and the sensuality plays pimp for intellectual perversions" (74); but isn't the function of self-referential writing precisely to strut in order to display its deceptive effects in awareness of its superficial optics of appearance?

The most striking aspect of Barker's critique is the glaring gender bias that organizes his thoughts. Emulating Smart's art of the metaphor, he offers a remedy for her ailing prose:

> You gotta put powder on and gild the eyelids and lacquer the fingernails and use a good lipstick BUT ALL THIS IS USELESS UNLESS THE MARRIAGE SERVICE TAKES PLACE BETWEEN ALL THIS LITERARY PARAPHERNALIA AND THE MASCULINE METAPHORICAL. At present you have an immense masculine metaphorical and dozens of cosmetics i.e. images vocabularies etc BUT NO BRIDE ... she is the story or drama or history or happenings or events or what have you. (76)

Barker's identification of the metaphor in terms of the masculine is a blatant appropriation of a tool he regards as his property. The metaphor is poetic and *his* trade, while the narrative process remains feminine and *her* trade. In his rush to teach and preach, Barker remains blind to the experimental constituent of Smart's poetic narrative. His question as to whether Smart's text has achieved the state of major or minor martyrdom will seem obscure to today's readers, but the way Smart handled his criticisms remains fascinating. For some reason, Barker concludes that her text creates a mere minor martyrdom. Smart did not passively accept this critique and—this is the point where things get very interesting—went on to counter Barker in her novel: "Why does he write 'minor' martyrdoms? Didn't the crucifixion only last three days? Is it the shortness of the days of torture or the fact that hope still breathes that lets him say minor? How can anything so total not be major?" (*By Grand Central Station* 86). By inserting Barker's text into her narrative, Elizabeth Smart transforms her writing into a dialogical and agonistic performance that allows her to inscribe and engender the conflict at the heart of her modernist endeavour.[11]

Smart constructed *By Grand Central Station* as a critique of T.S. Eliot's poetics of impersonality, and in this respect she belongs to a group of women who, according to Shari Benstock, "challenged the white, male, heterosexual ethic underlying the Modernist aesthetics of 'impersonality'" ("Authorizing the Autobiographical" 21). Eliot practised intertextuality as a means of evicting the Romantic self, whose suffering was then muffled by the noise of tradition. By contrast, Smart has a devious conception of intertextuality that questions this model of creativity, which is identified by Bonnie Kime Scott in *Refiguring Modernism* as a masculinist modernist poetics. The raison d'être of Smart's writing practice is to impregnate her textual allusions to tradition with a creative principle of jubilation that stems from her resolve to wrestle with the modernist angel.

It is thus difficult to endorse Podnieks's conclusion that, because Smart uses literary allusions to mediate the expression of emotion, her diary "inscribes the modernist aesthetic of detachment, whereby the author stands back, paring her fingernails while the quotations stand on their own" (68). This would be a plausible claim were it not for the fact, which Podnieks examines at length, that this use of intertextuality also occurs within the context of Smart's journal writing. The generic context makes all the difference, and, as Podnieks herself argues, Smart's use of the diary to blur the boundaries of art and life means that she remained on the margins of the modernist hardcore. In fact, her practice of autobiography recalls Daphne Marlatt's definition of the genre as "not separable from poetry ... [a] fictionalysis: a self-analysis that plays fictively with the primary images of one's life, a fiction that uncovers analytically that territory where fact and fiction coincide" ("Self-Representation" 204). The more obvious conclusion is that Smart's use of intertextuality actually enhances the expression of emotion in both her journals and her poetic narrative. We have here a perfect example of the extent to which Smart borrowed from modernist practices in order to conduct a critique of modernist assumptions. By splintering practice and ideological assumption, Smart succeeded in producing liminal texts bearing the contradictions that the clash with male modernism engendered. Smart's text begets the suffering self in all its "personality" and, as Cy-Thea Sand puts it, "the act of reading [the novel] is analogous to scraping one's hand along stucco" (11).

It is, however, this very pathos that has led critics like Denise A. Heaps to identify Smart as a blotch on the history of feminism. One can indeed feel exasperated when the narrator of the novel resigns herself to her predicament in the following terms: "I can do nothing, being paralyzed by doubt. I can only wait, like an egg for the twenty-first day, for him to arrive with all the west winds of irrefutable conviction" (*By Grand Central Station* 88). The scars that this gender conflict inflicted upon Smart the writer, in addition to the more general pressures of the age, can still be seen some forty years later when, in 1982, she published eleven poems, one of which is entitled "The Muse: His and Hers." In it, Smart broods upon the stereotypes she would have encountered as a writer: "Can women do? / Can women make? / When the womb rests / Animus awake?" (*In the Meantime* 27).

Smart was concerned, if not obsessed, with the way cultural biases concerning women's procreation got in the way of their creativity. I see her poetic narrative as an attempt to reclaim the power that sexuality, reproduction, and maternity give women, as is evidenced by the metaphors of ovulation, pregnancy, waters, blood, and birth pervading her poetic narrative. From a historical standpoint, her writings herald Hélène Cixous's *écriture feminine*, which calls for a "newly born woman" emerging out of a writing practice that would take the female body as its point of departure (37–42).[12] From a historical standpoint, one can envisage the writing of an international genealogy of *écriture feminine* that would include early examples like Smart's modernist writings and Cixous's provocative manifestos, and later writings like those of Eavan Boland, who has called for the eroticization of history: "the past needs us. That very past in poetry which simplified us as women and excluded us as poets now needs us to change it ... we need to change the past. Not by intellectualizing it. But by eroticising it" (335). One recognizes the same poetics in Smart's journals where she was already using a language that eroticizes selves and places. For instance, writing of Mexico, she states, "Why have I not spoken of Mexico? Because it has not made love to me" (*Necessary Secrets* 207). In another entry and referring to an exchange between herself and Paalen, the husband of her female lover, she also states, "I hung over the balcony thinking of Tristan and Isolde, but dared not mention them. I wanted to say at tea—O how I love *man*, and I love woman too. I love *love*" (214). The voice of her narrator is generous and presents itself as perpetual gift to whomever is capable of receiving it. "Her libido," to quote Cixous, "is cosmic, just as her unconscious is worldwide: her writing also can only go on and on, without ever inscribing or distinguishing contours, daring dizzying passages in other, fleeting and passionate dwellings within the hims and hers whom she inhabits" (44).[13] Also, Smart meant her new language to have political implications, and in the novel she uses female sexuality to challenge a patriarchal order of society. In part 6, the narrator proclaims,

> With [love] I can repopulate all the world. I can bring forth new worlds in underground shelters while the bombs are dropping above; I can do it in lifeboats as the ship goes down; I can do it in prisons without the guard's permission; and O, when I do it quietly in the lobby while the conference is going on, a lot of statesmen will emerge twirling their moustaches, and see the birth-blood, and know that they have been foiled. (*By Grand Central Station* 66)

The lines may sound naïve but they also anticipate feminist slogans of the second wave against the masculinist culture of war, violence, and phallocratic decision-making.

A Newly Born Woman

Smart's striving to create a feminine medium and her modernist affiliation combine to produce a specific temporality attuned to the self and the world she envisaged in her writing. It is frequently implied that her narrative is ahistorical and that she relegated World War Two to a blurred background in the story. Her unorthodox treatment of history may have led to critical oversight. In the following passage, the topic of war is sifted through a Gothic rhetoric:

> I have locked my door, but terror is ambushed outside. The eucalyptus tree batters the window, and I hear all smitten Europe wailing from the stream below. Malevolent ghosts appear at the black panes, unabashed by the pale crosses of the frame, for now Jesus Christ walks the waters of another planet, bleeding only history from his old wounds. (*By Grand Central Station* 32–33)

Far from being insignificant, the war is part of the temporality the narrator must fight in order to become a newly born woman. In the novel, war is associated with linear time and apocalyptic history: its outbreak always occurs at the end of a schedule driven by finality, and war itself develops with an awesome sense of inevitability even though it can always be ended. In the 23 September 1938 entry of her journal, Smart represents the problem in the following imaginary dialogue:

> "What do you think of the war scare
> Bill, my good man?"
> (I like to get the opinion of the people when I can)
> "Looks pretty bad. But I guess I'd do the same again,"
> . . .

> [Gaunt dreamers] rise trembling, they foretold him here
> The nerve-straining wait done
> They are relieved their roll of prophet is over
> And doom at last begun. (*Necessary Secrets* 177–78)

War is associated with teleological time and ready-made formulas. By contrast, Smart's text is engaged in a search for reality in the fugitive and the ephemeral. It is the role of language to reveal a new temporality that will provide epiphanies of feather-like reality:

> Living—that quickening and glow, the lovely instruments of love, dancing, laughing, talking, loving, swimming, lying in the sun expanded—But art—only the realization, capture and condensation of the MOMENT, any MOMENT, in any time or place (a lady's head like a bird bent, a oneness with a stone, Eva's feet like whipped but faithful dogs). Or pulling strange substitutes out of your own dark depths in lonely cells, in isolated towers. (*Necessary Secrets* 223)[14]

One might rush to the conclusion that Smart's approach to time and subjectivity is romantic, and the passionate characteristic of her writing has led Alice Van Wart to regard Smart as a writer with a "highly romantic sensibility searching for the vital moments in life that she believed could be found only in love, art, and the natural world" (24).[15] However, there are elements in the narrative that point to a different interpretation. The narrative does not present itself as the act of recollection in tranquility. In her ambivalent allegiance to modernism, Smart shares with Pound a fascination for the present. In January 1940, she records,

> I say I must rend the Now, the Now is only important—I can't reconstruct the past, and if I could I'm afraid of missing the present. The important juice-drops are small, but worth a million of the garrulous chaff that the will forces out when it says do this or do that … I want each word to be essence, irreplaceably and authentically the only only note. (*Necessary Secrets* 236).

In her analysis of Smart's journals, Podnieks demonstrates the extent to which Smart was using the genre as a construct for eventual publication.[16] With its vision and revisions, its fusion of the private and the public, the published journal is one step further from the lyrical "I" of Romantic poetry. The fusion of the public and the private does not go without a hitch as it forces the writer to face the world out there. Similarly, her poetic narrative is based on the tension between the awareness of history and culture on the one hand, and, on the other, the experiences of the personal self. The conclusion to the narrative does not celebrate the romantic lyrical "I"; instead, it presents North American popular culture as indifferent and callous in its ignorance of the search for the NOW.

To grasp Smart's endeavour, one needs to turn to another modernist writer. In her study of Gertrude Stein's practice of autobiography, Shirley Neuman emphasizes Stein's need to rid herself of the burden of the past: "Writing in Alice's person is one way of 'denuding' herself of time. Stein chooses to write autobiography by recreating in the narrative present another's mind as it hypothetically would remember and so avoids the preoccupation with personal chronology which tracing her own past in a more conventional manner would involve" (23). One chief technique in Stein's writing is the use of digression, which, since *Tristram Shandy*, has been used as a way of straying from chronology: "Toklas's divagations, as narrator, from the party, embody the 'continuous present' by conforming to the dictum that the narrative must move not by progression but by beginning again and again" (Neuman 24). In her autobiographical journals and poetic narrative, Elizabeth Smart is involved in the same search for being, even though her writing is markedly different from Stein's. In both cases, the aim is to create a type of language that will help circumvent linearity. This is where modern autobiography and the modernist project meet. The fashioning of a new language combines with an anti-chronological conception of time to create a new self that defines itself in terms of expanding, wave-like time. Neuman refers to Jean Starobinski's theory of autobiography, which confirms Smart's and Stein's predilection for the present as opposed to the past: "à l'autoréférence explicite de la narration elle-même, le style ajoute la valeur autoréférentielle implicite d'un mode singulier de l'élocution" (Neuman 11). Style is autobiographically significant because it gives birth and presence to the subject on the white page. We have here the reason why Smart's literary allusions do not land her in the cul-de-sac of impersonality. She taps the resources of intertextuality and rhetoric so as to give presence to the self on the page. In a famous passage, Smart states her poetics of the newly born woman:

> Drapery. What of drapery? I mean the oblique camouflaged form of putting the truth in a work of art. A poem, a note, a diary. These are the raw moments, the raw thoughts. I do not want, I am irritated with the devious method and hidden indirectness of the novel, for instance, or even the short story, or a play. Poems, notes, diaries, letters, or prose such as "The

House of Incest," in The Black Book, only meet my need ... Each word must rip virgin ground. No past effort must ease the birth. Rather than that, the haphazard note, the unborn child, the bottled embryo. (*Necessary Secrets* 201–2)

By Grand Central Station I Sat Down and Wept begets the newly born woman by maintaining an almost impossibly sublime rhetoric through most of the narrative.[17] The sublime takes the subject right out of the commonplace and clock-time. Smart achieves the sublime by using devices that allow her to tame the metonymic drive of her narrative. The first device is best described in her words when in her journal she refers to her habit of producing a "plot squashed into penny size" (*In the Meantime* 140). The shell of a narrative calendar can be deciphered through the references to months scattered here and there, which allow the reader to reconstitute the timeline of the basic plot. Events take place between the summer days preceding the war outbreak of 1939 and end with the period following the birth of the narrator's child the following summer. This timeline is far from being clear upon the first reading of a narrative that has been conceived in terms of temporal allusions to be tracked down by the reader. Having produced a minimalist plot, Smart proceeds to peg her metaphors on the metonymic line of her sentences. The effect of this rhetoric of accumulation is one of temporal expansion and dilation, which makes the birth of the new self possible.[18] The birth is painful for the reader who has to strive for meaning in a very dense and demanding text; her use of metaphor reminds one of the visual puzzles modernist painters were striving for and which are recalcitrant to normative perception. Smart's prose has the same effect on the reader, who tends either to see her sentences as made of blocks of words to be examined in its minutia, or to hear the flow of words before making out their semantic meaning.

The poetry of Smart's prose must therefore be understood in its reaction to the metonymic exigencies of the novelistic narrative. Other critics have documented additional poetic devices that allow us to say this is not a novel in the traditional sense of the term.[19] Smart's sentences have a rhythm that occasionally frolicks with the iambic pentameter. Van Wart notes the recurrence of zeugma, a rhetorical device producing a sense of syntactic disjunction as in Charles Dickens's "Miss Bolo ... went straight home, in a flood of tears and a sedan-chair" (553).[20] The figure is exemplified in the following passage: "And this, though shocking, enables me to understand, and myself rise as virile as a cobra, out of my loge, to assume control" (*By*

Grand Central Station 22). The juxtaposition of "understand" and "myself rise" constitutes the disjunction that characterizes a zeugma.

Smart's style is frequently associated with the art of the metaphor, but her style also owes its complexity to other figures of speech, such as the simile: "faint as hope, and definite as death, my possible phoenix of love is as bright as a totem-pole, in the morning, on the sky, breathing like a workman setting out on a job" (*By Grand Central Station* 36). Here the central metaphor of the phoenix of love is intensified by no less than four similes, two of which combine to form an antiphrastic introduction. Perhaps the most striking rhetorical aspect of the narrative is Smart's sustained use of hyperbole. Not only does the accretion of metaphors and similes produce a sense of surfeit, but the expression of emotion always reaches the highest octaves as in the following: "I do not bleed. The knife stuck in my flesh leaves only the hole that proves I am dead" (*By Grand Central Station* 86). At another point, she writes, "The pain was unbearable, but I did not want it to end: it had operatic grandeur. It lit up Grand Central Station like a Judgment Day" (*By Grand Central Station* 103). Questions are combined with apostrophes: "Where are we all headed for on the swollen river of my undammed grief? O hurricane, be decisive" (*By Grand Central Station* 104). The function of the narrative is to maintain the sublime as long as possible in the face of violence and the commonplace. By the end of the narrative, the narrator has lost her battle and has failed to meet the challenge of making love the lodestar of her vision. Passion has died, and the narrator is surrounded by the vulgar and the stereotypical, which have the last bathetic word: "I myself prefer Boulder Dam to Chartres Cathedral. I prefer dogs to children. I prefer corncobs to the genitals of the male. Everything's hotsy-totsy, dandy, everything's OK. It's in the bag. It can't miss" (*By Grand Central Station* 112). The Aristotelian machinery of plot has its revenge by driving the development of the love affair from beginning to end, that is to say from passion to betrayal, which coincides with the end of the experiment and the silencing of the narrator: "Every tear is wept and lies staining its falling place. I am without words" (*By Grand Central Station* 109).

Smart's Unwarranted Discourse of Passion

A contributor to the re-evaluation of female modernism, Suzanne Clark, has argued that women modernists wrote against a masculinist trend that cultivated the discourse of erotic love at the expense of the expression of love as sentiment. Clark regards the writings of Edna St. Vincent Millay, Kay Boyle, and Louise Bogan as the signs of "a contradiction *within* modernism" (5). I see Smart as subscribing to this "unwarranted discourse" (Clark 1), as well as exploring other meanings associated with love, including erotic love and maternal love. In a text written in 1939, "Dig a Grave and Let Us Bury Our Mother," Smart wrote, "Be sea, be sky, be wind. But I am not sea or sky or wind. I am this upright person thrust into the world too soon, still searching for the womb I lost. I suck my lover's lip frantically, as if it were a breast and I starved for milk" (*In the Meantime* 49). From a biographical standpoint, one might be tempted to relate this passage to Smart's first pregnancy, but the intriguing thing is that Smart's child was not born until a year later. If there is any biographical reference, it has to be Smart's relation to her own mother. Why does Smart appropriate for herself the language of maternity in order to describe the relation to the lover? Rosemary Sullivan has argued that Smart's approach to love is rooted in her relationship with her mother. Deprived of maternal love and searching for compensation, Smart did not fall in love with George Barker, "but with the passion itself" (112). Some of the statements in "Dig a Grave and Let Us Bury Our Mother" certainly give credence to Sullivan's interpretation and underscore the role of the mother figure in Smart's development: "I am escaping. I am putting miles of sea, continents of desert and impassable mountains between us. But her fatal electricity cannot be avoided. It penetrates every insulation. Now there are revengeful dreams where she catches me and drills her fierce will into my escaping life" (*In the Meantime* 43). In Smart's personal mythology, the mother is associated with class structure, for "she believed in the great class barriers" (*In the Meantime* 45). In the poetic narrative, the mother is omnipotent:[21] "my mother's clutch held me every way, with claws of biology and pity and hysterical hypnotism, and made me long for my annihilation. Can even Freud explain the terror of that clutch, the inescapability of its greed for authority, and why it was stronger than the North East wind, memory, reason, or Pre-Cambrian rock?" (*By Grand Central Station* 66).

Smart uses her reflection on motherhood to create a vocabulary to codify her idealistic search for plenitude. This search was still at the heart of her writing practice at the end of her career, as may be glimpsed in an entry of a late journal recounting a writing block Smart experienced in 1979. She writes, "What I want to explore is the severance, the necessary severance, of this wonderful completeness—in the womb, perfect, and even for many years after—a *passionate* connection" (*In the Meantime* 132). Each of these words is worth its weight in gold. Smart states concisely the elements of her poetic narrative, which, more than the account of a love affair, tells of a search for a state of plenitude that can only be compared to the totality that the womb offers and can only be described as passion. Further into the diary of this blockage, Smart adds,

> I wasn't going to write about my mother—only the *passionate* relationship—serving nature?—longer-lingering than the most *passionate* sexual love—and more abused ... It's easier to abandon your children than your mother—which is the memory of a hope of perfect human understanding, a oneness of course impossible, but a vivid unforgettable leaping hope, aroused again by *passionate* sexual love, but even that is easier to get over. (*In the Meantime* 146, 148; emphasis mine)

In quoting these poignant passages, I have italicized the word "passionate," which recurs four times, in order to bring out the fact that, in constructing her notion of passion, Smart establishes a bridge between the mother and the lover. In the journals as well as in the poetic narrative, sexual love is more than sexual love, and heightened passion functions as a polysemic term in her writings. I will begin by examining her discourse on passion as sexual love, then I will analyze the transition from the discourse of sexual love to that of mystical love, to argue finally that in her writings suffering is what the failure of mystical love entails.

Smart's account of erotic love participates in that part of the modernist movement that explored areas considered taboo. She belongs to the tradition initiated and developed by D.H. Lawrence, Anaïs Nin, Henry Miller, and Lawrence Durrell. At a time when the novel was inaccessible, she managed to find a copy of *Lady Chatterley's Lover* and offered a brief critical assessment of it in her journal. Thus, her narrative allusions to hot scenes of sexual attraction, homosexuality, and hermaphrodite lovers should be seen not only as a rebellion against Victorian puritanism but also as the desire to inscribe her text in an already established modernist tradition. The text slides from one type of love to the other without transition or judgement. Metaphors with erotic connotations spin away when it comes to the representation of her sexual lover who "has the innocent slipping advent of the next generation, which enters in one night of joy, and leaves a meadowful of lamenting milkmaids when its purpose is grown to fruit" (*By Grand Central Station* 22). The combination of a hyperbolic and incantatory style with a narrative that dilates and expands time indicates an aspiration to totality. It is this aspiration that differentiates Smart from male modernists such as

T.S. Eliot and Wyndham Lewis, whose idealistic quests often take the form of nostalgia short-circuited by irony and nihilism. Smart's idealism is lush and generous: "O the water of love that floods everything over, so that there is nothing the eye sees that is not covered in ... Everything flows like the Mississippi over a devastated earth, which drinks unsurfeited, and augments the liquid with waterfalls of gratitude ... the overflow drenches all my implements of trivial intercourse" (*By Grand Central Station* 39). In her poetic narrative, Smart offers the means to fertilize modernist deserts and wastelands.

In 1978, Michael Brian Oliver proposed to read the novel as "a rewriting of the Bible, in the tradition of William Blake. This is no simple love story, but a succinct and penetrating vision of reality, 'all there is' literally" (112).[22] Because the narrative remains open and exposed to the material reality of North American culture, Oliver concludes that Smart's vision is "extreme, but it is neither solipsistic nor mystical" (131); and yet the narrative uses a code that we usually associate with saints, mystics, and visionaries.[23] Notwithstanding the mythological reference, one thinks of St. Teresa's writings upon reading the following: "here I was taking the vomiting body of humanity to my bosom, living their greed over the last tutti-frutti cake, their fear, their imaginary ills, lulled in the very rough arms of father neptune himself" (*Necessary Secrets* 196). In part 7, the narrator identifies herself with the Christian martyr St. Christopher, whose name etymologically signifies the "bearer of Christ." This etymology has led to the creation of iconography representing a giant carrying the infant Christ on his back as exemplified by the famous woodcut of Buxheim's St. Christopher.[24] Smart's intertextual and intercultural reference to St. Christopher represents yet another instance of her endeavour to engender a form of modernism from the standpoint of a feminine revision of the world and culture.

The narrator is prepared to embrace the whole world in both its depressing and exciting manifestations: "Even in transient coffee-shops and hotels, or the gloom of taverns, the crooning of Bing Crosby out of a jukebox, and the bar-tender clanking glasses, achieve a perfect identity, a high round note of their own flavour, that makes me tearful with the gratitude of reception" (*By Grand Central Station* 43). These lines represent an even greater degree of affirmation than the pontifical profession of love reached in Auden's "September 1, 1939." Her mysticism is based on the aspiration to commune with life and nature, and in this scenario sexual love is the stepping stone to ecstasy. The narrative reaches an acme of mythopoeic empathy with nature: "But I have become a part of the earth: I am one of its waves flooding and leaping. I am the same tune now as the trees, hummingbirds, sky, fruits, vegetables in rows. I am all or any of these. I can metamorphose at will" (*By Grand Central Station* 42). The passion that Smart identifies with the mysteries of creation is also coterminous with the passion that she associates with creativity. The link between the two is made in a 1982 poem entitled "What Is Art? Said Doubting Tim":

> Dido cried, like a million others.
> But it isn't her tears
> That sear the years,
> Or pity for girls with married lovers
> That light up the crying I
> With the flash that's poetry:
> It's the passion one word has for another. (*In the Meantime* 36).

Here as in sexual love and maternal plenitude, "passion" is the key word that ensures the transition from one plane of existence to another.[25]

It is difficult to establish whether Smart's language of mysticism corresponds to a religious experience or to a code that would function the same way as her metaphors. Whatever the case, Julia Kristeva's theory of poetic language furthers our interpretation of this mystical discourse. Kristeva distinguishes between symbolic language and poetic language. The former is used to "express meaning in a communicable sentence between speakers" (131). It bears the marks of social and legislative constraints. Semiotic language precedes symbolic language: while symbolic language is characterized by the use of the sign, the signified object and the signifier (which are features of thetic consciousness), semiotic language reactivates the "repressed, instinctual, maternal element" (136) and characterizes the echolalia of infants. Semiotic language, which Kristeva describes as a "pulsation of sign and rhythm" (139), subverts the signified object in order to create a process of subjectivity. Smart's writing is characterized by what Kristeva identifies as the "undecidable process between sense and nonsense, between language and rhythm" (135). Sentences are heard before they are understood, as in, for example, the speaker's observation that "the texts are meaningless, they are the enemy's deception. My foot danced by mistake over the helpless, and bled no solace for my butchery" (*By Grand Central Station* 35). This surrealistic and poetic medium acts as suture between the evocation of passion as sexual love and passion as mystical love of the universe. Through and through, the echolalia resonates indicating a never-ending and "unsurfeited" search for the plenitude of the womb.

Like Ulysses, the reader may decide to weather the narrative, bound to the mast and deaf to the siren's song; or the reader may succumb until she or he stumbles on statements such as the following: "I am shot with wounds which have eyes that see a world of sorrow, always to be, panoramic and unhealable, and mouths that hang unspeakable in the sky of blood" (*By Grand Central Station* 23). The reader is momentarily caught off balance as the text shifts from the sublime to the Gothic representation of a masochistic delirium. Smart's text is surprisingly rife with Gothic references, which function like the uncontrolled jumps of a cardiogram.[26] These Gothic black marks signal a reversal in the thematic logic of her narrative, which from a mystical union with the pulse of the universe lapses into a state of severance and suffering. No longer mystical love, passion acquires the Christian connotation of suffering and endurance.

The breadth of Smart's experimental approach to narrative and language, the scope of her challenge to the masculinist poetics of impersonality, and the depth of her reflection on gender and the search for being all indicate that we have in *By Grand Central Station I Sat Down and Wept* not only a mature Canadian text but also a mature and sophisticated response to modernism. As important as Djuna Barnes, Anaïs Nin, H.D., Jean Rhys, Mina Loy, and Mary Butts, Smart belongs to what, in *The Gender of Modernism*, Bonnie Kime Scott refers to as the "tangled mesh of modernists" whereby "modernism" is conceived as the product of dialogical relations and counter-relations among writers of the same period (10). Smart's Canadian and centrifugal position contributes to this modernist mesh. It now remains to assess Elizabeth Smart's belated influence on the development of Canadian writing.

Notes

1 Here is a list of articles and essays published over that period, in chronological order: Michael B. Oliver's "Elizabeth Smart: Recognition" (1978); Barbara Godard's "Transgressions" (1979); Cy-Thea Sand's "The Novels of Elizabeth Smart: Biological Imperialism and the Trap of Language" (1983); Alice Van Wart's "*By Grand Central Station I Sat Down and Wept*: The Novel as a Poem" (1986); David Lobdell's "Eros in the Age of Anxiety: Elizabeth Smart and Louise Maheux-Forcier" (1990); Dee Horne's "Elizabeth Smart's Novel-Journal" (1991); Alice Van Wart's "'Life Out of Art': Elizabeth Smart's Early Journals" (1992); Denise A. Heaps's "The Inscription of 'Feminine *Jouissance*' in Elizabeth Smart's *By Grand Central Station I Sat Down and Wept*" (1994); Elizabeth Podnieks's "'Keep Out / Keep Out / Your Snooting Snout ... ':

The Irresistible Journals of Elizabeth Smart" (1996); and Rosemary Sullivan's "Tantalus Love" in *Labyrinth of Desire: Women, Passion and Romantic Obsession* (2001).
2. In "Eclectic Detachment: Aspects of Identity in Canadian Poetry," A.J.M. Smith refers to the Canadian poet as an "eclectic" poet able to draw on diverse cultures and traditions. While Godard's argument favours a centrifugal approach, Smith proposes a more centripetal view with the poet at the hub of an international culture.
3. Marilyn J. Rose, in her essay "Anne Marriott: Modernist on the Periphery," in this volume argues for a liminal and decentred modernism.
4. I will be referring to *By Grand Central Station I Sat Down and Wept* as a poetic narrative for reasons that will become clear as my argument develops. I have used four volumes in which Smart's journals are edited. These are *In the Meantime*, edited by Alice Van Wart; *Autobiographies*, edited by Christina Burridge; *Necessary Secrets*, edited by Alice Van Wart; and *On the Side of the Angels*, edited by Alice Van Wart.
5. See A.J.M. Smith, "Introduction to *The Book of Canadian Poetry*" (1943), in *On Poetry and Poets*, and George Woodcock, *George Woodcock's Introduction to Canadian Poetry* (1993).
6. See Moyes's paper in this volume, "Discontinuity, Intertextuality, and Literary History: Gail Scott's Reading of Gertrude Stein," and Rudy's "Women, Poetics and Canada before 1960: The Limits of Nationalism and Modernism"; both were originally delivered at the conference "'Wider Boundaries of Daring': The Modernist Impulse in Canadian Women's Poetry" in 2001.
7. Critics such as Brigid Brophy in her foreword to *By Grand Central Station I Sat Down and Wept* (9–10), Alice Van Wart ("*By Grand Central Station*" 44–45), and Elizabeth Podnieks (64–65) have documented Smart's intertextual references, ranging from Homer and the Bible to Joyce. In addition, Smart commented on her modernist readings in her journals.
8. In her introduction to *Essays on Life Writing: From Genre to Critical Practice,* Marlene Kadar proposes a new conception of the genre of autobiography or "life writing" that "would allow us to include metafiction and, even, narrative poetry; that would enable us to include both 'high' and 'non-high' forms of writing; that would let us reread the canon while inserting the prejudices of women, and women's 'styles'; and that would concede to unfinished or imperfect styles" (11). This new approach, which developed out of the gynocritical work of the seventies and eighties, can certainly help us grasp the singularity of Smart's text.
9. I wish to thank Belinda Beveridge, at Acadia University, for her research on Dorothy Dix. The website at the Austin Peay State University introducing the collection of Dorothy Dix's writings states, "As the forerunner of today's popular advice columnists, Elizabeth Meriwether Gilmer (1861–1951), writing under the pen name 'Dorothy Dix,' was America's highest paid and most widely read female journalist at the time of her death. Her advice on love and marriage was syndicated in newspapers around the world. One of her most famous columns was her *Dictates for a Happy Life*. With an estimated audience of 60 million readers, she became a popular and recognized figure on her travels abroad."
10. In this respect, Smart seems to belong to a historical and cultural generation of Canadian women whose relation to their mothers significantly shaped their development as female writers. In her analysis of the relation between Dorothy Livesay and her mother, Ann Martin argues in "The Writing Livesays" (elsewhere in this volume) that "family politics and literary politics converge in the overdetermined figure of the mother" in Livesay's autobiographical writings.

11 Throughout the pages of her journal, Smart reports on the tensions that her relationships engender. Whether she is dealing with Jean Varda, Wolfgang Paalen, or George Barker, she is engaged in a power relationship determined by masculine domination. For instance, in "The Little Cassis Book," she refers to the room Varda had reserved for her with a lock on the outside of the door (*Necessary Secrets* 191).

12 The argument that women modernists anticipated much of French feminism is well known and has already been put forward by Bonnie Kime Scott in her introduction to *The Gender of Modernism: A Critical Anthology* (13).

13 In "Gnosis," Donna Smyth also develops the theme of the kind of knowledge that bears the sign of female anatomy: "Gnosis: rock-a-bye in water womb. Amphibian ambiguity. Assertiveness-training will not save us. We struggle to breathe in the alien air" (86). In "The Inscription of 'Feminine Jouissance,'" Heaps links Smart's writing to Cixous's *écriture* of *jouissance*. However, she criticizes Smart for remaining indebted to a Judeo-Christian philosophy of sacrifice, guilt, and punishment. I would argue that we need to historicize our approach to Smart's texts, which show the signs of a subject caught up in the contradictions of her culture.

14 Decades later, in "Writing Our Way Through the Labyrinth," Daphne Marlatt would make the same critique of instrumental language and would propose a labyrinthine approach: "in a time when language has been appropriated by the Freudians as intrinsically phallic, it seems crucial to reclaim it through what we know of ourselves in relation to writing. Writing can scarcely be for women the act of the phallic signifier, its claim to singularity, the mark of the capital I (was here). Language is no 'tool' for us, no extension of ourselves, but something we are 'lost' inside of. Finding our way in a labyrinthine moving with the drift, slipping though claims to one-track meaning so that we can recover multiple related meanings, reading between the lines. Finding in write, rite, growing out of ar-, that fitting together at the root of read (we circle back), moving into related words for arm, shoulder (joint), harmony— the music of connection. Making our way through all parts of the figure, using our labyrinthine sense, we (w)rite our way ar- way, "reading" it, in intercommunicating passages" (46).

15 Shari Benstock's description of the encounter between women writers and modernism gives us more leeway: "The instability of the subject is nowhere more apparent than in women's writing of [the modernist] period, in texts by Djuna Barnes, Isak Dinesen, H.D., Mina Loy, Anaïs Nin, Jean Rhys, Gertrude Stein, and Virginia Woolf, writing that puts into question the most essential component of the autobiographical—the relation between 'self' and 'consciousness'" (21).

16 By contrast, in "Elizabeth Smart's Novel-Journal," Dee Horne argues that Smart's journals and novel-journal should be assessed on the basis of their truthfulness, credibility, and intimacy. However, as she herself shows, Smart's writing is highly elaborate and the product of stylistic work: "Smart uses juxtaposition, alliteration, allusion, repetition, rhythm, and cadence to approximate more closely through poetry the intensity of the narrator's feelings" (137).

17 Or what Van Wart in "*By Grand Central Station I Sat Down and Wept*: The Novel as a Poem" describes as the "extravagant" in Smart's narrative (40–41).

18 In her 9 October 1939 journal entry, Smart produces a comic example of style sagging under the weight of (mixed!) combined metaphors: "Saligmann and J.B. Neumann before lunch. His nose waits like a hawk to prey, and his glistening eyes are the clever boys of the class. But from their two pairs of eyes flow the most buoyant doves into the huge empty stadium of my ego" (*Necessary Secrets* 183).

19 In "Eros in the Age of Anxiety," David Lobdell also analyzes the poetic aspects of the narrative (65).
20 Bernard Dupriez defines zeugma as "a figure of syntax which consists in uniting several parts of a sentence by means of some common, non-repeated element. Zeugma includes both adjunction and disjunction" (475).
21 In a recent biography of Smart, Kim Echlin also underlines the lifelong, controlling role of Louie Smart with which, from "Dig a Grave and Let Us Bury Our Mother" to her 1977 journals, Elizabeth Smart struggled (Echlin 60–63, 208–16). The iconoclasm of Smart's writing on the subject endures: "So dig a grave and let us bury our mother, but not before we've murdered her" (qtd. in Echlin 211).
22 Oliver argues that Christian symbolism plays a major role in the novel by providing the ten sections of the poetic narrative with the structure of the ten stations along the Way of the Cross.
23 In *Women in the House of Fiction: Post-War Women Novelists*, Lorna Sage refers to St. Teresa of Avila as another intertextual reference in Smart's poetic narrative (55).
24 The coloured woodcut of St. Christopher in the Carthusian monastery in Buxheim, Germany, held at the John Rylands Library, Manchester, UK, was produced in 1423 by an unknown artist. For an electronic reproduction of the woodcut, consult "St. Christopher Woodcut" on the website *Art and Books: The Introduction of Printing*. For a further consideration of visual art in relation to Smart's experimental writing see my essay "Elizabeth Smart and Cecil Buller: Engendering Experimental Modernism," which supports the claims I make here.
25 One hears echoes of Whitman's voice: "These days all sky and sea are wild with innuendo and submerged life. The greens, blues, whites, half-greys, large embryonic clouds float with the unformed bigness of potentiality. The whitecaps of foam, the gulls' flight, the strong warm wet air, full of spring messages, go through everything, through every pore, the brain, the sex, the mouth, the hair. The soft wind ravishes, exhilarates, possesses. O to leap, to leave the endless becoming, to be sea, be sky, be wind. But whose will, though voracious for self-denial, can hasten the metamorphosis?" (*In the Meantime* 48).
26 Intertextual and generic references to Gothic are scattered throughout the text. Some of the numerous references are to be found on 23, 31, 32, 33, 34, 35, 55, 80, 89, 104, 105, and 110 of Smart's poetic narrative.

Works Cited

Art and Books: The Introduction of Printing. Home page. 11 August 2003 <www.csu.edu.au/faculty/arts/humss/art317/stchris.htm>.

Auden, W.H. "September 1, 1939." *The Collected Poetry of W.H. Auden*. New York: Random House, 1945. 57–59.

Benstock, Shari. "Authorizing the Autobiographical." *The Private Self: Theory and Practice of Women's Autobiographical Writings*. Ed. S. Benstock. Chapel Hill: U of North Carolina P, 1988. 10–33.

Boland, Eavan. "Letter to a Young Woman Poet." *By Herself: Women Reclaim Poetry*. Ed. Molly McQuade. St. Paul, MN: Graywolf, 2000. 331–44.

Brophy, Brigid. Foreword. *By Grand Central Station I Sat Down and Wept*. By Elizabeth Smart. London: HarperFlamingo, 1992. 7–13.

Cixous, Hélène. "The Newly Born Woman." *The Hélène Cixous Reader*. Ed. Susan Sellers. London: Routledge, 1994. 37–45.

Clark, Suzanne. *Sentimental Modernism: Women Writers and the Revolution of the Word*. Bloomington: Indiana UP, 1991.

Dickens, Charles. *The Pickwick Papers*. Ed. James Kinsley. Oxford: Clarendon, 1986.

Dupriez, Bernard. *A Dictionary of Literary Devices: Gradus, A–Z*. Trans. Albert W. Halsall. Toronto: U of Toronto P, 1991.

Echlin, Kim. *Elizabeth Smart: A Fugue Essay on Women and Creativity*. Toronto: Women's Press, 2004.

Filippo, Inga. *Dorothy Dix*. Felix G. Woodward Library, Austin Peay State University. 11 August 2003 <http://library.apsu.edu/dix/dix.htm>.

Godard, Barbara. "Ex-centriques, Eccentric, Avant-Garde: Women and Modernism in the Literatures of Canada." Tessera I/*Room of One's Own: A Feminist Journal of Literature and Criticism* 8.4 (January 1984): 57–75.

———. "Transgressions." *Fireweed* 5.6 (1979–80): 120–29.

Heaps, Denise A. "The Inscription of 'Feminine *Jouissance*' in Elizabeth Smart's *By Grand Central Station I Sat Down and Wept*." *Studies in Canadian Literature* 19.1 (1994): 142–55.

Horne, Dee. "Elizabeth Smart's Novel-Journal." *Studies in Canadian Literature* 16.2 (1991): 128–46.

Huyssen, Andreas. *After the Great Divide: Modernism, Mass Culture, Postmodernism*. Bloomington: Indiana UP, 1986.

Johansson, Brigitta. "Deconstructing Smart's *By Grand Central Station I Sat Down and Wept*." Paper delivered at "'Wider Boundaries of Daring': The Modernist Impulse in Canadian Women's Poetry." Conf. held at University of Windsor, Windsor, ON. 27 October 2001.

Kadar, Marlene. "Coming to Terms: Life Writing—From Genre to Critical Practice." *Essays on Life Writing: From Genre to Critical Practice*. Ed. M. Kadar. Toronto: U of Toronto P, 1992. 3–16.

Kristeva, Julia. *Desire in Language: A Semiotic Approach to Literature and Art*. Trans. Thomas Gora, Alice Jardine, and Leon S. Roudiez. New York: Columbia UP, 1980.

Lobdell, David. "Eros in the Age of Anxiety: Elizabeth Smart and Louise Maheux-Forcier." *Essays on Canadian Writing* 40 (Spring 1990): 57–79.

Marlatt, Daphne. "Self-Representation and Fictionalysis." *Collaboration in the Feminine: Writings on Women and Culture from Tessera*. Ed. Barbara Godard. Toronto: Second Story, 1994. 202–6.

———. "Writing Our Way Through the Labyrinth." *Collaboration in the Feminine: Writings on Women and Culture from Tessera*. Ed. Barbara Godard. Toronto: Second Story, 1994. 44–46.

Neuman, Shirley C. *Gertrude Stein: Autobiography and the Problem of Narration*. Victoria: University of Victoria, 1979.

Oliver, Michael Brian. "Elizabeth Smart: Recognition." *Essays in Canadian Writing* 12 (1978): 106–33.

Podnieks, Elizabeth. "'Keep Out / Keep Out / Your Snooting Snout ... ': The Irresistible Journals of Elizabeth Smart." *A/B: Auto/Biography Studies* 11.1 (Spring 1996): 56–81.

Quéma, Anne. "Elizabeth Smart and Cecil Buller: Engendering Experimental Modernism." *The Canadian Modernists Meet*. Ed. Dean Irvine. Ottawa: U of Ottawa P, 2005. 275–303.

Rudy, Susan. "Women, Poetics and Canada before 1960: The Limits of Nationalism and Modernism" Paper delivered at "'Wider Boundaries of Daring': The Modernist Impulse in Canadian Women's Poetry." Conf. held at University of Windsor, Windsor, ON. 27 October 2001.

Sage, Lorna. *Women in the House of Fiction: Post-War Women Novelists*. London: Routledge, 1992.

Sand, Cy-Thea. "The Novels of Elizabeth Smart: Biological Imperialism and the Trap of Language." *Canadian Woman Studies* 5.1 (Fall 1983): 11–14.

Scott, Bonnie Kime. Introduction. *The Gender of Modernism: A Critical Anthology*. Ed. Bonnie Kime Scott. Bloomington: Indiana UP, 1990. 1–18.

———. *Refiguring Modernism*. Bloomington: Indiana UP, 1995.

Smart, Elizabeth. *Autobiographies*. Ed. Christina Burridge. Vancouver: William Hoffer/Tanks, 1987.

———. *By Grand Central Station I Sat Down and Wept*. London: Flamingo, 1992.

———. *In the Meantime*. Ed. Alice Van Wart. Ottawa: Deneau, 1984.

———. *Necessary Secrets*. Ed. Alice Van Wart. Toronto: Deneau, 1988.

———. *On the Side of the Angels*. Ed. Alice Van Wart. London: HarperCollins, 1994.

Smith, A.J.M. "Eclectic Detachment: Aspects of Identity in Canadian Poetry." *Towards a View of Canadian Letters*. Vancouver: U of British Columbia P, 1973. 22–30.

———. "Introduction to *The Book of Canadian Poetry*." *On Poetry and Poets*. Toronto: McClelland and Stewart, 1977. 19–42.

Smyth, Donna. "Gnosis." *Collaboration in the Feminine*. Ed. Barbara Godard. Toronto: Second Story, 1994. 81–87.

Stevens, Peter, ed. *The McGill Movement*. Toronto: Ryerson, 1969.

Sullivan, Rosemary. "Tantalus Love." *Labyrinth of Desire: Women, Passion and Romantic Obsession*. Toronto: HarperFlamingo, 2001. 102–13.

Trehearne, Brian. *Aestheticism and the Canadian Modernists: Aspects of a Poetic Influence*. Kingston: McGill-Queen's UP, 1989.

———. *The Montreal Forties: Modernist Poetry in Transition*. Toronto: U of Toronto P, 1999.

Van Wart, Alice. "*By Grand Central Station I Sat Down and Wept*: The Novel as a Poem." *Studies in Canadian Literature* 11.1 (Spring 1986): 38–51.

———. "'Life out of Art': Elizabeth Smart's Early Journals." *Essays on Life Writing: From Genre to Critical Practice*. Ed. Marlene Kadar. Toronto: U of Toronto P, 1992. 21–27.

———. "Textual Matters." *Necessary Secrets*. Toronto: Deneau, 1988. n.p.

Willmott, Glenn. *Unreal Country: Modernity in the Canadian Novel in English*. Montreal: McGill-Queen's UP, 2002.

Woodcock, George. *George Woodcock's Introduction to Canadian Poetry*. Toronto: ECW, 1993.

Jay Macpherson's Modernism
MIRIAM NICHOLS

With her short rhyming poems, classical and Christian references, and quantitatively modest output, Jay Macpherson has remained at the edges of critical focus among interpreters of Canadian modernism. In look and feel, her work seems traditional rather than modernist, if by the latter we mean reflexivity, formal innovation, and a crisis of faith in master narratives.[1] *The Boatman* (1957) and *Welcoming Disaster* (1974)[2] loosely follow the trajectory of the quest myth—that narrative of narratives—to explore the possibility of a mythopoetic renewal of the Christian humanist vision; yet this project is complicated in the two collections by modernist scepticism and a woman-identified perspective. What marks Macpherson's work as modern is its reflexivity and suspension of origins; what marks the poems as proto-feminist is both a focus on the female content of traditional myths and a duplicity of tone that suggests distance from and dis-identification with the masculinist perspective embedded in these representations of women. Rather than simply dismiss the humanist tradition or assert a feminist revision of it, Macpherson offers a modernist mythopoetics that intricately combines irony and belief.

The central myth of *The Boatman* is the story of Noah. In Macpherson's hands, this is a narrative that works on many levels—cosmic, psychic, social, aesthetic—and therefore serves to reference key issues that arise from the mythopoetic strand of the modern. In the postwar period when the poems were written, poets had already lost the ease of a given habitude to a modern "flood" of social and intellectual changes that included a recent war, emerging social hetereogeneity, and the disenchantments of psychoanalysis, as well as ongoing philosophical and political challenges to the humanist tradition and the claims of reason.[3] Mythopoeisis represents one possible response to the modernist decentring of experience. If what we are and know constitutes a contingent perspective rather than reality as such, then our desire to connect, understand, and assign value to the things of the world may be addressed through the making of new relations rather than a fruitless quest for certitude. Poetic myth-making answers existential alienation and epistemological scepticism—major preoccupations of modernists from Joyce to Eliot to Stein—with art. At the social and psychological levels, however, this business of remaking the cultural imaginary raises some vexed questions that have occupied generations of postmodern and contemporary writers. How, for instance, might the social covenant—the arc (ark) between us—be redesigned in fractured, multi-perspectival societies? How might Othered social subjects (subjects assigned minority status through gender, race, or class) be re-created beyond the binary oppositions that have defined them? Macpherson's "Poor Child," a figure recurrent in various guises throughout the poems, is both an existential and social exile, an everyman or woman looking for a new world after the flood.

In *The Spirit of Solitude* (1982), a critical work on the romantic pastoral, Macpherson writes that the adequate response to exile or compulsory outsider status is inclusion: "The solution comes with the discovery that the alien or hostile is the excluded: that Nature, rather than the poet, is the creative Titan able to embrace all opposites as complements, and that imitation of her is not only the poet's task, but man's escape from solitude and madness" (36). I hear in this comment the plot of Macpherson's own poems: they propose an art that includes the hitherto excluded. The human universe may be renewed, the poems imply, if we relinquish our bad tendency to devalue, repress, or destroy what we deem alien. Both *The Boatman* and *Welcoming Disaster* follow this narrative line. Each presents a dystopic world and a quest for regeneration that takes the poet through psycho-mythical darkness toward new vision. The difference between the two books comes from a shift in emphasis and perspective: *The Boatman* gives us compelling images of the constructive possibilities of poeisis, while *Welcoming Disaster* confronts more directly some of the consequences of the desired inclusivity. A blurring of boundaries, for instance, makes the articulation of personal or cultural identity difficult, if not impossible, and the *Disaster* collection is haunted by the possibility of silence. *The Boatman* takes as a key image the little world of Noah's ark, an image that calls to mind the modernist's well-wrought urn. In *Welcoming Disaster*, the corresponding image is an umbrella, identified in "Umbrella Poem" with the world tree (*Poems Twice Told* [henceforth *PTT*] 90). In hindsight, the difference between the two images suggests the difference between a closed and an open world order, or a closed and an open kind of art. The (modernist) ark, as a metaphor of cultural rescue, has the limits of a closed form. If we think of creation at the level of species life, we can take the ark as encyclopedic, but as soon as we try to read it as a trope of community, we are reminded that it embraces only the exemplary members of each species. The (postmodern) umbrella, in contrast, is apparently open to all comers, but the shelter it offers is fragile and limited—forlornly inadequate to the flood.

In what is still the most extended study of Macpherson to date,[4] Lorraine Weir finds in *The Boatman* a reassertion of community, reading the poem itself as a sacramental site of communion between writer and reader.[5] In *Welcoming Disaster*, however, she sees an underworld of pain, guilt, and gendered silence from which there is no return. Suniti Namjoshi, in contrast, reads *Welcoming Disaster* as ultimately redemptive. W.J. Keith takes up a median position: he finds that *Welcoming Disaster* differs from *The Boatman* in that the former plays out as psychology rather than cosmology, and he associates the losses of *Disaster* with the processes of maturation rather than, as in Weir, the repression of women's experience. In my view, these conflicting readings point to a duplicity in the poems, which are reflexive *and* mythopoetic, centrifugal *and* centripetal, metaphorical *and* metonymical. The difference between the two books is a matter of degree and emphasis rather than of kind: *Welcoming Disaster* moves restlessly between the mythic, psychic, personal, existential, and domestic dimensions of the poet's imagination, and this movement extends the centripetal forces already at work in *The Boatman*. Taken together, the two collections create an intricate dance of possibility and disenchantment. Life persists past the destruction of particular worlds: comic renewal inheres in disaster; disaster lurks in comedy. In *The Spirit of Solitude*, Macpherson writes that the ark as an emblem is a benign version of the idealist's "palace of art," and she distinguishes it from those utopian creations that represent impossible states of perfection, tempting the artist to perversion (Nathaniel Hawthorne's short story "The Birthmark" is one of her examples [*PTT* 179]). The ark represents "the carrying over of existence from one kind of life to the next," she says, and while it is elegaic as the "sign of some overwhelming disaster in the past … it should look also to a new start, being a cradle of life as well as a coffin" (179). Macpherson's writing of the modern is similarly transitional: between the "already" of an older humanist order and the "not yet" of a new world not quite emerged, we are to set sail.

The Boatman

The Boatman is divided into six books or suites, as James Reaney calls them, and published with a seventh titled "Other Poems." In the first three, "Poor Child," "O Earth Return," and "The Plowman in Darkness," Macpherson gives us what she calls, in *The Spirit of Solitude,* "foul-weather" pastoral: pastoral scenes and figures from the postlapsarian world (6). Exile, within this classical–Christian narrative of paradise lost, is a chronic human condition, and this is where Macpherson begins in the "Poor Child" suite. The Child is the "royal goosegirl" of Grimm's tales as well as "Achilles sulking, Odysseus returned, / Philoctetes, Prufrock, and you and you" (*PTT* 12): the exiles are ancient and modern, figures of high myth as well as lowly folktale. What the Child wants is not "childhood's flowers but absolute return," to "swing in dark or water" (12). This longing to assuage the pain of individuation (or spiritual loss, or social alienation) in dissolution haunts the poems as unsayable darkness and silence: the "dark or water," the void that gapes under the ark. However, the poems balance this darkness with the mystic's vision of union with the divine: unknowing and ultimate knowing contrarily address the same condition of alienation. In the esoteric, Neoplatonic branch of the Christian tradition, the mystic accomplishes return through the meditative ingathering of the Many to the One. In the poems, however, *poiesis,* rather than mystical effort, performs a similar task: through art, we renew our vision of the earthly paradise, and we gather the Many into the ark.

Along with the "foul weather" poems that underscore the condition of exile—poems about pestilence, blizzards, ill winds, and the sickness of the earth—the "Poor Child" section includes two poems about art. The first is called "The Third Eye," and it conflates the visionary's eye with that of the artist whose creative "seeing" selects, assembles, and arranges the sensuous continuum into meaningful order:

> Of three eyes, I would still give two for one.
> The third eye clouds: its light is nearly gone.
> The two saw green, saw sky, saw people pass:
> The third eye saw through order like a glass

> To concentrate, refine and rarefy
> And make a Cosmos of miscellany.
> Sight, world and all to save alive that one
> Fading so fast! Ah love, its light is done. (*PTT* 13)

Although Macpherson depicts the eye as dimming here, its constructivist function is clear: the third eye sees relationship and form—"a Cosmos"—where the physical eyes see "miscellany." In "Cold Stone," the poem immediately following, Macpherson elaborates. The speaker lays her face against stone to find a new awareness of flesh, even as the stone begins to take on warmth:

> My returned self in cheek and hands
> Regards as yet not very far
> The leap from shape to living form;
> For where I rested, the stone is warm. (*PTT* 13)

The desired form emerges from the interplay between the "clear will" of the poet and the "unordered rigour" of the stone (*PTT* 13). Order, then, comes from the human reworking of nature into habitude—and habitude is the artist's answer to exile.

In addition to these two poems that address the creative process, the "Poor Child" suite includes a rather more tricky piece called "The Thread." This one consists of three strands. There is the thread of memory, which takes the speaker to "earlier places" at night through dreams; the "thread Night's daughters spin" binds all living things to their mortality; and the "daedal thread" is the one Ariadne gives to Theseus to help him return from the Cretan labyrinth (*PTT* 12). Memory and art-magic (a *techne*) are threads that pull against that other one that ties us to the "snipping Fate." Memory calls up the absent, unravelled self; poetic magic reweaves that life in mnemonic lines and rhythms, enabling the hero to navigate psycho-mythical labyrinths and return with monsters slain and knowledge of the descent intact. Translating Virgil in her book of Greek myths for children, Macpherson writes in the section on Theseus that "The descent to Avernus is easy; but to retrace your way and escape to the upper world, that is the difficulty" (*Four Ages of Man* 93). The poet-hero's task, like that of the mystic, is to make light what was dark: in mythopoetic terms, to draw both inner and outer worlds into the languaged universe; but the triple-ply thread that is supposed to guide also binds the poet to entropy and death—to unknowing—as well as to art-magic. Memory, as well, always cuts two ways: it makes the absent present, but it also presents the mind with absence. In *The Boatman*, the thread ties us to limit as well as possibility, and as we follow it through the different books of the collection, it draws us into a labyrinth rather than out of one.

The second book of *The Boatman*, "O Earth Return," replays the theme of exile in another key with a pantheon of female goddesses and Mothers—Eve, Sibylla, Eurynome, Sheba, Isis, Mary of Egypt, Earth. These mythical women have all been banished or repressed in various ways: Eve is a "lost girl gone under sea" (*PTT* 17), where she remains trapped while Adam wanders in a wasteland. Sibylla is suspended between life and death in her "pendant grave" (*PTT* 17). Eurynome lies "mortal" in the "snake's embrace" (*PTT* 17); Love languishes in Egypt, and Earth is forever separated from her Heavenly mate except in a fantasy realm beyond reason. Meanwhile, a "mystic Swan," cloistered in a "tower of ivory," bends to the "mirrored gaze" (*PTT* 20). In Mallarméan fashion, the swan of poetry regards herself while the female Earth figures suffer various states of insult;[6] yet the series ends with a poem about Time, a "day-labourer" on God's farm set to tend the living creatures, who carries a roosting phoenix on his arm. As the sleeping phoenix rustles her "warm feathers," we sense her keeping alive a creative potential that has fallen asleep in this bad world (*PTT* 20).

At this point, however, Macpherson lets the narrative thread tangle. In the next series, the tone and angle of vision shift. The mythic women of "Earth Return" reappear in a comic mode in "The Plowman in Darkness," no longer victims but comic, self-possessed libertines. Sibylla boasts about tricking a god and makes light of losing her youth (*PTT* 22); Eurynome extols the advantages of marrying snakes and urges the "squeamish" to do the same (*PTT* 22). Mary of Egypt recounts her younger years as a jolly prostitute (*PTT* 23), and a poem called "The Rymer" offers graveyard humour with an image of "Hell's Queen" as a corpse that somehow manages to decompose jauntily (*PTT* 23). Macpherson telescopes the contrast between the female figures in "Earth Return" and "The Plowman" in a final, untitled poem where Philomel, that classic figure of abused femininity, pours out her grief *"in barren waste"* in the first stanza, while her sister *"chatters, gabbles, all the day"* in the second (*PTT* 26; italics in the original).

Given the high seriousness of Macpherson's material, this shift to the comic is shocking. "The Plowman" series is in the middle of the collection, and if title and positioning are indicators, the series should have represented the lowest point in the journey. From one point of view, it does. The merry gabblers of "The Plowman" can be read as air-headed party girls or ladies of the night in a place of spiritual darkness. If we hear them this way, they are close to amoral nature in their sexual delights and therefore halves of a traditional, gendered mind and body opposition. From this perspective, female flesh has to reconnect with male mind, just as "quean Earth and her fancy-fellow Heaven" have to mate in order to renew the world in a place "out of reason's reach" in the "Earth Return" suite (*PTT* 19). From a woman-centred view, however, it is just as plausible to read the comic women as the "earthy" sides of their doubles in "Earth Return," a reading that would imply that the life of the body and senses is a part of what has been repressed or perverted to disastrous effect. Macpherson tells us that the "plowman," stubbing his toe in the dark, is "working up a / Snorting rage" (*PTT* 26), but it is difficult not to speculate that the rage may belong equally to the women of this section. If we compare Macpherson's comic treatment of sexuality with that of T.S. Eliot, for instance, the distinctiveness of "The Plowman" comes into focus. Macpherson summarizes Eliot's position in *Spirit of Solitude* where she writes of *The Waste Land* that "April is the cruelest month because the outward renewal of the earth is a mockery to the man whose state is spiritual death" (6); unlike Eliot, who registers "spiritual death" as sexual disgust (the typist's indifferent coupling with the "young man carbuncular," "Waste Land" 72), Macpherson's comic women suggest that the repression of earthiness is more cause than symptom. The narrative thread of the poems thus can take us in several directions: toward an Eliotian view of sexual perversity and spiritual loss, if we are inclined in that direction, or toward a celebration of female pleasure, precocity, and strength. If we follow this latter strand, then we also confront the possibility of finding ourselves at loose ends—of dis-identifying with the quest narrative of spiritual loss and regeneration, and the gendered dualism of mind and body that it presupposes.

Macpherson replays this theme of gendered oppositions in her fourth series. As if the darkness of "The Plowman" had induced sleep, and sleep dream, the figures of "The Sleepers" are in various states of suspended animation: they sleep, they dream, or they lose themselves in love-madness. This sober sequence is full of disjunction, especially between the sexes. "The Martyrs," for instance, refers to Aristophanes's well-known fable in Plato's *Symposium* of an original human race in which the sexes were joined in one body before they were divinely punished with separation for becoming too powerful: love, says the comic poet, is the desire for one's missing half. In Macpherson's poem, "The sexes waking, now separate and sore, / Enjoy conjunction not feasible before; / But never long enough, never near enough" (*PTT* 30). This pained division recurs in "The Garden of the Sexes," where the male is bound to a tree during the day and the female speaker "goes free" (*PTT* 30): at night, the situation is reversed. These poems underscore the gendered nature of the dualistic relations already at work in the poems between home and exile, health and sickness, earth and sky: binaries characterize the sickness of the waste world. In response, "The Sleepers" series directs us toward the realm of dream and imagination. Merlin holds Arthur and the "dragon crest" safe in his dreams "though [he sleeps] in a witche's arms" (*PTT* 32). Like the phoenix of "Earth Return," the community of the future, the *utopos* of the roundtable, is not dead but dormant. Significantly, the witch—that female feared and vilified historically for her healing arts and midwifery—enfolds and enables the male magus, artist of the public world. Equally suggestive is Macpherson's "caverned woman," inert like stone on the outside but inside alive with vision (*PTT* 33). Like the phoenix, this female figure keeps alive the possibility of a new human universe in the midst of dystopic conditions.

The promise of these first four books finds an answering imagery in the fifth, "The Boatman." The ark series begins with a poem in which the reader is an ark who is urged to "*get his beasts outside him*" so that they can re-enter two by two (*PTT* 37, italics in the original). Cathartic release of the repressed is to be followed by a gathering in. If oppositional relations characterize the modern wasteland, the ark extends its communal welcome to the formerly excluded. The poems that follow bear witness to the transformative powers of the mythopoetic imagination. Under Noah's shaping hand, the ark acquires a voice and begins to speak. It is a mediate and mediating vehicle, a metaphor of metaphor, that rejoins the sensible and intelligible, the tree from which it came and the conscious will of the man—and by extension, all the other binaries. The ark embodies art's measure and it keeps "the black sea"—the unformed, the raw mass—from "gap[ing] sheer" (*PTT* 39). These poems renew the aesthetic promise of "The Third Eye" and "Cold Stone" in suggesting that the human world is constituted by naming a sensual "miscellany" into languaged order and relationship. Deluged by a flood of sensation or confronted by a cosmos in disarray, the artist remakes the world. In "Ark Parting," the ark says to Noah,

> You dreamed it. From my ground
> You raised that flood, these fears.
> The creatures all but drowned
> Fled your well of tears. (*PTT* 40)

The flood is in the eye in this poem: when it recedes, "new-washed eyes" perceive "fresh shores" (*PTT* 40). The angle of vision is all. This "Boatman" section has a denouement in "Leviathan," and "The Anagogic Man." In the former, "Creation shines, as that first day / When God's Leviathan went forth to play" (*PTT* 42). The book ends with Noah as the Anagogic Man, in whose head, as in a golden bubble (the fragility of human constructs), all things are contained.

In a very shrewd and durable comment on *The Boatman*, James Reaney notices that Macpherson's art gives us "things inside other things" (29). He writes of the ark that it is "Leviathan within Leviathan": "it prophesies to Noah that one day he will swallow his own Ark, that is, make mental and controllable what was physical before and not so easily controlled" (33). Reaney sees a cosmos "completely metaphored" as the metapoetic end of the poems (28), although to my reading the artist's ark implies more than a static place of permanent arrival. Rather, it is a site of possibility and of spirit pacified in the thought of the ongoing redemptive labour open to humanity: the effort after an earthly paradise, once again.

This notion that life persists through the disintegration of one mode of the world and the birth of another is not only implied by the imagery of *The Boatman* but is also embedded in the structure of the poems. Formally, *The Boatman* offers three different temporal patterns, only one of which is linear as in the narrative I have been following. The imaginative triumph envisioned in "The Anagogic Man" is already there in "Cold Stone" of the "Poor Child" suite, suggesting that regeneration is immanent in historical processes rather than their end or result. "Poor Child" begins with a poem called "Ordinary People in the Last Days," which not only embeds an end in the beginning of the series, but also draws the apocalyptic moment into everyday life and implies that it is repeatable. In the "last days,"

> My mother was taken up to heaven in a pink cloud,
> My father prophesied,
> The unicorn yielded to my sweetheart,
> The white bull ran away with my sister,
> The dove descended on my brother,
> And a mouse ran away in my wainscot. (*PTT* 11)

The tone of these lines is neither flippant nor elevated: the mundane is not lifted by the eschatological and neither is the eschatological reduced. Rather the two levels of intensity come together in the same place: a world ends; life goes on. Not only does this perspective historicize things as they are and destabilize the metaphysics of origins, but it also implies a certain distance from and dis-identification with the *mundus*—the world—and its traumas. The world we inhabit is not definitive of human possibility, the poem seems to say, but is simply our current container.

This long view of things lets Macpherson engage a very complex sense of time. Her narrative line, for instance, is content as much as form. The quest unfolds within larger, containing temporalities (Reaney's "things inside other things"). "The child is mortal," Macpherson says, but "Poor Child / Creeps through centuries of bone" (*PTT* 12). It is as plausible to read the different sections of *The Boatman* as repetitions of each other as it is to see them as consecutive segments of a narrative because they replay similar material in different tones and at different levels of reference. Existential exile in "Poor Child" returns as gender antagonism and sexual repression in "O Earth Return" and "The Plowman." The ark poems replay "The Third Eye" and "Cold Stone." The "caverned woman" recalls the promise of the phoenix and genders the earlier image. As well, images of destruction, alienation, and disease are interspersed with those of renewal in all the books rather than arranged chronologically. Even in "The Blighted Spring" from "Poor Child," the waste world harbours "green and hopeful nests" of mistletoe (*PTT* 15). Whether the creative or destructive dominates depends on how we view the psycho-cosmic landscape and who traverses it. Do we lament the end of the world with Poor Child? Do we shrink it down in scale to the size of a mouse? Or do we laugh through it all with Macpherson's comic women? If we read the different books as tonal variations of each other, we may see them as manifesting alternating phases of entropy and renewal, one eclipsing the other as in the seasonal cycles: when the Plowman is in darkness, the Boatman is ascendent. However, if we focus even more closely on the poems, we can see that all possibilities are present simultaneously—that like "Ordinary People in the Last Days," last and first are contained in each poem. This spatialized temporality or aeon is immanent in the "dark or water" of "absolute return" (*PTT* 12) and in the black sea that sustains the ark. Typically, Macpherson's temporal containers turn out to be contained, so that we are led from narrative to aeon and then to that point where imagination fails. If we retain Immanuel Kant's faith in the supersensible, this mental process will take us to the sublime. If we do not, we will find ourselves sliding into the vertigo of post-foundational thinking, an endless regress (each container contained) or confronting the un-meaning of sheer matter (the "dark" that holds up the ark).[7]

Tellingly, Macpherson does not end *The Boatman* with "The Anagogic Man." Instead, she offers a much more ambiguous book of riddles in her sixth series, "The Fisherman." So, for instance, "That strong creature from before the Flood, / headless, sightless, without bone or blood" (*PTT* 44) turns out to be a storm; "A living tree that harbours / No singing-birds, no flowers" is coral (*PTT* 45). The Fisher is engaged in the hermeneutical task of deciphering the world, and insofar as he aims to take in the whole of things, he doubles the Anagogic Man who contains all of creation, as well as the Boatman who takes the world in through his ark/art and the Plowman who remakes the earth to his measure in furrows and fields—or would do if he were not in the dark. However, the Fisher's ability to contain is more precarious than that of the others. If it is not grounded, the practice of hermeneutics implies endless elaboration, rather than a narrative passage from one state to another or the rhythm of seasonal cycles. The title poem of the series brings out the difference between Fisher and Boatman in a mythic history of the world:

> The world was first a private park
> Until the angel, after dark,
> Scattered afar to wests and easts
> The lovers and the friendly beasts.
>
> And later still a home-made boat
> Contained Creation set afloat,
> No rift nor leak that might betray
> The creatures to a hostile day.
>
> But now beside the midnight lake
> One single fisher sits awake
> And casts and fights and hauls to land
> A myriad forms upon the sand. (*PTT* 49)

As I have suggested, the boat without "rift or leak" suggests a closed cosmos—a well-wrought urn. The "fisher of the fallen mind," however, is outside and open to whatever comes. He cannot, for instance, line his creatures up two by two or write a human universe in the furrows of the earth. His task is fraught with contingency because he must work with the fluid and the hidden, rather than the substantive, and without the mediation of a closed art form. Even though he manages to consume his catch—"sucks up / The lake and all that therein is / To slake that hungry gut of his"—he is himself in the end consumed. In the last lines of the poem, "God the Lord with patient grin / Lets down his hook and hoicks him in" (*PTT* 49). "Things inside other things" brings us finally to a container we cannot contain.

As I read "The Fisherman," the poem is a fable about our inability to establish foundations and thus a bold rewriting of the Fisher King story. In the grail romances, the knight who seeks the grail must ask the right question if the ailing Fisher King is to be healed of his wound, the wasteland regenerated, and the knight to experience the redemptive vision of the Grail.[8] The question is to take the form of a "what is it?": "What is the Holy Grail?" If the knight knows to ask, he frees the waters that will bring fertility to the wasteland. Macpherson's riddles also take the form of the "what is it" question, but in her version the results differ. Not only does a freeing of the waters seem like irony in a collection of poems that takes the flood as a key metaphor, but also the "myriad forms" the Fisher catches are more miscellany than cosmos. In fact, the various items riddled present the reader with a "myriad" (a storm, a mermaid, coral, a whale, the sun and moon), while the riddles themselves consist of little narratives that render these items more complex. Names, in other words, spill into a metonymic content that takes us back into the labyrinth of narratives and cycles that compose the historical world. Whatever contains that world is to us as the Fisher is to the fish, a denizen of another element that we cannot inhabit. For the "fisher of the fallen mind" there is blind faith in "God the Lord," or there is the world and its stories. The hermeneutical circle can elaborate a world into languaged being but can neither anchor it in certitude nor secure a cosmos against miscellany, metaphor against metonymy. This can be either a joyous proposition or a tragic one, depending on whether we embrace process and relativity as providing aspects of life or lament our loss of solid ground.

Welcoming Disaster

The tonal ambivalence of "welcoming" an event that one nonetheless calls a disaster characterizes the poems of Macpherson's 1974 collection. Loss of certitude exposes the fragility of our cultural habitude, and the invocation poems in the first section of the *Welcoming Disaster* collection show us this side of the modern experience. In "Lost Books and Dead Letters," the poet asks not to be "put to silence" (*PTT* 62), but it is not only the poet who is personally menaced, or menaced as a female writer: whole worlds fall silent in these opening poems. "The Oracle Declines" recalls the ruin of the Delphic oracle with the coming of Christianity, and the following poem, "'Still Waiting for the Spark from Heaven'" extends that entropy to the Christian world: the "Magian star" brings "news of nothingness, of night, / If any word at all" (*PTT* 64). In this poem, the poet turns to the muse because "Familiar oracles are dumb," but "No spark descends, no waters rise" (*PTT* 64). Memory is likened to a half-recovered Eurydice, veiled and silent, which puts the poet in the tragic position of the Orphic singer who cannot bring the lost Other (the self, the beloved, the world) into the light and life of poetic song. In the last poem of this first section, "Conjuring the Dead," the dead have no message and the living are too "dead-engrossed" to communicate. The would-be poet-magus is left "Stupid—cumbering the ground" (*PTT* 66), alone and without kin or commons, conjuring up dead and living souls who cannot, or will not, hear. In this keynote series of invocations, the elegaic dominates, implying failed communication and loss of world.

After the disastrous beginning, however, the plot of the collection repeats the descent and return of *The Boatman*. Like the earlier poems, *Welcoming Disaster* is divided into titled series: "Invocations," "The Way Down," "The Dark Side," "Recognitions," "Shadows Flee," and "Epilogue." In "The Way Down," as might be expected from the title, the poet moves through mythopsychic spaces of pain and loss, and while some of the old denizens of the underworld are there in the creator-destroyer goddesses—Inanna, Ereshkigal, Geshtinanna, Hecate—there is an emphasis on the psychological rather than the mythic: "First loves and oldest ... / Greed, pride and envy" (*PTT* 76). "The Dark Side" then takes the poet to the lowest point in the descent, down to a cellar where she finds her betrayed mother, sister, and brother, and below that, to the bottom of a well where she sees her own image "Lying with all that's lost" (*PTT* 83). Structurally "The Well" is the turning point: the poet sees Orion reflected in the well and the winter constellations rising like a stair. Book 4, "Recognitions," offers scenes that replay the theme of the Boatman: regeneration through inclusivity. In "Gathering In," the poet accepts all the creatures of her underworld—the "hurtful baby," the mermaid, the Medusa—including her own psychic monsters:

> Naked spectres, come for shrouding,
> Those I failed and snubbed and crossed,
> In the deadly waters crowding:
> Angel, let not one be lost. (*PTT* 89)

Again, the poetic quest brings the poet to face the alien and hostile. The fifth sequence of poems, "Shadows Flee," then gives us an image of cosmos that corresponds to and counters that of the ark. A world-tree, graphically represented as an umbrella in the line-drawing[9] that accompanies the poem, is "Rooftree—wordtree—/ space—time—friend—" (*PTT* 90), and it appears after the poet has accepted her "share in perdition" (*PTT* 76). This message is underscored by the graphic depiction of the symbols for male and female followed by the yin–yang emblem, all of them under the umbrella.

The possibility of a redemptive mythopoetic practice is thus immanent in pieces like "Umbrella Poem," just as alienation is ever-present in the more optative *Boatman*, but the tone of *Welcoming Disaster* is darker, and the collection includes poems that hint of intimate betrayals and social wrongs. The shift of attention from the "mythic, 'archetypal' ... hermetic, unifying, 'impersonal'" in *The Boatman*, to the "anthropological and psychological" in *Welcoming Disaster* (Keith 32) has some strong consequences. At the existential level, the human universe may be gathered under the common umbrella of species life, but if we turn from this high level of generality to particular historical worlds and social orders, the shareable becomes much harder to define, as contemporary writers have demonstrated.[10] What it means to cut loose from rationalist or metaphysical rubrics has occupied generations of writers throughout the modern and postmodern eras. The *shock* of that cut, however, is a distinctively modernist experience, and we can feel it in *Welcoming Disaster*. The collection begins to play out the implications of *The Boatman* at a level that is more often mundane than mythical and therefore closer to lived experience, closer to the bone.

The vulnerability of individuals to the psychic and social effects of modernity is poignantly illustrated in *Welcoming Disaster* in the Woolworth's teddy bear who guides the poet to the underworld and in the world-tree become umbrella. In "After the Explosion," the poet is "Back to the basics—sobbing in ... bed, and / Clutching [her] dolly" (*PTT* 80). Ted substitutes for Dumuzi, beloved of the goddess Inanna, just as the umbrella substitutes for the cosmos of the ark, but as substitutes, these frail technologies do little to assuage the pain of psychic individuation or social fragmentation. Throughout the collection, Ted fills in for "Him not there," but of course the absence is irreparable as we see finally in "Recognitions," where it is identified as an existential condition: "the primal wrong, / That rift in Being, Me" (*PTT* 87). As comforts—fragments shored against the ruins, to think of Eliot again ("Wasteland" 43)—a stuffed bear and an umbrella emphasize the smallness of the individual and the childishness of art in relation to the "disaster," rather than the heroism of the artist who, like Noah, sets out to save the world. Under the umbrella, there is, perhaps, some shelter, as indeed there may be comfort for the pain of childhood's losses in a teddy bear, but it is a chilly kind of comfort. On the one hand, the sought-after inclusivity of *The Boatman*'s artist requires a relaxing of boundaries, but on the other, a relaxing of boundaries implies the flooding out of habitude; and when the ground of the human becomes fluid, we literally do not know where we stand.

From the beginning of *Disaster*, this fluidity manifests as an instability of perspective. In "House Lights" from the series "Invocations," the poet places herself outside a lit house on a dark street as one of a "silent crowd" drawn by the light (*PTT* 65). In the next stanza, however, she imagines a "you" inside the house looking out and asks whether the second person might see the crowd or only his or her "own veiled look" (65). This question about whether the view would shift radically with the position of the seer and whether it would be reflexive or not suggests that neither inside nor outside (subjective nor objective) can be privileged. In the earlier collection, we have "things inside other things," but as micro- to macrocosm. In a conventionally "metaphored world," the two terms of the metaphor confirm resemblance over difference and, like John Donne's famous compass, come back home;[11] but as these poems illustrate, the modern is about losing the harmony of analogy, and a subsequent dispersal of metaphor into metonymy, resemblance into difference, a cosmos into miscellany. Ted-the-substitute, who is supposed to guide the poet between the in and out, the up and down of things, is an utter failure as a means of passage to the metaphored world. In "The Way Down," the poet buries Ted in a compost heap, committing him and herself to earth and presumably to the pastoral hope of regeneration. Natural cycles "should" be emblems of spiritual renewal; but as Weir has noticed, Ted is not *like* the natural world at all. He is, in fact, most unlike the fertility god for whom he substitutes (*Jay Macpherson* 27). Buried in "The Way Down," Ted pops up again in "Recognitions," where we discover he is "an alien in the earth" and cannot rot (*PTT* 87). When we last see him in the "Epilogue," he is worn and blank, as if his function as an emblem, along with his artificial fur, has simply gotten old. Unlike the ark, Ted is not a rich emblem of the mythopoetic. Commenting on D.C. Scott's "The Piper of Arll" in *Spirit of Solitude*, Macpherson says that the dream of art is to combine the durability of artifice with the fecundity of nature. This is what Scott imagines when he has the fairy ship, beloved of the Piper, sprouting Dionysian vines after it has been transformed into precious metals and gems ("Piper" 383–84). Ted, in comparison, is a parody.

If we turn from Ted to the female figures of *Welcoming Disaster*, the myths of betrayal and rivalry that attach to Inanna, Ereshkigal, and Geshtinanna emphasize divisiveness rather than harmony or continuity. Nature, as well, is "false mother" in "The Way Down," in a descent that ultimately leads to the painful image of the "maimed child, barbed mother" of "What Falada Said" (*PTT* 91). In the damaged child, an image Macpherson retains right into the "Epilogue" where the "maimed baby" shows through the bare patches on Ted, regeneration is crippled, as in the "blighted spring" of *The Boatman*. The baby, of course, is another version of Poor Child, returned on the psychic plane, while the "barbed mother" suggests the Medusa or destroyer face of the archetypal goddess. In a counter-image to the fierce mother, Macpherson also gives us a very placid-looking feeder-devourer that partially explicates her falsity. The drawing that accompanies "Palladia and Others" shows two serpents locked in a perfect circle, but the serpents have their eyes closed, indicating the suspension of conscious awareness (*PTT* 78). The analogy between human and non-human life again appears to be broken as it is in Ted: species life is not *like* the individuated life of the mind and spirit. Species live in cyclical time, individuals in linear narratives. Hence nature is "false mother" (*PTT* 79). What the triple goddess destroys at the level of the individual she can restore to the species; but in the psychic and social world, this is small comfort. In "Transformations," Macpherson evokes the great arc of the sky—the umbrella in its cosmic dimensions—when she has Ted turn into a constellation[12] ("See through leaves the heavens, where / Whirls in play a smallish Bear" [*PTT* 89]); but the celestial arc under which we all stand is very far away from the foul weather she conjures up for us here on earth.

The poem "Playing," from the sequence "Shadows Flee," brings home the intellectual and emotional impasses that come about when the metaphored world begins to come apart and analogies between the existential and social fail. Here, the poet imagines being stuck in a board game in which she has not moved from "Square One." "Square Two" in fact, "Never got marked on this / Board, and you knew—" (*PTT* 94). "Playing" is about movement in stasis. What the poet has been able to generate with the help of Ted are a number of substitutions and displacements, a "play" that does not go anywhere: underworld turns into psychic cellar, god into doll, creators into destroyers. Although this repetitive play is also the stuff of *The Boatman*, there the "things inside other things" emphasize cosmic harmony, and as long as we stay at the level of the existent, in the ark or golden bubble of Noah's anagogical head, we have an *imago mundi*, cunningly made. When we descend to the social and psychic, however, the bubble bursts into the half-arc of the umbrella and the "things" come loose.

Although I have emphasized the strong skeptical component of *Welcoming Disaster* to show the difference between this later collection and *The Boatman*, I do not think that it precludes the possibility of a mythopoetic practice. In "Old Age of the Teddy Bear" and "The End," both from "Epilogue," the poet tells us that Ted has run his course as a poetic device. "Magic like that runs out" (*PTT* 95), she says, but in the same poem she is told by her gods that the bear was never meant to be kept (95). *Welcoming Disaster*, like *The Boatman*, speaks of worlds ending and cultural forms breaking apart under the pressure of a hitherto alien content that includes not only the perennial demons of the psyche ("greed, pride and envy"), but also the return of a repressed and gendered Other. "Gathering In" urges the Angel, a creature usually neuter or male in literary tradition, to include "the mermaid, gaunt and bony." She is, the poet says, "Sister to Medusa stony—/ Now's the chance to do her right" (*PTT* 89), but the endings that this new inclusivity sets in motion take place within the larger spatialized temporality of the poems. Nothing in *Welcoming Disaster* implies full identification with any one of the narratives, and in poems like "Playing," there is that same sense of the aeon that lets Macpherson put her apocalypse first in *The Boatman*. Within the aeon, the play of forms and stories elaborates a space through repetition and substitution rather than narrative movement, and this leaves us with the possibility of life after death, so to speak, right here and now in the mundane. In a rhymed "Notes and Acknowledgements" on the last page of *Poems Twice Told*, Macpherson writes, "Major debts thus once more noted, / Muse, let's jump: our boat's re-floated" (96). The boat of the human universe floats on, and we can begin again, even if the poet herself bails. To my ear, both collections emphasize the need for new cultural narratives adequate to the reach for newness initiated in *The Boatman*, and not an ironic dismissal of poetic myth-making. In hindsight, this is to name the task that feminist writers have taken up in the three decades since *Welcoming Disaster* was published.

Weir has argued that Macpherson's poems are marked by gender in two ways: through the decentring of public meaning, and in the half-saying of women's experience.[13] Certainly there is a great welcoming of female energy in the "two-natured mothers" (*PTT* 89) of myth and legend, the creator-destroyer goddesses. Moreover, Macpherson's "gathering in" of these female figures in their abject, comic, and fierce aspects anticipates the work of feminist revisionists such as Annis Pratt. Pratt argues that the destroyer faces of archetypal female figures represent women's strength depicted from a fearful, masculinist perspective. These Medusa figures, Pratt says, are to be welcomed rather than shunned, as ways into female empowerment.[14] In their comic and fierce modes, the banished females of Macpherson's poems are potentially retrieved: certainly they are welcomed. As well, it is possible to perceive a "half-saying" of women's historical experience thinly veiled in these mythical figures: Sibylla caged, Eurynome subjected to the snake's embrace, Psyche abandoned. In the "Other Poems" that accompany *The Boatman* is a painful image of female abjection and entrapment: "A small damp female who applies / Nose, nipples, tummy flat against the glass / And weeps, and howls, and cries" (*PTT* 56). Despite the woman-oriented perspective, however, Macpherson's material remains canonical. Her women are victims, mothers, children, goddesses, or happy hookers, and when they are not abject or fierce, they win what pleasure and position they may through trickery or seduction, the traditional "feminine" weapons of the powerless. As well, Macpherson's attitude toward her strong comic figures is equivocal. "Hail Wedded Love" from *The Boatman*, a poem about the "joys of a harlot's wedding" concludes our glimpse of what sounds like a rollicking good time with these sober lines:

> Well, delight attend their pillow!
> And I'll go seek a bending willow
> To hang my silent harp upon
> Beside the river of Babylon. (24)

In my view, the more radical feminist promise of Macpherson's work comes in the suggestive imagery and treatment of the temporalities. Wasteland, flood, ark, umbrella, and teddy bear point to the malaise of a culture that needs to face what it has repressed and so reinvent itself. This has long been the focus of feminists such as Nicole Brossard or Daphne Marlatt in Canada, as well as that of theorists like Luce Irigaray, Hélène Cixous, and Julia Kristeva in France. All of these women have taken up the "flood" in various ways, reworking the metaphysics of substance into a language of the fluid, the in-between, the matrix, the preverbal, and the semiotic. In particular, Macpherson's treatment of time seems to anticipate Kristeva's discussion of cyclical and monumental temporality in relation to female subjectivity. Kristeva describes monumental time as "the aporia of the *chora*, matrix space, nourishing, unnameable, anterior to the One, to God and, consequently, defying metaphysics" (191). In Macpherson, there is the "dark or water" of "absolute return" (*PTT* 12) and the witch's arms, cradling the maker of kingdoms.

As suggestive as it is, however, Macpherson's vocabulary is not Kristeva's or Irigaray's or anyone else's, nor can I see any self-aware, concerted effort to defy metaphysics in the poems. Macpherson's "Fisherman" still leaves the door open a crack to faith in "God the Lord," even though it must be blind and therefore severed from the rational. In a poem called "The End," Ted has become dumb as his stuffing, and the silence that threatens the poet in "Invocations" finally arrives. This turning of the trope to materiality, this tumbling out of cosmos, brings us to the very edge of articulation. This is where the hard-headedness of Macpherson shows, her willingness to face a blank without trying to fill it in. It is also where later feminists have begun to reimagine the world again. To read Macpherson anachronistically through their work is, in my view, to go too far, to read beyond what the poems can sustain; yet it is clear that in a feminist context, as well as a modernist one, the ark is womb and tomb. In "The Old Age of the Teddy-Bear" from the "Epilogue" poems, the poet sees a "nameless maimed baby" peering out from the bare patches of the Ted:

> Something in both of us
> never got born:
> too late to hack it out,
> or to unlearn
> needed, familiar pain.
> Come, little thorn. (*PTT* 93)

As is the case so often with Macpherson, the lines are deceptively simple. What "never got born" is a present absence in these poems, palpable as pain—"maimed baby, barbed mother"—and waiting.

Notes

1. My characterization of modernism in this paper is meant to be proximate to that of Northrop Frye in "Improved Binoculars" (1967). Frye was Macpherson's colleague at the University of Toronto, an acknowledged mentor, and a consultant on the arrangement of the poems.
2. The publishing history of Macpherson's collections is as follows. *O Earth Return*, now reprinted as a section in *The Boatman*, first appeared in 1954. *The Boatman* followed from Oxford University Press in 1957, and won the Governor General's Award for poetry in 1958. *Welcoming Disaster* was first released privately by Saannes Publishing in 1974. Both collections were republished by Oxford in 1981 as *Poems Twice Told*. This later collection includes a revised edition (1968) of *The Boatman*. *Poems Twice Told* is the most readily available text and my source for all quotations from Macpherson's poetry in this commentary.
3. I have in mind the major architects of modernism: Sigmund Freud, Carl Jung, Friedrich Nietzsche, Martin Heidegger and the existential philosophers, and Karl Marx. These thinkers challenge the universality of reason and the centrality of the individual will in the shaping of the life world. As well, feminist writers such as Simone de Beauvoir, Virginia Woolf, Gertrude Stein, and Djuna Barnes undermine the neutrality of the male voice as they begin to self-consciously gender the modern experience.
4. Macpherson has not received any recent rereadings. Although she is included in Harold Bloom's collection of 2002, *American and Canadian Women Poets, 1930–Present*, she is represented there by two brief reviews reprinted from much earlier sources, one excerpted from Northrop Frye's review of recent poetry publications in the *University of Toronto Quarterly* (1958) and another from Margaret Atwood's *Second Words* (1982). Macpherson does not appear in Dean Irvine's edited collection, *The Canadian Modernists Meet* (2005).
5. According to Weir, "Reading, then, is a process of conversion for Macpherson in *The Boatman*, and the poem is an image and expression of the sacramental community—not a static artefact but a process of interaction, sharing, and exchange between poet and reader" (*Jay Macpherson* 16).
6. Reading Macpherson's "The Swan" through Mallarmé's "Le vierge, le vivace et le bel" leads me to draw out the reflexivity of her image in the lines of "The Swan," "The tower of ivory sways, / Gaze bends to mirrored gaze" (*PTT* 20). Mallarmé's swan, an ancient and disdainful beauty, regards itself in a frozen lake, "le transparent glacier" (44), akin to Macpherson's mirror. Mallarmé's poem asks if the beautiful today will shatter the frozen lake in which "un cynge d'autrefois" (44) is caught and doomed because it has not sung of life. The poet would be nothing, would disappear into his language, if he did not keep looking in the mirror. Overcoming the metaphysical is connected here to the shock of reflexivity.
7. Kant argues that we experience the sublime when we form a concept of the infinite but cannot create a corresponding mental image of it. By definition, the infinite is without limit and therefore without form. For Kant, this experience suggests the

superiority of the human mind over nature; in its ability to conceive of the infinite, the mind produces something that is nowhere to be found in nature. The sublime allows us an intuitive glimpse into the realm of the divine or "supersensible." See Book II, "Analytic of the Sublime," in *The Critique of Judgement* (90–203).

8   I refer to Jessie Weston's reading of the Grail legends in *From Ritual to Romance*, a source readily available to Macpherson.

9   On the drawings and their referencing of emblem books, see Weir in *Jay Macpherson and Her Works* (17–25).

10 Consider Homi Bhabha's argument in *The Location of Culture* against what Bhabha sees as the limits of liberal pluralism, such as that proposed in the political philosophies of Hannah Arendt and Richard Rorty after her. Liberalism, he says, assumes as common ground for recognition and inclusion of the Other "the consensual overlapping of 'final vocabularies' that allow imaginative identification with the other so long as certain words—'kindness, decency, dignity'—are held in common" (192). The subaltern, however, dislocates and reinscribes the terms of public discourse (192–97); he or she refuses recognition and refuses to recognize an unacknowledged demand for homogeneity embedded in rationalist ideas of the common. I do not mean to debate this complex argument here, but simply to point to one of the better known discussions of inclusivity as a social idea.

11 I refer to Donne's metaphor of the compass in "A Valediction: Forbidding Mourning." On taking leave of his beloved, the poet compares their two souls to the legs of a compass joined in movement.

12 As a constellation, Ted is both very far away and near since Macpherson puts the constellation "Bright, immortal, close and dear / As the eye's crystalline sphere" (*PTT* 89); but if the constellation is *in* the eye, then the point of view will determine who stands under this sky, who lives in this particular world. In *Boatman*, the ark tells Noah that the flood was *in* his eye: now the poet-artist has to see the consequences of that condition. The poem "Transformation" comes in the series called "Recognitions."

13 On "half-saying" see Weir in "Toward a Feminist Hermeneutics" (61).

14 See Pratt in *Dancing with Goddesses: Archetypes, Poetry and Empowerment*, particularly part 1, on Medusa.

Works Cited

Atwood, Margaret. "Jay Macpherson: *Poems Twice Told*." *Second Words: Selected Critical Prose*. Toronto: Anansi / Boston: Beacon, 1982. 407–11. Rpt. in Bloom 175–78.

Bhabha, Homi. *The Location of Culture*. London: Routledge, 1994.

Bloom, Harold, ed. *American and Canadian Women Poets, 1930–Present*. Philadelphia: Chelsea House, 2002.

Donne, John. *The Selected Poetry of Donne*. Ed. Marius Bewley. New York, London, Scarborough: New American Library, 1979.

Eliot, T.S. *The Waste Land and Other Poems*. 1940. London: Faber and Faber, 1983.

Frye, Northrop. "Improved Binoculars." *The Modern Century: The Whidden Lectures, 1967*. Toronto: Oxford UP, 1967. 50–86.

———. "Letters in Canada 1957: Poetry." *University of Toronto Quarterly* 27.4 (July 1958): 434–50; Rpt. as "Jay Macpherson: Poetry in Canada, 1957," in Bloom 169–74.
Irvine, Dean, ed. *The Canadian Modernists Meet.* Ottawa: U of Ottawa P, 2005.
Kant, Immanuel. *The Critique of Judgement.* Trans. James Creed Meredith. 1952. Oxford: Claredon Press, 1989.
Keith, W.J. "Jay Macpherson's *Welcoming Disaster*: A Reconsideration." *Canadian Poetry* 36 (Spring/Summer 1995): 32–43.
Kristeva, Julia. "Women's Time." Trans. Alice Jardine and Harry Blake. *The Kristeva Reader.* Ed. Toril Moi. New York: Columbia UP, 1986. 187–213.
Macpherson, Jay. *Four Ages of Man: The Classical Myths.* Toronto: Macmillan, 1962.
———. *Poems Twice Told:* The Boatman *and* Welcoming Disaster. Toronto: Oxford UP, 1981.
———. *The Spirit of Solitude: Conventions and Continuities in Late Romance.* London: Yale UP, 1982.
Mallarmé, Stéphane. "Le vierge, le vivace et le bel aujourd'hui …" / "Will New and Alive the Beautiful Today …" Trans. Patricia Terry and Maurice Z. Shroder. *Selected Poetry and Prose.* Ed. Mary Ann Caws. New York: New Directions, 1982. 44–47.
Namjoshi, Suniti. "In the Whale's Belly: Jay Macpherson's Poetry." *Canadian Literature* 79 (1978): 54–59.
Pratt, Annis. *Dancing with Goddesses: Archetypes, Poetry and Empowerment.* Bloomington: Indiana UP, 1994.
Reaney, James. "The Third Eye: Jay Macpherson's *The Boatman*." *Canadian Literature* 3 (1960): 23–34.
Scott, Duncan Campbell. "The Piper of Arll." *Literature in Canada.* Vol. 1. Ed. Douglas Daymond and Leslie Monkman. Toronto: Gage Publishing, 1978. 379–84.
Weir, Lorraine. *Jay Macpherson and Her Works.* Toronto: ECW, 1989.
———. "Toward a Feminist Hermeneutics: Jay Macpherson's *Welcoming Disaster.*" *Gynocritics/Gynocritiques: Feminist Approaches to the Writing of Canadian and Quebec Women.* Ed. Barbara Godard. Toronto: ECW, 1985. 59–70.
Weston, Jessie L. *From Ritual to Romance.* New York: Doubleday, 1957.

Word, I, and Other in Margaret Avison's Poetry

KATHERINE QUINSEY

> We can see here that whole notion that knowledge is always beginning anew, that we exist not in a state of knowing but in a state of not knowing, that we are constantly being born again into the world not knowing ... the title here ... points to knowledge as "found," not possessed. (bp Nichol, "Sketching" 113)

In the light of her winning the 2003 Griffin Prize for her collection *Concrete and Wild Carrot*, it is hard to remember that Margaret Avison started writing in the 1930s, contemporary with Auden, and that her early poetics were formulated in reviewing A.M. Klein, Dorothy Livesay, and Edith Sitwell in the 1940s. Avison's modernist poetic roots are deep, and the influence of T.S. Eliot, Ezra Pound, and especially of Gerard Manley Hopkins have long been noted in her work.[1] Avison's work embodies many central principles of poetic modernism: a revisionary focus on intense perceptive experience; aesthetic economy, challenging conventional linguistic expression; and the articulation, particularly in her early work, of human alienation and fragmented subjectivity. Her work, however, spans the modernist–postmodernist trajectory, through an art that pushes language to its limits and beyond, in an encompassing vision that rejects the centrality of human ways of knowing, inverts hierarchies of language, and breaks open conventional definitions of self and Other.[2]

Avison has a place in this volume as one of Canada's supreme poets, one who has distinctively widened the boundaries of Canadian women's poetry. More deeply, Avison's work not only widens but crosses, transcends, and blurs boundaries, both in its nature and in its major themes: boundaries between art and life, mind and body, subject and object, self and Other; between categories of society, and categories of being. Although her work cannot be said to engage issues of gender overtly, in some ways she anticipates the major theoretical concerns of recent gender and postcolonial studies, rejecting the centrality of traditional human ways of knowing, and privileging Otherness. More specifically, in her free play with language, in her understanding of the relation of language and self and body, in her intensity of detail and experience, and in her challenge to logocentric hierarchies of language and of being, her work can be said to evoke some core ideas of feminist theory. Particularly in her later writing, Avison redefines notions of the self–Other dynamic and the boundaries of self-identity, and privileges alterity across unusual categories.[3] Her challenge to assumptions of universality broadens the feminist context to a human, cosmic one, transcending boundaries not only between human cultural constructs but also between categories of being, between the inmost self and the uttermost Other. In her work, an urgent sense of social and environmental justice coincides with a radical faith in an encompassing, immanent, and transcendent Other who is also Self; it is this faith that underlies and empowers her poetic vision, with its challenge to the norms and hierarchies of conventional ways of knowing.

Any discussion of these issues in Avison must begin with her central concept of eye and I: the identification of seeing with being in her well-known image of the "optic heart," the bursting of generally accepted boundaries and frameworks of perception, and "the imagination's re-creation of the world of experience" (Redekop, *Margaret Avison* 3). In "Snow," she writes, "Nobody stuffs the world in at your eyes. / The optic heart must venture: a jail-break / and re-creation" (*Always Now* 1.69). The optic heart unites sense (eye) and inner being (heart) in a multi-dimensional, imaginative vision that breaks through conventional structures of perception and stretches/blurs/transcends the boundaries of sense perception. Seeing is linked to inner identity, being done by the "I" behind the eye.[4] Such seeing is a willed activity requiring conscious effort: "Nobody stuffs the world in at your eyes." Only you can do your seeing. Paradoxically, however, in order to see for yourself, you must venture both out of a self-centred point of view and out of the framework of things as seen "for" you by conventional boundaries and angles of perception, space–time co-ordination, categories of visual objects, and the like.

This is the jailbreak suggested in such early poems as "Geometaphysical" and "Perspective," and borne out in the surrealism of *Winter Sun* poems like "Snow" and "Jonathan, O Jonathan" (*Always Now* 1.69, 72).

The process questions the basis for Enlightenment modernity, or post-Renaissance Western subjectivity, that is, the link between individual perception and identity.[5] Avison's altered perception challenges the most basic assumptions of this world view and thus is fraught with primal fear, a fear that takes two forms: the fear of dissolution in leaving the security, however confining, of a self-defined world; and the paradoxical fear of being entombed in the self, unable either to absorb or to communicate the changed vision. This apprehension appears in the whirlpool of "The Swimmer's Moment" and in the poet of "Chronic," sequestered in her house made of old newspapers, "failing ... In credence of reality as others / Must know it" (*Always Now* 1.89, 60).

In the larger pattern of Avison's poetry, the fear of dissolution blends into an affirmation of re-creation.[6] The jailbreak becomes Avison's version of the Gospel paradox that one must lose one's life in order to find it. In order to be re-created, the seer must abandon self-definition and self-enclosure to be drawn out of the self, both into the world she perceives and into the source of that world's light—a process vividly described in "Psalm 19," where "fear" is to

> know longing for clear
> sunlight, to the last ribcorner
> and capillary—and wonder
> if, so known, a sighing-
> over-the-marshlands me
> might all evaporate, wisp away. (*Always Now* 1.162)

That fear proves instead the source of life, of re-creation "green / with life ... and thus, trusted to fire, drawn / towards an enduring sun."[7] Frequently, in Avison's later poetry, such as "March Morning," perception becomes an encounter, in which seer and thing seen may change places, or the boundaries between perceiver and perceived may blur; the eye participates in what it sees, and all the being is involved in the act:

> My heart branches,
> swells into bud and spray:
> heart-break. (*sunblue* 25)

Avison's poetry thus fundamentally challenges the conventional hierarchy between seer and thing seen, subject and object. For Avison, the ultimate Object of knowing is also the primary Subject, a transcendent Other who both encompasses and permeates the self, and, with the self, the creation in all its variety, breaking down divisions between self and Other, self and others.

In her earlier work, Avison's recurrent trope of discovery (astronomy and New World exploration, symbols for rapidly expanding frameworks of perception), which is her metaphoric critique of self-centred perception, interestingly anticipates the current re-examination of Western assumptions of the centrality and rights of the subject. One well-known example is her brilliant mocking of the assumption of the self at the centre, through the artifice of the vanishing point in classical painting, in the early poem "Perspective."[8] The same humanist assumptions of centrality are also queried in "Dispersed Titles," where the speaker asks a rhetorical question,

> Are they all only in
> those other hieroglyphs
> of the created, solitary brain?
> borne here in a man-toy?"[9]

She answers a few lines later with the declaration that the substance of history, human experience, cannot be contained in the individual, singular perception, in a mixing of metaphors that contrast essence and emptiness: "No pith of history will / be cratered in one skull" (*Always Now* 1.56).[10]

In Avison's later work, the vertiginous freeing of perception and the resultant act of discovery invert the power dynamic normally associated with the act of exploration and knowing. As suggested in the epigraph to this essay, for Avison knowledge is not something to be acquired and possessed; it is not an invasive act that objectifies what it thinks it knows (but thus does not know at all). Rather, knowledge is a "found" experience, an act of celebration and openness, a changing of the self. One knows, and is known in the process. The Discovered is much larger than the process of discovery, changing the one who discovers. In the recent poem "Prospecting," where the image of mining and exploration is applied to all human enquiry, experience, history, and the cosmos itself, at its heart (the "node") the process of discovery itself translates into the One discovered:

> For at the node
> all energies become
> that unrewarded effortless and
> ruthless kindness,
> Person. (*Concrete and Wild Carrot* 53)[11]

Avison's work also challenges the boundaries of the self, redefining the category of "subject" in all its senses. As indicated earlier, the feared dissolution of the perceiving self in "Psalm 19" becomes resolved as the act is not one of knowing a subject (object) but being known by an Other who is not object but Subject.

Characteristically, Avison's poetry plays with pronouns and shifts point of view, continually blurring the relationship between first and second, first and third person; a typical example occurs in the concluding poem of *Concrete and Wild Carrot*, which begins with an imperative addressed "To myself everywhere," blurring distinctions between the subjects and objects of global politics. A similar blurring occurs in the earlier poem "SKETCH: End of a day: Or, I as a blurry" (*sunblue* 19); as Nichol points out, the title is *not* an abbreviation of the first line of the poem ("I as a blurry groundhog bundling home"). Rather, the first line deliberately alters the meaning: "'I' is a concept not in focus, or perhaps composed of multiple elements that together blur it, or create a blur in their flickering back and forth" (114). The seeming syntactical break adds to the "blurriness" of the point of view, the eliding of animal and human in the first line: "I as a blurry groundhog bundling home / find autumn storeyed." The ambiguity in point of view continues: it is unclear whether one is at groundhog height or human height. Moreover, it does not matter, *because* autumn is "storeyed," from "leafstain" in the street to "disappearing clear," all perspectives equally present and valued, and because of the "creatureliness," the identity and perspective, shared with the groundhog.

The same ambiguity is applied more radically to the boundary between human and divine, created and uncreated, in the evocation of the subjectivity of the Incarnate God in the recent poem "On a Maundy Thursday Walk," which imagines the unimaginable intersection of human body and uncreated God, of "finely-tuned senses" and "a clear serene constancy." The Incarnation, that ultimate intersection of Self and Other that is at the heart of Christian redemption, is the "essential / pivot" (*Concrete and Wild Carrot* 71–72). Avison's poetry is thus intensely concerned with Otherness, with breaking down conventional self–Other boundaries—not only politically recognized ones like class, disability, appearance, and age (adult–child), but also conventional boundaries between categories of being: human–animal, animate–inanimate, created–uncreated. Avison's work insists on using alterity of perspective to challenge the assumed centrality of the self, erasing nominal boundaries not only between self and transcendent Other but also between self and other others—boundaries between the literate, middle-class self and those on the margins of society, boundaries between child and adult, animal and human. This challenge is rooted not only in Avison's theology and spiritual experience but also in her deep social commitment and longtime experience working among those least privileged in society. In "Searching and Sounding," the speaker *becomes* the down-and-out man in the rooming house or the drug-damaged youth; indeed, this identification is essential to the divine re-creation of her own self:

> But you have come and sounded
> a music around me, newly
>
> as though you can clear
> all tears from our eyes only
> if we sound the wells of weeping with
> another's heart, and hear
> another's music only. (*Always Now* 1.200)

Avison continually breaks through the "proscenium" arch of limited individual perspective, asserting the value, as well as the subjectivity, the knowableness, of Otherness. In "Scar-face," a man and his badly damaged outward face must "prow his life through / the flow and wash / of others' looks," but "His face is a good / face, looking-out-from" (72). Avison subverts the power dynamic of the gaze, asserts its doubleness, the doubleness of the "face" as that which is both "looked at" and "look[ed]-out-from," the I and eye behind the object of gaze.[12]

Another powerfully repeated experience in Avison's poetry is the crossing of child–adult, animal–human boundaries, inverting conventional power relationships, conventional assumptions about maturity, authority, perception, and worth. The child as emblem of imaginative vision is perhaps derived from Wordsworth and from Joycean epiphanic moments of perception, but also reflects the Genesis moment of joy at creation, with the underlying Gospel teaching that of such is the kingdom of heaven. Animals appear repeatedly in Avison's poetry as Other and yet related to human;

the poet enters into their alien perception, stressing the limits of the reasoning by which humans claim dominance and centrality. This is well exemplified in the title pun in "Seeing So Little," a dramatic monologue from poet to sparrow that acknowledges the limitations of the traditional subject–object dynamic of investigation:

> I do not want to face the fact that
> loving watching you, over
> ranges of long time, I
> learn so little—yet too much
> to "look you up." (*No Time* 61)

Similarly, in "Relating" (*Concrete and Wild Carrot* 22–23), the insect–human encounter as the poet watches ant on its "diligent" way focusses on both their respective alienness and their shared "creatureliness." Alien forms of perception and purpose (the "more segmented awarenesses" that intricately impel the ant's movement) are "beyond / this other living creature's grasp." Like the stars that cannot be seen in the morning, or the languages spoken by others that the poet has never learned herself, the ant may represent a communal world of being and knowledge far beyond any human perception:

> Is your being one
> pictograph, seed of a
> word, the gateway to
> a language nobody speaks?
> So none can read this
> unsegmented, unsmall,
> shared reality.

Both human and insect are linked to the "radii of power" (literally, beams of the midday sun; metaphorically, the creating and life-giving power of God) that shape their being and identity, focussing "down and in / on you and me over our / warped little shadows." The image evokes another relationship with Otherness beyond perceptive limits, yet an Otherness that relates, that accommodates, intimately (adjusting to the movement of both ant and poet in "this midday instant"). This leads the poem to conclude with the possibility of dialogue, where at the intersection of two separate paths, two alien beings might meet: "I greet you on your way. / You greet me too, departing?"

The permeability of boundaries between normally separate categories of being (animal, mineral, vegetable) has long been a key idea throughout Avison's work. Not only is it at the heart of the Christian notion of Incarnation and redemption, but it is also reflected in Avison's environmental philosophy, where a blurring and interpenetration of categories is essential to organic life and health, indeed to any identity. In "Two," she writes,

> Trees breathe for any
> who breathe to live.
>
> Stone makes every thing
> more what it is:
> sun-hot,
>
> late November bare,
> cold in an early April morning;
>
> age in being
> always. (*Concrete and Wild Carrot* 59)[13]

The unsettling of conventional categories and relations is embodied in Avison's poetic language and in the stylistic oddities of her poems: she forces the imagination and intellect to work and demands that the attentive reader accomplish the jailbreak herself. Avison's poetry demands "creative readers" as well as "creative writers" (Interview 25); it challenges and stretches the reader's own perception, eye and ear, and the boundaries of form and experience (cf. Mazoff 19, 48). Its time-space point of view moves through history and around the world; personal pronouns shift from first to third, the reference ambiguous, challenging notions of point of view, self, and perspective; metaphor is pushed beyond metaphor, as tenor and vehicle blur and unite; seer and thing seen interpenetrate. Ambiguities and interruptions in syntax and diction re-create the ambiguities of experience or point to experiences beyond words: concentrated, cryptic utterances or piled-up hyphenated clusters give the impression of language stretched over something too big for it, or of the attempt to convey a multiplicity of meaning and experience in which all levels are equally present and important. It is difficult to speak of imagery in Avison's poetry: in the act of the optic heart, metaphor and "reality" elide, and sign becomes one with the thing signified.

Avison has affinities with the poststructuralist (and feminist) challenge to conventional categories of language and the normal reader–writer contract, stretching the notion of text, breaking language open, pushing convention well beyond its limits, and using it joyously against itself. Unlike the endless spiral of poststructuralist linguistics, however, her language and vision are "cryptic" (another key word in Avison's lexicon), packing meaning in. In another form of the dissolving jailbreak, her work breaks linguistic construction open only to invoke unimaginable dimensions of meaning and reference—the uncircumferenced circle of "First."[14] For Avison, all language is alive, carrying a multiplicity of meanings past and present:

> a poet chooses to accept the full halo of values in the words he uses. He accepts the personal identity they reveal. He develops his sense of their echoes across developing centuries, the double or triple meanings, the suggestiveness of vowel-sound and rhythm. No potential effect of any word is irrelevant to the poem where it occurs. ("Muse of Danger" 148–49)

Earlier meanings, multiple meanings, live in a word; syntax is twisted and stretched to evoke new relationships and to alter structures of thought, perception, and experience, as Avison turns the power relations implicit in language inside out. Her play with language enacts a version of feminine *jouissance*, playing through multiplicity of reference, where meanings are open-ended and at play in the word, and syntactical and etymological relations are broken open and re-created. In "Focussing," for instance, she writes,

> Given is all there is and
> all is
> there is
> given here and
> who is roomy enough for all to get in all given
> forgiven and forgiving and given
> giving in and
> being given there
>
> all is
> here
>
> give (*No Time* 90)

This poem explores the redemptive heart of language as Avison uses it. It is substantive, not active, a realm of symbol such as Kristeva might suggest, intensely and redemptively playful, unearthing meanings as a child might, prior to the syntactical imperative of conquest, subject-verb-object. This is its main point, of course, encapsulated in the shift from the third-person, passive, past participle "given" to the infinitive—or command—"give."

Avison inverts the Derridean model of the primacy of writing and reference (the "erased trace"), privileging speech over writing. In her work, speech is primary and encompassing: "The word read by the living Word / sculptured its shaper's form," she writes in "The Bible to Be Believed" (*sunblue* 56–57). In "Light (I)," God "from elsewhere speaks," "breathes" life and "impasse-crumpled hope" (59); in "Listening," He accomplishes His work and is known through the voice (58). For Avison, as she writes in "Words," language is emphatically from the body, springing from the self in a very particular sense:

> The ancient, the new
> confused in speech,
> breathe on, involving
> heart-warmed lungs, the reflexes
> of uvula, shaping tongue, teeth, lips,
> ink, eyes, and de-
> ciphering heart. (*Always Now* 1.161)

Avison's thinking is reminiscent of Renaissance/classical rhetorical theory, where word and speech are closely identified with the self.[15] Writing is subordinate to speech here, listed with the oral, bodily media of language; more deeply, the imagery unites body, soul, self, again eliding categories. "Heart" has three meanings: physiological and emotional and intellectual, or perceptive ("heart-warmed lungs," "eyes, and de- / ciphering heart"). The union of word and flesh in this poem touches the core image of Incarnation, at the centre of Avison's ideas of art as well as life; Word becomes flesh, word and thought and act are one. Language is not a medium for something already complete but rather a means of creation in itself: "What happens, means," she observes in "The Bible to Be Believed" (*sunblue* 56).[16] Being and action fuse, as do metaphor and referent.

Bearing Avison's dictum about "creative readers" in mind, we will now turn to three poems that embody changing notions of language and form in Avison's work, and her challenge to notions of self and Other. The first two poems represent two poles: the early poem "Butterfly Bones: Sonnet Against Sonnets" emphasizes the repressive limitations of language and form, in terms reminiscent of the feminist critique of phallogocentrism, while "From Age to Age: Found Poem," published eighteen years later, sees naming not as restrictive but rather as celebratory, in a shared experience and wonder, through the eyes of a child. The third poem, "Alternative to Riots but All Citizens Must Play," which concludes Avison's *Concrete and Wild Carrot*, addresses contemporary issues of globalization, conflict, and culture, with an urgent call to abandon constructed notions of Otherness and self-identity.

"Butterfly Bones: Sonnet Against Sonnets" is a piece of technical virtuosity, which uses with great precision all the aspects of the traditional Shakespearean sonnet to examine the limitations both of poetic form and of traditional ways of knowing (*Always Now* 1.71). Of Avison's works this is the one that most exactly reflects many of the central concerns of later feminist and postcolonial theories of literature, knowledge, and learning. It pillories in itself that knowledge which is invasive and violent, which restricts, defines, and confines, which constricts and constructs the Other—which objectifies the Other in the act of defining, and so cannot "know" the Other at all. The "final stiffness" of the opening image of the sonnet links with the "sheened and rigid trophies" of both sonnet and butterfly to emphasize the effect of this objectification: the being closed off, impossible to open, permanently sealed in and isolated, its final stiffness being rigor mortis as well as artificial preservation of poisonous cyanide. The poem compares language, and poetic form in particular (with the sonnet as one of the strictest traditional exemplars of that form), to scientific and geographic exploration ("Plane dogsled and safari / assure continuing range," *Always Now* 1.71), and suggests that this kind of knowledge isn't knowledge at all. These preconceived notions and categories of definition—the "strange certainties" fulfilled by scientific experiment and poetic convention and represented by the "sheened and rigid" forms of the butterflies (and poems)—might "strike men blind" to larger, more real, ways of seeing. The "peering boys" of the butterfly trophies could also be seen as amusingly anticipating feminist critiques of masculinist modes of discourse and discovery, scientists and literary critics alike: their inherent phallogocentrism, their assumption of the right to look, to explore, to define, is reduced to the slightly prurient and immature image of boys looking into a jar of their own making. The glaring of the rigid objects, to them, confirms this centrality and "prove[s] / [the] strange certainties" (*Always Now* 1.71) of the assumptions underlying so-called scientific fact, the preconceived categories of knowledge that put humanity at the centre and in control.

The central structure of the poem, however, juxtaposes the subjectivity, or perspective, of both looker and looked at, breaking down the self–Other distinction; the shift at line 9 (the traditional transition point in the sonnet) moves from the perspectives of the human explorer/scientist/literary critic, to that of the insect in its most alienating form; the shift is further underlined through internal rhyme and the double meaning of such words as "stare" and "glare": "Cased in a white glare / these specimens stare for peering boys, to prove / strange certainties" (lines 2–4). Moreover, the earlier passages also suggest double meanings in the term "strange," repeated through the poem: the "strange certainties" are perhaps strange in that these certainties of humanistic centrality are not certain at all, or else there is another kind of strangeness that the butterfly/poems prove, a world beyond ordinary human perception. In the term "prove" the earlier meaning exists, whereby the trophies test, not demonstrate, these so-called certainties. The strangeness of humanistic assumptions, reaffirmed by "learning" to "leave all living stranger" could on another level refer to an entirely different strangeness that challenges those assumptions, and to a humbler kind of learning that opens rather than closes the mind.

It is notable that Avison rhymes "stranger" with "danger," the key term at the turning point of the poem, where it shifts to the butterfly's living point of view, the point of view that challenges human categories of perception. "Danger" becomes the transitional term in the sonnet—a term reminiscent (or anticipatory) of the danger inherent in the jailbreak, the abandoning of traditional categories of perception. This paradox is encapsulated in the transitional lines at the centre of the poem:

> Insect—or poem—waits for the fix, the frill
> precision can effect, brilliant with danger.
> What law and wonder the museum spectres
> bespeak is cryptic for the shivery wings (*Always Now* 1.71)

The "frill" of pinned, expanded wing or poetic image is "brilliant" (literally shining) "with danger" that is reinforced by the rhyme and is multiple in its implications: danger to the butterfly, to the life of the poem, or to the observer. The "law and wonder" evoke at first the idea of discipline (rule of law), then the wonder that breaks it open, suggesting instead a different kind of law by which the human observer will be judged; "cryptic," as suggested earlier, is a key term in Avison's lexicon, suggesting layers of vision and reference, as well as altered perception: "the world cut-diamond-eyed, those eyes' reflectors, / or herbal grass, sunned motes, fierce listening" (*Always Now* 1.71). These lines vividly describe the most alien aspect of insect life, the clustered eyes, and the "I" that looks out through those eyes, the alternate ways of perceiving, alien to humans. The image also suggests the looker–looked at dynamic again (the world as seen through the butterfly's eyes and other senses, the reflectors those eyes are in themselves, and the world as reflecting the butterfly's perception). It is the privileging of the human perspective, the "certainties" that are not, that has in fact killed human vision and reduced the butterfly (and the alternatives of poetic vision) to "sheened and rigid trophies," with the suggestion of violence and death, the ultimate objectification.

The final couplet, providing the twist or comment as conventional in the Shakespearean sonnet, focusses on the reasons for this blindness. Men are "blinded" by this objectifying, violent knowledge, for an originary reason— "Adam's lexicon locked within the mind" (*Always Now* 1.71) (which is syntactically linked to the butterfly trophies). However, the line suggests a double meaning: in traditional feminist thinking, Adam's act of naming the animals is the quintessentially masculinist act of definition, categorization, emblem of the phallogocentric word of law; but its other meaning here is the original language of new experience, the freshness of creation, an act of perception and celebration rather than of preconceived categories. The blindness results from its being locked within the mind, buried deep under the constructed, killing perspectives of the fallen world. The same doubleness applies to the poem itself, as the irony of the title carries through: the strict, pinned form itself opens up the "strangeness" and "danger" of alternate vision.

"From Age to Age: Found Poem," one of four poems on children at the end of *sunblue*, presents the re-creative process not through the poet's eyes alone but through her witness of a child reliving the perceptive moment of Genesis (*sunblue* 102). In these four poems, as in Avison's later work generally, the emblem of creative perception is the child, who is absorbed in what he or she sees, and who *is* in the act of seeing; perception and language come together in the eternal moment of Genesis, "when Adam names the animals" (*sunblue* 102), in an ongoing act of re-creation. This poem could be read with "Prelude," from Avison's first collection, *Winter Sun* (*Winter Sun* 9–11; *Always Now* 1.61–63), as it centres on an epiphanic moment of perception through the eyes of a child, follows the process of maturing perception, and, by the end, shows the potential or availability of such vision to all adults. This is also the poem whose title is referred to in the above epigraph from bp Nichol, as an example of knowledge not possessed (obtained, objectified) but found (experienced); unlike the consciously fashioned "Sonnet

Against Sonnets," this is a "Found Poem," an experience, not a "sheened and rigid" object of examination. The poem is "found" both by the child through the streetcar window and by the observer in the streetcar watching both child and poem: the finding itself re-enacts, from age to age, the moment of Adam's perception of creation in all its freshness.

Like much of *sunblue*, "From Age to Age: Found Poem" is "threaded through" with the elemental images of light and water—the original elements of Creation, which permeate the physical creation still, and which for Avison symbolize—even literally embody—God's transforming life in the world, there for the optic heart to see. The streetcar journey structures the poem as a maturing process, the day changing from bright morning to storm clouds and the reflective calm of evening, and the journey of life itself, from the child to the adults sealed in their cars. In one sense, the shades of the prison-house close in, as the child "ground[s]" his "elation and surprise," as "storm clouds ... eclipse" the sunlit waters, and as the "flashing, flowering ... fountains" give way to "reflective low waters." The voice of the poem is ambiguous, however. The question "is it all past?" leaves the matter open; and the "grounding" of wonder is not necessarily forgetting or devaluing it so much as internalizing it, absorbing it into the being, where such experience will be available to the adult. Windows appear throughout this poem. From Avison's earliest work, windows are an important symbol for perception, simply meaning what we look through. Here they are present not only in "the steady streetcar windows" through which the child (and the poet) looks on the stages of his journey, but also in the "windowed cars" linked by water and light—even in the "window squares / of the department stores," which look back at the streetcar, child, and poet (*sunblue* 102).

To follow this process more closely, I will begin with the moment of perception and recognition, which re-enacts the wonder of the day when the morning stars sang for joy: "the voice of the morning" sings again in the back of a Toronto streetcar. The moment of perception is also the moment of naming; perception and poetic language unite in the same act of re-creation, "as in the morning day / when Adam names the animals" (*sunblue* 102) There is a duality here, as in "Butterfly Bones," but with an opposite emphasis: where in that poem "Adam's lexicon" was equated syntactically with the "sheened and rigid trophies" of poetic form and was an act of naming that committed violence by capturing and fixating meaning, the morning voice in "From Age to Age: Found Poem" shows the act of naming to be celebratory and re-creative, both giving and receiving meaning in an open-ended, ongoing experience. In "the morning day / when Adam names the animals," the eternal present tense shows naming to be an ongoing and living process, not a fixed act of definition. The morning language does not pin down experience like a dead butterfly, but rather celebrates experience, opens up new experience, and enables the sharing of experience. This poem thus rejects the phallogocentric model of language as a construct aggressively imposed upon experience, to replace it with a view of language as a *means* of experience: the child is not asserting his power over the fountain, or inscribing himself and his subjectivity upon it; rather, he is responding to the fountain, recognizing its being, and celebrating that being through a name, and, through the name, sharing the wonder of that recognition. This experience challenges conventional categories in the eyes of the poet, as the "flashing, flowering ... fountains" cross boundaries of elements and types, and places her vision in the childlike state of openness, prior to the "honeycombing" of sense, the sterile construction of vision that occurs in adulthood (see "Prelude," also in *Winter Sun* [9–11], for Avison's further development of this idea).

As the child's perception matures and becomes more precise, "the light sharpens," and he attempts to communicate the experience, "Shaman di / dactic" like the poet, who both teaches, sharing knowledge, and works magic, initiating into mysteries. Time flows by, "stop succeeds stop," and the day matures still further, "flow[ing] over him"; yet this phrase can also describe the power of light in which the child's being is absorbed. Here is one of Avison's most precise descriptions of the full experience of re-creative perception: "The day flows over him. / He communes here, absorbing, confiding, / at one" (*sunblue* 102). Perception works two ways, both taking in the light, "absorbing" it, and giving out, "confiding" oneself to it; the perceiver is "at one" with what is perceived. Far from one committing an act against the Other, self against Other, both seer and thing seen *interact*; both are re-created by the light and by the word that shares in the creative power of the Word.[17]

"Is it all past? [as the streetcar presumably leaves the fountains behind]" (*sunblue* 102) is a question that echoes through time, addressed to us as well as to the poet herself; and the rest of the poem points, perhaps ambiguously, towards an answer. We live in a fallen world, where the storm clouds have eclipsed the blue and gold (emblematic colours in *sunblue* for the freshness of God's life in creation, in the air we breathe), but the clouds are dove grey, not threatening, suggesting Noah's messenger of peace and the brooding creative dove of the Holy Spirit. The child "ground[s]" his "elation and surprise," muting them perhaps, but also internalizing that initial response, possibly even confirming and firmly rooting it. "West farther still" we look beyond the streetcar journey, to a distance in both space and time (note the shift to the future tense here), and a broader view of "every windowed car" (*sunblue* 102). The car here is reminiscent of the plane in *sunblue* and Avison's later poetry (for example, "Light [II]" and "Light [III]"): a small, enclosed technological cell from which we peer out at the creation through small windows. Even these sealed-in cells have windows, however, and they are themselves "threaded through" by light and water. The "far lake light" and "reflective low waters" (*sunblue* 102) may be muted versions of the fountains, but the experience and re-creative power are still there, in memory and potential in the adult mind, and available to everyone. Every windowed car is threaded through by the same elements that played in the fountain of morning wonder. The same wonder is there to be rediscovered and to re-create the discoverer, "from age to age."

The poem that concludes the Griffin-winning *Concrete and Wild Carrot*, "Alternative to Riots but Every Citizen Must Play," returns emphatically to the theme of jailbreak, in imagery of contemporary global politics and conflict, but in a larger, eschatological context, digging through to the heart of the problem across the sweep of human history; humanity must abandon materialist, constructed, limited ways of knowing, false categories of perception centred on the self, for the unknown and ineffable, that which is beyond our immediate control and perception, "the / glory of / nothing to hold onto / but untried air currents." Only through this kind of freeing of perception and identity, through radical re-vision of the self–Other relationship at the individual level, can global transformation be accomplished—even if that transformation is at first infinitesimal, unseen, like a seed "germinating / in the darkness" (*Concrete and Wild Carrot* 81).

The poem begins by breaking down the self–Other distinction on which most human culture is founded, between first, second, and third person, calling "To myself everywhere" (77). The call to "Break / all our securities … break out! … Break in! Break up / all our so solid structures" (77, 81) and "Explore only the ranges / beyond our mastering" (77) is an urgent, now global, restatement of the need for jailbreak and re-creation. Avison suggests here wide-ranging issues, structures of human understanding across time and space: the cultural, economic, and political frameworks that provide self-definition and that are attempts to control our environment and the others within it, are seen as a limiting, false construct. Instead of providing safety ("security") and identity, they do just the opposite, putting the self in danger and blurring ("conglomerat[ing]") identity (79). The repeated word "security" also appears as "securities" (77), a financial pun, part of a thread of financial metaphors throughout the poem, metaphors where tenor and vehicle elide (the insecurity of securities is also true in the world of finance, as recent events in the stock market make clear). In the larger sense, "security" refers to the framework of perception, the determining of identity and relationship, by which we attempt to shape our world, which end up being shaped for us by forces beyond our control. It is this kind of "security" that must be broken out of, in order for the world to be re-created, and for humanity to be free.[18]

As in the early poem "Dispersed Titles" (*Winter Sun* 3–7; *Always Now* 1.55–59), Avison stretches the concept of "culture," playing here on the multiple meaning of the term: high art, cultural achievement; cultural/ethnic identity; and dominant culture that claims universality or invisibility, whether it is imperial Rome, financial empires, or the modern West. The "faceless, imperial (world-wide) / governance and its shimmery / statistical sheen" (*Concrete and Wild Carrot* 77) can refer to "culture" as imperialism, the global power that erases identity and turns people into numbers, be it imperial Rome or modern fiscal empires. The Rome–Greece succession denotes the roots of Western civilization and dominance, but also the image of imperial succession and military conquest, the imposition of power and control; even the memory-traces of ancient Grecian music are forgotten, an image of culture as experience giving way to culture as commodified object of conquest.

The theme of control and attempted control dominates the poem; all human culture and "achievement" are "imprisoned by / managed relationships / no-one can manage, quite" (77–78); human endeavour is trapped in a materialist framework of humanity's own making, a dynamic of power and dominance of one over another. Among the structures to be broken out of are those of politically and economically managed relationships, which tend to construct and efface (or deface) individual identity. Money becomes a miasma, a weather condition, erasing individual and collective difference:

> Money is no longer
> visible. Now
> it vapourizes and disperses somehow
> and settles over all of us.

> We turn into a monstrous
> sameness, a jumble
> within one skin,
> a skin pulled taut
> until it hurts
> the whole ungeographical
> world of us. (*Concrete and Wild Carrot* 78)

The "ungeographical / world of us" challenges national, spatial, and cultural divisions, but also refers to the non-material world of relationship; humanity is one body, an organic whole, but a "jumble," not orderly, constrained and confused by false structures and economy (tightness of the skin): in a Donnian image, the global and cultural and economic forces that hurt one, hurt and limit all.

The poem repeatedly critiques the various constructs by which humanity attempts to control the situation, as a false basis for security. In a metaphor from financial planning, it insists that we break free from "safe comprehensive arrangements" (79) that, like the "managed relationships" (77), are not fully comprehended either by controllers (another financial pun) or controlled. The exigencies of these structures have created false divisions and categories that actually homogenize identity ("signatures bespeaking persons") and difference:

> Once there were landscapes, features
> rugged outcroppings, signatures
> bespeaking persons. Now they all melt into
> categories, till conglomeration
> begins to make categories
> a fiction, although still
> a soothing one. (*Concrete and Wild Carrot* 79)

The imagery here is apocalyptic, suggesting an undoing of creation: continental drift is reversed, the shaping of the earth's crust undone. This cataclysmic, global, transhistorical wrongness is the context for all social and political pain. Both "secure" and "insecure" are caught up in a framework of disparity and of forces beyond their control: in a vivid description of (un)comfortable middle-class consciousness, "security shackles in shame and helplessness" when faced with the "insecure," who are "drained clean of / expecting, or of anything/ beyond the courage to go on / dully surviving" (79).

The self–Other conflict in global politics turns into another form of constructing identity that will falsify self and prove unsafe; minority politics can become as self-centred as dominant culture, falsely limiting perspective, defining vision, and leaving one open to assault from both without and within, blind and deaf to the voice of the Other:

> Beware of any notion of
> safety from having clustered under
> some forced, or chosen,
> minority. All of them are
> self-centred, all a
> security that blinds and deafens
> exposing flank, and heart
> to poisons from within as well. (*Concrete and Wild Carrot* 79–80)

To place one's security in these notions is to make one's home in a warscape, living in a land under conditions of terrorism, seen in the imagery of gas attacks ("lethal puffs ... out of a fair sky" [80]) and scattered gunfire amidst the rubble of walls that should have kept one safe. "Sanctuary" and "sheltering walls / have crumbled" (80): in the urgency of the call again, jailbreak forces itself upon us, and the security we base our lives on is in fact not only false but destructive. The image here works on two levels, literal and metaphoric, and the two are causally related, blurring metaphor and reality: on one level, the actual world conditions (war, terrorism, loss of homes) in which all must share ("myself everywhere"); and on another, the deeper belief systems, limited perceptive framework, that create and feed the forces shaping these conditions. Conventional attempts to control are beyond us, imaged in the ineffectual and unknowingly naked diplomats seeking a reasoned solution.

Those (like Avison's readers?) who claim to be part of the "bland" "majority" (80) of such moderation, reason, and toleration find that "sure / foundation ... wobbly" (80); it is subject to a kind of entropy, leading to paralysis in its motive force: "The animus keeps fading into / passivity" (80–81). Individuals who were once part of that toleration "straggl[e] off" into various false visions of redemption:

> Stop them! Disrupt these
> vanilla visions, spongy with
> yearnings, for prophesied
> pre-dawn light, this very day. (*Concrete and Wild Carrot* 81)

Avison skewers the "vanilla visions" (81) of liberals as well as religious fundamentalists who claim to know the day and the hour of the end-time for themselves, while in fact "nightfall is near" (81). This expression is open-ended, all meanings at play: the concept of global cataclysm coincides with the inevitable and necessary dissolution of those "so solid structures" (81) that define the perceptive universe, the dissolving of self-boundaries necessary for real encounter with the Other, which is an image of apocalypse in itself.[19] This is the jailbreak that must happen in both a global and an individual sense if there is to be re-creation.

As Avison returns to the urgent call to abandon our worldly notions of security, our limited concepts of selfhood and Otherness, she evokes images of trust instead of control, of encounter that is as unmistakable as a gunshot:

> Break in! Break up
> all our so solid structures for the
> glory of
> nothing to hold onto
> but untried air currents,
> the crack and ricochet
> of impact. (*Concrete and Wild Carrot* 81)

The image of flying on new air currents like a glider or a bird, trusting to the wind, echoes the "sighing ... me" of "Psalm 19" (*Dumbfounding* 24; *Always Now* 1.162), the loss of self that results in re-creation; but this is an unmistakable, even startling "impact"/encounter with the Other. Prepositional constructions open up the complex simplicity of what is required: we must "break in" [to ourselves, into life] and "break up" the encrusted, falsifying structures that prevent us from living.

The layering of paradoxes in Avison's final command to "Risk / survival" stretches language, eliding contrasting ideas, in such a way as to force the reader to enact that change of perception for herself:

> Risk
> survival! into
> some indestructible
> transmuted loss. (*Concrete and Wild Carrot* 81)

The contrasting, riddling terms (when is survival a risk? how can loss be indestructible? and also transmute?) are answered in the jailbreak paradox on both the individual and eschatological levels: in the Christian framework that is Avison's core of belief, heaven and earth will be created anew, but this change must be imaged and experienced now in each individual life. Life, identity, and self must be lost so as to be redemptively re-created. As in the paradox of jailbreak, the "loss" could be of securities, limited, "safe" visions of self and Other; such loss is "transmuted" into an "indestructible" gain, one that cannot be destroyed or taken. With the individual change ("every citizen must play"), the global change can begin, germinating like a seed in the darkness, in a Biblical reference to the kingdom of heaven growing from a tiny mustard seed, the universal from humble individual beginnings.

Thus in this final poem of Avison's late collection, divisions between universal and individual, global and personal, material and spiritual, are broken down—and the de-structuring and re-creation of conventional definitions and limits is urgently pressed. In the title of the poem ("Alternative to Riots but All Citizens Must Play"), "riots" are a response to forces beyond people's control, an image of global unrest and crisis. Change can only happen through a deeper change, an abandoning of self-centred perspective and an opening of the self to Otherness, divine, human, and natural—this is the "alternative." Global change can only be accomplished if each individual makes that change within: "all citizens must play." "Play" is a word with multiple meanings, a key term in poststructuralist discourse, but for Avison it suggests a deep and complex notion of joy combined with engagement (play as in "participate"). Finally, a "citizen" denotes a person with fundamental rights and responsibilities. Everyone has a role to play in the struggle of self and Other at the heart of the world's pain, and in the intersection of spiritual and material that Avison sees at the heart of existence. Only through radical re-visioning of self and other, a new eye and I (and you), can the new world begin, in the image of earliest, organic growth, a "slow / secret, gradual germinating / in the darkness" (81).

Notes

1 Initially by A.J.M. Smith; see Kent's introduction to *"Lighting up the terrain"* (iv–vi).
2 It is worth noting that Avison was the only Canadian invited to attend the gathering of "postmodernist" poets at the University of British Columbia in 1963—a distinction linked to the tributes to her by George Bowering and bp Nichol in Kent. I am indebted to Barbara Godard for this observation.
3 The concepts of Avison and otherness introduced in this essay are elaborated further in my study of Avison and ecopoetry, "'Our own little rollicking orb': Divinity, Ecology, and Otherness in Avison" (2006/2007), which focusses particularly on Avison's final collection, *Momentary Dark*. Avison's challenge to human-centred

perception and subjectivity, frequently articulated in her poetry through the natural world, reflects the fundamental principles of ecopoetics. Together with Robert Merrett's essay in the same issue of *Canadian Poetry*, this study shows that Avison could be considered one of Canada's most significant practitioners of ecopoetry in its most searching sense. While her ecopoetics are not linked to ecofeminism as such, one should also note her celebration of female friends (e.g., the Jo poems in *No Time*), and the vivid presence of these women and of female friendship in her poetry. There is room for a more specific study of the representation of gender and ideas of the feminine in Avison. The qualities of her work and her challenge to the modernist–postmodernist trajectory are also characteristic of feminine writing; it is now commonplace (though still not adequately recognized) that women's writing and women writers, at any given period in the construct of literary history, develop along a different trajectory, and challenge and question the male-centred norms on which those models are based. Modernism itself has been characterized as anticipating the issues and traits of contemporary feminist writing (Rado 4). See the discussion of Canadian women's writing and modernist–postmodernist trajectory in Lianne Moyes's essay in this volume.

4 Avison draws here on a central strand of modernism, the link between consciousness and identity: the Enlightenment eye/I central to both early and late modern intellectual history in the west. For an illuminating discussion of early modern philosophy around consciousness, embodiment, and identity in relation to literary modernism, see Karen Jacobs (9–18). A possibly related issue is that of subjectivity, dealing with the "I" in poetry, one of the earliest issues Avison had to deal with in writing. See her own account in the foreword to *Always Now* (14), and her advice to Gail Fox (57), on the principle of eschewing the confessional "I" in poetry. See also note 5 below.

5 See note 4 above. It is an irony that Avison uses the images of Enlightenment discovery—Copernican revolution, Tycho Brahe, global exploration—to challenge the very basis on which Enlightenment science, aesthetics, and socioeconomic structures are laid: individual subjectivity. The challenge also bears some resemblance to the feminist challenge to the essentially masculine subjectivity constructed by the Enlightenment observer.

6 Some years ago, in "The Dissolving Jail-Break in Avison," I wrote about the central imaginative process in Avison's work, the jailbreak and re-creation, and how this process itself becomes transformed through her work; in the religious and imaginative re-creation taking place, the venture and jailbreak themselves become radically transformed, dissolving into an "opening-out" (1990). Some passages of that essay are reprinted here.

7 It can be noted that both of these fears (the fear of self-dissolution and of entombed subjectivity), as well as the openness to redemption through accepting the loss of the self-defined ego boundaries, are qualities of the feminine. Relatedly, they are also an image of masculinist fear of the feminine, fear of loss of integrity, of self-definition, especially through union with an Other whose self is an openness, an expansion, a lack of closure and definition. Avison's image of God and the act of creation partakes of these qualities in many ways, primary and encompassing, ever open, not entombed or objectified—"the radium, / the all-swallowing moment" into which fragments must be drawn for wholeness. This is, however, a larger topic beyond the scope of this study.

8 George Bowering points out how in Avison's view our notions of time and space place self at the centre and reduce things distant (59). Bowering's observation is central to

this argument: Avison's challenge to perspective, her suggestion that it is a subjective construct, anticipate the basis for current postcolonial and gender criticism, the exposing of assumptions of Western or White male centrality, although she applies this more broadly to assumptions of human centrality.

9   Note the nicely gendered pun: born/"borne," "man's toy," a trivial object versus real birth, the Otherness of created being.

10 An excellent early reading of this poem can be found in J.M. Zezulka's "Refusing the Sweet Surrender" (1977). As Zezulka and Ernest Redekop (*Margaret Avison* 70) both point out, the poem also suggests that modern Western civilization is cut off from its own (Mediterranean) roots. I would add that this creates a sterile assumption of objectivity and neutrality, consistent with the Enlightenment secularist myth of scientific "truth" and Western assumptions of universality.

11 This can also be seen as Avison's answer to modernist alienation and fragmentation: rather than documenting each moment of individual subjectivity (as in the novel, e.g., Woolf or Joyce), we must look out, beyond the self, to an unimaginable reality. Where modernist art seeks to construct community and connection, Avison challenges construction, postulating a reality outside the self, powerful enough to overload the individual vision. The final lines of "Searching and Sounding" rewrite those of *The Waste Land*; rather than shoring up the fragments of experience and attempting to make sense of life as best we can, through art, we offer our fragments to One who is at both centre and margins, in the ongoing act of Creation: "GATHER my fragments towards / the radium, the / all-swallowing moment / once more" (*Always Now* 202).

12 Avison here exemplifies another key concept in feminist theory, particularly in film theory and performance studies; see Laura Mulvey's early work on the concept of woman as to-be-looked-at, and later work in performance theory examining the interaction of gazer/gazed at, the subjectivity of the actor as object, in the dynamic of the theatre (Straub, *Sexual Suspects*; Rosenthal 94–95).

13 Environmentalism in Avison's work is a topic in need of further study; God is immanent in the creation, and the natural order has a spiritual significance—for example, in "Orders of Trees," environmental pollution is linked with spiritual and moral pollution, resulting from the Fall. Avison critiques humanity's self-centred perspective by portraying artificial human order imposed on natural (*No Time* 62). Men have been "interpreters and spoilers" since Eden but there is, in "Light (III)," hope for redemption (*sunblue* 61).

14 Language, theology, and word in Avison are discussed by Mazoff (in terms of Iserian rhetoric), Jon Kertzer (7–26), David Jeffrey (58–77), and Ernest Redekop ("Word/word" 115–34).

15 As Avison puts it elsewhere, "A person's unique flesh-and-blood force is in his own words, in his way of sounding them and using them. His words reveal his family and the time and place he is abroad on the earth. The natural rhythm, the flow or biting off or slow shaping of word, reflect temperament and mood" ("Muse of Danger" 148). In "To Wilfred Cantwell Smith" similarly, writing is an extension of speech and language is interrelated with the organic, developing self:

> Our native language shapes us, does it not
> even as it shapes itself upon the page?
> The languages you've learned, in life and college,
> carve and emboss characters in your thought?
> ...

> Ink on white paper keeps informing those
> who learn, to listen long, until there glows
> within the friendly signs of being understood. (*Concrete and Wild Carrot* 67–68)

16 In general, Avison's organic, creative, non-hierarchical view of language, while reminiscent of earlier linguistic models such as that of Owen Barfield (see Kertzer's discussion in Kent [11–14]), is also comparable to feminist responses to Derrida's essentially masculinist linguistics.

17 In "Sun-Son light/Light: Avison's Elemental *sunblue*," Redekop explores this relation of the poetic word to God's creating word.

18 The poem's sweeping challenge to "structures" and "managed relationships" bears some resemblance to the feminist challenge to the "naturalness" of male domination that continues as the basis for most of the world's social, cultural, and economic systems. As elsewhere, however, Avison is applying this principle more deeply and broadly. At the core of her Christian beliefs is the need for a radically transformed vision of and relationship between the self and the Other (both divine and human, Other and others); this change at the individual level is what will, or may, bring about global change. The poem operates on a number of levels—global politics, socio-economic disparities, Christian eschatology—but at the same time it blurs the boundaries between those levels, seeing them as one, part of the same process.

19 This poem can be seen as Avison's response to both contemporary millenarianism and current global politics. She deliberately layers the two and challenges the assumptions underlying both; she replaces them with her own version of the apocalypse—the jailbreak and re-creation on both an individual and global level—that fundamentally changes the relationship between self and Other, self and others. Hence the reference to an unmistakable encounter or "impact," which suggests both the unmistakable nature of Christ's coming in Christian apocalyptic tradition and the powerful inner impact of change in vision at the individual level, upon direct encounter with the Other as opposed to one's constructed vision of the Other. The apocalypse (literally, unveiling, again suggesting transformed vision) must take place within, at the individual level, for any global re-creation to take place.

WORKS CITED

Avison, Margaret. *Always Now*. Vol. 1. Erin, ON: Porcupine's Quill, 2003. Rpt. of *Winter Sun* (1960) and *The Dumbfounding* (1966).
———. *Concrete and Wild Carrot*. London, ON: Brick, 2002.
———. *The Dumbfounding*. New York: Norton, 1966.
———. Interview. By Peggy Murray. *Toronto Telegram* 27 February 1961: 25.
———. "Muse of Danger." Kent 148–49.
———. *No Time*. Hansport, NS: Lancelot, 1989.
———. "Perspective." *Poetry* 70 (September 1947): 320–21.
———. *sunblue*. Hantsport, NS: Lancelot, 1978.
———. *Winter Sun*. Toronto: U of Toronto P, 1960.
———. Interview with Peggy Murray. *Toronto Telegram* 27 February 1961: 25.
Bowering, George. "Avison's Imitation of Christ the Artist." *Canadian Literature* 54 (Autumn 1972): 56–69.

Fox, Gail. "Dancing in the Dark [with journal selections]." Kent 55–57.
Jacobs, Karen. *The Eye's Mind: Literary Modernism and Visual Culture*. Ithaca, NY: Cornell UP, 2001.
Jeffrey, David. "Light, Stillness, and the Shaping Word: Conversion and the Poetic of Margaret Avison." Kent 58–77.
Kent, David A., ed. *"Lighting up the terrain": The Poetry of Margaret Avison*. Toronto: ECW, 1987.
Kertzer, Jon. "Margaret Avison and the Place of Meaning." Kent 7–26.
Mansbridge, Francis. "Margaret Avison: An Annotated Bibliography." *The Annotated Bibliography of Canada's Major Authors*. Ed. Robert Lecker and Jack David. Vol. 6. Toronto: ECW, 1985. 56.
Marsden, Jean. "Rape, Voyeurism, and the Restoration Stage." *Broken Boundaries: Women and Feminism in Restoration Drama*. Ed. Katherine M. Quinsey. Lexington: UP of Kentucky, 1996. 185–200.
Mazoff, C. D. *Waiting for the Son: Poetics/Theology/Rhetoric in Margaret Avison's* sunblue. Dunvegan, ON: Cormorant, 1989.
Merrett, Robert James. "Margaret Avison on Natural History: Ecological and Biblical Meditations." *Canadian Poetry* 59 (Fall 2006 / Winter 2007): 95–110.
Mulvey, Laura. "Afterthoughts on 'Visual Pleasure and Narrative Cinema' inspired by *Duel in the Sun*." *Framework* 6.15–17 (1981): 12–15. Rpt. in *Feminism and Film Theory*. Ed. Constance Penley. New York: Routledge, 1988. 69–79.
———. "Visual Pleasure and Narrative Cinema." *Screen* 16.3 (Autumn 1975): 6–18. Rpt. in *Feminism and Film Theory*. Ed. Constance Penley. New York: Routledge, 1988. 57–68.
Nichol, bp. "Sketching." Kent 111–14.
Quinsey, K. M. "The Dissolving Jail-Break in Avison." *Canadian Poetry* 25 (Winter 1990): 21–37.
———. "'Our own little rollicking orb': Divinity, Ecology, and Otherness in Avison." *Canadian Poetry* 59 (Fall 2006 / Winter 2007): 111–38.
Rado, Lisa, ed. *Rereading Modernism: New Directions in Feminist Criticism*. New York: Garland, 1994.
Redekop, Ernest. *Margaret Avison*. Toronto: Copp Clark, 1970.
———. "Sun-Son light/Light: Avison's elemental *Sunblue*." *Canadian Poetry* 7 (Fall/Winter 1980): 21–37.
———. "The Word/word in Avison's Poetry." Kent 115–34.
Rosenthal, Laura J. "'Trials of Manhood': Cibber, *The Dunciad*, and the Masculine Self." *"More Solid Learning": New Perspectives on Alexander Pope's Dunciad*. Ed. Catherine Ingrassia and Claudia N. Thomas. Lewisburg: Bucknell UP, 2000. 81–105.
Straub, Kristina. *Sexual Suspects: Eighteenth-Century Players and Sexual Ideology*. Princeton: Princeton UP, 1992.
Zezulka, J.M. "Refusing the Sweet Surrender: Margaret Avison's 'Dispersed Titles.'" *Canadian Poetry* 1 (Fall/Winter 1977): 44–53.

Reading P.K. Page in English/Italian; or, On the Politics of Translating Modernist Gender

ELENA BASILE

Can a translation bring to the fore aspects of an author's poetics otherwise unnoticed? How might an analysis of a translation help to draw attention not only to the tensions and contradictions in the way an author's work is circulated and received within a culture, but also to the ambiguous aspects of a poet's language, apparent only when it is filtered through the strictures of a different linguistic and cultural system? As I propose in this essay, analysis of Italian translations of P.K. Page's poetry enables a reinterpretation of her complexly gendered relation to modernism.

Rosa dei venti / Compass Rose is an English/Italian bilingual anthology of P.K. Page's poetry, published in 1998 by Longo Editore, a small Italian publishing house that specializes in visual art and poetry. The book was first launched in Canada in conjunction with an art exhibition sponsored by the Italian Institute of Culture in Toronto, but it has circulated primarily in Italy. I begin by mentioning the geographical and institutional sites of production and dissemination of this particular anthology of P.K. Page's work in order to contextualize the theoretical questions this essay intends to tackle: namely, what are the cultural politics of translating a Canadian modernist woman poet into Italian, that is, of translating a poet belonging to a minor Western literature into a relatively minor Western language? What are the critical stakes involved in the process, and how does this particular text address them? More generally, what role can bilingual editions of poetry play in fostering the formation of informed transnational audiences, that is, the formation of a diffuse transcultural awareness of the rhetorical "frayages" (Spivak, "Politics of Translation" 180) in/visibly regulating the production of meaning within and between languages?

This chapter will address these questions by combining a geopolitical and institutional account of the book's framing conditions of production and dissemination with an analysis of the interpretive tensions engendered by its textual strategies of translation. I will highlight the structural interdependence between these two aspects of the book, in particular expanding on how its conditions of production frame the ideological configurations of its bilingualism. My aim is to show how this text brings into relief a complex set of issues pertaining to cross-cultural interpretations of modernism and gender, here specifically related to the poetry of P.K. Page.

The Geopolitics of Publication

Rosa dei venti / Compass Rose is a book whose circumstances of production and dissemination bear witness to contemporary institutional networks of international cultural exchange. The central site of these networks is constituted by the Italian Institute of Culture in Toronto (IIC), which is the cultural branch of the Italian Consulate in Canada and is financed by the Italian government. The book's translator, Francesca Valente, was the institute's director when the book's launch took place in the IIC's own art gallery in October 1998. On that occasion, new work by Italian artist Mimmo Paladino was presented to provide a visual commentary on P.K. Page's poems; some of the manuscripts of the poems were also displayed. Although there exists a separate comprehensive catalogue of the exhibition dedicated to Paladino, *Rosa dei venti / Compass Rose* also contains some of his drawings. Strangely enough, no paintings or drawings by P.K. Page were shown at the exhibition or included in the book, even though Page's visual art stands in meaningful proximity to her poetry—both biographically[1] and aesthetically.[2] Explanations for this absence can only be conjectural, although it is likely that the editors considered it redundant to insert Page's visual art in a book belonging to a series whose defining feature is the cross-cultural pairing of an Italian visual artist with an English-Canadian poet. It is important to consider this publishing context (that is, the Peter Paul Bilingual Series of Canadian Contemporary Poetry), so as to illuminate further the contextual cultural politics surrounding the publication of *Rosa dei venti / Compass Rose*. The series was first established in 1993 by Francesca Valente and her husband Branko Gorjup, with the edition of Irving Layton's *Il cacciatore sconcertato / The Baffled Hunter*. A total of ten bilingual editions of anglophone Canadian poets, primarily translated by Valente herself, have appeared in the Peter Paul Series since 1993. Besides Irving Layton and P.K. Page, the other poets in the series are Gwendolyn MacEwen, Al Purdy, Margaret Atwood, Michael Ondaatje, Margaret Avison, Dennis Lee, Dionne Brand, and most recently Leonard Cohen. All of the publications are accompanied by the work of contemporary Italian visual artists.[3] The books were initially launched in Canada, in conjunction with the Italian artists' exhibitions, and received financial assistance from federal funding bodies, specifically, the Canada Council and the Canadian Department of Foreign Affairs. Although some of the texts in the series seem to enjoy some form of distribution in Canada by McArthur and Company (a HarperCollins agent), the books have circulated primarily in Italy, mostly among an educated audience of students and scholars of Canadian literature.[4]

This brief overview gives us a sense of the cultural project pursued by the IIC in the last decade and allows us to locate the international network of people and institutions framing the publication of Page's book. I insist on defining this network as *inter*national rather than *trans*national because the institutions involved officially represent, respectively, the Canadian and the Italian states, and their mode of exchange is regulated by assumptions of reciprocal commensurability based on parameters of nationally achieved cultural value. In this respect, it is important to pay attention to the choice of authors made, to the mode of cross-cultural collaboration being foregrounded, and to the sites of cultural dissemination being privileged. All of these factors frame the book's bilingualism and indirectly govern the stylistic and semantic trajectory of the translation.

With regards to the choice of authors, Valente and Gorjup's series seems to follow an interesting pattern of alternating gender and, at least for the first six publications, of pairing a male and a female poet according to the poets' peak period of recognition: modernists Irving Layton and P.K. Page were both made famous in the fifties; Gwendolyn McEwen and Al Purdy emerged in the sixties and established themselves in the seventies; Margaret Atwood's and Michael Ondaatje's fame, though bridging three decades, is very much contemporary. Afterwards, the criteria for choosing poets become somewhat less clear. The publication of Margaret Avison's poetry in 2003 could be read as a signal of the editors' renewed interest in Canadian modernism, although the poetry selection in the book is strongly weighted towards her post-conversion poetry. In 2005, it was the turn of

Dennis Lee, celebrated as a "protean" poet informed by an existential and political ethos turning mostly on questions of environmental and civic responsibility. Similarly, an intense political ethos hinging on questions of diaspora, globalization, and the violent contradictions of the contemporary cosmopolitan city characterizes the urgency pervading Dionne Brand's poetry published in 2007. The latest publication in the series, a selection of Leonard Cohen's poetry, can be read as part of the editors' ongoing commitment to translating voices with an international profile.

Words & Images, a celebratory anthology of the first ten volumes of the series, was launched in May 2008. In his introduction, Branko Gorjup articulates explicitly the editorial principles guiding his choices over fifteen years: a personal preference for certain poets, important voices in Canadian literary history, and poets not previously translated into Italian.[5] Mentioning the challenges in accounting fully for Canada's cultural diversity,[6] he refers to the racialized dimensions of contemporary Canadian poetry, manifest in the inclusion of Michael Ondaatje and Dionne Brand, but not to issues of gender, which remain implicit in the series in the alternation of male and female poets. The emphasis on history and biography in the series as a whole is reflected in each volume's critical introduction, which situates the poet's work within a narrative of English-Canadian literature where systemic questions of gender and poetic practice are muted within a framework outlining the individual writer's poetic career rather than within more complex analytical frames attending to the material and discursive conditions of her/his cultural production. In particular, with regard to the edition of P.K. Page's poetry, the relative absence of an explicit theorization of questions of gender, authorship, and literary history is also reflected in the translation itself, as we shall soon see.

If we now shift our attention to the mode of cultural exchange foregrounded by these books and their privileged sites of dissemination, two noticeable patterns emerge. First, the cross-cultural pairings of Italian and Canadian artists tend to be primarily regulated by considerations of each poet's and each artist's symbolic prestige within the frame of two separate national canons of cultural history. This separation of discrete national values tends to contain and freeze—rather than positively value and mobilize—both the internal dynamics of creative encounter between the actual artists' poetic and aesthetic visions, and the readers' (potentially transnational) interpretive experience. Second, the asymmetry between a Canadian one-time-only book launch linked to an art exhibition and the books' ongoing presence and distribution in Italy reveals a differential targeting of separately constituted national audiences. This differential targeting is predicated on liberal configurations of national culture, which silently omit the historical presence of a (subaltern) transnational reading constituency such as the Italian-Canadian one, and privilege an Italian reader based in Italy, specifically in an Italian university.

In the IIC's 1996 twentieth-anniversary book *Incontro*, Francesca Valente writes about the activities of her institute as characterized by a "reciprocal approach [committed] to negotiating an appropriate manner in which to present culture to another country, showing sensitivity to what the host country might find relevant to receive" (21). Valente does not expand on the kind of criteria used to evaluate "relevance" for the "host country." However, these latter become clear when leafing through the photos of Italian and Canadian celebrities hosted by the institute, photos that comprise the bulk of this celebratory book (21). While the list of names includes more and less famous people (from Umberto Eco and Margaret Atwood to Fulvio Tomizza and Janice Kulyk Keefer), the captions describing each person's cultural role and contribution to the institute's history carefully produce each name as the effect of a rigorous criterion of international selection and exchange based on the symbolic capital of the author-function as prestigious ambassador of national culture. What seems to count most are less the dynamic and creative effects constituting a transnational interpretive community engendered by cross-cultural collaborations—where the production of cultural value need not be primarily sustained by the legitimizing apparatuses of the nation-state—than the frozen representation of a domestic author's cultural prestige to a foreign audience.[7] This logic also seems to inform the bilingual publication I am presently analyzing. P.K. Page herself confirms this when commenting on how she came in contact with Italian artist Mimmo Paladino:

> With Paladino there is no collaboration at all, if collaboration means working together. I've never met Paladino. I've never spoken to him. I've never written to him. Francesca Valente, the director of the Istituto Italiano di Cultura, Toronto, gave him the poems that she translated into Italian and he came up with his images. It was the least personal collaboration of all. The most abstract really. (Bashford and Ruzesky 125–26)

Page's comment underscores the crucial role played by Francesca Valente—both translator and institutional patron—in fostering the intercultural dialogue between herself and Paladino. The proximity of the role of translator and institutional patron in the same person signals that this specific discursive formation impinges on the pragmatics of translation. As I have mentioned above, this discourse is heavily invested in the production and legitimization of official national cultures as discrete and relatively unified entities, whose reciprocal cultural exchanges are predicated on liberal fictions of international commensurability and equivalence, which tend to conceal, rather than expose, geopolitical asymmetries of power and symbolic capital both within and between national contexts.

Following in the wake of contemporary translation theory informed by a postcolonial sensibility, my analysis then seeks "to draw attention to [the] differentiating asymmetries of power that orient the social logic of translation in [this specific] linguistic pairing" (Godard, "Millennial Musings" 51). If, as Lawrence Venuti argues, translation always participates in a domesticizing impulse, in that it is bound to produce a domestic image of a foreign culture, in the case of this book, the series to which it belongs, and the artistic events that first launched it, such a domesticizing impulse works in two directions at once: one towards the production of the prestigious Italian visual artist in Canada, and the other towards the production of the prestigious Canadian poet in Italy. This double effect of translative domesticization is governed by a series of differentiated commensurabilities regulated both inter- and intranationally: internationally by the geopolitical status of each country's national languages; and intranationally by sociosymbolic hierarchies of linguistic competence and cultural value. At an international level, the pairing of an Italian *visual* artist with a Canadian *poet* and the production of a bilingual rather than a monolingual Italian edition signal the global pervasiveness of anglophone linguistic hegemony. On the one hand, the choice of an Italian *visual* artist implicitly points out the assumption of a monolingual anglophone audience, in that the language of line and colour can easily be assumed to transcend strictly linguistic boundaries. On the other hand, the keeping of the "original" English in the bilingual edition can be read as a symptom of the linguistic awareness of cultural relativity specific to speakers of minor languages—Italian being here a relatively minor language in the global economy of linguistic exchanges.

At an intranational level (Italian and Canadian), issues pertaining to social hierarchies of linguistic and cultural belonging come to the forefront when we consider how the selection of authors and the series' institutional sites of production and dissemination reveal the assumption of two separate national readership constituencies, characterized by class and ethnic privilege. These anthologies' ideal reader is someone whose relation to her second language is primarily regulated by formal schooling in a first-language environment—that is, an Italian reader who has learned English in the Italian school system—rather than by a minoritized familial immersion positioned against a linguistically different wider social context—this latter being the experience of so many Italian Canadians, the hyphenated, quasi-creolized subjects emerging from the histories of twentieth-century working-class migration. In other words, the series as a whole does not reckon with the historical existence of a specific transnational constituency of readers, whose subaltern history bears witness to the limits of liberal narratives of both Italian and Canadian national cultures.[8] The silent omission of the Italian-Canadian reading community from the horizon of publication also reveals a conventional liberal approach to issues of multiculturalism and diasporic literatures. Significantly, none of the authors chosen for the series is Italian-Canadian, and the two poets who could be taken to represent contemporary diasporic literary culture, Michael Ondaatje and Dionne Brand, are well on their way to achieving canonical status in Canada and have become well known in Italy thanks to the translation of their novels.

Bilingual Invisibility

The geopolitics of intra- and international cultural hegemony I have described so far contribute to a paradoxical aspect of these bilingual editions, and particularly of the text analyzed here. Despite their bilingualism, in fact, all the books are notable for the self-effacing character of their translations. With the exception of a very short translator's note to Avison's poems[9] and a short artist's statement by Giuseppe Zigaina in the anthology dedicated to Al Purdy, none of the paratextual apparatus of all nine publications (the critical introductions and the informal "Appreciations") make any explicit reference to the labour of translation—whether this be the interlingual translation of the Canadian poet or the intersemiotic translation performed by the Italian visual artists. This functional invisibility unwittingly stresses the symbolic primacy of the Canadian poet's "original" expressive genius, and inscribes translation as a self-effacing function of textual explication, primarily geared towards facilitating the reader's access to the source text, rather than towards a more dynamic experience of reading that would be as attentive to the effects of difference as to the effects of equivalence brought into relief by the encounter between the translated and the translating language. Interestingly enough, this framing inscription of translation as subordinate and derivative stands in visible contradiction to the material layout of the book, where the presence of English and Italian on the same page prompts a non-linear and comparative experience of reading that necessarily troubles the books' framing linguistic hierarchy. It is in the rifts of such a contradictory tension that I seek to posit my critical reading of the politics of translation orienting *Rosa dei venti / Compass Rose*.

The observations above become particularly obvious when skimming through P.K. Page's bilingual anthology. The book has no translator's foreword nor afterword, no commentary on the relations between Paladino's work and Page's poetry, and none of the seven introductory "Appreciations," including Branko Gorjup's critical foreword, make any remark either on the interlingual choices marking the Italian versions of Page's poetry, or on the intersemiotic significance of the relation between her texts and Paladino's paintings. The introductory "Appreciations" limit themselves to personal appraisals of Page's "gift" (14), and Gorjup's critical remarks, while providing an introduction to the poet's historical background and main poetic themes, make no reference at all to the difficulties and challenges the translator might have encountered, nor to her working criteria. Translation, in other words, permeates this book and yet it is made transparent by its subordination to the primacy of an author-function conceptualized within the romantic and pre-modernist tradition of singular expressive genius, rather than within a more complex framework that takes into account varying discursive contexts of authorial production and readerly interpretation. The effects of this subordination are multiple and operate on many levels, both cultural and textual. Culturally, the effect is one of framing the *value of the foreign* within a paradigm of domestic legitimization shaped by the institutional networks in which it is expected to be read. Here such networks are constituted by Italian academic courses in modern languages departments, where the study of a foreign language, despite the recent influence of cultural and postcolonial studies, remains institutionally rooted in the study of its national literature within a framework inherited by the nineteenth-century European systematization of comparative literature.[10] The mildly historicist interpretive frame utilized in Gorjup's introduction confirms this and suggests that the book's bilingualism serves primarily a pedagogical function geared towards referential explication and facilitation of the reader's access to the English text, rather than towards expressive reproduction, let alone creative displacement into a new language.

I mention these three different potential functions/effects of translation (referential explication, expressive reproduction, and creative displacement) for the purpose of marking a range of ideological positions vis-à-vis the pragmatics of transcultural exchange through translation. Whereas the practice of translation as referential explication reveals an implicit Lockeian assumption that language is a transparent communicative tool for social exchanges—where everything is subordinated to the search for *equivalent signifieds*—in the case of translation as expressive reproduction, primary attention is given to the connotative value of the signifier. More radically, when translation becomes a practice of creative displacement, what emerges is an attention to the performative effects produced by the open-ended play of signifiers within and between languages. These three positions roughly mark the difference between what I call an *empiricist*, a *romantic*, and a *(post)modernist* approach to language and to signifying practices. I suggest these three categories not for the purpose of marking sequential historical periods, but to signal their coexistence in contemporary practices of translation, where the prevalence of one approach over the other is defined by contextual considerations invariably linked to the politics of culture pursued by a translator, her publishing house, and the specific position this latter occupies in the juridical, economic, and symbolic configurations of the (dynamic) cultural field within which it seeks recognition (Bourdieu). In the case of this bilingual edition of a modernist English-Canadian woman poet, my critical argument is that the cultural politics of its mode of production sustain an empiricist—rarely romantic and never postmodern—mode of translation. The limits of this approach become particularly visible when evaluated against the contested interpretation of P.K. Page's own (gendered) modernist inscription of language and poetic practice.

Page's (Un)Gendered Modernism in Translation

The translation's empiricist tendency towards referential explication has the effect of producing an Italian image of P.K. Page that dilutes the impact of her modernist practices of signification and does not take into account her poetry's complex imagist inscription of gendered perception and agency. In the translation, this absence of a gendered analysis results in an unquestioned alignment with Italian hegemonic conventions of gender, and, generally, in conservative linguistic choices, which mobilize for the reader a very narrow range of domestic literary and cultural references. The most visible, if not the only, instance of mobilization of domestic literary references not surprisingly involves an intertextual reference to Italy's most canonical author: Dante. In "Photos of a Salt Mine," a poem from the early 1950s marking Page's transition from socially committed poetry to a more introspective one marked by references to the mystical tradition, the tension between an aesthetic apprehension of the mine's visual beauty and the horrific social reality of (child) labour exploitation is bridged by an explicit reference to Dante's *Inferno* in the poem's last stanza:

> Like Dante's vision of the nether hell
> men struggle with the bright cold fires of salt
> locked in the black inferno of the rock:
> the filter here not innocence but guilt. (*Compass Rose* 120)

The Italian version anticipates Page's explicit reference to Dante to the first line of the third stanza of the poem, where the word "stopes" is translated with "gironi," which is the technical term to indicate the concentric circles that structure the architecture of hell in *The Divine Comedy*. An Italian reader would immediately recognize the reference.

This is the only remarkable instance where the Italian translation makes a (timid) attempt to mobilize domestic literary and cultural references. Generally, the limits of what I have called the translation's empiricist approach become particularly visible when (a) the translation foregoes the possibility of exploiting Italian's higher degree of gender sensitivity, by resorting to the universal masculine even when the poetic *I* in much of Page's poetry could in Italian be rendered in the feminine; and (b) when it opts for *psychological* and *referentially oriented* interpretations of Page's lyrics, sometimes completely eliding the metapoetic implications of her imagist metaphors.

The poems "Foreigner," "The Travellers' Palm," and "Preparation" are apt illustrations of the translation's tendency to elide altogether—rather than highlight—the thorny interpretive issue of Page's configuration of a gendered poetic self within the modernist imperative of the poet's detachment and impersonality (Killian 86). All three poems were written in the 1960s, in the aftermath of Page's long silence and at the beginning of a new poetics no longer rigidly invested in upholding the credo of impersonality typical of the poems she had published in *Preview* and *Northern Review*, two little magazines most notably allied to a masculinist articulation of the modernist avant-garde (Irvine 26–27). Whereas the poems in *Preview* and *North-*

ern Review rarely ever contained references to the writing subject, "Foreigner," "The Travellers' Palm," and "Preparation" all have a self-reflexive aspect and make reference to the writing subject either through a self-address in the second person ("Preparation" and "Foreigner"), or through direct self-identification of the writing "I" ("The Travellers' Palm"). In all instances, the English does not specify the gender of the writing subject being referred to. Italian's grammatical gender sensitivity, however, requires that the gender of the writing subject be marked either in the masculine or in the feminine. The translator is thus constrained by the language to interpret the text in one direction or the other. She cannot fully reproduce the absence of gender determination present in the English text, and has to decide whether or not to highlight a gendered connection between the author and her work. This is not an easy decision to make, particularly if we consider, on the one hand, Page's reluctance to "claim her poetic vision as *belonging to a gendered self*" (Killian 97),[11] and, on the other, the double bind of a feminist approach to language, which constantly runs the risk of essentialism[12] in its attempts to subvert the universalizing claims of the masculine generic by purposefully marking the feminine. In translation, however, marking the gender of the speaker is also a crucial decision to make, particularly given the ongoing work of feminist critics, theorists, and translators to demonstrate how an approach that assumes the masculine as the unmarked paradigm of gender determination constitutes a powerful tool for the systemic reproduction of a phallocentric symbolic order.[13]

As we will see, the Italian translation elides these issues altogether and reverts to an unproblematic assumption of the masculine as a universal and paradigmatic gender category. Let us see what happens in each poem. The opening lines of "Foreigner" read: "Between strange walls / you, *foreigner*, walk in silence" (*Compass Rose* 86).[14] In English, one can only speculate as to the gender of the "foreigner," there being space for interpreting the "you" of the opening address as other than the writing self. However, the last four lines of the poem make an allusive reference to this "you" as a writing subject, thus allowing a reader to draw a (gendered) connection between the name of the author and the subject referred to in the poem:

> Now pressed in a corner *by words*
> you have no face
> and cry for love
> in the leaning tower of the self. (86)

The Italian translation, which cannot avoid gendering the poem's subject, chooses to translate "foreigner" with "stran*iero*" (masculine) rather than "stran*iera*" (feminine), consequently gendering the rest of the poem also in the masculine.

While "Foreigner" leaves room for interpretation as to who exactly the addressed "you" refers to, "Preparation" forcefully inscribes the address in the second person as an imperative self-address. Again, the English does not explicitly gender this "you," whereas in Italian a choice of gender has to be made, specifically when the verb is conjugated in the passive. Again the translation prefers the masculine. The first lines of the second, third, and fourth stanza respectively read

Prepare to be huge	Preparati ad essere grande
Be *prepared* to be small	Sii *preparato* ad essere *piccolo*
...	...
Be *prepared* to prepare	Sii *preparato* a preparare
for what you have dreamed	quello che sognavi
to burn and be *burned*	a bruciare e a essere *bruciato*
...	...
Be pre-pared. And pre-pare.	Sii pre-*parato*. E pre-para. (186–87)

"*Preparato*," "*piccolo*," "*bruciato*": for a feminist reader these modifiers gender the poet's self-address in the masculine while purporting to produce an impersonal, disinterested, and "universal" image of a poetic self.

Finally, "The Travellers' Palm" inscribes directly a writing "I" and qualifies it as "traveller" (*Compass Rose* 134). In this case, the Italian translation symptomatically reveals its pervasive assumption of the masculine as the unmarked paradigm of gender. Interestingly, there is an Italian word for "traveller" that reads the same both in the masculine and in the feminine, and the translation inconsistently uses such word in its title, but not in the body of the poem. The translation of the title reads "La palma dei *viandanti*." The singular of this noun, *viandante* stands both for the masculine and for the feminine. However, in the body of the poem, "traveller" is translated as "viaggiatore" (the feminine would be *viaggiatrice*), a more inconsistent choice if we consider that the word appears in a line that reads "for *me*, traveller / a well," where that "me" explicitly connects the "traveller" to the authorial self. Ironically enough, even if the translator had been unwilling to risk essentializing the gender of Page's authorial persona, she still had the choice of using the bivalent noun *viandante*.

Not surprisingly, the instances where the translation chooses to gender the poetic "I" in the feminine are those where Page either explicitly connotes it thus through signifiers that link femininity to archetypal images of fluidity and earth fertility (as in "Summer" and "After Rain"), or when the poem is more narrative in tone, and makes explicit reference to the "I" as an embodied, biographical entity ("Dwelling Place," "The Maze," "After Reading *Albino Pheasants* by Patrick Lane," "The Filled Pen," and "Ancestors"). For example, in "Summer" (*Compass Rose* 100) the line "my feminine fingers" explicitly marks the authorial persona and authorizes the translation to gender in the feminine all the other modifiers in the poem. In "Dwelling Place," it is the poem's explicitly deictic reference to the poet's own body that makes the translation opt for the feminine in gendering the speaking "I": "This habitation—bones, flesh and skin—/ where I reside" (158). The second line of the last stanza, "I, its inhabitant, indweller—eye," thus becomes in Italian "io, la su*a* abitante, inquilin*a*—un occhio" (158–59). In its gendering choices among different poems, the translation confirms the dominant symbolic alignment of the generic masculine with abstract universality and of the generic feminine with embodied biographical singularity.

Mimetic Modernism?

My critique in the examples above clearly sides with a postmodern sensibility, specifically informed by the notion of a feminist "womanhandling" (Godard, "Theorizing Feminist Discourse" 50) of the text in translation, which has been extensively practised and theorized by anglophone Canadian women writers and translators (Barbara Godard, Daphne Marlatt, Gail Scott, Di Brandt, Betsy Warland, and others), who are now actively reclaiming the cultural legacy of female modernism (the conference "Wider Boundaries of Daring" being part of this movement). My analysis so far might then be read as problematic, to the extent that it focusses more thoroughly on the signifying possibilities released by the gendered structure of the translating language, than on a historicized understanding of Page's participation in the impersonal (and thus implicitly masculine) paradigm of modernist poetics. However, notwithstanding new critical work that significantly re-evaluates the presence of a female line of modernist influence on Page's poetic practice,[15] the Italian translation in *Rosa dei venti* / *Compass Rose* also betrays a somewhat superficial reading of the poet's modernism, particularly of her early period (1940s and 1950s). Here, Page's use of imagist techniques of metaphoric condensation, while fully invested in an aesthetics of objective detachment, nonetheless conveys a specific understanding of gendered agency and of gender relations. Far from addressing the complex ways in which Page's particular brand of imagist modernism deeply encodes the interpenetration of material and symbolic conditions in the structuring of gender relations, the translation consistently takes explicative shortcuts, which tend to reduce the semantic density of formal choices to transparent statements of inner psychology.

The translation's elision of Page's modernist approach to issues of gendered agency and subjectivity is particularly visible in two of her early poems, "The Typists" and "After Rain." In "The Typists," the first lines read "They, *without message*, having read / the running words on their machines" (*Compass Rose* 80). These become in Italian "Leggendo *senza capire* / le parole che scorrono sulla macchina da scrivere" (81), which literally translates "[They] reading without understanding / the words that run on the typing machine." What in English is configured as the absence, in the typists, *of a content*, that is, of something meaningful to say—an absence that does not imply the absence of the ability *as such*—becomes in Italian the absence of an *ability to understand*. Such an interpretation, in implying a disparagingly psychological characterization of working-class women, implicitly assigns to the voice of the poet-observer an elitist posture of intellectual and class superiority. This, I would argue, is absent from the English version precisely because its impersonal account of the alienating tensions engendered by the typists' material working conditions avoids making explicit psychological statements.

The Italian shift from a parenthetic nominal clause to a subordinate prepositional clause holding an infinitive verb in the first line of "The Typists" also illustrates another tendency of the translation: it transforms Page's imagist preference for nominal and asyntactic sentences[16]—layered with an abundance of metaphors that insist on visual and spatial differences/distances—into verb-governed and syntactically complete sentences that tend to dilute the semantic density of Page's formal choices into a transparent explication of content. This interpretive shift is the more striking if we consider that there are no norms of syntax or grammar impeding the construction of nominal sentences in Italian. On the contrary, nominal sentences are far less tolerated in English than they are in Italian. In "After Rain" (*Compass Rose* 174), this tendency has again the effect of conveying a sense of psychologizing empathy in the Italian, where the English tends to stress relations of *alterity* and *distance* governed by differences of gender and class. The poem dramatically juxtaposes the author's (middle-class) "female whimsy," rendered happily "half drunk" by an aestheticized visual apprehension of a garden in disarray after the rain, against the pragmatic concern of her gardener Giovanni, rendered desolate by the same disarray she finds so enticing. Generally read as a turning point in Page's career (Irvine; Sullivan; Killian; Trehearne, *Montreal Forties*), the poem is striking for its subjective tone and for the poet's self-critical recognition of the limitations incurred by an aesthetics exclusively founded on the objectifying powers of the gaze. While all critics agree on these aspects of the poem, interpretations differ when it comes to assessing the poem's last stanza and its prayer for a "heart a size larger than seeing": is it a call for a "wholeness" inclusive of an emerging sense of mystical empathy and fluidity, which will become more evident in her subsequent poems (Sullivan 34, 42)? Or does it signal the poet's radical inability to overcome her own "aesthetic fixation" despite the brief record of sympathy with Giovanni's dolours (Trehearne, *Montreal Forties* 42)? The translation offers its own interpretive slant already in the second to last stanza, where the tension between self and Other, between the exclusivity and self-involvement of the poet's fantasy and the objective Otherness of the Other's suffering is underscored by the choice of signifiers such as "rim" and "hub" that mark self-enclosed and unbridgeable spatial distances (Sullivan 34). Let us see how the translation works. In English, the stanza reads,

> I suffer shame in all these images.
> The garden is primeval, Giovanni
> in soggy denim *squelches by my hub*,
> over his ruin
> shakes a doleful head.
> But he so beautiful and diademed,
> His long Italian hands so wrung with rain
> *I find his ache exists beyond my rim*
> And almost weep to see a broken man
> Made subject to my whim. (*Compass Rose* 174, 176)

In Italian:

> Provo vergogna per queste immagini.
> il giardino è primordiale, Giovanni
> in una fradicia tuta, *al mio fianco, struscia*

sulla sua rovina,
scuotendo il capo affranto.
Ma è così bello e cinto da diadema,
Le lunghe mani italiane *così straziate dalla pioggia*
Che sento il suo dolore traboccare
E quasi piango a vedere un uomo avvilito
Assoggettato al mio capriccio. (175, 177)

The Italian translation of "squelches by my hub" ("al mio fianco, struscia") transforms "hub" (in Italian *perno* or *fulcro*)[17] into "side" ("fianco"), significantly reducing thus the poem's emphasis on an unbridgeable spatial distance between two separate entities, each comprised of a centre (a "hub") and a periphery. Further on, the Italian version recomposes the broken syntax of the stanza's last sentence—"But he so beautiful ... I find he ..."—into a syntactically complete phrase, inclusive of copula and consecutive conjunction: "Ma é così bello ... che" (But he *is* so beautiful ... *that*). This prose-like explication of the broken syntax results in the turning line "I find his ache exists beyond my rim" being translated into "sento il suo dolore traboccare" (I feel his pain overflow). What in English is the sudden halt of an indicative statement of existential alterity becomes in Italian a syntactically prepared-for affective declaration of shareable empathy. As we have already seen in "The Typists," the translation here produces an effect of psychological realism, which is quite alien to Page's oeuvre as a whole, both from her strictly modernist phase and from her later one, characterized by a growing interest in mysticism. Such choices further reveal the pedagogical character of the translation, to the extent that they consistently recompose Page's fragmented syntax into a prose-like whole, primarily geared towards facilitating the English text's intelligibility rather than towards reproducing in Italian a similar expressive intensity.

The translation's explicative tendency also elides many of the metapoetic implications present in Page's careful wording of her visual metaphors. Specifically, the translation seems to be entirely unaware of how Page consistently relies on a vocabulary borrowed from painting and the visual arts in her metaphors. This choice has the crucial epistemic effect of connoting the human gaze, the "eye" as an active *inscriber* and thus *producer* of (worded) images, rather than just their passive *recorder*.[18] In "Only Child," for example, we encounter the word "stuccoed" in the last line of the fourth stanza, when we are first introduced to the child's alienating relation to his mother's words:

> By the pool she said, "Observe
> the canvasback's a diver," and her words
> *stuccoed* the slaty water of the lake. (*Compass Rose* 64)

Page's careful word choice is metavisual in essence, in that it conveys the child's experience of objective alienation through a precise reference to painterly techniques of mimetic reproduction. Page's choice here amounts to nothing less than a rigorous exploration of the effects of mimetic repetition/reproduction on human consciousness. In other words, we are here in full purview of the modernist critique of representation as a transparent reproduction of reality. The Italian version, however, misses the word's epistemic implications entirely, and translates "stuccoed" with "raggelavano" (froze), emphasizing again the child's emotional response within a framework of psychological transparent referentiality.

The elision of Page's metapoetic layering is also visible in the Italian versions of "Adolescence," "The Landlady," and "The Maze." In "Adolescence," the last lines of the first stanza read, "And white was mixed with all their colours / as if they drew it from the flowering trees" (*Compass Rose* 70). The Italian translates, "E il bianco si mischiava con tutti i loro colori / come se lo ricavassero dagli alberi in fiore" (71). The Italian choice of the verb *ricavare* for "to draw" considerably narrows the polysemic valency of the English word. The Italian *tracciare* would have easily conveyed such polysemy, without substantially altering the line's rhythm. Similarly, in "The Maze" the same word *tracciare* would have conveyed Page's emphasis on the act of painterly/writerly inscription at play in her attempt to reproduce her mystic vision. At the end of the second stanza, the poet writes, "I was tracing the spiral nebula in my head" (156). The Italian translates, "I was tracing" with "seguivo" (I followed), undoubtedly a less pregnant word than "tracing." Finally, in "The Landlady" (76–77), the highly visual English "stippled with curiosity" is translated as "fremente di curiosità" (quivering with curiosity). The poet's subtle reference to a precise painting technique could have easily been rendered in Italian by the word *punteggiata*. The translation instead returns to its usual penchant for using words connoting movement and direct access to inner psychology, where the English consistently underlines immobility and barely fathomable surfaces of seeing.

All of the observations I have made so far emphasize a certain degree of systemic convergence between the book's institutional conditions of production and dissemination, the critical framework of interpretation articulated by the book's paratextual apparatus (the six "Appreciations" and

Gorjup's critical introduction) and the interpretive trajectory of the translation itself. I have argued that a conventional frame of comparative literature hinging on the (Western liberal) fiction of discrete national cultures, together with a pre-modernist notion of authorship as singular expressive genius and the assumption of a non-specialized student readership, thoroughly contribute to the explicative and self-effacing character of the Italian versions of Page's poetry, paradoxically achieved despite the pervasiveness of translation in the book's self-presentation. I have noted the serious limitations of such an approach, particularly with regards to how it produces a domesticized (and domesticated) interpretation of Page's poetry that similarly elides both the question of the poet's modernist approach to gendered agency and the question of the epistemic implications of her imagist aesthetics. This aspect of my criticism has relied on what I have called a romantic approach to translation, in that my suggestions for alternative translations were mostly informed by a desire to reproduce in Italian the same expressive density as the original English version. This attention to the connotative dimensions of Page's choice of signifiers allowed me to question the translation's empiricist assumption of semantic stability in her poetry. Beyond this, my observations have also articulated a critique that moves towards a more open-ended approach to the question of translation, one which reads translation less as a self-effacing process of interpretive adequation to a normatively posited authorial intention, and more as an ideologically aware trajectory of interpretive manipulation, committed to making visible the manifold cultural and linguistic contexts within which its work takes place. Specifically, my critique of the translation's conservative interpretation of Page's ambiguous inscription of gender in "Preparation," "The Travellers' Palm," and "Foreigner" was premised neither on a retrieval of the author's original intentions, nor on a historicist reconstruction of her (non-feminist) cultural context (Trehearne, *Montreal Forties*), but on an ideological allegiance to a postmodern feminist project of linguistic change, one whose claim to revising the cultural legacy of modernist women writers is justified by the systemic persistence of phallogocentrism in contemporary transnational contexts.

I acknowledge, however, that despite the limitations inscribed in its inter- rather than transnational framework of production and dissemination, it was the book's bilingualism that first constituted for me the enabling occasion for pursuing this kind of critique. There is something to be said about the signifying possibilities released for the reader by finding herself confronted with a text in two languages at once. The visible, graphic symmetry of the bilingual inscription prompts a shuttle reading movement that goes in both directions, from Italian to English as much as from English to Italian. What this movement inevitably produces for the reader is an awareness not only of the implicit assumptions governing the translator's lexical, syntactic, and stylistic choices, but also a heightened awareness of the set of signifying constraints peculiar to each of the two languages: their strengths, their weaknesses, and where their proximity has the potential to generate unexpected semantic drifts between them. This is where bilingual editions constitute a particularly compelling editorial choice. Borrowing the term from Clifford Geertz, I would argue that the visible proximity of the translated and the translating language compels the reader to seek a "thick" approach to the poetry's expressive density, thus providing an ideal training ground for cultivating the kind of "transnational literacy" that for Gayatri Chakravorty Spivak ("Questioned on Translation" 15) constitutes the necessary means for a "persistent critique" of the ideology of general "permeability" (17) between languages brought about by anglophone hegemony in the global economy of linguistic exchanges. This essay has, after all, been one such exercise in cultivation.

Notes

1 Between the mid-fifties and the mid-sixties, P.K. Page stopped writing and started painting. Interestingly, her painting began during her sojourn as a Canadian ambassador's wife in Brazil—in a country, that is, that forced her to confront questions of translation, as she did not know Portuguese when she arrived there. I here tentatively suggest that her shift from poetry to painting might well be related to the difficult encounter with a foreign language and culture, and the crucial absence of a social context immediately receptive to her poetic communication. In other words, her poetic work migrated or "translated" (which etymologically means to carry through and/or over) into the realm of the visual at a point in the poet's life when her linguistic means showed their limitations and insufficiencies (see *Brazilian Journal*). In his introduction to *Compass Rose*, Branko Gorjup makes only a passing reference to her painting years.
2 The imagist influence on Page's poetry runs deep in her consistent use of synaesthetic metaphors that draw most of their signifying force from the visual, and from the techniques of visual arts in particular. In an essay focussed on Page's visual art, Barbara Godard argues that Page's emergence of a painterly self still invested in asking "writerly" questions about the "paradoxical status of both word and visual image as signs of reality" took place during a period "of personal transition when ... wordlessness threatened to unravel her very identity" ("Kinds of Osmosis" 66).
3 Irving Layton's *Il cacciatore sconcertato / The Baffled Hunter* (1993) contains drawing by Enzo Cucchi and "calligrammusic" by Marcello Panni. Gwendolyn MacEwen's *Il geroglifico finale / The Last Hieroglyph* (1997) has drawings by Sandro Chia. Margaret

Atwood's *Giochi di specchi / Tricks with Mirrors* (1999) contains watercolours by Luigi Ontani, and Al Purdy's *Pronuncia i nomi / Say the Names /* (1999) has drawings by Giuseppe Zigaina. Michael Ondaatje's poetry (*Notte senza scale / A Night Without a Staircase*) is accompanied by drawings and collages by Vettor Pisani (2001), and Margaret Avison's poems (*Il cuore che vede / The Optic Eye*) are accompanied by watercolours and graphic designs by Ubaldo Bartolini (2003). The most recent additions to the series—Dennis Lee's *Dimora del cuore / Heart Residence* (2005), Dionne Brand's *Luce ostinata / Tenacious Light* (2007), and Leonard Cohen's *La Solitudine della forza / The Solitude of Strength* (2008)—contain, respectively, drawings and graphic designs by Nunzio, drawings by Achille Perilli, and embossings on paper by Arnaldo Pomodoro.

4   As Branko Gorjup notes in his introduction to *Words & Images*, the celebratory anthology dedicated to the Peter Paul Series, interest in Canadian literature in Italy has been fostered and nurtured in Italian universities since the early 1960s "by aspiring academics who tired of an Anglo-American curriculum in English Studies" (14). The 1990s saw Canadian literature "burst onto the Italian stage," mostly thanks to commercial publishers successfully circulating fiction by Margaret Atwood, Michael Ondaatje, Ann-Marie MacDonald, Anne Michaels, Alistair MacLeod, Mordecai Richler, and others. The commercial success of these translations was also made possible by the policy of internationalization pursued by the Canada Council, which offers foreign publishers financial support when translating a Canadian author (Canada Council, International Publishing Grants). This has facilitated the growth of interest also in Canadian poetry, particularly thanks to an increasing number of Italian universities opening their own centres for Canadian studies and inviting authors "to give lectures and readings" (Gorjup, *Words & Images*, 14).

5   Among the poets already translated into Italian, Gorjup lists Earl Birney, George Bowering, Anne Michaels, and Anne Carson. He forgets to name Miriam Waddington and Elizabeth Smart, two modernist women poets published in Italian in recent years, the analysis of whose translation would provide an interesting point of comparison in the context of my own analysis of the translations of P.K. Page's poetry. Smart's masterpiece, *By Grand Central Station I Sat Down and Wept*, was first translated in 1971 for a major Italian publisher, Il Saggiatore. The translation, by Rodolfo Wilcock, contains a brief introduction by Cesare Garboli, one of Italy's major poetry critics. His introduction, however, is not intended for a specialized audience and reads as a generic review, more preoccupied with the author's biographical details than with providing any literary or historical context for the reader. A new edition of the same translation was reissued by Theoria in 1993, a much smaller publishing house. In 1993, there appeared also a translation of Smart's last book, *The Assumption of Rogues and Rascals* (trans. Alessandra Calanchi), by another small press, Il Melangolo. Both editions are meant for a general public and do not pay attention to issues of translation. A bilingual anthology of Miriam Waddington's poetry, "*Cercando fragole in giugno*" *e altre poesie*, however, was curated and translated by Daniela Fortezza for a university press in 1993. Hers is the only Italian scholarly edition of a Canadian modernist women poet that contains explicit references to the challenges of translation.

6   Gorjup mentions how "fully aware" he is "of the fact that it is almost impossible to create a representative view of the poetic landscape of a country [as] physically and culturally diverse as Canada," and reminds us that the series is a "work in progress," which will "continually readjust itself to the figure on the ground, responding to newer voices, while still reaching back into the past" (14).

7   Except for Ubaldo Bartolini, who is acknowledged and thanked for having produced new work specifically tailored to Margaret Avison's poetry, all of the other Italian artists in the series seem to have donated previously existing material for publication.
8   See Francesco Loriggio's collection *Social Pluralism and Literary History: The Literature of the Italian Immigration* (1996).
9   Interestingly, Avison is the only poet in the series described as having "a language-driven craft" (Gorjup, Introduction, *Il cuore che vede / The Optic Eye* 28), as if only a poet's linguistic difficulty would authorize the translator's higher degree of visibility in the text. However appropriate the remark is with regard to Avison's poetry, there are linguistic challenges facing the translators of each poet in the series, which inevitably bring difference to the fore in the passage between one language and another. It is thus baffling to read the translators of Avison's poetry apologetically articulate the difficult choices they had to make. Surely the translators made difficult choices when working on the other books, too!
10 For an introduction to the institutional history of comparative literature, see Susan Bassnett, *Comparative Literature: A Critical Introduction* (esp. 12–31).
11 Recently, Page seems to have forgone such a reluctance to claim a gendered poetic vision for herself. In "P.K. Page: Discovering a Modern Sensibility"—a paper presented at the "Wider Boundaries of Daring" conference and now included in this volume—Sandra Djwa convincingly reconstructs a female modernist genealogy of influence on Page's early literary education (especially Woolf and Mansfield) through oral testimony (interviews with the poet herself) and private writing (the poet's diaries and letters). Djwa's strategic use of "private" documents to account for the gendered literary legacy standing behind Page's most frequent metaphor for poetic inspiration (the "hidden room"), indirectly reconfigures the poet's allegiance to the "impersonal" imperatives of modernist poetics less as full ideological adherence than as the effect of a consciously assumed public persona in the midst of a male-dominated literary world. Laura Killian draws a similar conclusion when she argues through psychoanalysis that Page's hyperformalism can be read as a defence mechanism against being labelled a sentimental, and thus "feminine," poet.
12 That is, of reading the gendering of the authorial persona as an indexical sign, directly denoting her "sex."
13 On Italian critiques of the "neutral universal masculine" ("*il maschile neutro universale*") in language, see Patrizia Violi, *L'infinito singolare* (1986); Diotima, *Il pensiero della differenza sessuale* (1987); Luisa Muraro, *L'ordine simbolico della madre* (1991); and Bono and Kemp's edited collection *Italian Feminist Thought: A Reader* (1991). For Canadian feminist translation theory, see Godard (1989), Susanne de Lotbinière-Harwood, *Re-belle et infidèle / The Body Bilingual* (1991); Edwin Gentzler, *Contemporary Translation Theories* (1993); Sherry Simon, *Gender in Translation* (1996); and Luise Von Flotow, *Translation and Gender* (1997).
14 Unless otherwise noted, all italics in the poetry quotations are added.
15 See Djwa's article "P.K. Page: A Portrait of the Artist as a Young Woman" (2004) and her contribution to this volume.
16 For an analysis of the rhetorical strategies of imagist poetry, see John T. Gage, *In the Arresting Eye: The Rhetoric of Imagism* (1981). For a commentary on Page's early imagism, see Brian Trehearne, *The Montreal Forties: Modernist Poetry in Translation* (1999). Trehearne has more recently argued for recognizing the influence of Surrealism in Page's work, in particular the automatist principles of free association in Page's

preference for "parallelism and parataxis ... unashamed alliterations [and] associative chaining [of disparate signifiers]" ("P.K. Page and Surrealism" 50).

17 Both "fulcro" and "perno" are composed of two syllables, like "fianco." The choice of one of them would not have compromised the rhythm of the stanza, excluding thus the hypothesis that the translator might have had prosodic considerations in mind when choosing "fianco."

18 The problematic alignment of such an active inscription of the gaze with the masculine power of the phallus constitutes the central focus of Laura Killian's reading of P.K. Page. Killian does not expand on an interesting psychoanalytic (and specifically Lacanian) reading of Page's articulation of the gaze and of the field of vision throughout her artistic career, but I agree with her suggestion that the poet's fears of being dubbed "sentimental"—that is, of having her writerly skills collapsed into a generic appraisal of her "natural" gendered tendencies—contributed to the hypertrophic aspects of her formalism in her early poetry. In Lacanian terms, I would argue that her hyperformalism is symptomatic of Page's ambivalent relation to the (phallic) symbolic order legitimizing her cultural value as a poet. Conversely, this symptomatic attachment can also be read—as I suggest in my interpretation of "Only Child"—as an unwittingly rigorous exploration of the alienating powers of the phallic gaze, that is of the gaze that names. This exploration, I would add, is indifferent as to whether the subject perpetrating the gaze is gendered male or female; in "Only Child," for example, it is the mother that performs such a phallic function.

Works Cited

Atwood, Margaret. *Giochi di specchi / Tricks with Mirrors*. Ed. Branko Gorjup and Francesca Valente. Watercolours by Luigi Ontani. Trans. Laura Forconi, Caterina Ricciardi, and Francesca Valente. Ravenna: Longo Editore, 2000.

Avison, Margaret. *Il cuore che vede / The Optic Eye*. Ed. Branko Gorjup and Francesca Valente. Watercolours by Ubaldo Bartolini. Trans. Brunella Antomarini, Francesca Inghilleri, and Francesca Valente. Ravenna: Longo Editore, 2003.

Bashford, Lucy, and Jay Ruzesky. "Entranced: A Conversation with P.K. Page." In Rogers and Peace, eds. 110–128.

Bassnett, Susan. *Comparative Literature: A Critical Introduction*. Oxford: Blackwell, 1993.

Bono, Paola, and Sandra Kemp, eds. *Italian Feminist Thought: A Reader*. Oxford: Basil Blackwell, 1991.

Bourdieu, Pierre. *The Field of Cultural Production*. Ed. and intro. Randal Johnson. New York: Columbia UP, 1993.

Brand, Dionne. *Luce ostinata / Tenacious Light*. Ed. Branko Gorjup and Francesca Valente. Drawings by Achille Perilli. Intro. Janice Kulyk Keefer. Trans. Marco Fazzini, Sara Fruner, and Francesca Valente. Ravenna: Longo Editore, 2007.

Cohen, Leonard. *La solitudine della forza / The Solitude of Strength*. Ed. Branko Gorjup and Francesca Valente. Trans. Francesca Valente. Ravenna: Longo Editore, 2008.

Diotima. *Il pensiero della differenza sessuale*. Milano: Tartaruga Edizioni, 1987. 43–75.

Djwa, Sandra. "P.K. Page: A Portrait of the Artist as Woman." *Journal of Canadian Studies / Revue d'études canadiennes* 38.1 (Winter 2004): 5–22.

Gage, John T. *In the Arresting Eye: The Rhetoric of Imagism*. Baton Rouge: Louisiana State UP, 1981.

Geertz, Clifford. *The Interpretation of Cultures: Selected Essays*. New York: Basic Books, 1973.

Gentzler, Edwin. *Contemporary Translation Theories*. London: Routledge, 1993.

Godard, Barbara. "Kinds of Osmosis." *Journal of Canadian Studies / Revue d'études canadiennes* 38.1 (Winter 2004): 65–75.

———. "Millennial Musings on Translation." *La traduzione*. Ed. Susan Petrilli. Spec. issue of *Athanor: Semiotica, Filosofia, Arte, Letteratura* [Roma: Meltemi Editore] 10.2 (1999–2000): 46–56.

———. "Theorizing Feminist Discourse/Translation." *Tessera. La traduction au Feminine / Translating Women* 6 (Spring 1989): 42–53.

Gorjup, Branko. Introduction. *Il cuore che vede / The Optic Eye*. Margaret Avison. Ravenna: Longo Editore, 2003. 23–51.

———. Introduction. *Words & Images: A Celebratory Bilingual Anthology of Contemporary Poetry*. The Peter Paul Series of Canadian Contemporary Poetry 1993–2008. Ed. Branko Gorjup. Ravenna: Longo Editore, 2008.

———. "My Absolute Centre: Introduction to *Compass Rose* / Il mio centro assoluto: introduzione a *Rosa dei venti*." Page, *Compass Rose*, 30–47.

Irvine, Dean. "Two Giovannis: P.K. Page's Two Modernisms." *Journal of Canadian Studies / Revue d'études canadiennes* 38.1 (Winter 2004): 23–46.

Killian, Laura. "Poetry and the Modern Woman: P.K. Page and the Gender of Impersonality." *Canadian Literature* 150 (Autumn 1996): 86–105.

Layton, Irving. *Il cacciatore sconcertato / The Baffled Hunter*. Ed. Branko Gorjup and Francesca Valente. Illus. Enzo Cucchi. Calligrammusica by Marcello Panni. Trans. Francesca Valente. Ravenna: Longo Editore, 1993.

Lee, Dennis. *Dimora del cuore / Heart's Residence*. Ed. Branko Gorjup and Francesca Valente. Drawings by Nunzio. Trans. Laura Forconi, Caterina Ricciardi, and Francesca Valente. Ravenna: Longo Editore, 2005.

Loriggio, Francesco, ed. and intro. *Social Pluralism and Literary History: The Literature of the Italian Emigration*. Toronto: Guernica, 1996.

Lotbinière-Harwood, Susanne de. *Re-belle et infidèle: La traduction comme pratique de réécriture au féminin / The Body Bilingual: Translation as Rewriting in the Feminine*. Toronto: Women's Press / Montreal: Éditions du remue-ménage, 1991.

MacEwen, Gwendolyn. *Il geroglifico finale / The Last Hieroglyph*. Ed. Branko Gorjup. Drawings by Sandro Chia. Trans. Francesca Valente. Ravenna: Longo Editore, 1997.

Muraro, Luisa. *L'ordine simbolico della madre*. Roma: Editori Riuniti, 1991.

Ondaatje, Michael. *Notte senza scale / A Night Without a Staircase*. Ed. Branko Gorjup and Francesca Valente. Drawings and collages by Vettor Pisani.

Trans. Anna Maria Chiavatti and Francesca Valente. Ravenna: Longo Editore, 2001.

Page, P.K. *Brazilian Journal*. Toronto: Lester and Orpen Dennys, 1987.

———. *Rosa dei venti / Compass Rose*. Ed. Branko Gorjup. Illus. Mimmo Paladino. Trans. Francesca Valente. Calligrammusic by Harry Somers. Ravenna: Longo Editore, 1998.

Paladino, Mimmo, and P.K. Page. *Mimmo Paladino: Works on Paper Inspired by the Poetry of P.K. Page*. Toronto: Istituto Italiano di Cultura, 1998.

Purdy, Al. *Pronuncia i nomi / Say the Names*. Ed. Branko Gorjup. Illus. Giuseppe Zigaina. Trans. Laura Forconi, Caterina Ricciardi, and Francesca Valente. Ravenna: Longo Editore, 1999.

Reeves, John, and Istituto Italiano di Cultura. *Where Italy and Canada Meet, 1976–1996*. Toronto: Istituto Italiano di Cultura / Exile Editions, 1996.

Rogers, Linda, and Barbara Colebrook Peace, eds. *P.K. Page: Essays on Her Works*. Toronto: Guernica, 2001.

Simon, Sherry. *Gender in Translation: Cultural Identity and the Politics of Transmission*. New York: Routledge, 1996.

Smart, Elizabeth. *L'assunzione di farabutti e mascalzoni*. Translation of *The Assumption of the Rogues and the Rascals* (1978). Trans. Alessandra Calanchi. Genova: Il Melangolo, 1993.

———. *Sulle fiumane della Grand Central Station mi sono seduta e ho pianto*. Translation of *By Grand Central Station I Sat Down and Wept* (1945). Trans. Rodolfo Wilcock. Milano: Il Saggiatore, 1971. Rpt. Theoria Edizioni, 1993.

Spivak, Gayatri Chakravorty. "The Politics of Translation." *Outside in the Teaching Machine*. London: Routledge, 1993. 179–200.

———. "Questioned on Translation: Adrift." *Public Culture* 13.1 (2001): 13–22.

Sullivan, Rosemary. "A Size Larger Than Seeing: The Poetry of P.K. Page." *Canadian Literature* 79 (1978): 32–42.

Trehearne, Brian. *The Montreal Forties: Modernist Poetry in Transition*. Toronto: U of Toronto P, 1999.

———. "P.K. Page and Surrealism." *Journal of Canadian Studies / Revue d'études canadiennes* 38.1 (Winter 2004): 46–64.

Venuti, Lawrence. *The Scandals of Translation: Towards an Ethics of Difference*. New York: Routledge, 1998.

Violi, Patrizia. *L'infinito singolare: Considerazioni sulla differenza sessuale nel linguaggio*. Verona: Essedue edizioni, 1986.

Von Flotow, Luise. *Translation and Gender: Translating in the "Era of Feminism."* Manchester: St. Jerome, 1997.

Waddington, Miriam. *"Cercando fragole in giugno" e altre poesie*. Ed. and trans. Daniela Fortezza. Bologna: Editrice Clueb, 1993.

CONTRIBUTORS

ELENA BASILE teaches in the English department at York University, where she is completing her dissertation on questions of translation and experimental poetic practices. Recent publications include "Responding to the Enigmatic Address of the Other: A Psychoanalytical Approach to the Translator's Labour," *New Voices in Translation Studies* (2005), and "Itchy Language Scars: Thoughts on Translation as a Poetics of Cultural Healing," in *Traducciòn, Género y Postcolonialismo: De Signis; Publicaciòn de la Federaciòn Latinoamericana de Semiòtica* (Spring 2008).

DI BRANDT is the award-winning author and editor of more than a dozen books. Her poetry titles include *questions i asked my mother* (1987), *Agnes in the sky* (1990), *Jerusalem, beloved* (1995), *Now You Care* (2003), and *Speaking of Power: The Poetry of Di Brandt* (2006). Her prose titles include *Wild Mother Dancing: Maternal Narrative in Canadian Literature* (1993) and *So this is the world & here I am in it* (2007). Her libretto for *Emily, the Way You Are*, a one-woman opera about the life and work of Emily Carr, composed by Jana Skarecky, premiered at the McMichael Gallery, Kleinburg, Ontario, in April 2008. Her website address is www.dibrandt.ca. Di Brandt holds a Canada Research Chair at Brandon University, Manitoba.

PAULINE BUTLING taught Canadian Literature at Selkirk College in Castelgar, BC, David Thompson University Centre in Nelson, BC, and at the Alberta College of Art in Calgary. She currently lives in Vancouver, where she is writing a family history/memoir. Her publications include

Seeing in the Dark: The Poetry of Phyllis Webb (1997), *Poets Talk*, with Susan Rudy (2005), and *Writing in Our Time: Canada's Radical Poetries*, with Susan Rudy (2005).

SANDRA DJWA, Professor Emerita of Simon Fraser University, has written extensively on Canadian poetry and Canadian poets. Her books include *E.J. Pratt: The Evolutionary Vision* (1974), the *Complete Poems of E.J. Pratt*, 2 vols. (1989), and the *Selected Poems of E.J. Pratt* (1999), co-edited with Zailig Pollock and W.J. Keith. Her biographies include *F.R. Scott: The Politics of the Imagination* (1987), *F.R. Scott: Une vie* (translation 2001), and *Professing English: A Life of Roy Daniells* (2002), a mini-history of the discipline of English and the development of a Canadian literature. She is working on a biography of P.K. Page.

BINA TOLEDO FREIWALD, graduate program director and professor of English at Concordia University, teaches and researches on critical theory, contemporary women's writing across genres and national literatures, autobiographical practices, and identity discourses of gender, sexuality, and nation. Recent publications include chapters in *Identity, Community, Nation* (2002), *Postmodernism and the Ethical Subject* (2004), *Tracing the Autobiographical* (2005), *Unfitting Stories: Narrative Approaches to Disease, Disability, and Trauma* (2007), and *The Jewish Diaspora as a Paradigm* (2008). Her current research project is "Gender, Nation, and Self-Narration: The Construction of National and Diasporic Identities in Jewish Women's Life Narratives in Palestine/Israel and Canada."

BARBARA GODARD, Historica Chair of Canadian Literature at York University, has published widely on Canadian and Quebec literatures and on feminist and literary theory. Her translations and essays on translation theory have contributed to the "cultural turn" in translation studies. Among her publications are the edited volumes *Gynocritics/Gynocritiques: Feminist Approaches to the Writing of Canadian and Quebec Women* (1987); *Collaboration in the Feminine: Writings on Women and Culture from* Tessera (1994); *Intersexions: Issues of Race and Gender in Canadian Women's Writing* (1996); and *Re:Generations: Canadian Women Poets in Conversation*, with Di Brandt (2005). *Canadian Literature at the Crossroads of Language and Culture*, a volume of her essays, appeared in 2008. For more information, see her website at www.yorku.ca/bgodard/.

SARA JAMIESON is an assistant professor in the Department of English at Carleton University where her research interests include intersections of Victorian and modernist poetic practice in the work of twentieth-century Canadian women poets, as well as representations of aging in Canadian writing. She has published articles in *Canadian Literature*, *Canadian Poetry*, and *Studies in Canadian Literature*. She is currently working on a book manuscript entitled *Soundless Grieving: Women Poets, Mourning, and Modernism in Canada*.

PEGGY LYNN KELLY specializes in Canadian women's writing. She has published in *Atlantis*, *Open Letter*, *Canadian Poetry*, *Studies in Canadian Literature*, *Literary Encyclopedia Online*, *The History of the Book in Canada*, *Framing Our Past: Canadian Women's History in the Twentieth Century*, and *Limited Edition: Voices of Feminism, Voices of Women*. She is editor of the second edition of *Shackles* by Madge Macbeth (2005), and associate general editor for Tecumseh Press's Early Canadian Women Writers Series. Peggy Kelly teaches English literature and composition at Algonquin College and the University of Ottawa.

CHRISTINE KIM is an assistant professor in the Department of English at Simon Fraser University. Her teaching and research focus on Asian North American literature and theory, contemporary Canadian literature, and diasporic writing. She has published articles in *Mosaic*, *Open Letter*, and *Studies in Canadian Literature*. She is currently working on a book-length project titled *From Multiculturalism to Globalization: The Cultural Politics of Asian North American Writing*.

ANN MARTIN is an assistant professor in the Department of English at the University of Saskatchewan, where she teaches twentieth-century British literature. She is the author of *Red Riding Hood and the Wolf in Bed: Modernism's Fairy Tales* (2006), and is currently researching the role of the automobile in the fiction of Dorothy L. Sayers.

PAMELA MCCALLUM is professor of English at the University of Calgary. She recently co-edited, with Wendy Faith, *Linked Histories: Postcolonial Studies in a Global World* (2005) and published an edited and annotated edition of Raymond Williams's *Modern Tragedy* (2006). Her research interests are focussed on representations of history, materiality, and globalization in literature and other cultural texts.

KATHY MEZEI teaches in the Department of Humanities at Simon Fraser University. She has published articles on translation studies, Canadian literature, narrative theory, and modern British women writers, and has edited special issues on domestic space for *Signs* (2002) and *BC Studies* (2003–2004). Her translations of French and Quebec poets have appeared in *ellipse* and *La Traductière*. Her most recent book, co-written with Chiara Briganti, is *Domestic Modernism, the Inter-war Novel, and E.H. Young* (2006). She runs a website on domestic space at www.sfu.ca/domestic-space. She is a participant in the project *Bibliography of Comparative Studies in Canadian, Quebec and Foreign Literatures*, based at the Université de Sherbrooke (www.compcanlit.ca).

LIANNE MOYES, associate professor of English at Université de Montréal, specializes in Canadian and Quebec literature. She is editor of *Gail Scott: Essays on Her Works* (2002); co-editor, with Domenic A. Beneventi and Licia Canton, of *Adjacencies: Minority Writing in Canada* (2004); and, from 1993 to 2003, was co-editor of the bilingual feminist journal *Tessera*. Her work on Anglo-Montreal writing has appeared in *Études canadiennes*, *Voix et images*, and *Canadian Literature*, as well as in the collections *Un certain genre malgré tout: Pour une réflexion sur la différence sexuelle à l'oeuvre dans l'écriture* (2007), *Language Acts: Anglo-Québec Poetry, 1976 to the 21st Century* (2007), and *Trans.Can.Lit: Resituating Canadian Literature* (2007).

MIRIAM NICHOLS teaches contemporary literature and literary theory at the University College of the Fraser Valley. She has published numerous articles on Canadian and American poets and is the editor of *Even on Sunday: Essays, Readings and Archival Materials on the Poetry and Poetics of Robin Blaser* (2002). Recently she edited *The Fire: The Collected Essays of Robin Blaser* (2006) and *The Holy Forest: The Collected Poems of Robin Blaser* (2006). She is working on *Radical Affections*, a book that re-reads the poetry of Charles Olson, Robert Creeley, Robert Duncan, Jack Spicer, Robin Blaser and Susan Howe.

ANNE QUÉMA teaches at Acadia University. A specialist of theories of criticism and twentieth-century British literature, she has published *The Agon of Modernism: Wyndham Lewis's Allegories, Aesthetics, and Politics* (1999), as well as articles in *Contemporary Literary Criticism*, *English Studies in Canada*, *The Canadian Modernists Meet*, *Studies in Canadian Literature*, *Philosophy and Literature*, *West Coast Line*, *Gothic Studies*, and the *International Journal of Law in Context*. The recipient of a SSHRC grant, she is currently working on a project on contemporary twentieth-century Gothic fiction and English family law.

KATHERINE QUINSEY teaches at the University of Windsor, where she was the 2007 Humanities Research Fellow. She has published widely on seventeenth- and eighteenth-century poets, Canadian poet Margaret Avison, and Biblical tradition in English literature. She is editor of *Broken Boundaries: Women and Feminism in Restoration Drama* (1996) and *Lumen: Selected Proceedings of the Canadian Society for Eighteenth-Century Studies* (1998), and co-editor, with David Kent, of an issue of *Canadian Poetry* devoted to the work of Margaret Avison. Following her SSHRC-funded project, *Tempting Grace: The Religious Imagination of Alexander Pope*, and a related project, *Rhyme and Print: Pope, Poetry, and the Material Text*, she will research women and religion in England 1640–1740 for *Under the Veil: Faith, Freedom, and Feminism in Early Modern Britain*.

CANDIDA RIFKIND is an assistant professor in the Department of English at the University of Winnipeg, where she specializes in modernism, women writers, and Canadian popular culture. She has published articles in *Studies in Canadian Literature, Essays on Canadian Writing,* the *Journal of Canadian Studies, TOPIA: Canadian Journal of Cultural Studies / Revue d'études canadiennes, Open Letter,* and in the critical anthology, *The Canadian Modernists Meet* (2005). Her book *Comrades and Critics: Women, Literature, and the Left in 1930s Canada* appeared in 2009. She is currently conducting a major research project into popular and pulp fictions written in and about Canada in the twenties and thirties.

MARILYN ROSE is a professor in the Department of English Language and Literature and dean of Graduate Studies at Brock University. A specialist in Canadian literature, she has published and presented numerous conference papers on the work of Canadian women poets, including Anne Marriott, Lorna Crozier, P.K. Page, Florence Livesay, and Pauline Johnson, as well as on Canadian novelists such as Joy Kogawa and Sinclair Ross. With graduate student Erica Kelly, she developed and maintains a website on Canadian women poets at www.brocku.ca/canadian womenpoets. In addition, she participates in Brock's MA program in Popular Culture and, with Professor Jeannette Sloniowski, undertakes research in and maintains a scholarly website on the study of detective fiction at www.brocku.ca/crimefictioncanada.

INDEX

Abednego, 202–3, 205
Acker, Kathy, 166
Acorn, Milton, 104
Adachi, Ken, 225, 234
Aiken, Henry David, 246, 249, 249n13
Alan Crawley and Contemporary Verse (McCullagh), 50, 68n5, 69n13
Allan, Andrew, 214, 216–19, 221–24, 226, 231n28
Allan, Ted, 231n24, 233n46
A/long Prairie Lines (Lenoski), 154
Althusser, Louis, 111
Anderson, Patrick, 51–52, 69n13, 75, 77, 90, 93n32, 275, 278, 281–85, 288–89, 293n20
"Anne Marriott: Treading Water" (Nelson), 159n2
Annotated Bibliography of Canada's Major Authors (Frey), 249n11
Anthology (CBC), 226, 229n1
The Arcades Project (Benjamin), 177, 181
Archer, Violet, 227; "A Program of Songs and Piano Music," 234n62
Arendt, Hannah, 345n10
Armstrong, Jeannette, 13, 238
Arnason, David, 8, 15, 22–23, 39, 46, 234
art gallery: Leicester Galleries, 80, 90; National Gallery (Ottawa), 242; of Ontario, 144; Tate, 79; of Windsor 15, 22
Association of Canadian Radio Artists (ACRA), 230n12, 230n13
Atwood, Margaret, 13, 87, 160, 375, 377, 392n4, 394; *Giochi di specchi/Tricks with Mirrors*, 392n3; Introduction to *The Sun and the Moon*, 93n28, 93; "Jay Macpherson: *Poems Twice Told*," 345; letter to Polk and Gibson, 93n27; *New Oxford Book of Canadian Verse in English*, 7, 22, 119, 119n14, 154; *Second Words*, 344n4
Auden, W.H., 39, 76–77, 81, 91n1, 277, 286, 300, 347; "In Memory of W.B. Yeats," 292n4
"Authorizing the Autobiographical" (Benstock), 306, 320
Autobiographics: A Feminist Theory of Women's Self-Representation (Gilmore), 111
automatistes, 167
Avison, Margaret, 7, 20, 29, 75–76, 126, 347–71
Avison, Margaret, works: "Alternative to Riots but All Citizens Must Play," 356–57, 362, 367; *Always Now*, 348–50, 352, 356–59, 363, 368n4,

369n11, 370; "The Bible to Be Believed," 355–56; "Butterfly Bones: Sonnet Against Sonnets," 356–57, 359–60, 361; "Chronic," 349; *Concrete and Wild Carrot*, 347, 351, 353–54, 357, 362–66; "Danger," 358; "Light (I)," 356; "Dispersed Titles," 350, 363; *The Dumbfounding*, 366; "First," 355; "Focussing," 355; "Found Poem," 360; "From Age to Age: Found Poem," 356, 359–60; "Geometaphysical," 349; *Il cuore che vede/The Optic Eye*, 392n3, 393n9, 394; "Jonathan, O Jonathan," 349; "Light (II)," 361, 362, 369n13; "Light (III)," 362, 369; "Listening," 356; "March Morning," 349; *Momentary Dark*, 367n3; "Muse of Danger," 355, 369n15, 370; *No Time* 353, 369n13; "On a Maundy Thursday Walk," 351; "Order of Trees" 369n13; "Perspective," 349–50; "Prelude," 359, 361; "Prospecting," 350; "Psalm 19," 349, 366; "Relating," 353; "Scar-face," 352; "Searching and Sounding," 352, 369n11; "Seeing So Little," 353; "SKETCH: End of a day: Or, I as a blurry," 351; "Snow," 348–49; *sunblue*, 349, 351, 356, 359–62, 369n13; "The Swimmer's Moment," 349; "To Wilfred Cantwell Smith," 369n15; "Two," 354; *Winter Sun*, 359, 361, 363, 370; "Words," 355–56

Bachelard, Gaspard, 129, 132–33, 135, 143–44
Bailey, Anne Geddes, 69n13, 71, 118n5, 119n14, 151, 153, 160
Baird, Irene, 269, 270n1
Banting, Pamela, 37, 46, 62, 65, 71, 183
Barbour, Doug, 143–44
Barker, George, 20, 304–5, 313, 319n11
Barnes, Djuna, 9, 166, 168, 175, 303, 317, 319n15, 344n3
Barthes, Roland, 173
Bartolini, Ubaldo, 392n3, 393n7, 394
Basile, Elena, 20, 59
Bates, Maxwell, 79

Beardsley, Doug, 37
Beattie, Munro, 52, 66n1, 104, 119, 210
Belyea, A. Eleanor, 69n13
Benjamin, Jessica, 86
Benjamin, Walter, 171, 174, 177, 181–82, 202; "On Some Motifs in Baudelaire," 184
Bennett, Donna, 154, 160
Benstock, Shari, 11, 22, 319n15, 320
Bentley, D.M.R., 108, 119, 151, 160
Berland, Jody, 243; "Nationalism and the Modernist Legacy," 249
Berrigan, Father Daniel, 240, 246, 249
Bersianik, Louky, 167
"Between One Cliché and Another: Language in *The Double Hook*" (Godard), 167
Bhabha, Homi, 137–38, 143–44, 345, 345n10
Bible, 202, 315, 318n7, 367, 401
Birney, Earle, 55, 75, 128, 149, 217–18, 231n30, 233n57, 239–40, 244, 255, 392n5; "Canada: Case History," 268; "David," 218
"The Birthmark" (Hawthorne), 327
Bishop, Elizabeth: "North Haven," 293n14
Bissell, Claude, 153
Bissett, Amy, 227
Blais, Marie-Claire, 183n8
Blake, William, 79, 89, 315
Blanchot, Maurice, 174
Bloom, Harold, 38, 46, 292n6, 344n4
Boehrer, Bruce, 280, 293n17, 294
Boland, Eavan, 307, 320
A Book I Like (CBC), 224
The Book of Canadian Poetry (Smith), 75–76, 153, 155
boundary 2, 9
Bourdieu, Pierre, 54, 59, 63, 71, 234, 394
Bowering, George, 168, 367n2, 368n8, 370, 392n5
Bowles, Jane, 166, 175
Bowman, Louise Morey, 33, 39, 45n4, 92n2, 92n4, 154–55
Boylan, Charles Robert, 208, 210n4
Boyle, Harry, 215, 218, 230n14
Bradstreet, Anne, 277, 292n5

Brand, Dionne, 375, 376, 379; *Luce ostinata/Tenacious Light*, 392n3
Brandt, Di, 62, 66, 118n1, 119, 164, 166, 182–83, 230n19, 234, 270, 385
Brecht, Bertold: "An die Nachgeborenen," 206
Brewster, Elizabeth, 7, 16, 69n13, 75, 77, 92n2, 97–123, 147; Denham interview, 108, 120; fonds, 120; Freiwald interview, 99, 120; Frye review, 103; Pacey correspondence, 98, 118n1, 122
Brewster, Elizabeth, works: *Away from Home*, 97, 109, 112–15; "Beginning the Fifties," 108; *Bright Centre*, 97, 117–19; *The Burning Bush*, 114, 117, 119; "By the River Again," 117; "Chronology of Summer," 101, 119; "City Street," 103; *Collected Poems I and II*, 97, 102–3, 105, 108, 120; "Digging In," 108; "East Coast—Canada," 101–2, 119n10; *East Coast*, 97, 103–4, 120; *Entertaining Angels*, 108, 120; "Essence of Marigold," 115, 118n1, 120; "Garden Cantos: A Month of Poems," 112; *Garden of Sculpture*, 117, 120; "Granite Is Not Enough," 104; "Harvard-Radcliffe Daze," 98, 108; "Hilda Doolittle Analyzes Sigmund Freud," 108; *A House Full of Women*, 118n1, 120; "In the Library," 101, 104, 109, 119n10; *The Invention of Truth*, 97, 107, 111–16, 118n1, 120; "The I of the Observer," 111; *Lillooet*, 104, 119n11; "The Loneliness That Wrapped Her Round," 103; Manuscript Notebook, 117, 119n10; "Marching Feet," 107; "Mosaic of Dreams," 117; "November Sunday," 105; "On P.K. Irwin's Bright Centre," 118n1; *Passage of Summer*, 101, 104–6, 119–21; "Poem about a Summer," 108; "Poems for Psychoanalysis," 105; "Poems for Seven Decades," 98, 108; "Psychoanalyst," 108; "Roads," 103, 119n13; *Roads and Other Poems*, 104, 119n13; *Selected Poems*, 106; "Self-Reliance: To Ralph Waldo Emerson," 105; "Shock," 105; "Speeding Towards Strange Destinations," 101; *Spring Again*, 109, 112; *Sunrise North*, 104–5, 119n11; "Supposition," 104; "Taking Stock," 117; "Time and Tide," 109, 120; "Victorian Interlude," 110; "Visitations," 117; *Visitations*, 117; *The Way Home*, 109; *Wheel of Change*, 98, 108; "Winter Trying to Become Spring," 114; "Woman Talk," 109
Brick: A Literary Journal, 22n2
Brittain, Vera, 80
Broadcasting Act (Canada): of 1932, 216; of 1958, 230n20
Brophy, Brigid, 302, 318n7, 320; Foreword, *By Grand Central Station I Sat Down and Wept*, 318n7
Brossard, Nicole, 166–67, 343
Brown, Audrey Alexandra, 55, 92n3, 151
Brown, E.K., 153, 259, 267, 271
Brown, Russell, 154, 160; *Anthology of Canadian Literature in English*, 154
Burridge, Christina, 304, 318n4
Butling, Pauline, 7, 18, 50, 71, 220, 234, 249, 249n9, 254
"*By Grand Central Station I Sat Down and Wept*: The Novel as a Poem" (Van Wart), 317n1, 319n17

Call, F[rank] O[liver], 33, 40, 46, 154–55; Foreword, *Acanthus and Wild Grape*, 40, 46
Callaghan, Morley, 244, 255, 269
Cameron, Elspeth, 217, 234
Campbell, Allan, 222, 224
Campbell, Wanda, 5, 33, 46
"Canada's Modernist Legacy" (Berland), 243
Canadian Authors' Association, 3, 92n4, 105, 149
Canadian Broadcasting Corporation (CBC)/CBC Radio, 5, 6, 18, 149, 150, 152, 210, 213–36, 237–38, 240, 242–45, 247, 248n2, 248n3, 249n8, 254, 261–64, 265, 293n23, 294n23; Eastern Network, 222; Galapagos Expedition, 244; International Service, 215,

230n15; Pacific Network, 222, 225; Public Affairs Department, 224–35, 229n4, 237; Radio 1, 231n26, 295; Radio 2, 231n26; CBC Toronto, 234, 234n67; Western Network (CBC), 222. *See also* Dominion Network *and program names*
Canadian Forum, 103–4, 255, 260–66
Canadian Literature, 3, 105, 294, 370
The Canadian Modernists Meet (Irvine), 3, 10, 23, 33, 46, 100, 118, 142, 209, 270n1, 345n4
Canadian National Theatre on the Air (Fink), 218, 226, 230n22, 231n24
Canadian Poetry (UWO), 32, 46, 128, 269, 368n3
Canadian Poetry Magazine (CAA), 77, 149, 195
Canadian Short Stories (CBC), 224, 229n1
"Canadian Tradition and Canadian Literature," 257, 267, 270
Capital Culture (Berland and Hornstein), 249
Carman, Bliss, 69n13, 76; Bliss Carman Society of Fredericton, 118n5, 119; *The Pipes of Pan*, 76
Carmichael, Stokely, 240, 244–45, 249
Carr, E.H., 192
Carr, Emily, 39, 269; *Hundreds and Thousands*, 233n52; *The Book of Small*, 233n52, 234; *Pause*, 233n52
Carrington, Leonora, 22n2, 166
"A Case for Nationalized Broadcasting" (Spry), 264
Casey, Jane, 62, 64, 183
CBC. *See* Canadian Broadcasting Corporation
CBC Radio. *See* Canadian Broadcasting Corporation
CBC Times, 217, 227
CBC Summer Theatre, 232n41
CBR Vancouver (CBC), 213–14, 224–25, 231n31; *Opening Night* series, 214
CCF. *See* Cooperative Commonwealth Federation
Chekhov, Anton, 85, 92n21
"Childe Roland to the Dark Tower Came" (Browning), 136

Chisholm, Dianne, 169, 177–78, 181, 183
"Christ in Alabama" (Hughes), 201
Citizens' Forum (CBC), 244
Cixous, Hélène, 106, 307, 343
Clark, Suzanne, 312–13
Clarke, Austin, 240, 244–45, 249
Close-Up (CBC), 263
Cogswell, Fred, 67n5, 69n13
Cohen, Leonard, 168, 240, 375–76, 392n3; *La Solitudine della Forza/The Solitude of Strength*, 392n3
Coldwell, Joan, 125, 127–28, 133, 143–44; Introduction, *The Tightrope Walker*, 139, 144
Collins, William, 277, 292n4
Communist Party, 2, 4, 18, 193–96; bookstore, 193
Contemporary Verse (*CV*, 1941–52), 2, 6, 15–16, 49–52, 54–60, 63–64, 66, 66n1, 67, 67n1, 67n4, 68n7, 68n10, 68n11, 69n13, 69n15, 70n18, 71n20, 90, 93n32, 118n5, 129, 148–50, 152, 154–55, 159, 183n4
Contemporary Verse II: A Quarterly of Canadian Poetry Criticism (*CV/II*, 1975–84), 2, 15–16, 49–55, 58–66, 67n4, 70n19, 70n20, 71, 183n4, 234
Contemporary Verse 2 (*CV2*, 1985–), 2, 15–16, 49–50, 62–66, 67n4, 69n15, 70n17, 70n18, 70n19, 70n20, 71n23, 71, 166, 183n4; *The Feminism of Our Discontent* (*CV2* sp. issue), 69n15, 71
"A Conversation with P.K. Page," 281, 285
Cooley, Dennis, 203
Co-operative Commonwealth Federation (CCF), 6, 239, 248n7
Cotnoir, Louise, 167
Cranston, Maurice: "The Structuralism of Claude Lévi-Strauss," 247
Crawford, Isabella Valency, 53, 92n6
Crawley, Alan, 2, 49, 52, 59, 66n1, 69n13, 92n3, 127, 148, 149–51, 155
Creative Writing in Canada (Pacey), 50
Creeley, Robert, 237, 2428n3
criticism, schools of, 269; apocalyptic-mythic, 267; ecocriticism, 86; English

Practical Criticism, 207; historical-social, 267; New Criticism, 207, 210n4; poststructuralist, 207
Cruz, John, 201, 204
Cullen, Countee, 91, 194
cummings, e.e., 227
Cunard, Nancy, 198, 200
Cutler, James E., 198–99

"Daddy's Girl: Dorothy Livesay's Correspondence with Her Father" (Banting), 46
Daniells, Roy, 76, 91n11, 153
Dante: *The Inferno*, 382
David, Jack, 154, 160
Day-Lewis, Cecil, 39
de Beauvoir, Simone, 270, 344n3
Deichmann, Erica, 84, 92n18
de Lauretis, Teresa, 111, 164
Deleuze, Gilles, 126, 144
Denham, Paul, 101, 108, 195
Depression, 192, 198, 205, 217, 257
Derrida, Jacques, 300, 356, 370n16
Design for Murder (CBC), 217, 231n24
Dial, 32, 154
Dickinson, Emily, 39, 104–5, 133, 141, 229n3
"Dictates for a Happy Life" (Dix), 301, 318n9
Dilworth, Ira, 223, 225–26, 233n55, 234; Foreword, *The Book of Small*, 233n52
Discipline and Punish (Foucault), 199
Dix, Dorothy (Elizabeth Meriwether Gilmer), 301, 318n9
Djwa, Sandra (S.D.), 16, 67n4, 92n10, 92n11, 92n12, 92n14, 92n15, 92n16, 93n23, 93n24, 93n31, 94, 119n9, 281, 393n11, 393n15
Dobbs, Kildare, 127–28, 130
Dominion Network, 223, 230n22, 231n26; *It Happened Here*, 217, 231n24
"Domus and the Megalopolis" (Lyotard), 132, 145
Donne, John, 284, 339; *Complete Poetry*, 93; "The Ecstasy," 292n13; *Selected Poetry*, 345; "A Valediction: Forbidding Mourning," 345n11

Doolittle, Hilda. See H.D.
Dorothy Livesay (Thompson), 34
Dorothy Livesay and the CBC (Tiessen and Tiessen), 213, 229n6, 233n46
"Dorothy Livesay and the Rise of Modernism in Canada" (Arnason), 8, 22, 46
Dorothy Livesay: Patterns in a Poetic Life (Stevens), 34, 36
Dorothy Livesay's Poetics of Desire (McInnis), 46n5
Du Bois, W.E.B.: *The Souls of Black Folk*, 201
Dudek, Louis, 2, 4, 5, 67n1, 69n13, 100, 119n14, 127, 143–44, 154, 160, 239–40, 254, 295; letter to A. Wilson, 144; "The Role of Little Magazines in Canada," 51, 56, 72
Dumont, Marilyn, 13
Duncan, Robert, 240, 245, 248n3
Dupré, Louise, 167
Duras, Marguerite, 166
Durrell, Lawrence, 300, 314

"Earle Birney's Radio Dramas" (Fink), 223
Ecce Homo (Epstein), 80
"Editorial postscript" (Irvine), 193
"El Greco in Canada" (Godard), 167
Eliot, T.S., 9, 19, 75–77, 81, 98–99, 101, 108, 118n3, 118n4, 118n5, 129, 133, 172, 207, 210, 259, 291n2, 298, 300, 302, 304–5, 315, 326, 339, 345, 347; *Four Quartets*, 290; "Little Gidding," 290; J. Alfred Prufrock, 160, 328; "The Metaphysical Poets," 75; *The Rock*, 92n3; "Tradition and the Individual Talent," 75, 99; "*Ulysses*, Order, and Myth," 31; *The Waste Land*, 12, 31, 77, 92n3, 151, 276, 331, 339, 369n11; *The Waste Land and Other Poems*, 345
"Elizabeth Smart's Novel-Journal" (Horne), 317n1, 319n16
The English Elegy (Sacks), 291n3
Epstein, Jacob, 80
"Eros in the Age of Anxiety" (Lobdell), 317n1, 320n19

Essays on Life Writing (Kadar), 318n8
"The Evangelist" (Harris), 230n18
"Ex-centriques, Eccentric, Avant-Garde" (Godard), 9, 20, 167, 298
Exorcising Blackness (Harris), 198
Ezell, Margaret J.M., 170, 173, 183

Fairley, Barker, 255
Fairley, Margaret, 255
Fanon, Franz: *The Wretched of the Earth*, 245
Fee, Margery, 119n14, 228
"Feminism and Deconstruction" (Schenk), 277, 279, 281, 291n3, 292n5, 293n14
"Feminist Periodicals and the Production of Cultural Value" (Godard), 62–63
Ferne, Doris, 2, 49, 66n1, 68n12, 148, 155
The Fiddlehead, 69–71, 116, 118n5
Fiedler, Leslie, 245
Field, Joanna [Marion Milner], 83–84, 86–89
The Field of Cultural Production (Bourdieu), 59, 71, 234, 394
Finch, Robert, 5, 51–52, 67n2, 91n2, 100, 154–55
Fink, Howard, 216, 218, 223, 225–26, 229n6, 230n8, 230n22, 231n24
First Statement, 5, 15, 49–51, 53–54, 57, 68n9, 68n10, 71n20, 299, 304
Forster, E.M., 300
Foster, Clarise, 70n17, 70n18, 70n19
Foster, Robert, 61–62
Foucault, Michel, 97, 111, 172–73, 199
Fowler, Adrian, 61
Fowler Commission *Report* (Royal Commission on Broadcasting), 261–62
Francis, Wynne, 53–54, 67n1, 68n6
Freud, Sigmund, 37, 83–84, 108–9, 135–36, 143–44, 313, 344n3
Frick, Alice, 214, 219, 222–23, 227, 230n8, 230n10, 230n22
Frye, Northrop, 13, 153, 240, 254, 258, 267, 271n4, 344n4, 345–46; *The Bush Garden*, 103; "Improved Binoculars," 344n1, 345; "Letters in Canada" review, 103
Futurism, 12, 167

Gasparini, Len, 105, 110
Gauvreau, Claude, 167
Geddes, Gary: *15 Canadian Poets*, 2; *15 Poets x 3*, 7, 154; *20th Century Poetry and Poetics*, 7
The Gender of Modernism (Scott), 3, 24, 317, 319n12
Genovese, Eugene, 201–2
Gerson, Carol, 3, 15, 31–32, 39, 46, 100, 155, 160
Gibbs, Robert, 98, 105
Gilbert, Sandra, 3, 38, 46, 99, 292n7, 294
Gilman, Marvin, 195
Gilmer, Elizabeth Meriwether. *See* Dorothy Dix
Ginsberg, Allen, 237, 248n3
"A Girl" (Pound), 85
Gnarowski, Michael, 3, 5, 50–52, 67n1, 68n6, 100, 154, 160; Introduction to *New Provinces*, 52
Godard, Barbara, 9, 10, 15, 20, 22, 62–66, 118n1, 119, 142, 144, 164, 166–67, 172–73, 182–83, 209, 230n19, 232n45, 234, 270, 288, 293n15, 294, 298–99, 318n2, 367n2, 391n1, 393n13; "Intertextuality," 173; "Une littérature en devenir," 183; "Millennial Musings," 378; "Re: post," 183n12; "Theorizing Feminist Discourse/Translation," 385; "Transgressions," 317n1
Godard, Jean-Luc, 174
Gorjup, Branco, 374–76, 380, 390, 391n1, 392n4, 392n5, 392n6, 393n9, 394
Gothic, 308, 317, 320n26
Gould, Glenn, 240; "The Idea of North," 245
Governor General's Award for Poetry, 2, 7, 67n2, 150–51, 344n2
Gowan, Elsie Park, 223, 233n47
Gubar, Susan, 3, 38, 46, 99, 292n7, 294
Gustafson, Ralph, 119n14, 155, 160
Gwyn, Sandra, 31–32, 36, 271n3

Hale, Katherine, 33, 45n4
Harryman, Carla, 166, 168, 174
Hawthorne, Nathaniel, 327

H.D. (Hilda Doolittle), 20, 39, 77, 105, 108, 219, 293n18, 302–3, 317, 319n15; "Stars Wheel in Purple," 12
Heaps, Denise A., 306, 317n1, 319n13
Heidegger, Martin, 344n3
Hemingway, Ernest, 176, 300
Holiday, Billie, 210
Horner, Jan, 62, 183
Hudson, W.H.: *Green Mansions*, 80
Hughes, Langston, 194, 201
Hurston, Zora Neale, 194, 203–5, 208
Huxley, Aldous, 300

Ideas (CBC), 6, 18, 234n67, 238, 239–40, 244–45, 248n2, 249–52, 254; *The Best Ideas You'll Hear Tonight*, 238; "Money and Power" series, 244
Imagism, 2, 6, 7, 12–13, 15, 31–34, 39, 77, 92n6, 136, 151, 154, 159n6, 208, 302, 381–82, 385, 386, 390–91, 393
"The Inscription of 'Feminine *Jouissance*' in Elizabeth Smart's *By Grand Central Station I Sat Down and Wept*," 317n1, 319n13
In Search of Eros (Gibbs), 98
Irvine, Dean J., 3, 10, 22, 39, 46, 50, 60, 65, 93n25, 119n8, 121, 127–29, 142–46, 149, 161, 184–85, 193, 209, 212, 270n1, 272, 282, 293n16, 294, 322, 345n4, 346; Introduction to *The Canadian Modernists Meet*, 4; Introduction to *Heresies*, 129; "Little Histories," 159; "A Poetics of the Elemental Imagination," 139, 144n16
Irwin, P.K., 6, 118n1
Italian Institute of Culture, 373–75, 377

Jackson, John, 223, 225–26
Jake and the Kid (Mitchell), 231n23, 232n39
James, Henry, 78, 133
Jamieson, Sara, 19
Jay Macpherson and Her Works (Weir), 340, 344n5, 345n9
Johnson, E. Pauline (Tekahionwake), 13, 53

Johnson, Randal, 234, 394
Jones, D.G., 254
Jonson, Ben, 277, 282, 292n11; "To the Memory of my Beloved, the Author Mr. William Shakespeare," 292n4; "The Vision of Ben Jonson," 294
Journal of Canadian Studies/Revue d'études canadiennes, 6, 294
Joyce, James, 5, 118n4, 300, 318n7, 326, 352, 369n11
Jung, Carl G., 135, 143–44, 344n3

Kafka, Franz, 141
Kant, Immanuel, 334, 344n7
Kearns, Judith, 70n17, 70n19
Keats, John, 88, 93n29
Keefer, Janice Kulyk, 377, 394
Keith, W.J., 327, 338
Kelly, Peggy Lynn, 18, 51, 194, 230n19, 234, 239
Kennedy, Leo, 4, 49, 51–52, 154–55, 255
Kennedy, Paul, 238–39, 248n2
Kent, David, 367n1, 367n2, 370n16, 370
Kermode, Frank, 46, 271
Killian, Laura, 101, 291n2, 293n18, 294, 382–83, 387, 393n11, 394n18
Kim, Christine, 15, 20, 118n5, 183, 215, 298–99, 304
King, Martin Luther, Jr., 208, 210, 240, 245
Klein, A.M., 4, 51, 69n13, 76, 154, 255–57, 259–60, 267–68, 347; *The Second Scroll*, 257–58
Klinck, Carl F., 71, 119n14, 153, 267; *Literary History of Canada*, 52, 66n1, 104, 119, 153, 210; Conclusion, *LHC*, 271n4
Knister, Raymond, 34, 91n2, 155
Kristeva, Julia, 165–66, 173, 316, 343, 355
Kristjanson, Gustaf, 213–14, 220, 230n8, 230n9
Kristjanson, Guy, 230n8

Langbauer, Laurie, 129, 143
Lawrence, D.H., 77, 81, 84, 87–88, 298, 300, 314; *Collected Letters*, 80; *Lady Chatterley's Lover*, 314

Layton, Irving, 68n6, 69n13, 119n14; *Il cacciatore sconcertato/The Baffled Hunter*, 375, 391n3
The Learning Stage (CBC), 238
Lecker, Robert, 126, 143n2, 154, 271n4
Lefebvre, Henri, 127–29, 143
Levertov, Denise, 237
Lewis, Wyndham, 167, 219, 314
A Life of My Own (CBC), 213, 220, 221
A Life of One's Own (Field), 83, 86, 88
Lipking, Lawrence, 276–77, 292n4, 292n11, 293n21, 294
The Little Magazine in Canada 1920–80 (Norris), 54, 66
Livesay, Dorothy, 1–6, 8–18, 22, 29–32, 34–45, 46n5, 46n6, 46n7, 49, 53, 55, 58, 62, 66n1, 67n4, 68n7, 68n8, 68n10, 69n12, 69n13, 71n19, 71n20, 75–77, 91n2, 92n2, 92n3, 97, 109–10, 126, 147–48, 151–52, 154–55, 163–66, 191–236, 239, 254–56, 271n5, 272, 275–76, 278, 285–88, 293n16, 293n18, 294, 318n10, 347; Canadian Communist Party and, 194; Dorothy Livesay Papers 69n12; estate, 22; fonds, 293n16, 293n18; fonds 2024, 294; poetry read by John Drainie, 229n1
Livesay, Dorothy, correspondence: with CBC, 229n2, 229n3, 229n4, 230n10, 230n13, 230n15, 231n31, 232n33, 232n34, 232n25, 232n26, 232n37, 232n40, 232n41, 232n44, 233n48, 233n49, 233n50, 233n51, 233n52, 233n53, 233n54, 233n55, 233n56, 233n60, 233n61, 234n65, 234n66, 234n67; with Nixon, 232n42; with *Star Weekly*, 229n5; with Weaver, 229n1
Livesay, Dorothy, works: *Archive for Our Time: Previously Uncollected and Unpublished Poems*, 10, 22, 31; "Broadcast," 31; "Call My People Home," 224–26, 229n6; "City Wife," 41–42; *Collected Poems: The Two Seasons*, 36, 39, 41–43, 191; *The Colour of God's Face*, 224; "Day and Night," 18, 39, 191–92, 194–96, 202–5, 208–10, 231n27, 254; "Decadence in Modern Bourgeois Poetry," 5; "Disasters of the Sun," 227; "Documentary Poetry and the Canadian Tradition," 271n5; "Fire and Reason," 12; Foreword, *Alan Crawley and* Contemporary Verse, 50; "The Green Jacket," 230n15; *Green Pitcher*, 8, 154, 222; "Green Rain," 12; "The Halloweens," 36; "If the World Were Mine," 221, 229n6, 232n40, 232n41; "In Green Solariums," 43; "Journey," 42; *Journey with My Selves*, 37–39, 42, 46n6, 109, 192–93, 210; "Momatkum," 213–14, 220, 229n7; "Monition," 42; "New Jersey: 1935," 210n; "Old Man Dozing," 41; "Ontario Story," 218; "The Origin of the Family," 37; "The Other Side of the Street," 230n13; "The Other Side of the Wall," 293n18; "Our Painters, Writers and Musicians," 229n3; *Plainsongs*, 227; Preface, *Down Singing Centuries*, 38; "The Raw Edges," 231n27; "Soccer Game," 227; "Prophet of the New World," 231n27; *Right Hand Left Hand*, 5, 29, 39, 91n2, 192–94, 200, 209–10, 230n9, 232n40, 232n41; "Saguenay's Job," 214, 218, 230n11; *The Self-Completing Tree*, 37, 39, 217; *Signpost*, 8, 41, 44, 154, 227; "Song and Dance," 227; "Staccato," 41; "Statement for New Year's Day," 229n6; "The Three Emilys," 39; "Threshold," 41; "The Times Were Different," 193, 199, 232n40; *The Unquiet Bed*, 226; "The Uprooting," 35; "We Are Alone," 1, 11, 13, 22, 163; "West Coast: 1943," 231n27; "What Is the True Approach to Peace?" 229n6; *A Winnipeg Childhood*, 35; "Zambia," 231n27
Livesay, F[lorence] R[andal], 9, 15, 29–45, 45n2, 45n4, 46n7, 68n8, 91n2, 155, 227; "Canadian Poetry Today," 47; "Drugs: Vacation Requirements," 44; Gerson biographical sketch, 31–32, 40, 46; "Her Evening Out," 42; "In the Public Ward," 44; "The

Moon and the Morning Star," 32; "On the White Keys," 39; "Romance," 43; "Rondel," 33; *Savour of Salt*, 32, 42, 46n7; *Shepherd's Purse*, 32–33, 39, 41, 44, 47; "Short-Cuts," 41; *Songs of Ukraina*, 32, 36–37; "Time," 41; "Windows," 33
Livesay, John Frederick Bligh, 32, 34, 37, 92n3, 151
Livesay Collection (BPSC), 220n1, 229n1
Lobdell, David, 317n1, 320n19
Lowell, Amy, 33, 39, 147, 155, 293n14, 293n18
Lowry, Malcolm, 219
Loy, Mina, 293n18, 317, 319n15
Lyotard, Jean-François, 132, 135, 142

MacEwan, Gwendolyn: *Il geroglifico finale/The Last Hieroglyph*, 391n3
MacKay, L[ouis] A., 155, 269; *The Ill-Tempered Lover*, 263
Macpherson, Jay, 7, 20, 55, 104, 106, 325–46; Philomel and, 330
Macpherson, Jay, works: "After the Explosion," 338; "The Anagogic Man," 333, 335; "Ark Parting," 332–33; "The Blighted Spring," 334; *The Boatman*, 106, 325–28, 330, 337–42, 344n2, 345n5, 345n12; "Cold Stone," 329, 332, 334; "Conjuring the Dead," 337; "The Dark Side," 337; "The End," 341, 343; "Epilogue," 337, 340–41; "The Fisherman," 335–36; *Four Ages of Man: The Classical Myths*, 329; "The Garden of the Sexes," 332; "Gathering In," 338, 341; "Hail Wedded Love," 342; "House Lights," 339; "Invocations," 337, 339, 343; "Lost Books and Dead Letters," 337; "The Martyrs," 331; "O Earth Return," 328, 330–32, 334, 344n2; "Old Age of the Teddy-Bear," 341, 343; "The Oracle Declines," 337; "Ordinary People in the Last Days," 333–34; "Other Poems," 328, 342; "Palladia and Others," 340; "Playing" 340, 341; "The Plowman in Darkness," 328, 330–31, 334; *Poems Twice Told (The Boatman* and *Welcoming Disaster)*, 327–43, 344n2, 345n6, 345n12; "Poor Child," 326–27, 333–34; "Recognitions," 337, 339–40, 345n12; "The Rymer," 330; "Shadows Flee," 337–38, 340; "The Sleepers," 331–32; *The Spirit of Solitude*, 326–28, 331, 340, 346; "Square One," 341; "Square Two," 341; "Still Waiting for the Spark from Heaven," 337; "The Swan," 344n6; "The Thread," 329; "Transformations," 340, 345n12; "Umbrella Poem," 327, 338; "The Way Down," 337, 339–40; *Welcoming Disaster*, 325–27, 337–42, 344n2; "The Well," 337; "What Falada Said," 340
The Madwoman in the Attic (Gilbert and Gubar), 3, 38, 46, 294
Mallarmé, Stéphane, 292n4, 292n4, 330, 345n6
Mandel, Eli, 104, 254
Mansfield, Katherine, 16, 67n3, 76–78, 80–81, 84–87, 92n13, 92n18, 92n21, 300, 393n11; "At the Bay," 78, 94; *The Garden Party and Other Stories*, 94; *Journal*, 84; letter from D.H. Lawrence, 94; *Letters*, 84, 85, 94; *Scrapbook*, 84; *Stories*, 84
Margaret Avison (Redekop), 348, 369n10
Marlatt, Daphne, 9, 13, 64, 106, 306, 319n14, 343; *Frames of a Story*, 106; "Self-Representation and Fiction-analysis," 306
Marriott, Anne, 2, 7, 17, 29, 49, 66n1, 68n12, 75–76, 92n3, 147–62, 159–61, 269; fonds, 161
Marriott, Anne, works: *Aqua*, 147, 150, 154, 158, 161; "Barriers," 158; *Calling Adventurers!* 150, 161; *The Circular Coast*, 150, 157–59, 161; "Countries," 154; *Countries*, 148, 150, 161; "Full Circle," 158; *Letters from Some Islands*, 150, 157; "Living Under Water," 158; "Oregon" 157; "Prairie Graveyard," 154; *Salt Marsh*, 150–52, 161; *Sandstone and Other Poems*, 148, 150–52, 161; "Two Poems of Wall," 157; "The

Wind Our Enemy," 154; *The Wind Our Enemy*, 76, 92n3, 147–48, 150–51, 154
Martin, Ann, 15, 68n6, 209, 276, 318n10
Marx, Karl, 108–9, 246, 249n14, 269, 344n3
Massey Commission *Report*, 243
McCallum, Pamela, 18, 215, 254
McCullagh, Joan, 50, 53, 55, 67n5, 68n7, 69n13, 73
McGeer, Ada, 220–21, 229n2, 232n37
McInnis, Nadine, 4, 46n5
McLaren, Floris Clark, 2, 49, 66n1, 68n12, 69n13, 148, 155
McLuhan, Marshall, 19, 219, 238, 240, 248n2, 254, 265–66
McNeil, Bill, 215, 229n5
Mezei, Kathy, 9, 16, 64
Millay, Edna St. Vincent, 76–77, 313
Miller, Henry, 300, 314
Milton, John, 280, 287; "Lycidas," 293n17
Monro, Harold, 77, 80, 93n22
Monroe, Harriet, 33, 149, 155
Moore, Marianne, 147, 293n18
"A More Public Voice" (Thompson), 31, 37
Morningside (CBC), 210, 248n2
Mourning and Panegyric (Schenck), 275, 277, 292n6, 292n12
Moyes, Lianne, 17, 67n3, 71n21, 77, 299, 304, 318n6, 368n3; "Sex of a Clown: Gail Scott's *My Paris*," 183n11
Murdock, Graham, 226, 233n58

National Film Board of Canada, 148–49, 152, 271n5
Negro: Anthology (Cunard), 198, 200, 203, 210n6
Nelson, Cary, 201, 207–8
Neuman, Shirley, 107, 144, 310
New, W[illiam] H., 46, 216
Nichol, b.p., 7, 351, 359, 367n2; "Ontario Report," 61, 73; "Sketching," 347
Nichols, Miriam, 20
Nietzsche, Friedrich, 173, 344n3
Nin, Anaïs, 166, 300, 314, 317, 319n15
Nixon, Doug, 223, 225, 232n42

Norris, Ken, 33, 52, 54, 66n1, 70n20, 153
Northern Affairs department (Canada), 245
Northern Review, 5, 49, 67n2, 100, 382

Oliver, Michael Brian, 315, 317n1, 320n22
Ondaatje, Michael, 6, 7, 168, 375–76, 379, 392n4; *Notte senza scale/A Night Without a Staircase* 392n3

Paalen, Wolfgang, 307, 319n11
Pacey, Desmond, 50, 66n1, 69n13, 71n22, 98–99, 105–6, 118n2, 153, 161, 267; letter to Sherburn, 118n2; "The Poetry of Elizabeth Brewster," 105
Page, P.K., 5–7, 12 –13, 16, 19–21, 22n1, 29, 59, 66n1, 67n2, 68n7, 68n11, 69n13, 75, 77–91, 92n4, 92n5, 92n6, 92n7, 92n8, 92n9, 92n10, 92n11, 92n12, 92n14, 92n15, 92n16, 92n17, 92n18, 92n19, 92n20, 92n21, 93n26, 93n31, 93n32, 98–99, 115, 118n1, 119n9, 121, 126, 147, 164, 275–95, 373–77, 380–90, 391n1, 391n2, 392n5, 393n11, 393n16, 394n18; "Aunt Bibbi" and, 78–79; "Cullen" persona, 91; interview with Orange ("That's me, firing Salvador"), 281; and father, 78; fonds, 92n21; Woolf and, 80; Rogers interview, 293n23; Wachtel interview, 281; "Letter to *Northern Review*," 122; letter to Ethel Wilson, 73; letters to Dorothy Livesay, 293n16, 293n19
Page, P.K., works: "Adolescence," 389; "After Rain," 12, 77, 385; "After Reading *Albino Pheasants* by Patrick Lane," 385; "Ancestors," 385; "The Answer," 293n22; "Arras," 292n8; "Autumn," 92n9, 290; "A Bagatelle," 294n22; *Brazilian Journal*, 391n1; "But We Rhyme in Heaven," 275, 285, 288; *Collected Poems*, 81–82; "Dwelling Place," 385; "Ecce Homo," 78, 90; *Evening Dance of the Grey Flies*, 292n13; "The Filled Pen," 385; "The Flower Bed," 292n13;

"The Gold Sun," 292n8; *The Hidden Room*, 83, 91, 161, 282–84, 287, 289–90, 292n8, 293n13, 293n22, 293n22; *Hologram*, 92n9, 94, 275, 277–78, 280–81, 285, 286, 290, 291n1, 292n6; *A Kind of Fiction*, 118n1; "The Maze," 385, 389; "The Moon-Child," 93n25; "The Moth," 78–79; "Ours," 275, 281–82, 284, 288, 290, 292n13; "Photos of a Salt Mine," 382; "Portrait of Marina," 160n8; "Presences," 293n22; "Reflection," 86; *Rosa dei Venti/Compass Rose*, 21, 373–74, 380, 382–87, 389, 391n1; "The Stenographers," 75; "Stories of Snow," 12, 292n8; "Summer," 385; *The Sun and the Moon*, 82, 86, 88–90, 92n17, 93, 93n26, 93n27, 93n28; "To Katherine Mansfield," 92n21; "The Typists," 386, 388; "Victoria," 103, 115, 117

Paladino, Mimmo, 21, 374, 377, 380
Panorama (CBC), 229n3
"The Paris Arcades, the Ponte Vecchio and the Comma of Translation" (Simon), 169, 176
The Penguin Book of Canadian Verse (Gustafson), 119n14, 155
Peterson, Len, 221, 232n39, 232n41; "Burlap Bags," 222; "They're All Afraid," 222
Pickthall, Marjorie, 13, 45n4, 76, 92n2, 151
Pierce, Lorne, 92n3, 149, 151–53
"The Piper of Arll" (Scott), 340
Plato: *Phaedrus* 292n6; *The Symposium*, 331
Podnieks, Elizabeth, 300, 304–6, 309, 317n1, 318n7
Poetry (Chicago), 32–33, 45n4, 149, 154
Pollock, Zailig, 6, 233n59
Poor Splendid Wings: The Rossettis (Winwar), 81, 84, 95
"A Poor Thing but Our Own" (Pearson), 251
Porter, Cole: "Night and Day," 210, 212
Pound, Ezra, 5, 77, 85–86, 101, 108, 112, 129, 207, 240, 242, 249n11, 302, 309, 347; "In a Station of the Metro," 12

Powys, John Cowper: *Wolf Solent*, 86–87
Prairie Playhouse (CBC), 223, 230n8
Pratt, E.J., 4, 51–52, 61, 75–76, 92n3, 149, 153–54, 195, 269
Preview, 6, 15, 16, 49, 50–51, 53–54, 57, 66n1, 69n13, 71n20, 77, 90, 93n32, 100, 281–82, 299, 304, 382; "Statement," 93n33
Proust, Marcel, 133, 300
Purdy, Al: *Pronuncia i nomi/Say the Names*, 392n3

Quéma, Anne, 19, 119n9

Ramazani, Jahan, 276, 291n3; *Poetry and Mourning*, 277
Ransom, John Crowe, 207
Read, Sir Herbert, 247
Reaney, James, 104, 254, 267, 328, 333–34
Re-belle et infidèle/The Body Bilingual (Lotbinière-Harwood), 393n13
Redekop, Ernest, 348, 369n10, 369n14
Re:Generations (Brandt and Godard), 22n2, 22, 118n1, 119
Relke, Diana M.A., 13, 30, 41, 86
"Review of *Poems* by Robert Finch" (Sutherland), 67n1
Rhys, Jean, 303, 317, 319n15
Richards, I.A., 207
Richardson, Dorothy, 219
Richler, Mordecai, 224
Rifkind, Candida, 18, 45n1, 231n31, 239
Rilke, Rainer Maria, 79, 242, 300; "Autumn Day," 92n9
Ringelblum, Emmanuel: *Notes from the Warsaw Ghetto*, 258
The Road to Now (Williams), 210
Roberts, Sir Charles G.D., 119n12
Rogers, Linda, 22n1
Rogers, Shelagh, 294n22
Roll Jordan Roll (Genovese), 201
"A Roman Holiday" (Pickens), 200
Rooke, Constance, 88, 92n7, 93n29, 93n30
Rorty, Richard, 345n10
Rose, Marilyn J., 17, 45n2, 67n3, 147, 275, 318n3
Ross, Malcolm, 267

Ross, Sinclair, 269
Ross, W.W.E., 33, 75, 154–55
Rothschild, Joan, 232n43
Roy, Camille, 168, 183n7
Roy, Gabrielle, 9, 20, 183n8, 298
Royal Commission on Broadcasting, 1955–57 (Fowler Commission): report, 261, 271
Royal Commission on Canadian Broadcasting (1929): report, 242
Ruddick, Bruce, 69n13, 93n32
Rudy, Susan, 299, 318n6
Rutherford, Paul, 217–18, 230n22, 260, 263–64, 270n3
Ruzesky, Jay, 22n1

Sacks, Peter M., 276, 291n3
Sage, Lorna, 320n23
Said, Edward, 254–55
Sand, Cy-Thea, 306, 317n1
Sandburg, Carl, 195
Sandwell, B.K., 233n57
Sartre, Jean-Paul, 246
Saturday Afternoon at the Opera (CBC), 231n26
Saturday Night, 31–32, 233n57, 260, 265, 269, 271n3
Saul, John Ralston, 238
Schenck, Celeste M., 275–79, 281–82, 292n5, 292n6, 292n12, 293n14
Scott, Bonnie Kime, 3, 4, 317, 319n12; Introduction to *The Gender of Modernism*, 107; *Refiguring Modernism*, 99, 118n4, 306; "A Tangled Mesh of Modernists," 107, 172
Scott, D.C., 340
Scott, F.R., 2, 4, 8, 33, 49, 51–52, 54, 69n13, 75–77, 93n32, 100, 107, 111, 126, 153–55, 193, 239–40, 255, 269; "The Canadian Authors Meet," 3, 118n7; "Radio and Writers West Coast Replies," 231n30; "Trans Canada," 12. See also *New Provinces*
Scott, Gail, 9, 17, 67n3, 163–64, 166–74, 176–87, 291n2, 385
Scott, Gail, works: "Bottoms Up," 168, 185; "Intertexts," 175; "Miroirs inconstants," 167–69; "My Montréal:

Notes of an Anglo-Québécois Writer," 163, 167–71, 176, 179; *My Paris: A Novel*, 17, 171, 176–81; "The Porous Text," 168, 175, 179, 181; *Spaces Like Stairs: Essays*, 166, 168–69; *Spare Parts*, 166; "The Virgin Denotes," 167–68, 174–75; "What If the Writer Were in Bed? On Narrative," 174
Sexton, Anne: "Somewhere in Africa," 293n14
Shackles (Macbeth), 230n17
Shakespeare, William, 68n7, 240, 277, 357; *Hamlet*, 79
Shaw, George Bernard, 300; *Major Barbara*, 79
Shaw, Neufville, 69n13, 77, 93n32
Sidney, Sir Philip, 277
Sigourney, Lydia, 276
Simmel, Georg, 31, 137
Simon, Sherry, 169, 176, 181–82
Sitwell, Edith, 76, 229n3, 347
Skinner, Constance Lindsay, 13, 155
Smart, Elizabeth, 7, 9, 19, 167, 297–323
Smart, Elizabeth, works: *The Assumption of Rogues and Rascals*, 392n5; *Autobiographies*, 304, 318n4; *By Grand Central Station I Sat Down and Wept*, 9, 297–98, 300–3, 305, 307–8, 311–13, 315–17, 318n4, 318n7, 392n5; "Dig a Grave and Let Us Bury Our Mother," 313, 320n21; *In the Meantime*, 307, 310, 313–16, 318n4, 320n25; "The Little Cassis Book," 319n11; "The Muse: His and Hers," 307; "My Lover John," 301; *Necessary Secrets*, 309, 315, 318n4, 319n11, 319n18; *On the Side of the Angels*, 318n4; "What Is Art? Said Doubting Tim," 316
Smart, Patricia, 8, 13, 183n6
Smith, A.J.M., 33, 49, 51–53, 55–56, 66n1, 69n13, 75–77, 119, 126–28, 132, 149, 152–54, 216, 255, 266, 271n6, 291n2, 299, 318n2, 367n1; "Introduction: A Reading of Anne Wilkinson," 143n5; "Introduction to *The Book of Canadian Poetry*," 318n5; *New Provinces*, 2,

34, 51–53, 76, 153–54, 291n2, 304; *The Oxford Book of Canadian Verse in English and French*, 119n14, 155; "A Rejected Preface," 67n1; "Swift Current," 12
Smith, Kay, 84, 87, 92n4, 93n23
Smyth, Donna, 319n13
Souster, Raymond, 230n19
Spencer, Stanley: *Saint Francis and the Birds*, 80
Spender, Stephen, 39, 77, 300
Spivak, Gayatri Chakravorty, 21, 129, 174, 374; "Questioned on Translation," 391
Stage (CBC), 222, 226, 231n25
Starobinski, Jean, 310
Stein, Gertrude, 9, 17, 67n3, 163, 166–72, 177–82, 186–87, 298, 310, 319n15, 326, 344n3; "Ada," 178–79, 186; *Autobiography of Alice B. Toklas*, 176, 180; "Composition as Explanation," 172; "How Writing Is Written," 176, 180; *Paris France*, 176–77, 179; "Poetry and Grammar," 175–76; "Portraits and Repetition," 176, 179–80; "What Are Master-pieces?" 180
Stereo Morning (CBC), 248n2
Stevens, Peter, 34, 37, 229n7; *The McGill Movement*, 4, 304
Stevenson, Lionel: *Appraisals of Canadian Literature*, 267, 272
"Strange Fruit" (Holiday), 198, 210–11
Stringer, Arthur, 33, 39, 154
Studies in Canadian Literature (journal), 9, 142
Sullivan, Rosemary, 88, 92n7, 93n29, 93n30, 106, 122, 278, 280, 292n6, 313, 387; "Meeting in Mexico" (Sullivan), 22n2; *Poetry by Canadian Women*, 106, 154
Sutherland, John, 51, 66n1, 69n13, 100, 127–28, 153, 162, 267

Tamarack Review, 118n1, 143
Tardif, Thérèse, 9, 298
Tekahionwake (E. Pauline Johnson), 13
Tennyson, Alfred, Lord, 91, 135, 291n2, 292n9; "The Lady of Shalott," 136

Tessera, 9, 64, 65, 166, 168–69, 172
Théoret, France, 166–67, 183
"The Third Eye: Jay Macpherson's *The Boatman*" (Reaney), 328, 332, 334
Thompson, Lee Briscoe, 2, 4, 8, 31, 34, 229n7
Thomson, James, 277
Thurston, Michael, 205, 207, 212
Tiessen, Hildi Froese, and Paul Gerard Tiessen, 213, 219, 227, 229n6, 230n11, 232n32, 233n60
Toklas, Alice B., 178, 310
Town Meeting (CBC), 229n6
Trans-Canada Network, 217, 223, 224–26, 231n25, 231n26
Trehearne, Brian, 3, 22n2, 31, 33, 99–100, 159, 293n20, 387; *Aestheticism and the Canadian Modernists*, 4, 155, 299, 302; *The Montreal Forties*, 5, 99, 293n20, 302, 390, 393n16
Tristram Shandy (Sterne), 310
Twentieth Century Poetry (Monro), 77, 80, 85, 93n22

University of the Air (CBC), 237
University of Toronto Quarterly, 103, 153, 345n4

Valente, Francesca, 21, 374–75, 377
Van Wart, Alice, 300–1, 309, 317n1, 318n4, 318n7, 319n17
Varda, Jean, 304, 319n11
Varo, Remedios, 22n2
Vertov, Ziga: *Man with a Movie Camera*, 195
Vickery, Ann, 172–73
Vidler, Anthony, 131–32, 143
Villa-Lobos, Heitor, 244
Virgil, 276, 290, 293n21, 329

Wachtel, Eleanor, 248n4
Waddington, Miriam, 5, 7, 19, 29, 45n1, 69n13, 100, 166, 239, 253–71, 271n5, 271n6, 392n5; "English 649" (course), 268–69
Waddington, Miriam, works: *Apartment Seven*, 253, 257, 266, 268, 270; "Breaking with Tradition," 256;

"The Cloudless Day," 257; "Falling for a Magic Pot?" 266; "The Function of Folklore in the Poetry of A.M. Klein," 257; Introduction to *The Collected Poems of A.M. Klein*, 257; "Outsider: Growing Up in Canada," 266; "Radio and Television," 260; "Signs on a White Field: Klein's *Second Scroll*," 257–58; "Women and Writing," 270
Walker, Cheryl, 276
"Walking the Tightrope with Anne Wilkinson" (Coldwell), 125, 128, 133
Wallace, Bronwen, 293n15
Waste Heritage (Baird), 270n1
Watson, Sheila, 10, 20, 163–64, 166–67, 183, 216, 298, 304; *The Double Hook*, 9; *Four Stories*, 166; "Gertrude Stein: The Style Is the Machine," 167
Weaver, Carol Ann, 22, 153
Weaver, Robert, 154, 220, 224, 226, 228, 229n1, 229n3, 230n13, 233n61, 248n3
Webb, Phyllis, 5, 6, 13, 29, 58, 69n13, 73, 104, 126, 166, 220, 228, 237–52, 254–55; at Canadian Writers' Conference (1955), 248n8; fonds, 238, 248n3; "Intimations of Mortality" (Wachtel interview), 247, 248n4; "Scorpion and Bull" (project), 238, 239; Williamson interview, 240, 247
Webb, Phyllis, works: "Dostoyevsky," 241; *Even Your Right Eye*, 248n1; "Ezra Pound," 241; "Father," 241; Foreword, *Wilson's Bowl*, 241–42, 247; *Hanging Fire*, 242, 249n12; "Imperfect Sestina," 242; "Kropotkin," 241; Kropotkin poems, 242, 249n12; "Letters to Margaret Atwood," 241–42, 247; "Message Machine," 241; *Naked Poems*, 238, 251; *Nothing but Brushstrokes*, 248n12; "Poems of Failure," 241–42; "The Poet and the Publisher," 248n8; "The Poet, His Media, and the Public," 248n8; "Portraits," 241–42, 249n11; "The Question as an Instrument of Torture," 239; "Rilke," 241; *The Sea Is Also a Garden*, 248n1;

"Socrates," 241; *Talking*, 239, 242; "Vasarely," 241–42; *The Vision Tree*, 242; *Water and Light*, 242, 249n15; *Wilson's Bowl*, 241–42, 249n11
Wednesday Night (CBC), 217, 222, 225, 229n3, 230n14, 231n25
Weir, Lorraine, 327, 339, 345n5, 345n9, 345n12
West Coast Line, 23
Whitehouse, Raymond, 219, 223–25, 232n34, 232n35, 232n40, 232n41
Whitman, Walt, 195, 329n25
Whitney, Patricia, 293n20
"Why the CBC Must Be Dull" (McLuhan), 265
Wider Boundaries of Daring (conference/festival), 15, 22, 118, 144, 166, 234n62, 254, 270, 318n6, 321–22, 385, 393n11; *Awakenings*, 22; *Planet Earth*, 22
Wilde, Oscar, 300
Wilkinson, Anne, 7, 16, 29, 55, 125–46; fonds, 130, 143, 144; Osler family and, 125, 130, 134, 144
Wilkinson, Anne, works: "After Reading Kafka," 132, 140–41; "Amphibian Shores," 140; "The Autobiography," 135; "Black and White," 126; "Claustrophobia," 141–42; *Collected Poems/Prose Memoir*, 128, 141, 143, 146; "Dissection," 141; "Falling for a Magic Pot?" 266; "Fishwife," 140; "A Folk Tale: With a Warning to Lovers," 138; "Four Corners of My World," 132, 139; *The Hangman Ties the Holly*, 128; *Heresies: The Complete Poems*, 9, 10, 23, 126–27, 129, 131–33, 136, 138–42, 144–46; "Lake Song," 134, 139; "Lens," 126–27, 133; "Letter to My Children," 130; *Lions in the Way*, 130, 134, 136; "Nature Be Damned," 140; "Notes on Suburbia," 128; "One or Three or Two," 126, 130; "Poems from the Copy-Books," 127; "The Red and the Green," 126, 130; "Roches Point," 134; "A Sorrow of Stones," 134; "Still Life," 140; "Suburbia," 143; "Summer Acres," 133–34, 138; "Summer Storm,"

140–41; "Theme and Variation," 126; *The Tightrope Walker*, 126–28, 130, 133, 135, 137–41, 143–44; "Tower Lullaby" 135; "Virginia Woolf," 140
Williams, Dorothy W., 210n2
Williams, Raymond, 262
Williams, William Carlos, 11, 230n19
Willmott, Glen, 10, 300–1, 303
Wilson, Anne Elizabeth, 45n4
Wilson, Ethel, 68n11, 73; "Of Alan Crawley," 68n7
Wilson, Milton, 104, 153
Winwar, Francis, 81, 84
Wiseman, Adele, 269
"With all best wishes, high hopes, and thanks" (Knight), 249n8
Wittgenstein, Ludwig, 247
Wolfe, Morris, 215, 220n5
Wollstonecraft, Mary, 270
Women in the CBC (CBC), 220, 232n45
Women of the Left Bank (Benstock), 3, 22
"Women, Poetics and Canada before 1960" (Rudy), 318n6
Woodcock, George, 77, 104, 224–25, 246, 299, 318n5, 323
Woolf, Virginia, 4, 9, 16, 20, 38, 67n3, 76–77, 83–85, 87–88, 97, 107–10, 118, 119n9, 125, 133, 140–41, 166, 182–83, 219, 239, 248n6, 293n18, 300, 319n15, 344n3, 369n11, 393n11; *Orlando*, 109–10; *A Room of One's Own*, 81–84, 99, 101, 110, 182n3, 183n9; *Three Guineas*, 80; *The Waves*, 78, 80–81, 109; *A Writers' Diary*, 92n13
Wordsworth, William, 352; *The Prelude*, 115
world war: WWI, 11, 29 31, 71, 91n2, 100; WWII, 159, 216–18, 220, 222, 224, 230n11, 231n27, 244, 301, 303
Wreford, James, 69n13
Wright, Richard, 194
Writing in the Father's House (P. Smart), 13
"Writing Our Way Through the Labyrinth" (Marlatt), 319n14

Yeats, W.B., 76, 81, 240, 277, 286, 291, 294, 300; "The Tower," 136
Young, Tory, 198, 210n6

Zeiger, Melissa F., 279–80, 292n9, 293n14
Zezulka, J.M., 369n10
Zola, Émile, 248n5

www.ingramcontent.com/pod-product-compliance
Lightning Source LLC
Chambersburg PA
CBHW071145070526
44584CB00019B/2663